RACE, RIGHTS AND REPARATION
Law and the Japanese American Internment

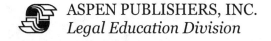 ASPEN PUBLISHERS, INC.
Legal Education Division

RACE, RIGHTS AND REPARATION
Law and the Japanese American Internment

Eric K. Yamamoto
University of Hawai'i
William S. Richardson School of Law

Margaret Chon
Seattle University
School of Law

Carol L. Izumi
George Washington University Law School

Jerry Kang
University of California, Los Angeles
School of Law

Frank H. Wu
Howard University
School of Law

ASPEN LAW & BUSINESS
A Division of Aspen Publishers, Inc.
Gaithersburg   New York

Printed in the United States of America

1 2 3 4 5 6 7 8 9 0

ISBN 0–7355–2393–2

Library of Congress Cataloging-in-Publication Data

Race, rights and reparation : law and the Japanese American internment /
 Erik K. Yamamoto . . . [et al.].
  p. cm.
 Includes index.
 ISBN 0-7355-2393-2
 1. Japanese Americans—Legal status, laws, etc. 2. Japanese Americans—Evacuation
and relocation, 1942-1945. 3. Japanese Americans—Civil rights. 4. Restitution—
United States. I. Yamamoto, Eric K., 1952-

 KF7224.5.R33 2001
 342.73'0873—dc21

                 2001022325

About Aspen Law & Business
Legal Education Division

With a dedication to preserving and strengthening the long-standing tradition of publishing excellence in legal education, Aspen Law & Business continues to provide the highest quality teaching and learning resources for today's law school community. Careful development, meticulous editing, and an unmatched responsiveness to the evolving needs of today's discerning educators combine in the creation of our outstanding casebooks, coursebooks, textbooks, and study aids.

ASPEN LAW & BUSINESS
A Division of Aspen Publishers, Inc.
A Wolters Kluwer Company
www.aspenpublishers.com

About the Authors

Eric K. Yamamoto is Professor of Law at the William S. Richardson School of Law, University of Hawai'i. He received his J.D. from Boalt Hall, University of California at Berkeley. He was in private practice in Hawai'i for seven years before beginning his teaching career in 1985. In 1983-1984, he served as a member of the *coram nobis* legal team reopening *Korematsu v. United States*. He has participated in the litigation of many civil rights and human rights cases.

Professor Yamamoto's scholarship includes his recent book, INTERRACIAL JUSTICE: CONFLICT AND RECONCILIATION IN POST-CIVIL RIGHTS AMERICA, and numerous articles on civil rights, complex litigation, critical race theory and indigenous peoples' justice. He is the senior legal advisor to the Native Hawaiian Advisory Council, is a member of the American Law Institute, and has served on the boards of the Legal Aid Society and the Journal of Legal Education.

Margaret Chon began teaching law at Syracuse University in 1991 and is currently associate professor at Seattle University School of Law. While in graduate and law schools, she co-taught an Asian American studies class, which was one of the first such classes offered at the University of Michigan. Her current scholarly interests include digital copyright as well as Asian Americans and law. She teaches or has taught administrative law, civil procedure, computers and the law, intellectual property law, Internet law, legal writing, professional responsibility, and race and law.

Following law school, Professor Chon worked at the U.S. Court of Appeals for the Third Circuit, as a staff attorney and then as clerk to the Honorable A. Leon Higginbotham, Jr. She then practiced intellectual property law with Schnader, Harrison, Segal & Lewis in Philadelphia, and served an administrative clerkship with the Honorable Dolores K. Sloviter of the U.S. Court of Appeals for the Third Circuit. She is a graduate of Cornell University College of Arts and Science (A.B. 1979), the University of Michigan School of Public Health (M.H.S.A. 1981) and the University of Michigan Law School (J.D. *cum laude* 1986). She has two children.

Carol L. Izumi is a graduate of Oberlin College and Georgetown University Law Center. She has been a member of the full-time faculty at George Washington University Law School since 1986 where she is a full Professor of Clinical Law. During her tenure at George Washington, Professor Izumi has been the director of two consumer law programs (mediation and litigation) and has taught upper level courses in alternative dispute resolution and trial practice. She currently runs the consumer clinic and teaches an academic course on mediation.

Professor Izumi is a nationally known dispute resolution academic and is invited to teach at law schools around the country. She is actively engaged as a certified mediator, arbitrator, and skills trainer. Her scholarly research and writing has been concentrated in these subject areas.

Professor Izumi has been active in Asian Pacific American organizations for many years. She was co-founder and president of the Asian American Law Students Association at Georgetown University Law Center and secretary of the founding Board of Directors of the Asian Pacific American Bar Association Educational Fund (AEF). She currently serves as Secretary of the Board of Directors of the Washington, D.C. chapter of the Japanese American Citizens League (JACL) and co-chairs the chapter's Education Committee. Professor Izumi has been the Faculty Advisor to the Asian Pacific American Law Students Association at George Washington since 1986.

Jerry Kang began teaching at UCLA School of Law in 1995 following a clerkship with Judge William A. Norris of the Ninth Circuit Court of Appeals and a year of information policy analysis at the National Telecommunications and Information Administration. He graduated *magna cum laude* from Harvard University (B.A. Physics) and Harvard Law School. During law school, he was a supervising editor of the Harvard Law Review and Special Assistant to Harvard University's Advisory Committee on Free Speech.

At UCLA, Professor Kang has pursued teaching and scholarly agendas in race and cyberspace. He teaches Civil Procedure, Asian American Jurisprudence, Communications Law and Policy, and Cyberlaw. He recently authored a casebook entitled COMMUNICATIONS LAW AND POLICY (Aspen 2001). On race, he has focused specifically on the Asian American community and has written about hate crimes and affirmative action. He is also active with numerous Asian Pacific American organizations, such as the UCLA Asian American Studies Center and the APA Legal Center in Los Angeles.

Frank H. Wu joined the faculty of Howard University School of Law in Washington, D.C., in 1995. He teaches in the Clinical Law Center and in traditional courses such as civil procedure. Professor Wu received his undergraduate degree in writing from Johns Hopkins University in Baltimore, Maryland, and his law degree from the University of Michigan. He served as a Teaching Fellow at Stanford University Law School. Before beginning his academic career, Professor Wu held a clerkship with the late United States district court judge Frank J. Battisti in Cleveland, Ohio. He then joined the civil litigation practice group at the law firm of Morrison & Foerster in San Francisco. While there, he devoted a quarter of his time to representation of indigent individuals. On leave of absence, Professor Wu worked as a campaign organizer with Californians United Against Proposition 187.

Professor Wu has written extensively on affirmative action and immigration. He has written on a regular basis for the New York Times Syndicate "New America" News Service and Asian Week. His work has appeared in The Washington Post, The Chronicle of Higher Education, and World Journal. He has also testified before Congress on affirmative action and appeared on numerous television and radio programs. He has served on the Board of Directors of the Asian Pacific American Bar Association Educational Fund (AEF), the Advisory Board of the Minority Fellows Program of the Washington Center, and the Professions Fellowship Selection Panel of the American Association of University Women.

To George and Tamiko Yamamoto for their love and support,

and

to Fred, Gordon and Min for the courage of their convictions.

Eric K. Yamamoto

To Wan Yong Chon and Keum Sook Chon, my parents, who made it possible for me to carry on the family privilege of teaching, writing and influencing future generations.

Margaret Chon

In memory of my parents Shinsuke Edwin Izumi and Misao Oshima Izumi, an Issei and Nisei of remarkable courage, fortitude and grace.

Carol L. Izumi

To Taera Lynn Kang.

Jerry Kang

To my parents Hai and Grace Wu.

Frank H. Wu

Summary of Contents

Contents

Part I: Context

Part II: Internment

Part III: Redress

Preface

The mass internment of Japanese Americans during World War II was one of the worst violations of civil liberties in the United States. The Japanese American redress movement of the 1980s produced an historically unique confession of racial wrongdoing by the federal government. At the heart of both the internment and redress stood the Rule of Law—its noble promises and wrenching failures in the context of war, race and politics. Given their significance, the internment and redress are obvious sites for intensive legal inquiry. Yet to date no comprehensive curricular materials—introductory essays, original documents, legal cases, commentary and in-depth study modules—exist to foster their critical examination and study. This book is one of first impression, in this and other ways.

AUDIENCE

Unlike many law textbooks, the book's comprehensive approach targets three audiences. First, it is aimed at law professors and law students across a spectrum of courses. Second, the book is written to be accessible to professors and students in graduate and upper-level undergraduate courses in Asian American Studies, African American Studies, Ethnic Studies, Political Science, Cultural Studies, Sociology and History. Third, it speaks to civil rights and other social justice advocates, or public intellectuals interested in an in-depth inquiry into the interplay of American culture, government politics, the courts and civil liberties. The book can be used as the primary text for a course on the internment and redress as well as a supplement for more general courses. Its chapters (or even parts of chapters) also can be studied separately.

THEMES

Again, departing from the usual legal casebook, which exists primarily to illustrate specific doctrinal points, this book is organized around three central themes. Suggested by the title, these are the concepts of race, rights and reparation—particularly as they shape the testing of civil liberties during wartime. Throughout each of the chapters, the notes and questions develop these foundational themes, and ask the reader to make connections across seemingly disparate historical events and legal decisions.

A major issue discussed in all the chapters of the book is the tension between civil rights, civil liberties and national security. Other questions explored include the racial components of legal or social decisions, and the extent to which the Constitution's equal protection clause protects the rights of racial minority groups. Yet another theme is the responsibility of governments to acknowledge human rights violations that have occurred in the past. All of these themes have tremendous contemporary significance. They are each treated in some detail in Chapter 1, to provide basic conceptual structure and vocabulary. And they are revisited in the last chapter, Chapter 7, in order to illustrate the ongoing social dialogue and debate about the proper balance among each of these different concepts.

PEDAGOGY

Legal education often encourages studying law in the absence of non-legal considerations. This book pays careful attention to both law—understood narrowly as the enforceable pronouncements of the executive, legislative and judicial branches—and to context—the combined influences of politics, economics and culture on race, law and liberty. Each chapter starts with a broad overview essay that provides historical and social context about Asians in America. Then each chapter presents carefully selected and edited cases, original materials, commentary and questions within a series of detailed, subject-area study modules to facilitate teacher-student-scholar interactions. To assist all readers, and especially non-law school readers, explanatory paragraphs interconnect the various study modules and provide clear, if brief, introductions to essential legal concepts, processes and terminology. Throughout, the book engages the critical faculties of all audiences by providing thematic overviews, striking details, technical analyses, socio-historical setting and provocative questions.

For law teachers, the pedagogical approach will seem simultaneously familiar and different. The case approach, combined with notes and questions, facilitates an interactive (so-called Socratic) dialogue with students. At the same time, this book presents these cases not only to illustrate legal doctrine, but also to teach about the impact of historical and political events on diverse areas of law typically not taught in a single class. The book treats subjects such as race relations and critical race theory; constitutional, criminal and national security law; criminal and civil procedure; professional ethics; evidence; legal history; and lawyering practice. A professor in the area of constitutional law, for example, might excerpt relevant portions of the book to supplement the standard, typically decontextualized caselaw treatment of the *Korematsu* and *Hirabayashi* cases.

This book is designed to support law professors who want to teach about an historically significant civil liberties and social justice challenge—the Japanese American internment and redress—by infusing it throughout the law school curriculum. Approaching the study of law through the lens of an issue, rather than through the lens of a specific legal rule, can involve students with their passion and political instincts, as well their analytical abilities. If teaching at its best is about engaging students' hearts and minds, and provoking stimulating debate, these materials are designed to facilitate just that.

For non-law professors or the law professor who teaches seminars in Asian American jurisprudence, or race and law, the book is organized chronologically. Used in a more linear fashion, the book should highlight law's relevance to different facets of the Japanese American internment and redress. Instead of an episodic, doctrinally specific approach to the internment, it will reveal how law is part of the overall social and political events of the day. Law then can be viewed and studied as an interconnected web embedded within social context. Legal doctrine itself is not compartmentalized, but seen as part of a seamless whole, a set of tools to address a social problem.

A few words about our racial terminology: We use the terms *White American* and *African American* to denote racial groups that currently are typically termed *White* and *Black*. Those of Asian and Latin American ancestry are termed, respectively, Asian Americans and Latinas/os. We employ these terms fully cognizant that race may be best understood as a social construct without fixed or scientific meaning and that our choice of terms may be controversial. Because we provide historical materials, the outdated terms *Caucasian*, *Negro* and *Oriental* are encountered in the text. The various meanings ascribed to these older, arguably offensive, terms are discussed within the book.

STRUCTURE

Except for Chapter 1, each of the chapters contains an overview section, which can be read simply to get a feel for the chapter's contents. Each overview is followed by a section of study modules designed to be separable from other parts of the book. These modules can be used in specific law school classes. Finally, each chapter ends with a list of additional readings, so that interested readers can continue study beyond the materials provided here.

Chapters 1 and 2 provide a thematic and historical introduction to the materials. They are a primer both to the theoretical perspectives as well as to the particular incarnations of race, rights, reparations and liberty in Asian American legal history.

Chapters 3 and 4 describe in detail the legal challenges to the internment as well as the experience of the internment from the perspectives of the internees. Chapters 5 and 6 discuss the Japanese American redress movement in particular, and reparations movements generally. The *coram nobis* cases are also examined in depth. Those cases reopened the original internment cases and culminated in judicial declarations of injustice that forged new understandings of the internment and the law ostensibly supporting it. The chapters also explore other redress efforts, including African American claims for reparations.

Finally, Chapter 7 provides contemporary case studies to aid the reader in applying the lessons of the internment and redress to current political and social controversies. This is a mindful attempt to link the internment and redress to analogous issues of other groups. Congress's purpose in establishing the Civil Liberties Public Education Fund, which provided support for this book, is

> to sponsor research and public educational activities . . . so that the events surrounding the evacuation, relocation, and internment of United States citizens and permanent resident aliens of Japanese ancestry will be remembered, and so that the causes and circumstances of this and similar events may be illuminated and understood. . . .

Public Law 100-383 (August 10, 1988); 50 U.S.C. app. 1989b-5.

May studying this past prevent similar tragedies in the future.

Eric K. Yamamoto

Margaret Chon

Carol L. Izumi

Jerry Kang

Frank H. Wu

April 2001

Acknowledgments

In preparing this work we accrued substantial debts. First, we thank the many people involved in research and administrative support. The following students assisted us in many ways: Christopher D. Anderson, Alicia Sakura Barron, Sara Bradley, Earl Bravo, Kakoli Caprihan, Josephine Chang, Sophia Chao, Victor Chen, Christina L. Collins, Lia Sheehan Dwight, Baoding Fan, Kim Haraughty, Naoko Inoue, Regan Iwao, Douglas Kobayashi, Michelle Kim, Soo Kim, Kelly Kunsch, Iris Lee, Joanne Lee, Phoebe Liu, Steven Liu, Kelsie Manner, Khoa Nguyen, May Nicholson, Shellie Kiyomi Park, Tracy Park, Jeffrey C. Pepe, Minh Pham, Julia Roig, Eugene Ryu, Susan Kiyomi Serrano, Maile Shimabukuro, Sonja Valant, Anna Lisa Vidad, Brett C. Vinson, Wendy S. Wall, Kiera Wong, Robert Yap, Ayanna Yonemura and Jonathan Yun. In particular, Susan Kiyomi Serrano contributed some valuable text for various chapters.

Moreover, the design and high quality of the book's format is due in large part to Tal Grietzer, whose careful attention, desktop publishing expertise and many extra hours of work ensured a superior result. Lauren St. Pierre and Laurie J. Sleeper assisted with word processing. The UCLA School of Law provided much of the technological support as well as other direct and indirect support for the final stages of the book production. Seattle University generously provided in kind contributions as well as a summer faculty fellowship award to Margaret Chon for mid-stage editing.

Second, we gratefully acknowledge the fiscal sponsorship and management assistance of the Asian Pacific American Bar Association Education Fund (AEF), a non-profit organization in Washington, D.C. offering public interest fellowships and educational opportunities for law students. This book does not necessarily reflect the views of the AEF.

Third, we appreciate the valuable input of our editorial consultants to the book: Professors K. Scott Wong and Lorraine K. Bannai. As well we thank those who allowed access to the archives of some primary source material used here: Alice Ito of the Densho Project and Marji Lee of the *Korematsu v. United States Coram Nobis* Case Collection, UCLA Asian American Studies Center, Asian American Movement Archives. We also appreciate the careful work of the Aspen editors, including Jessica Barmack, Melody Davies, Barbara Rappaport and Peggy Rehberger, as well as the enthusiasm of Lynn Churchill, our acquisitions editor.

Fourth, we acknowledge the authors of the following images and excerpts used in this volume with their permission or under government public domain:

Albers, Clem, photo (Los Angeles, California, 1942), War Relocation Authority.

Anderson, Nick, *Spy Scare Taints Lab's Atmosphere, Asian Americans Say Discrimination: Insensitive Remarks, Warnings Raise Fear of "Ethnic Profiling" Following Allegations of Chinese Espionage, Employees Say* (1999). Reprinted by permission of the Los Angeles Times Syndicate.

Asian American Journalists Association, *Coverage of Spying Allegations at Nuclear Labs* (1999). Reprinted by permission by the Asian American Journalists Association.

Bannai, Lorraine K., interview with Alice Ito and Margaret Chon (2000). Reprinted by permission of Densho: The Japanese American Legacy Project.

Bannai, Lorraine K. and Dale Minami, *Internment During World War II and Litigations* (1992). Reprinted by permission of Lorraine K. Bannai, Dale Minami and the Greenwood Publishing Group.

Brooks, Roy L. (ed.), WHEN SORRY ISN'T ENOUGH: THE CONTROVERSY OVER APOLOGIES AND REPARATIONS FOR HUMAN INJUSTICE (1999). Reprinted by permission of the New York University Press.

Broom, Leonard, and Ruth Riemer, REMOVAL AND RETURN: THE SOCIO-ECONOMIC EFFECTS OF THE WAR ON JAPANESE AMERICANS (1949). Reprinted by permission of the University of California Press.

Chew, Pat K., *Asian Americans: The "Reticent" Minority and Their Paradoxes* (1994). Reprinted by permission of Pat K. Chew.

Chin, Gabriel J., Sumi K. Cho, Jerry Kang and Frank H. Wu, BEYOND SELF-INTEREST: ASIAN AMERICANS TOWARD A COMMUNITY OF JUSTICE (1996). Reprinted by permission of the authors.

Cho, Sumi, *Whiteness Redeemed: Earl Warren, Internment and Brown v. Board of Education* (1999). Reprinted by permission of Sumi Cho and the Boston College Third World Law Journal/Boston College Law Review.

Collins, Donald E., NATIVE AMERICAN ALIENS: DISLOYALTY AND THE RENUNCIATION OF CITIZENSHIP BY JAPANESE AMERICANS DURING WORLD WAR II (1985). Reprinted by permission of Greenwood Publishing Group.

Dang, Janet, *API Lab Employees File Suit* (2000). Reprinted by permission of Asian Week.

Daniels, Roger, CONCENTRATION CAMPS, NORTH AMERICA: JAPANESE IN THE UNITED STATES AND CANADA DURING WORLD WAR II (1993). Reprinted by permission of the Krieger Publishing Company.

Daniels, Roger, AMERICAN CONCENTRATION CAMPS: A DOCUMENTARY HISTORY OF THE RELOCATION AND INCARCERATION OF JAPANESE AMERICANS, 1942-1945 (1989). Reprinted by permission of Roger Daniels and Garland Publishing Co.

Estrada, Richard, *Familiarity Doesn't Always Breed Friendship* (1999). Reprinted by permission of The Dallas Morning News.

Goldberg, Arthur, letter to William Marutani (1982). Reprinted by permission of the Goldberg family.

Gómez, Laura, photo (Fred and Kathryn Korematsu, 2000). Reprinted by permission of Laura Gómez.

Gott, Gil, *A Tale of New Precedents: Japanese American Internment as Foreign Affairs Law* (1999). Reprinted by permission of the Boston College Third World Law Journal/Boston College Law Review.

Hatamiya, Leslie T., RIGHTING A WRONG: JAPANESE AMERICANS AND THE PASSAGE OF THE CIVIL LIBERTIES ACT OF 1988 (1993). Reprinted by permission of Stanford University Press.

Hing, Bill Ong, MAKING AND REMAKING ASIAN AMERICA THROUGH IMMIGRATION POLICY, 1850-1990 (1993). Reprinted by permission of Stanford University Press.

Hirabayashi, Gordon, interview by Roger Daniels (1981). Reprinted by permission of Roger Daniels and the University of Washington Libraries.

Hirata, Mary, interview by Beth Kawahara (1998). Reprinted by permission of Densho: The Japanese American Legacy Project.

Hong, Joseph, *Racism Still on the Law Books*, Asian Week (2001). Reprinted by permission of Asian Week.

Hoshida, George, drawing, Looking at Center Picnic March 25, 1945, 1:15 p.m., 97.106.2EU (1945). Reprinted as a gift of June Hoshida Honma, Sandra Hoshida and Carole Hoshida Kanada, Japanese American National Museum.

Hosokawa, Bill, NISEI: THE QUIET AMERICANS (1969). Reprinted by permission of the University Press of Colorado.

Huie, Chris K.D., photos (various press conferences, 1983). Reprinted by permission of Chris K.D. Huie and courtesy of Donald Tamaki.

Iijima, Chris K., *Reparations and the "Model Minority" Ideology of Acquiescence: The Necessity to Refuse the Return to Original Humiliation* (1999). Reprinted by permission of the Boston College Third World Law Journal/Boston College Law Review.

Iritani, Frank and Joanne Iritani, map from ASIAN AMERICAN CURRICULUM PROJECT (1995). Reprinted by permission of Frank and Joanne Iritani.

Irons, Peter, JUSTICE DELAYED: THE RECORDS OF THE JAPANESE AMERICAN INTERNMENT CASES (1989). Reprinted by permission of the University Press of New England.

Irons, Peter, *Fancy Dancing in the Marble Palace* (1986). Reprinted by permission of the University of Minnesota Law School.

Irons, Peter, JUSTICE AT WAR: THE STORY OF THE JAPANESE AMERICAN INTERNMENT CASES (1983). Reprinted by permission of Oxford University Press, Inc.

Iwanaga, Leigh, photo (Fred Korematsu chatting with students, 1999). Reprinted by permission of Leigh Iwanaga.

Johnson, Julie, *President Signs Law to Redress Wartime Wrong*, (1988). Reprinted by permission of the New York Times.

Kim, Hyung-chan, ASIAN AMERICANS AND THE SUPREME COURT: A DOCUMENTARY HISTORY (1992). Reprinted by permission of Greenwood Press.

Korematsu family, photo (Korematsu family, 1940). Reprinted by permission of Fred Korematsu and courtesy of Donald Tamaki.

La Franiere, Sharon and George Larner, *U.S. Set to Photograph, Fingerprint All New Iraqi and Kuwaiti Visitors: Unusual Move Taken to Try to Counter Possible Terrorist Attacks* (1991). Reprinted by permission of The Washington Post.

Lange, Dorothea, photos ("Pledge of Allegiance," "Grandfather and Grandchildren," 1942), War Relocation Authority.

Law, Vincent, *Chinagate and Chinagoats* (1999). Reprinted by permission of about.com.

Lee, Russell, photo (Los Angeles, CA, 1942), Farm Security Administration.

Lin, Sam Chu, *Stanford Experts Criticize Cox Report, China Probe* (1999). Reprinted by permission of the Rafu Shimpo.

Little, Cheryl, *InterGroup Coalitions and Immigration Politics: The Haitian Experience in Florida* (1999). Reprinted by permission of the University of Miami Law Review.

Lopez, Frank, poster (Of Civil Wrongs and Rights, 2000). Reprinted by permission of Frank Lopez.

Lopez, Jose, photo (President Reagan signing reparations bill, 1988). Reprinted by permission of the New York Times.

Matsuoka, Kay, interview by Alice Ito (1999). Reprinted by permission of Densho: The Japanese American Legacy Project.

Matsuda, Mari J., *Foreword: McCarthyism, the Internment and the Contradictions of Power* (1998). Reprinted by permission of Mari J. Matsuda.

Matsuda, Mari J., *Looking to the Bottom: Critical Legal Studies and Reparations* (1987). Reprinted by permission of Mari J. Matsuda.

Matsumoto, Valerie J., FARMING THE HOME PLACE: A JAPANESE AMERICAN COMMUNITY IN CALIFORNIA, 1919-1982 (1993). Reprinted by permission of Cornell University Press.

McLemore, Henry, quote in the San Francisco Examiner (1942). Reprinted by permission of the San Francisco Examiner.

Mesler, Bill, *The Spy Who Wasn't* (1999). Reprinted by permission of The Nation.

Minami, Dale, memorandum to legal team (1983), handwritten notes of oral argument (1983), letter to Peggy Nagae (1984) and e-mail message to Margaret Chon (2001). Reprinted by permission of Dale Minami.

Minow, Martha, BETWEEN VENGEANCE AND FORGIVENESS: FACING HISTORY AFTER GENOCIDE AND MASS VIOLENCE (1998). Reprinted by permission of Martha Minow.

Miyatake, Henry, interview by Tom Ikeda (1999). Reprinted by permission of Densho: The Japanese American Legacy Project.

Mulhousen, Russ, photo (Fred Korematsu, Lorraine Bannai and Peter Irons, 1997). Reprinted by permission of Seattle University School of Law.

Museum of History & Industry, Seattle Post-Intelligencer Collection photos (Bainbridge Island evacuation, 1942). Reprinted by permission of the Museum of History & Industry and the Seattle Post-Intelligencer.

Myer, Dillon S., UPROOTED AMERICANS; THE JAPANESE AMERICANS AND THE WAR RELOCATION AUTHORITY DURING WORLD WAR II (1971). Reprinted by permission of the University of Arizona Press.

Nagae, Peggy, e-mail message to Margaret Chon (2001). Reprinted by permission of Peggy Nagae.

Nakano, Mei T., JAPANESE AMERICAN WOMEN: THREE GENERATIONS, 1890-1990 (1990). Reprinted by permission of Mina Press.

New York Times, Justice Black, *Champion of Civil Liberties for 34 Years on the Court, Dies at 85* (1971). Reprinted by permission of the New York Times.

Oh, Angela E., *Spy Charges Fueled Search for Scapegoats* (1999). Reprinted by permission of the Los Angeles Times Syndicate.

Oh, Reggie and Frank Wu, Essay, *The Evolution of Race in the Law: The Supreme Court Moves From Approving Internment of Japanese Americans to Disapproving Affirmative Action for Asian Americans* (1996). Reprinted by permission of the Michigan Journal of Race and Law.

Peretz, Martin, *Cambridge Diarist: Siege Mentality* (1998). Reprinted by permission of The New Republic.

Peterson, William, *Success Story, Japanese American Style* (1966). Reprinted by permission of the New York Times Magazine.

Rehnquist, William H., ALL THE LAWS BUT ONE: CIVIL LIBERTIES IN WARTIME (1998). Reprinted by permission of Random House/Knopf.

Risen, James, *Fund-Raising Figure Had Spy Case Role* (1999). Reprinted by permission of the New York Times.

Rooney, Andy, *Who Can Figure Out the Inscrutable Chinese* (1999). Reprinted by permission of Tribune Media Services.

Saito, Natsu Taylor, *Justice Held Hostage: U.S. Disregard for International Law in the World War II Internment of Japanese Peruvians-A Case Study* (1999). Reprinted by permission of Natsu Taylor Saito and the Boston College Third World Law Journal/Boston College Law Review.

Saito, Natsu Taylor, *Model Minority, Yellow Peril: Functions of "Foreignness" in the Construction of Asian American Legal Identity* (1997). Reprinted by permission of Natsu Taylor Saito.

Salyer, Lucy E., Laws Harsh As Tigers: Chinese Immigrants and the Shaping of Modern Immigration Law (1995). Reprinted by permission of University of North Carolina Press.

Sasaki, May, interview by Lori Hoshino (1997). Reprinted by permission of Densho: The Japanese American Legacy Project.

Shan, Jun, *Asian Americans Victimized?* (1999). Reprinted by permission of about.com.

Stewart, Francis, photo (Thaws at this Tule Lake Center, 1943), War Relocation Authority.

Ting, Jan C., *Other Than a Chinaman: How U.S. Immigration Law Resulted from and Still Reflects a Policy of Excluding and Restricting Asian Immigration* (1995). Reprinted by permission of the Temple Political and Civil Rights Law Review.

United States Commission on Wartime Relocation and Internment of Civilians. Personal Justice Denied: Report of the Commission on Wartime Relocation and Internment of Civilians (1997). Reprinted by permission of the Civil Liberties Public Education Fund and the University of Washington Press.

Wu, Frank H., *Spying Case Shouldn't Lead to Racial Stereotyping*, (1999). Reprinted by permission of the Sun-Sentinel.

Yamamoto, Eric K., *Racial Reparations: Japanese American Redress and African American Claims* (1999). Reprinted by permission of Eric K. Yamamoto.

Yamamoto, Eric K., *Race Apologies* (1997). Reprinted by permission of Eric K. Yamamoto.

Yamamoto, Eric K., *Friend, Foe or Something Else: Social Meanings of Redress and Reparations* (1993). Reprinted by permission of Eric K. Yamamoto.

Yamamoto, Eric K., *Efficiency's Threat to the Value of Accessible Courts for Minorities* (1990). Reprinted by permission of Eric K. Yamamoto.

Yamamoto, Eric K., Korematsu *Revisited: Correcting the Injustice of Extraordinary Government Excess and Lax Judicial Review—Time for a Better Accommodation of National Security Concerns and Civil Liberties* (1986). Reprinted by permission of Eric K. Yamamoto.

Yasui, Minoru, letter to Dale Minami (1984). Reprinted by permission of the family of Minoru Yasui.

Yen, Alfred C., *Introduction: The Importance of* Korematsu *Studies* (1999).

Young, Brigadier Peter, (ed.), The World Almanac of World War II: The Complete and Comprehensive Documentary of World War II (1992). Reprinted by permission of Primedia Reference Inc.

Finally, we are deeply grateful to the Civil Liberties Public Education Fund (CLPEF), whose generous funding made possible this inaugural book on law and the Japanese American internment. Any use of this book should acknowledge the CLPEF.

Of course, any errors are our own.

RACE, RIGHTS AND REPARATION
Law and the Japanese American Internment

Part I: Context

George Hoshida, Looking at Center Picnic (pen and ink drawing of Gila River internment camp), courtesy of the Japanese American National Museum.

Chapter 1 **RACE, RIGHTS AND REPARATION: AN OVERVIEW**

The legal machinations leading to the internment of 120,000 Japanese American citizens and legal permanent residents during World War II are much more than just unfortunate events affecting a small ethnic group within the United States. They implicate both the best and the most dangerous aspects of the American legal process for all Americans—the promise of equality and the precariousness of liberty in times of national stress. As legal scholar Mari Matsuda notes, "[t]he lens of the internment is exactly what we need to illuminate grand themes, connections, and a deep understanding of American consciousness," not only Japanese American or even Asian American consciousness. *All* Americans have a stake in understanding how and why the internment happened.

The U.S. Supreme Court decisions in the internment cases, and the 1980s' petitions for writ of error *coram nobis* ("in our presence"; petitions to obtain relief from a convicting court, based on errors of fact) reopening those same cases, are two sides of the same coin. The former upheld the Japanese American curfew and incarceration; the latter found that those original decisions were "manifestly unjust" because they were based on a factual record deliberately fabricated in key parts by high U.S. government officials and lawyers. The internment cases thus can be studied in two distinctly different ways. We could examine them as an isolated and perhaps even anachronistic set of judicial decisions impacting a minority group in some increasingly distant past, notable only for their still-cited technical legal rules (*e.g.*, "strict scrutiny" of racial classifications). Instead, we urge using these decisions as vehicles to address the law of the internment and redress through the following questions: What is race and when should it matter? Who benefits from constitutional safeguards: citizens or aliens, neither or both? How should we accommodate the tension between national security interests and the protection of personal freedom and the mandate of equality under the law? What roles do apologies and reparations play in rectifying historical injustice? Succinctly put, the Japanese American internment and redress raise issues that lie at the core of some of our most heated contemporary social justice debates.

Before proceeding, we want to identify our vantage point. We believe the internment was wrong. But we do not expect readers simply to accept our assessment. The cases, original documents, and commentary and questions presented throughout this book encourage readers to inquire critically and draw their own conclusions. For instance, we ask the reader to evaluate whether there are internal inconsistencies in the opinions, and to what extent inappropriate political considerations may have weighed in the justices' decisions. Like the U.S. Supreme Court itself fifty years later, we are critical of the Court's wartime decisions. We believe, however, that the judicial process in these cases ought not to be dismissed quickly as racist, if for no other reason than because to do so implies that the same thing could not happen again in our more "enlightened" world. To the contrary, the difficult questions raised by the cases about racial justice, national security and the equal protection of the laws are alive today and warrant careful attention.

Presented throughout this book are detailed primary source materials in the form of legal documents such as cases, briefs, evidence, and memoranda.

The centerpiece is the quartet of legal challenges to the military orders that resulted in the prolonged detention of an American minority group without individual charges or trial. Legal materials bearing the names of individuals engaging in acts of civil disobedience and legal resistance—Endo, Hirabayashi, Korematsu and Yasui—illuminate the history and politics of the moment.

And the converse is also true: historical, political and sociological context clarifies why lawyers and judges acted as they did at crucial junctures in the legal processes. Lawyers operate within a rhetorical framework that allows them only a limited set of arguments and that generally does not allow them to refer to external factors or to theoretical models. Some of these explanatory models—the best of which are as rigorous as legal doctrine—require that readers of judicial opinions (and lawyers practicing with such precedent) delve further than face value into the mechanics of legal decision-making. These twin interpretive processes—examining law's effect on politics as well as the political dimensions of law—are central to the necessarily complex discussions of the internment and redress and, just as important, their implications and lessons for other Americans.

These materials span over one hundred years—beginning with the legal response to the arrival of immigrants from Asia to America in the 19th century and ending with the recent federal prosecution of a Chinese American scientist for national security violations in the early 21st century. While the time frame covered by this book is broad, what emerges consistently throughout each of the chapters are questions about *race, rights and reparation*. We focus on each of these three themes here briefly. In so doing, we incorporate some theoretical models borrowed from legal scholars, legal historians, sociologists and political scientists, among others.

A. RACE

What part did legalized racial discrimination play in the internment of 120,000 Japanese Americans during World War II? To answer this question, we consider in more detail what we mean by the terms "race" and "racism," especially as they operated and still function in the American legal system.

Courts seldom define the term "race," despite the unfortunate fact that it is a highly relevant legal concept. Indeed, current views of race are a complex accumulation of natural scientific (what we term "biological race"), social scientific ("cultural race"), popular and other understandings of race. The exact mix of these components has always been in flux.

1. FROM BIOLOGICAL RACE TO CULTURAL RACE

That our nation was founded on a premise of racial difference and hierarchy is evidenced in the early writings of Thomas Jefferson, who posited a natural and inevitable difference between White Americans and their slaves:

> the real distinctions which nature has made; and many other circumstances, will divide us into parties, and produce convulsions which will probably

never end but in the extermination of one or the other race. To these objections, which are political, may be added others which are physical and moral.
The first difference which strikes us is that of color. . . . I advance it therefore
as a suspicion only, that the blacks, whether originally a distinct race or made
distinct by time and circumstances, are inferior to whites in the endowments
of both body and mind.

Thomas Jefferson, *Notes on the State of Virginia, Query XIV* (1787), *quoted
in* Juan F. Perea, Richard Delgado, Angela P. Harris & Stephanie Wildman,
RACE AND RACES: CASES AND RESOURCES FOR A DIVERSE AMERICA 100, 101
(2000).

Beginning in the mid-18th century, European scientists such as Johann
Friedrich Blumenbach began to categorize people into types, mimicking the
method that Carolus Linnaeus used to organize the plant world into different
species. By the mid-19th century, during the peak of European imperialism
and American slavery, race was based heavily on this method of cataloguing
physical differences among groups of people. The predominant view was
similar to Jefferson's: that race was a biological given and, importantly, predetermined one's "natural" place in a racial hierarchy. Biology-based differences were linked to differing mental capabilities and levels of cultural
achievements. Significantly, "scientific" groupings of people were used to
justify social pecking orders in which some groups were superior to or more
deserving than other groups.

Related to this was the idea that certain groups were so discrete that they
could, would or should not assimilate with other groups. As will be seen in
Chapter 2, in the so-called Chinese Exclusion Case, 130 U.S. 581 (1889), the
U.S. Supreme Court complained of "foreigners of a different race in this country, who will not assimilate with us." Thus, by the late 1800s, physical differences (as well as differences of national origin—a factor that will be discussed
later) between White Americans and other Americans functioned as markers
for the inevitability of inferiority and separateness. This strand of racial
thinking persists today under the rubric of "scientific racism." Challenges to
laws based on racial difference, while occasionally successful, had to overcome the prevailing world view that social difference based on racial difference was natural and, more important, fixed by biology.

Judges of the time did not distinguish much, if at all, between biology and
society or biology and culture. As seen by the above quotation, for example,
the Court did not inquire into the social barriers to assimilation by Chinese
immigrants. Nor was the Court later able to accept that a Japanese immigrant who had deliberately assimilated himself into White American culture
(by speaking English, etc.) could be thought of as "White," therefore fulfilling
the racial requirement for naturalization. Immigrants from Asia were
thought to be physically different from and hence culturally unassimilable to
European immigrants—and that was that. The legal system reinforced the
idea that race was the extrapolation of physical differences to seemingly
"natural" cultural traits and social hierarchies.

By the early 20th century, this determinate view of race had been challenged if not completely discredited by social scientists such as Franz Boas,
who argued that culture rather than biology best explained human difference.

The scientific project of identifying unchanging, mutually exclusive racial categories ultimately faltered due to internal illogic. As legal historian Peggy Pascoe points out, "culturalists delighted in pointing out the discrepancies between them, showing that scientific racists could not agree on such seemingly simple matters as how many races there were or what criteria—blood, skin color, hair type—best indicated race." Legal cases testing the meaning of "White" in various federal and state laws highlighted the absurdities of scientific racial classification (such as questions over whether dark-skinned Aryans such as South Asians were "White") and questioned the obvious racism embodied in biological race. Nonetheless, the concept of cultural race was not a complete panacea to the negative treatment of racial minorities.

The wartime internment cases discussed in Chapter 3 and revisited in Chapter 5 represent the complexities and contradictions of this ideological transition from the 19th century toward modern views of race. In these decisions, the U.S. Supreme Court by its words but not its actions rejected race-based legal classifications harmful to racial minorities, a conceptual aspect of these internment opinions that is a cornerstone of modern American civil rights law. Yet its failure adequately to ground its decisions upholding the curfew and internment in hard evidence of actual disloyalty meant that, in effect, Japanese Americans *were* "guilty" of disloyalty as a group. The Court accepted the premise that certain cultural characteristics of Japanese Americans allegedly predisposed them to espionage. Thus biology and cultural propensity were still rolled into one self-evident whole.

These uneven shifts in racial ideology can be seen too in legal arguments by lawyers involved in the internment cases. For example, the government's brief in *United States v. Hirabayashi*, 321 U.S. 81 (1943), noted the prevalence of legal and social discrimination against the Japanese in America, thus shifting the focus away from innate physical characteristics to structural reasons for their group identity. Nevertheless, the government then alleged that these *social* reasons were also evidence of the group's lack of loyalty. In their *amicus curiae* (friend of the court) brief, the Japanese American Citizen's League (JACL) pointed out that if past discrimination against a group is evidence of possible group disloyalty, then every despised immigrant group would be a national security risk. The JACL brief was a "Brandeis" brief, marshaling not only legal arguments but also social science evidence against the notion of separate races. The brief was over one hundred pages long; the table of citations alone was seven pages long. Only eleven cases were cited; the rest of the materials were various scientific and newspaper articles. However, while the Court may have rejected biological race as a basis for permissible government action, it ultimately accepted the government's conclusion of disloyalty, noting that the discrimination against the Japanese Americans had only "intensified their solidarity."

Law is itself a cultural process that both reflects and reinforces the racial categories defined initially outside of law. To the extent that the internment decisions are explicitly based on racial stereotyping, they are based on assumptions that most now see as undesirable and even unacceptable. However, in a powerful and reflexive dynamic, these internment decisions as well as other legal acts *contributed* to these stereotypes and assumptions.

2. ASIAN AMERICAN "RACIAL" DIFFERENCE

Since the mid-1800s, biological and cultural rationales for Asian American racial difference perpetuated a "forever foreign" image of Asians. As Asian Americanist historian Sucheng Chan states, the people of China were "nothing more than starving masses, beasts of burden, depraved heathens and opium addicts." Ronald Takaki, another historian, documents how

> [the] Chinese migrants found that racial qualities previously assigned to blacks quickly become "Chinese" characteristics. . . . White workers referred to the Chinese as "nagurs," and a magazine cartoon depicted the Chinese as a bloodsucking vampire with slanted eyes, a pigtail, dark skin, and thick lips. Like blacks, the Chinese were described as heathen, morally inferior, savage, childlike, and lustful. Chinese women were condemned as a "depraved class," and their depravity was associated with their physical appearance, which seemed to show "but a slight removal from the African race."

Ronald Takaki, STRANGERS FROM A DIFFERENT SHORE: A HISTORY OF ASIAN AMERICANS 101 (1989). Historian K. Scott Wong describes the "racial antipathy towards the Chinese, who were considered immoral and unclean, biologically inferior, and perhaps most important, unassimilable."

Each of these Asian Americanists has documented the importance of law in constructing and reinforcing Asian American inferiority. As Chapter 2 details, legal decisions involving Asian Americans were permeated from the very beginning with associations of outsiderness. The first racial bars to immigration were directed at Chinese and later Japanese immigrants. Significantly, these legal restrictions were justified by protean forms of national security arguments: inherent in sovereign power is the power to exclude potentially dangerous hordes of aliens at the border. (Some of these federal acts also included restrictions on admissible evidence, stemming from "loose notions" of truth supposedly held by Asian witnesses.) Even the right of Asian Americans to U.S. citizenship by birth after the ratification of the fourteenth amendment was questioned. Until legislation was passed in the 1940s and '50s, Asian Americans were not legally allowed to become naturalized citizens. Thus the early political status of Asian immigrants in America was marked by their exclusion from the realms of permanent residence, not to mention citizenship.

On the state and local levels, legalized discrimination against Asian Americans, especially in the Western states, contributed heavily to their political, economic and social exclusion. Early Chinese immigrants from the 1850s to 1900 were subjected to discriminatory legislation of all sorts: immigration taxes, occupational taxes, the so-called lodging house law and basket law and a host of other local regulations such as the laundry ordinance challenged successfully in *Yick Wo v. Hopkins,* discussed in Chapter 2. The 1879 California constitutional amendments included an explicit provision forbidding corporations to employ Chinese immigrants. Many historians have noted that the claims made about Asian immigrant unassimilability were rooted in popular fears of unfair competition (the flip side of the current model minority stereotype, discussed in Chapter 4). Some of the local restrictions on employment and ownership of property were based on citizenship status: For example, those who were ineligible for citizenship were subject to a higher miner's tax than White non-citizens who could naturalize. Combined, these laws had a powerful symbolic as well as material effect. They served to buttress the social understanding that Asian immigrants were not legitimate members of the social compact.

Asian immigrants initially resisted the process of being consolidated into a racial category of "yellow," "Asiatic," "Oriental" or (the typically preferred term now) "Asian American." Historian K. Scott Wong documents attempts by early educated Chinese immigrants to refute the damaging images of Chinese that circulated widely in print media, via articles printed in many of the same periodicals that published anti-Chinese tracts. And, later, Japanese immigrants tried to differentiate themselves from the earlier Chinese immigrants. However, these early attempts at what Professor Yen Espiritu has called "ethnic disidentification" did not succeed. For the most part, the early negative reaction by White Americans against Chinese immigrants was repeated against later Japanese, Korean, Filipino and South Asian immigrants. Assumptions were consistently made about the unassimilability and undesirability of all Asian immigrants. Thus, the xenophobic reasoning of the Chinese Exclusion Case (Asians as essentially unassimilable, foreign and sneaky) is echoed in the later internment cases, detailed in Chapter 3.

Overtly racist views about Japanese Americans during World War II must be linked to a powerful social process in which Americans from Asia were (and some say continue to be) regarded as not part of the national body. Justice Murphy's concurrence in *Hirabayashi, supra,* even noted

> the melancholy resemblance to the treatment accorded to members of the Jewish race in Germany and in other parts of Europe. The result is the creation in this country of two classes of citizens for the purposes of a critical and perilous hour—to sanction discrimination between groups of United States citizens on the basis of ancestry. In my opinion this goes to the brink of constitutional power. . . .

Arguably, the view of Germans or Italians as basically assimilable to the overall White American national paradigm (despite language and other cultural differences) mitigated what could have been similarly harsh treatment of these other American ethnic groups.

3. RACE: REPUDIATION OR REPETITION?

Just after the end of World War II, courts began consistently to reject the racist assumptions underlying biological race. As discussed in Chapter 4, civil rights cases brought by Japanese Americans immediately following the internment period challenged state alien land laws and legal restrictions on occupations such as fishing. These local discriminatory regulations depended on the racial bar provided by the federal naturalization statute. Barely a quarter century after the U.S. Supreme Court first deemed alien land laws constitutional in *Terrace v. Thompson,* 263 U.S. 197 (1923), it questioned their continuing legitimacy in Oyama v. California, 332 U.S. 633 (1948).

Courts were eager to repudiate the scientific racism that had resulted in the theory of Aryan supremacy against which the United States purportedly had fought in Europe. By this time as well, the social science literature included such influential studies as Gunnar Myrdal's AN AMERICAN DILEMMA, which documented the enduring racial inequality in the United States. This underlying ideological shift made it possible for civil rights plaintiffs to construct careful and (more often than not) successful challenges to legalized school segregation, anti-miscegenation laws, segregated public accommodations and other forms of overt racial discrimination. Civil rights successes in the second half of the 20th century included the Japanese American movement in support of redress and reparations, covered in Chapters 5, 6 and 7. Thus, in the 1987 *coram nobis* case, which vacated Gordon Hirabayashi's wartime conviction, the Ninth Circuit Court of Appeals stated that "the information now in the public record constitutes objective and irrefutable proof of the racial bias that was the cornerstone of the internment orders." In so stating, the court considered the undisguised racial animosity of the military leaders responsible for the wartime orders. This judicial pronouncement could be read as an utter repudiation of any remnant of biological racial thinking that might endorse white supremacy.

But if the courts swung away from legally endorsed scientific racism, what exactly have they swung toward? Race continues to pose a dilemma in judicial decision-making today, for racism and racial discrimination against minorities still exist, even if not in overt *de jure* forms. As well, there is an ongoing debate over the legality of remedies for past discrimination, such as affirmative action or attention to racial disparities in the criminal justice system. Modern thinking rejects the older views of race (present today in marginalized factions such as white supremacy groups or more respectable studies of IQ differences) as condemnable bigotry, but it still tolerates a wide range of activity that affects or defines race.

In the legal world, the majority of the current Supreme Court has endorsed a view of race that is often characterized as "color-blind," in reference to Justice Harlan's famous dissent in *Plessy v. Ferguson*, 163 U.S. 537 (1896). Under this color-blind view of race, it matters not whether race is biological, environmental, social, cultural or white supremacist, to name just a few of the possibilities. It could be all or none of the above. Rather, as legal historian Peggy Pascoe has noted, the significance of race has been "winnowed down to the single, powerfully persuasive belief that the eradication of racism depends on the deliberate non-recognition of race"—a philosophy that holds sway in both liberal and neoconservative forms today. In its most extreme manifestation, this color-blind view of race makes any racial classification legally suspect regardless of its actual social significance. This view of race is based on an assumption that racism consists of openly hateful dominative acts, easily identified and censured.

Rather than defining "racism" as an aberrant, irrational prejudice, much of the scholarly literature about race today documents more subtle, pervasive forms. For example, an aversive racist is one who believes in white race superiority but is not actively engaged in promoting it. He or she may avoid the problem by avoiding people of color. A focus on structural rather than individual causes of racism leads to the theory of institutional racism, in which racial hierarchy is part of the dominant cultural symbolic matrix; ordinary people, rather than being consciously prejudiced, simply participate in the culture of racism through their everyday practices. Some legal scholars, drawing on the work of social cognition theorists, posit the widespread existence of unintentional, unconscious racism. As legal scholar Charles Lawrence stated, "[t]o the extent that this cultural belief system has influenced all of us, we are all racists. At the same time, most of us are unaware of our racism. We do not recognize the ways in which our cultural experience has influenced our beliefs about race or the occasions on which those beliefs affect our actions." These theories are based on the assumption that racial stereotyping is a form of cognitive categorization rather than motivated necessarily by animus. Nonetheless, these psychological categories, according to legal theorist Linda Krieger, "operate absent intent to favor or disfavor a particular social group . . . even though they may operate beyond the reach of decision-maker self-awareness." According to Lawrence, when not challenged, "they seem part of the individual's rational ordering of her perceptions of the world."

Without an ongoing and deep understanding of race and racism, legal scholar Sumi Cho argues that a premature process of racial redemption can occur in which overt white supremacy is denounced but its operation in other forms is permitted and even endorsed. That is, rather than repudiating racism, courts may repeat it in disguised forms. As suggested by the wartime *Hirabayashi* case, *supra,* the early concepts of cultural race could be used to advance regressive legal arguments and social policy. Since then, nonbiological theories of race continued to become more complex and contested. For example, Nathan Glazer and others have suggested that ethnicity, which included both culture and biological descent, is a more significant category of analysis than race. Under one judicial version of this theory, all ethnic groups would assimilate ultimately into "just one race here . . . American"—a view set forth by Supreme Court Justice Scalia in *Adarand Constructors v. Pena*, 515 U.S. 200 (1995).

Rhetorical and analytical moves "beyond race" are embraced by so-called neoconservative legal scholars. These scholars view law as neutral and objective. For them, civil rights justice has been achieved, and any remaining racial injustice is a natural outcome of group competition. They claim that present inequality is not the result of discrimination because society no longer discriminates against people of color. According to some neoconservatives, continuing socioeconomic disadvantage for some racial groups is a result of cultural group deficiencies. Modern popular views of Asian Americans often reflect this perspective. For example, Asians are sometimes seen not as victims of discrimination (the "Miss Saigon syndrome"), or even as a "better" racial minority group than others (the "model minority myth," discussed in Chapter 4).

By contrast, the liberal civil rights paradigm is characterized by the belief that racial justice has not been achieved yet, but that we are nonetheless progressing toward a "nonracist, egalitarian society." For liberals, racism is an intentional and irrational deviation from otherwise neutral power distributions. A liberal may see the individual racial animus underlying state ballot measures such as Proposition 187 in California, which attempted to deny public benefits to legal permanent residents. However, because of the liberal's focus on the individual, he or she will downplay or misunderstand why so many Asian Americans are aliens rather than citizens, and thus systematically barred from full political and economic participation in this nation. As with the neoconservative perspective, the liberal view of race and law treats law as neutral and objective. Although liberals will acknowledge the need for race-conscious remedies in the face of discrimination, they view racism as an anomaly and thus, like neoconservatives, see color-blindness as part of an enlightened world view. As Professor Gary Peller aptly described the liberal mindset, "[o]nce we remove prejudice, reason will take its place; once we remove discrimination, neutrality will take its place; and once we remove segregation, integration will take its place."

Since the 1980s and '90s, critical legal scholars have offered strong critiques of the ostensible objectivity and neutrality of law and the legal process. These theoretical schools have drawn upon insights of legal realism from the 1930s and '40s. The legal realists argued that law was not an autonomous, self-contained discipline, nor was it objective. Law could be best understood by examining what judges (and law clerks) actually did as much as by looking at what they said they were doing. Legal realists thus looked beyond traditional scientific explanations of law and legal process, beyond the logic of the doctrine and reasoning expressed in published opinions. The influence of the legal realists has been so far-reaching that one legal scholar has astutely remarked that "we're all realists now."

Proponents of critical legal studies (CLS) agree with the realist insight that traditional scientific methods of legal reasoning (applying relevant rules to the facts to achieve accurate, consistent and just results) do not produce determinate or necessarily objective outcomes. Institutional and political judgments sometimes play a heavy role. CLS therefore posits that law and the legal process are largely a function of hidden politics. In significant cases, judges (and clerks) actually are engaged in political decision-making under the guise of legal objectivity. CLS observed that for these reasons legal decision-making tends to serve the interests of those in power while maintaining systemic legitimacy through the impression of legal neutrality. The judicial recognition and enforcement of rights of minorities are thus often little more than a ruse by those in power. Moreover, legal rules and categories are indeterminate; that is to say, legal doctrine itself does not lead logically to a single conclusion in any given case. Legal interpretation is highly manipulable. Cultural and political factors, rather than the reasoning that is offered by courts, may better explain outcomes.

Although the liberal and CLS schools of thought share the common goal of eradicating inequality, critical race theory (CRT) sharply challenges both paradigms as inadequate to address systemic and institutionalized racial oppression. CRT examines racial justice in connection with race, law and social structure. It recognizes that race is a social construction that plays an essential part in structuring and representing the social world. And Asian American critical race scholars, such as Robert Chang, argue that "while all disempowered groups have suffered from exclusion and marginalization, Asian Americans have been subject to unique forms." While CRT draws upon many of CLS's conclusions about law's indeterminacy, it disagrees with the CLS disparaging of legal rights. For critical race theorists such as Patricia Williams, the assertion of legal rights is indispensable for the definition, community and identity of people of color.

Critical race theorists attempt to re-center the significance of race, in response to its displacement by previous assimilationist social theories such as ethnicity theories and the color-blind jurisprudence that has emerged from those theories. For example, critical sociologists Michael Omi and Howard Winant define the term "racial formation" as the social processes of creating, inhabiting or transforming racial categories. Rather than being a thing, race is a process: an "unstable and 'decentered' complex of social meanings constantly being transformed by political struggle." Critical race scholar Neil Gotanda has developed a nuanced vocabulary of race, coining the term "historical race" to denote the historical experiences of subordination of a particular minority group. Historical race would encompass the observation that Asian Americans are viewed as outsiders: the reverse presumption accorded to most White Americans, who are thought automatically to belong regardless of the length of their generational ties to the United States. The majority of the current Supreme Court, by contrast, has adopted what Gotanda has termed "formal race," which reflects only skin color and descent and is unconnected to social context, history, culture, ability, disadvantage, wealth or language.

Legal scholars such as Gotanda and Frank Wu argue that American citizens of Asian descent are still viewed as inherently racially different. As evidence, they point to the continuing policy debates over the correct parameters of Asian immigration and naturalization in the 1996 Immigration Reform Act, the campaign finance reform scandals of the late 1990s, in which Asian nationals were often conflated with Asian Americans, and by the selective prosecution of nuclear scientist Wen Ho Lee, discussed in Chapter 7. Other contemporary issues discussed in Chapter 7 test both the limits of the prevailing color-blind view of race, and the usefulness of critical perspectives, given the Japanese American experience and those of other racialized minority groups such as Haitians, Native Hawaiians and others.

4. RACE AND THE JUDICIAL ROLE IN NATIONAL SECURITY CASES

National security is an ill-defined concept with highly elastic limits. Government definitions tend to be self-justifying. The very phrase "national security" is used only occasionally, but other closely related terms such as "military necessity," "war powers," and presidential status as "Commander in Chief" also are used in arguing that judicial review of official actions should be relaxed. These arguments raise foundational issues about the relationship between the Constitution and the judiciary.

Although national security is often raised in the context of wartime powers (particularly of the executive branch), the power of the federal government to secure national borders is also evident in Congress's power over immigration. The Chinese Exclusion Case stated:

> To give security against foreign aggression . . . is the highest duty of every nation . . . whether from the foreign nation acting in its national character or from vast hordes of its people crowding in upon us. . . . The existence of war would render the necessity of the proceeding only more obvious and pressing. The same necessity, in a less pressing degree, may arise when war does not exist. . . . In both cases its determination is conclusive upon the judiciary.

Chae Chan Ping v. United States, infra.

These early cases established the government's right to exclude foreigners as a sovereign prerogative that could be exercised even in peacetime, and that was vested in the political branches of government. In *United States v. Wong Kim Ark,* 169 U.S. 649 (1898), which decided that Chinese Americans were eligible for birthright citizenship under the fourteenth amendment, the dissent pointed to the multiple loyalties of Chinese Americans and vigorously argued that the children of aliens were tainted by their parents' ephemeral allegiance to the United States.

During World War I, Charles Evan Hughes (at various times New York governor, U.S. Cabinet member, Supreme Court Chief Justice and presidential candidate) argued in a major speech that "the power to wage war is the power to wage war successfully"—later quoted by the *Hirabayashi* court. Hughes explained that the Constitution grants the federal government powers that "may all be construed so as to avoid making the constitution self-destructive, so as to preserve the rights of the citizen from unwarrantable attack, while assuring beyond all hazard the common defense and the perpetuity of our liberties. These rest upon the preservation of the nation. . . . It has been said that the Constitution marches," he continued, "[s]o, also, we have a *fighting* Constitution."

If we have not only a Constitution but a "*fighting* Constitution," then the judiciary is necessarily beset by arguments over the contours of its authority. In a system of checks and balances, where each government branch ensures that the other branches exercise their constitutional powers appropriately, claims of national security shift government authority toward the political branches and away from an independent judiciary. Such a shift may be appropriate in situations that require quick government responses to real threats to the government's security. In other situations, it may lead to horrendous violations of civil liberties, where the political branches respond to popular opinion or naked political pressure rather than to genuine security threats. National security rationales for government action thus evoke contradictory judicial responses: National security is a reason for deferring to political branches (and military authorities); it also is the reason for greater skepticism toward the legislative and executive branches.

Such separation of powers considerations underlie most government assertions of national security or military necessity. Those considerations are complicated significantly when the security or necessity restrictions target a discrete minority group. Constitutional support for the government's war power collides with other constitutional concerns over civil liberties and protecting society's minorities from undue discrimination. As Jacobus ten Broek, Edward N. Barnhart and Floyd W. Matson observed shortly after World War II, "had the question simply been the validity of a universally (*i.e.,* non-racially) applied curfew or of the evacuation of *all* persons from a limited area threatened even remotely by invasion—a basic constitutional issue of fact would still have to be decided, but it is doubtful that there would have been much question about the power of the military to impose the restriction." Race, however, clearly was central to the government's decision to intern citizens and aliens of Japanese descent. In later chapters, we offer a general framework for assessing government claims of national security as justification for restricting the civil liberties Americans value so highly, especially when a discrete minority group is the target of government action.

B. RIGHTS

How effective was the assertion of constitutional rights in the face of the internment? To answer this question, we turn now to a brief historical overview of the most relevant concepts and rights involved in challenging the internment. Its focus is on the Chinese and Japanese Americans, who were the earliest Asian American immigrants to wield legal rights.

1. CONSTITUTIONAL RIGHTS: APPLICABLE TO ALL?

The U.S. Constitution, particularly its Bill of Rights and the post-Civil War amendments, is replete with sources of legal rights. Less noticed is the fact that almost none of these provisions refer to "citizens" or "race." Most of these rights inhere to "people" or "persons," or sometimes to "the accused" or "the party." Typical in wording is the first amendment right of "*the people* peaceably to assemble, and to petition the Government for redress of grievances." Similarly, the fourth amendment guarantees "the right of *people* to be secure in their persons . . . against unreasonable searches or seizures." With a few exceptions, such as the privileges and immunities clause of the fourteenth amendment or fifteenth amendment right to vote, constitutional rights do not distinguish between the rights of citizens and those of non-citizens. Nor, with the exception of the fifteenth amendment right to vote, is the term "race" found.

Yet it is still an open question whether the juridical "person" to whom these rights attach includes non-citizens or non-Whites. Currently, for example, the fourth amendment rights of undocumented immigrants (who are mostly non-White) are contested, with the U.S. Supreme Court stating that "the people" refers to "a class of persons who are part of a national community or who have otherwise developed sufficient connection with this country to be considered part of that community." Historically, 19th century federal immigration laws barring entry or even re-entry to Chinese immigrants were based on the rationale that people outside the borders of the United States were not those to whom certain constitutional rights apply, even if they had been once physically within the United States. The rights of non-citizens today are still heavily influenced by a tremendous deference by the courts to Congress's virtually unbridled authority over immigration under what has come to be known as the plenary power doctrine. Thus, although the surface text of the Constitution appears to apply to all human beings equally, the sub-text is quite different. Certain classes of people did not and still may not enjoy the full panoply of rights that it guarantees.

Moreover, citizenship status and other types of political inclusion had and still have a racial cast. Although it was not addressed as a right within the Constitution until the passage of the fourteenth amendment, citizenship was an important precondition to other political rights such as voting or access to the courts. On the federal level, decisions such as *Dred Scott v. Sanford*, 60 U.S. (19 How.) 393 (1857), reaffirmed the lack of federal citizenship status of African Americans prior to the Civil War. As Chief Justice Roger Taney infamously intoned, "[t]he words 'people of the United States' and 'citizens' are synonymous terms and mean the same thing. The question before us is, whether the class of persons [who are descendants of slaves] compose a portion of this people. . .? We think they are not, and that they are not included, and were not intended to be included, under the word 'citizens' in the Constitution. . . ." Native Americans and many non-White Latinas/os were also excluded from national or state citizenship, either by treaty, congressional fiat or state laws. Beginning in 1790, a long-standing racial bar in the federal naturalization statute limited naturalization to "free White persons." After 1870, Congress extended naturalization to "aliens of African nativity, and to persons of African descent," but it did not completely eliminate the color bar until the passage of the McCarran-Walter Act in 1952.

On the state level, political and economic rights were often tied to citizenship status. Thus, as stated earlier, the California legislature successfully extracted a differential tax on Chinese miners by levying at a higher rate foreigners ineligible for citizenship. The first California constitution had an explicit "white male citizen" voting requirement, and the state's 1880 constitution stated that " [n]o native of China, no idiot, insane person, or person convicted of any infamous crime . . . shall ever exercise the privileges of an elector in this State." California was notable also for its ban forbidding testimony against Whites by a "black or mulatto person, or Indian"—a racial bar that was extended by courts to include Chinese.

At the heart of constitutional civil rights law are the rights enunciated within the due process clauses of the fifth and fourteenth amendments to the U.S. Constitution, as well as the equal protection clause of the fourteenth amendment.[*] Initially, the fourteenth amendment was passed to secure rights for newly freed slaves as part of a flurry of post-Civil War Reconstruction legal activity.[†] The amendment was intended to address in part the

---

[*] These so-called Reconstruction amendments are set forth in full at:
<www.law.ucla.edu/faculty/kang/racerightsreparation>.

[†] The thirteenth amendment was adopted in 1865, ending slavery; the fourteenth amendment, with its due process and equal protection clauses, was ratified in 1867; the fifteenth amendment followed in 1870, formally extending the vote to African American

"black codes" adopted by the former Confederate states to limit the freedom, opportunities and status of emancipated African Americans. It declares that the states may neither "deprive any person of life, liberty or property without due process of law; nor deny any person within its jurisdiction the equal protection of the laws."[*] (Similarly, the due process clause of the fifth amendment, applicable to discriminatory treatment by federal government, states: "[N]or shall any person . . . be deprived of life, liberty, or property, without due process of law.") Significantly, the equal protection clause of the fourteenth amendment has been interpreted by the Supreme Court (in a process known as "reverse incorporation") to limit *both* federal and state government action. And when it comes to asking about the ability of the government to act in the face of an established right, the due process and equal protection clauses have become indistinguishable, although at the time of the internment cases, the check provided by the equal protection clause to federal power was less definite.

The congressional debates over the adoption of the fourteenth amendment revealed primary concern for African Americans, although they also recognized discrimination against Chinese immigrants on the West Coast.[†] While legislators disagreed about the amendment's intended effect on racial segregation, most concurred that the amendment protected slaves' newly gained freedom. The early cases interpreting the fourteenth amendment, however, provided little protection for African Americans. In *The Slaughter-House Cases*, 83 U.S. 36 (1873), the Supreme Court rejected a challenge to a Louisiana statute creating a slaughter-house monopoly. In doing so, the Court narrowly construed the provision of the amendment requiring the states to respect the "privileges and immunities" of citizens of the United States. In its five-to-four majority decision, the Court declared that states rather than the federal government bore primary responsibility for civil rights, adding that it doubted "whether any action of the State . . . directed by way of discrimination against the negroes as a class, or on account of their race, will ever be held to come within the purview of this provision."[‡] One

---

males. Together with the 1866 and 1870 civil rights acts and Reconstruction statutes, the adoption of these constitutional amendments worked fundamental, although in some instances short-lived, changes in the legal system.

[*] In addition, the fourteen amendment decreed that "all persons born or naturalized in the United States" were "citizens of the United States and the state wherein they reside," and it prohibited states from "abridging the privileges or immunities of citizens of the United States."

[†] This concern was expressed during the debates on the fourteenth amendment, the Burlingame Treaty (granting China "most favored nation status") and the 1870 Civil Rights Act. Legal historian Charles McClain suggests that the impetus for this civil rights act emerged in part from meetings between Chinese immigrant leaders and political leaders. *See* Charles J. McClain, *The Chinese Struggle for Civil Rights in Nineteenth Century America*, 72 CAL. L. REV. 529 (1984); Charles J. McClain, IN SEARCH OF EQUALITY: THE CHINESE STRUGGLE AGAINST DISCRIMINATION IN NINETEENTH-CENTURY AMERICA (1994).

[‡] Although *The Slaughter-House Cases* concerned the privileges or immunities clause, not the equal protection clause, some scholars have argued that *The Slaughter-House Cases* created a two-tiered system of judicial review based on the quotation above. These scholars have reasoned that the Court could be understood as declaring that the fourteenth

eminent constitutional scholar, Charles Black, characterized *The Slaugh-ter-House Cases* as "probably the worst holding, in its effect on human rights, ever uttered by the Supreme Court." It effectively rendered the privileges and immunities clause of the fourteenth amendment a dead letter for civil rights litigation. This clause was probably already of limited value to Asian Americans at the time because it applied only to "citizens."

Even when the Court protected the civil rights of racial minorities immediately after the Civil War, it did so in limited fashion. Most devastating, the Court struck down the federal Civil Rights Act of 1875, which had forbidden racial segregation in places open to the public. In *The Civil Rights Cases*, 109 U.S. 3 (1883), the Court held the Act could only proscribe government acts (public conduct); it could not under the authority of the fourteenth amendment regulate actions of individuals or businesses (private conduct) even if those actions occurred in public places.

2. ANTIDISCRIMINATION PROVISIONS AND ASIAN AMERICANS

During the Reconstruction period, Chinese Americans (and, later, Japanese Americans) opposed racial subordination through their aggressive legal challenges to discriminatory laws. As documented in detail by legal historian Charles J. McClain, early cases challenged the validity of the California laws barring Chinese testimony against White Americans. The equal protection clause, newly ratified, was construed broadly by some trial courts to apply to all "persons," including non-citizens such as Chinese immigrants, and to include the equal right to testify in court. However, in *People v. Brady*, 40 Cal. 198 (1871), the first such case to reach the California Supreme Court, the court found that the racial bar on testimony did not violate equal protection, reasoning that a Chinese victim and a White American victim each had equal means of proving the crime: Neither could rely on testimony by Chinese witnesses and both could rely on testimony by White witnesses.

Other cases brought by Chinese plaintiffs continued to push the boundaries of the equal protection clause, and some of them were heard by Supreme Court Justice Stephen Field in his capacity as an occasional circuit judge for the Ninth Circuit. One was a challenge to an order detaining female Chinese immigrants, alleged prostitutes, pending receipt of a $500 bond. *In re Ah Fong*, 1 F. Cas. 213 (1874), was argued on the grounds both that the power to regulate immigration was an exclusively federal power and that the order violated the equal protection clause. In his circuit court opinion, Justice Field held that the federal power occupied the field of immigration, and that the equal protection clause prohibited "discriminating and partial legislation, favoring particular persons, or against particular persons of the same class." Thus he found that equal protection applied not only to citizens but also to non-citizens.

In another legal challenge involving the interpretation of the equal protection clause, this time involving a queue-cutting ordinance that was obvi-

---

amendment offered scant protection for economic interests, but better protection for newly freed slaves. *See, e.g.*, Geoffrey R. Stone et al., CONSTITUTIONAL LAW at 508–09 (3d ed. 1996).

ously aimed only at Chinese immigrants, Justice Field opined that "when we take our seats on the bench we are not struck with blindness, and forbidden to know as judges what we see as men; and where an ordinance, though general in its terms, only operates upon a special race, sect or class, it being universally understood that it is to be enforced only against that race, set or class, we may justly conclude that it was the intention of the body adopting it that it should only have such operation, and treat it accordingly." *How Ah Kow v. Nunan*, 12 F. Cas. 252 (C.C.D. CAL 1879). Again, he found that the equal protection clause applied not just to citizens, but prohibited "hostile and discriminating legislation by a state against persons of any class, sect, creed, or nation, in whatever form it may be expressed." Justice Field is notable as well for the Supreme Court majority opinion in the Chinese Exclusion Case, discussed in Chapter 2. Like some other jurists of the time, he possessed disparate views toward Asian Americans—sometimes viewing them as unwelcome outsiders, at other times extending to them the same rights extended to White Americans.

These and other lower court decisions laid the groundwork for the U.S. Supreme Court's *Yick Wo v. Hopkins* opinion, detailed in Chapter 2. Significantly, the laundry ordinance in *Yick Wo* was not facially discriminatory, but it was found to be unconstitutional as applied, because it affected almost solely Chinese laundry owners. *Yick Wo* stands for the proposition, applicable to the later internment cases, that race is a problematic basis for government action. The question that the Court did not answer explicitly is why.

Key to deciding discrimination suits under modern equal protection jurisprudence is the "standard of judicial review" that a court chooses to review the government action. As set forth in Chapter 3, Gordon Hirabayashi had claimed that the curfew and exclusion orders endorsed by Congress "unconstitutionally discriminated between citizens of Japanese ancestry and those of other ancestries," in violation of his fifth amendment due process rights. This could be interpreted as raising a substantive due process claim (*e.g.*, a liberty deprivation), a procedural due process claim (no charges or trial, in violation of his due process rights), and possibly an equal protection claim (discriminatory denial of rights). The Court, briefly noting in its opinion the textual difference between an equal protection and a due process claim, held that Hirabayashi had not proven a constitutional violation. In doing so, however, it implied a rule of heightened skepticism toward government rationales for racial classifications, later enunciated in fuller form in *Korematsu*. The Court itself and most constitutional commentators locate in the *Hirabayashi* and *Korematsu* internment cases the origins of the strict scrutiny model of equal protection, in which suspect classifications such as race are subject to the most searching review by courts, as opposed to simply a review for rationality. The Supreme Court's handling of this threshold question in the internment cases marks these cases as landmarks and forms the historical basis for much of the current body of antidiscrimination law, even as the Court found no constitutional violation at the time it announced those legal rules. The many ironies associated with these decisions are explored further in Chapter 3.

The little-known invocation of the equal protection clause by Asian Americans thus demonstrates its power and its limitations. Early successful challenges to discriminatory California laws show the broad potential of the equal protection clause to prevent abusive government power against minority groups. They ultimately established that "person" in the equal protection clause was to be read broadly to include non-citizens, and that distinctions based on race were not wholly acceptable. Yet as the California Supreme Court's *Brady, supra,* opinion reveals, this was hardly a foregone conclusion given the prevailing anti-Chinese sentiment and the then-applicable deferential standard of review. Moreover, these decisions took place in the larger context of a post-Reconstruction roll-back of rights for African Americans, including the infamous U.S. Supreme Court decision of *Plessy v. Ferguson,* 163 U.S. 537 (1896), which endorsed the separate-but-equal doctrine. The Supreme Court's later internment decisions illustrate the spectacular failure of equal protection and due process rights to protect Japanese Americans, citizen and non-citizen alike, against the government's discriminatory treatment.

These cases also constitute a cluster of social acts by which Asian Americans actively resisted the imposition of stigmatizing racial categories through their assertion of legal rights. This is exemplified in the internment era not only by the civil disobedience of individual litigants such as Fred Korematsu, but also by the sometimes contradictory actions of the JACL, the fledgling organization that had formed to advance the interests of the second generation (Nisei). Initially, the JACL advised people to comply with the evacuation orders, and opposed any test litigation of those orders. These could be seen as assimilationist decisions. Ultimately, the JACL filed *amicus curiae* briefs in support of both Gordon Hirabayashi and Fred Korematsu in the U.S. Supreme Court. The JACL's briefs are notable not only for their antagonism to the government's use of racial classifications, but also for urging the Court to repudiate the biological underpinnings of race.

Asian American challenges to discriminatory laws did not end with the internment cases. Just after the end of the Second World War, Japanese Americans litigated all the way up to the U.S. Supreme Court cases involving discriminatory land laws and occupational laws. In striking down these laws, the Court cited to principles of equal protection enunciated in *Hirabayashi* and *Korematsu,* decided just a few years earlier. They seemed to apply strict scrutiny review in the way that its label implies: reviewing government actions based on race with greater skepticism. The successful post-war assertion of economic rights was part of a general expansion of civil rights under the so-called Warren Court, including the landmark *Brown v. Board of Education,* 332 U.S. 631 (1954). Yet these cases followed right on the heels of the failed invocation of liberty and procedural due process rights in the face of wartime stresses. This uneven process of vindicating constitutional rights for minority groups brings into question whether the concept of "rights" is an illusory promise or a reliable panacea. As critical race scholar Mari Matsuda has asked:

> How could anyone believe both of the following statements?:
>
> > 1) I have a right to participate equally in society with any other person.

2) Rights are whatever people in power say they are.

One of the primary lessons [that can be] learn[ed] from the experience of the bottom is that one can believe in both of those statements simultaneously, and that it may well be necessary to do so.

Mari Matsuda, Looking to the Bottom: Critical Legal Studies and Reparations," 22 Harv. C.R.-C.L. L. Rev. 323 (1987).

In the 1980s, the lawyers who fought for reparations understood both the potential for progressive and regressive judicial interpretations of civil rights. They petitioned to vacate wartime convictions in the same trial courts that had convicted Gordon Hirabayashi, Fred Korematsu and Minoru Yasui forty years earlier. These legal teams knew that their success depended on the shifting of public opinion about equality—shifts that had occurred over time, in part as a result of the broader civil rights movement in the 1960s and public concern about rights for racial minorities, as well as public willingness to act upon that concern. And despite the judicial repudiation of the factual underpinnings of these cases, the legal precedents established retain landmark doctrinal status, as will be discussed below as well as in Chapters 5 and 7.

3. RIGHTS: ELIMINATING DISCRIMINATION?

It is worthwhile to ask the same question of antidiscrimination *rights* that was asked earlier with respect to *race*: Do the courts' interpretations reveal an ongoing narrative of increasing sophistication, a triumphant trajectory toward eliminating discrimination? Or are we witnessing a more ambiguous legacy of rights asserted by and on behalf of racial minorities?

Since World War II, the internment cases have had an unusual career. They have been condemned by virtually all observers, including the executive and legislative branches of the federal government. The Commission on Wartime Relocation and Internment of Civilians (CWRIC) stated the consensus view that "[t]oday the decision in *Korematsu* lies overruled in the court of history." CWRIC also concluded that while the case had not been overruled in a technical sense, for "[e]ach part of the decision, questions of both factual review and legal principles, ha[ve] been discredited or abandoned." Respected jurists such as D.C. Circuit judges Harry Edwards and Patricia Wald have stated that *Korematsu* could not be regarded as persuasive precedent. The latter has written that, "[c]ertain Supreme Court rulings are so distasteful to some lower court judges that they will ask for their excision in a colleague's opinion if there is another more acceptable precedent for the same general proposition," citing to *Korematsu* as one of only two examples "of such pariahs."

Yet recently the Supreme Court has begun an effort to reclaim the internment cases as legal authority. Although it recently acknowledged making a "mistake" in those cases, the Court rehabilitated the reasoning of the cases even as it rejected their outcomes. In its 1995 decision of *Adarand Constructors v. Pena*, *supra*, the Court presented its most detailed analysis of strict scrutiny mechanics since *Korematsu*. The central holding of *Adarand* is that strict scrutiny is to be applied to evaluate federal affirmative action programs.

It illustrates the wide divergence of views about race and rights held by the current justices of the Supreme Court.

In her majority opinion in the *Adarand* case, discussed in more detail in Chapter 7, Justice Sandra Day O'Connor discusses the internment cases at length. The main thrust of her opinion is that any person, of whatever race, has the right to demand that government actors justify, under the strictest judicial scrutiny, any racial classification subjecting that person to unequal treatment.   Justice Antonin Scalia's concurring opinion states that "[i]ndividuals who have been wronged by racial discrimination should be made whole; but under our Constitution there can be no such thing as either a creditor race or a debtor race . . . we are just one race here. It is American." Similarly, Justice Clarence Thomas concurred with the view that "Government cannot make us equal; it can only recognize, respect, and protect us as equal under the law." As the *Adarand* majority's use of *Hirabayashi* and *Korematsu* demonstrates, the equal protection clause in the early 21st century has become less of a shield for racial minorities and more of a sword for White Americans. Critical race scholar Eric Yamamoto has observed that interpretations such as those in *Adarand* allow neoconservative lawyers and activists to argue for equality and against racism while seeking to maintain social structures that subordinate racial minorities.

These judicial opinions conflict with the liberal civil rights vision of a steady societal march towards eliminating racial inequality. Justice John Paul Stevens's *Adarand* dissent notes that "there is no moral equivalence between a policy that is designed to perpetuate a caste system and one that seeks to eradicate racial subordination." And in her dissent, Justice Ruth Bader Ginsburg states that the United States "suffers from the lingering effects of racial discrimination . . . because, for most of our Nation's history, the idea that 'we are just one race,' was not embraced. For generations, our lawmakers and judges were unprepared to say that there is in this land no superior race, no race inferior to any other." Neither Stevens nor Ginsburg are ready to concede that racial equality has already been achieved.

In cases involving facially neutral laws (that is, ones that make no textual reference to race), the current Supreme Court requires a showing of discriminatory purpose rather than discriminatory impact. To explain how the equal protection clause has evolved over time to reinforce rather than dismantle racial status relations, legal scholar Reva Siegel posits a theory of "preservation through transformation." She argues that "[e]fforts to reform a status regime bring about changes in its rule structure and justificatory rhetoric," and points out that "[i]n the very same era that the Court adopted the highly deferential [discriminatory purpose framework], it began steadily to increase its scrutiny of affirmative action policies—recently subjecting such policies to strict scrutiny." The net effect is to leave untouched many facially neutral laws that have racially disparate impact—such as the death penalty and other sentencing laws. At the same time, laws and policies that attempt to remedy historical segregation against minorities, by specifically targeting minority groups for affirmative treatment, now trigger a heightened judicial review.

Noted by Justice Stevens in his *Adarand* dissent, the current Court has "equate[d] remedial preferences with invidious discrimination, and ignore[d] the difference between . . . a No Trespassing sign and a welcome mat." So while the courts have rejected outright assertions of white supremacy (as in rejecting the outcome of the internment cases), legal rules have evolved into "natural" rhetorical rationales for limiting the rights of minority groups (as in the use of the internment cases to justify the current rollback of remedial programs). As a group of Asian American law professors wrote, the *Adarand* Court was essentially reasoning that "because we interned the Japanese Americans, we cannot have affirmative action for African Americans." All told—the color-blind judicial philosophy, the formal race view of race and the formal symmetry that *all* racial classifications are subject to searching review—the dominant interpretative choices by the courts form a powerful barrier to the assertion of constitutional antidiscrimination rights by racial minority groups.

In an increasingly multiracial America, the assertion of rights by a particular minority group may have unexpected consequences for others. For example, the successful quest for redress by Japanese Americans has both negative as well as positive effects on other minority groups. As legal scholar Eric Yamamoto points out, the message of redress could be salutary, vindicating the liberal civil rights vision of a march toward increasing racial justice. But redress triumph for Japanese Americans could also mask the denial of similar remedies for other groups, such as African Americans who have suffered historical injury, implying that they are less deserving. Chapter 6 reviews some of the implications of redress for other U.S. racial minorities such as Japanese Latin Americans, African Americans and Native Hawaiians, as well as other people such as black South Africans.

Moreover, many legal scholars have pointed out that traditional paradigms of civil rights law contemplate only Black and White racial groups. Asian Americans are neither black nor white. Unlike African Americans, Asian Americans are often treated as foreigners and may be excluded from a vigorous application of equal protection doctrines. Doctrinally, one distinction drawn to the disadvantage of Asian Americans appears to be the permissible line between citizens and foreigners. Equal protection claims based on alienage status are reviewed under a deferential rational-basis standard of review—or, even more problematic, under Congress's plenary power to regulate immigration. Of course, part of the discriminatory treatment of Asian Americans traditionally has been the very assumption that they are foreigners. Moreover, Asian Americans who in fact are citizens are conceived of as foreigners. According to legal scholar Neil Gotanda, Asian American racial categorization causes citizenship to be nullified. Gotanda's thesis about the constricted rights of racialized immigrant groups could be extended to other "foreigners" such as Haitians, Arab Americans or Latinas/os. Chapter 7 examines issues pertinent to the Haitian interdiction program of the 1980s and the Arab American internment plan of the 1990s.

4. CONFLICT? CONSTITUTIONAL RIGHTS AND NATIONAL SECURITY

The internment cases presented a dilemma. As a society we value highly our constitutional rights and civil liberties. Those rights and liberties are enshrined in the amendments to the Constitution. Courts are ultimately responsible for assuring, among other constitutional rights, due process and equal protection of the laws. At the same time, the nation's security is essential to its social and political survival, and courts must take seriously government claims of "military necessity." How should the courts respond when the government asserts military necessity or national security as its justification for restricting the civil liberties of American citizens or legal permanent residents?

The Supreme Court has never announced a comprehensive theory of national security law, particularly as it affects civilian (*i.e.,* non-military) citizens. But a judicial approach to the civil liberties and national security dilemma can be inferred from the various cases addressing these issues. We address these cases, ranging from the Reconstruction-era case *Ex Parte Milligan*, 4 Wall. 2 (1866), to the Vietnam-era *Pentagon Papers* case, 403 U.S. 713 (1971), in Chapter 3, section B.2, *infra*.

It bears noting that in 1943, the Justice Department presented an extraordinarily selective evidentiary record in support of the constitutionality of the internment. More than forty years after these original trials, the Japanese American community sought reparations for the internment, including a judicial declaration that the wartime internment cases were wrongly decided. Three separate U.S. district courts vacated the original criminal convictions on writs of error *coram nobis*, in part on evidence that government lawyers deliberately misled the Court about the factual foundation for the claims of "military necessity." These cases are discussed in detail in Chapter 5.

Despite these recent judicial rulings, which undermine the factual foundation for the wartime decisions, courts continue to cite *Korematsu* and *Hirabayashi* as binding precedent in both equal protection cases (discussed above) as well as national security cases. While national security interests may be articulated differently in the post-Cold War era than they were during World War II, they are still offered as justifications for various government restrictions of civil liberties of citizens. The threat of terrorist attacks, for example, has been advanced as a justification for curtailing the civil liberties of Arab Americans, which are evaluated in Chapter 7. In deciding these politically charged controversies, the Court has struggled to define its role as the "non-political" branch of government.

C. REPARATION

What roles do apologies and other forms of redress play in rectifying historical injustice, such as the internment of Japanese Americans? The United States' apology to and reparations for interned Japanese Americans galvanized reparations movements in America and abroad. It also helped stimulate development of reparations theory—that is, the philosophical and strategic bases for government redress.

Reparations theory is at its early stages of development, hence the brevity of this section. The worldwide explosion of reparations efforts largely commenced in the late 1980s. One aspect of emerging reparations theory is highly conceptual: It draws upon law, political theory, social psychology, theology and community studies. A second aspect of developing reparations theory is practical: It describes conditions necessary for the achievement of group redress and guides redress movements through political and legal shoals. Part III of this book examines both types of reparations theory through the lens of the Japanese American redress movement. The Japanese Americans' quest for redress is relevant to other groups such as African Americans who seek reparations for past injury.

Chapters 5 and 6 examine both the theoretical and practical dimensions of apologies and reparations, as well as the range of possible government and societal responses. Chapter 5 explores in great detail the first of four types of possible government redress: judicial declaration of injustice. In the 1980s, petitions for writ of error *coram nobis* were filed in three separate federal courts. All three cases succeeded in obtaining the remedy requested: vacating the original convictions of the three individuals who violated the government's laws relating to internment. No money damages were requested, nor were the government's offers of pardon accepted.

Chapter 6 focuses on judicial awards of monetary damages—specifically, the Japanese American internees' class action lawsuit for monetary compensation as well as the federal courts' use of procedural rules to preclude adjudication on the merits. As both Chapters 5 and 6 indicate, the judicial branch of government plays a major role in reparations: indeed, one can view the usual remedy in a typical personal injury civil lawsuit as a form of reparation. In its broadest sense, *"reparation"* is defined as the making of amends for wrong or injury done, although we refer to the term here more specifically to mean reparations by government for harm that it has inflicted on individuals and discrete groups, including nonjudicial action.

Chapter 6 also covers very broadly governmental redress through executive and legislative action. It first reproduces President Ford's order rescinding Executive Order 9066 and President Bush's apology to Japanese American internees, and compares these forms of apology to President Clinton's recent apology to Native Hawaiians for the overthrow of their government. It then sketches the political backdrop for Japanese American reparations, including the Congressional Commission's inquiry and report on reparations, and reproduces key portions of the 1988 Civil Liberties Act. Finally, it examines the implications of nonjudicial forms of redress—including their effects on Japanese American internees and their simultaneous uplifting and unsettling potential for other groups suffering historical injustice. It inquires into the claims for reparations by Japanese Latin Americans, African Americans, Native Hawaiians, South Africans and Korean sex slaves. We thus conclude the chapter with the reparations theory that is currently emerging from worldwide redress efforts.

So, as queried at the beginning of each section on race, rights and reparation:

•   *What part did legalized racial discrimination play in the internment of 120,000 Japanese Americans during World War II?*

•   *How effective was the assertion of constitutional rights in the face of the federal government's internment decisions?*

•   *What roles do apologies and other forms of redress play in rectifying historical injustice, such as the internment of Japanese Americans?*

As you delve into the following chapters, consider with care the possible answers. In short, we invite readers to join in the challenge of unraveling the many complexities of the Japanese American internment and redress cases.

D. ADDITIONAL READINGS

BOOKS

Angelo Ancheta, RACE, RIGHTS, AND THE ASIAN AMERICAN EXPERIENCE (1998).

Derrick A. Bell, Jr., RACE, RACISM AND AMERICAN LAW (1992).

Charles L. Black, Jr., A NEW BIRTH OF FREEDOM: HUMAN RIGHTS, NAME AND UNNAMED (1998).

Sucheng Chan, ASIAN AMERICANS: AN INTERPRETIVE HISTORY (1991).

ASIAN AMERICANS AND POLITICS: PERSPECTIVES, EXPERIENCES, PROSPECTS (Gordon H. Chang ed., 2001).

Robert S. Chang, DISORIENTED: ASIAN AMERICANS, LAW, AND THE NATION-STATE (1999).

Gabriel J. Chin, Sumi K. Cho, Jerry Kang and Frank H. Wu, BEYOND SELF-INTEREST: ASIAN AMERICANS TOWARD A COMMUNITY OF JUSTICE (1996).

Introduction *in* CRITICAL RACE THEORY: THE KEY WRITINGS THAT FORMED THE MOVEMENT (Kimberlé Crenshaw et al. eds., 1995).

JAPANESE AMERICANS: FROM RELOCATION TO REDRESS (Roger Daniels et al. eds., c.1986, 1991).

Roger Daniels, AMERICAN CONCENTRATION CAMPS: A DOCUMENTARY HISTORY OF THE RELOCATION AND INCARCERATION OF JAPANESE AMERICANS, 1942-1945 (1989).

Roger Daniels, ASIAN AMERICA: CHINESE AND JAPANESE IN THE UNITED STATES SINCE 1850 (1988).

Roger Daniels, CONCENTRATION CAMPS, NORTH AMERICA: JAPANESE IN THE UNITED STATES AND CANADA DURING WORLD WAR II (1981).

Roger Daniels, THE DECISION TO RELOCATE THE JAPANESE AMERICANS, (1975, 1986).

Roger Daniels, CONCENTRATION CAMPS USA: JAPANESE AMERICANS AND WORLD WAR II (1972).

Roger Daniels, PRISONERS WITHOUT TRIAL: JAPANESE AMERICANS IN WORLD WAR II, (1993).

CRITICAL RACE THEORY: THE CUTTING EDGE (Richard Delgado ed., 1995).

Yen Le Espiritu, ASIAN AMERICAN PANETHNICITY: BRIDGING INSTITUTIONS AND IDENTITIES (1992).

Bill Ong Hing, MAKING AND REMAKING ASIAN AMERICA THROUGH IMMIGRATION POLICY, 1850-1990 (1993).

ONLY WHAT WE COULD CARRY: THE JAPANESE AMERICAN INTERNMENT EXPERIENCE (Lawson Fusao Inada ed., 2000).

Peter Irons, JUSTICE DELAYED: THE RECORD OF THE JAPANESE AMERICANS INTERNMENT CASES (1989).

Peter Irons, JAPANESE AMERICANS: EVACUATION AND RELOCATION 1942-1945 (1983).

A LEGAL HISTORY OF ASIAN AMERICANS, 1790-1990 (Hyung-chan Kim ed., 1994).

ASIAN AMERICANS AND THE SUPREME COURT: A DOCUMENTARY HISTORY (Hyung-chan Kim ed., 1992).

Joel Kovel, WHITE RACISM: A PSYCHOHISTORY (1984).

LANDMARK BRIEFS AND ARGUMENTS OF THE SUPREME COURT OF THE UNITED STATES: CONSTITUTIONAL LAW (Philip B. Kurland and Gerhard Casper eds., 1975).

Lisa Lowe, IMMIGRANT ACTS: ON ASIAN AMERICAN CULTURAL POLITICS (1996).

Mari Matsuda, WHERE IS YOUR BODY? AND OTHER ESSAYS ON RACE, GENDER AND THE LAW (1996).

ASIAN AMERICANS AND THE LAW, HISTORICAL AND CONTEMPARY PERSPECTIVES (Charles McClain ed., 1994).

Charles J. McClain, IN SEARCH OF EQUALITY: THE CHINESE STRUGGLE AGAINST DISCRIMINATION IN NINETEENTH-CENTURY AMERICA (1994).

THE MASS INTERNMENT OF JAPANESE AMERICANS AND THE QUEST FOR LEGAL REDRESS (Charles McClain ed., 1994).

Gunnar Myrdal, AN AMERICAN DILEMMA: THE NEGRO PROBLEM AND MODERN DEMOCRACY (1997).

John Okada, NO-NO BOY (1981, c1976).

Michael Omi and Howard Winant, RACIAL FORMATION IN THE UNITED STATES: FROM THE 1960S TO THE 1990S (1994).

Lucius Outlaw, Toward a Critical Theory of "Race," in ANATOMY OF RACISM (David Theo Goldberg, ed., 1990).

Juan F. Perea, Richard Delgado, Angela P. Harris and Stephanie Wildman, RACE AND RACES: CASES AND RESOURCES FOR A DIVERSE AMERICA (2000).

Monica Sone, NISEI DAUGHTER (1979, C1953).

Geoffrey R. Stone et al., CONSTITUTIONAL LAW (3d ed. 1996).

Ronald Takaki, A DIFFERENT MIRROR: A HISTORY OF MULTICULTURAL AMERICA (1993).

Ronald Takaki, STRANGERS FROM A DIFFERENT SHORE: A HISTORY OF ASIAN AMERICANS (1989).

UNITED STATES WAR RELOCATION AUTHORITY, IMPOUNDED PEOPLE: JAPANESE-AMERICANS IN THE RELOCATION CENTERS (1969).

UNITED STATES WAR RELOCATION AUTHORITY: LEGAL AND CONSTITUTIONAL PHASES OF THE WRA PROGRAM (1946).

Michi Weglyn, YEARS OF INFAMY: THE UNTOLD STORY OF AMERICA'S CONCENTRATION CAMPS (1976).

William Wei, THE ASIAN AMERICAN MOVEMENT (1993).

Patricia J. Williams, THE ALCHEMY OF RACE AND RIGHTS: DIARY OF A LAW PROFESSOR (1991).

CRITICAL RACE FEMINISM: A READER (Adrien Katherine Wing ed., 1997).

K. Scott Wong, *Cultural Defenders and Brokers: Chinese Responses to the Anti-Chinese Movement, in* CLAIMING AMERICA: CONSTRUCTING CHINESE AMERICAN IDENTITIES DURING THE EXCLUSION ERA (K. Scott Wong and Sucheng Chan eds., 1998).

Tingfang Wu, AMERICA THROUGH THE SPECTACLES OF AN ORIENTAL DIPLOMAT (1997).

Eric Yamamoto, INTERRACIAL JUSTICE: CONFLICT AND RECONCILIATION IN POST-CIVIL RIGHTS AMERICA (1999).

LAW REVIEW ARTICLES AND OTHER SOURCES

Keith Aoki, *The Scholarship of Reconstruction and the Politics of Backlash*, 81 IOWA L. REV. 1467 (1996).

Derrick A. Bell, Jr., *Brown v. Board of Education and the Interest Convergence Dilemma*, 93 HARV. L. REV. 518 (1980).

Robert S. Chang, *Toward an Asian American Legal Scholarship: Critical Race Theory, Post-Structuralism, and Narrative Space*, 81 CAL. L. REV. 1243 (1993).

Pat K. Chew, *Asian Americans: The "Reticent" Minority and Their Paradoxes* 36 WM. & MARY L. REV. 1 (1994).

Gabriel J. Chin, *Is There A Plenary Power Doctrine? A Tentative Apology and Prediction for Our Strange But Unexceptional Constitutional Immigration Law,* 14 GEO. IMMIGR. L.J. 257 (2000).

Gabriel J. Chin, *The Plessy Myth: Justice Harlan and the Chinese Cases*, 82 IOWA L. REV. 151 (1996).

Sumi K. Cho, *Redeeming Whitness in the Shadow of Internment: Earl Warren, Brown, and a Theory of Racial Redemption*, 19 B. C. THIRD WORLD L.J., 40 B.C. L. REV. 73 (1998).

Margaret Chon, *On the Need for Asian American Story-Telling in Law: Ethnic Specimens, Native Informants, Storytelling and Silences*, 3 ASIAN PAC. AM. L.J. 4 (FALL 1995).

Neil Gotanda, *Critical Legal Studies, Critical Race Theory and Asian American Studies*, 21 AMERASIA J. 127 (1995).

Neil Gotanda, *A Critique of "Our Constitution Is Color-Blind,"* 44 STAN. L. REV. 1 (1991).

Neil Gotanda, *"Other NonWhites" in American Legal History: A Review of Justice at War*, 85 COLUM. L. REV. 1186 (1986).

Angela Harris, *The Jurisprudence of Reconstruction*, 82 CAL. L. REV. 741 (1995).

Thomas Wuil Joo, *New "Conspiracy Theory" of the Fourteenth Amendment: Nineteenth Century Chinese Civil Rights Cases and the Development of Substantive Due Process Jurisprudence*, 29 U.S.F. L. REV. 353 (1995).

Jerry Kang, *Negative Action Against Asian Americans: The Internal Instability of Dworkin's Defense of Affirmative Action*, 31 HARV. C.R.-C.L. L. REV. 1 (1996).

Linda Hamilton Krieger, *The Content of Our Categories: A Cognitive Bias Approach to Discrimination and Equal Employment Opportunity*, 47 STAN. L. REV. 1161 (1995).

Charles R. Lawrence III, *The Id, The Ego, and Equal Protection: Reckoning with Unconscious Racism*, 39 STAN. L. REV. 317 (1987).

Mari J. Matsuda, *Foreword: McCarthyism, the Internment and the Contradictions of Power*, 19 B. C. THIRD WORLD L.J., 40 B.C. L. REV. 9 (1998).

Mari J. Matsuda, *When the First Quail Calls: Multiple Consciousness as Jurisprudential Method*, 11 WOMEN'S RTS. L. REP. 7 (1989).

Mari J. Matsuda, *Looking to the Bottom: Critical Legal Studies and Reparations*, 22 HARV. C.R.-C.L. L. REV. 323 (1987).

Charles J. McClain, Jr., *Tortuous Path, Elusive Goal: The Asian Quest for American Citizenship*, 2 ASIAN L.J. 33 (1995).

Charles J. McClain, Jr., *The Chinese Struggle for Civil Rights in Nineteenth Century America: The First Phase, 1850-1870*, 72 CAL. L. REV. 529 (1984).

Hiroshi Motomura, *The Curious Evolution of Immigration Law: Procedural Surrogates for Substantive Constitutional Rights*, 92 COLUM. L. REV. 1625 (1992).

Reggie Oh & Frank Wu, *The Evolution of Race in the Law: The Supreme Court Moves from Approving Internment of Japanese Americans to Disap-

proving Affirmative Action for Asian Americans, 1 MICH. J. RACE & LAW 165 (1996).

Peggy Pascoe, *Miscegenation Law, Court Cases, and Ideologies of "Race" in Twentieth Century America*, J. AM. HIST. 44 (June 1996).

Gary Peller, *Race Consciousness*, 1990 DUKE L.J. 758 (1990).

Victor C. Romero, *The Domestic Fourth Amendment Rights of Undocumented Immigrants: On Guitterez and the Tort Law/Immigration Law Parallel*, 35 HARV. C.R.-C.L. L. REV. 57 (2000).

Reva Siegel, *Why Equal Protection No Longer Protects: The Evolving Forms of Status-Enforcing State Action*, 49 STAN. L. REV. 1111 (1997).

Joseph W. Singer, *Legal Realism Now*, 76 CAL. L. REV. 465 (1988).

John Hayakawa Torok, *Reconstruction and Racial Nativism: Chinese Immigrants and the Debates on the Thirteenth, Fourteenth, and Fifteenth Amendments and Civil Rights Laws*, 3 ASIAN L.J. 55 (1996).

Patricia M. Wald, *Judicial Opinion Writing: The Rhetoric of Results and the Results of Rhetoric: Judicial Writings*, 62 U. CHI. L. REV. 1371 (1995).

Frank H. Wu and May L. Nicholson, HAVE YOU NO DECENCY? AN ANALYSIS OF RACIAL ASPECTS OF MEDIA COVERAGE ON THE JOHN HUANG MATTER, ASIAN AMERICAN POLICY REVIEW VII (1997).

Frank H. Wu, *Changing America: Three Arguments About Asian Americans and the Law*, 45 AM. U. L. REV. 811 (1996).

Frank H. Wu, *The Limits of Borders: A Moderate Proposal for Immigration Reform*, 7 STAN. LAW & POL'Y REV. 35 (1996).

Frank H. Wu, *Neither Black Nor White: Asian Americans and Affirmative Action*, 15 B.C. Third World L.J. 225 (1995).

John R. Wunder, *The Chinese and the Courts in the Pacific Northwest: Justice Denied?*, 52 PAC. HIST. REV. 191 (1983).

Eric K. Yamamoto, *Critical Race Praxis: Race Theory and Political Lawyering Practice in Post-Civil Rights America*, 95 MICH. L. REV. 821 (1997).

Eric K. Yamamoto, *Rethinking Alliances: Agency, Responsibility and Interracial Justice*, 3 UCLA ASIAN PAC. AM. L.J. 33 (1995).

Eric K. Yamamoto, *Friend, Foe or Something Else: Social Meanings of Redress and Reparations*, 20 DENV. J. INT'L L. & POL'Y 223 (1992).

Eric K Yamamoto, Korematsu *Revisited: Correcting the Injustice of Extraordinary Government Excess and Lax Judicial Review—Time for a Better Accommodation of National Security Concerns and Civil Liberties*, 26 SANTA CLARA L. REV. 1 (1986).

Chapter 2 AN HISTORICAL INTRODUCTION

A. ASIAN AMERICAN LEGAL HISTORY: AN OVERVIEW*

How could we have interned 120,000 Japanese Americans during World War II? Answering this question is no simple task. And the complication starts nearly a century before the Second World War, in the larger history of how Asian peoples came to the United States and came to be treated. What follows is a very brief summary of Asian American history, up through the internment, with emphasis on the interaction between Asian America and American law. In examining this dialectic, we study how law and legal institutions affected the demographic and life possibilities of Asian Americans. Conversely, we explore how Americans of Asian descent affected the development of American law, through political struggle and constitutional litigation.

Although this casebook focuses on the internment of persons of Japanese ethnicity, this historical essay goes beyond the Japanese American experience. It does so because understanding the experience of other Asian ethnicities, who were similarly perceived as "Oriental,"† helps explain how and why the public demanded internment and why all branches of government complied. In the course of telling this story, we use the term "Asian American" broadly to include not only those Asians with U.S. citizenship but all Asians in America—citizens or not—who staked their futures and their children's futures in this country. More precise references to citizenship status is used where appropriate.

1. IMMIGRATION

Asian American legal history begins with a story of exclusion—physical exclusion by force of law—that took place within the context of manifest destiny. European settlers viewed America as a terrain to be transformed and claimed physically, culturally and economically. Yet the various agricultural and industrial projects of the Pacific frontier required an influx of non-European labor. Asians first began to arrive in the United States in substantial numbers in the mid-19th century.

Initially, these were *Chinese* immigrants, almost all adult males, who landed on the shores of Hawaii and California. Many were pushed out of China, from the Guangdong province, by conditions of war, economic depression and the declining Qing dynasty. At the same time, they were pulled to America by the hope and promise of economic opportunity. Initially, they were drawn to the United States by the allure of California's Gold Rush. Later, they were recruited as cheap labor—for example, to work the labor-intensive sugar plantations in Hawaii and to lay down the first intercon-

---

* This essay draws from a section of Gabriel Chin, Sumi Cho, Jerry Kang & Frank Wu, BEYOND SELF INTEREST (1996).

† The term "Oriental" is disfavored among many Asian Americans because the word carries connotations of exoticism, foreignness and mystery.

tinental railroad. As Asian American historian Ronald Takaki states, "of alien origin, they were brought here to serve as an 'internal colony'—non-whites allowed to enter as 'cheap' migratory laborers and members of a racially subordinated group, not future citizens of American society." Between 1840 and 1880, approximately 370,000 Chinese arrived in the United States. To get some sense of the relative size of the Chinese population, consider the following numbers. In 1870, the Chinese constituted 29 percent of the population in Idaho, 10 percent in Montana, and 9 percent in California. In California, they amounted to 25 percent of the workforce.

When the economy was booming, the Chinese were treated tolerably—as necessary, indeed useful, workers. But when the economy collapsed, as it did in 1873–1877 and 1883–1886, White American workers quickly scapegoated the "yellow" invasion of "coolie" labor. They complained that White American labor was debased by the Chinese, who were willing and able to work under horrendous conditions for little pay. Intolerant individuals took matters into their own violent hands. By one count, at least 300 murders of Chinese were documented in the West between 1860 and 1887. One historian notes that 88 Chinese were murdered in California in a single year, 1862. It is hard to know how many other deaths went unrecorded.

At other times, intolerance was expressed through local civic and political institutions, which attempted to make the lives of the Chinese so miserable that they would leave or not come in the first place. But state and federal courts sometimes struck down these attempts for violating federal treaties with China or trespassing on those foreign affairs and immigration powers reserved exclusively to the federal government. For example, in *Chy Lung v. Freeman*, 92 U.S. 275 (1876) the U.S. Supreme Court struck down a California immigration statute on federal supremacy grounds. Thus the anti-Chinese movement, if it were to succeed, had to shift from local and state levels to the federal plane.

In 1882, the movement succeeded in the enactment of the Chinese Exclusion Act, which halted the immigration of Chinese laborers for ten years. The Exclusion Act was the first federal law to restrict immigration on the basis of race. (Of course, because it applied only to laborers, the Act also discriminated on the basis of class.) Amendments and expansions of the Exclusion Act—passed in 1884, 1888 (Scott Act), 1892 (Geary Act), 1902, and finally 1904—resulted in the permanent exclusion of Chinese laborers and the summary deportation of Chinese in America found without proper identification. These attempts to stop Chinese immigration generated innumerable habeas corpus petitions—requests to release someone unlawfully detained—including two cases discussed in detail here, *Chae Chan Ping v. United States* and *Fong Yue Ting v. United States*. A number of these petitions were initially granted by federal district courts. They raised fundamental questions about federalism—the vertical division of power between federal and state governments—and separation of powers—the horizontal division of power between the political branches (the executive and the legislative) and the judiciary.

These exclusionary laws had their intended effect, and Chinese immigration abated from the 1880s onward. Employers, especially Hawaii plantation owners, who had relied on Chinese workers, needed another source of cheap, dependable labor. That source would be another Asian country, *Japan*. From 1880 to 1910, approximately 400,000 Japanese entered America. Notwithstanding their different ethnicity and nationality, most Americans viewed Japanese and Chinese as fungible, clumped together in a broader, racialized class—the "Oriental." Similar to what happened to the Chinese, resentment against the Japanese grew in proportion to their absolute numbers.

This nativist resentment was expressed through law, social prejudice and targeted violence. To take one important example, the City of San Francisco segregated Japanese pupils at the beginning of the 20th century. The actions of the San Francisco school board sparked an international crisis with Japan, which bristled at the segregation of its subjects. President Theodore Roosevelt could not casually dismiss Japan's protests because by then Japan had become a world-class military power. Although in 1853 Commodore Matthew Perry's gunboats had easily "opened up" Japan to Western powers, by 1895 Japan had defeated China in war; more important, in 1905 it had defeated Russia—a nation perceived as White and Western. Given its military strength, Japan could not be ignored. In the end, Roosevelt struck a political compromise with San Francisco: The Japanese pupils would be allowed to attend White American schools in exchange for Roosevelt's promise to decrease Japanese immigration. Roosevelt kept his promise and negotiated in 1907 and 1908 a "gentlemen's agreement" that limited the immigration of Japanese laborers, through informal arrangements, without passage of express (and thus more insulting) legislation.

What about the immigration patterns of Asian ethnic groups other than the Chinese and Japanese? The first appreciable amount of *Korean* immigration began in the early 1900s, with approximately 7,000 Koreans arriving, mostly to Hawaii again to work on the plantations. The immigration flow was brief—until 1905—when Japan made Korea its protectorate following the Russo-Japanese War. At that time, concerned about how its own subjects were treated in the United States, Japan ended all immigration from Korea. Five years later, Japan annexed Korea.

The total number of *South Asian* immigrants in the early 20th century was comparable to the magnitude of Korean immigration. The immigrants were primarily unskilled laborers, who eventually settled on the West Coast for agricultural work after laboring for the railroads and lumber mills. This immigration largely ended with the Immigration Act of 1917, which was prompted by both anti-Asian sentiment and a broader nativism against Southern and Eastern Europeans. In this Act, Congress created the Asiatic Barred Zone, which excluded most immigrants from an area encompassing India, Southeast Asia, and the Pacific Islands.

Seven years later, Congress took a more drastic step and instituted the national origins quota system, which sought to preserve American demographics as they were before substantial Asian and "undesirable" European entry. The Immigration Act of 1924 capped immigrants for any given nation to 2 percent of that nationality's population in 1890. In addition, the Act barred entry of all "aliens ineligible for citizenship." Since only Whites, persons of African descent and certain Mexicans* were then eligible for citizenship, this law effectively barred entry of Asians. This law cut off the substantial stream of Japanese immigration—principally wives and children of male laborers already in the United States—that had continued despite the gentlemen's agreement. Thus, in 1924, Asian immigration to the United States was substantially constrained.

An important exception was *Filipino* immigration, which started in 1900 and continued past 1924 until the 1930s, for a total of approximately 180,000 persons. Like the Chinese, Japanese and Koreans, Filipinos were recruited by the Hawaii sugar plantations to replace and discipline the workers who had come before them. The 1924 Act that ended almost all Asian immigration did not, however, apply to Filipinos because they were not technically "aliens." The United States had taken jurisdiction over the Philippines at the end of the Spanish-American War in 1898; consequently, Filipinos held "national," not "alien," status. But this loophole was soon closed. In 1934, Congress passed the Tydings-McDuffie Act, which accomplished two objectives. On the one hand, it promised Filipino independence twelve years later, a promise Congress later fulfilled. On the other hand, it stripped all Filipinos of national status and declared them aliens, which subjected them immediately to the exclusionary 1924 Act.

At the time of World War II, these Asian ethnicities—Chinese, Japanese, Filipino, Korean and Indian—were the only ones present in any appreciable numbers in the United States. All others were kept out. These exclusionary laws did not loosen until the mid-20th century. Most important, in 1952, Congress passed the McCarran-Walter Act, which erased some of the color bar from our immigration laws. But even the McCarran-Walter Act was not entirely racially neutral. Not until the comprehensive 1965 reform of our immigration laws, which abolished the 1924 national origins quota system and adopted uniform country quotas for immigration, did America end explicit racial discrimination against Asians. And that is when the demographics of Asian America begin to change radically, in absolute size and composition. To get some sense of the magnitude of change, consider the following data: In 1965, Asian Americans numbered 1 million; by 1990, they numbered 7 million (2.9% of the national population). Since 1965, after Mexico, the four countries that have sent the most immigrants to the United States are the Philippines, Korea, China and Vietnam. Finally, nearly all Southeast Asians—Vietnamese, Laotian, Cambodian, Hmong, and Thai—have arrived in the United States after 1975.

---

* According to the 1848 Treaty of Guadalupe Hildago, which concluded the United States-Mexican War, those Mexicans who resided on territory ceded to the United States could elect U.S. citizenship.

2. CITIZENSHIP

To be an American, an individual must not only be allowed to come to this nation's shores; he or she must also be able to become a citizen. Just as the law at times forbade most Asian immigrants from physical entry, it prevented those who had managed to arrive from naturalizing. The first federal naturalization statute, passed in 1790, restricted naturalization to "free White persons." This statute was amended in 1870, after the Civil War, to include persons of African descent. Because Asian immigrants were deemed to be neither White nor African, they could not become citizens under federal law.

Judges repeatedly recognized that Asian applicants for naturalization were qualified in every respect but one: They were not White. These lower court decisions culminated in a pair of Supreme Court cases examined in detail here: *United States v. Thind* and *Ozawa v. United States*. Naturalization rights were granted to Asians only in the mid-20th century: in 1943 for Chinese, in 1946 for Asian Indians and Filipinos, and in 1952 (McCarran-Walter Act) for all other Asians. The granting of these naturalization rights was prompted at least partly, perhaps mostly, by the political context of World War II and the Cold War. Recall that in World War II, China was an important ally, whereas Japan was an enemy. In its propaganda, Japan highlighted how persons of Asian descent were mistreated in America. It grew increasingly difficult for the United States to rebut such claims when federal law clearly exhibited racism against Asians, including our allied Chinese. When signing the 1943 Chinese Repealer (which repealed the Chinese Exclusion Acts and allowed Chinese to naturalize), President Franklin Roosevelt made clear that doing so was "important in the cause of winning the war." In sum, only a half century ago, America refused to let Asian immigrants into the fold of citizenship because they were viewed as an inferior race.

This does not mean, however, that there were no U.S. citizens of Asian descent prior to the mid-20th century. Ratified in 1868, the fourteenth amendment of the Constitution provided another path to citizenship—birth on American soil. The first sentence of the fourteenth amendment reads, "All persons born or naturalized in the United States, and subject to the jurisdiction thereof, are citizens of the United States and of the State wherein they reside." Despite this express declaration, the question whether Asians born in America would be American citizens remained controversial for three decades. Not until 1898 in *Wong Kim Ark v. United States*, examined in detail here, did the Supreme Court resolve this issue in favor of Asians. However, as recently as 1942, during the fervor of World War II, this principle of citizenship by birth was formally challenged in *Regan v. King*, 49 F. Supp. 222 (N.D. Cal. 1942), *aff'd*, 134 F.2d 413 (9th Cir. 1942), 319 U.S. 753 (1943), an attempt to strike all individuals of Japanese ancestry born in the United States from the voter rolls. Calls to eliminate the citizenship clause of the fourteenth amendment have recently resurfaced in response to undocumented Mexican immigration.

3. ECONOMIC DISCRIMINATION

So far, we have discussed how Asian Americans faced partially closed doors by being excluded physically at the national borders and politically from the community of citizenship. But many Asians managed to find their way into the United States and to set down roots through work, play, marriage, education and civic life. Regrettably, Asian Americans were denied equality in their exercise of these basic liberties. For instance, social and legal segregation meant that they could not live next to White Americans. Anti-miscegenation laws meant that they could not marry White Americans. School segregation often meant that they could not learn next to White Americans, or, more important, they could not take advantage of educational resources reserved solely for White Americans. Racist rules of evidence meant that Asians could not testify against White Americans in a court of law, making it difficult if not impossible to enforce the few rights they formally possessed. In sum, Asians were hampered in exercising not only many political rights, but also civil and social rights.

In addition, Asian Americans suffered widespread *de jure* (enforced by law) and *de facto* (enforced by custom and practice) discrimination in their attempt to work for a living. For instance, California enacted a miner's tax as early as in 1852, which required non-citizen miners to pay a monthly tax. In the 1880s, San Francisco manipulated its licensing authority to close Chinese laundries while allowing laundries owned by White Americans to remain open. Even up to the 1950s, California tried to bar alien Japanese (who by law could not naturalize) from fishing in state waters. Asian Americans challenged many of these restrictions in courts of law, often by hiring well-regarded White American attorneys to argue their cases. Sometimes they won. One successful legal challenge to these discriminatory laws was *Yick Wo v. Hopkins*, a landmark constitutional ruling that is examined in detail here. But these legal victories, when they came, could not provide Asian Americans truly equal economic opportunity. In reality, what was left for Asian Americans were second-rate business and service-oriented jobs. They were consigned to be launderers, gardeners and servants.

One type of economic discrimination that especially affected Japanese Americans was the various state alien land laws. Threatened by Japanese competition in farming, White American agricultural interests persuaded Western state governments to forbid "aliens ineligible for citizenship" (the code phrase for Asians) from owning land. California passed the first alien land law targeting the Japanese in 1913. By 1925, eight more states, including Washington and Oregon, would pass similar laws.

In *Terrace v. Thompson*, treated here in depth, the U.S. Supreme Court upheld the constitutionality of the Washington statute on the theory that it did not amount to racial or alienage discrimination. Moreover, the Court held that states may limit property ownership to their citizens. These alien land laws, while not always enforced, stayed on the books through the internment. Indeed, many state attorneys general began vigorous enforcement of these laws for the first time when Japanese Americans were incarcerated in internment camps. To add insult to injury, during World War II three more states passed alien land laws: Utah, Wyoming and Arkansas. (These three states were also sites of the internment camps for Japanese evacuated from the Western states during the war.)

These land laws would not be struck down by courts or revoked by legislatures until 1948, in a pair of cases examined in Chapter 4, *Takahashi v. Fish & Game Commission* and *Oyama v. California.* The Supreme Court—perhaps regretting its approval of the internment—signaled ambivalence toward its previous decisions that had approved the alien land laws. Reading this ambivalence as an invitation to reexamine these laws, state supreme courts finally began to strike down their laws as unconstitutional.

4. INTERNMENT

While most Americans are taught little about the general history of Asian exclusion at the geographical, political, economic and social borders of a community, many have heard about the Japanese American internment during World War II. A more detailed history of the internment process appears in Chapter 3; this brief summary is provided for context.

The bombing of Pearl Harbor on December 7, 1941, set in motion the eventual internment of nearly 120,000 persons of Japanese descent. Over two-thirds were American citizens, mostly young children born on American soil. After the devastating attack on Pearl Harbor, which killed more than 2,000 people and sank eleven Navy ships, America was frantic about its national security. Immediately, the Federal Bureau of Investigation, together with the Office of Naval Intelligence, rounded up thousands of Japanese American community leaders (estimates range from two to three thousand) and sent them to internment camps operated by the Immigration and Naturalization Service.

Soon, it became widely believed that Pearl Harbor succeeded because of Japanese American sabotage. Whipped up by prominent editorialists such as Walter Lippman and Westbrook Pegler, mainstream society readily accepted that the Japanese as a group posed a genuine terrorist threat. The fact that so many Japanese were American citizens made little difference because of the long-standing belief that "Orientals" were somehow inherently foreign and un-American. President Woodrow Wilson had said as much about the Japanese back in 1912: "We cannot make a homogeneous population out of a people who do not blend with the Caucasian race." This sentiment was repeated more crudely by General John L. DeWitt, head of the Western Defense Command, who ultimately recommended internment. As he put it, "A Jap's a Jap. . . . It makes no difference whether he is an American; theoretically he is still a Japanese and you can't change him. . . . You can't change him by giving him a piece of paper."

Like General DeWitt, much of the American public and its institutions did not distinguish between the enemy country of Japan and the Americans who happened to be of Japanese descent. By contrast, the government did distinguish German Americans and Italian Americans from the enemy states Germany and Italy. It is true that the Department of Justice arrested some German and Italian nationals;[*] however, each was provided a loyalty hearing under an adversarial process. It is also true that small numbers[†] of German and Italian Americans were excluded from their homes. However, despite some proposals to intern broadly persons of German and Italian descent, neither group of European Americans was subject to blanket removal from their homes and imprisonment in internment camps.

On February 19, 1942, President Franklin Roosevelt issued Executive Order 9066, which authorized military commanders in the West to issue whatever orders were necessary for national security. Significantly, the executive order made no mention of race or ethnicity. In March, Congress criminalized disobedience of military regulations issued pursuant to the executive order. The military soon issued *curfew* orders, which applied to all alien enemies—including Italian and German—and to all persons of Japanese descent, both aliens and citizens. Then the military issued *exclusion* orders, applicable to those of Japanese descent only. The latter orders forced families, with only a few days' notice, to report to specified locations with whatever they could carry, without details about where they were headed and for how long they would be away. They were shipped to temporary assembly centers, typically fairgrounds or racetracks operated by the Army. Finally, they were taken to *relocation* centers (also called internment or concentration camps) operated by the newly created War Relocation Authority. By 1942's end, nearly all Japanese on the West Coast had been interned in one of ten desolate desert camps, surrounded by barbed wire and armed sentries. A telling exception were the 150,000 Japanese in Hawaii, who were never subject to mass evacuation and internment because they constituted 37 percent of the total population and played a crucial role in the island's economy and practical functioning.

The Supreme Court affirmed the constitutionality of the curfew and exclusion orders imposed on persons of Japanese descent in various test cases involving second generation Japanese Americans Gordon Hirabayashi, Minoru Yasui and Fred Korematsu. The Court deferred to the government's claims of military necessity. Perhaps the Court was duped by the government's suppression of key evidence from the Office of Naval Intelligence, Federal Bureau of Investigation and Federal Communications Commission, all of which exculpated the Japanese Americans. On the other hand, even without such evidence, a dissenting Justice Murphy was not fooled: He called his brethren's majority opinion a fall into "the ugly abyss of racism." The governmental misconduct in suppressing and altering evidence during these internment cases led federal courts nearly a half century later to vacate the criminal convictions of Hirabayashi, Yasui and Korematsu, though the consti-

---

[*] As of February 16, 1942, 1,393 Germans and 264 Italians had been taken into Justice Department custody. These numbers compared to 2,192 Japanese in custody.

[†] Between August 1942 and July 1943, the Western Defense Command excluded 174 ethnically German and Italian persons, many of whom were citizens.

tutional principles announced in the *Korematsu* decision itself remained unaffected.

In 1982, the Commission on Wartime Relocation and Internment of Civilians, charged by Congress to study the internment concluded that the "broad historical causes which shaped these decisions were race prejudice, war hysteria and a failure of political leadership," not any genuine military necessity. In other words, it was a tragic wartime mistake. But as historian Roger Daniels has cautioned,

> the general tendency of educated Americans . . . to write the evacuation off as a "wartime mistake" is to obscure its true significance. Rather than a mistake . . . the legal atrocity which was committed against Japanese Americans was the logical outgrowth of over three centuries of American experience, an experience which taught Americans to regard the United States as a White man's country. . . .

Roger Daniels, CONCENTRATION CAMPS, NORTH AMERICA: JAPANESE IN THE UNITED STATES AND CANADA DURING WORLD WAR II xvi (1981).

Following the Commission report and during the debate over reparations for the internment survivors—most of whom lost their real and personal property, their livelihoods, their possessions and years of freedom—some members of Congress continued to insist that the internment was justified. Forgetting that most of those interned were American citizens, certain Congresspersons even argued that internment victims should not be compensated until the government of Japan compensated American veterans.

We have summarized Asian American legal history up through the internment and redress. In the rest of this chapter, we explore more deeply various sites of litigation that profoundly affected Asian American life from the 1850s to the 1940s: immigration, citizenship, and *de jure* discrimination.

B. STUDY MODULES

1. THE EXERCISE OF PLENARY POWER OVER IMMIGRATION

In the late 19th century, the visage of the illegal or unwanted immigrant was distinctly Chinese. Initially, the federal government's stance toward Chinese immigration was favorable. In 1868, China and the United States signed the Burlingame Treaty, which recognized the inherent and inalienable right of each nation's people to change home and allegiance. The treaty also explicitly recognized the mutual advantage of free migration for the purposes of curiosity and trade, or for the immigrants to become permanent residents.

Pressures to exclude the Chinese increased; thus the Burlingame Treaty was renegotiated in 1880 to allow the United States to restrict, but not completely ban, immigration of laborers. In return, the United States ensured that all Chinese already in America at the time of the treaty's signing could shuttle back and forth between the two countries as they pleased. Two years later, Congress exercised the option created by the 1880 renegotiation and passed the Chinese Exclusion Act, which barred entry of laborers for ten years. To get some sense of what fueled the exclusion movement, consider the sentiments expressed by California Senator John F. Miller during passage of the 1882 Exclusion Act:

> One complete man, the product of free institutions and high civilization, is worth more to the world than hundreds of barbarians. Upon what other theory can we justify the almost complete extermination of the Indian, the original possessor of all these States? I believe that one such man as Newton, or Franklin, or Lincoln, glorifies the creator of the world and benefits mankind more than all the Chinese who have lived, struggled and died on the banks of the Hoang Ho.

13 Cong. Rec. 1,487 (1882).

Unfortunately for the Chinese exclusionists, the 1882 Act failed to accomplish their aims. As promised in the 1880 treaty, the Act allowed those Chinese in the United States as of November 17, 1880—the treaty signing date—to go back and forth freely between the countries. Chinese who were stopped at the border claimed that they had resided in the United States before November 17, 1880, and thus, under the express terms of the 1882 Act, had the right to reenter. To close this loophole, in 1884 Congress passed a law that required a specific "reentry certificate" as the sole evidence of having been present in the United States as of the treaty's signing. But this attempted solution also failed. Chinese claimed—often truthfully, sometimes falsely—that they had resided in the United States as of November 17, 1880, but had departed to China before the reentry certificate requirement had been instituted in 1884. Thus they could not possess a certificate that did not exist when they had departed. In *Chew Heong v. United States*, 112 U.S. 536 (1884), the U.S. Supreme Court accepted this argument and explained that there would be no greater injustice than demanding the impossible.

Increasingly irritated by the Chinese immigration problem, in 1888 Congress passed the drastic Scott Act, the subject of the following case.

CHAE CHAN PING V. UNITED STATES (THE CHINESE EXCLUSION CASE)
130 U.S. 581 (1889)

Mr. Justice FIELD delivered the opinion of the Court.

The appeal involves a consideration of the validity of the act of Congress of October 1, 1888, prohibiting Chinese laborers from entering the United States who had departed before its passage, having a certificate issued under the act of 1882 as amended by the act of 1884, granting them permission to return.

It will serve to present with greater clearness the nature and force of the objections to the act, if a brief statement be made of the general character of the treaties between the two countries and of the legislation of Congress to carry them into execution.

[After mentioning the first treaty between the United States and China, concluded in 1844, the Court described the 1858 Treaty of Peace & Amity. The 1858 treaty] reiterated the pledges of peace and friendship between the two nations, renewed the promise of protection to all citizens of the United States in China peaceably attending to their affairs, and stipulated for security to Christians in the profession of their religion. Neither the treaty of 1844, nor that of 1858, touched upon the migration and emigration of the citizens and subjects of the two nations respectively from one country to the other. But in 1868 a great change in the relations of the two nations was made in that respect.... [A]dditional articles to the treaty of 1858 were agreed upon, which gave expression to the general desire that the two nations and their peoples should be drawn closer together.

Whatever modifications have since been made to these general provisions [of the 1868 treaty amendments] have been caused by a well-founded apprehension—from the experience of years—that a limitation to the immigration of certain classes from China was essential to the peace of the community on the Pacific Coast, and possibly to the preservation of our civilization there. A few words on this point may not be deemed inappropriate here, they being confined to matters of public notoriety, which have frequently been brought to the attention of Congress.

The discovery of gold in California in 1848, as is well known, was followed by a large immigration thither from all parts of the world, attracted not only by the hope of gain from the mines, but from the great prices paid for all kinds of labor. The news of the discovery penetrated China, and laborers came from there in great numbers, a few with their own means, but by far the greater number under contract with employers, for whose benefit they worked. These laborers readily secured employment, and, as domestic servants, and in various kinds of out-door work, proved to be exceedingly useful. For some years little opposition was made to them except when they sought to work in the mines, but, as their numbers increased, they began to engage in various mechanical pursuits and trades, and thus came in competition with our artisans and mechanics, as well as our laborers in the field.

The competition steadily increased as the laborers came in crowds on each steamer that arrived from China, or Hong Kong, an adjacent English port. They were generally industrious and frugal. Not being accompanied by families, except in rare instances, their expenses were small; and they were content with the simplest fare, such as would not suffice for our laborers and artisans. The competition between them and our people was for this reason altogether in their favor, and the consequent irritation, proportionately deep and bitter, was followed, in many cases, by open conflicts, to the great disturbance of the public peace.

The differences of race added greatly to the difficulties of the situation. Notwithstanding the favorable provisions of the new articles of the treaty of 1868, by which all the privileges, immunities, and exemptions were extended to subjects of China in the United States which were accorded to citizens or subjects of the most favored nation, they remained strangers in the land, residing apart by themselves, and adhering to the customs and usages of their own country. It seemed impossible for them to assimilate with our people or to make any change in their habits or modes of living. As they grew in numbers each year the people of the coast saw, or believed they saw, in the facility of immigration, and in the crowded millions of China, where population presses upon the means of subsistence, great danger that at no distant day that portion of our country would be overrun by them unless prompt action was taken to restrict their immigration. The people there accordingly petitioned earnestly for protective legislation.

In December, 1878, the convention which framed the present constitution of California, being in session, took this subject up, and memorialized Congress upon it, setting forth, in substance, that the presence of Chinese laborers had a baneful effect upon the material interests of the State, and upon public morals; that their immigration was in numbers approaching the character of an Oriental invasion, and was a menace to our civilization; that the discontent from this cause was not confined to any political party, or to any class or nationality, but was well-nigh universal; that they retained the habits and customs of their own country, and in fact constituted a Chinese settlement within the State, without any interest in our country or its institutions; and praying Congress to take measures to prevent their further immigration. This memorial was presented to Congress in February, 1879.

So urgent and constant were the prayers for relief against existing and anticipated evils, both from the public authorities of the Pacific Coast and from private individuals, that Congress was impelled to act on the subject . . . [T]he supplementary treaty of November 17, 1880, was concluded and ratified in May of the following year. It declares in its first article that "Whenever, in the opinion of the Government of the United States, the coming of Chinese laborers to the United States, or their residence therein, affects or threatens to affect the interests of that country, or to endanger the good order of the said country or of any locality within the territory thereof, the Government of China agrees that the Government of the United States may regulate, limit, or suspend such coming or residence, but may not absolutely prohibit it.["]

On the 6th of May, 1882, an act of Congress was approved, to carry this supplementary treaty into effect. It is entitled "An act to execute certain treaty stipulations relating to Chinese."

The enforcement of this act with respect to laborers who were in the United States on November 17, 1880, was attended with great embarrassment, from the suspicious nature, in many instances, of the testimony offered to establish the residence of the parties, arising from the loose notions entertained by the witnesses of the obligation of an oath. This fact led to a desire for further legislation restricting the evidence receivable, and the amendatory act of July 5, 1884, was accordingly passed. The committee of the House of Representatives on foreign affairs, to whom the original bill was referred, in reporting it back, recommending its passage, stated that there had been such manifold evasions, as well as attempted evasions, of the act of 1882, that it had failed to meet the demands which called it into existence. To obviate the difficulties attending its enforcement the amendatory act of 1884 declared that the certificate which the laborer must obtain "shall be the only evidence permissible to establish his right of re-entry" into the United States.

This act was held by this court not to require the certificate from laborers who were in the United States on the 17th of November, 1880, who had departed out of the country before May 6, 1882, and remained out until after July 5, 1884. *Chew Heong v. United States*, 112 U.S. 536. The same difficulties and embarrassments continued with respect to the proof of their former residence. Parties were able to pass successfully the required examination as to their residence before November 17, 1880, who, it was generally believed, had never visited our shores. To prevent the possibility of the policy of excluding Chinese laborers being evaded, the act of October 1, 1888, the validity of which is the subject of consideration in this case, was passed. . . . It is as follows:

> "Be it enacted by the Senate and House of Representatives of the United States of America in Congress assembled, That from and after the passage of this act, it shall be unlawful for any Chinese laborer who shall at any time heretofore have been, or who may now or hereafter be, a resident within the United States, and who shall have departed, or shall depart therefrom, and shall not have returned before the passage of this act, to return to, or remain in, the United States.["]
>
> "SEC. 2. That no certificates of identity provided for in the fourth and fifth sections of the act to which this is a supplement shall hereafter be issued; and every certificate heretofore issued in pursuance thereof is hereby declared void and of no effect, and the Chinese laborer claiming admission by virtue thereof shall not be permitted to enter the United States. ["]
>
> "SEC. 4. That all such part or parts of the act to which this is a supplement as are inconsistent herewith are hereby repealed.["]

The validity of this act, as already mentioned, is assailed, as being in effect an expulsion from the country of Chinese laborers in violation of existing treaties between the United States and the government of China, and of rights vested in them under the laws of Congress. . . . It must be conceded that the act of 1888 is in contravention of express stipulations of the treaty of 1868 and of the supplemental treaty of 1880, but it is not on that account invalid or to be restricted in its enforcement. The treaties were of no greater legal obligation than the act of Congress.

The question whether our government is justified in disregarding its engagements with another nation is not one for the determination of the courts.

This court is not a censor of the morals of other departments of the government; it is not invested with any authority to pass judgment upon the motives of their conduct. When once it is established that Congress possesses the power to pass an act, our province ends with its construction, and its application to cases as they are presented for determination. . . . [T]he province of the courts is to pass upon the validity of laws, not to make them, and when their validity is established, to declare their meaning and apply their provisions. All else lies beyond their domain.

There being nothing in the treaties between China and the United States to impair the validity of the act of Congress of October 1, 1888, was it on any other ground beyond the competency of Congress to pass it? If so, it must be because it was not within the power of Congress to prohibit Chinese laborers who had at the time departed from the United States, or should subsequently depart, from returning to the United States. Those laborers are not citizens of the United States; they are aliens. That the government of the United States, through the action of the legislative department, can exclude aliens from its territory is a proposition which we do not think open to controversy. Jurisdiction over its own territory to that extent is an incident of every independent nation. It is a part of its independence. If it could not exclude aliens it would be to that extent subject to the control of another power.

To preserve its independence, and give security against foreign aggression and encroachment, is the highest duty of every nation, and to attain these ends nearly all other considerations are to be subordinated. It matters not in what form such aggression and encroachment come, whether from the foreign nation acting in its national character or from vast hordes of its people crowding in upon us. The government, possessing the powers which are to be exercised for protection and security, is clothed with authority to determine the occasion on which the powers shall be called forth; and its determination, so far as the subjects affected are concerned, are necessarily conclusive upon all its departments and officers. If, therefore, the government of the United States, through its legislative department, considers the presence of foreigners of a different race in this country, who will not assimilate with us, to be dangerous to its peace and security, their exclusion is not to be stayed because at the time there are no actual hostilities with the nation of which the foreigners are subjects. The existence of war would render the necessity of the proceeding only more obvious and pressing. The same necessity, in a less pressing degree, may arise when war does not exist, and the same authority which adjudges the necessity in one case must also determine it in the other. In both cases its determination is conclusive upon the judiciary. If the government of the country of which the foreigners excluded are subjects is dissatisfied with this action it can make complaint to the executive head of our government, or resort to any other measure which, in its judgment, its interests or dignity may demand; and there lies its only remedy.

The power of exclusion of foreigners being an incident of sovereignty belonging to the government of the United States, as a part of those sovereign powers delegated by the Constitution, the right to its exercise at any time when, in the judgment of the government, the interests of the country require it, cannot be granted away or restrained on behalf of any one. The powers of government are delegated in trust to the United States, and are incapable of transfer to any other parties. They cannot be abandoned or surrendered. Nor can their exercise be hampered, when needed for the public good, by any considerations of private interest. The exercise of these public trusts is not the subject of barter or contract.

Whatever license, therefore, Chinese laborers may have obtained, previous to the act of October 1, 1888, to return to the United States after their departure, is held at the will of the government, revocable at any time, at its pleasure. Whether a proper consideration by our government of its previous laws, or a proper respect for the nation whose subjects are affected by its action, ought to have qualified its inhibition and made it applicable only to persons departing from the country after the passage of the act, are not questions for judicial determination. If there be nay just ground of complaint on the part of China, it must be made to the political department of our government, which is alone competent to act upon the subject. The rights and interests created by a treaty, which have become so vested that its expiration or abrogation will not destroy or impair them, are such as are connected with and lie in property, capable of sale and transfer or other disposition, not such as are personal and untransferable in their character.

Order affirmed.

NOTES AND QUESTIONS

1. Racialized thinking: In the history provided by Justice Field, he makes clear that "[t]he differences of race added greatly to the difficulties of the situation." In other words, the Chinese immigration issue was not only about economic competition or political relations between China and the United States. Instead, it was about race. Drawing upon the vocabulary and concepts in Chapter 1, what conception of race do you think Justice Field held? Was its fixed or fluid, biological or social?

2. The Chinese as a race: In providing the history and context of this case, how does the Supreme Court characterize the Chinese race? What are its core qualities, both positive and negative? Pay close attention to the language used and the characteristics emphasized.

3. The legal question: What was the central legal issue? First, make sure you understand precisely what the Scott Act did. Was the central issue whether the 1888 Scott Act contravened the terms of the 1868 Burlingame Treaty as modified in 1880? Or was the issue whether Congress had the constitutional power to enact the Scott Act, regardless of whether it breached prior treaties?

4. National security: The Supreme Court concludes that Congress had that power. Specifically, that power is located in Congress's ability to exclude aliens in the pursuit of national security.

    a. Framing the debate: Do you think it odd that an immigration case not during wartime or any of military urgency is framed in national security terms?

    b. A threatening race: Try to link up how the Chinese were characterized as a race and the Court's anxieties about national security. What specific aspects about the Chinese make them such potent threats?

    c. Judicial deference to national security assessments: What is the Court's stance toward reviewing congressional decisions about national security? Is this a practical, sensible view given the institutional limitations of the judiciary? Recall that courts typically find facts pursuant to an elaborate process, which includes complicated rules of procedure, rules of evidence, and burdens of proof—all driven by the adversarial process of dueling parties. In addition, judges are not military experts, cannot independently investigate facts, and cannot receive information in a timely manner. Keep these factors in mind, for they resurface prominently in the internment cases.

5. Do things change? To what extent have the views of Chinese or other Asian ethnicities as a racial group changed after a century? For example, are Asian Americans still viewed as forever foreign? Asian Americans frequently comment that when they are asked "where are you from?," the questioner demands the name of an Asian country. Consider also increased resentment against Asian immigration. The following e-mail message circulated widely around the Internet in 1998:

> One reason ethnic pressures become so overbearing on our American culture that the numbers of these non-European foreigners has exploded. Ethnic politicians use these numbers as weapons against us. I also work in Fremont as an electrical engineer.

> On my 9-mile drive to work through Fremont's streets every morning, I see elderly Asian immigrants EVERYWHERE. They waddle around, bent over, bowlegged, tired- and confused-looking. They don't speak English, don't know a damn thing about our country, and have no desire to ever learn. And yet these creatures, with their ever-growing numbers, keep White Americans from being considered to be on the Fremont school board. This is outrageous! . . .

> These numbers multiply . . . the ultimate result for Americans like us is disenfranchisement, dispossession, displacement, higher housing prices, fewer housing options, less open space, more traffic, shopping malls that get asianized, and cultural annihilation.

E-mail from Lee Quarrier to "mailing list" at www.instanet.com (March 1998).

6. The Scott Act's impact: The enforcement of the Scott Act prevented between 20,000 to 30,000 Chinese—who had reasonably relied on their ability to return to America—from reentering the United States. Those with immediate family or more than $1,000 of property in the United States were allowed to return six years later, pursuant to an 1894 treaty.

7. Links between the legal treatment of Chinese and Japanese immigrants: Although significant Japanese immigration did not begin until the 1880s, the legal decisions involving Chinese and Japanese immigrants were linked together quickly. In *Nishimura Ekiu v. United States*, 142 U.S. 651 (1892), the Commissioner of Immigration of the State of California refused to let a Japanese woman land because he determined that she would be a "public charge." At that time, federal law instructed that "persons likely to become a public charge" be sent back to their country of origin. Nishimura filed a *habeas corpus* petition, which requests a federal court to free the petitioner from illegal governmental detention. She argued that she was eligible to enter the United States and that leaving the final judgment of whether she was or was not likely to be a "public charge" to the Commissioner of Immigration, without any possibility of judicial review, violated her constitutional due process rights.

The Supreme Court rejected Nishimura's petition. It held that Congress, by statute, had made the Commissioner of Immigration the sole and exclusive judge of whether someone was a "public charge." Moreover, doing so was perfectly constitutional:

> It is not within the province of the judiciary to order that foreigners who had never been naturalized, nor acquired any domicile or residence within the United States, nor even been admitted into the country pursuant to law, shall be permitted to enter, in opposition to the constitutional and lawful measures of the legislative and executive branches of the national government. As

to such persons, the decisions of executive or administrative officers, acting within the powers expressly conferred by Congress, are due process of law.

Nishimura Ekiu v. United States, 142 U.S. 651, 660 (1892). *Nishimura Ekiu* is an important addition to *Chae Chan Ping.* In *Chae Chan Ping,* the Court held that Congress and the executive had power over *substantive* immigration policies, such as whether to exclude Chinese laborers. In *Nishimura Ekiu,* the Court held that Congress and the executive also enjoyed power over the fact-finding *procedures* critical to determining whether a person has the right to land according to the substance of immigration law.

   8. Deportation and the Geary Act: In 1892, the same year *Nishimura Ekiu* was decided, the Geary Act extended the 1882 Exclusion Act for another ten years. It also created a registration requirement for all Chinese laborers within the United States. They had to obtain a certificate of residence from the collector of internal revenue within one year of the Act's passage. Those found without a certificate bore the burden of demonstrating through "at least one credible white witness" that they were legal residents. The constitutionality of the Geary Act is addressed in the following case.

FONG YUE TING V. UNITED STATES
149 U.S. 698 (1893)

Mr. Justice GRAY, after stating the facts, delivered the opinion of the Court.

   In the recent case of *Nishimura Ekiu v. United States,* 142 U.S. 651, 659 [(1892)],* the court . . . said: "It is an accepted maxim of international law, that every sovereign nation has the power, as inherent in sovereignty, and essential to self-preservation, to forbid the entrance of foreigners within its dominions, or to admit them only in such cases and upon such conditions as it may see fit to prescribe. In the United States, this power is vested in the national government, to which the Constitution has committed the entire control of international relations, in peace as well as in war. It belongs to the political department of the government, and may be exercised either through treaties made by the President and Senate, or through statutes enacted by Congress."

   The same views were more fully expounded in the earlier case of *Chae Chan Ping v. United States,* 130 U.S. 581 [(1889)], in which the validity of a former act of Congress, excluding Chinese laborers from the United States, under the circumstances therein stated, was affirmed. . . . [In *Chae Chan Ping,*] [t]he court then went on to say: "To preserve its independence, and give security against foreign aggression and encroachment, is the highest duty of every nation, and to attain these ends nearly all other considerations are to be subordinated."

   _____

   * In the Immigration Act of 1891, Congress abrogated existing contracts with state commissioners to enforce immigration laws and consolidated the enforcement powers back into federal officials. The Act also eliminated all judicial review of fact-finding performed by federal immigration officials. In *Ekiu,* the Court held that this elimination of judicial review was constitutional.—ED.

The right of a nation to expel or deport foreigners, who have not been naturalized or taken any steps towards becoming citizens of the country, rests upon the same grounds, and is as absolute and unqualified as the right to prohibit and prevent their entrance into the country.

The right to exclude or to expel all aliens, or any class of aliens, absolutely or upon certain conditions, in war or in peace, being an inherent and inalienable right of every sovereign and independent nation, essential to its safety, its independence and its welfare, the question now before the court is whether the manner in which Congress has exercised this right in sections 6 and 7 of the act of 1892 is consistent with the Constitution.

In exercising the great power which the people of the United States, by establishing a written Constitution as the supreme and paramount law, have vested in this court, of determining, whenever the question is properly brought before it, whether the acts of the legislature or of the executive are consistent with the Constitution, it behooves the court to be careful that it does not undertake to pass upon political questions, the final decision of which has been committed by the Constitution to the other departments of the government.

The power to exclude or to expel aliens, being a power affecting international relations, is vested in the political departments of the government, and is to be regulated by treaty or by act of Congress, and to be executed by the executive authority according to the regulations so established, except so far as the judicial department has been authorized by treaty or by statute, or is required by the paramount law of the Constitution, to intervene.

In Nishimura Ekiu's case, it was adjudged that, although Congress might, if it saw fit, authorize the courts to investigate and ascertain the facts upon which the alien's right to land was made by the statutes to depend, yet Congress might intrust the final determination of those facts to an executive officer, and that, if it did so, his order was due process of law, and no other tribunal, unless expressly authorized by law to do so, was at liberty to reexamine the evidence on which he acted, or to controvert its sufficiency.

The power to exclude aliens and the power to expel them rest upon one foundation, are derived from one source, are supported by the same reasons, and are in truth but parts of one and the same power.

The power of Congress, therefore, to expel, like the power to exclude aliens, or any specified class of aliens, from the country, may be exercised entirely through executive officers; or Congress may call in the aid of the judiciary to ascertain any contested facts on which an alien's right to be in the country has been made by Congress to depend.

Congress, having the right, as it may see fit, to expel aliens of a particular class, or to permit them to remain, has undoubtedly the right to provide a system of registration and identification of the members of that class within the country, and to take all proper means to carry out the system which it provides.

This section [6 of the 1892 Act] proceeds to enact that any Chinese laborer within the limits of the United States, who shall neglect, fail or refuse to apply for a certificate of residence within the year, or who shall afterwards be found within the jurisdiction of the United States without such a certificate, "shall be deemed and adjudged to be unlawfully within the United States." The meaning of this clause, as shown by those which follow, is not that this fact shall thereupon be held to be conclusively established against him, but only that the want of a certificate shall be prima facie evidence that he is not entitled to remain in the United States; for the section goes on to direct that he "may be arrested by any customs official, collector of internal revenue or his deputies, United States marshal or his deputies, and taken before a United States judge;" and that it shall thereupon be the duty of the judge to order that the laborer "be deported from the United States" to China, (or to any other country which he is a citizen or subject of, and which does not demand any tax as a condition of his removal to it,) "unless he shall establish clearly, to the satisfaction of said judge, that by reason of accident, sickness or other unavoidable cause, he has been unable to procure his certificate, and to the satisfaction of the court, and by at least one credible white witness, that he was a resident of the United States at the time of the passage of this act; and if, upon the hearing, it shall appear that he is so entitled to a certificate, it shall be granted upon his paying the cost. Should it appear that said China-man had procured a certificate which has been lost or destroyed, he shall be detained and judgment suspended a reasonable time to enable him to procure a duplicate from the officer granting it; and in such cases the cost of said arrest and trial shall be in the discretion of the court."

The provision which puts the burden of proof upon him of rebutting the presumption arising from his having no certificate, as well as the requirement of proof, "by at least one credible white witness, that he was a resident of the United States at the time of the passage of this act," is within the acknowledged power of every legislature to prescribe the evidence which shall be received, and the effect of that evidence, in the courts of its own government. The competency of all witnesses, without regard to their color, to testify in the courts of the United States, rests on acts of Congress, which Congress may at its discretion modify or repeal. The reason for requiring a Chinese alien, claiming the privilege of remaining in the United States, to prove the fact of his residence here, at the time of the passage of the act, "by at least one credible white witness," may have been the experience of Congress, as mentioned by Mr. Justice Field in Chae Chan Ping's case that the enforcement of former acts, under which the testimony of Chinese persons was admitted to prove similar facts, "was attended with great embarrassment, from the suspicious nature, in many instances, of the testimony offered to establish the residence of the parties, arising from the loose notions entertained by the witnesses of the obligation of an oath." And this requirement, not allowing such a fact to be proved solely by the testimony of aliens in a like situation, or of the same race, is quite analogous to the provision, which has existed for seventy-seven years in the naturalization laws, by which aliens applying for naturalization must prove their residence within the limits and under the jurisdiction of the United States, for five years next preceding, "by the oath or affirmation of citizens of the United States." Acts of March 22, 1816, c. 32, § 2, 3 Stat. 259.

The order of deportation is not a punishment for crime. It is not a banishment, in the sense in which that word is often applied to the expulsion of a citizen from his country by way of punishment. It is but a method of enforcing the return to his own country of an alien who has not complied with the conditions upon the performance of which the government of the nation, acting within its constitutional authority and through the proper departments, has determined that his continuing to reside here shall depend. He has not, therefore, been deprived of life, liberty or property, without due process of law; and the provisions of the Constitution, securing the right of trial by jury, and prohibiting unreasonable searches and seizures, and cruel and unusual punishments, have no application.

Mr. Justice BREWER dissenting.

I rest my dissent on three propositions: First, that the persons against whom the penalties of section 6 of the act of 1892 are directed are persons lawfully residing within the United States; secondly, that as such they are within the protection of the Constitution, and secured by its guarantees against oppression and wrong; and, third, that section 6 deprives them of liberty and imposes punishment without due process of law, and in disregard of constitutional guarantees, especially those found in the Fourth, Fifth, Sixth, and Eighth Articles of the Amendments.

[N]o act has [yet] been passed denying the right of those laborers who had once lawfully entered the country to remain, and they are here not as travellers or only temporarily. We must take judicial notice of that which is disclosed by the census, and which is also a matter of common knowledge. There are 100,000 and more of these persons living in this country, making their homes here, and striving by their labor to earn a livelihood. They are not travellers, but resident aliens.

These appellants, therefore, are lawfully within the United States, and are here as residents, and not as travellers. They have lived in this country, respectively, since 1879, 1877, and 1874—almost as long a time as some of those who were members of the Congress that passed this act of punishment and expulsion.

That those who have become domiciled in a country are entitled to a more distinct and larger measure of protection than those who are simply passing through, or temporarily in it, has long been recognized by the law of nations.

It is said that the power here asserted [to deport summarily] is inherent in sovereignty. This doctrine of powers inherent in sovereignty is one both indefinite and dangerous. Where are the limits to such powers to be found, and by whom are they to be pronounced? Is it within legislative capacity to declare the limits? If so, then the mere assertion of an inherent power creates it, and despotism exists. May the courts establish the boundaries? Whence do they obtain the authority for this? Shall they look to the practices of other nations to ascertain the limits? The governments of other nations have elastic powers—ours is fixed and bounded by a written constitution. The expulsion of a race may be within the inherent powers of a despotism. History, before the adoption of this Constitution, was not destitute of examples of the exercise of such a power; and its framers were familiar with history, and wisely as it seems to me, they gave to this government no general power to banish. Banishment may be resorted to as punishment for crime; but among the powers reserved to the people and not delegated to the government is that of determining whether whole classes in our midst shall, for no crime but that of their race and birthplace, be driven from our territory.

Whatever may be true as to exclusion, and as to that see *Chinese Exclusion* case and *Nishimura Ekiu v. United States*, I deny that there is any arbitrary and unrestrained power to banish residents, even resident aliens. What, it may be asked, is the reason for any difference? The answer is obvious. The Constitution has no extraterritorial effect, and those who have not come lawfully within our territory cannot claim any protection from its provisions. And it may be that the national government, having full control of all matters relating to other nations, has the power to build, as it were, a Chinese wall around our borders and absolutely forbid aliens to enter. But the Constitution has potency everywhere within the limits of our territory, and the powers which the national government may exercise within such limits are those, and only those, given to it by that instrument. Now, the power to remove resident aliens is, confessedly, not expressed. Even if it be among the powers implied, yet still it can be exercised only in subordination to the limitations and restrictions imposed by the Constitution.

I pass, therefore, to the consideration of my third proposition: Section 6 deprives of "life, liberty, and property without due process of law." It imposes punishment without a trial, and punishment cruel and severe. It places the liberty of one individual subject to the unrestrained control of another.

Once more: Supposing a Chinaman from San Francisco, having obtained a certificate, should go to New York or other place in pursuit of work, and on the way his certificate be lost or destroyed. He is subject to arrest and detention, the cost of which is in the discretion of the court, and judgment of deportation will be suspended a reasonable time to enable him to obtain a duplicate from the officer granting it. In other words, he cannot move about in safety without carrying with him this certificate. The situation was well described by Senator Sherman in the debate in the Senate: "They are here ticket-of-leave men; precisely as, under the Australian law, a convict is allowed to go at large upon a ticket-of-leave, these people are to be allowed to go at large and earn their livelihood, but they must have their tickets-of-leave in their possession." And he added: "This inaugurates in our system of government a new departure; one, I believe, never before practised, although it was suggested in conference that some rules had been adopted in slavery times to secure the peace of society."

It is true this statute is directed only against the obnoxious Chinese; but if the power exists, who shall say it will not be exercised tomorrow against other classes and other people? If the guarantees of these amendments can be thus ignored in order to get rid of this distasteful class, what security have others that a like disregard of its provisions may not be resorted to?

In the *Yick Wo* case [(1886)], in which was presented a municipal ordinance, fair on its face, but contrived to work oppression to a few engaged in a single occupation, this court saw no difficulty in finding a constitutional barrier to such injustice. But this greater wrong, by which a hundred thousand people are subject to arrest and forcible deportation from the country, is beyond the reach of the protecting power of the Constitution.

In view of this enactment of the highest legislative body of the foremost Christian nation, may not the thoughtful Chinese disciple of Confucius fairly ask, Why do they send missionaries here?

Mr. Justice FIELD dissenting.

I had the honor to be the organ of the court in announcing this opinion and judgment [in *Chae Chan Ping*, affirming Congress's power to exclude Chinese aliens]. I still adhere to the views there expressed in all particulars; but between legislation for the exclusion of Chinese persons—that is, to prevent them from entering the country—and legislation for the deportation of those who have acquired a residence in the country under a treaty with China, there is a wide and essential difference.

[Justice Field proceeded to criticize the Alien & Sedition Act of 1798.] I repeat the statement, that in no other instance has the deportation of friendly aliens been advocated as a lawful measure by any department of our government. And it will surprise most people to learn that any such dangerous and despotic power lies in our government—a power which will authorize it to expel at pleasure, in time of peace, the whole body of friendly foreigners of any country domiciled herein by its permission, a power which can be brought into exercise whenever it may suit the pleasure of Congress, and be enforced without regard to the guarantees of the Constitution intended for the protection of the rights of all persons in their liberty and property. Is it possible that Congress can, at its pleasure, in disregard of the guarantees of the Constitution, expel at any time the Irish, German, French, and English who may have taken up their residence here on the invitation of the government, while we are at peace with the countries from which they came, simply on the ground that they have not been naturalized?

Aliens from countries at peace with us, domiciled within our country by its consent, are entitled to all the guaranties for the protection of their persons and property which are secured to native-born citizens. The moment any human being from a country at peace with us comes within the jurisdiction of the United States, with their consent—and such consent will always be implied when not expressly withheld, and in the case of the Chinese laborers before us was in terms given by the treaty referred to—he becomes subject to all their laws, is amenable to their punishment and entitled to their protection. Arbitrary and despotic power can no more be exercised over them with reference to their persons and property, than over the persons and property of native-born citizens. They differ only from citizens in that they cannot vote or hold any public office. As men having our common humanity, they are protected by all the guaranties of the Constitution. To hold that they are subject to any different law or are less protected in any particular than other persons, is in my judgment to ignore the teachings of our history, the practice of our government, and the language of our Constitution.

Let us test this doctrine by an illustration. If a foreigner who resides in the country by its consent commits a public offence, is he subject to be cut down, maltreated, imprisoned, or put to death by violence, without accusation made, trial had, and judgment of an established tribunal following the regular forms of judicial procedure? If any rule in the administration of justice is to be omitted or discarded in his case, what rule is it to be? If one rule may lawfully be laid aside in his case, another rule may also be laid aside, and all rules may be discarded. In such instances a rule of evidence may be set aside in one case, a rule of pleading in another; the testimony of eye-witnesses may be rejected and hearsay adopted, or no evidence at all may be received, but simply an inspection of the accused, as is often the case in tribunals of Asiatic countries where personal caprice and not settled rules prevail. That would be to establish a pure, simple, undisguised despotism and tyranny with respect to foreigners resident in the country by its consent, and such an exercise of power is not permissible under our Constitution. Arbitrary and tyrannical power has no place in our system.

There is no dispute about the power of Congress to prevent the landing of aliens in the country; the question is as to the power of Congress to deport them without regard to the guaranties of the Constitution. The Statement that in England the power to expel aliens has always been recognized and often exercised, and the only question that has ever been as to this power is whether it could be exercised by the King without the consent of Parliament, is, I think, not strictly accurate. It may be admitted that the power had been exercised by the various governments of Europe. Spain expelled the Moors; England in the reign of Edward I, banished fifteen thousand Jews; and Louis XIV, in 1685, by revoking the Edict of Nantes, which gave religious liberty to Protestants in France, drove out the Huguenots. Nor does such severity of European governments belong only to the distant past. Within three years Russia has banished many thousands of Jews, and apparently intends the expulsion of the whole race—an act of barbarity which has aroused the indignation of all Christendom. [A]ll the instances mentioned have been condemned for their barbarity and cruelty, and no power to perpetrate such barbarity is to be implied from the nature of our government, and certainly is not found in any delegated powers under the Constitution.

The punishment is beyond all reason in its severity. It is out of all proportion to the alleged offence. It is cruel and unusual. As to its cruelty, nothing can exceed a forcible deportation from a country of one's residence, and the breaking up of all the relations of friendship, family, and business there contracted. The laborer may be seized at a distance from his home, family and his business, and taken before the judge for his condemnation, without permission to visit his home, see his family, or complete any unfinished business. . . .

I cannot but regard the decision as a blow against constitutional liberty, when it declares that Congress has the right to disregard the guaranties of the Constitution intended for the protection of all men, domiciled in the country with the consent of the government, in their rights of person and property. How far will its legislation go? The unnaturalized resident feels it to-day, but if Congress can disregard the guaranties with respect to any one domiciled in this country with its consent, it may disregard the guaranties with respect to naturalized citizens. What assurance have we that it may not declare that naturalized citizens of a particular country cannot remain in the United States after a certain day, unless they have in their possession a certificate that they are of good moral character and attached to the principles of our

Constitution, which certificate they must obtain from a collector of internal revenue upon the testimony of at least one competent witness of a class or nationality to be designated by the government?

What answer could the naturalized citizen in that case make to his arrest for deportation, which cannot be urged in behalf of the Chinese laborers of today?

NOTES AND QUESTIONS

1.   Understanding the Geary Act: What precisely did the Geary Act accomplish in substance and in procedure? In what ways did it differ from the Scott Act passed four years earlier?

2.   Substantive power: One way to challenge a statute is to argue that Congress lacked the constitutional power to enact the statute. Our federal government is a government of "limited powers." Accordingly, for every exercise of federal power, there must be some source of that power in the U.S. Constitution. So, according to the majority, where does the power to *deport* aliens come from? Is this the same source as the power to *exclude* aliens? What are the dissenting justices' views on this issue?

3.   Adequate procedures: What procedures were envisioned in the deportation process? According to the majority, were these procedures adequate to the task? Again, what did the dissenting justices think?

4.   Chinese as a race redux: Recall how the Chinese were constructed as a racial group back in *Chae Chan Ping*. We see similar constructions in the majority opinion, but surprisingly different ones in the dissenting opinions. Try to identify relevant language in all three opinions.

5.   Understanding the dissents:

a.   The puzzling Justice Field: It would be grand error to think that the dissenters thought that the Chinese were equal to White Americans. Take Justice Field for example. Although he dissented in this case, he authored the majority opinion in *Chae Chan Ping*, which cavalierly shut out tens of thousands of Chinese from reentry. His true feelings about the Chinese are displayed in his private correspondence:

> The manners, habits, mode of living, and everything connected with the Chinese prevent the possibility of their ever assimilating with our people. They are a different race, and, even if they could assimilate, assimilation would not be desirable. If they are permitted to come here, there will be at all times conflicts arising out of the antagonism of the races which would only tend to disturb public order and mar the progress of the country. . . . I belong to the class, who repudiate the doctrine that this country was made for the people of all races. On the contrary, I think it is for our race—the Caucasian race.

Hyung-Chan Kim, ASIAN AMERICANS AND THE SUPREME COURT: A DOCUMENTARY HISTORY 81 (1992) (quoting letter from Stephen Field to John Norton Pomeroy, April 14, 1882). What then could possibly explain the following language in Justice Field's dissent?

> As men having our common humanity, [the Chinese] are protected by all the guaranties of the Constitution. To hold that they are subject to any different

law or are less protected in any particular than other persons, is in my judgment to ignore the teachings of our history, the practice of our government, and the language of our Constitution.

Fong Yue Ting, supra.

b. Reconciling *Chae Chan Ping* and the dissents: In fact, all dissenters in this case joined the unanimous majority in *Chae Chan Ping*. What explains their radically disparate response to the exclusion at issue in *Chae Chan Ping* as opposed to the deportation at issue in *Fong Yue Ting*? In other words, for the dissenters, is there some moral or practical principle, formal rule of law or political explanation that distinguishes *Chae Chan Ping* from *Fong Yue Ting*? Do you agree? Should legal protections depend so much on whether an individual has gained a physical toehold in the United States, as the dissenters suggest?

6. Due process and fact-finding procedures: Another case, one concerning Japanese immigration, deserves mention: *Yamataya v. Fisher*, 189 U.S. 86 (1903) (the Japanese Immigrant Case). Yamataya had somehow entered the United States but was soon captured by the immigration inspector. The inspector determined that she was a "public charge" and ordered her deported. Yamataya filed a *habeas corpus* petition with the federal district court, in which she argued that she was lawfully in the United States and that the inspector's findings were made without procedural due process (adequate procedural safeguards for accuracy). On appeal, the Supreme Court pulled slightly back from its earlier holding in *Nishimura Ekiu*. At least for those persons already in the United States, subject to a deportation hearing, some minimal amount of process is constitutionally required. As the court wrote:

> [I]t is not competent for . . . any executive officer . . . arbitrarily to cause an alien, who has entered the country, and has become subject in all respects to its jurisdiction, and a part of its population, although alleged to be illegally here, to be taken into custody and deported without giving him all opportunity to be heard upon the questions involving his right to be and remain in the United States. No such arbitrary power can exist where the principles involved in due process of law are recognized.

Yamataya, 189 U.S. at 101.

Nevertheless, the Court held that Yamataya was given a sufficient opportunity to be heard, notwithstanding her lack of legal counsel and her inability to understand English. According to the Court, if her lack of English skills "put her at some disadvantage . . . that was her misfortune, and constitutes no reason, under the acts of Congress, or under any rule of law, for the intervention of the court by *habeas corpus*." *Id.* at 316.

7. The plenary power doctrine: These four cases—*Chae Chan Ping*, *Nishimura Ekiu*, *Fong Yue Ting*, *Yamataya*—constitute the original case law foundations of the "plenary power doctrine." As described by immigration scholar Hiroshi Motomura, the

> plenary power doctrine's contours have changed over the years, but in general the doctrine declares that Congress and the executive branch have broad and often exclusive authority over immigration decisions. Accordingly, courts should only rarely, if ever, and in limited fashion, entertain constitu-

tional challenges to decisions about which aliens should be admitted or expelled.

Hiroshi Motomura, *Immigration Law After a Century of Plenary Power:
Phantom Constitutional Norms and Statutory Interpretation*, 100 YALE L.J.
545, 547 (1990).

Because of this doctrine, due process and other constitutional limitations
on government action do not automatically apply to the immigration arena.
Accordingly, although the legislative and executive branches cannot ordinarily discriminate on the basis of race, ethnicity, gender, legitimacy and ideology, they can do so in the field of immigration. In sum, these immigration
cases are not only important markers in Asian American legal history but are
the building blocks of an important, controversial power still exercised by the
federal government.

8. The present impact: What, if any, impacts do Asian Americans
experience today because of these exclusionary laws? Professor Gabriel J.
Chin argues that one plain fact is that there are fewer Americans of Asian
descent now in the United States than there would have been otherwise:

> Numbers mean power, or at least, potential power. . . . In the United States
> today, there are more Jews than there are in Israel, more persons of Irish de-
> scent than there are in Ireland, and more than half as many people of English
> and German descent as there are residents of England and Germany. Amer-
> ica is one of the largest Latino countries in the world, and the American
> population of African ancestry is larger than the population of twenty-nine of
> the thirty-five African nations. But, though half the world is Asian, in this
> "nation of immigrants," there are fewer Asian Americans than there are resi-
> dents of a single large Asian city such as Bombay or Jakarta.

Gabriel J. Chin, *Segregation's Last Stronghold: Race Discrimination and the
Constitutional Law of Immigration*, 46 UCLA L. REV. 1, 40 (October, 1998).
What does this mean today for political power? Professor Chin notes that the
Civil Rights Act of 1991 was drafted so that it would not apply to a single civil
rights law suit then pending, *Wards Cove Packing Co. v. Atonio*, 490 U.S.
642 (1989). The plaintiffs in this case were Asian Americans. Chin notes:

> It was not arbitrary that a suit involving Asian Americans, rather than mem-
> bers of some other group, was used as a bargaining chip. It is hard to imag-
> ine the Congressional Black Caucus agreeing to give up an important lawsuit,
> for example, the litigation over systematic discrimination against African
> Americans at the Denny's restaurant chain, in order to get the bill passed. If
> the Congressional Asian Pacific American Caucus were a large group, it
> would not have voluntarily sacrificed a case so prominent in the
> Asian-American community.

Chin, supra at 42–43.

2. CITIZENSHIP THROUGH NATURALIZATION

Notwithstanding the laws that excluded Asians from American shores,
many persons of Asian descent found themselves physically in America. To
enter the political community, however, they needed citizenship. Citizenship
on the federal and state levels determined whether one could vote, hold po-

litical office and have access to courts. There are only two ways to obtain U.S. citizenship: by naturalization and by birth on American soil. In this module, we examine citizenship through naturalization.

Article II of the U.S. Constitution delegates to the Congress the power to create uniform rules of naturalization (art. II § 8). Congress exercised this power in 1790 when it enacted the first federal naturalization statute. This statute restricted naturalization to only "free White persons." After the Civil War and the enactment of the fourteenth amendment, persons of African descent were allowed into the fold. But what about Asians? A pair of cases that reached the Supreme Court in 1922 and 1923, *Ozawa v. United States* and *United States v. Thind*, provided decisive answers, in the negative.

As you read these two cases, consider the historical context in the early 20th century. Anti-Asian sentiments were strongly felt. In 1917, the Asiatic Barred Zone ended immigration from various Asian nations such as India. In 1924 (two years after *Ozawa*, one year after *Thind*), Congress adopted the national origins quota system, which ended nearly all legal Asian immigration.

OZAWA v. UNITED STATES
260 U.S. 178 (1922)

Mr. Justice SUTHERLAND delivered the opinion of the Court.

The appellant is a person of the Japanese race born in Japan. He applied, on October 16, 1914, to the United States District Court for the Territory of Hawaii to be admitted as a citizen of the United States. His petition was opposed by the United States District Attorney for the District of Hawaii. Including the period of his residence in Hawaii, appellant had continuously resided in the United States for twenty years. He was a graduate of the Berkeley, California, High School, had been nearly three years a student in the University of California, had educated his children in American schools, his family had attended American churches and he had maintained the use of the English language in his home. That he was well qualified by character and education for citizenship is conceded.

These questions for purposes of discussion may be briefly restated:

1. Is the Naturalization Act of June 29, 1906, limited by the provisions of § 2169 of the Revised Statutes of the United States?

2. If so limited, is the appellant eligible to naturalization under that section?

[Ozawa's first argument was that the comprehensive Nationalization Act of 1906 instituted uniform rules of naturalization, without any racial restriction. Although § 2169 of the Revised Statutes did contain a racial restriction, Ozawa argued that by its very terms, that section applied only to Title XXX, of which the 1906 Act was not a part.]

In all of the Naturalization Acts from 1790 to 1906 the privilege of naturalization was confined to "White persons" (with the addition in 1870 of those of African nativity and descent), although the exact wording of the various statutes was not always the same. If Congress in 1906 desired to alter a rule so well and so long established, it may be assumed that its purpose would have been definitely disclosed and its legislation to that end put in unmistakable terms.

We are asked [by Ozawa] to conclude that Congress, without the consideration or recommendation of any committee, without a suggestion as to the effect, or a word of debate as to the desirability, of so fundamental a change, nevertheless . . . has radically modified a statute always theretofore maintained and considered as of great importance. It is inconceivable that a rule in force from the beginning of the Government, a part of our history as well as our law, welded into the structure of our national polity by a century of legislative and administrative acts and judicial decisions, would have been deprived of its force in such dubious and casual fashion. We are, therefore, constrained to hold that the Act of 1906 is limited by the provisions of § 2169 of the Revised Statutes.

Second. This brings us to inquire whether, under § 2169, the appellant is eligible to naturalization.

On behalf of the appellant it is urged that we should give to this phrase the meaning which it had in the minds of its original framers in 1790 and that it was employed by them for the sole purpose of excluding the black or African race and the Indians then inhabiting this country. It may be true that these two races were alone thought of as being excluded, but to say that they were the only ones within the intent of the statute would be to ignore the affirmative form of the legislation. The provision is not that Negroes and Indians shall be excluded but it is, in effect, that only free white persons shall be included. The intention was to confer the privilege of citizenship upon that class of persons whom the fathers knew as white, and to deny it to all who could not be so classified. It is not enough to say that the framers did not have in mind the brown or yellow races of Asia. It is necessary to go farther and be able to say that had these particular races been suggested the language of the act would have been so varied as to include them within its privileges. . . . If it be assumed that the opinion of the framers was that the only persons who would fall outside the designation "white" were Negroes and Indians, this would go no farther than to demonstrate their lack of sufficient information to enable them to foresee precisely who would be excluded by that term in the subsequent administration of the statute. It is not important in construing their words to consider the extent of their ethnological knowledge or whether they thought that under the statute the only persons who would be denied naturalization would be Negroes and Indians. It is sufficient to ascertain whom they intended to include and having ascertained that it follows, as a necessary corollary, that all others are to be excluded.

The question then is, Who are comprehended within the phrase "free white persons?" Undoubtedly the word "free" was originally used in recognition of the fact that slavery then existed and that some white persons occupied that status. The word, however, has long since ceased to have any practical significance and may now be disregarded.

We have been furnished with elaborate briefs in which the meaning of the words "white person" is discussed with ability and at length, both from the standpoint of judicial decision and from that of the science of ethnology. It does not seem to us necessary, however, to follow counsel in their extensive researches in these fields. It is sufficient to note the fact that these decisions are, in substance, to the effect that the words import a racial and not an individual test, and with this conclusion, fortified as it is by reason and authority, we entirely agree. Manifestly, the test afforded by the mere color of the skin of each individual is impracticable as that differs greatly among persons of the same race, even among Anglo-Saxons, ranging by imperceptible gradations from the fair blond to the swarthy brunette, the latter being darker than many of the lighter hued persons of the brown or yellow races. Hence to adopt the color test alone would result in a confused overlapping of races and a gradual merging of one into the other, without any practical line of separation.

Beginning with the decision of Circuit Judge Sawyer, in *In re Ah Yup*, 5 Sawy. 155 (1878), the federal and state courts, in an almost unbroken line, have held that the words "white person" were meant to indicate only a person of what is popularly known as the Caucasian race. Among these decisions, see for example: *In re Camille*, 6 Fed. 256 [(1880)]; *In re Saito*, 62 Fed. 126 [(1894)]; *In re Nian*, 6 Utah 259 [(1889)]; *In re Kumagai*, 163 Fed. 922 [(1908)]; *In re Yamashita*, 30 Wash. 234, 237 [(1902)]; *In re Ellis*, 179 Fed. 1002 [(1910)]; *In re Mozumdar*, 207 Fed. 115, 117 [(1931)]; *In re Singh*, 257 Fed. 209, 211–212 [(1919)]; and *Petition of Charr*, 273 Fed. 207 [(1921)]. With the conclusion reached in these several decisions we see no reason to differ. Moreover, that conclusion has become so well established by judicial and executive concurrence and legislative acquiescence that we should not at this late day feel at liberty to disturb it, in the absence of reasons far more cogent than any that have been suggested.

The determination that the words "white person" are synonymous with the words "a person of the Caucasian race" simplifies the problem, although it does not entirely dispose of it. Controversies have arisen and will no doubt arise again in respect of the proper classification of individuals in border line cases. The effect of the conclusion that the words "white person" mean a Caucasian is not to establish a sharp line of demarcation between those who are entitled and those who are not entitled to naturalization, but rather a zone of more or less debatable ground outside of which, upon the one hand, are those clearly eligible, and outside of which, upon the other hand, are those clearly ineligible for citizenship. Individual cases falling within this zone must be determined as they arise from time to time by what this Court has called, in another connection "the gradual process of judicial inclusion and exclusion."

The appellant, in the case now under consideration, however, is clearly of a race which is not Caucasian and therefore belongs entirely outside the zone on the negative side. A large number of the federal and state courts have so decided and we find no reported case definitely to the contrary. These decisions are sustained by numerous scientific authorities, which we do not deem it necessary to review. We think these decisions are right and so hold.

The briefs filed on behalf of appellant refer in complimentary terms to the culture and enlightenment of the Japanese people, and with this estimate we have no reason to disagree; but these are matters which cannot enter into our consideration of the questions here at issue. We have no function in the matter other than to ascertain the will of Congress and declare it. Of course there is not implied—either in the legislation or in our interpretation of it—any suggestion of individual unworthiness or racial inferiority. These considerations are in no manner involved.

UNITED STATES V. THIND
261 U.S. 204 (1923)

Mr. Justice SUTHERLAND delivered the opinion of the Court.

[The central question presented was: "Is a high caste Hindu of full Indian blood, born at Amrit Sar, Punjab, India, a white person within the meaning of section 2169, Revised Statutes?"]

Section 2169, Revised Statutes, provides that the provisions of the Naturalization Act "shall apply to aliens, being free white persons, and to aliens of African nativity and to persons of African descent."

If the applicant is a white person within the meaning of this section he is entitled to naturalization; otherwise not. In *Ozawa v. United States*, 260 U.S. 178, we had occasion to consider the application of these words to the case of a cultivated Japanese and were constrained to hold that he was not within their meaning. . . . Following a long line of decisions of the lower federal courts, we held that the words imported a racial and not an individual test and were meant to indicate only persons of what is popularly known as the Caucasian race. But as there pointed out, the conclusion that the phrase "white persons" and the word "Caucasian" are synonymous does not end the matter. It enabled us to dispose of the problem as it was there presented, since the applicant for citizenship clearly fell outside the zone of debatable ground on the negative side; but the decision still left the question to be dealt with, in doubtful and different cases, by the "process of judicial inclusion and exclusion." Mere ability on the part of an applicant for naturalization to establish a line of descent from a Caucasian ancestor will not ipso facto and necessarily conclude the inquiry. "Caucasian" is a conventional word of much flexibility, as a study of the literature dealing with racial questions will disclose, and while it and the words "white persons" are treated as synonymous for the purposes of that case, they are not of identical meaning. . . .

In the endeavor to ascertain the meaning of the statute we must not fail to keep in mind that it does not employ the word "Caucasian" but the words "white persons," and these are words of common speech and not of scientific origin. The word "Caucasian" not only was not employed in the law but was probably wholly unfamiliar to the original framers of the statute in 1790. When we employ it we do so as an aid to the ascertainment of the legislative intent and not as an invariable substitute for the statutory words. Indeed, as used in the science of ethnology, the connotation of the word is by no means clear and the use of it in its scientific sense as an equivalent for the words of the statute, other considerations aside, would simply mean the substitution of one perplexity for another. But in this country, during the last half century especially, the word by common usage has acquired a popular meaning, not clearly defined to be sure, but sufficiently so to enable us to say that its popular as distinguished from its scientific application is of appreciably narrower scope. It is in the popular sense of the word, therefore, that we employ it as an aid to the construction of the statute, for it would be obviously illogical to convert words of common speech used in a statute into words of scientific terminology when neither the latter nor the science for whose purposes they were coined was within the contemplation of the framers of the statute or of the people for whom it was framed. The words of the statute are to be interpreted in accordance with the understanding of the common man from whose vocabulary they were taken.

They imply, as we have said, a racial test; but the term "race" is one which, for the practical purposes of the statute, must be applied to a group of living persons now possessing in common the requisite characteristics, not to groups of persons who are supposed to be or really are descended from some remote, common ancestor, but who, whether they both resemble him to a greater or less extent, have, at any rate, ceased altogether to resemble one another. It may be true that the blond Scandinavian and the brown Hindu have a common ancestor in the dim reaches of antiquity, but the average man knows perfectly well that there are unmistakable and profound differences between them today; and it is not impossible, if that common ancestor could be materialized in the flesh, we should discover that he was himself sufficiently differentiated from both of his descendants to preclude his racial classification with either. The question for determination is not, therefore, whether by the speculative processes of ethnological reasoning we may present a probability to the scientific mind that they have the same origin, but whether we can satisfy the common understanding that they are now the same or sufficiently the same to justify the interpreters of a statute—written in the words of common speech, for common understanding, by unscientific men—in classifying them together in the statutory category as white persons. In 1790 the Adamite theory of creation—which gave a common ancestor to all mankind—was generally accepted, and it is not at all probable that it was intended by the legislators of that day to submit the question of the application of the words "white persons" to the mere test of an indefinitely remote common ancestry, without regard to the extent of the subsequent divergence of the various branches from such common ancestry or from one another.

The eligibility of this applicant for citizenship is based on the sole fact that he is of high caste Hindu stock, born in Punjab, one of the extreme northwestern districts of India, and classified by certain scientific authorities as of the Caucasian or Aryan race. The Aryan theory as a racial basis seems to be discredited by most, if not all, modern writers on the subject of ethnology. A review of their contentions would serve no useful purpose. It is enough to refer to the works of Deniker (Races of Man, 317), Keane (Man: Past and Present, 445–6), Huxley (Man's Place in Nature, 278) and to the Dictionary of Races, Senate Document No. 662, 61st Cong., 3d sess., 1910–1911, p. 17.

The term "Aryan" has to do with linguistic and not at all with physical characteristics, and it would seem reasonably clear that mere resemblance in language, indicating a common linguistic root buried in remotely ancient soil, is altogether inadequate to prove common racial origin. There is, and can be, no assurance that the so-called Aryan language was not spoken by a variety of races living in proximity to one another. Our own history has witnessed the adoption of the English tongue by millions of Negroes, whose descendants can never be classified racially with the descendants of white persons notwithstanding both may speak a common root language.

The word "Caucasian" is in scarcely better repute. It is at best a conventional term, with an altogether fortuitous origin,[2] which, under scientific manipulation, has come to include far more than the unscientific mind suspects. According to Keane, for example, (The World's Peoples, 24, 28, 307, et seq.) it includes not only the Hindu but some of the Polynesians,[3] (that is the Maori, Tahitians, Samoans, Hawaiians and others), the Hamites of Africa, upon the ground of the Caucasic cast of their features, though in color they range from brown to black. We venture to think that the average well informed white American would learn with some degree of astonishment that the race to which he belongs is made up of such heterogeneous elements.[4]

The various authorities are in irreconcilable disagreement as to what constitutes a proper racial division. For instance, Blumenbach has five races; Keane following Linnaeus, four; Deniker, twenty-nine. The explanation probably is that "the innumerable varieties of mankind run into one another by insensible degrees," and to arrange them in sharply bounded divisions is an undertaking of such uncertainty that common agreement is practically impossible.

It may be, therefore, that a given group cannot be properly assigned to any of the enumerated grand racial divisions. The type may have been so changed by intermixture of blood as to justify an intermediate classification. Something very like this has actually taken place in India. Thus, in Hindustan and Berar there was such an intermixture of the "Aryan" invader with the darkskinned Dravidian.

In the Punjab and Rajputana, while the invaders seem to have met with more success in the effort to preserve their racial purity, intermarriages did occur producing an intermingling of the two and destroying to a greater or less degree the purity of the "Aryan" blood. The rules of caste, while calculated to prevent this intermixture, seem not to have been entirely successful.[9]

---

[2] Encyclopaedia Britannica (11th ed.), p. 113: "The ill-chosen name of Caucasian, invented by Blumenbach in allusion to a South Caucasian skull of specially typical proportions, and applied by him to the so-called white races, is still current; it brings into one race peoples such as the Arabs and Swedes, although these are scarcely less different than the Americans and Malays, who are set down as two distinct races. Again, two of the best-marked varieties of mankind are the Australians and the Bushmen, neither of whom, however, seems to have a natural place in Blumenbach's series."

[3] The United States Bureau of Immigration classifies all Pacific Islanders as belonging to the "Mongolic grand division." Dictionary of Races, supra, p. 102.

[4] Keane himself says that the Caucasic division of the human family is "in point of fact the most debatable field in the whole range of anthropological studies." Man: Past and Present, p. 444.

[9] 13 Encyclopaedia Britannica, p. 503: "In spite, however, of the artificial restrictions placed on the intermarrying of the castes, the mingling of the two races seems to have proceeded at a tolerably rapid rate. Indeed, the paucity of women of the Aryan stock would probably render these mixed unions almost a necessity from the very outset; and the

It does not seem necessary to pursue the matter of scientific classification further. We are unable to agree with the District Court, or with other lower federal courts, in the conclusion that a native Hindu is eligible for naturalization under § 2169. The words of familiar speech, which were used by the original framers of the law, were intended to include only the type of man whom they knew as white. The immigration of that day was almost exclusively from the British Isles and Northwestern Europe, whence they and their forbears had come. When they extended the privilege of American citizenship to "any alien, being a free white person," it was these immigrants—bone of their bone and flesh of their flesh—and their kind whom they must have had affirmatively in mind. The succeeding years brought immigrants from Eastern, Southern and Middle Europe, among them the Slavs and the dark-eyed, swarthy people of Alpine and Mediterranean stock, and these were received as unquestionably akin to those already here and readily amalgamated with them. It was the descendants of these, and other immigrants of like origin, who constituted the white population of the country when § 2169, reenacting the naturalization test of 1790, was adopted; and there is no reason to doubt, with like intent and meaning.

What we now hold is that the words "free white persons" are words of common speech, to be interpreted in accordance with the understanding of the common man, synonymous with the word "Caucasian" only as that word is popularly understood. As so understood and used, whatever may be the speculations of the ethnologist, it does not include the body of people to whom the appellee belongs. It is a matter of familiar observation and knowledge that the physical group characteristics of the Hindus render them readily distinguishable from the various groups of persons in this country commonly recognized as white. The children of English, French, German, Italian, Scandinavian, and other Europe parentage quickly merge into the mass of our population and lose the distinctive hallmarks of their European origin. On the other hand, it cannot be doubted that the children born in this country of Hindu parents would retain indefinitely the clear evidence of their ancestry. It is very far from our thought to suggest the slightest question of racial superiority or inferiority. What we suggest is merely racial difference, and it is of such character and extent that the great body of our people instinctively recognize it and reject the thought of assimilation.

It is not without significance in this connection that Congress, by the Act of February 5, 1917, has now excluded from admission into this country all natives of Asia within designated limits of latitude and longitude, including the whole of India. This not only constitutes conclusive evidence of the congressional attitude of opposition to Asiatic immigration generally, but is persuasive of a similar attitude toward Asiatic naturalization as well, since it is not likely that Congress would be willing to accept as citizens a class of persons whom it rejects as immigrants.

---

vaunted purity of blood which the caste rules were calculated to perpetuate can scarcely have remained of more than a relative degree even in the case of the Brahman caste."

NOTES AND QUESTIONS

1. Doctrinal consistency: In both *Ozawa* and *Thind*, the Court struggles with the relationship between the word "White" in the naturalization statute and the pseudo-scientific classification "Caucasian." Is the Court's analysis of this relationship the same in both cases? If different, are they consistent?

2. Legal definition of "race": After *Ozawa* and *Thind*, what is the legal definition of "race"? Is it essentially phenotype (skin color, rough morphology), genotype (genetic ancestry), behavior (culture, traditions), ideology (religion, political beliefs) or some combination of all of these?

3. Separate but equal: In both *Ozawa* and *Thind*, the Court declares that it means no disrespect in concluding that Japanese and Indians are not White and thus ineligible for naturalization. For example, in *Ozawa*, the Court states:

> Of course there is not implied—either in the legislation or in our interpretation of it—any suggestion of individual unworthiness or racial inferiority. These considerations are in no manner involved.

Similarly, in *Thind*, the Court writes:

> It is very far from our thought to suggest the slightest question of racial superiority or inferiority. What we suggest is merely racial difference, and it is of such character and extent that the great body of our people instinctively recognize it and reject the thought of assimilation.

Is the Court sincere? If so, is the Court deluded? If the Court is disingenuous, why does it include these disclaimers? Would these justices, if they were legislators voting on a similar policy, feel compelled to make the same disclaimers? What does this say about the role and functioning of these two branches of government?

4. Race and social choice: Note the legal arguments regarding assimilation that Takao Ozawa made on his own behalf. Could he have provided any additional evidence that would have persuaded the Court of his sincere desire to reject being "Japanese" in favor of being "American"? Or was Ozawa's sincere commitment to be "American" and not Japanese fundamentally irrelevant?

5. Tails I win, heads you lose: In his argument to be classified as White, Ozawa emphasized that

> [i]n name, General Benedict Arnold was an American, but at heart he was a traitor. In name, I am not an American, but at heart I am a true American. I set forth the following facts which will sufficiently prove this. (1) I did not report my name, my marriage, or the names of my children to the Japanese Consulate in Honolulu; notwithstanding all Japanese subjects are requested to do so. These matters were reported to the American government. (2) I do not have any connection with any Japanese churches or schools, or any Japanese organizations here or elsewhere. (3) I am sending my children to an American church and American school in place of a Japanese one. (4) Most of the time I use the American (English) language at home, so that my children cannot speak the Japanese language. (5) I educated myself in American schools for nearly eleven years by supporting myself. (6) I have

lived continuously within the United States for over twenty-eight years. (7) I chose as my wife one educated in American schools . . . instead of one educated in Japan. (8) I have steadily prepared to return the kindness which our Uncle Sam has extended me . . . so it is my honest hope to do something good to the United States before I bid a farewell to this world.

Ian Haney López, WHITE BY LAW: THE LEGAL CONSTRUCTION OF RACE 80 (1996), quoting from Yuji Ichioka, *The Early Japanese Immigrant Quest for Citizenship: The Background of the 1922 Ozawa Case*, 4 AMERASIA 1, 11 (1977).

Still, these arguments were to no avail. Later, in the wartime cases, the Supreme Court relied on evidence of Japanese schools in the United States and Japanese education abroad as indicia of possible disloyalty. Why would the judiciary ignore such evidence (*i.e.*, not sending one's children to Japanese schools in the United States) in the context of naturalization but rely on such evidence (*i.e.*, sending one's children to Japanese schools in the United States) in the context of internment?

6. Hard cases: If you think that persons of Japanese and Indian descent are easy cases (in other words, they are clearly not White), what do you think about Armenians? In *In re Halladjian*, 174 F. 834 (1st Cir. D. Mass. 1909), the United States contended that the petitioners belonged to the "Yellow" race. The court showed remarkably sophisticated skepticism about the very existence of a European or Yellow race. Nonetheless, when push came to shove, it found persuasive what it considered to be unanimous ethnographic consensus that Armenians were White. Interestingly, the court also appealed to the original meaning of the term "White" in the naturalization statute. It concluded as follows:

> From all these illustrations, which have been taken almost at random, it appears that the word "white" has been used in colonial practice, in the federal statutes, and in the publications of the government to designate persons not otherwise classified. The census of 1900 makes this clear by its express mention of Africans, Indians, Chinese, and Japanese, leaving whites as a catch-all word to include everybody else. A similar use appears 130 years earlier from the provincial census of Massachusetts taken in 1768, where "French neutrals" are not reckoned as white persons, notwithstanding their white complexion. Negroes have never been reckoned as whites; Indians but seldom. At one time Chinese and Japanese were deemed to be white, but are not usually so reckoned today. In passing the act of 1790 Congress did not concern itself particularly with Armenians, Turks, Hindoos, or Chinese. Very few of them were in the country, or were coming to it, yet the census taken in that year shows that everybody but a Negro or an Indian was classed as a white person. This was the practice of the federal courts. While an exhaustive search of the voluminous records of this court, sitting as a court of naturalization, has been impossible, yet some early instances have been found where not only western Asiatics, but even Chinese, were admitted to naturalization. After the majority of American had come to believe that great differences separated the Chinese, and later the Japanese, from other immigrants, these persons were no longer classified as white; but while the scope of its inclusion has thus been somewhat reduced, "white" is still the catch-all word which includes all persons not otherwise classified.

Id. at 843–44. What does this passage suggest about how society constructs and manipulates racial categories? Can a whole race of people pass from White to non-White? Can you think of examples of the reverse transformation? Is the view that Asian Americans are the "model minority" part of a reverse process through which a whole race is passing into Whiteness?

3. CITIZENSHIP THROUGH BIRTH ON AMERICAN SOIL

Remarkably, the original Constitution failed to define a concept as fundamental as citizenship. The original document addressed citizenship in three places: Article I's length of citizenship requirement for Congresspersons (art. I, §§ 2, 3); and Article II's natural-born citizenship requirement for the President (art. II, § 1); Article II's delegation to Congress the power to create uniform rules of naturalization (art. II, § 8). However, not until the ratification of the fourteenth amendment was an explicit, constitutional definition of "citizenship" introduced.

The first sentence of the fourteenth amendment reads: "All persons born or naturalized in the United States, and subject to the jurisdiction thereof, are citizens of the United States and of the State wherein they reside." To understand its significance, one must understand this clause's relationship to the infamous *Dred Scott v. Sanford*, 19 How. 393 (1857). Scott, whose slavery status was at issue, claimed that he became a free man by being brought into the free territory of Illinois. He sued for freedom in federal court. Federal courts are courts of limited jurisdiction. They can only hear certain types of cases outlined in Article III of the Constitution and in various federal statutes. Subject matter jurisdiction in this case was alleged on diversity of citizenship (*i.e.*, a citizen of one state was suing a citizen of another state). *See* 28 U.S.C. § 1332. Scott claimed to be a citizen of Illinois, the defendant Sanford a citizen of New York.

The Court ruled that no subject matter jurisdiction existed because no Black person such as Scott could be a "citizen" as understood in the Constitution. After this threshold ruling that the Court lacked power to decide this case, the Court did not have to go any further. Indeed, courts are not supposed to reach issues that are unnecessary to deciding a case. Nonetheless, the Court reached the merits anyway and struck down the Missouri Compromise.

The Civil War raged from 1861 to 1865. At its end, Reconstruction began. One legal element of Reconstruction was the passage of the Civil Rights Act of 1866. That Act made clear that a human being such as Scott was a U.S. citizen by virtue of his birth on American soil. For fear that the Act would be deemed unconstitutional, among other reasons, the fourteenth amendment was crafted and ratified in 1868.[*] Although the wording concerning citizen-

---

[*] The relevant portions of the fourteenth amendment are:
Amendment XIV
Section 1. All persons born or naturalized in the United States, and subject to the jurisdiction thereof, are citizens of the United States and of the state wherein they reside.

ship by birth was changed slightly from the Civil Rights Act to the fourteenth amendment, the purpose was the same. How, then, would this clause be applied to Asians? Would Asians born on American soil be allowed to join the political community?

UNITED STATES V. WONG KIM ARK
169 U.S. 649 (1898)

Mr. Justice GRAY, after stating the case, delivered the opinion of the Court.

Wong Kim Ark was born in 1873 in the city of San Francisco, in the State of California and United States of America, and was and is a laborer. His father and mother were persons of Chinese descent, and subjects of the Emperor of China; they were at the time of his birth domiciled residents of the United States, having previously established and still enjoying a permanent domicil and residence therein at San Francisco; they continued to reside and remain in the United States until 1890, when they departed for China; and during all the time of their residence in the United States they were engaged in business, and were never employed in any diplomatic or official capacity under the Emperor of China. Wong Kim Ark, ever since his birth, has had but one residence, to wit, in California, within the United States, and has there resided, claiming to be a citizen of the United States, and has never lost or changed that residence, or gained or acquired another residence; and neither he, nor his parents acting for him, ever renounced his allegiance to the United States, or did or committed any act or thing to exclude him therefrom.

In 1890 (when he must have been about seventeen years of age) he departed for China on a temporary visit and with the intention of returning to the United States, and did return thereto by sea in the same year, and was permitted by the collector of customs to enter the United States, upon the sole ground that he was a native-born citizen of the United States. After such return, he remained in the United States, claiming to be a citizen thereof, until 1894, when he (being about twenty-one years of age, but whether a little above or a little under that age does not appear) again departed for China on a temporary visit and with the intention of returning to the United States; and he did return thereto by sea in August, 1895, and applied to the collector of customs for permission to land; and was denied such permission, upon the sole ground that he was not a citizen of the United States.

It is conceded that, if he is a citizen of the United States, the acts of Congress, known as the Chinese Exclusion Acts, prohibiting persons of the Chinese race, and especially Chinese laborers, from coming into the United States, do not and cannot apply to him.

Section 5. The Congress shall have power to enforce, by appropriate legislation, the provisions of this article.
The full text of the fourteenth amendment is available at:
<www.law.ucla.edu/faculty/kang/racerightsreparation>—ED.

I.

The Constitution of the United States, as originally adopted, uses the words "citizen of the United States," and "natural-born citizen of the United States." The Constitution nowhere defines the meaning of these words, either by way of inclusion or of exclusion, except in so far as this is done by the affirmative declaration [in the fourteenth amendment] that "all persons born or naturalized in the United States, and subject to the jurisdiction thereof, are citizens of the United States." In this, as in other respects, it must be interpreted in the light of the common law, the principles and history of which were familiarly known to the framers of the Constitution.

II.

The fundamental principle of the common law with regard to English nationality was birth within the allegiance, also called "ligealty," "obedience," "faith" or "power," of the King.

[B]y the law of England for the last three centuries, beginning before the settlement of this country, and continuing to the present day, aliens, while residing in the dominions possessed by the Crown of England, were within the allegiance, the obedience, the faith or loyalty, the protection, the power, the jurisdiction, of the English Sovereign; and therefore every child born in England of alien parents was a natural-born subject, unless the child of an ambassador or other diplomatic agent of a foreign State, or of an alien enemy in hostile occupation of the place where the child was born.

III.

The same rule was in force in all the English Colonies upon this continent down to the time of the Declaration of Independence, and in the United States afterwards, and continued to prevail under the Constitution as originally established.

In *Dred Scott v. Sandford*, (1857) 19 How. 393, Mr. Justice Curtis said: "The first section of the second article of the Constitution uses the language, 'a natural-born citizen.' It thus assumes that citizenship may be acquired by birth. Undoubtedly, this language of the Constitution was used in reference to that principle of public law, well understood in this country at the time of the adoption of the Constitution, which referred citizenship to the place of birth." 19 How. 576. And to this extent no different opinion was expressed or intimated by any of the other judges.

IV.

[In this section, the Court discusses Roman law and customary international law.] Here is nothing to countenance the theory that a general rule of citizenship by blood or descent has displaced in this country the fundamental rule of citizenship by birth within its sovereignty.

V.

In the fore front, both of the Fourteenth Amendment of the Constitution, and of the Civil Rights Act of 1866, the fundamental principle of citizenship by birth within the dominion was reaffirmed in the most explicit and comprehensive terms.

The first section of the Fourteenth Amendment of the Constitution begins with the words, "All persons born or naturalized in the United States, and subject to the jurisdiction thereof, are citizens of the United States and of the State wherein they reside.". . . Its main purpose doubtless was, as has been often recognized by this court, to establish the citizenship of free negroes, which had been denied in the opinion delivered by Chief Justice Taney in *Dred Scott v. Sandford*, (1857); and to put it beyond doubt that all blacks, as well as whites, born or naturalized within the jurisdiction of the United States, are citizens of the United States. *The Slaughter house Cases*, (1873) 16 Wall. 36, 73; *Strauder v. West Virginia*, (1879) 100 U.S. 303, 306; *Ex parte Virginia*, (1879) 100 U.S. 339, 345; *Neal v. Delaware*, (1880) 103 U.S. 370, 386; *Elk v. Wilkins*, (1884) 112 U.S. 94, 101. But the opening words, "All persons born," are general, not to say universal, restricted only by place and jurisdiction, and not by color or race—as was clearly recognized in all the opinions delivered in *The Slaughterhouse Cases*, above cited.

Mr. Justice Miller, delivering the [*Slaughterhouse*] opinion of the majority of the court, after observing that the Thirteenth, Fourteenth and Fifteenth Articles of Amendment of the Constitution were all addressed to the grievances of the negro race, and were designed to remedy them, continued as follows: "We do not say that no one else but the negro can share in this protection. Both the language and spirit of these Articles are to have their fair and just weight in any question of construction. Undoubtedly, while negro slavery alone was in the mind of the Congress which proposed the Thirteenth Article, it forbids any other kind of slavery, now or hereafter. If Mexican peonage or the Chinese coolie labor system shall develop slavery of the Mexican or Chinese race within our territory, this Amendment may safely be trusted to make it void. And so if other rights are assailed by the States, which properly and necessarily fall within the protection of these Articles, that protection will apply, though the party interested may not be of African descent."

And in treating of the first clause of the Fourteenth Amendment, he said: "The distinction between citizenship of the United States and citizenship of a State is clearly recognized and established. Not only may a man be a citizen of the United States without being a citizen of a State, but an important element is necessary to convert the former into the latter. He must reside within the State to make him a citizen of it, but it is only necessary that he should be born or naturalized in the United States to be a citizen of the Union."

The only adjudication that has been made by this court upon the meaning of the clause, "and subject to the jurisdiction thereof," in the leading provision of the Fourteenth Amendment, is *Elk v. Wilkins*, 112 U.S. 94, in which it was decided that an Indian born a member of one of the Indian tribes within the United States, which still existed and was recognized as an Indian tribe by the United States, who had voluntarily separated himself from his tribe, and taken up his residence among the white citizens of a State, but who did not appear to have been naturalized, or taxed, or in any way recognized or treated as a citizen, either by the United States or by the State, was not a citizen of the

United States, as a person born in the United States, "and subject to the jurisdiction thereof," within the meaning of the clause in question.

That decision was placed upon the grounds [that]... "Indians born within the territorial limits of the United States, members of, and owing immediate allegiance to, one of the Indian tribes (an alien, though dependent, power), although in a geographical sense born in the United States, are no more 'born in the United States, and subject to the jurisdiction thereof,' within the meaning of the first section of the Fourteenth Amendment, than the children of subjects of any foreign government born within the domain of that government, or the children born within the United States of ambassadors or other public ministers of foreign nations."

The decision in *Elk v. Wilkins* concerned only members of the Indian tribes within the United States, and had no tendency to deny citizenship to children born in the United States of foreign parents of Caucasian, African or Mongolian descent, not in the diplomatic service of a foreign country.

The real object of the Fourteenth Amendment of the Constitution, in qualifying the words, "All persons born in the United States," by the addition, "and subject to the jurisdiction thereof," would appear to have been to exclude, by the fewest and fittest words, (besides children of members of the Indian tribes, standing in a peculiar relation to the National Government, unknown to the common law,) the two classes of cases—children born of alien enemies in hostile occupation, and children of diplomatic representatives of a foreign State—both of which, as has already been shown, by the law of England, and by our own law, from the time of the first settlement of the English colonies in America, had been recognized exceptions to the fundamental rule of citizenship by birth within the country. *Calvin's Case*, 7 Rep. 1, 18b; Cockburn on Nationality, 7; Dicey Conflict of Laws, 177; *Inglis v. Sailors' Snug Harbor*, 3 Pet. 99, 155; 2 Kent Com. 39, 42.

The foregoing considerations and authorities irresistibly lead us to these conclusions: The Fourteenth Amendment affirms the ancient and fundamental rule of citizenship by birth within the territory, in the allegiance and under the protection of the country, including all children here born of resident aliens, with the exceptions or qualifications (as old as the rule itself) of children of foreign sovereigns or their ministers, or born on foreign public ships, or of enemies within and during a hostile occupation of part of our territory, and with the single additional exception of children of members of the Indian tribes owing direct allegiance to their several tribes. The Amendment, in clear words and in manifest intent, includes the children born, within the territory of the United States, of all other persons, of whatever race or color, domiciled within the United States. Every citizen or subject of another country, while domiciled here, is within the allegiance and the protection, and consequently subject to the jurisdiction, of the United States.

To hold that the Fourteenth Amendment of the Constitution excludes from citizenship the children, born in the United States, of citizens or subjects of other countries, would be to deny citizenship to thousands of persons of English, Scotch, Irish, German or other European parentage, who have always been considered and treated as citizens of the United States.

VI.

Whatever considerations, in the absence of a controlling provision of the Constitution, might influence the legislative or the executive branch of the Government to decline to admit persons of the Chinese race to the status of citizens of the United States, there are none that can constrain or permit the judiciary to refuse to give full effect to the peremptory and explicit language of the Fourteenth Amendment, which declares and ordains that "All persons born or naturalized in the United States, and subject to the jurisdiction thereof, are citizens of the United States."

The decision in *Yick Wo v. Hopkins*, indeed, did not directly pass upon the effect of these words in the Fourteenth Amendment, but turned upon subsequent provisions of the same section. But, as already observed, it is impossible to attribute to the words, "subject to the jurisdiction thereof," that is to say, of the United States, at the beginning, a less comprehensive meaning than to the words "within its jurisdiction," that is of the State, at the end of the same section; or to hold that persons, who are indisputably "within the jurisdiction" of the State, are not "subject to the jurisdiction" of the Nation.*

It necessarily follows that persons born in China, subjects of the Emperor of China, but domiciled in the United States, having been adjudged, in *Yick Wo v. Hopkins*, to be within the jurisdiction of the State, within the meaning of the concluding sentence, must be held to be subject to the jurisdiction of the United States, within the meaning of the first sentence of this section of the Constitution; and their children, "born in the United States," cannot be less "subject to the jurisdiction thereof."

During the debates in the Senate in January and February, 1866, upon the Civil Rights Bill, Mr. Trumbull, the chairman of the committee which reported the bill, moved to amend the first sentence thereof so as to read, "All persons born in the United States, and not subject to any foreign power, are hereby declared to be citizens of the United States, without distinction of color." Mr. Cowan, of Pennsylvania, asked, "Whether it will not have the effect of naturalizing the children of Chinese and Gypsies, born in this country?" Mr. Trumbull answered, "Undoubtedly;" and asked, "Is not the child born in this country of German parents a citizen?" Mr. Cowan replied, "The children of German parents are citizens; but Germans are not Chinese." Mr. Trumbull rejoined: "The law makes no such distinction; and the child of an Asiatic is just as much a citizen as the child of a European." Mr. Reverdy Johnson suggested that the words, "without distinction of color," should be omitted as unnecessary; and said: "The amendment, as it stands, is that all persons born in the United States, and not subject to a foreign power, shall, by virtue of birth, be citizens. To that I am willing to consent; and that comprehends all persons, without any reference to race or color, who may be so born." And Mr. Trumbull agreed that striking out those words would make

---

* The phrase "within its jurisdiction" comes from another portion of the Fourteenth Amendment, which states: "[N]or shall any State deprive any person of life, liberty or property without due process of law, nor deny to any person within its jurisdiction the equal protection of the laws."—ED.

no difference in the meaning, but thought it better that they should be retained, to remove all possible doubt.

The Fourteenth Amendment of the Constitution, as originally framed by the House of Representatives, lacked the opening sentence. When it came before the Senate in May, 1866, Mr. Howard, of Michigan, moved to amend by prefixing the sentence in its present form, (less the words "or naturalized,") and reading, "All persons born in the United States, and subject to the jurisdiction thereof, are citizens of the United States and of the State wherein they reside." Mr. Cowan objected, upon the ground that the Mongolian race ought to be excluded; and said: "Is the child of the Chinese immigrant in California a citizen?" "I do not know how my honorable friend from California looks upon Chinese, but I do know how some of his fellow-citizens regard them. I have no doubt that now they are useful, and I have no doubt that within proper restraints, allowing that State and the other Pacific States to manage them as they may see fit, they may be useful; but I would not tie their hands by the Constitution of the United States so as to prevent them hereafter from dealing with them as in their wisdom they see fit." Mr. Conness, of California, replied: "The proposition before us relates simply, in that respect, to the children begotten of Chinese parents in California, and it is proposed to declare that they shall be citizens. We have declared that by law; now it is proposed to incorporate the same provision in the fundamental instrument of the Nation. I am in favor of doing so. I voted for the proposition to declare that the children of all parentage whatever, born in California, should be regarded and treated as citizens of the United States, entitled to equal civil rights with other citizens of the United States.... We are entirely ready to accept the provision proposed in this Constitutional Amendment, that the children born here of Mongolian parents shall be declared by the Constitution of the United States to be entitled to civil rights and to equal protection before the law with others." It does not appear to have been suggested, in either House of Congress, that children born in the United States of Chinese parents would not come within the terms and effect of the leading sentence of the Fourteenth Amendment.

Doubtless, the intention of the Congress which framed and of the States which adopted this Amendment of the Constitution must be sought in the words of the Amendment; and the debates in Congress are not admissible as evidence to control the meaning of those words. But the statements above quoted are valuable as contemporaneous opinions of jurists and statesmen upon the legal meaning of the words themselves; and are, at the least, interesting as showing that the application of the Amendment to the Chinese race was considered and not overlooked.

The Fourteenth Amendment of the Constitution, in the declaration that "all persons born or naturalized in the United States, and subject to the jurisdiction thereof, are citizens of the United States and of the State wherein they reside," contemplates two sources of citizenship, and two only: birth and naturalization. Citizenship by naturalization can only be acquired by naturalization under the authority and in the forms of law. But citizenship by birth is established by the mere fact of birth under the circumstances defined in the Constitution. Every person born in the United States, and subject to the jurisdiction thereof, becomes at once a citizen of the United States, and needs no naturalization.

The power of naturalization, vested in Congress by the Constitution, is a power to confer citizenship, not a power to take it away. . . . The Fourteenth Amendment, while it leaves the power, where it was before, in Congress, to regulate naturalization, has conferred no authority upon Congress to restrict the effect of birth, declared by the Constitution to constitute a sufficient and complete right to citizenship.

VII.

Upon the facts agreed in this case, the American citizenship which Wong Kim Ark acquired by birth within the United States has not been lost or taken away by anything happening since his birth.

Order affirmed.

Mr. Chief Justice FULLER, with whom concurred Mr. Justice HARLAN, dissenting.

The framers of the Constitution were familiar with the distinctions between the Roman law and the feudal law, between obligations based on territoriality and those based on the personal and invisible character of origin, and there is nothing to show that in the matter of nationality they intended to adhere to principles derived from regal government, which they had just assisted in overthrowing.

Manifestly, when the sovereignty of the Crown was thrown off and an independent government established, every rule of the common law and every statute of England obtaining in the Colonies, in derogation of the principles on which the new government was founded, was abrogated. The English common law rule recognized no exception in the instance of birth during the mere temporary or accidental sojourn of the parents.

But a different view as to the effect of permanent abode on nationality has been expressed in this country. In his work on Conflict of Laws, § 48, Mr. Justice Story, treating the subject as one of public law, said: "Persons who are born in a country are generally deemed to be citizens of that country. A reasonable qualification of the rule would seem to be that it should not apply to the children of parents who were *in itinere* in the country, or who were abiding there for temporary purposes, as for health or curiosity, or occasional business. It would be difficult, however, to assert that in the present state of public law such a qualification is universally established."

Undoubtedly all persons born in a country are presumptively citizens thereof, but the presumption is not irrebuttable.

In his Lectures on Constitutional Law, p. 279, Mr. Justice Miller remarked: "If a stranger or traveller passing through, or temporarily residing in this country, who has not himself been naturalized, and who claims to owe no allegiance to our Government, has a child born here which goes out of the country with its father, such child is not a citizen of the United States, because it was not subject to its jurisdiction."

The Civil Rights Act became a law April 9, 1866, and provided: "That all persons born in the United States and not subject to any foreign power, excluding Indians not taxed, are hereby declared to be citizens of the United States." The words "not subject to any foreign power" do not in themselves refer to mere territorial jurisdiction, for the persons referred to are persons born in the United States. All such persons are undoubtedly subject to the territorial jurisdiction of the United States, and yet the act concedes that nevertheless they may be subject to the political jurisdiction of a foreign government. In other words, by the terms of the act all persons born in the United States, and not owing allegiance to any foreign power, are citizens.

If the act of 1866 had not contained the words, "and not subject to any foreign power," the children neither of public ministers nor of aliens in territory in hostile occupation would have been included within its terms on any proper construction, for their birth would not have subjected them to ties of allegiance, whether local and temporary, or general and permanent. There was no necessity as to them for the insertion of the words although they were embraced by them.

But there were others in respect of whom the exception was needed, namely, the children of aliens, whose parents owed local and temporary allegiance merely, remaining subject to a foreign power by virtue of the tie of permanent allegiance, which they had not severed by formal abjuration or equivalent conduct, and some of whom were not permitted to do so if they would.

And it was to prevent the acquisition of citizenship by the children of such aliens merely by birth within the geographical limits of the United States that the words were inserted.

Two months after the statute was enacted, on June 16, 1866, the Fourteenth Amendment was proposed, and declared ratified July 28, 1868.

[I]n *Elk v. Wilkins*, 112 U.S. 94, 101, where the subject received great consideration . . . it was said:

> The section contemplates two sources of citizenship, and two sources only: birth and naturalization. The persons declared to be citizens are "all persons born or naturalized in the United States, and subject to the jurisdiction thereof." The evident meaning of these last words is, not merely subject in some respect or degree to the jurisdiction of the United States, but completely subject to their political jurisdiction, and owing them direct and immediate allegiance.

To be "completely subject" to the political jurisdiction of the United States is to be in no respect or degree subject to the political jurisdiction of any other government.

Now I take it that the children of aliens, whose parents have not only not renounced their allegiance to their native country, but are forbidden by its system of government, as well as by its positive laws, from doing so, and are not permitted to acquire another citizenship by the laws of the country into which they come, must necessarily remain themselves subject to the same sovereignty as their parents, and cannot, in the nature of things, be, any more than their parents, completely subject to the jurisdiction of such other country.

Generally speaking, I understand the subjects of the Emperor of China— that ancient Empire, with its history of thousands of years and its unbroken continuity in belief, traditions and government, in spite of revolutions and changes of dynasty—to be bound to him by every conception of duty and by every principle of their religion, of which filial piety is the first and greatest commandment; and formerly, perhaps still, their penal laws denounced the severest penalties on those who renounced their country and allegiance, and their abettors; and, in effect, held the relatives at home of Chinese in foreign lands as hostages for their loyalty.[1] And whatever concession may have been made by treaty in the direction of admitting the right of expatriation in some sense, they seem in the United States to have remained pilgrims and sojourners as all their fathers were. 149 U.S. at 717. At all events, they have never been allowed by our laws to acquire our nationality, and, except in sporadic instances, do not appear ever to have desired to do so.

The Fourteenth Amendment was not designed to accord citizenship to persons so situated and to cut off the legislative power from dealing with the subject.

The right of a nation to expel or deport foreigners who have not been naturalized or taken any steps toward becoming citizens of a country, is as absolute and unqualified as the right to prohibit and prevent their entrance into the country.

But can the persons expelled be subjected to "cruel and unusual punishments" in the process of expulsion, as would be the case if children born to them in this country were separated from them on their departure, because citizens of the United States? Was it intended by this amendment to tear up parental relations by the roots?

It is not to be admitted that the children of persons so situated [the Chinese] become citizens by the accident of birth. On the contrary, I am of opinion that the President and Senate by treaty, and the Congress by naturalization, have the power, notwithstanding the Fourteenth Amendment, to prescribe that all persons of a particular race, or their children, cannot become citizens, and that it results that the consent to allow such persons to come into and reside within our geographical limits does not carry with it the imposition of citizenship upon children born to them while in this country under such consent, in spite of treaty and statute.

In other words, the Fourteenth Amendment does not exclude from citizenship by birth children born in the United States of parents permanently located therein, and who might themselves become citizens; nor, on the other hand, does it arbitrarily make citizens of children born in the United States of parents who, according to the will of their native government and of this Government, are and must remain aliens.

Tested by this rule, Wong Kim Ark never became and is not a citizen of the United States, and the order of the District Court should be reversed.

---

[1] The fundamental laws of China have remained practically unchanged since the second century before Christ. The statutes have from time to time undergone modifications, but there does not seem to be any English or French translation of the Chinese Penal Code later than that by Staunton, published in 1810. That code provided: "All persons renouncing their country and allegiance, or devising the means thereof, shall be beheaded. . . ."

I am authorized to say that Mr. Justice Harlan concurs in this dissent.

NOTES AND QUESTIONS

1. Interpreting text: The legal issue in this case is the interpretation of the phrase "subject to the jurisdiction thereof" in the fourteenth amendment. What this phrase means may turn on the interpretive methodology used to divine its meaning. Consider, for example, how judges interpret statutes passed by legislatures. Often, they rely on the plain language of the statutory text (the so-called plain-meaning approach). Another method looks at other court decisions interpreting the same statute (known as judicial precedent). Courts also sometimes rely on statements of record made during the legislature's deliberations prior to enacting the statute into law (known as legislative history). And they will try to interpret statutes to further the social policies that they think underlie the particular legislation and to avoid terrible policy consequences. At issue here is not a statute but a constitutional amendment, which might lend itself to still other methods of interpretation. In this case, which interpretive methodology (or methodologies) was emphasized by the Court?

2. The dissent: In your own words, articulate the single best argument that the dissent has against Wong Kim Ark's claim to citizenship. As a factual matter, it is uncontested that Wong Kim Ark was born on American soil. But why then was he not subject to the jurisdiction of the United States?

3. Justice Harlan: Justice Harlan is extolled for dissenting from the infamous *Plessy v. Ferguson*, 163 U.S. 537 (1896), in which the Supreme Court upheld the constitutionality of segregated train cars. In his dissent, he rejected the doctrine of "separate but equal" established seventy years before *Brown v. Board of Education*, 347 U.S. 483 (1954) (formally ending segregated education). Specifically, Justice Harlan is praised for being color-blind and therefore putatively non-racist. But in his *Plessy* dissent, Justice Harlan had a line that has until recently been edited out of the leading constitutional law casebooks: "There is a race so different from our own that we do not permit those belonging to it to become citizens of the United States. . . . I allude to the Chinese race." *Id.* at 561. Harlan's point was this: If we allow even the Chinese—who are not allowed to become citizens—to ride trains with Whites, why do we not allow Blacks to do the same, who are, after all, American citizens. What are we to make of his dissent in *Plessy,* especially given his joining the dissent in *Wong Kim Ark* two years later?

4. Continuing challenges to citizenship: Citizenship by birth was challenged in 1942 by the Native Sons of the Golden West, who petitioned to strike all Japanese born in the United States to alien parents from the voter rolls. *See Regan v. King*, 49 F. Supp. 222 (N.D. Cal. 1942). At this time, the United States was at war with Japan, anti-Japanese sentiments were rabid and the internment process had already begun. The district court rejected the plaintiff's request on the clear authority of *Wong Kim Ark*.

5. Current debates: Citizenship by birth has been challenged even more recently. Some complain that undocumented pregnant Mexican women are crossing the border to have their children on U.S. soil. For example, House Representative Elton Gallegly (R-Cal.) has called for an amendment to the U.S. Constitution that would delete the citizenship clause of the fourteenth amendment. He wrote:

> The enactment of major immigration reforms during the 1980's and 1990's attests to our continuing strong commitment to the melting-pot credo, and our belief that newcomers legally entering our shores will benefit America's economy and its social and cultural heritage. . . . We must recognize, however, . . . in many parts of this country, especially in California, our cities and towns are being overrun with immigrants, both legal and undocumented, who pose major economic and law enforcement problems for local governments, and place an added burden on their already strained budgets.

139 CONG. REC. H 1005 (vol.139, No.24 March 3, 1993).

4. THE RIGHT TO WORK: LAUNDRY ORDINANCES AND YICK WO V. HOPKINS

As explained above, the Chinese first came to the United States in the 1850s to work the sugar plantations in Hawaii and to strike gold in California. On the mainland, by the mid-1860s, it had become increasingly difficult to survive as a miner. Consequently, many Chinese became low wage earners working in miscellaneous fields. Between 1865 and 1869, a great many Chinese (up to 12,000 at one point) labored for the Central Pacific Railroad. Under brutal conditions, they laid track from Sacramento, California, to Promontory Point, Utah, to help complete the first transcontinental railroad. Upon completing the railroad, many Chinese returned to San Francisco to enter manufacturing jobs, agriculture and self-employment, including laundries.

The laundry business was one of the few entrepreneurial opportunities left open to the Chinese. A laundry required a relatively small capital outlay and allowed Chinese with few other skills to eke out a living. Quickly, the commercial laundry industry claimed a large percentage of adult male Chinese laborers. In 1870, in San Francisco, there were approximately 1,300 Chinese laundrymen, which amounted to 12 percent of the city's entire Chinese population. By 1900, the census reported that 25 percent of all employed Chinese males in the United States were launderers, with 18 percent in agriculture and 14 percent working as household servants.

Starting in 1873, the City of San Francisco passed numerous ordinances targeting Chinese laundries. These ordinances were worded neutrally, without specific mention of the Chinese; for example, they taxed all laundries that did not use a horse and wagon, or they required all laundries made of wooden structures to undergo special licensing procedures. In practice, however, these facially neutral ordinances were crafted specifically to harass the Chinese and were enforced accordingly.

Many of these ordinances were struck down by state and federal courts as unfair, oppressive regulations that went beyond the powers of city and county governments. On the other hand, other ordinances were accepted as reasonable exercises of a state's police power. For example, in *Soon Hing v. Crow-*

ley, 113 U.S. 703 (1885), the Supreme Court addressed an ordinance that required laundries to close at night. The Court accepted the general rule as one enacted without racial animus, and that was a reasonable police regulation for the city's safety and welfare. Another such ordinance, which required all laundries housed in wooden buildings to receive a license from the board of supervisors to continue operation, was the subject of the well-known *Yick Wo v. Hopkins* case. It was challenged under the equal protection clause of the fourteenth amendment, which states: "Nor shall any State deprive any person of life, liberty, or property without due process of law; nor deny to any person within its jurisdiction the equal protection of the laws."

YICK WO V. HOPKINS
118 U.S. 356 (1886)

Mr. Justice MATTHEWS delivered the opinion of the Court.

We are . . . constrained, at the outset, to differ from the Supreme Court of California upon the real meaning of the ordinances in question. That court considered these ordinances as vesting in the board of supervisors a not unusual discretion in granting or withholding their assent to the use of wooden buildings as laundries, to be exercised in reference to the circumstances of each case, with a view to the protection of the public against the dangers of fire. We are not able to concur in that interpretation of the power conferred upon the supervisors. There is nothing in the ordinances which points to such a regulation of the business of keeping and conducting laundries. They seem intended to confer, and actually do confer, not a discretion to be exercised upon a consideration of the circumstances of each case, but a naked and arbitrary power to give or withhold consent, not only as to places, but as to persons. So that, if an applicant for such consent, being in every way a competent and qualified person, and having complied with every reasonable condition demanded by any public interest, should, failing to obtain the requisite consent of the supervisors to the prosecution of his business, apply for redress by the judicial process of mandamus, to require the supervisors to consider and act upon his case, it would be a sufficient answer for them to say that the law had conferred upon them authority to withhold their assent, without reason and without responsibility. The power given to them is not confided to their discretion in the legal sense of that term, but is granted to their mere will. It is purely arbitrary, and acknowledges neither guidance nor restraint.

This erroneous view of the ordinances in question led the Supreme Court of California into the further error of holding that they were justified by the decisions of this court in the cases of *Barbier v. Connolly*, 113 U.S. 27 [(1885)], and *Soon Hing v. Crowley*, 113 U.S. 703 [(1885)]. In both of these cases the ordinance involved was simply a prohibition to carry on the washing and ironing of clothes in public laundries and washhouses, within certain prescribed limits of the city and county of San Francisco, from ten o'clock at night until six o'clock in the morning of the following day. This provision was held to be purely a police regulation, within the competency of any municipality possessed of the ordinary powers belonging to such bodies; a necessary measure of precaution in a city composed largely of wooden buildings like San Francisco, in the application of which there was no invidious discrimination against any one within the prescribed limits, all persons engaged in the same business being treated alike, and subject to the same restrictions, and entitled to the same privileges, under similar conditions.

For these reasons, that ordinance was adjudged not to be within the prohibitions of the Fourteenth Amendment to the Constitution of the United States, which, it was said, in the first case cited, "undoubtedly intended not only that there should be no arbitrary deprivation of life or liberty, or arbitrary spoliation of property, but that equal protection and security should be given to all under like circumstances in the enjoyment of their personal and civil rights; that all persons should be equally entitled to pursue their happiness and acquire and enjoy property; that they should have like access to the courts of the country for the protection of their persons and property, the prevention and redress of wrongs, and the enforcement of contracts; that no impediment should be interposed to the pursuits of any one, except as applied to the same pursuits by others under like circumstances; that no greater burdens should be laid upon one than are laid upon others in the same calling and condition; and that in the administration of criminal justice no different or higher punishment should be imposed upon one than such as is prescribed to all for like offences. . . . Class legislation, discriminating against some and favoring others, is prohibited, but legislation which, in carrying out a public purpose, is limited in its application, if within the sphere of its operation it affects alike all persons similarly situated, is not within the amendment."

The ordinance drawn in question in the present case is of a very different character. It does not prescribe a rule and conditions for the regulation of the use of property for laundry purposes, to which all similarly situated may conform. It allows without restriction the use for such purposes of buildings of brick or stone; but, as to wooden buildings, constituting nearly all those in previous use, it divides the owners or occupiers into two classes, not having respect to their personal character and qualifications for the business, nor the situation and nature and adaptation of the buildings themselves, but merely by an arbitrary line, on one side of which are those who are permitted to pursue their industry by the mere will and consent of the supervisors, and on the other those from whom that consent is withheld, at their mere will and pleasure. And both classes are alike only in this, that they are tenants at will, under the supervisors, of their means of living. The ordinance, therefore, also differs from the not unusual case, where discretion is lodged by law in public officers or bodies to grant or withhold licenses to keep taverns, or places for the sale of spirituous liquors, and the like, when one of the conditions is that the applicant shall be a fit person for the exercise of the privilege, because in such cases the fact of fitness is submitted to the judgment of the officer, and calls for the exercise of a discretion of a judicial nature.

The rights of the petitioners, as affected by the proceedings of which they complain, are not less, because they are aliens and subjects of the Emperor of China.

The Fourteenth Amendment to the Constitution is not confined to the protection of citizens. It says: "Nor shall any State deprive any person of life, liberty, or property without due process of law; nor deny to any person within its jurisdiction the equal protection of the laws." These provisions are universal in their application, to all persons within the territorial jurisdiction, without regard to any differences of race, of color, or of nationality; and the equal protection of the laws is a pledge of the protection of equal laws. The questions we have to consider and decide in these cases, therefore, are to be treated as involving the rights of every citizen of the United States equally with those of the strangers and aliens who now invoke the jurisdiction of the court.

It is contended on the part of the petitioners, that the ordinances for violations of which they are severally sentenced to imprisonment, are void on their face, as being within the prohibitions of the Fourteenth Amendment; and, in the alternative, if not so, that they are void by reason of their administration, operating unequally, so as to punish in the present petitioners what is permitted to others as lawful, without any distinction of circumstances—an unjust and illegal discrimination, it is claimed, which, though not made expressly by the ordinances is made possible by them.

When we consider the nature and the theory of our institutions of government, the principles upon which they are supposed to rest, and review the history of their development, we are constrained to conclude that they do not mean to leave room for the play and action of purely personal and arbitrary power. Sovereignty itself is, of course, not subject to law, for it is the author and source of law; but in our system, while sovereign powers are delegated to the agencies of government, sovereignty itself remains with the people, by whom and for whom all government exists and acts. And the law is the definition and limitation of power. It is, indeed, quite true, that there must always be lodged somewhere, and in some person or body, the authority of final decision; and in many cases of mere administration the responsibility is purely political, no appeal lying except to the ultimate tribunal of the public judgment, exercised either in the pressure of opinion or by means of the suffrage. But the fundamental rights to life, liberty, and the pursuit of happiness, considered as individual possessions, are secured by those maxims of constitutional law which are the monuments showing the victorious progress of the race in securing to men the blessings of civilization under the reign of just and equal laws, so that, in the famous language of the Massachusetts Bill of Rights, the government of the commonwealth "may be a government of laws and not of men." For, the very idea that one man may be compelled to hold his life, or the means of living, or any material right essential to the enjoyment of life, at the mere will of another, seems to be intolerable in any country where freedom prevails, as being the essence of slavery itself.

There are many illustrations that might be given of this truth, which would make manifest that it was self-evident in the light of our system of jurisprudence. The case of the political franchise of voting is one. Though not regarded strictly as a natural right, but as a privilege merely conceded by society according to its will, under certain conditions, nevertheless it is regarded as a fundamental political right, because preservative of all rights.

This conclusion, and the reasoning on which it is based, are deductions from the face of the ordinance, as to its necessary tendency and ultimate actual operation. In the present cases we are not obliged to reason from the probable to the actual, and pass upon the validity of the ordinances complained of, as tried merely by the opportunities which their terms afford, of unequal and unjust discrimination in their administration. For the cases present the ordinances in actual operation, and the facts shown establish an administration directed so exclusively against a particular class of persons as to warrant and require the conclusion, that, whatever may have been the intent of the ordinances as adopted, they are applied by the public authorities charged with their administration, and thus representing the State itself, with a mind so unequal and oppressive as to amount to a practical denial by the State of that equal protection of the laws which is secured to the petitioners, as to all other persons, by the broad and benign provisions of the Fourteenth Amendment to the Constitution of the United States. Though the law itself be fair on its face and impartial in appearance, yet, if it is applied and administered by public authority with an evil eye and an unequal hand, so as practically to make unjust and illegal discriminations between persons in similar circumstances, material to their rights, the denial of equal justice is still within the prohibition of the Constitution. This principle of interpretation has been sanctioned by this court in *Henderson v. Mayor of New York*, 92 U.S. 259 [(1876)]; *Chy Lung v. Freeman*, 92 U.S. 275 [(1876)]; *Ex parte Virginia*, 100 U.S. 339 [(1880)]; *Neal v. Delaware*, 103 U.S. 370 [(1881)]; and *Soon Hing v. Crowley*, 113 U.S. 703 [(1885)].

The present cases, as shown by the facts disclosed in the record, are within this class. It appears that both petitioners have complied with every requisite, deemed by the law or by the public officers charged with its administration, necessary for the protection of neighboring property from fire, or as a precaution against injury to the public health. No reason whatever, except the will of the supervisors, is assigned why they should not be permitted to carry on, in the accustomed manner, their harmless and useful occupation, on which they depend for a livelihood. And while this consent of the supervisors is withheld from them and from two hundred others who have also petitioned, all of whom happen to be Chinese subjects, eighty others, not Chinese subjects, are permitted to carry on the same business under similar conditions. The fact of this discrimination is admitted. No reason for it is shown, and the conclusion cannot be resisted, that no reason for it exists except hostility to the race and nationality to which the petitioners belong, and which in the eye of the law is not justified. The discrimination is, therefore, illegal, and the public administration which enforces it is a denial of the equal protection of the laws and a violation of the Fourteenth Amendment of the Constitution. The imprisonment of the petitioners is, therefore, illegal, and they must be discharged.

NOTES AND QUESTIONS

1. Asian American civil rights plaintiffs: You might wonder how *Yick Wo* (which may have been the name of the laundry, not the proprietor) had the resources to mount a Supreme Court challenge. The resources were provided by a laundry guild called the Tung Hing Tong. This guild regulated the Chinese laundries and by 1885 represented 300 of them. The guild retained prominent, well-paid, White American attorneys to argue their cases, a tactic that flustered the San Francisco attorneys. Consider, for example, the briefing of the case in the Supreme Court. *Yick Wo*'s brief was a lean 13 pages. The city's brief was a meandering 111 pages with the following apologia and accusation:

> Were it not for the wealth and power of the Tung Hing Tong and the brilliant talent of opposing counsel, this argument should have been much shorter. It is not the fault of the respondent that the petitioner has hung the dragon flag of the Chinese empire over his door, and dared the municipality of San Francisco to touch it. . . . Strip this case of its imported features; disconnect it with the Tung Hing Tong; remove the disturbing elements of luminaries of the law of superior ability distributing themselves on . . . pages of printed matter, and we might have submitted our case without briefs and without argument.

Respondent's Brief, *Yick Wo. v. Hopkins*, at 103-4 (1886), *reprinted in* Philip B. Kurland, and Gerhard Casper (ed.), Landmark Briefs and Arguments of the Supreme Court of the United States: Constitutional Law 131-132 (1975).

2. Revising history: In omitted portions of the opinion, the Court made reference to a civil rights statute concerning equal contracting rights, section 1977 of the Revised Statutes, which is currently codified at 42 U.S.C. § 1981. In *Runyon v. McCrary*, 427 U.S. 160 (1976), the Court interpreted this statute to be derived from section 1 of the Civil Rights Act of 1866. In fact, as legal historian Charles McClain has shown, it is a codification of section 16 of the Civil Rights Act of 1870, which was passed explicitly to benefit the Chinese.* This is one example of how Asian Americans' role in the development of our civil rights law has been misremembered or ignored.

3. Civil rights law, judicial interests and economic ideology: Lawyers cite to *Yick Wo* for the legal proposition that facially neutral rules applied invidiously against a racial group violate the equal protection of the laws guaranteed by the Constitution. One view, then, of *Yick Wo* is of an early judicial impulse toward racial equality. There are other, less sanguine, views. Consider this:

> [T]he Chinese rights jurisprudence culminating in *Yick Wo* was possible only because the interests of Chinese aliens in fighting state discrimination converged with the interests of the federal judiciary in extending the Fourteenth Amendment to protect economic interests from state interference. The anachronistic reading of *Yick Wo* as a harbinger of the civil rights movement threatens to obscure from the American conscience a long and ugly era of racial hatred. The legal discrimination produced by this hatred was tempered only by self-interest and not by a desire for brotherhood.

Thomas Wuil Joo, *New "Conspiracy Theory" of the Fourteenth Amendment: Nineteenth Century Chinese Civil Rights Cases and the Development of Sub-*

---

* *See* Charles J. McClain Jr., *The Chinese Struggle for Civil Rights in Nineteenth Century America: The First Phase*, 1850-1870, 72 Cal. L. Rev. 529, 530-31 (1984).

stantive Due Process Jurisprudence, 29 U.S.F. L. REV. 353, 355 (1995). Contrast this critical view with the following:

> The Chinese laundry decisions rest ultimately of course on a general concept of equal protection. . . . They are also a tribute to judicial willingness to defend the rights of unpopular minorities in the face of popular pressure. But they are too, in an important sense, an enduring tribute to what we may call the judicial Jacksonianism of the post-Civil War period. As the historian Carl Degler points out, the cardinal principle of Jacksonianism, a dominant strain in American political thought throughout the nineteenth century, was economic freedom or, more precisely, freedom from economic discrimination by government. Boiled down to its essence the Jacksonian credo said "that no one should obtain rights or privileges from government which no one else enjoyed. In practice this meant that the state should not favor one class or individual over any other in economic endeavors." A major corollary of this principle was that individuals should be free from the effects of legislative favoritism as they sought to advance themselves economically through the pursuit of one of the so-called ordinary trades or avocations of life.

Charles J. McClain, IN SEARCH OF EQUALITY: THE CHINESE STRUGGLE AGAINST DISCRIMINATION IN NINETEENTH-CENTURY AMERICA 130–31 (1994).

5. THE RIGHT TO OWN PROPERTY: ALIEN LAND LAWS AND *TERRACE V. THOMPSON*

In the early 20th century in California, Japanese Americans enjoyed great success in certain forms of intensive truck farming. As they purchased more land and flourished economically, White American resentment began to increase. From 1907 to 1911, the California legislature considered numerous bills to constrain alien ownership of land. Political pressure from Presidents Theodore Roosevelt and William Howard Taft kept the bills from being enacted into law. However, by 1913, the resentment had grown too strong for then President Woodrow Wilson to stop the passage of California's alien land law.

In 1913, California passed its alien land law, the first alien land law in the nation motivated by anti-Japanese sentiments.[*] The law granted all aliens

---

[*] Earlier land laws were passed in the 19th century that disfavored the Chinese. For example, the 1859 Oregon Constitution stated explicitly: "No Chinaman, not a resident of the state at the adoption of [this] Constitution, shall ever hold any real estate or mining claim. . . ." Mark L. Lazarus, III, *An Historical Analysis of Alien Land Law: Washington Territory & State* 1853-1889, 12 U. PUGET SOUND L. REV. 197, 217 (1989) (quoting OR. CONST. art. XV, § 8 (1859, repealed 1946)). In 1879, the California Constitution extended land rights to aliens who were of the "white race or of African descent" but left the rights of those ineligible for citizenship unprotected by the state constitution. *See id.* at 216 (quoting CAL. CONST. art. I, § 17 (1879, amended 1954, repealed 1974)). Similarly, motivated by anti-Chinese sentiment, the territorial legislature of Washington in 1886 ensured broad property rights to aliens except those aliens incapable of becoming citizens. When Washington joined the Union in 1889, its constitution severely constrained ownership of property by aliens except by those who in good faith had declared their intention to become citizens. One commentator has argued, however, that this provision was less motivated by race than by the general fear of nonresident alien land holdings. *See id.* at 232-233.

eligible for citizenship plenary property rights but permitted aliens ineligible for citizenship (that is, those who could not be naturalized as "free White persons") to enjoy only those property rights guaranteed by treaty. Not coincidentally, the Treaty of 1911 between the United States and Japan made no mention of protecting agricultural property rights of the Japanese residing in the United States. In 1920, Californians voted by popular initiative to close certain loopholes left open in the 1913 law. Legal scholar Keith Aoki notes that this initiative "passed with a decisive majority in every county in California," and

> barred guardianships and trusteeships in the name of 'aliens ineligible to citizenship,' . . . barred all leases of agricultural land, barred corporations with a majority of shareholders who were 'aliens ineligible to citizenship' from owning agricultural land, and classified sharecropping contracts as 'interests in land.'. . . It drastically reduced Japanese-owned acreage.

Keith Aoki, *No Right to Own?: The Early Twentieth-Century "Alien Land Laws" as a Prelude to Internment,*" 19 B.C. THIRD WORLD L.J. 37 (1998); 40 B.C. L. REV. 37, 57, 59 (1998).

Any lingering doubt about the ineligibility for citizenship of Japanese immigrants was resolved with the 1922 *Ozawa v. United States* decision. By 1925, Arizona (1917), Louisiana (1921), Washington (1921),[*] New Mexico (1922), Idaho, Montana, Oregon (1923), and Kansas (1925) had all passed alien land laws. The Supreme Court first ruled on the constitutionality of these land laws in 1923.

TERRACE V. THOMPSON
263 U.S. 197 (1923)

Mr. Justice BUTLER delivered the opinion of the Court.

Appellants brought this suit to enjoin the Attorney General of Washington from enforcing the Anti-Alien Land Law of that State, c. 50, Laws, 1921, on the grounds that it is in conflict with the due process and equal protection clauses of the Fourteenth Amendment. . . .

[The Court also addressed arguments based on a treaty between the United States and Japan, and on the California Constitution.]

The appellants are residents of Washington. The Terraces are citizens of the United States and of Washington. Nakatsuka was born in Japan of Japanese parents and is a subject of the Emperor of Japan. The Terraces are the owners of a tract of land in King County which is particularly adapted to raising vegetables, and which for a number of years had been devoted to that and other agricultural purposes. The complaint alleges that Nakatsuka is a capable farmer and will be a desirable tenant of the land; that the Terraces desire to lease their land to him for the period of five years; that he desires to accept such lease, and that the lease would be made but for the act complained of.

---

[*] The 1921 Act closed various loopholes in the 1889 state constitution. As to the 1921 statute, there is no doubt that the "Japanese problem" was foremost in the legislators' minds.

Section 33[1] of Article II of the Constitution of Washington prohibits the ownership of land by aliens other than those who in good faith have declared intention to become citizens of the United States, except in certain instances not here involved. The act[2] provides in substance that any such alien shall not own, take, have or hold the legal or equitable title, or right to any benefit of any land as defined in the act, and that land conveyed to or for the use of aliens in violation of the state constitution or of the act shall thereby be forfeited to the state. And it is made a gross misdemeanor, punishable by fine or imprisonment or both, knowingly to transfer land or the right to the control, possession or use of land to such an alien. It is also made a gross misdemeanor for any such alien having title to such land or the control, possession or use thereof, to refuse to disclose to the Attorney General or the prosecuting attorney the nature and extent of his interest in the land. The Attorney General and the prosecuting attorneys of the several counties are charged with the enforcement of the act.

The Terraces' property rights in the land include the right to use, lease and dispose of it for lawful purposes (*Buchanan v. Warley*, 245 U.S. 60, 74 [(1917)]), and the Constitution protects these essential attributes of property (*Holden v. Hardy*, 169 U.S. 366, 391 [(1898)]), and also protects Nakatsuka in his right to earn a livelihood by following the ordinary occupations of life. *Truax v. Raich*, [239 U.S. 33 (1915)]; *Meyer v. Nebraska*, 262 U.S. 390

---

[1] Section 33. The ownership of lands by aliens, other than those who in good faith have declared their intention to become citizens of the United States, is prohibited in this State, except where acquired by inheritance, under mortgage or in good faith in the ordinary course of justice in the collection of debts; and all conveyances of land hereafter made to any alien directly or in trust for such alien shall be void: Provided, That the provisions of this section shall not apply to lands containing valuable deposits of minerals, metals, iron, coal, or fire-clay, and the necessary land for mills and machinery to be used in the development thereof and the manufacture of the products therefrom. Every corporation, the majority of the capital stock of which is owned by aliens, shall be considered an alien for the purposes of this prohibition.

[2] Section 1. In this act, unless the context otherwise requires,

(a) "Alien" does not include an alien who has in good faith declared his intention to become a citizen of the United States, but does include all other aliens and all corporations and other organized groups of persons a majority of whose capital stock is owned or controlled by aliens or a majority of whose members are aliens;

(b) "Land" does not include lands containing valuable deposits of minerals, metals, iron, coal or fire-clay or the necessary land for mills and machinery to be used in the development thereof and the manufacture of the products therefrom, but does include every other kind of land and every interest therein and right to the control, possession, use, enjoyment, rents, issues or profits thereof. . . .

(d) To "own" means to have the legal or equitable title to or the right to any benefit of;

(e) "Title" includes every kind of legal or equitable title;

Section 2. An alien shall not own land or take or hold title thereto. No person shall take or hold land or title to land for an alien. Land now held by or for aliens in violation of the constitution of the state is forfeited to and declared to be the property of the state. Land hereafter conveyed to or for the use of aliens in violation of the constitution or of this act shall thereby be forfeited to and become the property of the state.

[(1923)]. If, as claimed, the state act is repugnant to the due process and equal protection clauses of the Fourteenth Amendment, then its enforcement will deprive the owners of their right to lease their land to Nakatsuka, and deprive him of his right to pursue the occupation of farmer, and the threat to enforce it constitutes a continuing unlawful restriction upon and infringement of the rights of appellants, as to which they have no remedy at law which is as practical, efficient or adequate as the remedy in equity.

Appellants contend that the act contravenes the due process clause in that it prohibits the owners from making lawful disposition or use of their land, and makes it a criminal offense for them to lease it to the alien, and prohibits him from following the occupation of farmer; and they contend that it is repugnant to the equal protection clause in that aliens are divided into two classes,—those who may and those who may not become citizens, one class being permitted, while the other is forbidden, to own land as defined.

Alien inhabitants of a State, as well as all other persons within its jurisdiction, may invoke the protection of these clauses. *Yick Wo v. Hopkins,* 118 U.S. 356, 369 [(1886)]; *Truax v. Raich, supra,* 39. The Fourteenth Amendment, as against the arbitrary and capricious or unjustly discriminatory action of the State, protects the owners in their right to lease and dispose of their land for lawful purposes and the alien resident in his right to earn a living by following ordinary occupations of the community, but it does not take away from the State those powers of police that were reserved at the time of the adoption of the Constitution. *Barbier v. Connolly,* 113 U.S. 27 [(1885)]. And in the exercise of such powers the State has wide discretion in determining its own public policy and what measures are necessary for its own protection and properly to promote the safety, peace and good order of its people.

And, while Congress has exclusive jurisdiction over immigration, naturalization and the disposal of the public domain, each State, in the absence of any treaty provision to the contrary, has power to deny to aliens the right to own land within its borders. *Hauenstein v. Lynham,* 100 U.S. 483, 484, 488 [(1880)]; *Blythe v. Hinckley,* 180 U.S. 333, 340 [(1901)]. . . .

State legislation applying alike and equally to all aliens, withholding from them the right to own land, cannot be said to be capricious or to amount to an arbitrary deprivation of liberty or property, or to transgress the due process clause.

This brings us to a consideration of appellants' contention that the act contravenes the equal protection clause. That clause secures equal protection to all in the enjoyment of their rights under like circumstances. But this does not forbid every distinction in the law of a State between citizens and aliens resident therein.

By the statute in question all aliens who have not in good faith declared intention to become citizens of the United States, as specified in § 1 (a), are called "aliens," and it is provided that they shall not "own" "land," as defined in clauses (d) and (b) of § 1 respectively. The class so created includes all, but is not limited to, aliens not eligible to become citizens. Eligible aliens who have not declared their intention to become citizens are included, and the act provides that unless declarants be admitted to citizenship within seven years after the declaration is made, bad faith will be presumed. This leaves the class permitted so to own land made up of citizens and aliens who may, and who intend to, become citizens, and who in good faith have made the declaration required by the naturalization laws. The inclusion of good faith declarants in the same class with citizens does not unjustly discriminate against aliens who are ineligible or against eligible aliens who have failed to declare their intention. The classification is based on eligibility and purpose to naturalize. Eligible aliens are free white persons and persons of African nativity or descent. Congress is not trammeled, and it may grant or withhold the privilege of naturalization upon any grounds or without any reason, as it sees fit. But it is not to be supposed that its acts defining eligibility are arbitrary or unsupported by reasonable considerations of public policy. The State properly may assume that the considerations upon which Congress made such classification are substantial and reasonable. Generally speaking, the natives of European countries are eligible. Japanese, Chinese and Malays are not. Appellants' contention that the state act discriminates arbitrarily against Nakatsuka and other ineligible aliens because of their race and color is without foundation. All persons of whatever color or race who have not declared their intention in good faith to become citizens are prohibited from so owning agricultural lands. Two classes of aliens inevitably result from the naturalization laws,—those who may and those who may not become citizens. The rule established by Congress on this subject, in and of itself, furnishes a reasonable basis for classification in a state law withholding from aliens the privilege of land ownership as defined in the act. We agree with the court below (274 Fed. 841, 849) that:

> It is obvious that one who is not a citizen and cannot become one lacks an interest in, and the power to effectually work for the welfare of, the state, and, so lacking, the state may rightfully deny him the right to own and lease real estate within its boundaries. If one incapable of citizenship may lease or own real estate, it is within the realm of possibility that every foot of land within the state might pass to the ownership or possession of noncitizens. And we think it is clearly within the power of the State to include nondeclarant eligible aliens and ineligible aliens in the same prohibited class. Reasons supporting discrimination against aliens who may but who will not naturalize are obvious.

Truax v. Raich, supra, does not support the appellants' contention. . . . In the opinion it was pointed out that the legislation there in question did not relate to the devolution of real property, but that the discrimination was imposed upon the conduct of ordinary private enterprise covering the entire field of industry with the exception of enterprises that were relatively very small. It was said that the right to work for a living in the common occupations of the community is a part of the freedom which it was the purpose of the Fourteenth Amendment to secure.

In the case before us, the thing forbidden is very different. It is not an opportunity to earn a living in common occupations of the community, but it is the privilege of owning or controlling agricultural land within the State. The quality and allegiance of those who own, occupy and use the farm lands within its borders are matters of highest importance and affect the safety and power of the State itself.

The Terraces, who are citizens, have no right safeguarded by the Fourteenth Amendment to lease their land to aliens lawfully forbidden to take or have such lease. The state act is not repugnant to the equal protection clause and does not contravene the Fourteenth Amendment.

The decree of the District Court is affirmed.

Mr. Justice McReynolds and Mr. Justice Brandeis think there is no justiciable question involved and that the case should have been dismissed on that ground.

Mr. Justice Sutherland took no part in the consideration or decision of this case.

Notes and Questions

1. **Other cases:** The same day that the Court handed down *Terrace v. Thompson*, it decided *Porterfield v. Webb*, 263 U.S. 225 (1923), which upheld California's version of the alien land law. Creative end-runs attempted by Japanese Americans around the alien land laws were subsequently squelched. *See, e.g., Webb v. O'Brien*, 263 U.S. 313 (1923) (share-cropping agreements with Japanese tenant farmers); *Frick v. Webb*, 263 U.S. 326 (1923) (Japanese ownership of shares in agribusiness); *Cockrill v. California*, 268 U.S. 258 (1925) (land purchased through a White agent for the citizen children of Japanese aliens).

2. **Policy behind alien land laws:** To get some sense of the motivations of the alien land law, consider the public comments of Attorney General Ulysses S. Webb, one of the authors of the law in 1913, in a speech before the Commonwealth Club of San Francisco:

> The fundamental basis of all legislation upon this subject, State and Federal, has been, and is, race undesirability. It is unimportant and foreign to the question under discussion whether a particular race is inferior. The simple and single question is, is the race desirable. . . . [The alien land law] seeks to limit their presence by curtailing their privileges which they may enjoy here; for they will not come in large numbers and long abide with us if they may not acquire land. And it seeks to limit the numbers who will come by limiting the opportunities for their activity here when they arrive.

Oyama, 332 U.S. at 657 (quoting Yamato Ichihashi, Japanese in the United States 275 (1932), quoting Ulysses S. Webb, speech before the Commonwealth Club of San Francisco on August 9, 1913).

In addition to White supremacy, naked economic self-interest also played an important role. Consider, again, the comments of Webb made to the Supreme Court in his brief in *Frick v. Webb*, 263 U.S. 326 (1923):

> It was the purpose of those who understood the situation to prohibit the enjoyment or possession of, or dominion over, the agricultural lands of the State by aliens ineligible to citizenship,—in a practical way to prevent ruinous competition by the Oriental farmer against the American farmer.

Dudley O. McGovney, *The Anti-Japanese Land Laws of California and Ten Other States*, 35 California Law Review 7, 47 (1947).

3. Race and alienage: Note the interplay between race and alienage discrimination. The Court's opinion seems to suggest that race discrimination is not generally acceptable, whereas alienage discrimination is generally acceptable. What explains the difference in legal and moral terms? How does your analysis change when you consider that naturalization was not open to all races? Or that the state legislatures used alienage as a proxy for race? As in *Yick Wo*, these statutes did not discriminate facially against Asian immigrants; however, as applied, they had a disproportionate impact on non-White American immigrants.

4. Bootstrapping argument: Note how the State of Washington bootstraps its justification for treating aliens ineligible for citizenship differently from other aliens because Congress chose to do the same in its naturalization statute. The Court accepts this argument and writes, "[t]he rule established by Congress on this subject, in and of itself, furnishes a reasonable basis for classification in a state law withholding from aliens the privilege of land ownership as defined in the act." This rationale would be rejected 25 years later in *Takahashi v. Fish & Game Commission* and *Oyama v. California*, which are discussed in Chapter 4.

5. Escheat actions: While Japanese Americans were interned during World War II, three more states passed alien land laws: Utah, Wyoming and Arkansas. The Arkansas legislature did not bother using the code phrase "aliens ineligible for citizenship." Instead, they stated bluntly that "no Japanese or a descendant of a Japanese shall ever purchase or hold title to any lands in the State of Arkansas." Moreover, as Chapter 4 details, many states' attorneys general commenced escheat actions—law suits to revert real property to state ownership because of the lack of a lawful owner—while Japanese American owners were locked up in distant camps. These alien land laws would not be struck down or repealed until after World War II, when the U.S. Supreme Court signaled constitutional concerns about them in *Oyama v. California*, discussed in Chapter 4.

6. Race, not class: Finally, consider the class issues embedded within the historical development of Chinese and Japanese Americans into a racial group. Professor Alexander Saxton argues that Chinese immigrants became the "indispensable enemy" against which the white working class of disparate ethnic backgrounds and economic interests could unite. Instead of allying themselves with Chinese workers along class lines, European American workers opted to make alliances along racial lines. Alexander Saxton, THE INDISPENSABLE ENEMY: LABOR AND THE NATI-CHINESE MOVEMENT IN CALIFORNIA (1971). Professor Yen Espiritu reminds us that the same labor organizations that rallied successfully against Chinese immigrants in California then turned their efforts against Japanese immigrants. Yen Espiritu, ASIAN AMERICAN PANETHNICITY: BRIDGING INSTITUTIONS AND IDENTITIES (1992).

C. ADDITIONAL READINGS

BOOKS

Carey McWilliams, FACTORIES IN THE FIELD (1971).

Sucheng Chan, ASIAN AMERICANS: AN INTERPRETIVE HISTORY (1991).

Sucheng Chan, THIS BITTERSWEET SOIL: THE CHINESE IN CALIFORNIA AGRICULTURE, 1860–1910 (1986).

Gabriel Chin, Sumi Cho, Jerry Kang & Frank Wu, BEYOND SELF INTEREST (1996).

JAPANESE AMERICANS: FROM RELOCATION TO REDRESS (Roger Daniels et al. eds., c.1986, 1991).

Roger Daniels, ASIAN AMERICA: CHINESE AND JAPANESE IN THE UNITED STATES SINCE 1850 (1988).

Yen Espiritu, ASIAN AMERICAN PANETHNICITY: BRIDGING INSTITUTIONS AND IDENTITIES (1992).

Peter Irons, JUSTICE AT WAR: THE STORY OF THE JAPANESE AMERICAN INTERNMENT CASES (1983).

ASIAN AMERICANS AND THE SUPREME COURT: A DOCUMENTARY HISTORY (Hyung-Chan Kim ed., 1992).

Ian Haney López, WHITE BY LAW: THE LEGAL CONSTRUCTION OF RACE 80 (1996).

Charles McClain, IN SEARCH OF EQUALITY: THE CHINESE STRUGGLE AGAINST DISCRIMINATION IN NINETEENTH-CENTURY AMERICA (1994).

Carey McWilliams, PREJUDICE: JAPANESE-AMERICANS: SYMBOL OF RACIAL INTOLERANCE (1944).

Lucy E. Salyer, LAWS HARSH AS TIGERS: CHINESE IMMIGRANTS AND THE SHAPING OF MODERN IMMIGRATION LAW (1995).

Alexander Saxton, THE INDISPENSABLE ENEMY: LABOR AND THE NATI-CHINESE MOVEMENT IN CALIFORNIA (1971)

Peter H. Schuck, & Rogers M. Smith, CITIZENSHIP WITHOUT CONSENT: ILLEGAL ALIENS IN THE AMERICAN POLICY (1985).

Rogers M. Smith, CIVIC IDEALS: CONFLICTING VISIONS OF CITIZENSHIP IN U.S. HISTORY (1997).

Ronald Takaki, STRANGERS FROM A DIFFERENT SHORT: A HISTORY OF ASIAN AMERICANS (1989).

United States Commission on Wartime Relocation and Internment of Civilians, PERSONAL JUSTICE DENIED: REPORT OF THE COMMISSION ON WARTIME RELOCATION AND INTERNMENT OF CIVILIANS (1997).

LAW REVIEW ARTICLES AND OTHER SOURCES

Keith Aoki, *No Right to Own?: The Early Twentieth-Century "Alien Land Laws" as a Prelude to Internment,* 19 B.C. THIRD WORLD L.J. 37 (1998); 40 B.C. L. REVIEW 37 (1998).

Robert S. Chang, *Toward an Asian American Legal Scholarship: Critical Race Theory, Post-Structuralism, and Narrative Space,* 81 CAL. L. REV. 1243 (1993).

Gabriel J. Chin, *Segregation's Last Stronghold: Race Discrimination and the Constitutional Law of Immigration,* 46 UCLA L. REV. 1, 40 (October, 1998).

Christian Fritz, *A Nineteenth Century "Habeas Corpus Mill": The Chinese Before the Federal Courts in California,* 32 AMERICAN JOURNAL OF LEGAL HISTORY 347 (1988).

Yuji Ichioka, *The Early Japanese Immigrant Quest for Citizenship: The Background of the 1922 Ozawa Case,* 4 AMERASIA 1, (1977).

Thomas Wuil Joo, *New "Conspiracy Theory" of the Fourteenth Amendment: Nineteenth Century Chinese Civil Rights Cases and the Development of Substantive Due Process Jurisprudence,* 29 U.S.F. L. REV. 353 (1995).

Rep. Gallegly, IT IS TIME TO AMEND OUR BIRTHRIGHT CITIZENSHIP LAWS, 139 CONG. REC. H 1005 (vol.139, No.24 March 3, 1993).

Dudley O. McGovney, *The Anti-Japanese Land Laws of California and Ten Other States,* 35 CAL. L. REV. 7 (1947).

Hiroshi Motomura, *Immigration Law After a Century of Plenary Power: Phantom Constitutional Norms and Statutory Interpretation,* 100 YALE L.J. 545 (1990).

Part II: Internment

Looking at Center
Picnic
3-25-45 1:15 PM.
97-TOG-2E11

Chapter 3 THE INTERNMENT CASES

A. FROM PEARL HARBOR TO THE ASSEMBLY CENTERS: AN OVERVIEW

How did the internment of over 120,000 Americans of Japanese descent occur? To promote clarity, in reading these cases it is useful to note that the internment process can be divided into three parts. First, military orders imposed a nighttime *curfew* on Japanese Americans. It was the curfew that Gordon Hirabayashi and Minoru Yasui tested. Second, the orders implemented *exclusion*. It was the initial order to report to an assembly center to prepare for exclusion that both Hirabayashi and Fred Korematsu violated. Third, without explicitly so stating, the orders created the conditions of continued *detention*. It was not until Mitsuye Endo filed her *habeas corpus* petition that the Court addressed the legality of that ultimate result. Together, these phases—the curfew, exclusion and continued detention, all without charges or trial—constituted what we call the internment. However, well before the internment process officially began, Americans of Japanese descent were targeted both formally and informally.

1. BEFORE PEARL HARBOR

Well before the bombing of Pearl Harbor, the federal government prepared for possible conflict with Japan. In the late 1930s, the Justice Department compiled a list of Japanese resident aliens* who were potentially "subversive" and "dangerous." Designated the "ABC" list for its categories— "A" for "known dangerous" aliens; "B," "potentially dangerous" and "C," persons who "were watched because of their pro-Japanese inclinations and propagandist activities"—more than 2,000 Japanese immigrants were identified by name. Among them were leaders of Japanese American civic groups, businessmen, language teachers, Buddhist priests, and martial arts instructors. This list constituted nearly the entire leadership of first-generation West Coast Japanese Americans.

The government also engaged in counter-espionage. In March 1941, Lieutenant Commander Kenneth D. Ringle of Naval Intelligence was chosen by President Roosevelt to investigate the West Coast "Japanese Problem." Ringle broke into the Japanese Consulate in Los Angeles and recovered extensive information, including lists of Japanese sympathizers and agents. These leads helped uncover an espionage operation led by Itaru Tachibana, a Japanese naval officer posing as a language student. Shortly after the break-in, Tachibana and his agents were incarcerated.

After these arrests, military intelligence and the FBI disagreed about how much espionage threat remained. Military intelligence maintained that a credible threat persisted although even they concluded that Japanese espio-

---

* As Chapter 1 points out, federal law prohibited the first generation of Japanese immigrants from naturalizing because they were not "free White persons."

nage would likely have minimal impact. By contrast, FBI Director J. Edgar Hoover believed that the military overstated the risks.

The federal government also conducted broader studies of Japanese American loyalty. One early inquiry was conducted by Curtis B. Munson, a Chicago businessman working freelance for the White House. Munson's report was colorful and contradictory. He warned that "there are still Japanese in the United States who will tie dynamite around their waist and make a human bomb out of themselves" and he was "horrified to note that dams, bridges, harbors, power stations, etc. are wholly unguarded everywhere." Yet he did not recommend detention of Japanese Americans as a group. In an extensive memo, he wrote to Roosevelt, "[w]e do not believe that they would be any more disloyal than any other group in the United States with whom we went to war. Those being here are on a spot and they know it."

Finally, the Justice Department and the War Department developed specific contingency plans. In March 1941, they reached a secret agreement to coordinate an internment of "enemy aliens." The agreement called for "transferring enemy aliens to the custody of military authorities for permanent detention." The departments, however, did not contemplate mass detention, and their agreement explicitly provided for arrest under warrant issued by a federal prosecutor, a preliminary hearing and a Justice Department determination of each individual's loyalty. In this initial agreement, citizens were distinguished from aliens.

2. THE BOMBING OF PEARL HARBOR

On December 7, 1941, the Japanese Navy attacked Pearl Harbor, shocking military leaders and the American public. Military authorities earlier appeared confident that the United States mainland would be safe from attack. While German submarines had come perilously close to shore in their attacks on East Coast commercial shipping, the West Coast seemed secure from such threats.

On the very day of the Pearl Harbor attack, the Justice Department immediately arrested enemy aliens, most of whom were Japanese. The initial arrests took into custody more than 2,000 individuals. In accordance with the Justice and War Departments' plan, enemy alien review boards quickly processed these people through individual loyalty hearings. Two-thirds of the Japanese aliens but less than half of the German and Italian aliens were then detained in Immigration and Naturalization Service internment camps in Montana, New Mexico and North Dakota.

By December 10, just three days after Pearl Harbor, FBI Director Hoover reported that "practically all" of the persons whom the FBI had intended to arrest had been taken into custody. However, on that same day, the head of the Western Defense Command (covering the western portion of the United States), Lieutenant General John L. DeWitt, began to raise "certain questions relative to the problem of apprehension, segregation and detention of Japanese in the San Francisco Bay Area."

Exacerbating military anxieties, between December 17 and December 23, Japanese submarines sank two tankers and damaged one freighter along the

West Coast. General DeWitt feared that Japanese Americans were aiding the submarines by signaling them from shore. By December 19, DeWitt advocated "collect[ing] all alien subjects fourteen years of age and over, of enemy nations and remov[ing] them to the Zone of the Interior." Still, throughout the month of December, there was no government-wide consensus. Even as General DeWitt was starting to envision mass internment, U.S. Attorney General Francis Biddle was assuring the public that arrested aliens were given individualized assessments and that "[n]o alien was apprehended, and none will be, on the score of nationality alone."

But with the new year and the declaration of war, public opinion began to turn squarely against Japanese Americans. As documented by the Commission on Wartime Relocation and Internment of Civilians (CWRIC) in PERSONAL JUSTICE DENIED: REPORT OF THE COMMISSION ON WARTIME RELOCATION AND INTERNMENT OF CIVILIANS (PERSONAL JUSTICE DENIED),

> On January 2 the Joint Immigration Committee [of the California legislature] sent a manifesto to California newspapers which summed up the historical catalogue of charges against the ethnic Japanese. It put them in the new context of reported fifth column activity in Hawaii and the Philippines and a war that turned the Japanese into a problem for the nation, not California alone. Repeating the fundamental claim that the ethnic Japanese are "totally unassimilable," the manifesto declared that "those born in this country are American citizens by right of birth, but they are also Japanese citizens, liable . . . to be called to bear arms for their Emperor, either in front of, or behind, enemy lines." Japanese language schools were attacked as "a blind to cover instruction similar to that received by a young student in Japan—that his is a superior race, the divinity of the Japanese Emperor, the loyalty that every Japanese, wherever born, or residing, owes his Emperor and Japan." In these attacks the Joint Immigration Committee had the support of the Native Sons and Daughters of the Golden West and the California Department of the American Legion, which in January began to demand that "all Japanese who are known to hold dual citizenship . . . be placed in concentration camps." By early February, Earl Warren, then Attorney General of California, and U.S. Webb, a former Attorney General and co-author of the Alien Land Law, were actively advising the Joint Immigration Committee how to persuade the federal government that all ethnic Japanese should be removed from the West Coast. . . .

PERSONAL JUSTICE DENIED at 67–68. Old-standing prejudices, often driven by economic self-interest, came to the forefront. For example, a White American manager of the Salinas Vegetable Grower-Shipper Association announced:

> We're charged with wanting to get rid of the Japs for selfish reasons. We might as well be honest. We do. It's a question of whether the white man lives on the Pacific Coast or the brown man. They came into this valley to work, and they stayed to take over. . . . If all the Japs were removed tomorrow, we'd never miss them in two weeks, because the white farmers can take over and produce everything the Jap grows. And we don't want them back when the war ends, either.

Frank J. Taylor, "The People Nobody Wants," 214 Saturday Evening Post 24, 66 (May 9, 1942), quoted in *Korematsu v. United States, infra* (Justice Murphy, dissenting).

Such views gained legitimacy with the January release of a report commissioned by President Roosevelt. Authored hastily by Supreme Court Justice Owen Roberts, the Roberts Commission report concluded that Japanese living in America had committed espionage, contributing to the Pearl Harbor disaster. As early as December 9th, a nationally syndicated newspaper columnist, Westbrook Pegler, had suggested concentration camps for "alien Japanese" as well as disloyal Italian and German Americans. After the Roberts report, the idea of mass internment caught on. For example, Henry McLemore, in a January 29, 1942, column in the San Francisco Examiner wrote: "I am for the immediate removal of every Japanese on the West Coast to a point deep in the interior. I don't mean a nice part of the interior either. Herd 'em up, pack 'em off and give 'em the inside room in the badlands. . . . Personally, I hate the Japanese. And that goes for all of them."

The Roberts report laid some blame for Pearl Harbor on military negligence, and these criticisms affected General DeWitt. DeWitt made clear that he was "not going to be a second General Short," referring to a Pearl Harbor commander whose career had ended in disgrace. Over time, DeWitt would claim forthrightly the racial justifications for his "final recommendation." DeWitt is well known for stating publicly that "a Jap's a Jap." Although German and Italian immigrants could be treated as individuals, he made clear that the Japanese—immigrants and citizens alike—were something special:

> I have little confidence that the enemy aliens are law abiding or loyal in any sense of the word. Some of them, yes; many, no. Particularly the Japanese, I have no confidence in their loyalty whatsoever. I am speaking now of the *native born* Japanese—117,000—and 42,000 in California alone. . . . *In the war in which we are now engaged racial affinities are not severed by migration. The Japanese race is an enemy race and while many second and third generation Japanese born on United States soil, possessed of United States citizenship have become "Americanized" the racial strains are undiluted.* . . .

> I have the mission of defending this coast and securing vital installations. The danger of the Japanese was, and is now—if they are permitted to come back—espionage and sabotage. *It makes no difference whether he is an American citizen, he is still a Japanese. American citizenship does not necessarily determine loyalty.* . . .

> *You needn't worry about the Italians at all except in certain cases. Also, the same for the Germans except in individual cases. But we must worry about the Japanese all the time until he is wiped off the map.* Sabotage and espionage will make problems as long as he is allowed in this area—problems which I don't want to have to worry about.

CWRIC, PERSONAL JUSTICE DENIED at 65–66, 66 (emphasis added, quoting transcript of meeting in DeWitt's office, Jan. 4, 1942; testimony before House Naval Affairs Subcommittee, April 13, 1943).

General DeWitt's views were amplified through prominent newspaper journalists. By February, the popular syndicated columnist Walter Lippman, considerably more liberal than Pegler, also recommended internment. Before he published his editorial, Lippman had met with DeWitt, whose arguments Lippman would parrot to his readers. To civilian government officials, the widely circulated Lippman essay confirmed popular sentiments favoring internment. On February 13, DeWitt made his "final recommendation" on the "Evacuation of Japanese and Other Subversive Persons from the Pacific Coast." In it, he claimed again that Japanese ethnicity determined loyalty, supporting this claim with "indications that these [potential enemies] are organized and ready for concerted action at a favorable opportunity. The very fact that no sabotage has taken place to date is a disturbing and confirming indication that such action will be taken."

3. MILITARY, EXECUTIVE AND CONGRESSIONAL ACTION

Certain high-ranking government officials such as Attorney General Biddle opposed the evacuation of Japanese Americans. Nonetheless, on February 19, President Roosevelt signed Executive Order 9066 granting the military the power to exclude persons from specified areas. On its face, the order made no mention of the Japanese.

Executive Order—No. 9066
Authorizing the Secretary of War and to Prescribe Military Areas

Whereas the successful prosecution of the war requires every possible protection against espionage and against sabotage to national defense material, national defense premises, and national defense utilities:

Now, therefore, by virtue of the authority vested in me as President of the United States, and Commander in Chief of the Army and Navy, I hereby authorize and direct the Secretary of War, and the Military Commanders who he may from time to time designate, whenever he or any designated Commander deems such action necessary or desirable, to prescribe military areas in such places and of such extent as he or the appropriate Military Commander may determine, from which any or all persons may be excluded, and with respect to which, the right of any person to enter, remain in, or leave shall be subject to whatever restrictions the Secretary of War or the appropriate Military Commander may impose in his discretion.

I hereby further authorize and direct the Secretary of War and the said Military Commanders to take such other steps as he or the appropriate Military Commander may deem advisable to enforce compliance with the restrictions applicable to each Military area hereinabove authorized to be designated, including the use of Federal troops and other Federal Agencies, with authority to accept assistance of state and local agencies.

I hereby further authorize and direct all Executive Departments, independent establishments and other Federal Agencies to assist the Secretary of War or the said Military Commanders in carrying out this Executive Order, including the furnishing of medical aid, hospitalization, food, clothing, transportation, use of land, shelter, and other supplies, equipment utilities, facilities, and services.

The White House

February 19, 1942

In quick succession, General DeWitt issued various military orders that eventually led to the mass detention of approximately 120,000 people of Japanese descent. In early March, he issued public proclamations that designated Military Areas #1 and #2,* warned about future evacuation, and encouraged voluntary resettlement outside of Military Area #1.

Then, on March 21, 1942, Congress passed Public Law 503, which criminalized violations of duly authorized military orders. Congress had been conducting hearings throughout February and March in San Francisco, Portland, Seattle and Los Angeles. Chaired by Representative John Tolan of California, these Tolan Committee "National Defense Migration" hearings generated many witnesses sympathetic to European aliens but almost none favorable to Japanese Americans and Japanese immigrants. With the passage of Public Law 503, both the executive and legislative branches stood together behind the exclusion and evacuation.

Three days after the law's enactment, General DeWitt began issuing a series of 108 Civilian Exclusion Orders. Japanese communities were given seven days to evacuate. They were shipped first to sixteen different assembly centers operated by the Army, such as the Puyallup racetrack in Washington and the Santa Anita racetrack in Southern California. Afterwards, they would be moved to more permanent relocation centers run by a civilian agency call the War Relocation Authority (WRA), created by executive order on March 18. There, most of them would remain for several years, behind barbed wire and watched by armed guards. With the military in the lead, the executive branch following, and, finally, Congress attaching federal criminal penalties to disobedience, all but one branch of government—the judiciary—had approved the internment process. Outside the camps, the Supreme Court began to consider the cases that challenged the internment.

4. LITIGATION

Each of the four test cases against the government's internment orders originated independently of the others. Each of them raised different procedural and substantive claims. Each was tried by a different court. Yet they eventually became essential pieces of a single whole. At the appeals level, for example, oral arguments before the Court of Appeals for the Ninth Circuit *en banc* on the *Yasui*, *Korematsu* and *Hirabayashi* cases were heard on the same day, and that court eventually certified legal questions in all three cases together to the U.S. Supreme Court. The defense strategies in these individual cases were loosely coordinated and were all subject to contradictory interventions by both the national and local chapters of the American Civil Liberties Union (ACLU) as well as the Japanese American Citizen's League (JACL). Interestingly, the government's lawyers were also riven by internal disagreements about ethical, political and legal strategy choices. The U.S.

---

* Military Area #1 included the western half of Washington, Oregon and California, as well as the southern part of Arizona. Military Area #2 included the remaining portions of all these states. In the end, all Japanese in Military Area #1 were evacuated. All Japanese in California, in both Areas #1 and #2, were eventually evacuated.

Supreme Court's opinions carefully layered each decision on the reasoning of ones issued before it. Those interested in a detailed historical account of these cases should refer to Peter Irons, JUSTICE AT WAR: THE STORY OF THE JAPANESE AMERICAN INTERNMENT CASES. Here, the focus is on how these cases influenced and were influenced by concepts of race, rights and liberty prevalent at the time.

B. STUDY MODULES

In the following study modules, we challenge the reader to analyze with rigor the basic framework for legal decision-making in these and other civil rights cases: how the U.S. Supreme Court chooses levels of judicial review in constitutional cases, how each type of judicial scrutiny affects case outcomes and what standards of judicial review the Court articulated and actually applied in the internment cases. Constitutional rights such as due process or equal protection are subject to claims of national security, and thus it is important to examine the complex interplay between civil liberties and military necessity. Finally, the reader is invited to consider the effect of factors such as racial prejudice on the legal process. In summary, these modules explore how and why a racial minority group, having experienced harsh discrimination and facing imprisonment during wartime without charges or trial, turned to the Constitution and the courts for help—and largely failed to receive it.

1. EQUAL PROTECTION: THE CURFEW CASES

At the heart of civil rights law lies the right to equal protection of the laws, guaranteed by the U.S. Constitution. This guarantee of equal protection is found explicitly in the fourteenth amendment of the Constitution, ratified after the Civil War, which reads "nor shall any State . . . deny to any person within its jurisdiction the *equal protection of the laws*."*

An equal protection argument claims that the government should not be treating the aggrieved individual differently from others. However, not all differences in treatment amount to a constitutional violation because good reasons may justify that differential treatment. For example, under our current income tax system, people who make more money are taxed at a higher percentage of their income. This difference in treatment does not violate the equal protection rights of high income earners because the government has sufficiently good reasons to adopt a graduated income tax.

In deciding equal protection cases, the court must therefore determine whether some difference in treatment is sufficiently justified. Under current

---

* Emphasis added. Although the fourteenth amendment applies only to state governments, essentially the same requirements had been read into the fifth amendment's due process clause, which applies to the federal government. The fourteenth amendment and the fifth amendment began to converge most clearly when the Supreme Court decided *Brown v. Board Education, 347 U.S. 483 (1954)*, and its companion case, *Bolling v. Sharpe*, 347 U.S. 497 (1954).

constitutional doctrine, courts analyze the problem in two steps. First, the court decides the appropriate level of scrutiny. Second, it determines whether under that standard of review the government has satisfied the requirements of what is known as "means-ends" scrutiny.

Level of scrutiny. To simplify somewhat, under current doctrine there are three different levels of scrutiny: strict, intermediate and mere rationality. These levels of scrutiny apply different amounts of deference to government action. Strict scrutiny, for instance, is very skeptical and is likely to result in constitutional invalidation. By contrast, mere rationality scrutiny acts mostly as a rubber stamp.

What determines which level of scrutiny is appropriate? Among other factors, any government action that intentionally treats individuals differently on the basis of a suspect classification, which includes ethnicity and race, is given strict scrutiny. By contrast, most government decisions regarding economic matters—as in the example of the graduated income tax—are reviewed under the mere rationality level of scrutiny.

Means-ends analysis. Once the level of scrutiny has been selected, the government decision must be tested in the following manner. First, the purpose of the differential treatment must satisfy some normative standard. For strict scrutiny, the ends sought by the government must be "compelling." By contrast, for mere rationality scrutiny, the ends must be merely "legitimate." Second, the means adopted by the government must further those ends according to some normative standard. For strict scrutiny, the means must be "narrowly tailored" to furthering that compelling interest. If the means selected are poorly chosen—for example, if they are substantially over-inclusive, under-inclusive, or both—the court will strike down the government action as invalid. By contrast, for mere rationality scrutiny, as long as the means are "reasonably related" to the legitimate interest, courts will not second-guess the other branches.

This brief and stylized overview of equal protection law can only be made sense of by reading numerous equal protection cases—the subject of good constitutional law classes. However, a rule of thumb can be provided: Intentionally treating individuals differently on the basis of race or ethnicity warrants strict scrutiny, which means that the different treatment must be narrowly tailored to a compelling government interest—something hard to demonstrate.

In applying this rule of thumb to the internment cases, make sure not to commit the error of anachronism. Equal protection jurisprudence in the 1940s did not look like equal protection jurisprudence does in the 21st century. Indeed, the basic analytical machinery of giving suspect classifications heightened scrutiny was first developed in protean form in the internment cases themselves. Accordingly, the Court's analyses will not neatly correspond to the doctrinal description just provided.

a. HIRABAYASHI V. UNITED STATES—THE CURFEW, PART I

(i) BACKGROUND

The internment was a process, not a single event. Although the events leading to the incarceration of Japanese Americans at the assembly centers occurred quickly, they were neither immediate nor simultaneous.

On March 24, 1942, General DeWitt issued Public Proclamation No. 3—imposing a curfew on all enemy aliens (which included Japanese, Italians and Germans) *as well as citizens* of only Japanese descent. Three days later, he issued Public Proclamation No. 4, known as the "freeze order," which prohibited enemy aliens from voluntarily leaving the designated military areas. At the same time, DeWitt started issuing Civilian Exclusion Orders that required Japanese American households within particular geographical areas to report to assembly centers. The Civilian Exclusion Order that applied to Gordon Hirabayashi was issued on May 10, 1942.

Even at the time General Dewitt issued his Civilian Exclusion Orders, it was clear that "exclusion" meant more than simply that. Despite consideration of "voluntary" evacuation, in which Japanese Americans would leave the West Coast but remain otherwise at liberty, "exclusion" meant confinement at assembly centers and subsequently detention in the more permanent internment camps. By the time the Supreme Court heard oral argument in the cases, the internment camps were a reality.

On May 16, Gordon Hirabayashi turned himself into FBI headquarters to challenge the exclusion order, in a calculated act of civil disobedience. In Hirabayashi's own words, as related to historian Roger Daniels,

> I think having had to confront a position that was not popular—certainly not popular among the Japanese, had I consulted them—was the position of being a conscientious objector.... But having done that[,] ... having taken this stand and seeking advice and so on, ... I no longer feel that I'm just doing an isolated lonely stance; even though it's a minority, I'm a part of a movement. So I became familiar with the respectability of standing on principle even if it goes against some order of the day.... From that introduction, it would only take a certain kind of sensitive jarring for me to relate the curfew situation to a position of objection, even though ... I had initially intended to go along with it. There was no intellectual exercise of objecting to it at the beginning. But as the issues came up, and I had to confront it, you know, it just hit me. Having confronted it that way, I couldn't justify it in the line of certain other positions I'd been taking. I'd have to sort of plow up all ... kinds of fundamental beliefs that gave me energy and motive to live a certain way.... So the alternative was to confront the government on this....
>
> Regarding the curfew, I just took a citizen's position and felt that I'm not going to have anything more to do with it, which is the position that all non-Japanese took. I mean, they didn't have to abide by it, so they didn't do anything about it. So I just said, I'm going to live like an ordinary American, and left it up to the government; if they wanted to pick me up, okay. We'll face it then. So I just ignored it, and nothing happened. The exclusion order is something different, because everybody's being removed. If I was roaming

the streets, sooner or later—sooner probably—I'd be accosted and picked up. So rather than to run into that . . . I just made arrangements with Arthur Barnett to meet me the morning after the last busload of Japanese left, and he'd drive me over to the FBI.

Gordon Hirabayashi, interviewed by Roger Daniels, Feb. 9, 1981, University of Washington Libraries.

Public Law 503 made it a federal crime to disobey any duly authorized military order. Hirabayashi's intent was to challenge the *exclusion* order; however, when he turned himself in, he brought along a personal journal. Entries in that journal made clear that Hirabayashi had also been violating the earlier *curfew* order, in addition to the exclusion order. Consequently, Hirabayashi was charged with two counts: first, failing to obey the exclusion order; second, disobeying the curfew.

PETER IRONS, JUSTICE AT WAR
89–92

Gordon Hirabayashi grew up in an unconventional family. He was born in 1918 in Auburn, a town twenty miles south of Seattle where his father ran a roadside fruit market. Hirabayashi absorbed the pacifism of his parents, Japanese natives who belong to a sect called "Friends of the World." Similar in organizational form and beliefs to the Quakers, of which it is a Japanese offshoot, this group worshipped without ministers and rejected military service and war. Eager for contact with young people outside the small Japanese American community in his home town, Hirabayashi served as president of the nondenominational Auburn Christian Fellowship during his high school years.

When he entered the University of Washington in Seattle in 1937, Hirabayashi became active in the student religious and social-action groups that contended with the dominant fraternity and sorority atmosphere of the conservative campus. He assumed a leadership role in the YMCA and the Japanese Student's Club, and also joined the Seattle chapter of the Japanese American Citizens League. Shopping around for a religious home Hirabayashi and his roommate, Bill Makino, attended in turn the University Temple ("because they had an excellent choir"), the Unitarian Church, and finally the University Quaker Meeting. "We liked that setting," he recalled. "We found ourselves gravitating over there more frequently, and after a while we weren't shopping around."

As a YMCA officer, Hirabayashi traveled to New York City in the summer of 1940 to attend the "President's School" held jointly at Columbia University and the affiliate Union Theological Seminary. Here he was exposed in seminars and discussions to the social activism and pacifism preached by A.J. Muste, Evan Thomas (brother of Socialist Party leader Norman Thomas), and John Nevin Sayre, all members of the pacifist Fellowship of Reconciliation (FOR). This experience proved to be a turning point in the young student's life.

"I guess I was ready for that philosophy," Hirabayashi later said. Hirabayashi joined the FOR, which advocated nonviolent but militant resistance to war and military service, during his summer in New York. On his return to Seattle, he registered with his local draft board as a conscientious objector and was granted that status without objection.

Precarious family finances had forced Hirabayashi to alternate quarters of study at the University with work as a houseboy and farmhand during his first two years of school. At the age of twenty-four, he had just begun his senior year when the curfew on Japanese Americans became effective in March 1942. . . . The issuance of the first Civilian Exclusion Order on March 29, which required the evacuation of the Japanese American residents of Bainbridge Island, prompted Hirabayashi to drop out of school. "I knew I wasn't going to be around very long," he recalled, "so I just didn't register for the spring quarter and volunteered with the fledgling American Friends Service Committee (AFSC) in Seattle." Headquartered in Philadelphia, the AFSC was the social-service branch of the Quakers. Working with AFSC director Floyd Schmoe, Hirabayashi helped Japanese American families subject to exclusion orders in finding storage space for their furniture and in transporting them to the Puyallup Fairgrounds. . . .

Like all Japanese Americans, Hirabayashi had been subject to General DeWitt's curfew order since March 28, 1942. He obeyed the curfew until the evening of May 4, unaware of Min Yasui's challenge to it more than a month before. "I was expected like every citizen to obey the law, and I did," he recalled. "There were twelve of us living in the YMCA dorm, and they all became my volunteer timekeepers—'Hey, it's five minutes to eight, Gordy'—and I'd dash back from the library or the coffeeshop. One of the times I stopped and said, 'Why the hell am I running back? Am I an American or not? Why am I running back and nobody else is?'"

During the weeks that preceded the order to evacuate the University District, Hirabayashi and Makino talked for hours about a joint stand against evacuation. Both young men encountered opposition from their parents. Hirabayashi later recounted these arguments: "My mother said 'I know you're right, I agree with you and I admire this stand of yours. But we don't know if we'll ever see each other again. Why stick to a principle? Stick with us.'" She used tears and everything, but I couldn't do it. Dad was physically able, so I didn't have that worry. But Bill was the only son of parents who were at least ten years older than my parents and this pressure was very strong. I didn't want to have someone who would be having remorse all the way through, and I figured we were going to have serious problems. . . . He thought about it and decided he'd just have to stick with his family."

Before he made a final decision to resist, Hirabayashi sought legal advice from Arthur Barnett, a thirty-five-year-old lawyer and fellow member of the Friends Meeting. Word of his stand also reached Mary Farquharson, a lawyer who represented the University District in the state senate. Although not a Quaker, her efforts on behalf of interned Japanese Americans kept her in touch with Arthur Barnett. . . .

"Mary Farquharson came to see me," Hirabayashi recalled. "She said, 'I'm checking up on a rumor that you are intending to object to evacuation; is that true?' I said, 'Yes, I've already made a stand, and I've written a state-ment.' She said, 'Are you planning to make a test case of this?' 'Well, I know that's a possibility,' I said, 'but I don't know very much about law and I don't have any money. I'm making a personal stand. I don't know what's going to happen as a result of it and I've made no plans.' 'If you've made no plans,' she said, 'there's a group here including myself who are very upset about what's happening to our civil liberties and the status of citizenship. We've been looking for a case to object to these things and we haven't been able to find one. Do you have any objections to a group of us using your case as a vehicle to fight for citizens' rights?'"

Farquharson quickly organized an informal committee to provide legal advice and to raise money for bail in anticipation of his arrest.

When he and Barnett arrived at the FBI office on May 16, Hirabayashi in-tended simply to initiate a test case of the evacuation order. Had he not brought with him a briefcase that contained his incriminating diary, it is un-likely the FBI would have learned of his repeated curfew violations. FBI agent Manion, however, confiscated the briefcase. After filing the complaint charging Hirabayashi with violation of the evacuation order, and taking him to the King County Jail, Manion went through the briefcase and discovered the diary.

(ii) THE CASE

Through state representative Mary Farquharson and the local Seattle chapter of the ACLU, Hirabayashi obtained the legal services of Frank L. Wal-ters, a local corporate attorney. The ACLU's national board would oppose the local's representation of Hirabayashi at the appeals level, but ultimately itself undertook to represent him at the U.S. Supreme Court proceedings.

At trial in Seattle, in October 1942, the government prosecutors called Hirabayashi's father as their first witness in a failed effort to present a less than sympathetic figure. Hirabayashi himself served as a volunteer inter-preter for the court. Undermining the prosecution's claims about any cul-tural ties to Japan, Hirabayashi then admitted that he was not up to the job of interpreter because his Japanese language skills were too poor. Other than those minor gaffes, though, the government case proceeded smoothly. Hira-bayashi admitted both the curfew and exclusion violations. Although Walters appealed to the jury not to convict on the basis of unjust laws, the jury re-turned a guilty verdict in ten minutes. Initially, Hirabayashi was sentenced to consecutive sentences totaling less than ninety days, but he asked for a longer sentence so that he could do road work rather than serve his time in jail. The judge obliged, and sentenced Hirabayashi to ninety days on each count, to be served concurrently.

The case was appealed to the Ninth Circuit Court of Appeals on the issue of whether the federal government had violated the fifth amendment's re-quirement that equal burdens should be imposed on all classes of citizens. However, instead of deciding the appeal itself, the court certified the case (along with the *Korematsu* and *Yasui* cases, argued the same day) directly to the Supreme Court.* As drafted by the appeals court, the legal issues certified in *Hirabayashi* included the constitutionality of Public Law 503 and of General DeWitt's curfew and evacuation orders.

Hirabayashi's local lawyers gave up control over their Supreme Court brief to the national ACLU and became bound by the ACLU resolution that forbade any constitutional attack on Executive Order 9066. The brief focused primarily on a doctrine known as the non-delegation doctrine, which forbids Congress from delegating its authority to agencies without providing adequate standards. The argument that General DeWitt's orders unconstitutionally singled out Japanese Americans occupied only two pages of the brief. Because there was no Supreme Court precedent, none could be cited in support of the following proposition: "[T]he holdings in these earlier cases that race constituted 'an improper basis of classification' under state law should be extended to the requirement by the Fifth Amendment's due process clause that similar classifications by the federal government have a 'reasonable basis' in fact." However, the local ACLU and national JACL both filed *amicus* briefs pressing the discrimination argument.

Starting on May 10, 1943, and continuing to the next day, the Supreme Court heard oral arguments not only in *Hirabayashi* but also in *Yasui* and *Korematsu*. Six weeks later, on June 21, the Court issued its *Hirabayashi* ruling, the reasoning of which would be crucial for subsequent opinions.

HIRABAYASHI V. UNITED STATES

320 U.S. 81 (1943)[†]

Mr. Chief Justice STONE delivered the opinion of the Court.

Appellant, an American citizen of Japanese ancestry, was convicted in the district court of violating the Act of Congress of March 21, 1942, which makes it a misdemeanor knowingly to disregard restrictions made applicable by a military commander to persons in a military area prescribed by him as such, all as authorized by an Executive Order of the President.

The questions for our decision are whether the particular restriction violated, namely that all persons of Japanese ancestry residing in such an area be within their place of residence daily between the hours of 8:00 p.m. and 6:00 a.m., was adopted by the military commander in the exercise of an unconstitutional delegation by Congress of its legislative power, and whether the restriction unconstitutionally discriminated between citizens of Japanese ancestry and those of other ancestries in violation of the Fifth Amendment.

The indictment is in two counts. The second charges that appellant, being a person of Japanese ancestry, had on a specified date, contrary to a restriction promulgated by the military commander of the Western Defense

---

* See 28 U.S.C. § 1254(2) (permitting certification by Court of Appeals of questions of law to the Supreme Court, which may require entire record to be sent up for decision of the entire case).

† The full text of this and the other principal opinions can be found at: <www.law.ucla.edu/faculty/kang/racerightsreparation>.

Command, Fourth Army, failed to remain in his place of residence in the designated military area between the hours of 8:00 o'clock p. m. and 6:00 a.m. The first count charges that appellant, on May 11 and 12, 1942, had, contrary to a Civilian Exclusion Order issued by the military commander, failed to report to the Civil Control Station within the designated area, it appearing that appellant's required presence there was a preliminary step to the exclusion from that area of persons of Japanese ancestry.

[A]ppellant asserted that the indictment should be dismissed because he was an American citizen who had never been a subject of and had never borne allegiance to the Empire of Japan, and also because the Act of March 21, 1942, was an unconstitutional delegation of Congressional power. On the trial to a jury it appeared that appellant was born in Seattle in 1918, of Japanese parents who had come from Japan to the United States, and who had never afterward returned to Japan; that he was educated in the Washington public schools and at the time of his arrest was a senior in the University of Washington; that he had never been in Japan or had any association with Japanese residing there.

The jury returned a verdict of guilty on both counts and appellant was sentenced to imprisonment for a term of three months on each, the sentences to run concurrently.

Since the sentences of three months each imposed by the district court on the two counts were ordered to run concurrently, it will be unnecessary to consider questions raised with respect to the first count if we find that the conviction on the second count, for violation of the curfew order, must be sustained.

The curfew order which appellant violated, and to which the sanction prescribed by the Act of Congress has been deemed to attach, purported to be issued pursuant to an Executive Order of the President. In passing upon the authority of the military commander to make and execute the order, it becomes necessary to consider in some detail the official action which preceded or accompanied the order and from which it derives its purported authority.

On December 8, 1941, one day after the bombing of Pearl Harbor by a Japanese air force, Congress declared war against Japan. On February 19, 1942, the President promulgated Executive Order No. 9066. The Order recited that "the successful prosecution of the war requires every possible protection against espionage and against sabotage to national-defense material, national-defense premises, and national-defense utilities." By virtue of the authority vested in him as President and as Commander in Chief of the Army and Navy, the President purported to "authorize and direct the Secretary of War, and the Military Commanders whom he may from time to time designate, whenever he or any designated Commander deems such action necessary or desirable, to prescribe military areas in such places and of such extent as he or the appropriate Military Commander may determine, from which any or all persons may be excluded, and with respect to which, the right of any person to enter, remain in, or leave shall be subject to whatever restrictions the Secretary of War or the appropriate Military Commander may impose in his discretion."

On February 20, 1942, the Secretary of War designated Lt. General J. L. DeWitt as Military Commander of the Western Defense Command ... to carry out there the duties prescribed by Executive Order No. 9066. On March 2, 1942, General DeWitt promulgated Public Proclamation No. 1. The proclamation recited that the entire Pacific Coast "by its geographical location is particularly subject to attack, to attempted invasion by the armed forces of nations with which the United States is now at war, and, in connection therewith, is subject to espionage and acts of sabotage, thereby requiring the adoption of military measures necessary to establish safeguards against such enemy operations." It stated that "the present situation requires as a matter of military necessity the establishment in the territory embraced by the Western Defense Command of Military Areas and Zones thereof"; it specified and designated as military areas certain areas within the Western Defense Command; and it declared that "such persons or classes of persons as the situation may require" would, by subsequent proclamation, be excluded from certain of these areas, but might be permitted to enter or remain in certain others, under regulations and restrictions to be later prescribed.

An Executive Order of the President, No. 9102, of March 18, 1942, established the War Relocation Authority, in the Office for Emergency Management of the Executive Office of the President; it authorized the Director of War Relocation Authority to formulate and effectuate a program for the removal, relocation, maintenance and supervision of persons designated under Executive Order No. 9066.

Congress, by the Act of March 21, 1942, provided: "That whoever shall enter, remain in, leave, or commit any act in any military area or military zone prescribed, under the authority of an Executive order of the President, by the Secretary of War, or by any military commander designated by the Secretary of War, contrary to the restrictions applicable to any such area or zone or contrary to the order of the Secretary of War or any such military commander, shall, if it appears that he knew or should have known of the existence and extent of the restrictions or order and that his act was in violation thereof, be guilty of a misdemeanor and upon conviction shall be liable" to fine or imprisonment, or both.

Three days later, on March 24, 1942, General DeWitt issued Public Proclamation No. 3. After referring to the previous designation of military areas by Public Proclamations Nos. 1 and 2, it recited that "... the present situation within these Military Areas and Zones requires as a matter of military necessity the establishment of certain regulations pertaining to all enemy aliens and all persons of Japanese ancestry within said Military Areas and Zones...." It accordingly declared and established that from and after March 27, 1942, "all alien Japanese, all alien Germans, all alien Italians, and all persons of Japanese ancestry residing or being within the geographical limits of Military Area No. 1 ... shall be within their place of residence between the hours of 8:00 P.M. and 6:00 A.M., which period is hereinafter referred to as the hours of curfew." It also imposed certain other restrictions on persons of Japanese ancestry, and provided that any person violating the regulations would be subject to the criminal penalties provided by the Act of Congress of March 21, 1942.

Beginning on March 24, 1942, the military commander issued a series of Civilian Exclusion Orders pursuant to the provisions of Public Proclamation No. 1. Each such order related to a specified area within the territory of his command. The order applicable to appellant was Civilian Exclusion Order No. 57 of May 10, 1942. It directed that from and after 12:00 noon, May 16, 1942, all persons of Japanese ancestry, both alien and non-alien, be excluded from a specified portion of Military Area No. 1 in Seattle, including appellant's place of residence, and it required a member of each family, and each individual living alone, affected by the order to report on May 11 or May 12 to a designated Civil Control Station in Seattle. Meanwhile the military commander had issued Public Proclamation No. 4 of March 27, 1942, which recited the necessity of providing for the orderly evacuation and resettlement of Japanese within the area, and prohibited all alien Japanese and all persons of Japanese ancestry from leaving the military area until future orders should permit.

Appellant does not deny that he knowingly failed to obey the curfew order as charged in the second count of the indictment, or that the order was authorized by the terms of Executive Order No. 9066, or that the challenged Act of Congress purports to punish with criminal penalties disobedience of such an order. His contentions are only that Congress unconstitutionally delegated its legislative power to the military commander by authorizing him to impose the challenged regulation, and that, even if the regulation were in other respects lawfully authorized, the Fifth Amendment prohibits the discrimination made between citizens of Japanese descent and those of other ancestry.

It will be evident from the legislative history that the Act of March 21, 1942, contemplated and authorized the curfew order which we have before us.

The Chairman of the Senate Military Affairs Committee explained on the floor of the Senate that the purpose of the proposed legislation was to provide means of enforcement of curfew orders and other military orders made pursuant to Executive Order No. 9066. He read General DeWitt's Public Proclamation No. 1, and statements from newspaper reports that "evacuation of the first Japanese aliens and American-born Japanese" was about to begin. He also stated to the Senate that "reasons for suspected widespread fifth-column activity among Japanese" were to be found in the system of dual citizenship which Japan deemed applicable to American-born Japanese, and in the propaganda disseminated by Japanese consuls, Buddhist priests and other leaders, among American-born children of Japanese. Such was stated to be the explanation of the contemplated evacuation from the Pacific Coast area of persons of Japanese ancestry, citizens as well as aliens. Congress also had before it the Preliminary Report of a House Committee investigating national defense migration, of March 19, 1942, which approved the provisions of Executive Order No. 9066, and which recommended the evacuation, from military areas established under the Order, of all persons of Japanese ancestry, including citizens. The proposed legislation provided criminal sanctions for violation of orders, in terms broad enough to include the curfew order now before us, and the legislative history demonstrates that Congress was advised that curfew orders were among those intended, and was advised also that regulation of citizen and alien Japanese alike was contemplated.

The conclusion is inescapable that Congress, by the Act of March 21, 1942, ratified and confirmed Executive Order No. 9066. The question is . . . whether, acting in cooperation, Congress and the Executive have constitutional authority to impose the curfew restriction here complained of. We must consider also whether, acting together, Congress and the Executive could leave it to the designated military commander to appraise the relevant conditions and on the basis of that appraisal to say whether, under the circumstances, the time and place were appropriate for the promulgation of the curfew order and whether the order itself was an appropriate means of carrying out the Executive Order for the "protection against espionage and against sabotage" to national defense materials, premises and utilities. For reasons presently to be stated, we conclude that it was within the constitutional power of Congress and the executive arm of the Government to prescribe this curfew order for the period under consideration and that its promulgation by the military commander involved no unlawful delegation of legislative power.

Executive Order No. 9066, promulgated in time of war for the declared purpose of prosecuting the war by protecting national defense resources from sabotage and espionage, and the Act of March 21, 1942, ratifying and confirming the Executive Order, were each an exercise of the power to wage war conferred on the Congress and on the President, as Commander in Chief of the armed forces, by Articles I and II of the Constitution. We have no occasion to consider whether the President, acting alone, could lawfully have made the curfew order in question, or have authorized others to make it. For the President's action has the support of the Act of Congress, and we are immediately concerned with the question whether it is within the constitutional power of the national government, through the joint action of Congress and the Executive, to impose this restriction as an emergency war measure. The exercise of that power here involves no question of martial law or trial by military tribunal. *Cf. Ex parte Milligan,* 4 Wall 2 [(1866)]. Appellant has been tried and convicted in the civil courts and has been subjected to penalties prescribed by Congress for the acts committed.

The war power of the national government is "the power to wage war successfully." *See* Charles Evans Hughes, War Powers Under the Constitution, 42 A.B.A. Rep. 232, 238. It extends to every matter and activity so related to war as substantially to affect its conduct and progress. The power is not restricted to the winning of victories in the field and the repulse of enemy forces. It embraces every phase of the national defense, including the protection of war materials and the members of the armed forces from injury and from the dangers which attend the rise, prosecution and progress of war. Since the Constitution commits to the Executive and to Congress the exercise of the war power in all the vicissitudes and conditions of warfare, it has necessarily given them wide scope for the exercise of judgment and discretion in determining the nature and extent of the threatened injury or danger and in the selection of the means for resisting it. Where, as they did here, the conditions call for the exercise of judgment and discretion and for the choice of means by those branches of the Government on which the Constitution has placed the responsibility of war-making, it is not for any court to sit in review of the wisdom of their action or substitute its judgment for theirs.

The actions taken must be appraised in the light of the conditions with which the President and Congress were confronted in the early months of 1942, many of which, since disclosed, were then peculiarly within the knowledge of the military authorities. On December 7, 1941, the Japanese air forces had attacked the United States Naval Base at Pearl Harbor without warning, at the very hour when Japanese diplomatic representatives were conducting negotiations with our State Department ostensibly for the peaceful settlement of differences between the two countries. Simultaneously or nearly so, the Japanese attacked Malaysia, Hong Kong, the Philippines, and Wake and Midway Islands. On the following day their army invaded Thailand. Shortly afterwards they sank two British battleships. On December 13th, Guam was taken. On December 24th and 25th they captured Wake Island and occupied Hong Kong. On January 2, 1942, Manila fell, and on February 10th Singapore, Britain's great naval base in the East, was taken. On February 27th the battle of the Java Sea resulted in a disastrous naval defeat to the United Nations. By the 9th of March Japanese forces had established control over the Netherlands East Indies; Rangoon and Burma were occupied; Bataan and Corregidor were under attack.

Although the results of the attack on Pearl Harbor were not fully disclosed until much later, it was known that the damage was extensive, and that the Japanese by their successes had gained a naval superiority over our forces in the Pacific which might enable them to seize Pearl Harbor, our largest naval base and the last stronghold of defense lying between Japan and the west coast. That reasonably prudent men charged with the responsibility of our national defense had ample ground for concluding that they must face the danger of invasion, take measures against it, and in making the choice of measures consider our internal situation, cannot be doubted.

The challenged orders were defense measures for the avowed purpose of safeguarding the military area in question, at a time of threatened air raids and invasion by the Japanese forces, from the danger of sabotage and espionage. As the curfew was made applicable to citizens residing in the area only if they were of Japanese ancestry, our inquiry must be whether in the light of all the facts and circumstances there was any substantial basis for the conclusion, in which Congress and the military commander united, that the curfew as applied was a protective measure necessary to meet the threat of sabotage and espionage which would substantially affect the war effort and which might reasonably be expected to aid a threatened enemy invasion. The alternative which appellant insists must be accepted is for the military authorities to impose the curfew on all citizens within the military area, or on none. In a case of threatened danger requiring prompt action, it is a choice between inflicting obviously needless hardship on the many, or sitting passive and unresisting in the presence of the threat. We think that constitutional government, in time of war, is not so powerless and does not compel so hard a choice if those charged with the responsibility of our national defense have reasonable ground for believing that the threat is real.

When the orders were promulgated there was a vast concentration, within Military Areas Nos. 1 and 2, of installations and facilities for the production of military equipment, especially ships and airplanes. Important Army and Navy bases were located in California and Washington. Approximately one-fourth of the total value of the major aircraft contracts then let by Government procurement officers were to be performed in the State of California. California ranked second, and Washington fifth, of all the states of the Union with respect to the value of shipbuilding contracts to be performed.

In the critical days of March 1942, the danger to our war production by sabotage and espionage in this area seems obvious. The German invasion of the Western European countries had given ample warning to the world of the menace of the "fifth column." Espionage by persons in sympathy with the Japanese Government had been found to have been particularly effective in the surprise attack on Pearl Harbor. At a time of threatened Japanese attack upon this country, the nature of our inhabitants' attachments to the Japanese enemy was consequently a matter of grave concern. Of the 126,000 persons of Japanese descent in the United States, citizens and non-citizens, approximately 112,000 resided in California, Oregon and Washington at the time of the adoption of the military regulations. Of these approximately two-thirds are citizens because born in the United States. Not only did the great majority of such persons reside within the Pacific Coast states but they were concentrated in or near three of the large cities, Seattle, Portland and Los Angeles, all in Military Area No. 1.

There is support for the view that social, economic and political conditions which have prevailed since the close of the last century, when the Japanese began to come to this country in substantial numbers, have intensified their solidarity and have in large measure prevented their assimilation as an integral part of the white population.[4] In addition, large numbers of children of Japanese parentage are sent to Japanese language schools outside the regular hours of public schools in the locality. Some of these schools are generally believed to be sources of Japanese nationalistic propaganda, cultivating allegiance to Japan. Considerable numbers, estimated to be approximately 10,000, of American-born children of Japanese parentage have been sent to Japan for all or a part of their education.

Congress and the Executive, including the military commander, could have attributed special significance, in its bearing on the loyalties of persons of Japanese descent, to the maintenance by Japan of its system of dual citizenship. Children born in the United States of Japanese alien parents, and especially those children born before December 1, 1924, are under many circumstances deemed, by Japanese law, to be citizens of Japan. No official

---

[4] Federal legislation has denied to the Japanese citizenship by naturalization and the Immigration Act of 1924 excluded them from admission into the United States. State legislation has denied to alien Japanese the privilege of owning land. It has also sought to prohibit intermarriage of persons of Japanese race with Caucasians. Persons of Japanese descent have often been unable to secure professional or skilled employment except in association with others of that descent, and sufficient employment opportunities of this character have not been available.

census of those whom Japan regards as having thus retained Japanese citizenship is available, but there is ground for the belief that the number is large.

The large number of resident alien Japanese, approximately one-third of all Japanese inhabitants of the country, are of mature years and occupy positions of influence in Japanese communities. The association of influential Japanese residents with Japanese Consulates has been deemed a ready means for the dissemination of propaganda and for the maintenance of the influence of the Japanese Government with the Japanese population in this country.

As a result of all these conditions affecting the life of the Japanese, both aliens and citizens, in the Pacific Coast area, there has been relatively little social intercourse between them and the white population. The restrictions, both practical and legal, affecting the privileges and opportunities afforded to persons of Japanese extraction residing in the United States, have been sources of irritation and may well have tended to increase their isolation, and in many instances their attachments to Japan and its institutions.

Viewing these data in all their aspects, Congress and the Executive could reasonably have concluded that these conditions have encouraged the continued attachment of members of this group to Japan and Japanese institutions. These are only some of the many considerations which those charged with the responsibility for the national defense could take into account in determining the nature and extent of the danger of espionage and sabotage, in the event of invasion or air raid attack. The extent of that danger could be definitely known only after the event and after it was too late to meet it. Whatever views we may entertain regarding the loyalty to this country of the citizens of Japanese ancestry, we cannot reject as unfounded the judgment of the military authorities and of Congress that there were disloyal members of that population, whose number and strength could not be precisely and quickly ascertained. We cannot say that the war-making branches of the Government did not have ground for believing that in a critical hour such persons could not readily be isolated and separately dealt with, and constituted a menace to the national defense and safety, which demanded that prompt and adequate measures be taken to guard against it.

Appellant does not deny that, given the danger, a curfew was an appropriate measure against sabotage. It is an obvious protection against the perpetration of sabotage most readily committed during the hours of darkness. If it was an appropriate exercise of the war power its validity is not impaired because it has restricted the citizen's liberty. Like every military control of the population of a dangerous zone in war time, it necessarily involves some infringement of individual liberty, just as does the police establishment of fire lines during a fire, or the confinement of people to their houses during an air raid alarm—neither of which could be thought to be an infringement of constitutional right. Like them, the validity of the restraints of the curfew order depends on all the conditions which obtain at the time the curfew is imposed and which support the order imposing it.

But appellant insists that the exercise of the power is inappropriate and unconstitutional because it discriminates against citizens of Japanese ancestry, in violation of the Fifth Amendment. The Fifth Amendment contains no equal protection clause and it restrains only such discriminatory legislation by Congress as amounts to a denial of due process. *Detroit Bank v. United States*, 317 U.S. 329, 337–38 [(1943)]. Congress may hit at a particular danger where it is seen, without providing for others which are not so evident or so urgent.

Distinctions between citizens solely because of their ancestry are by their very nature odious to a free people whose institutions are founded upon the doctrine of equality. For that reason, legislative classification or discrimination based on race alone has often been held to be a denial of equal protection. *Yick Wo v. Hopkins*, 118 U.S. 356 [(1886)]; *Yu Cong Eng v. Trinidad*, 271 U.S. 500 [(1926)]; *Hill v. Texas*, 316 U.S. 400 [(1942)]. We may assume that these considerations would be controlling here were it not for the fact that the danger of espionage and sabotage, in time of war and of threatened invasion, calls upon the military authorities to scrutinize every relevant fact bearing on the loyalty of populations in the danger areas. Because racial discriminations are in most circumstances irrelevant and therefore prohibited, it by no means follows that, in dealing with the perils of war, Congress and the Executive are wholly precluded from taking into account those facts and circumstances which are relevant to measures for our national defense and for the successful prosecution of the war, and which may in fact place citizens of one ancestry in a different category from others. "We must never forget, that it is a constitution we are expounding," "a constitution intended to endure for ages to come, and, consequently, to be adapted to the various crises of human affairs." *McCulloch v. Maryland*, 4 Wheat. 316, 407, 415 [(1819)]. The adoption by Government, in the crisis of war and of threatened invasion, of measures for the public safety, based upon the recognition of facts and circumstances which indicate that a group of one national extraction may menace that safety more than others, is not wholly beyond the limits of the Constitution and is not to be condemned merely because in other and in most circumstances racial distinctions are irrelevant.

Here the aim of Congress and the Executive was the protection against sabotage of war materials and utilities in areas thought to be in danger of Japanese invasion and air attack. We have stated in detail facts and circumstances with respect to the American citizens of Japanese ancestry residing on the Pacific Coast which support the judgment of the war-waging branches of the Government that some restrictive measure was urgent. We cannot say that these facts and circumstances, considered in the particular war setting, could afford no ground for differentiating citizens of Japanese ancestry from other groups in the United States. The fact alone that attack on our shores was threatened by Japan rather than another enemy power set these citizens apart from others who have no particular associations with Japan.

Our investigation here does not go beyond the inquiry whether, in the light of all the relevant circumstances preceding and attending their promulgation, the challenged orders and statute afforded a reasonable basis for the action taken in imposing the curfew. We cannot close our eyes to the fact, demonstrated by experience, that in time of war residents having ethnic affiliations with an invading enemy may be a greater source of danger than those of a different ancestry. Nor can we deny that Congress, and the military authorities acting with its authorization, have constitutional power to appraise the danger in the light of facts of public notoriety. We need not now attempt to define the ultimate boundaries of the war power. We decide only the issue as we have defined it—we decide only that the curfew order as applied, and at the time it was applied, was within the boundaries of the war power. In this case it is enough that circumstances within the knowledge of those charged with the responsibility for maintaining the national defense afforded a rational basis for the decision which they made. Whether we would have made it is irrelevant.

The conviction under the second count is without constitutional infirmity. Hence we have no occasion to review the conviction on the first count since, as already stated, the sentences on the two counts are to run concurrently and conviction on the second is sufficient to sustain the sentence. For this reason also it is unnecessary to consider the Government's argument that compliance with the order to report at the Civilian Control Station did not necessarily entail confinement in a relocation center.

Affirmed.

Mr. Justice DOUGLAS, concurring:

While I concur in the result and agree substantially with the opinion of the Court, I wish to add a few words to indicate what for me is the narrow ground of decision.

After the disastrous bombing of Pearl Harbor the military had a grave problem on its hands. The threat of Japanese invasion of the west coast was not fanciful but real. The presence of many thousands of aliens and citizens of Japanese ancestry in or near to the key points along that coast line aroused special concern in those charged with the defense of the country. They believed that not only among aliens but also among citizens of Japanese ancestry there were those who would give aid and comfort to the Japanese invader and act as a fifth column before and during an invasion. If the military were right in their belief that among citizens of Japanese ancestry there was an actual or incipient fifth column, we were indeed faced with the imminent threat of a dire emergency. We must credit the military with as much good faith in that belief as we would any other public official acting pursuant to his duties. We cannot possibly know all the facts which lay behind that decision. Some of them may have been as intangible and as imponderable as the factors which influence personal or business decisions in daily life. The point is that we cannot sit in judgment on the military requirements of that hour. Where the orders under the present Act have some relation to "protection against espionage and against sabotage," our task is at an end.

Much of the argument assumes that as a matter of policy it might have been wiser for the military to have dealt with these people on an individual basis and through the process of investigation and hearings separated those who were loyal from those who were not. But the wisdom or expediency of the decision which was made is not for us to review. Nor are we warranted where national survival is at stake in insisting that those orders should not have been applied to anyone without some evidence of his disloyalty. The orders as applied to the petitioner are not to be tested by the substantial evidence rule. Peacetime procedures do not necessarily fit wartime needs. It is said that if citizens of Japanese ancestry were generally disloyal, treatment on a group basis might be justified. But there is no difference in power when the number of those who are finally shown to be disloyal or suspect is reduced to a small per cent. The sorting process might indeed be as time-consuming whether those who were disloyal or suspect constituted nine or ninety-nine per cent. And the pinch of the order on the loyal citizens would be as great in any case. But where the peril is great and the time is short, temporary treatment on a group basis may be the only practicable expedient whatever the ultimate percentage of those who are detained for cause. Nor should the military be required to wait until espionage or sabotage becomes effective before it moves.

It is true that we might now say that there was ample time to handle the problem on the individual rather than the group basis. But military decisions must be made without the benefit of hindsight. The orders must be judged as of the date when the decision to issue them was made.

Since we cannot override the military judgment which lay behind these orders, it seems to me necessary to concede that the army had the power to deal temporarily with these people on a group basis. Petitioner therefore was not justified in disobeying the orders.

But I think it important to emphasize that we are dealing here with a problem of loyalty not assimilation. Loyalty is a matter of mind and of heart not of race. That indeed is the history of America. Moreover, guilt is personal under our constitutional system. Detention for reasonable cause is one thing. Detention on account of ancestry is another.

There are other instances in the law where one must obey an order before he can attack as erroneous the classification in which he has been placed. Thus it is commonly held that one who is a conscientious objector has no privilege to defy the Selective Service Act and to refuse or fail to be inducted. He must submit to the law. But that line of authority holds that after induction he may obtain through *habeas corpus* a hearing on the legality of his classification by the draft board.

Mr. Justice MURPHY, concurring:

It is not to be doubted that the action taken by the military commander in pursuance of the authority conferred upon him was taken in complete good faith and in the firm conviction that it was required by considerations of public safety and military security. Neither is it doubted that the Congress and the Executive working together may generally employ such measures as are necessary and appropriate to provide for the common defense and to wage war "with all the force necessary to make it effective." *United States v. Macintosh*, 283 U.S. 605, 622. This includes authority to exercise measures of control over persons and property which would not in all cases be permissible in normal times.

It does not follow, however, that the broad guaranties of the Bill of Rights and other provisions of the Constitution protecting essential liberties are suspended by the mere existence of a state of war. It has been frequently stated and recognized by this Court that the war power, like the other great substantive powers of government, is subject to the limitations of the Constitution. *See Ex parte Milligan,* 4 Wall. 2. We give great deference to the judgment of the Congress and of the military authorities as to what is necessary in the effective prosecution of the war, but we can never forget that there are constitutional boundaries which it is our duty to uphold. It would not be supposed, for instance, that public elections could be suspended or that the prerogatives of the courts could be set aside, or that persons not charged with offenses against the law of war could be deprived of due process of law and the benefits of trial by jury, in the absence of a valid declaration of martial law. *Cf. Ex parte Milligan, supra.*

Distinctions based on color and ancestry are utterly inconsistent with our traditions and ideals. They are at variance with the principles for which we are now waging war. We cannot close our eyes to the fact that for centuries the Old World has been torn by racial and religious conflicts and has suffered the worst kind of anguish because of inequality of treatment for different groups. There was one law for one and a different law for another. Nothing is written more firmly into our law than the compact of the Plymouth voyagers to have just and equal laws. To say that any group cannot be assimilated is to admit that the great American experiment has failed, that our way of life has failed when confronted with the normal attachment of certain groups to the lands of their forefathers. As a nation we embrace many groups, some of them among the oldest settlements in our midst, which have isolated themselves for religious and cultural reasons.

Today is the first time, so far as I am aware, that we have sustained a substantial restriction of the personal liberty of citizens of the United States based upon the accident of race or ancestry. Under the curfew order here challenged no less than 70,000 American citizens have been placed under a special ban and deprived of their liberty because of their particular racial inheritance. In this sense it bears a melancholy resemblance to the treatment accorded to members of the Jewish race in Germany and in other parts of Europe. The result is the creation in this country of two classes of citizens for the purposes of a critical and perilous hour—to sanction discrimination between groups of United States citizens on the basis of ancestry. In my opinion this goes to the very brink of constitutional power.

Except under conditions of great emergency a regulation of this kind applicable solely to citizens of a particular racial extraction would not be regarded as in accord with the requirement of due process of law contained in the Fifth Amendment. We have consistently held that attempts to apply regulatory action to particular groups solely on the basis of racial distinction or classification is not in accordance with due process of law as prescribed by the Fifth and Fourteenth Amendments. It is true that the Fifth Amendment, unlike the Fourteenth, contains no guarantee of equal protection of the laws. It by no means follows, however, that there may not be discrimination of such an injurious character in the application of laws as to amount to a denial of due process of law as that term is used in the Fifth Amendment.[2]

In voting for affirmance of the judgment I do not wish to be understood as intimating that the military authorities in time of war are subject to no restraints whatsoever, or that they are free to impose any restrictions they may choose on the rights and liberties of individual citizens or groups of citizens in those places which may be designated as "military areas." While this Court sits, it has the inescapable duty of seeing that the mandates of the Constitution are obeyed. That duty exists in time of war as well as in time of peace, and in its performance we must not forget that few indeed have been the invasions upon essential liberties which have not been accompanied by pleas of urgent necessity advanced in good faith by responsible men.

Nor do I mean to intimate that citizens of a particular racial group whose freedom may be curtailed within an area threatened with attack should be generally prevented from leaving the area and going at large in other areas that are not in danger of attack and where special precautions are not needed. Their status as citizens, though subject to requirements of national security and military necessity, should at all times be accorded the fullest consideration and respect. When the danger is past, the restrictions imposed on them should be promptly removed and their freedom of action fully restored.[*]

NOTES AND QUESTIONS

The following notes and questions span the technical to the contextual. The first set addresses the legal questions both answered and avoided by the Supreme Court in *Hirabayashi*. The second group examines critically *Hirabayashi*'s effect on equal protection legal doctrine, and the third places the Court's decision within a broader social and political context.

WHAT THE COURT DECIDED

1. Threshold issue: As the opinion makes clear, Hirabayashi was convicted on two separate counts: violation of the curfew order and violation of an evacuation order. The Court, however, addresses the constitutionality of only the curfew order. If you were a Supreme Court Justice, what pragmatic or political considerations would lead you to address only the curfew violation? Of course, judges cannot generally offer solely pragmatic or political justifications for their decisions. Instead, or at least in addition, they must provide doctrinal justifications. What aspect of Hirabayashi's sentencing allowed the Court to do doctrinally what a majority of the justices thought to be sensible practically?

---

[2] For instance, if persons of an accused's race were systematically excluded from a jury in a federal court, any conviction undoubtedly would be considered a violation of the requirement of due process of law, even though the ground commonly stated for setting aside convictions so obtained in state courts is denial of equal protection of the laws.

[*] [The concurring opinion of Justice Rutledge has been omitted.—ED.]

2. Mapping the constitutional arguments: According to the Court, Hirabayashi raised two types of constitutional arguments—one about power, the other about discrimination. Specifically, he challenged the curfew and exclusion orders as "unconstitutional delegation[s] by Congress of its legislative power" and as "unconstitutional[] discriminat[ions] between citizens of Japanese ancestry and those of other ancestries in violation of the Fifth Amendment."

3. Power

a. A government of limited powers: The federal government is a government of limited powers. When the United States was created, the federal government was granted only a specifically delimited set of powers in the U.S. Constitution. Thus, although state governments enjoy a general "police power" to act in a general public interest, all federal government actions must stem from some specific grant of power identified in the Constitution. Does the federal government lack the affirmative power to issue and enforce the orders under which Hirabayashi was convicted? What does the majority think? What portions of the Constitution, if any, give the federal government the affirmative power to do what it did?

b. Nondelegation doctrine: A related argument focused on the congressional delegation of power to the military. In the 1930s, the Supreme Court introduced the "nondelegation doctrine," which stated that Congress could not delegate broad, unspecified legislative powers to an agency. Instead, any delegation of legislative power had to be constrained by sufficiently specific substantive standards. Although agencies could find particular facts, which would trigger different substantive results, the basic substantive rule had to be specified by Congress. In omitted portions of the opinion, the Court rejected Hirabayashi's nondelegation doctrine argument. The Court conceded that Public Law 503 contained no explicit substantive standard. However, the Court explained that the Act must be read in light of the Executive Order 9066, as well as General DeWitt's Public Proclamations, both of which preceded the congressional Act. Read in their light, the Court identified an implicit substantive standard of protection against "espionage and sabotage":

> It is true that the Act does not in terms establish a particular standard to which orders of the military commander are to conform, or require findings to be made as a prerequisite to any order. But the Executive Order, the Proclamations and the statute are not to be read in isolation from each other. They were parts of a single program and must be judged as such. The Act of March 21, 1942, was an adoption by Congress of the Executive Order and of the Proclamations. The Proclamations themselves followed a standard authorized by the Executive Order—the necessity of protecting military resources in the designated areas against espionage and sabotage. And by the Act, Congress gave its approval to that standard.

Hirabayashi, 320 U.S. at 103.

Do you find this decision to view the Executive Order, Public Proclamations and the statute as all parts of a coordinated, organic program odd when the Court decided to do just the opposite when it carefully separated the curfew order from the evacuation order?

EQUAL PROTECTION AND THE STRICT SCRUTINY STANDARD OF REVIEW

4. Standard of judicial review: Earlier, we set forth the basic doctrinal machinery of current equal protection analysis: A court first determines the appropriate level of scrutiny: strict, intermediate, mere rationality. Next, the Court decides whether the government action satisfies means-ends analysis: For example, under strict scrutiny, the ends pursued must be "compelling" and the means must be "narrowly tailored." That said, the *Hirabayashi* opinion does not neatly follow any such algorithm. To expect it to do so would be to commit the error of anachronism, because the specific operation of means-ends analysis was not made clear by the court until much later.

So, reviewing the opinion on its own terms, is there any language that resembles a "standard of review" for disparate treatment on the basis of race? Consider the following:

> Distinctions between citizens solely because of their ancestry are by their very nature odious to a free people whose institutions are founded upon the doctrine of equality. For that reason, legislative classification or discrimination based on race alone has often been held to be a denial of equal protection. *Yick Wo v. Hopkins.*

Hirabayashi, supra. Is there any other language that more accurately captures the Court's standard of review?

5. Deference to military necessity: The above quotation continues: "We may assume that these considerations would be controlling here were it not for the fact that the danger of espionage and sabotage, in time of war and of threatened invasion. . . ." In other words, even though race-based discriminations are "odious to a free people," (thereby raising the level of judicial scrutiny), decisions made in the face of military necessity warrant deference (lowering the level of judicial scrutiny). Try to identify language in the majority opinion that fleshes out the degree of deference that exigent circumstances (compelling ends?) of war and military necessity require. The role that "military necessity" arguments should play in equal protection cases is discussed further in the next study module.

6. A good enough reason?: At bottom, was there good enough reason to justify a curfew on all individuals of Japanese descent, immigrant and citizen alike? The basic reasoning seems to be that individuals of Japanese descent pose a greater threat than other individuals of assisting the Japanese Empire in espionage or terrorism. Is this a reasonable generalization? Since no generalization is ever perfectly accurate, how correct must the generalization be before it is constitutionally acceptable? Should race-based generalizations be especially suspect?

7. The evidence: The Court concluded that "We cannot say that the war-making branches of the Government *did not have ground* for believing that in a critical hour such persons could not readily be isolated and separately dealt with, and constituted a menace to the national defense and safety." The evidentiary basis for the government's *ground* consisted of the following possible sources:

- DeWitt's Public Proclamations ("The proclamation recited that the entire Pacific Coast 'by its geographical location is particularly subject to attack, to attempted invasion by the armed forces of nations with which the United States is now at war, and, in connection therewith, is subject to espionage and acts of sabotage, thereby requiring the adoption of military measures necessary to establish safeguards against such enemy operations'"), *Hirabayashi, supra*;

- DeWitt's House testimony ("He also stated to the Senate that 'reasons for suspected widespread fifth-column activity among Japanese' were to be found in the system of dual citizenship which Japan deemed applicable to American-born Japanese, and in the propaganda disseminated by Japanese consuls, Buddhist priests and other leaders, among American-born children of Japanese. Such was stated to be the explanation of the contemplated evacuation from the Pacific Coast area of persons of Japanese ancestry, citizens as well as aliens."), *id.*;

- The Tolan Committee House Report ("Congress also had before it the Preliminary Report of a House Committee investigating national defense migration, of March 19, 1942, which approved the provisions of Executive Order No. 9066, and which recommended the evacuation, from military areas established under the Order, of all persons of Japanese ancestry, including citizens.), *id.*; and

- The Roberts Report ("Espionage by persons in sympathy with the Japanese Government had been found to have been particularly effective in the surprise attack on Pearl Harbor."). *Id.*

How solid is this evidence? Would it matter to you that many of these sources were never formally admitted into evidence at Hirabayashi's trial? This issue is discussed further in Chapter 5.

A DEEPER LOOK AT CONTEXT

8. Rationalizing race: The government argued in its brief:

These facts, which should be considered in determining the constitutionality of the Act of March 21, 1942, as here applied, embrace the general military, political, economic, and social conditions under which the challenged orders were issued. These historical facts, which we shall endeavor to set forth, are of the type that are traditionally susceptible of judicial notice in considering constitutional questions, and in particular, many of these facts appear in official documents, such as the contemporary Tolan Committee's reports, which are peculiarly within the realm of judicial notice. . . .

The reaction of the Japanese to their lack of assimilation and to their treatment is a question which of course does not admit of any precise answer. It is entirely possible that an unknown number of the Japanese may lack to some extent a feeling of loyalty toward the United States as a result of their treatment, and may feel a consequent tie to Japan, a heightened sense of racial solidarity, and a compensatory feeling of racial pride or pride in Japan's achievements.

40 LANDMARK BRIEFS AND ARGUMENTS OF THE SUPREME COURT OF THE UNITED STATES: CONSTITUTIONAL LAW 289, 299 (Philip B. Kurland and Gerhard Casper, eds., 1975).

In its *amicus curiae* brief, the Japanese American Citizens League countered:

> One other rationalization, and a most ominous one, for approving discriminatory evacuation, exists. It is said that since persons of Japanese ancestry have been discriminated against, legally and socially, in American life, they bear resentment against this country and would be likely to retaliate by betraying our west coast to an invader. . . .

> Fortunately the forces of evil, past and present, are not as all-powerful as the superficial would like to think. They have not succeeded in isolating these people or in alienating them from the main stream of American life. . . .

Id. at 489.

What stories are being told by these briefs? Why were the government's arguments more persuasive to the Court? Why do you think the Court was reticent to examine the issue of "race" in its opinion, given that it was deciding a case that was grounded on a claim of racial discrimination? How could it take judicial notice of certain allegedly racial characteristics without squarely confronting the issue of race?

9. Race, legal measures and unassimilability: In footnote 4 of the opinion and the accompanying text, the Court explains that because the Japanese had not "assimilated," they posed a greater military threat. Surprisingly, the Court does not place blame solely on the Japanese for being aloof and cliquish—for example, by sending their children back to Japan for schooling. In addition, the Court recognizes that mainstream society, through racially discriminatory laws, kept Japanese Americans at a distance. Because Japanese Americans were not allowed into the fold of American society, the Court explains that it is reasonable to be more skeptical about their loyalty. On the one hand, this seems to be obviously true: Any society that stigmatizes a group should not be surprised if that group shows more hostility, or at least more skepticism, toward that society. On the other hand, this seems to put the Japanese Americans into a Catch-22. Put bluntly, does the majority justify current racist actions on the basis of generalizations that are "reasonable" only because of previous racist actions?

10. The politics of drafting: Justices Douglas and Murphy originally prepared their concurring opinions in *Hirabayashi* as dissents. Justice Felix Frankfurter eventually prevailed upon both of his colleagues to change their initial views and to join the majority's judgment. Concurrences, though, indicate some divergence from the majority's analysis.

a. Justice Douglas: When *Hirabayashi* was decided, Justice Douglas was a junior member of the Court who had not yet established his reputation for outspoken liberal opinions. What does Douglas's opinion add? He explains that sorting the loyal from disloyal would have been very time-consuming, and that time was of the essence. Would the majority agree or disagree? He further writes that this is a problem of "loyalty not assimilation," and that guilt is personal, not ancestral. Again, would the majority agree or disagree? Finally, at the end of his opinion, he makes a muted reference to the writ of *habeas corpus*, which is a way for an individual to petition a court to ask for release from illegal government detention. (We discuss the mechanics further *infra*, with respect to the *Endo* case.) What might Justice Douglas have been thinking? When *Hirabayashi* was decided, over 100,000 individuals of Japanese descent were interned. Was he envisioning that each individual would have to file a separate *habeas corpus* petition for release? How feasible is that?

b. Justice Murphy: Murphy, a former attorney general who started the precursor to the Civil Rights division of the Justice Department, actually circulated his draft dissent. But upon Justice Felix Frankfurter's strong urging, the dissent was converted into a concurrence. Reread Justice Murphy's opinion and imagine how it might be converted back into a dissent. Further, after reading his dissent in *Korematsu, infra*, note how Justice Murphy's dissent builds on his concurrence here.

11. Race and national origin: Alien Italians and alien Germans, like alien Japanese, were subject to Public Proclamation 3, the curfew order. However, the only American citizens also subject to this order were of Japanese descent. What legal arguments could be made to support the inclusion of alien Germans and Italians? Is national origin, regardless of racial classification, an accurate proxy for greater risk of disloyalty? If so, can one show discrimination based on national origin?

How does race complicate the national origin analysis? Could it be argued that the government curfew order should be subject to even stricter scrutiny when applied to racial minorities than when applied to European American groups where the possibility of racial prejudice is not at issue? If so, perhaps it is even bizarre in retrospect that the Court upheld a curfew as applied to the racial minority group and, in particular, to American citizens of that racial minority group.

12. Kiplingesque folklore?: Even at the time of these decisions, contemporaneous observers found them indefensible. Eugene Rostow, Dean of Yale Law School and later Undersecretary of State during the Johnson Administration, called the internment cases "a disaster." Shortly after the end of the war, he observed that the internment "rest[ed] on five propositions of the utmost potential menace":

> (1) Protective custody, extending over three or four years, is a permitted form of imprisonment in the United States; (2) political opinions, not criminal acts, may contain enough clear and present danger to justify such imprisonment; (3) men, women and children of a given ethnic group, both Americans and resident aliens, can be presumed to possess the kind of dangerous ideas which require their imprisonment; (4) in time of war or emergency the military, perhaps without even the concurrence of the legislature, can decide what political opinions require imprisonment, and which ethnic groups are infected with them; and (5) the decision of the military can be carried out without indictment, trial, examination, jury, the confrontation of witnesses, counsel for the defense, the privileged against self-incrimination, or any of the other safeguards of the Bill of Rights.

Eugene V. Rostow, "The Japanese American Cases—A Disaster," 54 *Yale L.J.* 489, 532 (1945). Rostow called the Supreme Court's treatment of the facts as "Kiplingesque folklore about East and West." He observed that there had been no evidence taken on Japanese Americans as a group nor on loyalty of Japanese Americans as individuals. Reviewing the DeWitt Final Report, Rostow concluded that the basis for the decisions had been "ignorant race prejudice."

b. YASUI V. UNITED STATES—THE CURFEW, PART II

(i) BACKGROUND

Unlike Hirabayashi, who was a pacifist, Yasui was an Army officer. A member of the reserves, Yasui tried unsuccessfully to report for active duty after the bombing of Pearl Harbor.

PETER IRONS, JUSTICE AT WAR
81–85

One minute after midnight on March 28, 1942, Japanese Americans on the West Coast became subject to criminal penalties for violation of the curfew imposed by General DeWitt on "all persons of Japanese ancestry." Later that same day, five hours after the 6:00 p.m. curfew took effect, Minoru Yasui walked into a Portland, Oregon, police station and demanded to be arrested for curfew violation. This early act of resistance gave Yasui the distinction of raising the first legal test of DeWitt's orders among the entire Japanese American population.

Min Yasui was in many ways an unlikely candidate for this distinction. The path that ended in the Portland drunk tank on that Saturday night had passed through training as an Army officer, education as a lawyer, employment in a Japanese consular office, and active involvement in the Japanese American Citizens League. In pursuing his challenge to the Supreme Court, Yasui nonetheless accepted the basic legality of Roosevelt's executive order and the congressional statute that enforced it. Even the ordeal of nine months in solitary confinement failed to shake Yasui's avowed "110 percent" patriotism and his commitment to military obedience. In a final touch of irony, Yasui volunteered his services to the Justice Department in a futile campaign to dissuade imprisoned Japanese American draft resisters from continuing their own objections to military orders.

Perhaps the best explanation for the apparent contradiction between Yasui's roles as a law violator and law enforcer lies in his thoroughly American upbringing. Born in October 1916 to parents who settled in Hood River Oregon, after their migration from Japan, Min Yasui was the second of seven children. Masuo Yasui raised his children as Methodists, sent them to public schools, and put them all through college. The owner of an apple orchard in the fertile Hood River Valley, Masuo was accepted into the largely white leadership of the apple growers' association, while at the same time he acted as a defender of the six hundred Japanese Americans in the valley. As a youngster, Min attended the local Japanese language school for three summers but never achieved fluency in his ancestral tongue. Even then he was a stubborn student. "I was kicked out before I finished Book Three for being a bad boy," he later said with obvious relish.

Min entered the University of Oregon at Eugene in 1933. After two years of compulsory military training, he volunteered for the final two years of reserve officer training. Forced to wait until his twenty-first birthday, he received a commission as Second Lieutenant in the Army Infantry Reserve on December 8, 1937. Min then entered the University's law school, where he studied under Wayne Morse, the nation's youngest law school dean and later a maverick member of the United States Senate. Morse later provided an incisive but telling thumbnail sketch of Yasui's personality in a 1943 letter to ACLU director Roger Baldwin. He held a "relatively high opinion" of Yasui as a law student, Morse wrote, "but on many occasions I detected a streak of blind stubbornness in him. . . ."

Yasui found it difficult to land a job as a lawyer following his law school graduation in 1939. His father, who had been decorated by the Japanese government for his leadership of the Hood River Valley community, was a close friend of the Japanese consul in Portland. Through the intercession of his father, Yasui secured a position as an attaché of the Japanese consulate in Chicago. As an American citizen, he duly registered with the State Department as a foreign agent.

The day after Pearl Harbor, while the Japanese consul hurriedly burned cables and codes, Yasui received a telegram from his father: "NOW THAT THIS COUNTRY IS AT WAR AND NEEDS YOU, AND SINCE YOU ARE TRAINED AS AN OFFICER, I AS YOUR FATHER URGE YOU TO ENLIST IMMEDIATELY." Responding to this parental request on his own patriotic impulse, Yasui immediately resigned his consular post. When he went to the Chicago railroad station to buy a ticket to Portland, he discovered that the agents would not sell a ticket to anyone of Oriental appearance. Only after he received a telegram from the Army a few days later, ordering him to report for duty at the Vancouver barracks cross the Columbia River from Portland, was Yasui able to buy a train ticket. When he reported to Fort Vancouver, Yasui was placed in command of a platoon of soldiers. The next day, before his formal induction, Army officers told Yasui he was unacceptable for service and ordered him off the base. He returned eight times to Fort Vancouver with an offer to serve and was turned away each time.

A few days after he rejoined his family, Yasui's father was arrested for membership in the "ABC" list and sent to the Justice Department internment camp in Missoula, Montana. At loose ends after his father's arrest and his rejection by the Army Yasui moved from Hood River to Portland and hung out his shingle as a lawyer.

Within two weeks of Min Yasui's return from Missoula to Portland, President Roosevelt signed Executive Order 9066. "A lot of rumors were flying back and forth," Yasui recalled. "They were going to take the Nisei, they were going to draft everybody and put them into labor camps, all sorts of rumors." Hoping even before the curfew and the first evacuation orders to find a legal means to block internment, Yasui consulted Earl F. Bernard, a leading Portland lawyer and at the time only a casual acquaintance. Bernard, a stolid and conservative lawyer in his early fifties, advised Yasui that no challenge was possible until the government issued orders backed with criminal penalties. However, Bernard did offer to represent Yasui in the event that he later raised a challenge to the anticipated orders.

Meeting with fellow Nisei in Portland, Yasui plotted a strategy to find an appealing test case. "We were going to find a Nisei who'd served in the Army and had an honorable discharge, with two or three little kids, and we thought that would be an ideal test case. So I talked to my friends, but none of them were willing to undertake it. I had a few bucks, so I said, 'Look, I'll put up the money, you guys be the guinea pigs.' But it's hard to tear yourself away from your family and friends. I knew I was not an ideal test case, but somebody had to do it."

Yasui did not wait for the evacuation orders he felt were inevitable. He had no quarrel with the curfew order on general principle, or with one applied only to aliens. "But Military Order Number 3 applied to all persons of Japanese ancestry. I said, 'There the general is wrong, because it makes distinctions between citizens on the basis of ancestry.' That order infringed on my rights as a citizen."

Yasui wasted no time in offering himself as a test case. "I had my secretary call the police on March 28th, a Saturday night, and report that 'There's a Japanese walking up and down the streets, arrest him.' I had an awful time getting arrested. I was getting tired walking around town, and I approached a policeman at eleven o'clock at night. I pulled out this order that said all persons of Japanese ancestry must be in their place of abode, and I pulled out my birth certificate and said, 'Look, I'm a person of Japanese ancestry, arrest me.' And the policeman said, 'Run along home, you'll get in trouble.' I actually had to go down to the Second Avenue police station and talk to the sergeant and tell him what I wanted to do. He said, 'sure, we'll oblige you.' So they threw me in the drunk tank until Monday morning, which was a miserable experience." In his eagerness to institute a test case, Yasui forgot that persons arrested on Friday and Saturday nights languished in the lockup over the weekend. He remained behind bars until Earl Bernard arrived on Monday morning to bail him out.

(ii) THE CASE

Yasui's trial differed from Hirabayashi's trial. Appearing in June 1942 in Portland, Oregon, Yasui's lawyer, Earl Bernard, chose to waive Yasui's right to a jury trial, opting instead for a bench trial before Judge James A. Fee. Their anticipation that Judge Fee would be independent-minded proved partially accurate.

Although the ACLU briefly considered entering the case, it refrained because it regarded Yasui as a less than ideal plaintiff. Due to his employment at the Japanese Consulate in Chicago, which entailed registering as a "propaganda agent" on behalf of the Japanese government, Yasui was unable to make the same claim as many other Japanese Americans, who could honestly deny any connection with an enemy nation. The JACL also opposed the *Ya-*

sui test case. At the time, the JACL was strongly encouraging compliance with military orders. Its leadership feared that Yasui would set a bad example. Later, the JACL and Yasui would make amends, as Yasui worked to dissuade draft resistance among Japanese Americans.

At trial, the government lawyers requested that the court take judicial notice of various facts purporting to demonstrate that Japanese Americans were likely to be disloyal. Central to their strategy was a racial characteristics argument: the intertwined claims, prepared with the help of the War Relocation Authority, that Japanese Americans were biologically predisposed to side with the Japanese government and that Japanese Americans were essentially different from White Americans. The government argued that the military had already determined that in the event of invasion, Japanese Americans might help Japanese soldiers, and that individual assessments of Japanese American loyalty would be made difficult by psychological differences between White Americans and Japanese Americans. They further offered a protective custody justification: The internment actually benefited Japanese Americans by protecting them from vigilantism and private violence.

In the midst of the proceedings, Judge Fee suddenly took over the cross-examination of Yasui. Fee asked a series of questions about the Shinto religion. His inquiries ranged from "what is Shinto?" and "do you give adherence to its precepts?" to "was not Shinto practiced in your household?" and whether Yasui "accept[ed] divine pretensions on the part of the Emperor of Japan." When Yasui answered consistently that he, as well as his parents, were Methodists, Fee responded by asking Yasui if he "believe[d] in the sanctity of an oath." Fee asked Yasui to recite his oath as an Army officer and whether he felt he should obey curfew orders.

After the trial was over, Fee issued a written opinion much longer than the Supreme Court's subsequent opinion. Fee reached a pair of conclusions. Initially, he held that the curfew orders were unconstitutional as applied to U.S. citizens. However, he also found that Yasui had indirectly renounced his U.S. citizenship. Taken together, these conclusions allowed Fee to hold that Yasui was guilty as charged.

Fee wrote:

> The question now before this court is whether a military commander has the right to legislate and pass statutes defining crimes which will be enforced by the civil courts. . . . It is axiomatic that so long as no form of military jurisdiction is in force over the particular locality or person, the civil law will prevail.

> There are valid reasons for control of citizens of Japanese ancestry, but the test is color and race. An equally valid foundation can be found for control of persons of Italian, German and Irish ancestry. . . . But the history of this country contains too many examples of loyalty of persons of foreign extraction to justify any blanket treatment.

United States v. Yasui, 48 F. Supp. 40, 53 (D. Ore. 1942).

Fee discounted actions Yasui had taken as a child, such as visiting relatives in Japan and attending a language school, before turning to his conclusion:

The record shows that the father of the defendant was decorated by the Emperor of Japan. Within a few months after Yasui had been admitted to the Bar of the State of Oregon, he was, at the instigation of his father, employed by the Consulate General of Japan at Chicago.

While so employed, Yasui followed the orders of the Consulate General of Japan and made speeches, setting forth the philosophy and purposes of the military caste of Japan as propaganda agent for the Emperor. While in this position, he was registered twice by the Consulate General as a propaganda agent for a foreign power, pursuant to the regulations issued by the State Department of the United States. It is true that he testifies that there was an American citizen named Murphy, presumably not of Japanese extraction, who was employed in the same work, but we are not concerned here with the employment of Murphy or his purposes or the innocence of his intention. . . .

Yasui remained as a propaganda agent until after the declaration of war by this country against Japan and after the treacherous attack by the armed forces of Japan upon territory of the United States in the Islands of the Pacific.

The court thus concludes from these evidences that defendant made an election and chose allegiance to the Emperor of Japan, rather than citizenship in the United States at his majority.

Yasui, supra at 55.

The Ninth Circuit appeals court heard oral argument on the same day in the *Hirabayashi, Yasui* and *Korematsu* cases and subsequently certified legal questions for all three cases to the Supreme Court. In Yasui's case, the issues certified and argued were the constitutionality of the curfew order and whether Yasui had renounced his citizenship. The government conceded in its Supreme Court brief that the trial judge had wrongly decided the citizenship issue. At oral argument, Yasui's lawyers pressed the claim (not made in the *Hirabayashi* oral argument the same day) that nothing in Executive Order 9066 or Public Law 503 authorized Japanese American citizens to be singled out. Their argument emphasized the more extreme statements made by General DeWitt, including his remark to a congressional committee one month earlier that "a Jap's a Jap."

The Court issued its the *Hirabayashi* and *Yasui* opinions on the same day.

YASUI v. UNITED STATES
320 U.S. 115 (1943)

Mr. Chief Justice STONE delivered the opinion of the Court.

Appellant, an American-born person of Japanese ancestry, was convicted in the district court of an offense defined by the Act of March 21, 1942. The indictment charged him with violation, on March 28, 1942, of a curfew order made applicable to Portland, Oregon, by Public Proclamation No. 3, issued by Lt. General J.L. DeWitt on March 24, 1942. The validity of the curfew was considered in the *Hirabayashi* case, and this case presents the same issues as the conviction on Count 2 of the indictment in that case.

From the evidence it appeared that appellant was born in Oregon in 1916 of alien parents; that when he was eight years old he spent a summer in Japan; that he attended the public schools in Oregon, and also, for about three years, a Japanese language school; that he later attended the University of Oregon, from which he received A.B. and LL.B. degrees; that he was a member of the bar of Oregon, and a second lieutenant in the Army of the United States, Infantry Reserve; that he had been employed by the Japanese Consulate in Chicago, but had resigned on December 8, 1941, and immediately offered his services to the military authorities; that he had discussed with an agent of the Federal Bureau of Investigation the advisability of testing the constitutionality of the curfew; and that when he violated the curfew order he requested that he be arrested so that he could test its constitutionality.

The district court ruled that the Act of March 21, 1942, was unconstitutional as applied to American citizens, but held that appellant, by reason of his course of conduct, must be deemed to have renounced his American citizenship. The Government does not undertake to support the conviction on that ground, since no such issue was tendered by the Government, although appellant testified at the trial that he had not renounced his citizenship. Since we hold, as in the *Hirabayashi* case, that the curfew order was valid as applied to citizens, it follows that appellant's citizenship was not relevant to the issue tendered by the Government and the conviction must be sustained for the reasons stated in the *Hirabayashi* case.

But as the sentence of one year's imprisonment—the maximum permitted by the statute—was imposed after the finding that appellant was not a citizen, and as the Government states that it has not and does not now controvert his citizenship, the case is an appropriate one for resentence in the light of these circumstances. The conviction will be sustained but the judgment will be vacated and the cause remanded to the district court for resentence of appellant, and to afford that court opportunity to strike its findings as to appellant's loss of United States citizenship.

So ordered.

NOTES AND QUESTIONS

1. **Brevity explained:** In contrast to the *Hirabayashi* opinion, the *Yasui* opinion is quite short. The simple explanation is that the decision in *Hirabayashi* applies squarely to the question presented in *Yasui*. Moreover, the government conceded that Yasui did not lose his American citizenship simply by working for the Japanese Consulate.

2. **Ambivalence of national organizations:** Litigation support for the test cases was provided by the ACLU and the JACL. However, Yasui's case did not receive the same support that Hirabayashi's did.

a. **The ACLU:** Legal historian Peter Irons notes that the ACLU was not interested in taking this case because of Yasui's connection with the Japanese Consulate. (By the way, do you think that many jobs were open to a Japanese American attorney at the time?) By contrast, the ACLU was involved in Hirabayashi's case, as well as Korematsu's and Endo's, in lesser capacities. The specific details are not as important as the general tension between the national ACLU office and regional offices on the West Coast. The national board of the ACLU, populated by Roosevelt loyalists, prohibited any direct constitutional challenge to Executive Order 9066. This caused various splits with local lawyers and chapters representing Hirabayashi and Korematsu at trial and on appeal to the Ninth Circuit. At the Supreme Court level, however, the national office took over the *Hirabayashi* case and made sure not to challenge Roosevelt's actions directly. Instead, as described earlier, they focused their efforts on the nondelegation doctrine.

b. The JACL: The JACL was an influential social organization of Japanese Americans who held citizenship. The JACL vigorously resisted litigation challenging the internment, even though two of the protesters, Yasui and Hirabayashi, were JACL members, and Endo's lawyer had first been recruited by JACL president Saburo Kido. William Minoru Hohri writes that Mike Masaoka, the first executive director of the JACL, cited ten reasons for opposing Yasui's test case and any others like it:

1. cooperation in the war effort;

2. the JACL and its members had pledged total cooperation to the President;

3. cooperation with Federal Authorities will cause reciprocal cooperation;

4. our contribution to the war effort is to accept all army regulations and orders;

5. public opinion is opposed to any challenges of the Army and its authority;

6. we might win the case, but lose goodwill in the process;

7. any challenge might result in retaliation by the Army;

8. Attorney General Biddle said there was little chance the courts would challenge the military's authority;

9. the ACLU decided against a test case and they are the champions of civil liberties;

10. unfavorable publicity as seen in the headlines from the Yasui case.

William Minoru Hohri, REPAIRING AMERICA: AN ACCOUNT OF THE MOVEMENT FOR JAPANESE-AMERICAN REDRESS 45 (1988).

Michi Weglyn writes that, just before World War II, the "Japanese American Citizens League (JACL), . . . [i]n an eagerness to gain white approbation, and moved by the deep and unselfish ideals of the Republic, . . . had early taken the route of superpatriotism, leading in time to a near-systematic disavowal of things Japanese." Historian Sucheng Chan documents that the JACL "never criticized racism, although they worked hard to challenge discriminatory laws. They successfully obtained naturalization rights for some 500 Issei veterans of World War I and helped to get the Cable Act, which affected Japanese as much as Chinese, repealed. So far as they participated in domestic electoral politics, a majority of the JACL members were Republican."

One possible response to unwelcome racial grouping is to hyper-assimilate in order to prove one's loyalty to the dominant culture. If that is a discernible social process, then why did it fail to support Yasui, who was a staunch patriot?

2. NATIONAL SECURITY RESTRICTIONS OF CIVIL LIBERTIES: THE EXCLUSION CASE

a. HISTORICAL ORIGINS: JUDICIAL REVIEW OF MILITARY CONTROL OVER CIVILIANS

A Reconstruction era case, *Ex parte Milligan*, 4 Wall. 2 (1866), contained the most directly relevant legal precedent for *Hirabayashi* and *Korematsu*. Milligan was an abolitionist who was not a member of the armed forces. He had been arrested in Indiana and charged with treason. A civilian grand jury declined to indict him. Nevertheless, a military commission tried and convicted him and imposed the death sentence. The Supreme Court overturned the conviction.

> The controlling question in the case is this: had the military commission jurisdiction, legally, to try and sentence him? . . .

> No graver question was ever considered by this court, nor one which more nearly concerns the rights of the whole people; for it is the birthright of every American [civilian] citizen when charged with crime, to be tried and punished according to law.

> [The laws] applicable to this case are found in that clause of the original Constitution which says, "That the trial of all crimes, except in case of impeachment, shall be by jury."

> One of the plainest constitutional provisions was, therefore, infringed when Milligan was tried by a court not ordained and established by Congress.

> It is claimed that martial law covers with its broad mantle the proceedings of this military commission. . . . If this position is sound to the extent claimed, then when war exists, . . . the [military commander can] on plea of necessity, with the approval of the Executive, substitute military force for and to the exclusion of the laws, and punish all persons, as he thinks right and proper, without fixed or certain rules. . . . If true, republican government is a failure, and there is an end of liberty regulated by law.

Ex parte Milligan, 4 Wall at 118-19, 122, 124. The *Milligan* case is susceptible to varying interpretations. If *Milligan* stands for the narrow proposition that the military courts lack authority over civilians (even if martial law has been declared), then it may not apply at all to the internment cases, which involved conviction by non-military courts. Apparently, this is how the *Hirabayashi* majority chose to interpret this important precedent.

If, however, *Milligan* stands for the broader proposition that, even during time of war the government must prove the existence of a bona fide "military necessity" in order to deprive civilians of their protected liberties, then it would provide a stronger basis for scrutinizing the internment. As Justice Murphy's concurrence in *Hirabayashi* stated, "[T]he war power, like the other great substantive powers of government, is subject to the limitations of the Constitution. . . . It would not be supposed . . . that the prerogatives of the courts could be set aside, or that persons not charged with offenses against the law of war could be deprived of due process of law and the benefits of trial by jury, in the absence of a valid declaration of martial law." Indeed, the

Court in *Milligan* described its role in those circumstances as one of "watchful care" over the liberties of civilians.

b. NATIONAL SECURITY DOCTRINE SINCE WORLD WAR II

Congress has not formally declared war since 1941. Nevertheless, on numerous occasions, both political branches and the military have asserted national security as the justification for restricting civil liberties of Americans. Conceptually, cases tend to fall along a spectrum, from military policies that directly regulate military personnel to political actions that only indirectly relate to military interests. The position of a particular case on this spectrum is likely to determine a court's standard of review and thus the outcome of the case.

On one end of the spectrum, the Court has been extremely deferential to government action where it has viewed the challenged action as a congressional exercise of its powers over military personnel. For example, in *Rostker v. Goldberg*, 453 U.S. 57 (1981), upholding a congressional decision to exclude women from the military draft, the Court held that "[perhaps] in no other area has the Court accorded Congress greater deference." The Court added that not only is "the scope of Congress' constitutional power in this area broad, but the lack of competence on the part of the courts is marked." Similarly, in *Goldman v. Weinberger*, 475 U.S. 503 (1986), the Court upheld military personnel regulations that prohibited an Orthodox Jewish officer from wearing a yarmulke (religious skullcap). In rejecting a first amendment religion clause challenge to the rule, the Court reiterated that it "[had] repeatedly held that 'the military is, by necessity, a specialized society separate from civilian society.'" For that reason, the Court stated, "[C]ourts must give great deference to the professional judgment of military authorities concerning the relative importance of a particular military interest."

On the other end of the spectrum, the Court has disapproved of presidential actions taken in the name of national security but not directly related to military personnel or operations. Less than a decade after the internment cases, the Court decided the so-called *Steel Seizure* case, *Youngstown Sheet & Tube Co. v. Sawyer*, 343 U.S. 579 (1952). During the (undeclared) Korean War, President Truman surmised that a labor dispute between unions and steel mill owners would disrupt the production of steel needed by the military. When a nationwide strike loomed, the President ordered the Treasury Secretary to seize and operate the mills. The mill owners obtained a federal district court injunction stopping the executive seizure and operation of the mills.

Justice Hugo Black, author of the earlier *Korematsu* majority opinion, wrote an expedited majority opinion affirming the trial court's injunction. Black explained that the presidential power must flow from the Constitution or congressional lawmaking. Cases "upholding broad powers in military commanders engaged in day-to-day fighting in a theatre of war . . . need not concern us here," he wrote. "[W]e cannot with faithfulness to our constitutional system hold that the Commander in Chief . . . has the ultimate power as such to take possession of private property in order to keep labor disputes from stopping production.... That is a job for the nation's lawmakers, not for its military authorities."

Justice Jackson's influential concurring opinion first observed that the President acted without the support of Congress. He then criticized the President's effort to proffer some source of executive authority through the "loose and irresponsible use of adjectives" such as "'inherent' powers, 'implied' powers, 'incidental' powers, 'plenary' powers, 'war' powers and 'emergency' powers." In the absence of bona fide military necessity or national emergency, he reasoned, the executive branch lacked unilateral authority to seize and operate privately owned steel mills. (And, indeed, the strike lasted six weeks, and the military continued its operations without interruption.)

More recently, in *New York Times Co. v. United States*, 403 U.S. 713 (1971), the so-called *Pentagon Papers* case, the Court again considered national security arguments justifying otherwise impermissible government restrictions on the press's freedom of speech. The Nixon Administration sought to enjoin the New York Times from publishing internal documents of the Defense Department. The papers, obtained by Daniel Ellsberg, a former Pentagon employee, detailed the origins of the Vietnam War. At the time of potential publication, domestic protests against the war were at their peak. The Court held that the first amendment freedom of the press could not be defeated by the government's unsubstantiated contention that it was protecting "vital" national security interests.

In deciding these post-internment cases, the Court appears to be relying on an important conceptual distinction: It distinguished military control over *military* personnel and operations from military (and executive) control over *civilians* for asserted reasons of national security. This distinction, first made over 150 years ago in *Ex parte Milligan*, was a significant factor in the internment cases.

c. AN APPROACH FOR SCRUTINIZING CLAIMS OF NATIONAL SECURITY

In *Hirabayashi*, the majority acknowledged the government's military concerns but not the Japanese Americans' civil liberties. How did the Court address the tension between ostensible military needs and civilian liberties? According to what approach?

This section explores these questions and their legal and political implications. Before embarking on that exploration, consider the following proposed judicial approach for scrutinizing government claims of military necessity or national security as justification for restricting the civil liberties of Americans.

ERIC K. YAMAMOTO, KOREMATSU REVISITED—CORRECTING THE
INJUSTICE OF EXTRAORDINARY GOVERNMENT EXCESS AND LAX
JUDICIAL REVIEW: TIME FOR A BETTER ACCOMMODATION OF
NATIONAL SECURITY CONCERNS AND CIVIL LIBERTIES

26 Santa Clara L. Rev. 1, 51-59 (1986)

When the government asserts military necessity or national security as
justification, it asserts that "although this restriction would be impermissible
under ordinary conditions, the existence of extraordinary danger to the nation . . . compels it and thus legitimates it." Judicial inquiry therefore should
focus first on the danger: whether credible information establishes that
Americans intentionally or otherwise pose a danger to legitimate government
security interests. If the danger exists, then the government has a compelling
interest in eliminating it, and the inquiry shifts to the tailoring of the restriction to the danger. These determinations are essentially factual. They can be
made in most instances on the basis of proffered evidence according to judicially manageable standards, with due concern to the sensitivity of national
security information.

Existence of the Danger

Courts have a long history of adjudging the existence of *bona fide* danger,
whether the initial determination is made by the military, the executive
branch or Congress . . . [I]n a variety of situations the Supreme Court has
shown an inclination to review congressional and executive determinations of
necessity, whether in examining the factual foundation of the asserted exigency or in defining the limits to the government's self-protective powers.

Most recently, in *New York Times Co. v. United States*, the Court rejected
the President's claim that the executive branch, under its war and foreign policy powers and "in the name of national security" could prohibit the publication of the classified Pentagon Papers. Justice Brennan [wrote] that the first
amendment tolerates no prior judicial restraint on the press predicated on
the mere surmise or conjecture that untoward consequences may result. He
declared that although an earlier case [appeared to have] created a narrow
exception when the "nation is at war," prior restraint should be deemed
proper only upon "governmental allegation and proof that publication must
inevitably, directly, and immediately cause the occurrence of an event kin-
dred to imperiling the safety of a transport already at sea. . . . In no event
may mere conclusions be sufficient." . . .

Less Restrictive Alternatives

Judicial review of less restrictive alternatives is now a generally accepted
principle. The Supreme Court has undertaken that analysis in many con-
texts: under the equal protection clause in applying a strict scrutiny standard
of review, under the commerce clause, under the contracts clause, under the
first amendment, and in other situations.

The general analytical approach to less restrictive alternatives is substantially unaltered by the infusion of national defense or security concerns. Indeed, the Court has applied "less drastic impact" and "no greater than
essential" standards in several cases involving national security restrictions

imposed on first and fifth amendment freedoms. Restrictiveness can be assessed through analysis of over-inclusiveness—is the restriction so broad that it catches not only individuals who pose a threat to the government's security but also those who do not? Restrictiveness can also be assessed through analysis of overkill—does the restriction of those posing some threat go beyond what is necessary to meet the danger? If the answer is affirmative in either situation, the inquiry proceeds to whether the restriction can be reformulated in concept to cure the problems of over-inclusiveness or overkill. If it can, the final query is whether the narrowed restriction effectively meets the danger.

This determination does not entail a detailed projection of the restriction's effect on all possible situations. Rather it simply assures that the reformulated restriction is designed in concept to achieve "the same basic purpose" as the original restriction. The court does not approve the specific structure and operation of any alternative. It merely sets the conceptual guidelines that the Constitution will tolerate and leaves implementation to the political branches. The court thus avoids advisory opinions and immersion into a quicksand of technical detail and political policy.

In light of Yamamoto's proposed framework, consider the *Korematsu* case below, keeping squarely in mind the role of the judiciary with respect to executive and legislative claims of military necessity.

d. KOREMATSU V. UNITED STATES: THE EXCLUSION

(i) BACKGROUND

PETER IRONS, JUSTICE AT WAR
93–96

The third Japanese American whose violation of DeWitt's orders reached the Supreme Court had not intended to offer himself as the subject of a test case. On the afternoon of May 30, 1942, the police in San Leandro California, picked up a young man walking down the street with his girlfriend. Under questioning by Lieutenant A.B. Poulsen at the San Leandro police headquarters, the young man produced a draft registration card that identified him as "Clyde Sarah."

The suspect claimed to be of Spanish-Hawaiian origin. He had been born in Las Vegas, the suspect told Poulsen, and his parents had been killed in a fire that burned their house to the ground. The young man's story quickly fell apart. He spoke no Spanish, and his draft card had been clumsily altered with ink eradicator.

Poulsen could not persuade the suspect to reveal his name, although he did admit that he was of Japanese descent. His identity came out by chance: "One of the girls who worked in the office seemed to recognize me, and so I finally said who I was." The slim young man told Poulsen that his name was Fred Toyosaburo Korematsu. He was a welder and had lived until recently in nearby Oakland, where he had been born in 1919, with his Japanese-born parents and three brothers. Korematsu told Poulsen that the other members of his family had reported to the Tanforan assembly center—located south of San Francisco in a converted race track—three weeks earlier on May 9. This was the effective date of Exclusion Order No. 34, to which all Japanese Americans who lived in Oakland and San Leandro were subject.

Apprehended and turned over to the FBI, Korematsu became a cooperative prisoner who no longer held back the details of his life or of his violation. After graduation from Oakland High School in 1938, Korematsu told [the FBI that] he entered Los Angeles City College but dropped out after only one month for financial reasons. He then attended the Master School of Welding in Oakland and worked as a shipyard welder following this training. . . . Korematsu had belonged to the Boiler Makers Union, which expelled its members of Japanese descent after the Pearl Harbor attack. He lost his shipyard job as a result and had worked before his evacuation order at a series of short-term welding jobs.

The Navy turned down his attempt to volunteer for service in June 1941. The next month, he was classified 4-F by his draft board because of gastric ulcers.

What gave Korematsu confidence that he would not be recognized in San Leandro as a Japanese American, three weeks after the evacuation deadline? Mansfield's initial report to FBI headquarters illustrated why this confidence was misplaced. The report described Korematsu as a member of the "yellow race" and included this observation: "Scars or marks—Cut scar on the forehead, lump between eyebrows on nose." Asked about these recent scars, Korematsu confessed that he had undergone plastic surgery in an effort to conceal his racial identity.

Korematsu further explained his motivations. He said, "I stayed in Oakland to earn enough money to take my girl with me to the Middle West. Her name is Miss Ida Boitano. She is a different nationality—Italian. Between the time I left home and the date before evacuation I lived 2 weeks in San Francisco during an operation on my face and 2 weeks in Oakland with a friend. The operation was for the purpose of changing my appearance so that I would not be subjected to ostracism when my girl and I went East."

FBI agents also questioned Ida Boitano, who expressed remorse about her relationship with Fred Korematsu. "She said that she was originally engaged to subject and had intended to marry him," the agents reported, "but that she now realized that such a marriage was impossible and that she had made a big mistake, particularly after the law regarding evacuation went into effect."

(ii) THE CASE

As the Seattle ACLU branch did for Gordon Hirabayashi, the San Francisco branch recruited a local lawyer, Wayne Collins, to represent Fred Korematsu. And like Min Yasui had done earlier, Korematsu opted to waive his right to a jury trial. Because of an earlier demurrer to the indictment, which was denied, the only issues at trial were the factual ones of whether General DeWitt's orders applied to Korematsu and whether he had violated them. Korematsu testified in his own behalf that he had a lack of attachment to Japanese culture. The judge found him guilty, and sentenced him to a five year probationary term, but then declined to impose the sentence. This left Korematsu's case in legal limbo, resulting in a question of whether the probationary sentence constituted an appealable judgment.

On appeal, the Ninth Circuit certified this question to the Supreme Court, and the Supreme Court issued its first *Korematsu* opinion three weeks before its *Hirabayashi* and *Yasui* opinions—on June 1, 1943. Finding the order final and appealable, the Court remanded the case back to the court of appeals for a decision on the constitutionality of the exclusion order. These procedural issues allowed the Court to avoid ruling on the merits of the exclusion and, importantly, delayed this ruling for over an additional year. When the *Korematsu* case made its way back up to the Supreme Court, it was paired with the *Endo* case, which squarely challenged the detention of Japanese American citizens. Both opinions were issued in December 1944, one day after the executive branch announced an end to detention.

Although by this point the ACLU no longer represented Korematsu, it filed an *amicus* brief asserting that: "The issue in this case is the validity of military detention under armed guard of civilian citizens of Japanese ancestry." And the JACL filed an *amicus* brief authored by the same anthropologist lawyer who wrote the earlier Hirabayashi *amicus* brief. Numbering over 200 pages and citing to 300 academic works, it attacked General DeWitt's final report as thinly disguised scientific racism.

KOREMATSU v. UNITED STATES

323 U.S. 214 (1944)

Mr. Justice BLACK delivered the opinion of the Court.

The petitioner, an American citizen of Japanese descent, was convicted in a federal district court for remaining in San Leandro, California, a "Military Area," contrary to Civilian Exclusion Order No. 34 of the Commanding General of the Western Command, U.S. Army, which directed that after May 9, 1942, all persons of Japanese ancestry should be excluded from that area. No question was raised as to petitioner's loyalty to the United States. The Circuit Court of Appeals affirmed, and the importance of the constitutional question involved caused us to grant certiorari.

It should be noted, to begin with, that all legal restrictions which curtail the civil rights of a single racial group are immediately suspect. That is not to say that all such restrictions are unconstitutional. It is to say that courts must subject them to the most rigid scrutiny. Pressing public necessity may sometimes justify the existence of such restrictions; racial antagonism never can.

In the instant case prosecution of the petitioner was begun by information charging violation of an Act of Congress, of March 21, 1942, which provides that:

. . . whoever shall enter, remain in, leave, or commit any act in any military area or military zone prescribed, under the authority of an Executive order of the President, by the Secretary of War, or by any military commander designated by the Secretary of War, contrary to the restrictions applicable to any such area or zone or contrary to the order of the Secretary of War or any such military commander, shall, if it appears that he knew or should have known of the existence and extent of the restrictions or order and that his act was in violation thereof, be guilty of a misdemeanor and upon conviction shall be liable to a fine of not to exceed $ 5,000 or to imprisonment for not more than one year, or both, for each offense.

Exclusion Order No. 34, which the petitioner knowingly and admittedly violated, was one of a number of military orders and proclamations, all of which were substantially based upon Executive Order No. 9066. That order, issued after we were at war with Japan, declared that "the successful prosecution of the war requires every possible protection against espionage and against sabotage to national-defense material, national-defense premises, and national-defense utilities. . . ."

One of the series of orders and proclamations, a curfew order, which like the exclusion order here was promulgated pursuant to Executive Order 9066, subjected all persons of Japanese ancestry in prescribed West Coast military areas to remain in their residences from 8 p.m. to 6 a.m. As is the case with the exclusion order here, that prior curfew order was designed as a "protection against espionage and against sabotage." In *Hirabayashi v. United States*, we sustained a conviction obtained for violation of the curfew order. The Hirabayashi conviction and this one thus rest on the same 1942 Congressional Act and the same basic executive and military orders, all of which orders were aimed at the twin dangers of espionage and sabotage.

In the light of the principles we announced in the *Hirabayashi* case, we are unable to conclude that it was beyond the war power of Congress and the Executive to exclude those of Japanese ancestry from the West Coast war area at the time they did. True, exclusion from the area in which one's home is located is a far greater deprivation than constant confinement to the home from 8 p.m. to 6 a.m. Nothing short of apprehension by the proper military authorities of the gravest imminent danger to the public safety can constitutionally justify either. But exclusion from a threatened area, no less than curfew, has a definite and close relationship to the prevention of espionage and sabotage. The military authorities, charged with the primary responsibility of defending our shores, concluded that curfew provided inadequate protection and ordered exclusion. They did so, as pointed out in our *Hirabayashi* opinion, in accordance with Congressional authority to the military to say who should, and who should not, remain in the threatened areas.

In this case the petitioner challenges the assumptions upon which we rested our conclusions in the *Hirabayashi* case. He also urges that by May 1942, when Order No. 34 was promulgated, all danger of Japanese invasion of the West Coast had disappeared. After careful consideration of these contentions we are compelled to reject them.

Here, as in the *Hirabayashi* case, ". . . we cannot reject as unfounded the judgment of the military authorities and of Congress that there were disloyal members of that population, whose number and strength could not be precisely and quickly ascertained. . . ."

Like curfew, exclusion of those of Japanese origin was deemed necessary because of the presence of an unascertained number of disloyal members of the group, most of whom we have no doubt were loyal to this country. It was because we could not reject the finding of the military authorities that it was impossible to bring about an immediate segregation of the disloyal from the loyal that we sustained the validity of the curfew order as applying to the whole group. In the instant case, temporary exclusion of the entire group was rested by the military on the same ground. The judgment that exclusion of the whole group was for the same reason a military imperative answers the contention that the exclusion was in the nature of group punishment based on antagonism to those of Japanese origin.

We uphold the exclusion order as of the time it was made and when the petitioner violated it. *Cf. Chastleton Corporation v. Sinclair*, 264 U.S. 543 [(1924)], 547; *Block v. Hirsh*, 256 U.S. 135, 154–5 [(1921)]. In doing so, we are not unmindful of the hardships imposed by it upon a large group of American citizens. *Cf. Ex parte Kawato*, 317 U.S. 69, 73 [(1942)]. But hardships are part of war, and war is an aggregation of hardships. All citizens alike, both in and out of uniform, feel the impact of war in greater or lesser measure. Citizenship has its responsibilities as well as its privileges, and in time of war the burden is always heavier. Compulsory exclusion of large groups of citizens from their homes, except under circumstances of direst emergency and peril, is inconsistent with our basic governmental institutions. But when under conditions of modern warfare our shores are threatened by hostile forces, the power to protect must be commensurate with the threatened danger.

It is argued that on May 30, 1942, the date the petitioner was charged with remaining in the prohibited area, there were conflicting orders outstanding, forbidding him both to leave the area and to remain there. Of course, a person cannot be convicted for doing the very thing which it is a crime to fail to do. But the outstanding orders here contained no such contradictory commands.

It is now argued that the validity of the exclusion order cannot be considered apart from the orders requiring him, after departure from the area, to report and to remain in an assembly or relocation center. The contention is that we must treat these separate orders as one and inseparable; that, for this reason, if detention in the assembly or relocation center would have illegally deprived the petitioner of his liberty, the exclusion order and his conviction under it cannot stand.

We are thus being asked to pass at this time upon the whole subsequent detention program in both assembly and relocation centers, although the only issues framed at the trial related to petitioner's remaining in the prohibited area in violation of the exclusion order. Had petitioner here left the prohibited area and gone to an assembly center we cannot say either as a matter of fact or law that his presence in that center would have resulted in his detention in a relocation center. These separate requirements were that those of Japanese ancestry (1) depart from the area; (2) report to and temporarily remain in an assembly center; (3) go under military control to a relocation center there to remain for an indeterminate period until released conditionally or unconditionally by the military authorities. Each of these requirements, it will be noted, imposed distinct duties in connection with the separate steps in a complete evacuation program. Had Congress directly incorporated into one Act the language of these separate orders, and provided sanctions for their violations, disobedience of any one would have constituted a separate offense. There is no reason why violations of these orders, insofar as they were promulgated pursuant to Congressional enactment, should not be treated as separate offenses.

The *Endo* case graphically illustrates the difference between the validity of an order to exclude and the validity of a detention order after exclusion has been effected.

Since the petitioner has not been convicted of failing to report or to remain in an assembly or relocation center, we cannot in this case determine the validity of those separate provisions of the order. It is sufficient here for us to pass upon the order which petitioner violated. To do more would be to go beyond the issues raised, and to decide momentous questions not contained within the framework of the pleadings or the evidence in this case. It will be time enough to decide the serious constitutional issues which petitioner seeks to raise when an assembly or relocation order is applied or is certain to be applied to him, and we have its terms before us.

It is said that we are dealing here with the case of imprisonment of a citizen in a concentration camp solely because of his ancestry, without evidence or inquiry concerning his loyalty and good disposition towards the United States. Our task would be simple, our duty clear, were this a case involving the imprisonment of a loyal citizen in a concentration camp because of racial prejudice. Regardless of the true nature of the assembly and relocation centers—and we deem it unjustifiable to call them concentration camps with all the ugly connotations that term implies—we are dealing specifically with nothing but an exclusion order. To cast this case into outlines of racial prejudice, without reference to the real military dangers which were presented, merely confuses the issue. Korematsu was not excluded from the Military Area because of hostility to him or his race. He was excluded because we are at war with the Japanese Empire, because the properly constituted military authorities feared an invasion of our West Coast and felt constrained to take proper security measures, because they decided that the military urgency of the situation demanded that all citizens of Japanese ancestry be segregated from the West Coast temporarily, and finally, because Congress, reposing its confidence in this time of war in our military leaders—as inevitably it must—determined that they should have the power to do just this. There was evidence of disloyalty on the part of some, the military authorities considered that the need for action was great, and time was short. We cannot—by availing ourselves of the calm perspective of hindsight—now say that at that time these actions were unjustified.

Affirmed.

Mr. Justice FRANKFURTER, concurring.

The provisions of the Constitution which confer on the Congress and the President powers to enable this country to wage war are as much part of the Constitution as provisions looking to a nation at peace. And we have had recent occasion to quote approvingly the statement of former Chief Justice Hughes that the war power of the Government is "the power to wage war successfully." *Hirabayashi v. United States.* Therefore, the validity of action under the war power must be judged wholly in the context of war. That action is not to be stigmatized as lawless because like action in times of peace would be lawless.

Mr. Justice ROBERTS, dissenting.

I dissent, because I think the indisputable facts exhibit a clear violation of Constitutional rights.

This is not a case of keeping people off the streets at night as was *Hirabayashi v. United States*, nor a case of temporary exclusion of a citizen from an area for his own safety or that of the community, nor a case of offering him an opportunity to go temporarily out of an area where his presence might cause danger to himself or to his fellows. On the contrary, it is the case of convicting a citizen as a punishment for not submitting to imprisonment in a concentration camp, based on his ancestry, and solely because of his ancestry, without evidence or inquiry concerning his loyalty and good disposition towards the United States. If this be a correct statement of the facts disclosed by this record, and facts of which we take judicial notice, I need hardly labor the conclusion that Constitutional rights have been violated.

The Government's argument, and the opinion of the court, in my judgment, erroneously divide that which is single and indivisible and thus make the case appear as if the petitioner violated a Military Order, sanctioned by Act of Congress, which excluded him from his home, by refusing voluntarily to leave and, so, knowingly and intentionally, defying the order and the Act of Congress.

The petitioner, a resident of San Leandro, Alameda County, California, is a native of the United States of Japanese ancestry who, according to the uncontradicted evidence, is a loyal citizen of the nation.

A chronological recitation of events will make it plain that the petitioner's supposed offense did not, in truth, consist in his refusal voluntarily to leave the area which included his home in obedience to the order excluding him therefrom. Critical attention must be given to the dates and sequence of events.

[After a brief history, Justice Roberts continued:]

March 24, 1942, General DeWitt began to issue a series of exclusion orders relating to specified areas.

March 27, 1942, by Proclamation No. 4, the General recited that "it is necessary, in order to provide for the welfare and to insure the orderly evacuation and resettlement of Japanese voluntarily migrating from Military Area No. 1, to restrict and regulate such migration"; and ordered that, as of March 29, 1942, "all alien Japanese and persons of Japanese ancestry who are within the limits of Military Area No. 1, be and they are hereby prohibited from leaving that area for any purpose until and to the extent that a future proclamation or order of this headquarters shall so permit or direct."

No order had been made excluding the petitioner from the area in which he lived. By Proclamation No. 4 he was, after March 29, 1942, confined to the limits of Area No. 1. If the Executive Order No. 9066 and the Act of Congress meant what they said, to leave that area, in the face of Proclamation No. 4, would be to commit a misdemeanor.

May 3, 1942, General DeWitt issued Civilian Exclusion Order No. 346 providing that, after 12 o'clock May 8, 1942, all persons of Japanese ancestry, both alien and nonalien, were to be excluded from a described portion of Military Area No. 1, which included the County of Alameda, California. The order required a responsible member of each family and each individual living alone to report, at a time set, at a Civil Control Station for instructions to go to an Assembly Center, and added that any person failing to comply with the provisions of the order who was found in the described area after the date set would be liable to prosecution under the Act of March 21, 1942. It is important to note that the order, by its express terms, had no application to persons within the bounds "of an established Assembly Center pursuant to instructions from this Headquarters. . . ." The obvious purpose of the orders made, taken together, was to drive all citizens of Japanese ancestry into Assembly Centers within the zones of their residence, under pain of criminal prosecution. The predicament in which the petitioner thus found himself was this: He was forbidden, by Military Order, to leave the zone in which he lived; he was forbidden, by Military Order, after a date fixed, to be found within that zone unless he were in an Assembly Center located in that zone. General DeWitt's report to the Secretary of War concerning the programme of evacuation and relocation of Japanese makes it entirely clear, if it were necessary to refer to that document,—and, in the light of the above recitation, I think it is not,—that an Assembly Center was a euphemism for a prison. No person within such a center was permitted to leave except by Military Order.

In the dilemma that he dare not remain in his home, or voluntarily leave the area, without incurring criminal penalties, and that the only way he could avoid punishment was to go to an Assembly Center and submit himself to military imprisonment, the petitioner did nothing.

The Government has argued this case as if the only order outstanding at the time the petitioner was arrested and informed against was Exclusion Order No. 34 ordering him to leave the area in which he resided, which was the basis of the information against him. That argument has evidently been effective. The opinion refers to the *Hirabayashi* case, to show that this court has sustained the validity of a curfew order in an emergency. The argument then is that exclusion from a given area of danger, while somewhat more sweeping than a curfew regulation, is of the same nature,—a temporary expedient made necessary by a sudden emergency. This, I think, is a substitution of an hypothetical case for the case actually before the court. I might agree with the court's disposition of the hypothetical case. The liberty of every American citizen freely to come and to go must frequently, in the face of sudden danger, be temporarily limited or suspended. The civil authorities must often resort to the expedient of excluding citizens temporarily from a locality.

The drawing of fire lines in the case of a conflagration, the removal of persons from the area where a pestilence has broken out, are familiar examples. If the exclusion worked by Exclusion Order No. 34 were of that nature the *Hirabayashi* case would be authority for sustaining it. But the facts above recited, and those set forth in *Ex parte Endo*, show that the exclusion was but a part of an over-all plan for forcible detention. This case cannot, therefore, be decided on any such narrow ground as the possible validity of a Temporary Exclusion Order under which the residents of an area are given an opportunity to leave and go elsewhere in their native land outside the boundaries of a military area. To make the case turn on any such assumption is to shut our eyes to reality.

I had supposed that if a citizen was constrained by two laws, or two orders having the force of law, and obedience to one would violate the other, to punish him for violation of either would deny him due process of law. And I had supposed that under these circumstances a conviction for violating one of the orders could not stand.

We cannot shut our eyes to the fact that had the petitioner attempted to violate Proclamation No. 4 and leave the military area in which he lived he would have been arrested and tried and convicted for violation of Proclamation No. 4. The two conflicting orders, one which commanded him to stay and the other which commanded him to go, were nothing but a cleverly devised trap to accomplish the real purpose of the military authority, which was to lock him up in a concentration camp. The only course by which the petitioner could avoid arrest and prosecution was to go to that camp according to instructions to be given him when he reported at a Civil Control Center. We know that is the fact. Why should we set up a figmentary and artificial situation instead of addressing ourselves to the actualities of the case?

I would reverse the judgment of conviction.

Mr. Justice MURPHY, dissenting.

This exclusion of "all persons of Japanese ancestry, both alien and non-alien," from the Pacific Coast area on a plea of military necessity in the absence of martial law ought not to be approved. Such exclusion goes over "the very brink of constitutional power" and falls into the ugly abyss of racism.

In dealing with matters relating to the prosecution and progress of a war, we must accord great respect and consideration to the judgments of the military authorities who are on the scene and who have full knowledge of the military facts. The scope of their discretion must, as a matter of necessity and common sense, be wide. And their judgments ought not to be overruled lightly by those whose training and duties ill-equip them to deal intelligently with matters so vital to the physical security of the nation.

At the same time, however, it is essential that there be definite limits to military discretion, especially where martial law has not been declared. Individuals must not be left impoverished of their constitutional rights on a plea of military necessity that has neither substance nor support. Thus, like other claims conflicting with the asserted constitutional rights of the individual, the military claim must subject itself to the judicial process of having its reasonableness determined and its conflicts with other interests reconciled. "What are the allowable limits of military discretion, and whether or not they have been overstepped in a particular case, are judicial questions." *Sterling v. Constantin*, 287 U.S. 378, 401 [(1932)].

The judicial test of whether the Government, on a plea of military necessity, can validly deprive an individual of any of his constitutional rights is whether the deprivation is reasonably related to a public danger that is so "immediate, imminent, and impending" as not to admit of delay and not to permit the intervention of ordinary constitutional processes to alleviate the danger. Civilian Exclusion Order No. 34, banishing from a prescribed area of the Pacific Coast "all persons of Japanese ancestry, both alien and non-alien," clearly does not meet that test. Being an obvious racial discrimination, the order deprives all those within its scope of the equal protection of the laws as guaranteed by the Fifth Amendment. It further deprives these individuals of their constitutional rights to live and work where they will, to establish a home where they choose and to move about freely. In excommunicating them without benefit of hearings, this order also deprives them of all their constitutional rights to procedural due process. Yet no reasonable relation to an "immediate, imminent, and impending" public danger is evident to support this racial restriction which is one of the most sweeping and complete deprivations of constitutional rights in the history of this nation in the absence of martial law.

It must be conceded that the military and naval situation in the spring of 1942 was such as to generate a very real fear of invasion of the Pacific Coast, accompanied by fears of sabotage and espionage in that area. The military command was therefore justified in adopting all reasonable means necessary to combat these dangers. In adjudging the military action taken in light of the then apparent dangers, we must not erect too high or too meticulous standards; it is necessary only that the action have some reasonable relation to the removal of the dangers of invasion, sabotage and espionage. But the exclusion, either temporarily or permanently, of all persons with Japanese blood in their veins has no such reasonable relation. And that relation is lacking because the exclusion order necessarily must rely for its reasonableness upon the assumption that all persons of Japanese ancestry may have a dangerous tendency to commit sabotage and espionage and to aid our Japanese enemy in other ways. It is difficult to believe that reason, logic or experience could be marshaled in support of such an assumption.

That this forced exclusion was the result in good measure of this erroneous assumption of racial guilt rather than bona fide military necessity is evidenced by the Commanding General's Final Report on the evacuation from the Pacific Coast area. In it he refers to all individuals of Japanese descent as "subversive," as belonging to "an enemy race" whose "racial strains are undiluted," and as constituting "over 112,000 potential enemies . . . at large today" along the Pacific Coast.[2] In support of this blanket condemnation of all per-

---

[2] Further evidence of the Commanding General's attitude toward individuals of Japanese ancestry is revealed in his voluntary testimony on April 13, 1943, in San Francisco

sons of Japanese descent, however, no reliable evidence is cited to show that such individuals were generally disloyal, or had generally so conducted themselves in this area as to constitute a special menace to defense installations or war industries, or had otherwise by their behavior furnished reasonable ground for their exclusion as a group.

Justification for the exclusion is sought, instead, mainly upon questionable racial and sociological grounds not ordinarily within the realm of expert military judgment, supplemented by certain semi-military conclusions drawn from an unwarranted use of circumstantial evidence. Individuals of Japanese ancestry are condemned because they are said to be "a large, unassimilated, tightly knit racial group, bound to an enemy nation by strong ties of race, culture, custom and religion."[4] They are claimed to be given to "emperor worshipping ceremonies"[5] and to "dual citizenship."[6] Japanese language schools and allegedly pro-Japanese organizations are cited as evidence of possible group disloyalty,[7] together with facts as to certain persons being educated and residing at length in Japan. It is intimated that many of these individuals de-

---

before the House Naval Affairs Subcommittee to Investigate Congested Areas, Part 3, pp. 739-40 (78th Cong., 1st Sess.):

"I don't want any of them [persons of Japanese ancestry] here. They are a dangerous element. There is no way to determine their loyalty. The west coast contains too many vital installations essential to the defense of the country to allow any Japanese on this coast. . . . The danger of the Japanese was, and is now— if they are permitted to come back—espionage and sabotage. It makes no difference whether he is an American citizen, he is still a Japanese. American citizenship does not necessarily determine loyalty. . . . But we must worry about the Japanese all the time until he is wiped off the map. Sabotage and espionage will make problems as long as he is allowed in this area. . . ."

[4] To the extent that assimilation is a problem, it is largely the result of certain social customs and laws of the American general public. Studies demonstrate that persons of Japanese descent are readily susceptible to integration in our society if given the opportunity. Strong, The Second-Generation Japanese Problem (1934); Smith, Americans in Process (1937); Mears, Resident Orientals on the American Pacific Coast (1928); Millis, The Japanese Problem in the United States (1942). The failure to accomplish an ideal status of assimilation, therefore, cannot be charged to the refusal of these persons to become Americanized or to their loyalty to Japan. And the retention by some persons of certain customs and religious practices of their ancestors is no criterion of their loyalty to the United States.

[5] Final Report, pp. 10-11. No sinister correlation between the emperor worshipping activities and disloyalty to America was shown.

[6] Final Report, p. 22. The charge of "dual citizenship" springs from a misunderstanding of the simple fact that Japan in the past used the doctrine of *jus sanguinis*, as she had a right to do under international law, and claimed as her citizens all persons born of Japanese nationals wherever located. Japan has greatly modified this doctrine, however, by allowing all Japanese born in the United States to renounce any claim of dual citizenship and by releasing her claim as to all born in the United States after 1925. See Freeman, Genesis, Exodus, and Leviticus: Genealogy, Evacuation, and Law, 28 Cornell L.Q. 414, 447-8, and authorities there cited; McWilliams, Prejudice, 123-4 (1944).

[7] Final Report, pp. 12-13. We have had various foreign language schools in this country for generations without considering their existence as ground for racial discrimination. No subversive activities or teachings have been shown in connection with the Japanese schools. McWilliams, Prejudice, 121-3 (1944).

liberately resided "adjacent to strategic points," thus enabling them "to carry into execution a tremendous program of sabotage on a mass scale should any considerable number of them have been inclined to do so."[9] The need for protective custody is also asserted. The report refers without identity to "numerous incidents of violence" as well as to other admittedly unverified or cumulative incidents. From this, plus certain other events not shown to have been connected with the Japanese Americans, it is concluded that the "situation was fraught with danger to the Japanese population itself" and that the general public "was ready to take matters into its own hands."[10] Finally, it is intimated, though not directly charged or proved, that persons of Japanese ancestry were responsible for three minor isolated shellings and bombings of the Pacific Coast area,[11] as well as for unidentified radio transmissions and night signaling.

The main reasons relied upon by those responsible for the forced evacuation, therefore, do not prove a reasonable relation between the group characteristics of Japanese Americans and the dangers of invasion, sabotage and espionage. The reasons appear, instead, to be largely an accumulation of much of the misinformation, half-truths and insinuations that for years have been directed against Japanese Americans by people with racial and economic prejudices—the same people who have been among the foremost advocates of the evacuation.[12] A military judgment based upon such racial and

[9] Final Report, p. 10; see also pp. vii, 9, 15-17. This insinuation, based purely upon speculation and circumstantial evidence, completely overlooks the fact that the main geographic pattern of Japanese population was fixed many years ago with reference to economic, social and soil conditions. Limited occupational outlets and social pressures encouraged their concentration near their initial points of entry on the Pacific Coast. That these points may now be near certain strategic military and industrial areas is no proof of a diabolical purpose on the part of Japanese Americans. See McWilliams, Prejudice, 119-121 (1944); House Report No. 2124 (77th Cong., 2d Sess.), 59-93.

[10] Final Report, pp. 8-9. This dangerous doctrine of protective custody, as proved by recent European history, should have absolutely no standing as an excuse for the deprivation of the rights of minority groups. See House Report No. 1911 (77th Cong., 2d Sess.) 1-2. Cf. House Report No. 2124 (77th Cong., 2d Sess.) 145-7. In this instance, moreover, there are only two minor instances of violence on record involving persons of Japanese ancestry. McWilliams, What About Our Japanese-Americans? 8 (Public Affairs Pamphlets, No. 91, 1944).

[11] Final Report, p. 18. One of these incidents (the reputed dropping of incendiary bombs on an Oregon forest) occurred on Sept. 9, 1942—a considerable time after the Japanese Americans had been evacuated from their homes and placed in Assembly Centers. See New York Times, Sept. 15, 1942, at 1, col. 3.

[12] Special interest groups were extremely active in applying pressure for mass evacuation. See House Report No. 2124 (77th Cong., 2d Sess.) 154-6; McWilliams, Prejudice, 126-8 (1944). Mr. Austin E. Anson, managing secretary of the Salinas Vegetable Grower-Shipper Association, has frankly admitted that "We're charged with wanting to get rid of the Japs for selfish reasons. . . . We do. It's a question of whether the white man lives on the Pacific Coast or the brown men. They came into this valley to work, and they stayed to take over. . . . They undersell the white man in the markets. . . . They work their women and children while the white farmer has to pay wages for his help. If all the Japs were removed tomorrow, we'd never miss them in two weeks, because the white farmers

sociological considerations is not entitled to the great weight ordinarily given the judgments based upon strictly military considerations. Especially is this so when every charge relative to race, religion, culture, geographical location, and legal and economic status has been substantially discredited by independent studies made by experts in these matters.

The military necessity which is essential to the validity of the evacuation order thus resolves itself into a few intimations that certain individuals actively aided the enemy, from which it is inferred that the entire group of Japanese Americans could not be trusted to be or remain loyal to the United States. No one denies, of course, that there were some disloyal persons of Japanese descent on the Pacific Coast who did all in their power to aid their ancestral land. Similar disloyal activities have been engaged in by many persons of German, Italian and even more pioneer stock in our country. But to infer that examples of individual disloyalty prove group disloyalty and justify discriminatory action against the entire group is to deny that under our system of law individual guilt is the sole basis for deprivation of rights. Moreover, this inference, which is at the very heart of the evacuation orders, has been used in support of the abhorrent and despicable treatment of minority groups by the dictatorial tyrannies which this nation is now pledged to destroy. To give constitutional sanction to that inference in this case, however well-intentioned may have been the military command on the Pacific Coast, is to adopt one of the cruelest of the rationales used by our enemies to destroy the dignity of the individual and to encourage and open the door to discriminatory actions against other minority groups in the passions of tomorrow. No adequate reason is given for the failure to treat these Japanese Americans on an individual basis by holding investigations and hearings to separate the loyal from the disloyal, as was done in the case of persons of German and Italian ancestry. *See* House Report No. 2124 (77th Cong., 2d Sess.) 247–52. It is asserted merely that the loyalties of this group "were unknown and time was of the essence." Yet nearly four months elapsed after Pearl Harbor before the first exclusion order was issued; nearly eight months went by until the last order was issued; and the last of these "subversive" persons was not actually removed until almost eleven months had elapsed. Leisure and deliberation seem to have been more of the essence than speed. And the fact that conditions were not such as to warrant a declaration of martial law adds strength to the belief that the factors of time and military necessity were not as urgent as they have been represented to be.

Moreover, there was no adequate proof that the Federal Bureau of Investigation and the military and naval intelligence services did not have the espionage and sabotage situation well in hand during this long period. Nor is there any denial of the fact that not one person of Japanese ancestry was accused or convicted of espionage or sabotage after Pearl Harbor while they

---

can take over and produce everything the Jap grows. And we don't want them back when the war ends, either." Quoted by Taylor in his article *The People Nobody Wants*, 214 Sat. Eve. Post 24, 66 (May 9, 1942).

were still free,[15] a fact which is some evidence of the loyalty of the vast majority of these individuals and of the effectiveness of the established methods of combating these evils. It seems incredible that under these circumstances it would have been impossible to hold loyalty hearings for the mere 112,000 persons involved—or at least for the 70,000 American citizens—especially when a large part of this number represented children and elderly men and women.[16] Any inconvenience that may have accompanied an attempt to conform to procedural due process cannot be said to justify violations of constitutional rights of individuals.

I dissent, therefore, from this legalization of racism. Racial discrimination in any form and in any degree has no justifiable part whatever in our democratic way of life. It is unattractive in any setting but it is utterly revolting among a free people who have embraced the principles set forth in the Constitution of the United States. All residents of this nation are kin in some way by blood or culture to a foreign land. Yet they are primarily and necessarily a part of the new and distinct civilization of the United States. They must accordingly be treated at all times as the heirs of the American experiment and as entitled to all the rights and freedoms guaranteed by the Constitution.

Mr. Justice JACKSON, dissenting.

Korematsu was born on our soil, of parents born in Japan. The Constitution makes him a citizen of the United States by nativity and a citizen of California by residence. No claim is made that he is not loyal to this country. There is no suggestion that apart from the matter involved here he is not law-abiding and well disposed. Korematsu, however, has been convicted of an act not commonly a crime. It consists merely of being present in the state whereof he is a citizen, near the place where he was born, and where all his life he has lived.

Even more unusual is the series of military orders which made this conduct a crime. They forbid such a one to remain, and they also forbid him to leave. They were so drawn that the only way Korematsu could avoid violation was to give himself up to the military authority. This meant submission to custody, examination, and transportation out of the territory, to be followed by indeterminate confinement in detention camps.

---

[15] The Final Report, p. 34, makes the amazing statement that as of February 14, 1942, "The very fact that no sabotage has taken place to date is a disturbing and confirming indication that such action will be taken." Apparently, in the minds of the military leaders, there was no way that the Japanese Americans could escape the suspicion of sabotage.

[16] During a period of six months, the 112 alien tribunals or hearing boards set up by the British Government shortly after the outbreak of the present war summoned and examined approximately 74,000 German and Austrian aliens. These tribunals determined whether each individual enemy alien was a real enemy of the Allies or only a "friendly enemy." About 64,000 were freed from internment and from any special restrictions, and only 2,000 were interned. Kempner, "The Enemy Alien Problem in the Present War," 34 Amer. Journ. of Int. Law 443, 444-46; House Report No. 2124 (77th Cong., 2d Sess.), 280-1.

A citizen's presence in the locality, however, was made a crime only if his parents were of Japanese birth. Had Korematsu been one of four—the others being, say, a German alien enemy, an Italian alien enemy, and a citizen of American-born ancestors, convicted of treason but out on parole—only Korematsu's presence would have violated the order. The difference between their innocence and his crime would result, not from anything he did, said, or thought, different than they, but only in that he was born of different racial stock.

Now, if any fundamental assumption underlies our system, it is that guilt is personal and not inheritable. Even if all of one's antecedents had been convicted of treason, the Constitution forbids its penalties to be visited upon him, for it provides that "no attainder of treason shall work corruption of blood, or forfeiture except during the life of the person attained." But here is an attempt to make an otherwise innocent act a crime merely because this prisoner is the son of parents as to whom he had no choice, and belongs to a race from which there is no way to resign. If Congress in peace-time legislation should enact such a criminal law, I should suppose this Court would refuse to enforce it.

But the "law" which this prisoner is convicted of disregarding is not found in an act of Congress, but in a military order. Neither the Act of Congress nor the Executive Order of the President, nor both together, would afford a basis for this conviction. It rests on the orders of General DeWitt. And it is said that if the military commander had reasonable military grounds for promulgating the orders, they are constitutional and become law, and the Court is required to enforce them. There are several reasons why I cannot subscribe to this doctrine.

It would be impracticable and dangerous idealism to expect or insist that each specific military command in an area of probable operations will conform to conventional tests of constitutionality. When an area is so beset that it must be put under military control at all, the paramount consideration is that its measures be successful, rather than legal. The armed services must protect a society, not merely its Constitution. The very essence of the military job is to marshal physical force, to remove every obstacle to its effectiveness, to give it every strategic advantage. Defense measures will not, and often should not, be held within the limits that bind civil authority in peace. No court can require such a commander in such circumstances to act as a reasonable man; he may be unreasonably cautious and exacting. Perhaps he should be. But a commander in temporarily focusing the life of a community on defense is carrying out a military program; he is not making law in the sense the courts know the term. He issues orders, and they may have a certain authority as military commands, although they may be very bad as constitutional law.

But if we cannot confine military expedients by the Constitution, neither would I distort the Constitution to approve all that the military may deem expedient. That is what the Court appears to be doing, whether consciously or not. I cannot say, from any evidence before me, that the orders of General DeWitt were not reasonably expedient military precautions, nor could I say that they were. But even if they were permissible military procedures, I deny that it follows that they are constitutional. If, as the Court holds, it does follow, then we may as well say that any military order will be constitutional and have done with it.

The limitation under which courts always will labor in examining the necessity for a military order are illustrated by this case. How does the Court know that these orders have a reasonable basis in necessity? No evidence whatever on that subject has been taken by this or any other court. There is sharp controversy as to the credibility of the DeWitt report. So the Court, having no real evidence before it, has no choice but to accept General DeWitt's own unsworn, self-serving statement, untested by any cross-examination, that what he did was reasonable. And thus it will always be when courts try to look into the reasonableness of a military order.

In the very nature of things, military decisions are not susceptible of intelligent judicial appraisal. They do not pretend to rest on evidence, but are made on information that often would not be admissible and on assumptions that could not be proved. Information in support of an order could not be disclosed to courts without danger that it would reach the enemy. Neither can courts act on communications made in confidence. Hence courts can never have any real alternative to accepting the mere declaration of the authority that issued the order that it was reasonably necessary from a military viewpoint.

Much is said of the danger to liberty from the Army program for deporting and detaining these citizens of Japanese extraction. But a judicial construction of the due process clause that will sustain this order is a far more subtle blow to liberty than the promulgation of the order itself. A military order, however unconstitutional, is not apt to last longer than the military emergency. Even during that period a succeeding commander may revoke it all. But once a judicial opinion rationalizes such an order to show that it conforms to the Constitution, or rather rationalizes the Constitution to show that the Constitution sanctions such an order, the Court for all time has validated the principle of racial discrimination in criminal procedure and of transplanting American citizens. The principle then lies about like a loaded weapon ready for the hand of any authority that can bring forward a plausible claim of an urgent need. Every repetition imbeds that principle more deeply in our law and thinking and expands it to new purposes. All who observe the work of courts are familiar with what Judge Cardozo described as "the tendency of a principle to expand itself to the limit of its logic." A military commander may overstep the bounds of constitutionality, and it is an incident. But if we review and approve, that passing incident becomes the doctrine of the Constitution. There it has a generative power of its own, and all that it creates will be in its own image. Nothing better illustrates this danger than does the Court's opinion in this case.

It argues that we are bound to uphold the conviction of Korematsu because we upheld one in *Hirabayashi v. United States*, 320 U.S. 81, when we sustained these orders in so far as they applied a curfew requirement to a citizen of Japanese ancestry. I think we should learn something from that experience.

In that case we were urged to consider only the curfew feature, that being all that technically was involved, because it was the only count necessary to sustain Hirabayashi's conviction and sentence. We yielded, and the Chief Justice guarded the opinion as carefully as language will do. He said: "Our investigation here does not go beyond the inquiry whether, in the light of all the relevant circumstances preceding and attending their promulgation, the challenged orders and statute afforded a reasonable basis for the action taken in imposing the curfew." 320 U.S. 81 at 101. "We decide only the issue as we have defined it—we decide only that the curfew order as applied, and at the time it was applied, was within the boundaries of the war power." 320 U.S. 81 at 102. And again: "It is unnecessary to consider whether or to what extent such findings would support orders differing from the curfew order." 320 U.S. 81 at 105. However, in spite of our limiting words we did validate a discrimination on the basis of ancestry for mild and temporary deprivation of liberty. Now the principle of racial discrimination is pushed from support of mild measures to very harsh ones, and from temporary deprivations to indeterminate ones. And the precedent which it is said requires us to do so is *Hirabayashi*. The Court is now saying that in *Hirabayashi* we did decide the very things we there said we were not deciding. Because we said that these citizens could be made to stay in their homes during the hours of dark, it is said we must require them to leave home entirely; and if that, we are told they may also be taken into custody for deportation; and if that, it is argued they may also be held for some undetermined time in detention camps. How far the principle of this case would be extended before plausible reasons would play out, I do not know.

My duties as a justice as I see them do not require me to make a military judgment as to whether General DeWitt's evacuation and detention program was a reasonable military necessity. I do not suggest that the courts should have attempted to interfere with the Army in carrying out its task. But I do not think they may be asked to execute a military expedient that has no place in law under the Constitution. I would reverse the judgment and discharge the prisoner.

Notes and Questions

The following notes and questions probe more deeply the judiciary's role in addressing the tension between an individual's civil liberties and government's claims of military necessity or national security to justify curtailing those liberties. As with the earlier module involving *Hirabayashi* and *Yasui*, this module addresses the impact of the internment cases on anti-discrimination law, as well as the effect of social and political context on the Court's decision-making.

What the Court Decided

At the threshold, courts must decide what to decide. Lawyers argue over what a case is about in order to shape the judge's views on which legal principles apply and the jurors' views on what results they ought to reach. Even after a case ends, lawyers and judges argue about what issues were actually decided in an effort to shape its future value as precedent. In both *Hirabaya-shi* and *Korematsu*, the justices disagreed about the issues before them.

1. What were the issues before the Court?: At the outset, imagine that you were Fred Korematsu's attorney in 1944. Discuss how you might have framed the legal issues persuasively and powerfully to a court. At stake was not only Korematsu's freedom, but the freedom of 120,000 persons of Japanese ancestry, the majority of whom were American citizens like Korematsu. How would you link this individual's claim to the situation of those others? What rights could you assert on behalf of yourself and others?

Now imagine that you were the government's attorney. Discuss what military concerns might have loomed large during the first months of U.S. involvement in World War II.

Your arguments may benefit from the earlier chapters' discussions of anti-Asian sentiment on the West Coast. Consider also the impact of popular opinion at the time on the persuasiveness of certain types of arguments.

2. Exclusion or incarceration?: How did the Court frame the legal issues? And how did the dissenters re-frame those same issues? Consider the following example. Was Korematsu arrested solely for failing to abide by the military's order excluding Japanese Americans from designated areas? The specific order violated did not mention detention.

Korematsu's lawyers sought to define the main issue in terms of the legality of the internment itself. Almost all Japanese Americans initially excluded from West Coast areas were, under threat of force, detained and then immediately interned. In his dissent, Justice Roberts agreed with this framing of the issue.[*] To ignore the linkage of the exclusion orders to the internment, in his words, "is to shut our eyes to reality." For Korematsu's lawyers and Justice Roberts, therefore, the case was about the incarceration or internment of a racial group without charges or trial.[†]

How did the *Korematsu* majority frame the same facts? Consider the following passage of the majority's opinion:

> [the] contention [is] . . . that we must treat these separate orders as one and inseparable; that, for this reason, if detention in the assembly or relocation center would have illegally deprived the petitioner of his liberty, the exclusion order and his conviction under it cannot stand. . . . Since the petitioner

---

[*] Justice Roberts' dissent explained that under the March 27 "Freeze Order," Korematsu was forbidden to leave the military area. Under the May 3 Exclusion Order, Korematsu was required to report for evacuation, which would almost certainly have resulted in his placement inside an internment camp. Justice Roberts believed that the orders were contradictory: Korematsu could neither leave the area nor have stayed in his home; he appears to have had no option—other than submitting to evacuation and then detention. Note that the Freeze Order explicitly stated that it would remain effective until superseded by a later order; the specific Exclusion Order applicable to Korematsu was just such a later order.

[†] This position initially appeared to persuade Justice Douglas. He completed a dissenting opinion, noting that "removal to an Assembly Center had become merely the first stage in a trip to a Relocation Center." For unknown reasons, Justice Douglas later withdrew this dissent and joined the majority.

has not been convicted of failing to report or to remain in an assembly or re-location center, we cannot in this case determine the validity of those separate provisions of the order. It is sufficient here for us to pass upon the order which petitioner violated. To do more would be to go beyond the issues raised, and to decide momentous questions not contained within the framework of the pleadings or the evidence in this case.

Korematsu, supra. Does the majority opinion indicate that the government successfully framed the legal question in narrow factual terms?

Recall that in the earlier *Hirabayashi* and *Yasui* decisions, the Court avoided ruling on the legality of the internment by characterizing those cases as "curfew" cases. In *Korematsu*, by defining the issue solely in terms of the military exclusion orders, did the Court once again avoid the issue most important to 100,000 incarcerated Japanese Americans: whether the Constitution permitted their indefinite detention in U.S. internment camps? How could this issue have been raised squarely? Remember that Korematsu did not deliberately set out to be a "test case."

NATIONAL SECURITY AND CIVIL LIBERTIES

We revisit here the topics introduced at the beginning of this study module: the differing judicial approaches to review of national security restrictions of civilian civil liberties. These notes and questions are intended to catalyze discussion of the appropriate judicial role in reviewing national security restrictions of civil liberties—in light of the influences of politics, culture and economics on judicial decision making.

3. Judicial review of military necessity claims—revisiting the historical rationales: The *Korematsu* majority described itself as compelled by military necessity to legitimate the exclusion. Yet the Court, by its own words, did not then and does not now accept as dispositive the government's mere invocation of "military necessity" or "national security." The question therefore is not whether the courts should ever intervene in political/military decisions restricting civil liberties, but rather when.

Read broadly, the internment cases appear to give government authorities a "military necessity" trump card to defeat even long-recognized civil liberties—at least if Congress has declared war and the executive and legislative branches are supportive. The *Steel Seizure* and the *Pentagon Papers* cases, discussed *supra* at section B.2.b, suggest that judicial intervention is appropriate where military necessity is unproven—at least in times of undeclared war and where Congress has not acted in concert with the executive.

In section B.2.c *supra*, Professor Yamamoto suggests a return to the "watchful care" role first enunciated in *Ex parte Milligan* in light of the documented political and military excesses during the internment period. Eric K. Yamamoto, *Korematsu Revisited, Time for a Better Accommodation of National Security Concerns and Civil Liberties, supra.* Revisit the internment cases with this proposed "watchful care" standard.

The justices anxiously assessed the institutional role of the courts vis-à-vis military operations targeting civilian citizens outside the theatre of war. Especially difficult for the Supreme Court was whether courts are competent to second-guess the judgments of the military. The Court was also concerned that its orders to the contrary of executive or military decisions might be disregarded to the detriment of its institutional authority. Justice Black expressed the strongest view. He argued to his colleagues that the Court could not review any military actions taken during wartime. Justice Black drafted a passage about judicial review that was not published but which conveyed his absolutist position:

> When an enemy Army imminently threatens a particular area of our country with invasion, the immediate responsibility for defense must necessarily rest on those who direct our armed forces. . . . Purely military orders, limited to the comings and goings of occupants of an area which may at any minute become an active war zone, call for the exercise of a military, not a judicial judgment. . . . Therefore, I find it unnecessary to appraise possible reasons which might have prompted the order to be issued in the form it was. It is enough for me that both Congress and the Commander-in-Chief of the Army made a decision that the regulation as made was necessary to provide for the common defense in an area in which no man could say whether or when armed invaders would appear.

Roger K. Newman, HUGO BLACK: A BIOGRAPHY 315 (1994).

Justice Jackson believed the internment was wrong as a matter of law and his dissent characterized the majority's approval of the military orders without proof of necessity as "a loaded weapon ready for the hand of any authority that can bring forward a plausible claim of an urgent need." Yet Jackson also believed that the courts could play only a limited role in reviewing military decisions. As he stated at the end of his dissent:

> My duties as a justice as I see them do not require me to make a military judgment as to whether General DeWitt's evacuation and detention program was a reasonable military necessity. I do not suggest that the courts should have attempted to interfere with the Army in carrying out its task. But I do not think they may be asked to execute a military expedient that has no place in law under the Constitution.

Korematsu, supra (Jackson, dissenting). As Professor Currie summed up, "Justice Jackson waxed eloquent over the unconstitutionality of the exclusion provision itself, although he emphatically refused to decide whether or not it was [unlawful]."

Does a "fighting Constitution" mean that the political branches and military should be allowed to wage war utterly without judicial interference? What if the government's restriction of civil liberties targets a politically vulnerable minority group outside the theatre of conflict largely for racist and economic reasons? Does the Constitution permit and indeed require a more elaborate assessment of proffered national security concerns that restrict civilian liberties? What would a "watchful care" standard have required the courts to do in the internment cases? Are courts competent to make the requisite judgments? And with what consequences in terms of legitimacy? Might the other branches of government depend on the judiciary to do the right thing despite populist pressure? Remember that federal judges have life tenure and cannot be removed except upon impeachment. Thus they are politically more protected than the other two representative branches of government.

Many of these questions concerning judicial review will come up again in Chapter 5, in light of the revelations of the *Korematsu* and *Hirabayashi co-ram nobis* litigations.

4. Contemporary views of national security: Chief Justices Warren and Rehnquist: Although most contemporary observers are sharply critical of the Court's handling of *Hirabayashi* and *Korematsu*, the internment cases continue to find defenders among prominent jurists. Chief Justices Earl Warren and William Rehnquist have weighed in with interpretations of the internment cases that, in the words of Professor Fred Yen, "praise [them] with faint damnation."

As California Attorney General, Earl Warren strongly supported the internment. He later authored *Brown v. Board of Education* and earned the reputation as the head of a liberal activist court supportive of civil rights. Although Warren later expressed regrets about the internment and his pivotal role, he nevertheless defended *Korematsu* as late as 1962, arguing that

> [w]ar is, of course, a pathological condition for our Nation. Military judgments sometimes breed action that, in more stable times, would be regarded as abhorrent. . . . Judges cannot detach themselves from such judgments, although by hindsight, from the vantage point of more tranquil times, they might conclude that some actions advanced in the name of national survival had in fact overridden the strictures of due process.

Earl Warren, *The Bill of Rights and the Military,* 37 N.Y.U. L. Rev. 181, 191-92 (1962). Warren, however, also acknowledged criticism of the internment cases:

> Whatever the correct view of the specific holding of those cases . . . there are some circumstances in which the Court will, in effect, conclude that it is simply not in a position to reject descriptions by the Executive of the degree of military necessity.

Id. at 192. He concluded with a kind of admission: "the fact that the Court rules in a case like *Hirabayashi* that a given program is constitutional, does not necessarily answer the question whether, in a broader sense, it actually is." *Id.*

More recently, Chief Justice William Rehnquist analyzed the Court's treatment of civil liberties during military conflict. Rehnquist makes the following philosophical observation about a muted judicial role in reviewing military necessity restrictions of civil liberties.

> An entirely separate and important philosophical question is whether occasional presidential excesses and judicial restraint in wartime are desirable or undesirable. . . . [T]here is every reason to believe that the historic trend against the least justified of the curtailments of civil liberty in wartime will continue in the future. It is neither desirable nor remotely likely that civil liberty will occupy as favored a position in wartime as it does in peacetime. But it is both desirable and likely that more careful attention will be paid by the courts to the basis for the government's claims of necessity as a basis for curtailing civil liberty. The laws will thus not be silent in time of war, but they will speak with a somewhat different voice.

William H. Rehnquist, ALL THE LAWS BUT ONE: CIVIL LIBERTIES IN WARTIME 224–25 (1998). He believes that politicians and the military are less inclined to act in derogation of civil liberties in the future, as they have done in the past, and that judges now may be more vigorous in reviewing their actions. But how vigorous? And in what kind of "different voice"?

While Chief Justice Rehnquist acknowledges the general postwar judgment that the internment was an injustice to loyal Japanese Americans, he observes that the military "was surely going to err on the side of caution" because of Pearl Harbor. He concurs in retrospect with "the necessity for prompt action" as "cogently stated by the Court in its *Hirabayashi* opinion." Without acknowledging the military's obligation to uphold the Constitution, he makes what sounds like a startling assertion—that the military leaders "were not entrusted with the protection of anyone's civil liberty; their job was making sure that vital areas were as secure as possible from espionage and sabotage." What is the sitting Chief Justice of the United States saying about the military's loyalty to the Constitution?

Chief Justice Rehnquist also argues that the internment was proper as to the first generation Japanese immigrants, or Issei, because they were "enemy aliens," without addressing the racial bar to their naturalization that ensured that they would remain foreign nationals even if politically loyal and culturally assimilated. He also concludes that the Japanese immigrants were different from German and Italian aliens, because of geographic concentration near sensitive sites.

Surprisingly, however, Chief Justice Rehnquist completely ignores the revelations and outcomes of the *coram nobis* litigation and the 1983 findings of the Congressional Commission on Wartime Relocation and Internment. As will be discussed in Chapter 5, unequivocal evidence was uncovered during the 1980s that several of the highest-ranking government officials during World War II suppressed critical evidence and misrepresented key facts to the Supreme Court about the "military necessity" justification for the internment.

With all this in mind, compare ᵗChief Justice Rehnquist's arguments to Professor Yamamoto's framework in the introduction to this study module, *supra* section B.2.c. Consider how Rehnquist describes the tension between equal protection on the one hand and national security on the other hand. Do Rehnquist's views echo those of Justices Black or Jackson? If, as Chief Justice, Rehnquist believes that "there is no reason to think that . . . future Justices of the Supreme Court will decide questions differently than their predecessors," then what does that suggest about the malleability of this area of the law? About the Court's duty to define the Constitution?

Consider, for example, the rhetoric of military necessity in the immigration context. The power to regulate immigration, like the power to make war, is characterized as an essential aspect of sovereignty, affecting the foundation of the political system. Some extreme restrictionists in the immigration debate today also characterize non-white immigration and particularly Latina/o immigration in the Southwest as a "peaceful invasion" or an appropriation of territory. Does the military necessity argument extend to immigration control? If so, what results would accrue from the different approaches to claims of national security?

EQUAL PROTECTION AND THE STRICT SCRUTINY STANDARD OF REVIEW REVISITED

Most courts and academic commentators have agreed upon key aspects of *Korematsu*: The strict scrutiny standard of judicial review had its genesis in *Korematsu*, and strict scrutiny remains good law. Beyond these basic points, however, the "long shadow" of *Korematsu*[*] has been given relatively little careful scholarly attention until recently.

Even at the level of "black letter" legal doctrine, *Korematsu* is more complex than it seems. Consider what the majority opinion states about equal protection law. The *Korematsu* Court appeared to contradict itself in two important respects. First, it announced strict scrutiny as the standard for evaluating racial classifications, but then it declared that the case was not about race. Second, the Court stated that it would strictly scrutinize the government's military orders, but then it proceeded to defer to the government's assertion of military necessity as justification for the orders. These apparent contradictions are examined below.

5. Racial prejudice?: At the outset, the majority announced the standard of judicial review seemingly governing the case. "[A]ll legal restrictions which curtail the civil rights of a single racial group are immediately suspect. That is not to say that all such restrictions are unconstitutional. It is to say that courts must subject them to the most rigid scrutiny." But the majority then appeared to backtrack on the particulars. "To cast this case into outlines of racial prejudice, without reference to the real military dangers which were presented, merely confuses the issue. Korematsu was not excluded from the Military Area because of hostility to him or his race."

Did the Court contradict itself? How could the majority say that the case was not about prejudice against a racial group? What determinations must the majority have made in order to conclude that racial classifications warranted strict judicial scrutiny but that Korematsu's case did not involve "racial prejudice"? That it did not involve race?

Curiously, the majority opinion did not address, much less dispute, the strong dissents by Justices Murphy and Jackson. Both dissents asserted that the exclusion orders were grounded in racism. (Indeed, Justice Murphy's dissent appears to be the first express Supreme Court reference to "racism" in an opinion.) How did these dissents characterize the racial dimension of the case? Is it fair to say that the majority's opinion is internally inconsistent? Why?

6. Strict (or lax) scrutiny?: The second contradiction emerges in the Court's articulation of a strict scrutiny standard of review and its apparent application of something far less exacting. As explored in the previous module, the Court had applied a deferential standard of review to the military orders and accompanying federal statutes in *Hirabayashi* a year earlier. In the related *Korematsu* case, the Court appeared to break from *Hirabayashi* and articulate a very different substantive standard: Instead of simply allowing

---

[*] *Symposium: The Long Shadow of Korematsu*, 19 B.C. THIRD WORLD L.J. (1998); 40 B.C. L. REV. (1998).

Congress to act reasonably, it subjected Congress and the military's actions "to the most rigid scrutiny." But what standard of review did the Court apply—that is, how exacting was its scrutiny in fact?

7. **Compelling ends?:** Under the modern form of strict scrutiny, the ends must be more than rational; they must be compelling. Did the *Korematsu* majority follow the modern test? Did it closely scrutinize the government's ends? Consider the majority's statement that "[n]othing short of apprehension by the proper military authorities of the gravest imminent danger to the public safety can constitutionally justify either." It defined "danger" by alluding to acts of espionage and sabotage by West Coast Japanese Americans. Is the prevention of possible espionage and sabotage, especially during wartime, always a compelling government interest?

If espionage and sabotage actually posed "the gravest imminent danger to public safety," as the majority put it, then the government surely would have had a compelling interest in preventing these acts of disloyalty. But how does a court know if a particular racial group poses an imminent threat of this sort? What kind of evidence supports the otherwise abstract contention that the nation's security is in immediate jeopardy? More specifically, what kind of information should justify judicial reliance on a military conclusion that an entire racial minority group posed a threat of espionage and sabotage? And from what sources and framework of analysis?

Review the *Korematsu* majority opinion to determine if the Court engaged in an independent review of the evidence about actual risk of espionage or sabotage posed by Japanese Americans. List facts in favor of the majority and dissents' positions regarding the conclusions of military authorities. They seem to tell completely different stories about the same group of people: Japanese Americans.

a. **Judicial notice of group loyalty:** Dale Minami and Professor Lori Bannai, two lawyers who worked on the later *Korematsu coram nobis* case, had this to say about the Court's reliance on evidence of racial propensity:

> The Japanese American internment cases illustrate a highly unusual use of the doctrine of judicial notice. The "facts" the government sought to establish were certain racial characteristics of Japanese Americans that, the government argued, predisposed them to espionage and sabotage. First, it does not seem appropriate that these "facts" could be established as true by means of judicial notice. For example, one of the "facts" asserted and ultimately relied upon by the Court was that "large numbers of children of Japanese parentage are sent to Japanese language schools ... some of these schools are generally believed to be sources of Japanese nationalistic propaganda, cultivating allegiance to Japan." Aside from the fact that the numbers of Japanese American children attending Japanese school might be disputable, it hardly seems it could have been a matter of general knowledge or indisputable that Japanese language schools were sources of Japanese propaganda. Second, the government was not using the doctrine to establish "facts" at all, but was using it to establish a *conclusion* that Japanese Americans constituted a threat, itself a disputable conclusion. For example, rather than simply trying to establish that Japanese American children attended Japanese language school, the government was asserting that attending such schools showed a high predisposition to espionage and sabotage. The doctrine notice

was therefore being applied to establish propositions as indisputable fact that were not factual and were highly disputable. Ironically, the architect of the judicial notice manipulation, Nanette Dembitz, later wrote a law review article condemning the very use of judicial notice by the Court which she had earlier advocated.

Using judicial notice as the vehicle for accepting certain "racial characteristics" of Japanese Americans, and, lacking any direct evidence that Japanese Americans presented threats of espionage or sabotage, the Court then adopted the government's theory that such certain "racial characteristics" indicated potential disloyalty.

Lorraine K. Bannai & Dale Minami, *Internment During World War II*, ASIAN AMERICANS AND THE SUPREME COURT (Hyung-chan Kim ed. 1992).

Based on this evidence, were Congress and the executive reasonable in concluding that Japanese Americans were loyal to Japan?

b. Other evidence of disloyalty: What was the evidence of disloyalty available at the time the military authorities acted in 1942 and at the time the Court considered the case in 1944? Immediately following the Pearl Harbor attack, political and military leaders expressed fear of a Japanese military invasion of the U.S. mainland. This chapter's overview and first study module summarized some of the information generated by military intelligence, the FBI, independent operative Munson, General DeWitt and the Tolan Committee. At oral argument, the Justice Department represented to the Court that "the Japanese army could take everything west of the Rockies if they chose to land."

And what about a threat of espionage and sabotage by West Coast Japanese Americans in support of such an attack? What evidence did military and political decision-makers have about this possible risk? Here, very quickly, the public record becomes murky. Publicly, General DeWitt maintained that Japanese Americans had committed acts of espionage and sabotage—for example, using on-shore radios and lights to send signals to off-shore submarines.

What the public record at the time did not reflect, however, were the reports of all of the government intelligence services involved in investigating possible acts of espionage and sabotage by Japanese Americans—reports by the FBI, Federal Communications Commission and Office of Naval Intelligence. Those investigative reports, sent directly to General DeWitt, unequivocally rejected the military's assertions about Japanese American espionage and sabotage. Equally important, those reports concluded that there was no basis for mass evacuation or internment of persons of Japanese ancestry on the West Coast. This evidence, some of which was withheld from the Supreme Court, is discussed in great detail in Chapter 5.

8. Narrowly tailored means?: Under the modern form of strict scrutiny, a compelling government interest alone is insufficient to sustain the challenged government action. The Court currently also requires that proof that the means devised are narrowly tailored to meet the government's goals.

The *Korematsu* majority stated that "exclusion from a threatened area, no less than curfew, has a definite and close relationship to the prevention of espionage and sabotage." Does "a definite and close relationship" to the chosen ends imply a narrow tailoring? How do the dissents characterize the relationship of the means (exclusion and detention) used by the government to the end of national security? Even Justice Murphy, who dissented against validation of the exclusion, argued for a relaxed means test, at least during times of war—the selected means had to have only "some reasonable relation to the removal of the dangers of invasion, sabotage and espionage."

How carefully did the Court scrutinize the exclusion: the "means" selected by the government for dealing with the ostensible threat of espionage and sabotage to West Coast military defense areas? Did it discuss other less drastic (and therefore more narrowly tailored) options, such as individual hearings of those among the group suspected of disloyalty? The British government employed that approach with over 50,000 persons, as did the United States in Hawaii with over 2,000 persons shortly after Pearl Harbor. German and Italian aliens suspected of espionage or sabotage in the United States received individual hearings or trials.

The U.S. Office of Naval Intelligence, assigned by President Roosevelt to investigate the West Coast "Japanese Question" concluded in early 1942 that no mass internment of Japanese Americans was warranted and that any question of disloyalty involving Japanese immigrants or Japanese Americans could and should be handled "on an individual basis." What if this report had been part of the evidentiary record presented to the *Korematsu* Court? Might the Court have ruled differently? Or would the Court likely have upheld the constitutionality of the Japanese American exclusion in any event? On what stated grounds?

What if the government had devised a classification based on alienage (and not race)? If, for example, all aliens from enemy countries (including Germany and Italy) had been excluded, then would that classification be more narrowly tailored to prevent espionage and sabotage? What if the military had retained a racial classification but added an alienage component, so that only Japanese aliens in the United States (and not Japanese Americans) were targeted? In assessing either of these options for addressing the issue of disloyalty, recall that U.S. naturalization laws prohibited Japanese in America from becoming citizens.

Recall also that the government initially considered both of these schemes. The first military orders applied to all enemy aliens regardless of race. Why didn't the Court consider these alternatives to be evidence of lesser restrictive means to accomplish the government ends than the wholesale exclusion of those of Japanese descent?

Korematsu's attorneys made a strategic concession regarding the earlier cases of *Hirabayashi* and *Yasui*: that the ends (public safety after dark) might have justified the means (curfew). They then argued, however, that the possible validity of a curfew did not necessarily legitimate the far more drastic means (exclusion and incarceration) addressed in the later *Korematsu* and *Endo* cases. In his dissent, Justice Roberts embraced this argument. He indicated that although *Hirabayashi* and *Yasui* were properly decided, they did not dictate the result in *Korematsu*. Similarly, Justice Jackson asserted at the justices' decision-making conference when they discussed *Korematsu,* "I stop at *Hirabayashi.*"

A DEEPER LOOK AT CONTEXT

The *Korematsu* majority equated the exclusion and curfew, treating *Hirabayashi* as precedent. Why? Was the Court persuaded that there was no difference between a nighttime curfew restriction and the indefinite mass exclusion of the members of one racial group from their homes and workplaces? What else might have influenced the majority's thinking? In order to answer these questions, let's take a deeper look at context.

9. The limits of logic: The lawyers for Mitsuye Endo, Gordon Hirabayashi and Fred Korematsu, and Min Yasui knew that real people were suffering very real harms on account of their race. The lawyers, however, could not simply protest the government's actions as unjust and injurious to their clients. They had to state legal claims and fashion legal arguments in light of the factual circumstances and relevant legal principles. However, the logical analysis of legal doctrines is necessary but not sufficient for an understanding of the internment cases—or, for that matter, any socially significant legal decision. The cultural and political dimensions of the internment also must be examined. In this section, we ask you to consider the internment cases in a broader context by examining the impact on these decisions of the war, longstanding economic tensions, the justices' own personal views, the cultural ideologies of the day and racism.

a. The war: The developments on the battlefield, and the accompanying shifts in public perception, offer a means of sorting through the judicial rhetoric in the four internment cases. When the internment started, the military objectives were daunting. When the early pair of cases (*Hirabayashi* and *Yasui*) were considered by the Supreme Court in 1943, fighting in the Pacific was fierce and U.S. success was by no means assured. But by the time the later pair of cases (*Korematsu* and *Endo*) were decided in late 1944, the allied forces were achieving spectacular battlefield successes, and the nation was far more confident about victory overseas and its security domestically.

Do these historical developments perhaps explain why the court issued a unanimous opinion in the first pair of cases but was splintered in the second pair?

b. Economic competition: The political background to the internment, discussed during the Tolan Committee hearings and mentioned in the dissenting opinions, suggests that White American businessmen preferred to be rid of Japanese American economic competition, perceived and real. The *Korematsu* majority mentioned this argument in passing. Justice Murphy's dissent specifically raised the issue of racial and economic motivations. He noted that "special interest groups were extremely active in applying pressure for mass evacuation," pointing to White agricultural businesses that sought to exclude Japanese Americans to eliminate economic competition.

c. The justices: The internment decisions profoundly disturbed several of the justices long after the war. One biographer of Justice Rutledge observed, "[h]e gave all, and he had much to give," adding that the internment cases presented "some of the problems which pushed Wiley Rutledge along the path to his premature grave." Speaking with Chief Justice Stone, Justice Rutledge said of *Hirabayashi*, "I have had more anguish over this case than any I have decided, save possibly one death case in the Court of Appeals." Another biographer revealed that "by the end of the war, it sometimes seemed that the justices were as exhausted by their internal feuds as by their Court calendar." With the internment cases as major contributing factors, Justice Roberts had come to so dislike the other justices he would not dine with them and finally resigned.

The complex interplay between judicial role-playing and personal opinion is illustrated by Justice Black, author of the majority opinion in *Korematsu*. He defended the decision until his death. In an interview with The New York Times, granted on the condition it be published posthumously, he said:

> I would do precisely the same thing today, in any part of the country. I would probably issue the same order were I President. We had a situation where we were at war. People were rightly fearful of the Japanese in Los Angeles, many loyal to the United States, many undoubtedly not, having dual citizenship—lots of them.
>
> They all look alike to a person not a Jap. Had they attacked our shores you'd have a large number fighting with the Japanese troops. And a lot of innocent Japanese Americans would have been shot in the panic. Under these circumstances I saw nothing wrong with moving them away from the danger area.

Justice Black, Champion of Civil Liberties for 34 Years on the Court, Dies at 85, NEW YORK TIMES, September 26, 1971 at 76.

Elsewhere, Justice Black remarked that the internment was appropriate because "a particular race was the threatening invader." How can later courts reconcile Justice Black's reasoning in the case, which appears to rely on careful step-by-step analysis, with his later statements about Japanese Americans, which appear to be little more than outright prejudice? Can they? Should they even try?

Justice William O. Douglas vacillated between calling his internment vote "one of my mistakes" and acknowledged the pull of politics in law:

> The Court does move with political trends, as the philosophy of newly appointed Justices commonly reflects a trend. And community attitudes are not without their effect. The Court is not isolated from life. Its members are very much a part of the community and know the fears, anxieties, cravings and wishes of their neighbors. That does not mean that community attitudes are necessarily translated by mysterious osmosis into new judicial doctrine. It does mean that the state of public opinion will often make the Court cautious when it should be bold. . . . The state of public opinion may lead it to find many reasons for not taking up a controversial issue at the time. In the privacy of the Conference [among the justices], that is often called "judicial statesmanship."

WILLIAM O. DOUGLAS, THE AUTOBIOGRAPHY OF WILLIAM O. DOUGLAS: THE COURT YEARS, 1939–1975 38 (1980) (recalling that *Korematsu* "was very much discussed, very much considered, very much debated up and down the halls of the corridor of the Court").

In addition to relying on the formal evidentiary trial record, the justices relied on their personal experiences and, for some, information from *ex parte* (private) contacts with government officials. Such private contacts are generally considered off-limits. The historical record nevertheless reflects instances of justices obtaining relevant information not in the litigation record from government officials or friends with a direct interest in the pending cases.

Justice Black and his wife visited socially with General DeWitt and his wife well before World War II. They reportedly discussed the West Coast situation and Japanese Americans. As discussed earlier, during his testimony to Congress in 1942, DeWitt revealed the depth of his belief in the inherent disloyalty of all persons of Japanese ancestry, including American citizens by birth.

Justice Frankfurter helped John McCloy obtain his job as Assistant Secretary of War at the War Department, and the two maintained regular contact while McCloy was actively involved in defending the legality of the internment. Justice Frankfurter, as a sitting justice, also remained heavily involved with the Roosevelt administration.

With these personal views and relationships in mind, how should we understand in retrospect the majority's proffered strict scrutiny analysis in *Korematsu*? Is it more or less defensible on the grounds of logic? Of context? Did their personal views perhaps create filters through which they received information about the Japanese American community?

d. Cultural ideologies: The justices in the majority also seemed to ignore the available *amicus* briefs that portrayed Japanese Americans more completely as a community. By contrast, the detailed footnotes to Justice Murphy's dissent were based largely on those *amicus* briefs. For example, in footnote four, he states that "[t]o the extent that assimilation is a problem, it is largely the result of social customs and laws of the American general public. . . . The failure to accomplish an ideal status of assimilation, therefore, cannot be charged to the refusal of these persons to become Americanized or to their loyalty to Japan." In his handwritten margin notes on the draft *Hirabayashi* opinion, Murphy had also criticized the majority's focus on supposed cultural indicators of disloyalty.

The *Korematsu* majority's opinion deferred to the military's sweeping conclusions about Japanese American disloyalty. How does this deference comport with the strict scrutiny standard of review articulated at the outset of Justice Black's opinion? To what extent might the justices' personal experiences, political ties and assent to majoritarian interpretations of cultural behavior have influenced how "strictly" the Court construed the evidence and assessed the Justice Department's legal arguments?

Do the facts in Justice Murphy's dissent effectively refute the basis for the majority's decision, or do they represent inappropriate judicial second-guessing of military decision-making?

The Court did not consider, and may not have been in a position to fully appreciate, the deceptions of the Justice Department and War Department concerning the evidence of military necessity. As uncovered via the *coram nobis* litigation of the 1980s, evidence withheld from the Court included intelligence reports that concluded in early 1942 that no mass internment of Japanese Americans was warranted. These evidentiary omissions will be discussed further in Chapter 5.

   e. Racism?: Recall the recurring image of Chinese or Japanese immigrants as inherently unassimilable. The associations rolled up into the "forever foreign" stereotype of Asian immigrants include at least the following strands: (1) heightened national security concerns with respect to Asian immigrants compared to European immigrant groups; (2) the heightened impact of the political power of the country of origin on activities of Asian nationals in the United States, compared to European nationals; (3) conflation of Asian nationals with Asian Americans; and (4) fear of a numerical takeover by Asian over European immigrants. Could these ideas, introduced in the mid-1800s, still circulate and influence judicial thinking in the mid-1900s?

   f. Coalition: W.E.B. Dubois, writing from his Amsterdam News column, "As the Crow Flies," had this to say in 1944 about the internment in general:

> Most people do not realize that outbreaks of so-called "racial hate" are practically always organized and not spontaneous. The driving out of people of Japanese descent on the West coast was not only the attempt to confiscate their savings without return, but to foment and prolong racial antagonism.

Professor Devon W. Carbado explores Black civil rights responses to Japanese American internment in the context of examining the possibilities for meaningful coalition building between people of color. *Race, Law, & Citizenship: Black Civil Rights Response to Japanese American Internment* (forthcoming). He argues that the nature and extent of Black civil activism on behalf of Japanese Americans relates to, but is not completely explained by, the specific ways in which Black American citizenship was legally delimited under the Jim Crow laws. He points out, for example, that the NAACP did not file an *amicus* brief in any of the internment cases but that the Black press (such as the DuBois excerpt above) did voice some opposition against the internment. Why do you think Black Americans might/might not have intervened on behalf of Japanese Americans? To the extent that you think that Black Americans would/could have intervened, what forms of interventions would you expect?

   10. The internment cases today: As discussed in greater detail in Chapter 7, in the 1995 case of *Adarand Constructors v. Pena*, Justice O'Connor interpreted the *Hirabayashi—Korematsu* pair of cases as having announced an equal protection "heightened scrutiny" analysis applicable to federal government at the same time it "inexplicably" failed to apply it.

   After studying the context of the *Hirabayashi* and *Korematsu* decisions, how would you, as a law clerk to Justice O'Connor, explain the "inexplicable"? Note that the *Adarand* Court held that a federal affirmative action program violated the equal protection clause.

3. POLITICS AND LEGAL PROCESS: THE DETENTION CASE

The last of the internment cases was markedly different from the prior three. Like thousands of Japanese Americans, Mitsuye Endo had been neither charged with nor convicted of any criminal conduct. She nonetheless had been imprisoned in an internment camp. Endo complied with the military orders throughout while simultaneously arguing that the orders violated the Constitution. Rather than challenging a criminal conviction, she entered the judicial system by filing a petition for a writ of *habeas corpus*, seeking liberation from wrongful detention.

The *Endo* case more than the others reveals the politics of procedure. Lawyers know that the procedural rules followed by lawyers in court sometimes can be manipulated to affect substantive outcomes; strategy and procedure can shape litigation results. In the *Endo* litigation, the strategic procedural maneuvers occurred on two distinct levels: within the legal doctrine and behind the scenes. We discuss the open deception before addressing the hidden history.

a. *EX PARTE ENDO*: THE DETENTION

(i) BACKGROUND

PETER IRONS, JUSTICE AT WAR
99–103

A fourth Japanese American joined these three young men in bringing a challenge to General DeWitt's orders before the Supreme Court. Mitsuye Endo differed from them, however, not only in sex but in the form of her challenge. Endo did not test the curfew and exclusion orders that preceded internment, nor did she risk the criminal penalties. Her challenge to internment began after she reported to the Tanforan assembly center and was based on the civil procedure of a *habeas corpus* petition. Despite a lengthy delay in the lower courts, the petition brought on behalf of Mitsuye Endo eventually forced the Supreme Court to confront the internment issue directly.

Endo's case actually began several months before she reported to Tanforan, and well before the decision to intern Japanese Americans had been made. James Purcell, a thirty-six-year-old San Francisco lawyer, received a telephone call late in January 1942 from his friend, [JACL President] Saburo Kido. The two lawyers had worked together on earlier cases that involved Japanese American clients.

Days after President Roosevelt signed Executive Order 9066 on February 19, Nisei employees [in the California civil service system] were "advised" to stay home from work, although they were not formally dismissed. On April 13, Wayne Miller, secretary of the personnel board, sent to each Nisei employee an identical seven-page statement of charges. Cast in the form of an indictment, the board's statement alleged "failure of good behavior, fraud in securing employment, incompetency, inefficiency, and acts incompatible with and inimical to the public service" as grounds for dismissal.

All of the charged Nisei employees were native-born American citizens, a requirement of California law. Each was nonetheless first charged with being "a citizen of the Empire of Japan, and a subject of the Emperor of Japan." Each "defendant" in the dismissal proceedings was additionally charged with the ability to "read and write the Japanese language," having attended "a Japanese school conducted by the officials of the Buddhist Church," and with being "a member and officer of certain Japanese organizations" which were "violently opposed to the Democratic form of Government of the United States and to its principles." The necessary exposure of the public to state employees of Japanese descent, claimed the personnel board had "created discord, hostility, unfriendliness, opposition, antagonism, disharmony [and] truculency. . . ."

The patent absurdity of such broadside charges encouraged Purcell to believe that "we'd have no difficulty meeting the charges as they were originally filed." Before Purcell completed the complaint he planned to file on behalf of his new clients, they had been forced by DeWitt's orders to report to assembly centers along with all the other Japanese Americans who lived in California.

Faced with this situation, Purcell visited those of his clients who were held in the Tanforan assembly center, located in a converted racetrack near San Francisco. The conditions under which his clients were held appalled Purcell and sparked his sensitivity to injustice. "I grew up in Folsom prison," he later said. "My father was a guard there. I know a prison when I see it, and Tanforan was a prison with watch towers and guns."

Purcell finally picked out Mitsuye Endo as "perfect type" of plaintiff for a *habeas corpus* petition. A twenty-two-year-old clerical worker in the California Department of Motor Vehicles in Sacramento, Endo had been raised as a Methodist, did not speak or read Japanese, and had never visited Japan. Best of all, she had a brother serving in the Army. Purcell had not previously met with Mitsuye Endo and secured permission to file suit in her behalf by correspondence.

Purcell met his client only once during the entire course of her case, during an interrogation conducted by [War Relocation Authority] solicitor Philip Glick. Glick offered to release her from internment in return for an agreement that she would not return to the "restricted area" of the West Coast which included all of California. Despite this offer to escape from internment, made as part of the government's effort to avoid a Supreme Court test of its powers to detain Japanese Americans, Endo refused to abandon her legal challenge and remained behind barbed wire for another two years.

(ii) THE CASE

The *Endo* case was procedurally different from the other three internment cases because it arose from a *habeas corpus* petition. The writ of *habeas corpus*, known at common as "the Great Writ," is an order from a court literally directing a prison-keeper to bring forth the body of the captive. The petition is essentially a request to the government to release someone unlawfully detained—typically as a result of an unconstitutional criminal conviction. It functions as the final legal safeguard protecting a person from being improperly deprived of liberty. Because of both the importance of the writ and their experience with its availability being suspended for dubious purposes, the drafters of the Constitution explicitly preserved this right in the Constitution.

The petition for a writ of *habeas corpus* is distinct from the prosecution of criminal charges. It is a later proceeding, civil in nature, following incarceration. It allows the petitioner to raise constitutional arguments against the initial proceedings, renew claims of innocence or both.

Throughout the lower court litigation, the government knew that Endo's case was the most likely to result in a finding of unconstitutionality. Justice Department lawyers who were opposed to the internment from the outset even began to strategize with the ACLU to present Endo's case in the best possible light, which included being argued at the same time as the second *Korematsu* appeal. Although the Supreme Court accepted certification of four questions in the spring of 1944, the Court delayed argument in both cases until its subsequent October term.

Arguing on behalf of the government, Solicitor General Fahy conceded that there was no authority in Public Law 503 for the detention of Japanese Americans. This strategic concession appeared to present the Court with an easy decision on the merits. Nevertheless, the Court's opinion is contradictory and even problematic.

EX PARTE ENDO
323 U.S. 283 (1944)

Mr. Justice DOUGLAS delivered the opinion of the Court.

The history of the evacuation of Japanese aliens and citizens of Japanese ancestry from the Pacific coastal regions, following the Japanese attack on our Naval Base at Pearl Harbor on December 7, 1941, and the declaration of war against Japan on December 8, 1941, has been reviewed in Hirabayashi v. United States.

The program of the War Relocation Authority is said to have three main features: (1) the maintenance of Relocation Centers as interim places of residence for evacuees; (2) the segregation of loyal from disloyal evacuees; (3) the continued detention of the disloyal and so far as possible the relocation of the loyal in selected communities. [The indefinite leave procedure] presently provides as follows:

Application for leave clearance is required. An investigation of the applicant is made for the purpose of ascertaining "the probable effect upon the war program and upon the public peace and security of issuing indefinite leave" to the applicant.[10] The grant of leave clearance does not authorize departure

---

[10] Nine factors are specified each of which is "regarded by intelligence agencies as sufficient to warrant a recommendation that leave clearance be denied unless there is an adequate explanation." These include, among others, a failure or refusal to swear unqualified allegiance to the United States and to forswear any form of allegiance to the Japanese Em-

from the Relocation Center. Application for indefinite leave must also be made. Indefinite leave may be granted under 14 specified conditions. For example, it may be granted (1) where the applicant proposes to accept an employment offer or an offer of support that has been investigated and approved by the Authority; or (2) where the applicant does not intend to work but has "adequate financial resources to take care of himself" and a Relocation Officer has investigated and approved "public sentiment at his proposed destination;" or (3) where the applicant has made arrangements to live at a hotel or in a private home approved by a Relocation Officer while arranging for employment; or (4) where the applicant proposes to accept employment by a federal or local governmental agency; or (5) where the applicant is going to live with designated classes of relatives.

But even if an applicant meets those requirements, no leave will issue when the proposed place of residence or employment is within a locality where it has been ascertained that "community sentiment is unfavorable" or when the applicant plans to go to an area which has been closed by the Authority to the issuance of indefinite leave. Nor will such leave issue if the area where the applicant plans to reside or work is one which has not been cleared for relocation.[13] Moreover, the applicant agrees to give the Authority prompt notice of any change of employment or residence. And the indefinite leave which is granted does not permit entry into a prohibited military area, including those from which these people were evacuated.

Mitsuye Endo made application for leave clearance on February 19, 1943, after the petition was filed in the District Court. Leave clearance was granted her on August 16, 1943. But she made no application for indefinite leave.

Her petition for a writ of *habeas corpus* alleges that she is a loyal and law-abiding citizen of the United States, that no charge has been made against her, that she is being unlawfully detained, and that she is confined in the Relocation Center under armed guard and held there against her will.

It is conceded by the Department of Justice and by the War Relocation Authority that appellant is a loyal and law-abiding citizen. They make no claim that she is detained on any charge or that she is even suspected of disloyalty. Moreover, they do not contend that she may be held any longer in the Relocation Center. They concede that it is beyond the power of the War Relocation Authority to detain citizens against whom no charges of disloyalty or subversiveness have been made for a period longer than that necessary to separate the loyal from the disloyal and to provide the necessary guidance for relocation. But they maintain that detention for an additional period after

---

peror or any other foreign government, power, or organization; a request for repatriation or expatriation whether or not subsequently retracted; military training in Japan; employment on Japanese naval vessels; three trips to Japan after the age of six, except in the case of seamen whose trips were confined to ports of call; an organizer, agent, member, or contributor to specified organizations which intelligence agencies consider subversive.

[13] The War Relocation Authority also recommends communities in which an evacuee will be accepted, renders aid in finding employment opportunities, and provides cash grants, if needed, to assist the evacuee in reaching a specified destination and in becoming established there. The Authority has established eight area offices and twenty-six district offices to help carry out the relocation program.

leave clearance has been granted is an essential step in the evacuation program. Reliance for that conclusion is placed on the following circumstances. As stated by General DeWitt in his report to the Chief of Staff:

> Essentially, military necessity required only that the Japanese population be removed from the coastal area and dispersed in the interior, where the danger of action in concert during any attempted enemy raids along the coast, or in advance thereof as preparation for a full scale attack, would be eliminated.

We are of the view that Mitsuye Endo should be given her liberty. In reaching that conclusion we do not come to the underlying constitutional issues which have been argued. For we conclude that, whatever power the War Relocation Authority may have to detain other classes of citizens, it has no authority to subject citizens who are concededly loyal to its leave procedure.

It should be noted at the outset that we do not have here a question such as was presented in *Ex parte Milligan*, 4 Wall. 2, or in *Ex parte Quirin*, 317 U.S. 1, where the jurisdiction of military tribunals to try persons according to the law of war was challenged in *habeas corpus* proceedings. Mitsuye Endo is detained by a civilian agency, the War Relocation Authority, not by the military. Moreover, the evacuation program was not left exclusively to the military; the Authority was given a large measure of responsibility for its execution and Congress made its enforcement subject to civil penalties by the Act of March 21, 1942. Accordingly, no questions of military law are involved.

We approach the construction of Executive Order No. 9066 as we would approach the construction of legislation in this field. That Executive Order must indeed be considered along with the Act of March 21, 1942, which ratified and confirmed it (*Hirabayashi v. United States*) as the Order and the statute together laid such basis as there is for participation by civil agencies of the federal government in the evacuation program. The Constitution is as specific in its enumeration of many of the civil rights of the individual as it is in its enumeration of the powers of his government. Thus it has prescribed procedural safeguards surrounding the arrest, detention and conviction of individuals. Some of these are contained in the Sixth Amendment, compliance with which is essential if convictions are to be sustained. And the Fifth Amendment provides that no person shall be deprived of liberty (as well as life or property) without due process of law. Moreover, as a further safeguard against invasion of the basic civil rights of the individual it is provided in Art. I, SS 9 of the Constitution that "The Privilege of the Writ of *Habeas Corpus* shall not be suspended, unless when in Cases of Rebellion or Invasion the public Safety may require it." *See Ex parte Milligan.*

We mention these constitutional provisions not to stir the constitutional issues which have been argued at the bar but to indicate the approach which we think should be made to an Act of Congress or an order of the Chief Executive that touches the sensitive area of rights specifically guaranteed by the Constitution. This Court has quite consistently given a narrower scope for the operation of the presumption of constitutionality when legislation appeared on its face to violate a specific prohibition of the Constitution. We have likewise favored that interpretation of legislation which gives it the greater chance of surviving the test of constitutionality. Those analogies are suggestive here. We must assume that the Chief Executive and members of

Congress, as well as the courts, are sensitive to and respectful of the liberties of the citizen. In interpreting a wartime measure we must assume that their purpose was to allow for the greatest possible accommodation between those liberties and the exigencies of war. We must assume, when asked to find implied powers in a grant of legislative or executive authority, that the law makers intended to place no greater restraint on the citizen than was clearly and unmistakably indicated by the language they used.

A citizen who is concededly loyal presents no problem of espionage or sabotage. Loyalty is a matter of the heart and mind, not of race, creed, or color. He who is loyal is by definition not a spy or a saboteur. When the power to detain is derived from the power to protect the war effort against espionage and sabotage, detention which has no relationship to that objective is unauthorized.

Nor may the power to detain an admittedly loyal citizen or to grant him a conditional release be implied as a useful or convenient step in the evacuation program, whatever authority might be implied in case of those whose loyalty was not conceded or established. If we assume (as we do) that the original evacuation was justified, its lawful character was derived from the fact that it was an espionage and sabotage measure, not that there was community hostility to this group of American citizens. The evacuation program rested explicitly on the former ground not on the latter as the underlying legislation shows.

Mitsuye Endo is entitled to an unconditional release by the War Relocation Authority.

Reversed.

Mr. Justice MURPHY, concurring.

I join in the opinion of the Court, but I am of the view that detention in Relocation Centers of persons of Japanese ancestry regardless of loyalty is not only unauthorized by Congress or the Executive but is another example of the unconstitutional resort to racism inherent in the entire evacuation program. As stated more fully in my dissenting opinion in *Korematsu v. United States*, racial discrimination of this nature bears no reasonable relation to military necessity and is utterly foreign to the ideals and traditions of the American people.

If, as I believe, the military orders excluding her from California were invalid at the time they were issued, they are increasingly objectionable at this late date, when the threat of invasion of the Pacific Coast and the fears of sabotage and espionage have greatly diminished.

Mr. Justice ROBERTS.

I concur in the result but I cannot agree with the reasons stated in the opinion of the court for reaching that result.

As in *Korematsu v. United States,* the court endeavors to avoid constitutional issues which are necessarily involved.

I conclude . . . that the court is squarely faced with a serious constitutional question,—whether the relator's detention violated the guarantees of the Bill of Rights of the federal Constitution and especially the guarantee of due process of law. There can be but one answer to that question. An admittedly loyal citizen has been deprived of her liberty for a period of years. Under the Constitution she should be free to come and go as she pleases. Instead, her liberty of motion and other innocent activities have been prohibited and conditioned. She should be discharged.

NOTES AND QUESTIONS

THE POLITICS OF LEGAL PROCESS

To see the procedural manipulation in *Endo*, recall *Hirabayashi* and *Yasui*, which were already decided, and *Korematsu*, which was decided simultaneously. Endo filed her *habeas corpus* petition at the same level of the judicial system as the other cases: in a trial court. There, the presiding judge held Endo's petition in abeyance until *Hirabayashi* and *Yasui* were decided. He then summarily dismissed the petition.

1. What the Court decided: As discussed, concerning *Hirabayashi* and *Yasui*, the Court employed a technique of piecemeal resolution. It treated each aspect of the internment in isolation rather than evaluating the sequence of events as a whole. This choice was explicit in the decisions themselves. In *Hirabayashi*, the majority explicitly addressed only Hirabayashi's conviction on the curfew count, not his conviction for failing to report for evacuation. The concurrences emphasized what Justice Douglas called "the narrow ground of decision." In *Yasui*, the majority relied on *Hirabayashi*.

Then, in *Korematsu*, the Court addressed only evacuation (or exclusion), not detention (or imprisonment). The Court stated, "[i]t will be time enough to decide the serious constitutional issues which petitioner seeks to raise when an assembly or relocation order is applied or is certain to be applied to him, and we have its terms before us."

When that time arrived, what did the Court decide—by its own terms? Does its choice tend to support or undermine the notion that legal doctrines are fixed and offer complete explanations of decisions? In the end, did the Court ever consider the constitutionality of internment as a whole, or the detention in particular? Or did its decisions leave uncertain the internment, between lawfulness and lawlessness?

2. What the Court did not decide: Consider how in *Endo* Justice Douglas avoided the constitutional issue by grounding the decision solely in the statute. Justice Douglas reasoned that the President and the Congress should be given the benefit of the doubt. He assumed that they meant to pursue policies within the constitutional limits, for "the law makers intended to place no greater restraint on the citizen than was clearly and unmistakably indicated by the language they used."

For his part, Justice Douglas later characterized *Endo* as mitigating *Korematsu*: The Court refused to approve of the detention of concededly loyal persons on the basis of their ancestry. Regardless of the Court's ruling in *Korematsu*, an individual who was subject to an Exclusion Order could have contested the ultimate result of detention in an internment camp through a petition for a writ of *habeas corpus*. Justice Douglas himself had suggested as much in his concurring opinion in *Hirabayashi*.

Yet did the possibility of individual *habeas corpus* relief really mitigate the constitutional problem? Can a defendant be deprived of her constitutional rights at trial solely because she may later seek *habeas corpus* relief from wrongful imprisonment? For the internment, Justice Douglas appeared to hold out *habeas corpus* as an exclusive remedy. What are the implications?

In the end, did the Court again manage to avoid ruling on the constitutionality of the internment—even as to concededly loyal individuals?

3. Timing of the decisions: Another aspect of process manipulation in *Endo* lies in the timing of its opinions. The *Korematsu* case was already before the Supreme Court for the second time (following the decision on finality of the conviction and remand) when the *Endo* case was ready for argument at the court of appeals in the spring of 1944. Recognizing the similar issues presented by *Korematsu* and *Endo*, Circuit Judge Denman certified the latter case directly to the Supreme Court.

By then, the scheduled period for oral argument in the *Korematsu* case had passed. It would have been possible, though, to have both cases argued before the close of the term, or it would have been possible to have proceeded with *Korematsu* alone. Instead, the Court announced in the spring that it would postpone both cases while 100,000 persons of Japanese ancestry remained incarcerated. The Court chose to hear the cases together in the fall of 1944. The Court would take its recess before considering the cases; the presidential elections would be over. By then, ending the internment by judicial decree would have limited political repercussions.

During the summer, the Roosevelt Administration—including its Cabinet members—debated the end of internment. Legal historian Peter Irons reported that "Roosevelt rejected proposals to end internment." Reviewing details of meetings during which numerous proposals were considered for concluding the internment, and weighed against their likely political consequences as well as their effect on the pending cases, Irons concluded that the events "illustrate in its most naked form the dominance of politics over law when the two collide." He further concluded that it was nothing less than "political pressure" in the form of a presidential election that delayed issuance of the *Korematsu* and *Endo* opinions and "held up release of Japanese Americans."

The net result was that, while the *Hirabayashi* and *Yasui* cases had been decided quickly, the *Korematsu* and *Endo* cases were delayed needlessly. And even after they were argued, the Court waited again.

Release of the *Endo* opinion was delayed to allow the Roosevelt Administration the opportunity to make an announcement of its decision to close the internment camps. As early as November 28, Justice Douglas asked the Chief Justice to release the *Endo* opinion. The Chief Justice and Justice Frankfurter, however, were working with the executive branch to time the decision to its advantage. Historians Irons and Roger Daniels have reported circumstantial evidence of communications between the justices and Assistant Secretary of War McCloy on the specific subject of timing the *Korematsu* and *Endo* decisions. The judicial delay and likely coordination with the executive branch gave the President rather than the Court the opportunity formally to end the internment. The decisions were issued on December 18, 1944—one day after the War Department announced the imminent release of the internees.

What do the details of the timing suggest about the *Endo* decision? About the confluence of insider politics and the framing, outcome and publicizing of some judicial decisions?

OTHER INTERNEES OR INAPPROPRIATE COMPARISONS?

4. Germans and Italians: Japanese Americans were not the only citizens who could be characterized as racially affiliated with enemy nations. Italian Americans and German Americans shared that status. The received view has been that Japanese residents of the United States were treated differently from Italian and German residents of the United States: as a group rather than as individuals, without respect to the line between citizen and alien, and without any hearings. In the earliest phases of post-Pearl Harbor activity, however, some Italian and German immigrants were treated in the same manner as the Issei. For instance, the order to turn in firearms, explosives, ammunition and weapons was directed at all citizens of Japanese, Italian and German ancestry alike. Moreover, there were proposals for an internment of Italian and German immigrants. In successful opposition, the image of famed baseball player Joe DiMaggio's family being mistreated was invoked.

The CWRIC report PERSONAL JUSTICE DENIED took seriously the issue of Italian Americans and German Americans. It explained that the Italian Americans were dismissed as not likely treacherous—in Roosevelt's words, "a lot of opera singers." In a chapter on German Americans, the report detailed the actual threat posed by German U-boats to Atlantic shipping; the submarines had sunk 13 ships with 95,000 gross tons of cargo in January 1942 alone—"Japanese attacks on the West Coast were insignificant by comparison." Aside from racial prejudice, the Commission mentioned "two typical explanations of the divergent treatment of the two ethnic groups." The German American population was over 6 million if all families with at least one German-born parent were counted. And they wielded political clout.

Revisionist historians recently have used oral histories to challenge both the conventional opinion of the era that the internment was right as well as the contemporary view that it was wrong. As academic activists, they have sought to make up not only for original mistreatment of the individuals involved but also for the exclusion of those persons from later efforts of redress.

"Truth does not suffer assumptions gladly," wrote Stephen C. Fox, one of the leading figures in the new wave. Reviewing in detail the government decision-making after Pearl Harbor, Fox portrays a confused struggle between civilian and military authorities on opposite coasts rather than any systematic effort to target persons of Japanese descent. He suggests it was "the very large number of Germans and Italians and the extent of their assimilation to American society, in sharp contrast with the Japanese" that led to the disparate treatment, but he notes that the absence of greater numbers of Japanese Americans can be traced directly to racially exclusive immigration policies.

Other scholarly commentators have greeted the assertions with skepticism. Jeffrey L. Sammons, a professor of German history writing in a leading journal, THE GERMAN QUARTERLY, stated, "I attempted to check the references" of the research on German Americans, and "some were non-existent, and those I was able to find did not support the claimed argument or were not of scholarly standing." Commenting on the most rigorous account, a monograph by Timothy Holian based on a Ph.D dissertation, Sammons questions as based on unreliable documentation the figure of 10,905 internees of German descent, along with the estimate that the majority of internees (56 percent) were of European heritage. Sammons also points out that the very active pro-Nazi Bund brought out 25,000 or more to its rallies, "more than twice as many as those who are said to have been interned," emphasizing that "no evidence has yet been brought forward that, except for the minor children of enemy aliens, *any German-Americans were interned during World War II.*"

Ironically, the treatment of persons of German origin during military conflict was much worse during World War I. The anti-German sentiments lingered long afterward, resulting in social ostracization and forced assimilation for one of the largest White ethnic groups. Prohibitions on teaching foreign languages, which had an anti-German motivation, were struck down by the Supreme Court in *Meyer v. Nebraska*, 262 U.S 390 (1923).

While it cannot be considered a parallel to internment, German prisoners of war were transported to the United States for incarceration. Their treatment provoked anger on the part of African Americans in the South, who believed that German enemies, because they were White, were given greater consideration than the African Americans were under the harsh Jim Crow system of segregation.

5. Distinguishing Japanese: How important are these comparisons to analysis of the internment? Would the internment be constitutional if German Americans and Italian Americans also were included? How does the distinction between German and German Americans, if it is accepted as a critique of revisionist work, apply to Japanese and Japanese Americans?

Was there a principled basis for distinguishing between Japanese Americans and German and Italian American individuals at the time of the internment? At the time of reparations?

In politics, how is it possible to evaluate competing claims about historical truth? Are either legislatures or courts ideal institutions for doing so?

C. ADDITIONAL READINGS

BOOKS

Hannah Arendt, THE ORIGINS OF TOTALITARIANISM (1973).

Leonard Baker, BRANDEIS AND FRANKFURTER: A DUAL BIOGRAPHY (1984).

Derrick Bell, FACES AT THE BOTTOM OF THE WELL: THE PERMANENCE OF RACISM (1992).

Ed Cray, CHIEF JUSTICE: A BIOGRAPHY OF EARL WARREN (1997).

CRITICAL RACE THEORY: THE KEY WRITINGS THAT FORMED THE MOVEMENT (Kimberlé Crenshaw et al. eds., 1995).

Philip Bobbitt, CONSTITUTIONAL INTERPRETATION (1991).

Roger Daniels, CONCENTRATION CAMPS, NORTH AMERICA: JAPANESE IN THE UNITED STATES AND CANADA DURING WORLD WAR II (1981).

AMERICAN CONCENTRATION CAMPS: A DOCUMENTARY HISTORY OF THE RE-LOCATION AND INCARCERATION OF JAPANESE AMERICANS, 1942-1945 (Roger Daniels ed., 1989).

JAPANESE AMERICANS: FROM RELOCATION TO REDRESS (Roger Daniels, et al. eds., c.1986, 1991).

William O. Douglas, THE COURT YEARS, 1939-1975: THE AUTOBIOGRAPHY OF WILLIAM O. DOUGLAS (1980).

Gerald T. Dunne, HUGO BLACK AND THE JUDICIAL REVOLUTION (1977).

THE DOUGLAS OPINIONS (Vern Countryman ed., 1977).

Sidney Fine, FRANK MURPHY: THE WASHINGTON YEARS (1984).

Louis Fisher & Neal Devins, POLITICAL DYNAMICS OF CONSTITUTIONAL LAW (1992).

Gerald Gunther & Kathleen Sullivan, CONSTITUTIONAL LAW (1997).

Samuel Joseph Konefsky, CHIEF JUSTICE STONE AND THE SUPREME COURT (prefatory note by Charles A. Beard 1945).

LANDMARK BRIEFS AND ARGUMENTS OF THE SUPREME COURT OF THE UNITED STATES: CONSTITUTIONAL LAW (Philip B. Kurland and Gerhard Casper eds., 1975).

Fowler V. Harper, JUSTICE RUTLEDGE AND THE BRIGHT CONSTELLATION (1965).

William Minoru Hohri, REPAIRING AMERICA: AN ACCOUNT OF THE MOVE-MENT FOR JAPANESE-AMERICAN REDRESS (1984).

Peter Irons, THE COURAGE OF THEIR CONVICTIONS (1988).

Peter Irons, JUSTICE AT WAR: THE STORY OF THE JAPANESE AMERICAN IN-TERNMENT CASES (1983).

Harry H.L. Kitano, GENERATIONS AND IDENTITY: THE JAPANESE AMERICAN (1993).

Joseph P. Lash (assisted by Jonathan Lash), FROM THE DIARIES OF FELIX FRANKFURTER: WITH A BIOGRAPHICAL ESSAY AND NOTES (1975).

Mike Masaoka with Bill Hosokawa, THEY CALL ME MOSES MASAOKA: AN AMERICAN SAGA (1987).

Alpheus Thomas Mason, HARLAN FISKE STONE: PILLAR OF THE LAW (1956).

POWER AND POLICY IN QUEST OF THE LAW: ESSAYS IN HONOR OF EUGENE VICTOR ROSTOW (Myres S. McDougal ed., 1986).

Charles J. McClain, IN SEARCH OF EQUALITY: THE CHINESE STRUGGLE AGAINST DISCRIMINATION IN NINETEENTH-CENTURY AMERICA (1994).

Elting Elmore Morison, TURMOIL AND TRADITION: A STUDY OF THE LIFE AND TIMES OF HENRY L. STIMSON (1960).

Gunnar Myrdal, AN AMERICAN DILEMMA (1998).

Roger K. Newman, HUGO BLACK: A BIOGRAPHY (1994).

William H. Rehnquist, ALL THE LAWS BUT ONE: CIVIL LIBERTIES IN WAR-TIME (1998).

Clinton Lawrence Rossiter, THE SUPREME COURT AND THE COMMANDER IN CHIEF (1976).

DISPASSIONATE JUSTICE, A SYNTHESIS OF THE JUDICIAL OPINIONS OF ROBERT H. JACKSON (Glendon Schubert ed., 1969).

Bernard Schwartz, SUPER CHIEF, EARL WARREN AND HIS SUPREME COURT: A JUDICIAL BIOGRAPHY (1983).

Peter M. Shane & Harold H. Bruff, SEPARATION OF POWERS LAW: CASES AND MATERIALS (1996).

James F. Simon, INDEPENDENT JOURNEY: THE LIFE OF WILLIAM O. DOUGLAS (1980).

Ronald Steel, WALTER LIPPMANN AND THE AMERICAN CENTURY (1980).

HUGO BLACK AND THE SUPREME COURT: A SYMPOSIUM (Stephen Parks Strickland ed., 1967).

Paul R. Spickard, JAPANESE AMERICANS: THE FORMATION AND TRANSFORMATIONS OF AN ETHNIC GROUP (1996).

Jere Takahashi, NISEI/SANSEI: SHIFTING JAPANESE AMERICAN IDENTITIES AND POLITICS (ASIAN AMERICAN HISTORY AND CULTURE) (1997).

Jacobus Ten Broek, Edward N. Barnhart & Floyd W. Matson, PREJUDICE, WAR, AND THE CONSTITUTION (1970).

Helen Shirley Thomas, FELIX FRANKFURTER: SCHOLAR ON THE BENCH (1960).

Laurence H. Tribe, AMERICAN CONSTITUTIONAL LAW (1988).

THE DOUGLAS LETTERS: SELECTIONS FROM THE PRIVATE PAPERS OF JUSTICE WILLIAM O. DOUGLAS (with an introduction by Melvin I. Urofsky ed., with the assistance of Philip E. Urofsky 1987).

Melvin I. Urofsky, FELIX FRANKFURTER, JUDICIAL RESTRAINT AND INDIVIDUAL LIBERTIES (1991).

THE SUPREME COURT JUSTICES: A BIOGRAPHICAL DICTIONARY (Melvin I. Urofsky ed., 1994).

United States Commission on Wartime Relocation and Internment of Civilians, PERSONAL JUSTICE DENIED: REPORT OF THE COMMISSION ON WARTIME RELOCATION AND INTERNMENT OF CIVILIANS (1997).

Samuel Walker, IN DEFENSE OF AMERICAN LIBERTIES: A HISTORY OF THE ACLU (1990).

G. Edward White, EARL WARREN: A PUBLIC LIFE (1982).

Robert A. Wilson and Bill Hosokawa, EAST TO AMERICA: A HISTORY OF THE JAPANESE IN THE UNITED STATES (1980).

LAW REVIEW ARTICLES AND OTHER SOURCES

Maurice Alexandre, *Wartime Control of Japanese-Americans*, 28 COR-NELL L.Q. 385 (1943).

John H. Burma, *Leadership Problems of Japanese Americans*, 37 SOCI-OLOGY AND SOCIAL RESEARCH 157 (1953).

David P. Currie, *The Constitution in the Supreme Court: The Second World War, 1941-1946*, 37 Cath. U. L. Rev. 1 (1987).

Charles Fairman, *The Law of Martial Rule and the National Emergency*, 55 HARV. L. REV. 1253 (1942).

Harrop Freeman, *Genesis, Exodus and Leviticus: Genealogy, Evacuation, and Law*, 28 CORNELL L.Q. 414 (1943).

Stephen Fox, *General John DeWitt and the Proposed Internment of German and Italian Americans During World War II*, PACIFIC HISTORICAL REVIEW, v. 57 (Nov. 1988): *The Unknown Internment: An Oral History of the Relocation of Italian Americans During World War II* (1990).

Robert H. Jackson, *Wartime Security and Liberty Under Law*, 1 BUFF. L. REV. 116 (1951).

Justice Black, Champion of Civil Liberties for 34 Years on the Court, Dies at 85, NEW YORK TIMES, September 26, 1971.

Charles Evans Hughes, *War Powers Under the Constitution*, 42 A.B.A. REP. 232 (1917).

Robert M.W. Kempner, *The Enemy Alien Problem in the Present War*, 34 AM. J. INTL. L. 443 (1940).

Pedro Loureiro, *Japanese Espionage and American Countermeasures in Pre-Pearl Harbor California*, 3 THE JOURNAL OF AMERICAN-EAST ASIAN RELATIONS 197 (1994).

Walter Lippman, NEW YORK HERALD TRIBUNE, February 12, 1942.

Charles J. McClain, Jr., *The Chinese Struggle for Civil Rights in Nineteenth Century America: The First Phase, 1850-1870*, 72 CALIF. L. REV. 529 (1984).

Memorandum on C.B. Munson's Report *Japanese on the West Coast* (November 7, 1941).

Martin Peret, *Cambridge Diarist: Siege Mentality*, THE NEW REPUBLIC, November 30, 1998.

Eugene V. Rostow, *The Japanese American Cases—A Disaster*, 54 YALE L.J. 489 (1945).

Jeffrey L. Sammons, *Were German Americans Interned During World War II? A Question Concerning Scholarly Standards and Integrity*, THE GERMAN QUARTERLY, v. 71 (Winter 1998).

A Symposium on Constitutional Rights in Wartime, 29 IOWA L. REV. 3 (1944).

Symposium: The Long Shadow of Korematsu, 19 B.C. THIRD WORLD L.J. (1998); 40 B.C. L. REV. 1–535 (1998).

Frank J. Taylor, *The People Nobody Wants*, 214 SATURDAY EVENING POST 24 (May 9, 1942).

Tolan Committee, *Preliminary Report and Recommendations* (March 19, 1942).

War Relocation Authority, U.S. Dept. of the Interior, Legal and Constitutional Phases of the WRA Program (1946).

Eric K. Yamamoto, *Korematsu Revisited—Correcting the Injustice of Extraordinary Government Excess and Lax Judicial Review: Time for a Better Accommodation of National Security Concerns and Civil Liberties*, 26 SANTA CLARA L. REV. 1 (1986).

WESTERN DEFENSE COMMAND AND FOURTH ARMY
WARTIME CIVIL CONTROL ADMINISTRATION
Presidio of San Francisco, California
May 3, 1942

INSTRUCTIONS
TO ALL PERSONS OF
JAPANESE
ANCESTRY
Living in the Following Area:

All of that portion of the City of Los Angeles, State of California, within that boundary beginning at the point at which North Figueroa Street meets a line following the middle of the Los Angeles River; thence southerly and following the said line to East First Street; thence westerly on East First Street to Alameda Street; thence southerly on Alameda Street to East Third Street; thence northwesterly on East Third Street to Main Street; thence northerly on Main Street to First Street; thence northwesterly on First Street to Figueroa Street; thence northeasterly on Figueroa Street to the point of beginning.

Pursuant to the provisions of Civilian Exclusion Order No. 33, this Headquarters, dated May 3, 1942, all persons of Japanese ancestry, both alien and non-alien, will be evacuated from the above area by 12 o'clock noon, P. W. T., Saturday, May 9, 1942.

No Japanese person living in the above area will be permitted to change residence after 12 o'clock noon, P. W. T., Sunday, May 3, 1942, without obtaining special permission from the representative of the Commanding General, Southern California Sector, at the Civil Control Station located at:

Japanese Union Church,
120 North San Pedro Street,
Los Angeles, California.

Such permits will only be granted for the purpose of uniting members of a family, or in cases of grave emergency.

The Civil Control Station is equipped to assist the Japanese population affected by this evacuation in the following ways:

1. Give advice and instructions on the evacuation.
2. Provide services with respect to the management, leasing, sale, storage or other disposition of most kinds of property, such as real estate, business and professional equipment, household goods, boats, automobiles and livestock.
3. Provide temporary residence elsewhere for all Japanese in family groups.
4. Transport persons and a limited amount of clothing and equipment to their new residence.

The Following Instructions Must Be Observed:

1. A responsible member of each family, preferably the head of the family, or the person in whose name most of the property is held, and each individual living alone, will report to the Civil Control Station to receive further instructions. This must be done between 8:00 A. M. and 5:00 P. M. on Monday, May 4, 1942, or between 8:00 A. M. and 5:00 P. M. on Tuesday, May 5, 1942.
2. Evacuees must carry with them on departure for the Assembly Center, the following property:
 (a) Bedding and linens (no mattress) for each member of the family;
 (b) Toilet articles for each member of the family;
 (c) Extra clothing for each member of the family;
 (d) Sufficient knives, forks, spoons, plates, bowls and cups for each member of the family;
 (e) Essential personal effects for each member of the family.

All items carried will be securely packaged, tied and plainly marked with the name of the owner and numbered in accordance with instructions obtained at the Civil Control Station. The size and number of packages is limited to that which can be carried by the individual or family group.

3. No pets of any kind will be permitted.
4. No personal items and no household goods will be shipped to the Assembly Center.
5. The United States Government through its agencies will provide for the storage, at the sole risk of the owner, of the more substantial household items, such as iceboxes, washing machines, pianos and other heavy furniture. Cooking utensils and other small items will be accepted for storage if crated, packed and plainly marked with the name and address of the owner. Only one name and address will be used by a given family.
6. Each family, and individual living alone, will be furnished transportation to the Assembly Center or will be authorized to travel by private automobile in a supervised group. All instructions pertaining to the movement will be obtained at the Civil Control Station.

Go to the Civil Control Station between the hours of 8:00 A. M. and 5:00 P. M., Monday, May 4, 1942, or between the hours of 8:00 A. M. and 5:00 P. M., Tuesday, May 5, 1942, to receive further instructions.

J. L. DeWITT
Lieutenant General, U. S. Army
Commanding

SEE CIVILIAN EXCLUSION ORDER NO. 33.

"Pledge of allegiance at Rafael Weill Elementary School, a few weeks prior to evacuation."
San Francisco, California, April 20, 1942.

Dorothea Lange, WRA.

Los Angeles, California, April, 1942.
Russell Lee, FSA.

Newspaper clipping of Bainbridge Island evacuees walking to train, watched by crowd on overpass.
Courtesy of the Museum of History & Industry, Seattle Post-Intelligencer Collection.
Reproduced from PAPER TRAIL TO INTERNMENT, collected by Yoriko Watanabe Sasaki.

Bainbridge Island, Washington, March 30, 1942.

Museum of History & Industry, Seattle Post-Intelligencer Collection, courtesy of the
Museum of History & Industry, Seattle.

Bainbridge Island ferry dock, Washington, March 30, 1942.
Museum of History & Industry, Seattle Post-Intelligencer Collection, courtesy of the
Museum of History & Industry, Seattle.

"Grandfather and grandchildren awaiting evacuation bus. The grandfather conducted a dyeing and cleaning business. The family unit is preserved during evacuation and at War Relocation Authority centers. . . ."
Hayward, California, May 8, 1942.

Dorothea Lange, WRA.

Los Angeles, California, April, 1942.
Clem Albers, WRA.

"Thaws at this Tule Lake Center turn the streets and firebreaks into seas of mud. . . ."
Newell, California, February 2, 1943.

Francis Stewart, WRA.

Sign on a barbershop in this small town near the Colorado River Relocation Center.
Parker, Arizona, circa 1945.

Photographer unknown, WRA.

Japanese repatriates embarking for Japan.
Seattle, Washington November 24, 1945.

Photographer unknown, WRA.

Colorado River Relocation Center.
Poston, Arizona, 1944.
Photographer unknown, WRA.

Chapter 4 THE INTERNMENT CAMPS

A. FROM THE ASSEMBLY CENTERS TO RESETTLEMENT: OVERVIEW

How did the 120,000 persons of Japanese descent, including over 80,000 American citizens, respond to the internment? We examine here the experience of living in the internment camps, the various types of leave permitted to the internees, some difficulties encountered both within the camps and upon resettlement and, ultimately, some of the legal issues arising after the internment ended. Our primary lens is the difference, created and enforced by law, between citizen and non-citizen. This difference played itself out not only in the responses by government to the Japanese attack on Pearl Harbor, but also in the political and legal choices of the internees themselves.

Recall that the *Wong Kim Ark* case bestowed citizenship upon those born within the borders of the United States. The significant American-born Japanese population existing by the 1940s reacted to the internment with various strategies of compliance and resistance. And the government's repeated assertions that the loyalty of those of Japanese descent could not be determined contradicted its actions in administering the various loyalty questionnaires in the camps.

Between the spring of 1942, when Executive Order 9066 was issued, and the fall of 1946, when the last of those detained were released, movement both into and out of internment camps was dictated by a series of legal orders. The internees were first moved into temporary assembly centers and from there to ten permanent relocation centers (or internment camps). Some moved out of the internment camps for purposes of military service, wartime employment or schooling. Others were moved among the camps due to the segregation of loyal from allegedly disloyal internees. And, beginning in 1945, when the relocation program was officially terminated, former internees resettled into their previous places of residence or migrated outward to new homes. Much of this chapter focuses on intergenerational and other differences among the internees. Within the Japanese American community, *Issei* means first-generation Japanese American, born and substantially raised in Japan. *Nisei* are second-generation Japanese American, born in the United States. *Kibei* are *Nisei* who were sent to Japan for education. (In all, 120,313 people were under WRA control.[*])

---

[*] Of these, 90,491 were transferred from assembly centers; 17,491 were taken directly from their homes; 5,918 were born to imprisoned parents; 1,735 were transferred from INS internment camps; 1,579 were moved there after being sent from assembly centers to work crops; 1,275 were transferred from penal and medical institutions; 1,118 were taken from Hawaii; and 219, mostly non-Japanese spouses, entered voluntarily.

After internment, 54,127 returned to the West Coast; 52,798 relocated to the interior; 4,724 moved (or were moved) to Japan; 3,121 were sent to INS internment camps; 2,355 joined the armed forces; 1,862 died during imprisonment; 1,322 were sent to institutions; and 4 were classified as "unauthorized departures."

As discussed in Chapter 3, the term *assembly centers* refers only to the sixteen temporary centers situated on race tracks or fairgrounds, and operated by the Army—indicated by the small squares on the map[*] below. From these temporary assembly centers, Japanese Americans were moved to sites of indefinite detention, placed in ten desolate locations—indicated in large squares on the map—throughout the United States. These were officially called *relocation centers.* In addition, the U.S. Justice Department operated twenty-seven other *internment camps*—indicated by the map's crosses—for certain aliens residing in the United States who were considered leaders of the Japanese American community, as well as the approximately 2300 "dangerous persons" of Japanese ancestry taken from twelve Latin American countries by the U.S. State and Justice Departments. Finally, there were so-called *citizen isolation camps*, which were penal colonies for U.S. citizens, indicated by the triangles below.

Historians refer to the relocation centers as *internment camps* or *concentration camps.* The use of the latter term in reference to the relocation centers has raised controversy because it is closely associated with the Nazi death camps of World War II. Linguistically, the term apparently originates from camps established by Britain to intern civilians in the Boer War (1899–1902). Historically, President Roosevelt, Dillon Myer (who succeeded Milton Eisenhower, Dwight Eisenhower's older brother, as director of the War Relocation Authority) and the justices in the *Korematsu* case referred to the relocation centers as concentration camps. We use the term *"internment camps"* here to refer to these relocation centers.

From Roger Daniels, The Forced Migrations of West Coast Japanese Americans, 1942-46: A Quantitative Note in JAPANESE AMERICANS: FROM RELOCATION TO REDRESS, Roger Daniels, Sandra C. Taylor, and Harry H.L. Kitano, eds. 1986.

[*] Reproduced from <http://www.geocities.com/Athens/8420/camps.html>; adapted from Frank and Joanne Iritani, TEN VISITS, Asian American Curriculum Project, Inc. (1995).

1. MOVEMENT INTO AND OUT OF THE CAMPS

As Japanese Americans were transferred from the temporary assembly centers to internment camps, political control of the Japanese Americans transferred from the Wartime Civil Control Administration ("WCCA"—the civilian branch of the Army's Western Defense Command) to the entirely civilian agency, the War Relocation Authority ("WRA"). Created by Executive Order 9012 on March 18, 1942, the WRA's mandate was to "formulate and effectuate a program for the removal, from [designated areas] of the persons or classes of persons designated . . . and for their relocation, maintenance, and supervision." At its helm was Milton Eisenhower, older brother of Dwight Eisenhower.

Initially, Eisenhower favored the idea of immediately resettling Japanese Americans in the intermountain states. But at a governors' conference held on April 7, 1942, he faced enormous resistance. For example, Governor Nels Smith of Wyoming advocated placing Japanese Americans in "concentration camps." He further warned that if they were allowed to resettle freely in his state, "[t]here would be Japs hanging from every pine tree." When alerted to the questionable constitutionality of indefinite detention, Governor Herbert Maw of Utah replied that, if necessary, "the constitution could be changed" to allow for internment.

After the governors' conference, the WRA realized that it would have to adopt an internment camp approach. The camps were scattered through California (Manzanar, Tule Lake), Idaho (Minidoka), Utah (Topaz), Arizona (Poston, Gila River), Wyoming (Heart Mountain), Colorado (Granada), and Arkansas (Jerome, Rohwer). Eight camps were in deserts. Many of the internees suffered not only from extreme heat and dust storms but also from extreme cold during winter. The two Arkansas camps were situated in swampland with inadequate drainage.

In these forsaken places, fenced in by barbed wire and guarded by armed sentries in watchtowers, uprooted people of Japanese descent did whatever it took to survive. The locations hardly resembled the WRA's euphemistic label "relocation centers." In many ways, the camps were prison-like. Internees were held against their will, contained within armed facilities, and were deprived of freedom of movement and liberty. The conditions were less than ideal for meeting even basic needs such as food, shelter, clothing and health care. As the internees settled into camps, they had to make the camps minimally habitable for human beings.

The early hostile reaction of the governors dashed any hopes for quick resettlement. According to Dillon Myer, who succeeded Eisenhower, the latter had concluded from the governors' conference that any "large-scale relocation outside of camps would not be feasible for a considerable period." Yet both the WRA and the War Department alike had interests in allowing the Japanese Americans to leave the internment camps. Some internees were soon allowed to leave under certain circumstances.

As early as 1942, the WRA allowed internees to leave the camps to engage in certain prescribed activities, such as farming, education and permanent employment. By 1943, the WRA had designated five categories of internees who would be allowed to leave the camps for specific purposes: 1) seasonal leave workers; 2) students; 3) those who found nonseasonal employment; 4) armed services volunteers; and 5) individuals thought to be disloyal to the United States, labeled "disaffected" and removed to segregated camps or prisons. The release of agricultural workers and students involved only temporary departure from the camps and was an obvious and easy policy to promote. Thus those who fell within these first two categories were allowed to leave within the early months of their incarceration. The third and fourth categories involved the permanent release of internees into the community, inspiring much apprehension on the part of non-Japanese Americans.

The WRA devised a conservative approach to integrating the internees back into the community, with two basic goals: 1) to infuse the war effort with hardworking, skilled Nisei labor; and 2) to break up ethnic centers such as "Japantowns" in San Francisco and Los Angeles. During the same period, the War Department changed its views on the participation of Japanese Americans in the armed forces. Although initially Japanese Americans were neither drafted nor allowed to volunteer for military combat, the War Department quickly saw the advantages of allowing their participation. In response to these various interests, the two agencies eventually developed leave policies, which in turn generated tensions among the internees, expressed both internally within the community and externally at government authorities.

The WRA designed and administered various leave policies to reintegrate internees into the general population. The mutual interests of the WRA in administering its leave program and the War Department in ascertaining viable recruits culminated in the creation of the "Application for Leave Clearance" (Leave Clearance questionnaire). This application, which more resembled a questionnaire, was given not only to draft-age males, but also to Nisei women over the age of 17 and all Issei. As well, Selective Service Form 304A was administered to draft-age males. Leaving the camps involved the processing of individual leave applications, which was time-consuming from the perspective of the agencies and highly intrusive from the perspective of the applicants.

The Leave Clearance questionnaire was intended to separate disloyal from loyal internees and to facilitate the movement of loyal internees out of the internment camps. However, they raised many issues for the internees and generated tremendous tension within the camps. For example, some of the questions smacked of a continued racial stigma imposed upon the group (*e.g.*, "Will you assist in the general resettlement program by staying away from large groups of Japanese?"), and raised the issue of what an appropriate response would be to the forms' categorical choices. Moreover, the questions were often poorly or ambiguously worded, and had different meanings for Issei (who were unable because of the racial bar on naturalization to become American citizens) compared to Nisei (who had citizenship by birth).

Two such questions (numbered 27 and 28 in the Selective Service questionnaire and with identical versions in the Leave Clearance questionnaire), became highly controversial within the internment camps:

> Are you willing to serve in the armed forces of the United States on combat duty whenever ordered?
>
> Will you swear unqualified allegiance to the United States of America and faithfully defend the United States from any or all attack by foreign or domestic forces, and forswear any form of allegiance or obedience to the Japanese emperor, to any other foreign government, power or organization?

Whether Issei or Nisei, a negative response to those two questions could result in segregation on grounds of disloyalty. Yet for Issei, a positive response to the second question could also result in being stateless—because of the racial bar to naturalization in the United States and the renunciation of Japanese citizenship. Protests from a group of Issei resulted in a revision of the second question to "Will you swear to abide by the laws of the United States and to take no action which would in any way interfere with the war effort in the United States?" This revision, however, came too late for many already subject to the loyalty review process.

Based on positive responses to both questions 27 and 28, some Nisei were eventually allowed to leave for voluntary military service. They joined either the Military Intelligence Language School, the 100th Battalion of the Hawai'i National Guard, or the 442nd Regimental Combat Team. Nisei in the military distinguished themselves by their unmistakably outstanding performance. Their military records were crucial to combatting prejudice against Japanese Americans at home, both during and after the war. Ironically, however, the latter two units were segregated, composed entirely of Japanese American soldiers.

Those considered disloyal based on responses to the questionnaires were eventually moved to the Tule Lake internment camp. Their responses (combined in some cases with a renunciation of their citizenship) later formed the basis for denaturalization proceedings. Those Nisei who answered "no" and "no" to questions 27 and 28 in the Selective Service questionnaire became known as the "No-No Boys." Moreover, there was organized resistance to the military's draft effort, based in part on the principle that people interned without charges or trial by their government should not be expected to fight for that same government in a military conflict.

As seen in Chapter 3, the Supreme Court's 1944 decision in *Ex parte Endo* found that the WRA had no authority to subject a loyal U.S. citizen to its leave procedure. After the *Endo* decision, the WRA announced its plan to close the camps. From 1945 to 1946, the remainder of the internees were faced with the prospect of relocating back into communities that had turned their backs on them previously or that were still actively hostile despite the cessation of the war. The internment caused tremendous social dislocation of the various Japanese communities in the United States.

The U.S. Supreme Court never squarely reached the constitutionality of detaining American citizens of Japanese descent and permanent resident aliens who were loyal to the United States. However, this four-year group detention without probable cause, charges or trial was followed by a legal period of relative liberalization, in which Japanese aliens established through litigation their constitutional rights of equal protection—ironically, established through Hirabayashi, Yasui and Korematsu's failed attempts at challenging the constitutionality of the internment itself.

After the war's end, former internees established their rights to live, work and be treated fairly. Although many more Nisei than Issei were willing to resettle into new areas, all faced economic and cultural hardship. Among other factors, staggering property losses had been incurred because of the hurried evacuation and continued detention. Some Issei trying to re-establish their livelihoods encountered local resistance, such as California laws that denied fishing licenses to Japanese aliens. Moreover, during the internment period, a few state attorneys general had instituted escheat actions (the transfer of property formerly owned by individuals or entities to the state) against Japanese Americans holding title to real property, claiming that these property owners had violated the various alien land laws in effect in the Western states. As seen in Chapter 2, these laws had been found constitutional by the U.S. Supreme Court in *Terrace v. Thompson*.

Many laws discriminating against Asian Americans had piggybacked on the legal status difference between those aliens eligible and those ineligible for citizenship by naturalization. For example, the so-called anti-Japanese or alien land laws applied not only to Japanese Americans but to all ineligible Asians. With the end of the war and of the internment, the U.S. Supreme Court and other courts began to erode the constitutional basis for these laws, in cases such as *Takahashi v. Fish and Game Commission*, 334 U.S. 410 (1948), and *Oyama v. California*, 332 U.S. 633 (1948), both discussed *infra*.

Finally, former internees grappled with initial remedial compensation measures in the Evacuation Claims Act of 1948 that fell far short of the actual economic damages incurred. The Act only compensated well-documented property losses, and that did not even begin to measure the pain and suffering entailed. The period from 1942–1952 thus represents an important transition phase from the discriminatory government acts examined in Chapters 1 and 2 to a period of partial government regret and reparations. The latter did not reach its full expression until after the civil rights movement, discussed more fully in later chapters.

The internment camp period largely preceded the coming of age for the second generation (the Nisei), and the emergence of a third generation (the Sansei) middle class. These rapid post-war changes in social, economic and political climates for Japanese Americans are explored in detail at the end of this chapter.

2. THE ASSEMBLY CENTERS

From March through August 1942, groups of Japanese Americans left their homes for temporary assembly centers, where they remained for an average of 100 days before being moved again to the internment camps. All but three of the sixteen centers were in California; most were located on fairgrounds or racetracks.

May K. Sasaki, Interview by Lori Hoshino

Oct. 28, 1997, Densho: Japanese American Legacy Project[*]

LH: Do you recall any description of what it looked like when you got to the bus?

MS: Oh well, all I remember is that one morning we were told to get ready and get our things and we were supposed to all meet at this bus stop and then I was startled because there was so many other of my friends were there too. And oh, this is going to be fun. And we got in the bus and I remember—see, bus rides were fun for me 'cause I didn't have those things too often, so the only thing that's really foreboding about it as I recall is that there were all these uniformed soldiers around us. And I wondered about that because that hadn't occurred either, but I just thought well. . . .

LH: Do you recall if they were armed?

MS: Yes, yeah. All the soldiers we saw were armed. Anyway, we got on the bus and then we all went to a point where—we didn't go straight to Puyallup, the assembly center. We were then dropped off at another point where a larger group of us were there by then. And then we were all tagged with tags, you know, that told us our family and things like that and information so that if any of us got lost, if families got lost, they could find each other I guess. And at that time, I believe they must have already assigned the areas, the areas A, B, C that I recall in Puyallup, that we were assigned to Area B.

LH: So you arrived at Puyallup. When you entered, do you recall any of the way it looked?

MS: Well, you know it was a former fairgrounds, which I had never been there before, so I didn't know but the one thing I remembered was the animal smells, you know, that's how fairs are. You have your animal smells. I remembered that. That was very different for me, and then the living quarters were of course some of the stalls and some of the buildings. But we had one of the row of stalls and so therefore the smells were greater there. And I remember that there were cots and, for some reason, some kind of mattress. It wasn't the kind of mattress I was used to but and then army blankets. And then we had the bare lightbulb hanging from the ceiling. And each stall is yea big, and there weren't ceilings. They did not come to the top of the walls, excuse me, didn't come to the ceilings. So you could see all the way across. If you climbed up on something high, you could see all the way to the other end, and [your] voice traveled all the way through.

LH: So you're all there together with your mother, your father, your two brothers, and yourself. And in a barrack?

MS: Yes, we had one. It wasn't even a barrack—it was a stall. It literally was a stall, and they told us it was temporary, so they just had to get us all assembled there so that they'll know which camps we're going to. So we had an idea that this was temporary and that's where we're supposed to get ready for this. . . .

---

[*] *Densho: The Japanese American Legacy Project* is a digital archive of videotaped interviews, photographs, documents, and other materials relating to the Japanese American experience. Additional information on the project is available at www.densho.org.

LH: Is there any other memory that sticks out in your mind about that time?

MS: Well, one of the things that I thought were kind of strange was that we had the barbed wire fencing all around the fairgrounds. And there was a road that passed by close to the fairgrounds. And they would bring busloads of non-Japanese people, and they would actually let them off and let them look at us like we were, you know, like we were caged animals. And I used to remember why are they doing that? But they actually came and looked at us while we were behind barbed wire fencing there. That was a little bit weird for me. I just remember we used to do gyrations. [Laughs]

LH: That's the first mention I've heard of these tour buses.

MS: Yeah. Well, they were either tour buses or buses that happened to stop by 'cause we were right along the main drag. And they actually let the people off and let them look at us and they'd go back. And I could hear them saying some things, you know, not quite understanding but just knowing that they were looking at us. So we must have been some kind of attraction for this group to come and look at us.

LH: And they were up against the barbed wire?

MS: Well, they didn't come too close to us 'cause we were near the wire and I think they were a little bit worried about what we might do.

MARY HIRATA, INTERVIEW BY BETH KAWAHARA

Mar. 27, 1998, Densho: Japanese American Legacy Project

BK: Okay. So then, you were all sent to Puyallup, and you were describing, a little bit, about how six of you were in that one apartment or one room. Was it an actual apartment, or. . .?

MH: No it was just a room. Where the grass came up through the floor, well, it always used to make me laugh. Of course, I guess we all went through it. . . . And that's all, the room was only wide, long enough to hold two beds together, foot by, to make the length. So the boys were on one side, and Mom and Dad and I were on the other side.

BK: So . . . I'm just trying to visualize this again. The walls of the Puyallup only went so high.

MH: I think they only went about eight feet, didn't they?

BK: Right.

MH: And so, all the way down, from one end to the other. I don't even remember how many were there, in this one barrack, but you could hear everything. You couldn't yell at anybody, you couldn't scream at anybody. If you did, everybody down the road heard it. And I think, that was the hardest part. Even where my sister was, in a horse stall, their partitions only went up so many feet, and they had a curfew there, so the . . . it happened to be that all the young people were in these horse stalls. So her and their neighbor, they figured out a way to have a ladder that would go over the top, so they'd go over to play cards, and they could get to the kids in a hurry if they heard one of the kids.

BK: Because they had a ladder from one . . .

MH: To the other.

BK: To the other.

MH: Can you imagine?

BK: No. [Laughs] Talk about the privacy, right? For a young couple? [Laughs] . . .

BK: What was a typical day like for you, while you were in Puyallup?

MH: One thing I remember is we wanted to learn the Morse code. We had a lot of Boy Scouts, of course, and so a bunch of us girls would get on one side, with maybe one or two of the boys to teach us, and the other boys would be on the other side of the grandstand. And then we only did it one day, because they told us, "No more." That we couldn't learn . . . they had these funny white hats that they would use as the signals. And after that, we'd look up on top of the grandstand, and there were machine guns. So, of course, we never did that again.

BK: What was your feelings, at that point, knowing that the machine guns were surrounding the camp? I mean, did you have any kind of fear?

MH: Well, I think I feared, but then, I don't know, I figured everybody else was in it. So that wasn't . . . of course, we weren't there that long anyway, only about three months, I believe.

3. CAMP LIFE

The internment camps were hardly the recreational "summer" camps connoted by their name. Although some former internees have downplayed the seriousness of the conditions at the camps, others

> Evacuees could not afford to meet even their minimal needs inside the centers. Sometimes the barest essentials in the Sears catalogue, such as shoes for the children, were out of reach. Meeting their outside obligations, such as mortgage payments, was impossible unless they already had savings.
> PERSONAL JUSTICE DENIED 167.

remember camp life as harsh or traumatic. As mentioned earlier, most internment camps were set in inhospitable sites such as harsh desert or swampland, and their facilities were constructed hastily. As reported to the United States Commission on Wartime Relocation and Internment of Civilians (CWRIC) in PERSONAL JUSTICE DENIED: REPORT OF THE COMMISSION ON WARTIME RELOCATION AND INTERNMENT OF CIVILIANS (PERSONAL JUSTICE DENIED):

> "So much of our work was done sloppily," Dean Meeker testified of Heart Mountain: "We all knew that there was no way anyone accustomed to California weather could possibly survive a Wyoming winter in those barracks. If they were from California, they probably didn't even own the proper clothing for a winter in Cody."

> The Arkansas camps had equally unpleasant weather. Winters were cold and snowy while summers were unbearably hot and humid, heavy with chiggers and clouds of mosquitos.

CWRIC, PERSONAL JUSTICE DENIED 159, 162.

a. HOUSING AND FACILITIES

As in the assembly centers, the living facilities in the internment camps were organized in barracks, composed of four to six rooms. Each room (ranging from 20 by 16 to 20 by 25 feet) housed at least one family. Eating, bathing, laundry and recreation facilities were communal.

Food was a huge concern for the interned population. Unrest at at least four camps was related to the quantity, quality and distribution of food. There were insufficient amounts of food, particularly for those who engaged in physical labor and for small infants whose parents did not have the means to purchase specialized foods. The shortages were exacerbated by some non-Japanese camp workers who stole food intended for internees. Moreover, the kind of food that was offered to the internees initially was of very poor quality. As told to Mei Nakano, "most evacuees, especially urbanites, had never partaken of foods like liver, hearts, tripe and the like before. What the quartermaster corps (which procured camp food) referred to as "edible offal," the evacuees acidly called "awful edibles." Mei T. Nakano, JAPANESE AMERICAN WOMEN: THREE GENERATIONS 1890–1990 144 (1990) ("JAPANESE AMERICAN WOMEN"). By the end of the internment years, most camps were almost self-sufficient in vegetable production, and produced much of their own meat as well.

The internment disrupted the traditional family structures. The generational divide between Issei and Nisei, already apparent from the Americanization of the second generation, was exacerbated by the loss in status of the Issei breadwinner. In the communal mess halls, children no longer felt obligated to eat with parents. Family living quarters were so small that social get-togethers could only be held outside the home. Intimacy within spousal relationships was extremely difficult if not impossible to maintain. Those families with babies were afraid of disturbing other members of the family, or other families.

Inadequate medical facilities and human resources contributed to poor and even life-threatening health care. Dr. Yoshiye Togasaki, who dealt with medical problems in both Manzanar and Tule Lake, recalled that "We had five doctors to take care of 10,000 people. There were open sewers; the barracks had no water, no stoves. And we had young families, many with new babies, and no vaccines, or DPT shots, or sanitary conditions for making baby formulas."

KAY MATSUOKA, INTERVIEW BY ALICE ITO
Dec. 29–30, 1999, Densho: Japanese American Legacy Project

AI: So tell me a little bit more about Jack and the emergency [truck] eventually came at. . .?

KM: It eventually came, but it's one of these paneled, kind of a, they called it panel truck. And, you know, it's better than walking to the hospital, I guess. [Laughs] And I went. And he was the first isolated case in camp and so they put him in this abandoned post office building, which was first used [and] the [] camp outgrew it so they had us move. And it was a small place, like the size of a, how you say now—? Like a barrack, of a half of a barrack, regular half of a barrack. And it had a divided into two portions, a little cubby hole. And then I was able to visit him with a mask on and through the cubbyhole, because they were afraid. And then I was visiting long enough that the nurse's aide came to bring his lunch. And the nurse's aide would just take it and shove it to him and go out. And well, I felt like she, he was a leper or something. And it was really sad. And 'course nobody would come to visit him because they were afraid to, that he might be contagious.

> June Tsutsui (Amache):
> The photograph of my first-born son's grave brings painfully vivid memories of his loss at birth in camp. I carried my baby full-term but the camp's inadequate medical care, including the doctor's late arrival, intensified a complex birth. A better-staffed hospital environment might have prevented the hemorrhaging aggravated by a hasty, fatal delivery on a hard flat table while I endured indescribable pain.
> JAPANESE AMERICAN WOMEN 150.

Probably was. So I really forgotten how long he was in there. But eventually, the real hospital in camp two finally got built up and finished, and so he was transferred. That was a really big hospital then.

AI: But for some time, he was stuck in this . . .

KM: Yeah, yeah.

AI: . . . isolated room . . .

KM: Yeah.

AI: . . . in the abandoned post office?

KM: Uh-huh. But it was, it kinda hurt me, and it made me feel very sad, too, because when I lost all my friends that used to come and see me, nobody came. And then, especially when they, all the nurse's aide would go to any other wards, but they wouldn't come to the TB ward. And that's what really, you know 'cause we were all in together as a result of the war. All fellow member, and it, that kinda really hurt me.

AI: And why was that, that they were not coming?

KM: Well, they'd rather go to other wards because they didn't want to be—think they were afraid. But then there again, I really don't remember how long I helped. Those times just kinda . . .

AI: But then eventually the hospital was finished . . .

KM: Yeah.

AI: . . . and he was transferred over. . .?

KM: So all the wards were all separated. And then you get kinda used to the daily habits. So it wasn't bad. And I, today now, after we got out of camp, my husband and I, oh frequently say, "You know, if this happened when we were outside the camp, it would've cost us a bundle," 'cause he was in there twenty months. So our first part of our marriage we were separated because of the sickness. So we were together three months under the circumstances of living with all these in-laws and by-laws, [Laughs] and then he got sick, and he, we were separated.

AI: For twenty months . . .

KM: Twenty months. Yeah.

AI: . . . while he was in the TB ward.

b. EMPLOYMENT

According to WRA policy, internees received food, shelter, medical care and education without charge. The pay scale for those working at the centers ranged from $12 to $16 a month, at a time when monthly pay for comparable outside jobs could be ten times higher. Token unemployment compensation payments were made to employable internees.

> *The WRA, determined to strive for communities that would be as self-sufficient as possible, wanted to avoid creating a permanently dependent population like the Indians. Therefore, the WRA approach to employment (as to many other issues) became a compromise—expecting and encouraging evacuees to work while denying them freedom of choice or incentives to perform. Needless to say, the result satisfied no one.*
> PERSONAL JUSTICE DENIED 165.

Within each internment camp, most workers engaged in food preparation, winterization and so on. Over the years, as stated above, internment camps produced almost enough food to feed the internees. In addition, some camps engaged in industrial work for "export" products, including camouflage nets and silkscreen posters. Others turned to meeting the internal needs of the camps through such industries as sewing and woodworking.

c. EDUCATION

The internment camps were not built with schools in mind. Initially, camps did not have facilities, including rooms and furniture, not to mention books. Even by the end of the internment period, camps were lacking in basic textbooks and supplies.

Recruiting and training teachers was a constant problem. Few evacuees were certified, because teaching opportunities before the war were scarce for those of Japanese ancestry. It was difficult to recruit outside teachers because of the centers' harsh living conditions, and staff turnover was high. Thus, many evacuees with two or more years of college became "assistant teachers" who in some cases assumed a full teaching load.

In the camps, Japanese Americans faced a form of segregated education much harsher than ever before. Nevertheless, the schools strove to encourage cultural assimilation and acceptance of the "American" values of democracy and liberty. The irony was extraordinary.

d. LAW WITHIN THE CAMPS

The WRA decided to observe "standards of treatment at least substantially equivalent to those guaranteed by the [Geneva] Convention" with respect to sanitation, medical care, housing, religious freedom and recreation,

> if only to avoid giving the Japanese Government any pretext for reprisal in the treatment of American civilians in the hands of the Japanese. . . . [T]here were varying degrees of departure from the literal requirements of the Convention. . . . Thus, the per capita food ration . . . never equalled in cost that provided members of the armed forces.

U.S. Department of Interior, LEGAL AND CONSTITUTIONAL PHASES OF THE WRA PROGRAM, PART II: LEGAL CONSIDERATIONS IN THE DEVELOPMENT OF CENTER MANAGEMENT POLICIES 18–19 (1946).

State criminal, family and domestic relations and probate laws were applied as if the evacuees were temporary residents; however, state licensing laws were not enforced. Since doctors, dentists, optometrists, nurses and members of other regulated occupations were drawn from the evacuee population, "their competency and qualifications were deemed sufficient by the Authority." Although the Geneva Convention prohibited confinement over 30 days at a time and the transfer of prisoners of war to prisons or penitentiaries, the WRA authorized confinement up to 90 days per offense in local jails outside the internment centers.

A framework was established for an evacuee government structure, including election and organization of a "representative legislative body" known as a "community council" with the government functions of legislative and judicial branches, subject to approval by the project director. The councils acted mainly to facilitate communication between the WRA administrators and evacuees in making recommendations or presenting complaints. "Block managers," who acted as liaisons with residential block residents, performed tasks such as distributing supplies, conducting census, maintaining records and other tasks. The government's plan originally included arbitration for private disputes; however, evacuees tended to resolve these matters privately between disputants.

> The police force (known as internal security officers) at each center was directly responsible to the project director.... The force consisted of a chief of internal security, several other Caucasian officers, and evacuees. These officers had the usual functions of police officers.... In the case of an offense that was a felony under State law, the project director was required to turn the offender over to the appropriate State law enforcement officer, unless it was agreed between them that the case could be better handled on the center.... In the field of misdemeanors, the project director could elect to try them as a violation of the center regulations or refer them to the appropriate law enforcing agency, except that, where the offense was a violation of a community council regulation, the offender was to be tried before the evacuee judicial commission.... Reliance on State and local authorities for law and order enforcement in the centers would have been unwieldy and fraught with administrative hazard. The centers were located in relatively poor and very sparsely settled counties ... and prompt handling of the disciplinary cases would have been difficult. Prejudice and suspicion against the evacuees was prevalent; there was a strong likelihood that local law enforcement officials would be influenced by this sentiment to deal more strictly with offenders among evacuees than the offenses warranted.

U.S. Department of Interior, *supra* at 18–36.

e. TENSIONS WITHIN THE CAMPS

As noted earlier, the internment camps were ringed by barbed-wire fences punctuated with guard towers. The internees were guarded by the U.S. Army, which assumed control over traffic and goods in and out of the camps. Many incidents of military overreaching have since been documented. Various internees were shot and even killed, in situations where the military claimed to be preventing escape or never provided a satisfactory explanation.

CWRIC, PERSONAL JUSTICE DENIED

158–180 (1997)

Discontent over camp living conditions was inevitable. . . . At the root of it all, evacuees resented being prisoners against whom no crime was charged and for whom there was no recourse. . . . [However, n]ot all hostility was directed at the WRA; tensions among evacuees also began to surface. Conflicts between Issei and Nisei arose. Most difficult was coping with the WRA-mandated "self-government," which specified that only citizens could serve on community councils. Parallel organizations, like competing block manager groups made up largely of Issei, heightened conflicts.

There were also conflicts between early and later arrivals. Early arrivals tended to be young, aggressive people who had volunteered to open the centers. They were accused of having taken the best jobs, often the level of administration just below WRA staff. Charges of corruption, incompetence and, most divisive, collaboration began to grow.

> *Even when the guards were not shooting, their presence had a lasting impact. As George Takei described it: . . .*
> *"I remember the sight of high guard towers. I remember soldiers carrying rifles, and I remember being afraid."*
> PERSONAL JUSTICE DENIED 176.

The same kinds of problems developed between JACL leaders, who were often favored by center administrators, and other evacuees, particularly the Kibei, who were denied some of the rights (such as student leave) that other evacuees received. Some JACL leaders blamed the Issei and Kibei for camp disturbances and charged them with being "disloyal." In fact, [Mike] Masaoka [then president of the JACL] volunteered to [Dillon] Myer [the administrator of the WRA] that JACL leaders might identify the "known agitators" at the camps so that the WRA could separate them from the rest of the evacuees. Some evacuees felt that the JACL had sold out the cause of Japanese Americans.

As tension grew, anyone perceived as close to the administration became suspect as an *inu* or dog. At Manzanar, a group called the Black Dragons surfaced, a handful of profascist enthusiasts for Imperial Japan. Among other activities, the Black Dragons instigated rock-throwing at the camouflage-net workers and beat those they considered *inu*. Other gangs, too, were involved in beatings. As the leave program got under way, draining the centers of many of the most constructively aggressive young men, the gangs grew.

Finally came the crises at Poston and Manzanar. Although these were the only two major confrontations (except at Tule Lake after the segregation), beatings and hostilities continued.

Incidents at Poston and Manzanar. At Poston on November 1, 1942, an evacuee who had cooperated with the WRA and was suspected of being an "informer" was beaten by a group of unidentified men. Evacuee police arrested two men on suspicion and held them at the FBI's request while the beating was investigated. After the two had been detained two days, a group of older evacuees asked their release; the request was refused. The next day, a crowd of about 1,000 demanded the release of the prisoners as did the community council. When their request was refused, the council resigned. Although one suspect was released after the FBI investigation, the other was held to be tried in the county court.

The evacuees formed a leadership committee which decreed a general strike and organized pickets surrounding the center's jail to prevent removal of the detained man. On November 23, an agreement was finally reached in which the prisoner was released to custody of two evacuee lawyers pending trial, and the emergency leaders agreed to help stop the beatings and try to establish better rapport with the administration.

> As Grace Nakamura testified: "I ran and became one of the curious spectators. The MP fired shots into the defenseless crowd. A classmate, Jimmy Ito, was shot and killed. It was a terrifying experience." PERSONAL JUSTICE DENIED 179.

On December 5, 1942, at Manzanar, a suspected "informer" was assaulted by six masked men. From the hospital he said he could identify one of the attackers, who was arrested and jailed outside the center. The next day a mass meeting was held to protest the arrest. The crowd decided to try to negotiate with the project director, appointing a committee of five. Meanwhile, the project director had asked military police to stand by. At first the director refused to negotiate. Later he agreed to do so and thought he had reached a compromise: the suspect would be returned and tried at the center and evacuees would cooperate on various future matters. Under the agreement, the suspect was returned to the center jail.

Later that day, the crowd reassembled. They demanded the suspect's release and made plans to get ten or eleven other suspected "informers." At this point, the project director called in the military police. When the crowd refused to disperse, the MPs threw tear gas. The crowd formed again as soon as the gas had blown away. When a person in the crowd started an empty car and headed it toward a machine gun, the MPs opened fire. Two evacuees were killed and nine wounded.

4. JAPANESE OUTSIDE THE MAINLAND UNITED STATES

The Territory of Alaska was placed under the Western Defense Command on December 12, 1941. Executive Order 9066 was cited as authority to declare it a military area by reason of its strategic geographic location. All "persons of the Japanese race of greater than half blood and all males of the Japanese race over 16 years of age of half blood" were removed; 145 persons of Japanese ancestry were turned over to the Wartime Civil Control Administration, 121 American-born and 24 foreign-born.

Although viewed suspiciously, Hawaiian Japanese were subjected to a different regime. Of the nearly 158,000 ethnic Japanese, including 35,000 Japanese aliens and 68,000 individuals having dual citizenship, less than 2,000 were taken into custody. Grounds for suspicion and investigation included being a Japanese language teacher, priest, commercial fisherman, or export-import merchant, and many were released without being taken into custody. Hearing boards, which some detainees felt were "pro forma," were appointed to try detainees. Many detainees, mostly curfew violators, were eventually released or paroled without restriction.

In Hawai'i, the U.S. military issued numerous orders, proclamations, directives, and regulations to control the civilian population. Many of these applied to all residents: a territory-wide curfew and censorship of all means of communication, requiring residents to carry identification cards at all times, suspension of foreign language broadcasts. However, some orders were specifically directed at Japanese aliens: travel required the Provost Marshal General's approval, buying or selling liquor was prohibited, no change of residence or occupation nor assembly of groups exceeding ten persons was allowed. Citizens of Japanese, German and Italian ancestry were ordered to turn in firearms, explosives, ammunition and weapons. Many orders remained in effect until the war's end.

Provost courts supplanted civil courts, and the military administered criminal law; jury trials and the summoning of grand juries were prohibited. During the course of the war, however, the military slowly relinquished some control over the civilian government, initially allowing civil courts to entertain certain civil matters as agents of the military governor. By the beginning of September 1942, civil court jurisdiction was extended to jury trials, and the Departments of War, Justice and Interior agreed upon restoration of a number of civil rights. In March 1943, although martial law was still in effect, civil courts were finally given jurisdiction over all violations except those relating to military violations.

Two petitioners who were independently tried and sentenced to imprisonment by military tribunals challenged the validity of their trials and convictions. The Supreme Court, in *Duncan v. Kahanamoku*, 327 U.S. 304 (1946), held that the implementation of martial law did not bestow upon military tribunals the power to supplant courts of law providing established procedural safeguards. The reach of this decision extended beyond the Hawaiian judicial system, effectively overruling one of the major predicates of the decision in *Korematsu v. United States*, 323 U.S. 214 (1944), *i.e.*, deference to the military. In light of the attack on Hawai'i, the argument for upholding military control over civilians would seem to have been more compelling in *Duncan* than in *Korematsu*. The end result, however, once again exemplified the differences in treatment between the Japanese in Hawai'i and the mainland.

> In the sense that the civil courts were replaced by the military, intrusion into normal civil life was greater [in Hawai'i] than on the West Coast, but insofar as military courts operated to find and punish personal guilt, the deviation from the constitutional norm was less than in the exclusion.

PERSONAL JUSTICE DENIED 281.

Immediately after the bombing of Pearl Harbor, a state of martial law was declared in the territory of Hawai'i, affecting over 421,000 persons. The Army closed schools, rationed gasoline and controlled food sales. Under martial law, Hawai'i's government and judicial system temporarily fell under military rule. Presidential Proclamation No. 2627 formally ended martial law on October 24, 1944. Now designated a military area, Hawai'i received a series of security orders and special orders as replacements for the general military orders, and the civilian population continued to be ruled under restrictive orders throughout the War.

Over 2,000 Latin Americans of Japanese ancestry were uprooted and put into U.S. relocation centers. Nearly 80 percent of them were from Peru, which was home to about 25,000 ethnic Japanese. The remainder were from a dozen other countries; Bolivia, Colombia, Costa Rica, Dominican Republic, Ecuador, Panama, Venezuela, El Salvador, Guatemala, Haiti, Honduras and Nicaragua cooperated with the U.S. effort. One of the largest concentrations of Japanese was in Brazil (250,000–300,000). Japanese Brazilians as a whole, like the Hawaiians, were left largely at liberty. Mexico created a 62-mile zone along the coast and U.S. border, forced Japanese to liquidate property and moved them inland to resettle in one of two cities—Guadalajara or Mexico City. Cuba sent adult male Japanese to Havana but allowed women and children to remain at home.

As part of the British Commonwealth, Canada entered World War II in 1939 against Germany. There were less than 25,000 Canadian Japanese: 16 percent were naturalized Canadians, 58 percent were native born, 26 percent were Japanese nationals. The Canadian government employed the military necessity rationale to set up "protected areas" in British Columbia, the home province of 95 percent of the ethnic Japanese in the country, and, with their own version of EO 9066, decreed that "every person of Japanese race shall leave the protected area." The majority were herded into "Interior Housing Centres" located in six old mining towns in the interior of British Columbia and two new towns; almost one-half in the housing centres were under age 18. The Canadian government also employed incentives to move the interned population outside of British Columbia; eventually 4,800 were dispersed into Alberta, Saskatchewan and Manitoba. On March 12, 1945, the Department of Labour published notice that "Japanese Canadians who want to remain in Canada should now reestablish themselves East of the Rockies as the best evidence of their intentions to cooperate with the Government policy of dispersal." In a policy quite similar to that in the United States, the Canadian government encouraged voluntary repatriation. Almost 49 percent applied: 6,966 adults and 3,817 dependent children (about two-thirds eventually withdrew their applications). Before the policy was withdrawn, over 4,000 had left for Japan.

After the war broke out, approximately 30,000 Japanese Americans were stranded in Japan. Frank Chuman describes so-called "strandees" as American citizens of Japanese ancestry who had gone to Japan for a variety of reasons (family visits, education, business, religion, travel) and had not returned before the outbreak of the war. These Americans endured food, fuel and clothing shortages along with others in Japan (due to the long war waged against China). In addition, they faced harassment, suspicion, discrimination and victimization at the hands of the Japanese due to their U.S. nationality. The U.S. Ambassador to Japan, Joseph W. Grew, warned American citizens in the early 1940s of the threat of war and urged them to arrange for return to the United States. While hundreds of Americans heeded this advice, many were unable to book passage and were stranded in Japan for the duration of the war. When the war ended with Japan's surrender on August 15, 1945, strandees applied for new passports to the American consul in Tokyo. Passports were denied to hundreds of these applicants on the ground that they lost American citizenship by holding dual Japanese citizenship during wartime. Their plight is discussed further in the following study modules.

B. STUDY MODULES

Some internees migrated out of the camps almost as soon as (or sometimes even before) they moved in, if they were students or could work as seasonal agricultural laborers. Soon thereafter, the WRA implemented leave policies designed to separate loyal from disloyal internees, so as to facilitate leave for military service and civilian resettlement. The first study module explores these efforts, along with the subsequent segregation of "disloyal" as well as the release of "loyal" Nisei men. It addresses attempts by internees to overcome the presumption of disloyalty that led to their incarceration in the first place. The second study module describes organized resistance efforts in two of the internment camps, Tule Lake and Heart Mountain. It also covers the government's role in some internees' decisions to renounce their U.S. citizenship. The third study module examines the legal shift occurring towards the end of the war, beginning with the evacuees' release after the *Endo* decision. It also considers post-World War II shifts in both judicial and legislative decisions, including some recognition of the discriminatory treatment suffered by those of Japanese descent. The fourth and final study module covers the demographic and cultural changes in the Japanese American population after World War II.

1. ALIENS AND CITIZENS

Before incarceration in the internment camps, no individual determinations were made that an evacuee actually posed a danger to the nation's security due to disloyalty. We examine here the limited options presented to internees who overcame this presumption of disloyalty and were allowed to leave the internment camps through military service, seasonal work in the agricultural sector and employment or education in non-exclusion areas. In all, about 33,000 Japanese Americans served in the military, and approximately 40,000 left the camps for various forms of employment or education.

a. ECONOMIC FACTORS AND LEAVE

As noted in Chapter 3, popular opinion strongly favored the internment "solution" not just because of the fear of sabotage but also for economic reasons. People of Japanese ancestry had established a strong presence in the agricultural sectors of the Western states, leading to resentment on the part of White American settlers. Journalist Bill Hosokawa observed:

> A surprisingly large number of witnesses [to the Tolan Committee] based their arguments for evacuation on the contention that removal of Japanese

would not hurt the West Coast economy. Most outspoken were representatives of a variety of farm organizations—the Western Growers Protective Association, the Grower-Shipper Vegetable Association in the Salinas Valley, the California Farm Bureau Federation, and others—who obviously would profit by the elimination of competition by Japanese growers. The fact that so much stress was placed on the possible economic effects of evacuation lent weight to the Nisei charge that powerful interests who would benefit by the expulsion of Japanese had a big part in forcing the decision.

Bill Hosokawa, NISEI: THE QUIET AMERICANS (1969).

The situation in Hawai'i most clearly revealed the extent to which mass internment was motivated by economic pressures. As described in the previous section, the Japanese in the territory of Hawai'i were not herded *en masse* into concentration camps during the war. Despite the large numbers of Japanese, no massive evacuation or relocation program occurred for several reasons. First, the numbers were too large. Japanese constituted over 30 percent of the population. Their removal would have crippled the workforce and disrupted the island's economy and infrastructure. With their strong ties to the community, many islanders spoke out in favor of the Japanese.

Soon after evacuation on the West Coast was initiated, requests for farm laborers began flooding the WRA's San Francisco regional office and intensified over the next few months. WRA officials realized they were sitting on a large and idle pool of Japanese American workers. Necessity and demand led to the development of seasonal leave—"seasonal" because it was based on the needs of the various agricultural seasons and harvest periods. The WRA secured an agreement with state officials that the workers' safety would be guaranteed; that transportation to and from the centers would be furnished by the employers; that released internees would be paid prevailing wages but would not replace local labor; and that the U.S. Employment Service would provide no-cost housing for the workers near their employment. Workers lived near the farms, worked for a period of weeks or months depending on the harvest season, and then returned to the camps to await the next agricultural opening. By mid-October, 1942 the demand for seasonal workers became so great that 10,000 evacuees were on seasonal leave in Oregon, Utah, Idaho and California. Requests were so continuously high that the WRA was criticized for not providing enough workers.

In addition, even before the evacuation into assembly centers was complete, some organizations expressed concern over the 2,400 Nisei who were forced to leave the colleges and universities on the West Coast. The next leave program to be developed after seasonal leave policy was one to allow interned college students to return to school. From June 1942 to June 1946, students registered with the National Japanese American Student Relocation Council by completing a lengthy questionnaire indicating the backgrounds and aspirations of the applicants. The questionnaire, scholastic transcripts and letters of recommendation were analyzed to determine the students' academic standing, special talents and evidence of adequate social adjustment to American life. If a student received a high rating and passed the necessary government requirements and investigation, the Council placement office tried to find a suitable opening.

In September 1942, only about 250 internees left the camps under the student leave policy. Some parents were concerned about the dangers to their children on the "outside," and many Nisei did not have the determination or initiative to fight their parents about their education. Eventually, the number of students who resettled reached 4,300. The students were scattered throughout the country, which furthered the overriding WRA policy of avoiding geographic concentrations of Japanese Americans.

The first official policy statement regarding resettlement of evacuees was issued on July 20, 1942. The leave outlined in this policy was only available to American-born Nisei who had never studied in Japan and who could prove they had a firm offer of employment. This employment could come from many different sources: Factories made requests for workers; religious organizations helped connect internees with employers; and family or friends outside the evacuated area helped locate possible job offers. The leave policy was so cautiously designed and implemented that many applications for employment leave were denied. Long delays in processing individual requests often resulted in the employment offer being rescinded, and many evacuees simply did not bother applying.

When Dillon Myer took over as WRA director, he initiated new liberalized leave regulations in October 1942. The regulations allowed for flexible short-term leave for personal matters (for medical reasons or matters regarding personal property or business); however, this type of leave was not publicized to internees or often granted. Myer's policies also outlined the possibilities for indefinite leave. In order to be approved for this type of permanent relocation, the applicant had to meet four requirements: that he or she (1) had a definite job offer or other means of support; (2) was not a danger to national security; (3) would have an acceptable community presence; and (4) agreed to keep the WRA informed of any changes in address. Formal steps in an evacuee's application for release began with the FBI security check, followed by an individual application-for-leave permit. Then, individual camp directors evaluated each candidate's work in camp and assessed the sentiment of the community where the candidate wished to resettle.

Although this offered an opportunity for internees to escape their desolate captivity, it was often difficult to identify or solicit employment while confined within the isolated camps. Sometimes former internees who had secured outside employment would send word back to the camps of possible job opportunities, but the evacuees often had to wait for employers to come to them. Moreover, working conditions varied tremendously, with some employers mistreating and otherwise exploiting this source of cheap labor. Over 80 percent of those who left for jobs under this program were Nisei between the ages of 15–35. Sixty percent were men. By the end of 1944, 35,989 Japanese Americans left the camps for jobs available in agriculture, railroad, mining, fruit/vegetable picking and canning, hotel and restaurant service, clerical work and domestic help. Those who left camp in 1942, 1943 or even early 1944, fared better in the employment market than those forced to leave in late 1944 and 1945.

b. LEAVE FOR MILITARY SERVICE

At the beginning of hostilities with Japan, the War Department declared Nisei unacceptable for service in the armed forces, and they were exempted from the draft. Most of the 6,000 Nisei already in the service were immediately dismissed. This exclusion policy was soon seen as untenable, however, as the military realized its need for Japanese speakers for interpreters, scouts and surveillance. Also, the WRA pressed the War Department to allow Nisei to volunteer for the armed services, and the JACL passed a resolution in 1942 strongly favoring the right of Nisei to serve in the military.

In response to the various pressures, Secretary of War Henry L. Stimson announced plans in early 1943 to organize a volunteer Japanese American unit and to require all Nisei males at the relocation centers to register for the draft. About 2,355 Nisei joined the army. Others enlisted after they left the camps under the indefinite leave program. During the war period, 25,000 Nisei were registered, and more than 21,000 were inducted. Counting not only draftees but volunteers and pre-Pearl Harbor enlistees maintained in the service after the outbreak of the war, a total of 33,000 Japanese Americans served in the army during World War II.

CWRIC, PERSONAL JUSTICE DENIED
254–60 (1997)

(A) THE MILITARY INTELLIGENCE SERVICE LANGUAGE SCHOOL

In the spring of 1941, a few alert Army intelligence officers realized that, if war came, the Army would need Japanese language interpreters and translators. After much delay, Lieut. Col. John Weckerling and Capt. Kai Rasmussen won approval to start a small school for training persons with some background in Japanese.... When the school closed in 1946,... it had trained 6,000 men. Of these, 3,700 served in combat areas before the Japanese surrender. Ironically, the often-mistrusted Kibei—Japanese Americans who had received formal education in Japan—proved most qualified for the interpreter's task; most Nisei had too little facility with Japanese to be useful. As Mark Murakami pointed out:

> [On] the one hand the Japanese Americans were condemned for having the linguistic and cultural knowledge of Japanese, and on the other hand the knowledge they had was capitalized on and used as a secret weapon by the Army and Naval Intelligence.

After the surrender, MISLS shifted to civil matters, and its graduates helped to occupy and reconstruct Japan. Despite their importance—General Willoughby, MacArthur's chief of intelligence, has said that the work of the Nisei MIS shortened the Pacific war by two years—these accomplishments got little publicity; most were classified information during the war. Instead, the highly-publicized exploits of the 100th Battalion and 442nd Regimental Combat Team in Europe first helped to show where Nisei loyalty clearly lay.

(B)   THE 100TH BATTALION

The 100th Battalion began as part of the Hawai'i National Guard. As evacuation plans were formulated on the mainland, the War Department also debated the best way to handle ethnic Japanese in Hawai'i. On February 1, 1942, Hawaiian Commander Lieut. General Delos Emmons learned to his dismay that the War Department wanted to release the Nisei from active duty. He needed the manpower and had been impressed with the desire of many Hawaiian Nisei to prove their loyalty. After much discussion, Emmons recommended that a special Nisei Battalion be formed and removed to the mainland; General Marshall concurred. By June 5, 1942, 1,432 men—soon to be known as the 100th Battalion—had sailed. . . .

[After training and a short stint in] North Africa, the 100th immediately went north to Italy, promptly going into combat at Salerno on September 26. From then until March 1944, the 100th plunged into the bloody campaign which moved the Allies slowly up the Italian peninsula. The 100th suffered heavy casualties; 78 men were killed and 239 wounded or injured in the first month and a half alone. By the time the 100th finally pulled out, its effective strength was down to 521 men. The battalion had earned 900 Purple Hearts and the nickname "Purple Heart Battalion." . . .

(C)   THE 442ND REGIMENTAL COMBAT TEAM

While the 100th Battalion fought its way through Italy, the 442nd Regimental Combat Team had been formed and trained in Camp Shelby. Composed of volunteers from Hawai'i and the mainland, many of whom came directly from relocation centers, the team trained from October 1943 to February 1944. Small groups left regularly to replace men from the 100th [in Italy]. . . .

In seven major campaigns, the 442nd took 9,486 casualties—more than 300 percent of its original infantry strength, including 600 killed. More than 18,000 men served in the unit. Commenting on the painful loss of many fellow Nisei in the European theater, Masato Nakagawa admitted that "it was a high price to pay," but "[i]t was to prove our loyalty which was by no means an easy [task]." The 442nd was one of the war's most decorated combat teams, receiving seven Presidential Distinguished Unit Citations and earning 18,143 individual decorations—including one Congressional Medal of Honor, 47 Distinguished Service Crosses, 350 Silver Stars, 810 Bronze Stars and more than 3,600 Purple Hearts. As President Truman told members of the 442nd as he fastened the Presidential Unit banner to their regimental colors, these Nisei fought "not only the enemy, but prejudice." . . .

c. THE LOYALTY REVIEW PROGRAM

From the very beginning of its administration, the WRA grappled with the reintegration of internees into the general population. In short order, the WRA was joined by the War Department, which sought to restore the Nisei's eligibility for the Selective Service Program. The military remained suspicious of the Japanese population, but also realized that many Nisei were eager for the opportunity to defend their country and to prove their loyalty. In January 1943, the Secretary of War announced the creation of an all-Nisei combat unit, and registration efforts in the camps ensued. All male Nisei of draft age were asked to fill out a special questionnaire designed to test their loyalty and willingness to serve in the armed forces.

Dillon Myer believed that a mass registration effort of this type could also benefit the WRA's relocation policies by circumventing the need for individual leave application processes. Thus the WRA and the War Department joined forces to administer a loyalty questionnaire (Selective Service Questionnaire) to draft-age Nisei men and eventually to all other adults in the centers, including Issei and women (Leave Clearance Questionnaire).

Responses from draft-eligible males were sent to military intelligence to decide who should be inducted. The remaining questionnaires were evaluated by the FBI and Naval Intelligence and were then forwarded to the Western Defense Command for investigation. On the basis of these findings, a determination was made whether the applicant could be released from the internment centers or cleared for possible work in a war production facility. This loyalty review and release program was vigorously opposed by Lieutenant General John Dewitt, who continued to maintain that loyalty could not be determined.

Although the questionnaires were designed to help internees and move them out of the camps quickly, they became one of the most divisive and wrenching episodes of the internment. As discussed earlier in this overview section, the two particularly controversial questions on the Selective Service questionnaire were questions 27 ("Are you willing to serve in the armed forces of the United States on combat duty, wherever ordered?") and 28 ("Will you swear unqualified allegiance to the United States of America and faithfully defend the United States from any or all attack by foreign or domestic forces, and forswear any form of allegiance or obedience to the Japanese emperor, or any other foreign government, power, or organization?"). These questions had their counterparts in the original Leave Clearance questionnaire administered to non-draft-eligible internees.

If either question was answered in the negative, an evacuee was viewed with suspicion, determined to be disloyal, and possibly eventually segregated from the other internees. Dillon Myer himself noted that Number 28 was poorly drafted and impossible for Issei to answer because they were ineligible by law for U.S. citizenship, so forswearing allegiance to Japan would leave them with no country. Many internees were angry and frustrated, and there were many reasons for answering no to both questions. As mentioned earlier, the mostly young men who answered "no-no" to these questions were commonly referred to as "no-no boys."

SELECTED QUESTIONS FROM THE LEAVE CLEARANCE QUESTIONNAIRE

reproduced from Michi Weglyn, YEARS OF INFAMY: THE UNTOLD STORY OF AMERICA'S CONCENTRATION CAMPS 196–199 (1976)

The purpose of this interview is to provide the W.R.A. with the assurance that in permitting your leave from this center, it is doing the best thing for the United States as a whole and for you as an individual.

Before questioning you any further, we would like to ask if you have any objection to signing a Pledge of Allegiance to the United States.

Do you object to taking an oath that you will tell the truth and nothing but the truth in this interview?

Did you belong to any Japanese organizations?

Did you attend a Japanese Language School?

Where did you get your education?

Have you at any time been a resident or visitor to Japan? If so, give inclusive dates.

Have you ever asked for repatriation?

Give the names of your parents.

When did they immigrate to the United States?

Do you have any relatives in Japan?

Are any relatives serving in the Japanese Army?

Are any relatives serving in the Armed forces of the United States?

Will you voluntarily remain out of the States of Arizona, Nevada, Utah until such time that public opinion makes you more welcome?

What is your plan for mixing into the community to which you will resettle?

Will you assist in the general resettlement program by staying away from large groups of Japanese?

Will you avoid the use of the Japanese language except when necessary?

Will you for the duration of the war, avoid the organization of any typically Japanese clubs, associations, etc?

Will you try to develop such American habits which will cause you to be accepted readily into American social groups?

Are you willing to serve in the Armed Forces of the United States if called upon by Selective Service to do so?

Are you willing to serve in war production?

Are you willing to give information to the proper authorities regarding any subversive activity which you might note or which you might be informed about directly or indirectly, both in the relocation centers and in the communities in which you are resettling?

Would you consider an informer of this nature an "Inu"? (Stoolpigeon)

Will you accept a position at a lower than standard wage? How will you find out what standard wages are?

Will you conform to the customs and dress of your new home?

Will you make every effort to represent all that is good, reliable, and honest in the Japanese Americans?

Have you been associated with any radical groups, clubs, or gangs which have been accused of anti-social conduct within the center?

Give 5 references of people who can vouch for your conduct in the center other than members of your family. Include at least 2 representatives of the administration.

Can you furnish any proof that you have always been loyal to the United States?

What do you think of the Segregation of the loyal from the disloyal in the relocation centers?

What do you think of the United States in general?

What effect has the report of any Japanese victory in the Pacific and in the Far East had upon your thinking?

Why are you requesting leave?

What would you do if you found a shortwave set, both sending and receiving or either, in your neighbor's apartment?

Do you think that you are "losing face" by cooperating with the United States?

Do you believe in the divine origin of the Japanese race?

What would you consider a disloyal act to the United States?

What do you think loyalty to Japan would demand of a person in the centers under the present conditions?

What is your opinion of dual citizenship?

Have you been associated with any groups whose membership is made up of those who have the majority of "No" answers on the Army Questionnaire?

What, in your opinion, did the "Yes" answer imply?

CWRIC, PERSONAL JUSTICE DENIED

218 (1997)

[A] vexing problem for DeWitt was the possible effect of the loyalty program on the evacuated area. The plan itself was silent on this point, but a Nisei certified loyal by the government could hardly be considered too dangerous to return to the West Coast. If exclusion of the loyal were to end, DeWitt's judgment would be publicly reversed and, particularly on the West Coast, the War Department might look very foolish for spending millions of dollars on relocation camps and uprooting the lives of thousands of people. It would, as [Col.] Bendetsen [from the War Department] put it, be "confess[ing] an original mistake of terrifically horrible proportions."

[] If, on the other hand, the exclusion policy were not ended, then the loyalty review plan would be logically inconsistent. Bendetsen discussed this with Captain Hall, [Assistant War Secretary] McCloy's assistant:

Bendetsen: How could you keep him out of the evacuated zone, if you said he was [loyal enough] to work in a war plant?

Hall: [The program is] . . . going to be limited to the areas outside of the evacuated area.

Bendetsen: How can you be consistent—do one and say that he can't come in the other?

Hall: Simply sensitivity of the West Coast to enemy attack. The reasons justifying the original evacuation still exist in certain degree.

Bendetsen: No, I don't see how they do . . . [t]he plan says that you assume that one of the reasons for evacuation was that there was no time to determine loyalty. One of the primary reasons. So that now that you decide that you can determine loyalty you've erased that reason, haven't you?

Hall: Well not necessarily. As far as the loyalty of this fellow is concerned, we feel that he is completely loyal. But because of certain military considerations partly responsible for the evacuation, we feel at least for the present he should not go back into the evacuated area.

Bendetsen: Kind of beats the devil around the bush, doesn't it?

NOTES AND QUESTIONS

1. What's in a name?: What are the values or interests that ought to be considered in deciding to use the term "concentration camp"? Besides linguistic and historical accuracy, what about the impact on Jewish Americans who believe that using this term makes light of the Holocaust? What about the impact on Japanese Americans who believe that the term "relocation centers" is a gross euphemism? When is it appropriate for one group to tell another group how it should remember its own stories of oppression?

The debate over the appropriateness of the term "concentration camp" turns partly on one's judgment of how bad camp life actually was. Consider the comments of Ken Masugi:

> While one should not be indifferent to the suffering caused by relocation, any property lost, and the proper indignation felt by the American citizens whose loyalty was questioned, one should never forget that this relocation of 90 percent of all ethnic Japanese in the U.S. took place in time of war which involved drastic upheavals throughout society. A glance at the smiling faces in photos of the semi-pro baseball team, scout troops, and dance band in *The Minidoka Interlude*, the yearbook of the Hunt, Idaho, relocation center (where my parents spent part of the war years) persuades one that "concentration camp" is at the very least a misnomer. For the evacuees, movement in and out of the centers was casual. Private car ownership was permitted. Jobs were made available. Provision was made for property to be moved from home to the centers.

Ken Masugi, "The Duties of Citizenship," 18 NEW PERSPECTIVES 3 (Winter/Spring 1996).

2. Ethnicity-based loyalty: The fallacy of the evacuation rationale is glaring when you compare the treatment of Japanese Americans in diverse geographic areas. If persons of Japanese ancestry were disloyal and untrustworthy due to racial heritage, why would Japanese Americans outside Military Area No. 1 and the California part of Military Area No. 2, the evacuated zones, be allowed to live in what has been described as "nervous liberty"? While 89 percent of the Japanese American population lived in the evacuated areas, the remainder were not subject to restrictions on movement and incarceration during the war. Moreover, when evacuees left the internment centers to relocate in East Coast and Midwestern cities, they remained in "constructive custody" of the Army. They were subject to reporting requirements, limits on association and other restrictions. The WRA took the position that even outside the camps, those granted leave could be "recovered" by the Authority.

By the same token, if internment was justified due to the large concentration of suspicious and potentially dangerous individuals of Japanese ancestry on the West Coast, why would the Hawaiian Japanese be spared mass internment? They made up a far larger percentage of the islands' population compared to Japanese Americans in California, exceeded them by 30 percent in a head count and were closer in proximity to Imperial Japan.

3. Loyalty, freedom of association and surveillance: The WRA sought to spread evacuees throughout the Midwest and East in order to disperse large congregations of Japanese Americans. This policy was carried over into the student leave program, which scattered students to various colleges throughout the nonevacuated states. Although Dillon Myer commented that the WRA was engaged in "democracy in relocation," the WRA exerted total control over where internees would be allowed to live and the conditions after their release. The situation was nearly analogous to parole programs out of criminal institutions. As Richard Drinnon noted:

> What [Myer] proposed to melt or boil away was the cultural heritage of his redistributed "evacuees." They would know nothing else but mainstream Anglo-American culture because his removal program set Issei against Nisei, sliced into kin and generational groupings, and scattered the severed members like leaves blown by prevailing westerlies.

> [T]he great social-engineering experiment of rounding up, penning, and strewing was less than half successful from the keepers' point of view. Despite all the relocation machinery, propaganda and badgering to move east, about 57,000 former inmates crossed back over the mountains; only about 50,000 resettled east of the Sierras. Yet the enormity of the scattering that did take place had racist and totalitarian implications of a piece with the antecedent exclusion and incarceration. Through Myer's executive agency the Roosevelt administration told citizens where they might live, what to do for a living, how to dress, how to behave, how to talk, and with whom to associate.

Richard Drinnon, KEEPER OF THE CONCENTRATION CAMPS: DILLON S. MYER AND AMERICAN RACISM 42–54 (1987).

What public policies and legal authority would allow an individual who has not been convicted of a crime to be subject to continuous surveillance and reporting requirements?

4. Loyalty and military service: A major rationale for the internment was "military necessity" to prevent acts of sabotage and espionage by presumptively disloyal members of a particular ethnic group. General DeWitt had insisted that Japanese descendants' loyalty could not be tested. How does that notion of loyalty square with recruiting Nisei for highly sensitive military intelligence operations?

Nisei were brought into the military not only to serve manpower needs but also for propaganda purposes. International pressure contributed to the decision to allow Nisei in the U.S. armed services. Japan maintained that the United States was waging a racial war and pointed to internment of Japanese Americans to support that allegation. To combat the criticism, the military did an "about-face" and not only allowed Nisei to serve but also began drafting men from the internment camps. In addition, a public relations campaign was waged to pay homage to the Nisei bravery in combat. The WRA publicized Nisei battle heroism to help ease racial tension at home. However, even outstanding military records did not insulate Nisei veterans from racial discrimination. As reported by Mitsuo Usui to the CWRIC:

> Coming home, I was boarding a bus on Olympic Boulevard. A lady sitting in the front row of the bus, saw me and said, "Damn Jap." Here I was a proud American soldier, just coming back with my new uniform and new paratrooper boots, with all my campaign medals and awards, proudly displayed on my chest, and this? The bus driver upon hearing this remark, stopped the bus and said, "Lady, apologize to this American soldier or get off my bus"— she got off the bus.

Embarrassed by the situation, I turned around to thank the bus driver. He said that's okay, buddy, everything is going to be okay from now on out. Encouraged by his comment, I thanked him and as I was turning away, I noticed a discharge pin on his lapel.

CWRIC, PERSONAL JUSTICE DENIED 259–60. What does this anecdote reveal about the symbolic and other values of military service?

5. Minorities and military service: Professor Mari Matsuda has drawn parallels between the Nisei soldiers and Black soldiers during the Civil War, both of whom "felt that their willingness to die for their country would help establish their loyalty and worth as human beings." Compare the military's segregation of Blacks with that of Japanese Americans during World War II. Were the same rationales applicable? Was the loyalty of African American soldiers at issue? In cases of sexual orientation discrimination in the military, Professor Kenneth L. Karst has argued that the Court has erred in applying rational basis review rather than a heightened standard.

6. Loyalty and leave: The Leave Clearance questionnaire purported to do what the Western Defense Command said could not be done—determine the loyalty of inmates. As discussed, the original justification for the exclusion policy was based on Dewitt's assertion that a "Jap is a Jap," and that loyalty could not be ascertained. The leave program was a shift away from this original view that individual loyalty was not determinable. Does its creation cast doubt on the War Department's original position? Why or why not?

7. Proof of loyalty: How can an individual prove loyalty? Is it the absence of disloyalty? Can actions be required of Americans to prove loyalty? In other words, should we presume citizens to be loyal unless disproved? What about aliens? How much proof should be required?

What might be some of the differences between Issei and Nisei regarding the "correct" responses to the loyalty questionnaires? How might the lack of opportunity to become citizens have affected the "forever foreign" status and thus the responses of Issei? Conversely, how might birthright citizenship have affected the way Nisei interpreted and reacted to those same questions? We will revisit these questions at the end of the next study module.

8. Loyalty oaths foreshadowed: Notwithstanding the indignities that the Japanese Americans suffered, they were expected to be loyal, productive and compliant citizens. Consider, for example, the oath they were asked to sign upon entering Poston in Arizona:

> I swear loyalty to the United States and enlist in the War Relocation Work Corps for the duration of the war and 14 days thereafter in order to contribute to the needs of the nation and in order to earn a livelihood for myself and my dependents. I will accept whatever pay, unspecified at the present time, the War Relocation Authority determines, and I will observe all rules and regulations.

INSIDE AN AMERICAN CONCENTRATION CAMP: JAPANESE AMERICAN RESISTANCE AT POSTON 34–35 (Richard S. Nishimoto and Lane Ryo Hirabayashi, eds. 1995). Considering the circumstances surrounding the signing of this oath, what moral or legal weight should such a promise have? This type of question arises again with respect to Japanese American requests to renounce U.S. citizenship, to which we now turn.

2. RESISTANCE IN THE CAMPS

The loyalty questionnaires added to the already heavy insult of the internment. Many internees opposed efforts by the government to obtain responses, and some resisted in other ways.

The government's insistence on testing the loyalty of each member of the community may have been an attempt to further dismantle the Japanese American community after the physical dismantling represented by the evacuation. As you work through the following materials, consider the impact of the questionnaires: Might they create cleavages within the internee population along the lines of parent/child, soldier/resister or alien/citizen?

CWRIC, PERSONAL JUSTICE DENIED
192–194 (1997)

It became rapidly apparent that the government had not thought through the implications of the loyalty review program. Not only was the program forced on the evacuees with no notice and with few answers to important questions, but the documents themselves were flawed. The evacuees did not know how their responses would be used. Particularly critical to the Issei was Question 28 on loyalty. The question was both unfair and unanswerable because it called upon the Issei to renounce their Japanese nationality, although they were barred by law from becoming United States citizens. To answer it affirmatively, they argued, would have made them "men without a country." On the other hand, answering it negatively might well bring separation from one's family and attract suspicion to oneself as a security risk. The WRA quickly corrected the question to avoid forcing Issei to make such a Hobson's choice, but suspicion and distrust lingered. There was confusion about the program and its basic intent. The document for Issei and women was titled "Application for Leave Clearance." Did this mean, asked many, that they would be forced to leave the center? They had lost their homes and property; with no assets were they now to be abandoned by the government in hostile communities? One evacuee described this dilemma:

> One can understand a situation of the head of a household, his livelihood taken away, having to face the possibility of earning a living for his family in some strange city. The temptation to declare a "no," "no" position [to Questions 27 and 28] just to maintain the dependent life style in the camps was very strong indeed. In such cases the issue is survival, not loyalty.

The Nisei too doubted the government's good faith and were wary of the program. The same Army and country confining them and their families behind barbed wire now asked Japanese Americans to volunteer to fight for principles of liberty, justice and equal protection under the law. To some, the segregated combat unit, although signifying the restoration of some of their rights as citizens, also continued discrimination. While German and Italian Americans were drafted by normal procedures through the Selective Service System, Japanese Americans were stigmatized by their classification as enemy aliens.

Others had different problems with Question 27. A "yes" answer might be interpreted as volunteering. A number of those who were loyal would stop short of enlisting in the military. With dependents at home and perhaps relatives in Japan who might suffer reprisals if they were known to have enlisted, some could not easily say "yes" to Question 27.

Finally, many were obligated to care for aging parents who were becoming more dependent and fearful in the camps' isolated confinement. If they were separated on the basis of differing answers, who would tend the Issei? Some felt they had to comply with parents who demanded that they maintain family solidarity.

> My father was no longer willing to venture out from camp to a society from which he had been expelled and whose business was demolished. [To him, it was clear that] the questionnaire was to be used to force him out of the camp. . . . The other, the bind that I was in, was to try and make a resolution in which I would pay homage and honor to my parents so that I would not break up the family and yet try to figure out how to give expression to my own future.

The Nisei, too, had problems with Question 28, the loyalty question. Some saw it as a trick question: "forswearing" their allegiance to the Japanese Emperor required admitting that they had once had such an allegiance.

> Not only had our government disregarded our citizenship but put us behind barbed wire, but now was asking these same citizens to foreswear [sic] allegiance to the Emperor of Japan and to swear allegiance to the United States as if at one time all of us had sworn allegiance to the Japanese Emperor.

Then, there was the insult of being asked to fill out another questionnaire which implicitly doubted one's loyalty. To many, their earlier compliance with the orders to evacuate and to be confined in the relocation centers had sufficiently shown their loyalty.

Still, despite reservations, most answered that they were loyal. Some retained their faith in the United States; some felt that, whatever happened, their future lay here; some simply wanted to leave camp.

> [M]y family all wrote "yes, yes." There is a Japanese saying, "umino-oya-yori mo sodate no oya," meaning, "your adoptive parents are your real parents."

> [I]n my case I registered "yes, yes" because I felt that this is the only country I have.

In those centers where good relations between government authorities and evacuees had fostered a sense of trust in the government, a higher proportion of evacuees were willing to state their loyalty. Minidoka, Idaho, for example, had the highest number of positive responses. There, the project director consulted with a number of Issei leaders before any meetings on the loyalty questionnaire. Some of the Issei participated in the meetings, and thorough discussion followed.

At the other extreme was Tule Lake. There, discussion was cursory and no time was allowed for discussion from the floor. When registration was to begin, many evacuees were unwilling to fill out questionnaires. After the administration announced that registration was compulsory, there were still refusals and resistance. Gangs formed to prevent others from registering and, eventually, a group of resisters were removed from the center. Finally, the community council and Issei planning board resigned.

Suspicious of the government's motives and intentions, some saw the questionnaires as a trap. Unrest simmered at almost every relocation center, and isolated incidents of violence or friction erupted. The loyalty questionnaires placed additional stress upon the internees along generational lines— separating those who were unable to become citizens due to the race-based naturalization laws from those who had birthright citizenship. They also fractured the Nisei generation, dividing those citizens who wanted to prove their loyalty by cooperating with the government and those who resisted the sorting of "loyal" from "disloyal." The most notable episodes of internee disaffection and dissension occurred at the Heart Mountain and Tule Lake internment camps.

a. THE HEART MOUNTAIN DRAFT RESISTERS

Just after the war began, the War Department declared Nisei unacceptable for military service by changing their Selective Service classification from 1-A to 4-C—"enemy alien." Like the disloyalty label, this across-the-board change applied to Japanese Americans rather than being based on individual determinations.

On January 24, 1944, the military reclassified Nisei back to 1-A, again an across-the-board shift. The inconsistency of the "loyalty" notion was apparent: Based on no evidence or review, the Selective Service authorities determined that Japanese Americans of military age were once again worthy of and subjected to the draft.

After Selective Service requirements were reinstituted for Nisei, a vocal group at the Heart Mountain internment camp formed the "Fair Play Committee." These draft-eligible men advocated resisting the draft until their rights as citizens were restored. More than 700 men from that camp did report for physicals, and 385 were inducted. However, a total of 85 men were convicted for draft resistance at Heart Mountain.

The contradictions and unfairness of the situation were acutely presented in the prosecution of draft resisters. The defendants maintained that their evacuation and detention were unlawful. They were willing to enter the armed services once the wrong done to them was corrected and their rights as citizens were restored. They also cited first amendment rights of free speech, press and assemblage.

The WRA took the leader of the committee, Kiyoshi Okamoto, into custody and transferred him to Tule Lake as "disloyal." Okamoto was convicted along with other leaders of the committee for conspiracy to counsel, aid and abet evacuees to defy draft orders. The convicted defendants were sentenced to prison terms ranging from two to four years. On appeal, however, the appeals court relied on an earlier case involving German Americans who insisted on retaining aspects of their ethnic identification by resisting the draft. *United States v. Okamoto*, 152 F.2d 905 (9th Cir. 1945)(quoting *Keegan v.*

United States, 325 U.S. 478, 493-494 (1945)). It quoted the earlier decision: "One with innocent motives, who honestly believes a law is unconstitutional and, therefore, not obligatory, may well counsel that the law shall not be obeyed; that its command shall be resisted until a court shall have held it valid. . . ." *Id.* at 908. The appeals court vacated the *Okamoto* convictions and remanded the case, ruling that the trial court should not have refused to give the same instruction to the *Okamoto* jury.

Sixty-three evacuees at Heart Mountain were prosecuted for violating the Selective Training and Service Act. Being within draft age, they were reclassified from 4-C to 1-A and ordered to report for pre-induction physical examinations. The defendants argued that the government had discriminated against them by classifying them as 4-C and removing them to relocation centers; their loyalty had been questioned without reason; and they should not be made to serve in the military until their citizenship status was clarified. The convicting court stated without irony:

> Certainly it cannot be effectively contended that if they had been found disloyal to this country and still bore allegiance to the country of their ancestors they would be thought to be desirable soldiers in the branches of the service fighting for our National existence. When, therefore, they were placed in 1-A and ordered to report for pre-induction physical examination, their pure American citizenship was established beyond question. If they are truly loyal American citizens they should, at least when they have become recognized as such, embrace the opportunity to discharge the duties of citizens by offering themselves in the cause of our National defense.

United States v. Fujii, 55 F. Supp. 928, 932 (D. Wyo. 1944). The trial court cited *Hirabayashi*, noting the Supreme Court's support for the military necessity rationale for the government's curfew orders, although noting that it "does not pass upon the legality of the removal and relocation." Adding to the multiple ironies, the appellate court stated that the defendants should have reported for induction and thereafter asserted a claim of exemption from military service by writ of *habeas corpus*, citing *Endo* as relevant precedent.

In 1947, President Truman pardoned the resisters of their convictions, but the stigma still stung many of them for most of their adulthood. Most internees believed that the resisters were disloyal and should have gone along with the JACL agenda of encouraging military service. This rift within the Nisei community remained largely beneath the surface but for many, particularly the resisters and veterans, ill feelings lingered for decades. It wasn't until the redress movement in the 1980s, discussed in Chapter 6, that some open discussion about the principles and resolve of the draft resisters began. In 1988, the JACL passed a resolution apologizing to the draft resisters and seeking to promote reconciliation.

b. THE TULE LAKE SEGREGANTS

As described earlier, political pressure mounted during the spring of 1943 to segregate "loyal" from "disloyal" internees. Besides determining who could leave the camps, the Leave Clearance questionnaire was also used to determine who should be segregated and who should continue to be incarcerated. The WRA began shifting those thought to be disloyal out of the camps and to the Tule Lake internment camp. This policy would seriously undermine DeWitt's initial premise that loyalty could not be tested, and he strongly opposed segregation. However, members of Congress recommended it; WRA project directors supported it and the primary mouthpiece for internees, the JACL, strongly favored it.

CWRIC, PERSONAL JUSTICE DENIED
208–212 (1997)

Tule Lake was chosen as the segregation center because it was a large facility and already housed many potential segregants. Five groups would be segregated:

- those who had applied for expatriation or repatriation to Japan and not withdrawn their application before July 1, 1943;

- those who answered "no" to the loyalty question or refused to answer it during registration and had not changed their answers;

- those who were denied leave clearance due to some accumulation of adverse evidence in their records;

- aliens from Department of Justice internment camps whom that agency recommended for detention; and

- family members of segregants who chose to remain with the family.

Tule Lake's population and restrictive policies guaranteed conflict there. The first incident was a labor dispute when on October 7, 1943 the administration fired 43 coal workers. No one would take the vacant positions. On October 12, the administration reinstated the workers and made other concessions. Three days later an accident touched off a strike when a truck carrying a work crew to the project farm overturned, killing one worker and injuring several. Dissident leaders used the incident to begin a strike of agricultural workers for more safety precautions. The next week a committee presented demands to the project director including a demand for "resegregation"—separating those who preferred the Japanese way of life from those at Tule Lake for other reasons. The committee also requested physical improvements and staff changes. The work stoppage among the farm workers was not resolved. On October 28, the administration announced it was firing the farm employees and bringing in a group of "loyal" evacuees from other camps. Compounding the insult, food from evacuee warehouses was requisitioned to feed the new farm workers.

On November 1, while Myer was visiting the camp, a large group gathered and the committee demanded to talk to him. During their discussion, another group of evacuees had visited the hospital and ended up beating the chief medical officer. Eventually, Myer addressed the full group and the gathering dispersed.

Several days later, on November 4, the explosion came. A gang moved into the administrative area to prevent the removal of food for volunteer farm workers from other centers. They fought with the internal security force and a staff member was injured. When the rioters moved toward the project director's house, the military guard was called in.

The Army retained control of Tule Lake until January 15, 1944. The period was one of "turmoil, idleness, impoverishment, and uncertainty. . . ." The partial strike continued and the stockade's population grew. Although there were no more major outbursts, the distinction sharpened between "loyal and disloyal," and suspicion of collaborators and informers flourished.

c. THE RENUNCIANTS

In response to the dissidents at Tule Lake, Congress enacted the Amendment to the Nationality Act of 1940, which allowed the disaffected Japanese Americans to renounce their U.S. citizenship. President Roosevelt signed it into law on July 1, 1944. The amendment authorized

> [m]aking in the United States a formal written renunciation of nationality in such form as may be prescribed by and before such officer as may be designated by, the Attorney General, whenever the United States shall be in a state of war

and further that

> the Attorney General shall approve such renunciation as not contrary to the interests of national defense.

According to the official JACL newspaper, *Pacific Citizen,*

> Attorney General Biddle testified that there were between "300 and 1000" persons of Japanese ancestry at the Tule Lake segregation center who had expressed a desire to renounce their citizenship and have asked [for] expatriation. It was stressed that the measure signed by President Roosevelt was designed to deal specifically with the group of between "300 and 1000" citizens of Japanese ancestry at the Tule Lake segregation center.

Frank F. Chuman, THE BAMBOO PEOPLE: THE LAW AND JAPANESE-AMERICANS 267–68 (1976).

Prior to this enactment, no legal mechanism existed to renounce one's citizenship. Ninety-five percent of the total 5,700 applications came from Tule Lake. An academic observer of Tule Lake, Professor Donald Collins, viewed the renunciation of citizenship as a cumulative process, including the stigma of disloyalty resulting from the registration and segregation processes; the pressures of internee extremists groups; the failure of the government to stop or punish the pressure groups; the demoralizing effect of four years in the centers; and beatings of evacuees by European American personnel. "[F]or almost four years, their experience had been of a nature calculated to make them lose faith in America and blight their conception of the value of American citizenship."

After the exclusion order was rescinded, Tuleans also faced the real or imaginary prospects of violence or impoverishment on the "outside," and many saw renunciation as the only way to stay in the safety of their camp homes. Rumors spread in the camps that renouncing one's citizenship would be the safest way to keep Nisei and Issei together as families. Widespread fear of the draft and family separation caused many young people to renounce.

When the war ended, President Truman signed an executive order which made the renunciants subject to deportation to Japan. However, after the atomic bomb had been dropped and the threat of anti-Japanese violence at home diminished, many Japanese Americans did not want to repatriate to Japan. Many contended that their renunciations were the result of misinformation and coercion. Some even argued temporary insanity caused by the hysterical circumstances in the center. Only 2,280 renunciants were granted exemptions.

According to a 1959 statement made by then U.S. Attorney General Roberts, 5,409 of the over 5,700 Nisei who had renounced their citizenship had asked that it be returned. Almost 5,000 had by that time recovered their citizenship.

Wayne Collins, a White American attorney who had been involved in the *Korematsu* litigation, believed that renunciation under detention was unconstitutional. In 1948, he argued successfully before the courts that the deportation order should be overturned due to duress and intimidation. Except for the 1,004 children who were held to have unconstitutionally renounced, Collins individually processed affidavits for the remaining 3,300 adults. The last case was not processed until 1968. The *Acheson* decision describes why the renunciations were not considered by the courts to be "voluntary." This finding is important because a constitutional right such as the right of citizenship can only be waived voluntarily.

ACHESON V. MURAKAMI

176 F.2d 953 (9th Cir. 1949)

DENMAN, Chief Judge.

The Secretary of State appeals from a judgment cancelling the renunciations of citizenship by appellees, American born of Japanese descent, made while incarcerated at Tule Lake. The district court found that the renunciations were "not as a result of their free and intelligent choice but rather because of mental fear, intimidation and coercions depriving them of the free exercise of their will, [and] said purported renunciations are void and of no force or effect."

Underlying all the particular factors so found as leading to a condition of mind and spirit of the American citizens imprisoned at Tule Lake Center, which make the renunciations of citizenship not the free and intelligent choice of appellees, is the unnecessarily cruel and inhuman treatment of these citizens (a) in the manner of their deportation for imprisonment and (b) in their incarceration for over two and a half years under conditions in major respects as degrading as those of a penitentiary and in important respects worse than in any federal penitentiary, and (c) in applying to them the Nazi-like doctrine of inherited racial enmity, stated by the Commanding General ordering the deportations as the major reason for that action.

Since the records of this court show the government is contesting some four thousand similar cases of deportees who are seeking identical relief, we are giving consideration to these uncontested underlying facts, certain to have their effect upon the minds of the mass of deportees incarcerated at Tule Lake.

In considering the effect of the government's treatment on the minds of our deported fellow citizens, those litigating here and many others found to be loyal Americans, it must be remembered how highly educated are the Nisei, the 70,000 native born Japanese. According to the Army's statistical division, Bulletin 11 of March 15, 1943, the educational level of the Nisei exceeded that of the native whites of native parentage in the four Western States. It is not surprising that such eminent educators as Robert Gordon Sproul, President of the University of California, protested the Nisei deportations and the De Witt doctrine of inherited racial enmity, later discussed.

A. The racial deportation. Its unnecessary hardships and cruelty as affecting the attitude of scores of thousands of loyal Americans towards their citizenship in a country so ordering them into imprisonment. . . .

B. The incarceration at the Tule Lake stockade. Its effect upon the minds of our fellow citizens as to the value of their citizenship.

The barbed wire stockade surrounding the 18,000 people there was like that of the prison camps of the Germans. There were the same turrets for the soldiers and the same machine guns for those who might attempt to climb the high wiring.

As if to drive it in to their already shocked spirits that their treatment was to be like criminals in a penitentiary, they were paid the prison wage of $12 a month to the unskilled and $16 to those skilled, while their free fellow citizens, working beside them, were paid the prevailing $12 to $20 per day of their respective trades. No federal penitentiary so treats its adult prisoners. Here were the children and babies as well. . . .

The sole money contribution of the government for its forced unemployment of its citizens is a so-called "unemployment compensation" of $4.25 to $4.75 per month. This against such compensation for free fellow citizens based upon their going wage, amounting in California to $20 per week.

C. General De Witt's doctrine of enemy racism inherited by blood strain. Its paramount effect on the minds of the imprisoned citizens.

The identity of this doctrine with that of the Hitler generals towards those having blood strains of a western Asiatic race as justifying the gas chambers of Dachau must have been realized by the educated Tule Lake prisoners of Japanese blood strain. The German mob's cry of "der Jude" and "the Jap is a Jap" to be "wiped off the map" have a not remote relationship in the minds of scores of thousands of Nisei, whose constant loyalty has at last been recognized, though the map referred to may have been the area of exclusion. . . .

Fear of reprisal if one failed to renounce his citizenship was for some the final pressure causing such renunciations. Such violence continuing over a year is another of the worse than penitentiary conditions considered *supra*. . . .

The above facts in evidence add to our conclusion that the ultimate fact found of renunciation because of mental fear, intimidation and coercion necessarily follows from the probative facts.

NOTES AND QUESTIONS

1. **Loyalty and civil disobedience:** Imagine that you are an internee who is convinced that the presumption of disloyalty made by the military is a violation of your constitutional rights. Attempt to answer some of the questions in the Leave Clearance questionnaire, as well as questions 27 and 28.

Considering the context within which these questions were asked, what weight should your answers have? Should these answers, standing alone, be grounds for removing you to a high security internment camp?

2. **Segregation and due process:** There were serious consequences to internees who were labeled among the "disaffected" and shipped off to Tule Lake. What procedural protections would you want to apply to the removal in question 1? A hearing? Representation by a lawyer? Opportunities for discovery and other fact-finding? A full-fledged trial? What level of due process should we expect under our Constitution?

3. **Renunciation and due process:** Under modern immigration law, there are only two ways to lose American citizenship. One is by revocation of naturalization, which applies only to former aliens who became naturalized U.S. citizens but, for some reason, whose naturalization was later determined to be invalid. The other is through expatriation, commission of specified acts deemed by statute to strip the actor of citizenship. Expatriation applies to all U.S. citizens without regard to how they originally received their U.S. citizenship. The concept of "expatriation" is differentiated from the international concept of "denationalization," in that expatriation under U.S. law requires the express manifest consent of the citizen, whereas "denationalization" is usually defined as the deprivation of nationality by the unilateral act of the State.

Could a finding of manifest consent be made here, under the circumstances? What evidence is relevant to this question? Voting in a foreign country's elections? Travel or previous residence in another country? Being drafted by a foreign government? Failure to appear at trial in the United States? Each of these factors was considered by various courts in renunciation cases.

4. **Person without a country:** The U.S. government deemed all renunciants Japanese aliens. However, the Ninth Circuit reasoned in 1951 that "mere renunciation of one citizenship does not of itself create another," *Barber v. Tadayasu Abo*, 186 F.2d 775, 777 (9th Cir. 1951), and required the district court to look beyond the pleadings to findings of Japanese law on this issue of fact.

In addition to the "invitation" to Japanese American internees to renounce their citizenship, the U.S. government was involved in the actions by the Peruvian government in the latter's decision to strip Japanese Peruvians of Peruvian citizenship. These government actions, and the internment of Peruvian Japanese in U.S. internment camps, are discussed in Chapter 6.

5. **Strandees:** The Nationality Act of 1940 at Section 401 (a) through (j) listed ten different ways in which a citizen can lose nationality by engaging in activity in a foreign state, including serving in the armed forces, voting in a political election, and committing an act of treason against the United States.

Many of the litigants who contested determinations that they lost citizenship based on this statutory section were strandees—that is, Japanese Americans who were stranded in Japan during the war.

The most famous strandee was Iva Ikuko Toguri (later D'Aquino after her marriage to Felipe D'Aquino, a Portuguese national, in Japan) who was born in Los Angeles in 1916. Toguri received her B.A. in zoology from UCLA in 1940 and continued postgraduate studies there with the goal of attending medical school. Her hopes were dashed, however, due to discrimination against female and Japanese applicants. In July 1941, Toguri went to Japan at the behest of her family to care for an ailing aunt. Toguri was anxious to get back to the States; she tried to return by steamship leaving December 2, 1941, but her travel documents were inexplicably delayed. She renounced the Japanese citizenship conferred upon her (which she never wanted) by removing her name from the family registry in the birthplace of her Issei father and, despite pressure from Japanese authorities, she refused to renounce her U.S. citizenship. As an American, she was denied a food ration card, and she became sick with malnutrition and disease. Trapped in Japan as an enemy alien, her money ran out and she had difficulty securing employment. She eventually landed a job as a clerk-typist at Radio Tokyo because of her English language skills. She was selected by Major Charles Cousens, an Australian POW who wrote the scripts, to serve as one of over 20 female disk jockey/announcers on a show titled "Zero Hour," which was broadcast to Allied soldiers in the Pacific.

By all accounts, Toguri did not fit the description of the mythical siren "Tokyo Rose," identified by GIs as a sexy female voice who taunted her listeners with pro-Japanese propaganda. An exhaustive investigation conducted by the military, FBI and prosecutors during her 12-month imprisonment in Japan (without counsel or other due process considerations) resulted in a recommendation not to prosecute. However, the prevailing anti-Japanese fervor and media pressure (led by Walter Winchell and nativist groups) resulted in her arrest and transfer to San Francisco to stand trial for treason. In 1949, after fifty-six days the jury returned a guilty verdict on one of the less serious charges of the eight-count indictment in the longest, most expensive trial in U.S. history at that time. She was sentenced to ten years and was fined $10,000; she served six and a half years in a federal penitentiary, lost her citizenship and was unable to be reunited with her husband, who was barred from the United States.

The JACL, shamed by its silence during the "Tokyo Rose" circus, passed a national resolution in 1969 and issued a formal apology to Toguri in 1974. Along with reporters, civil libertarians, government officials, historians, columnists and other supporters, the JACL pressed for a pardon from Presidents Eisenhower, Johnson, and Nixon. On January 19, 1977, his last day in office, President Gerald Ford granted Toguri a full and unconditional pardon, which allowed her to regain her American citizenship. Speaking to a reporter in 1991, Toguri said, "My mother died in an internment camp in 1942. And what happened to me during and after the war put a tremendous strain on the rest of my family. No, I'm not really bitter, but I'd like to see the truth told once and for all . . . not for myself so much, but so that people in this country will learn what happened to Americans of Japanese ancestry back then."

3. GOVERNMENTAL REGRET?: CITIZENSHIP STATUS AND CONSTITUTIONAL RIGHTS

The cases and materials here examine the legally and socially significant distinction made between alien and citizen. Because of the racial bars to naturalization at the federal level, states were able to pass discriminatory laws by relying on terms associated with alienage rather than race. Yet a high correlation existed between these two categories. The first section below examines the differential impact of the government's resettlement policies on the choices made by Issei versus Nisei. The next two sections revisit issues first introduced in Chapter 2—that is, the rights of aliens to own property and to work freely. All three modules examine the impact of overlooking the constitutional rights of aliens.

a. THE END OF DETENTION AND THE BEGINNING OF RESETTLEMENT

After winning the crucial November election assuring his fourth term, President Roosevelt no longer resisted Secretary Stimson's recommendation for rescinding the West Coast exclusion. On Sunday, December 17, 1944, just hours before the Supreme Court handed down (on December 18) the *Korematsu* and *Endo* decisions, General DeWitt's orders were rescinded. The military finally conceded that "the military situation no longer justifies the mass exclusion of persons of Japanese ancestry from the Western Defense Command," a total reversal of DeWitt's position. Certificates of Exemption began to be issued allowing evacuees who passed security investigations to return to the West Coast permanently. Applications were low at first because evacuees feared community reaction. As documented in the CWRIC report, PERSONAL JUSTICE DENIED, "[f]or many, leaving the camps was as traumatic as entering them."

Simultaneously, the WRA announced its termination policy that all centers under WRA jurisdiction were to be emptied within a half year to a year's time. At this time, about 80,000 people were still incarcerated. To encourage voluntary resettlement, WRA offered incentives of $50 per person, $75 with one dependent, for a maximum of $100 per family. The amounts were later revised to a one-way bus ticket, $3-per-day stipend for the journey, and $25 per person.

There were mixed feelings among the camp-dwellers about the WRA's termination policy. Many internees had heard so many horror stories about violence to Japanese Americans that they were afraid to leave the camps. After losing all their financial security, many internees saw no way of supporting themselves and had nowhere to go. To counter the WRA's push for resettlement, a self-appointed group in the Minidoka camp sent a document titled "Spiritual and Mental Welfare of Evacuee Resident" to the Spanish Consul (who handled communications with the Japanese government). The manuscript was an expression of active resistance to resettlement policy. Overall, internees felt ambivalent about assimilation, their ability to resettle, the effects of institutionalized camp life, their dependence on government assistance, national prejudice and the restoration of civil status. Many Issei were afraid to leave, and Nisei were reluctant to be separated from their parents.

Generational differences were acutely revealed when internees were asked whether they were ready to leave the camps: Issei answered 18 percent yes and 75 percent no, while Nisei answered 63 percent yes and 28 percent no. Issei looked to the government for restitution of their property losses, and felt the government should be responsible for their livelihood until they decided to resettle. They largely wanted to return to former residences in the West, while Nisei were more willing to resettle elsewhere in the United States.

On February 16, 1945, an all-center evacuee conference was held in Salt Lake City. Thirty Japanese American representative internees from seven camps attended. Out of this meeting the representatives produced the following "statement of facts":

LETTER TO DILLON S. MYER

War Relocation Authority, from Masuru Narahara, All Center Conference

February 24, 1945

Mr. Dillon S. Myer, National Director
War Relocation Authority
Washington, D.C.

Dear Mr. Myer:

We of Japanese ancestry residing within these United States feel that the people of this country, generally, have accepted us on the strength of our record as law-abiding residents during the past fifty and more years. We have engaged in farming, commerce, fishing, industry, etc., as operators and laborers, and so have established foundations in this country.

The outbreak of hostilities between the United States and Japan in 1941, was followed, in 1942, by the War Department's order that all of us who resided within the West Coast area, inclusive of American citizens as well as Japanese nationals, be forcibly evacuated. We suffered extreme shock and mental anguish, as well as substantial material losses. The foundations we had created by years of toil were almost completely wiped away. We have existed these past almost three years within the confines of barbed wire fences, within camps located in desert wilderness.

On December 7, 1944, the Western Defense Command announced the rescinding of the exclusion order. At the same time the War Relocation Authority announced that all our camps would be closed by not later than January 2, 1946.

Surveys of general opinion among center residents as a result of the foregoing dual announcements disclosed that fact that due to their present economic status, their fear of violence and discrimination on the outside, etc., the majority were not in a position to make plans either for relocation or for return to their former homes on the West Coast, under present conditions and under currently available facilities and assistance provided by the WRA and other agencies.

As a natural consequence, this, the All Center Conference, was decided upon. Delegates representing seven relocation centers met from February 16 to February 24, 1945, at Salt Lake City. After serious deliberation, mindful of our grave responsibility to do our utmost for the best welfare of 75,000 people, we now make the fervent appeal that the WRA centers be kept open for the duration of [the] war and for some time thereafter as may be needed, and further, be operated with a view to providing residents with necessities, facilities and services on at least on equal level as in the past.

We, hereinunder submit a statement of acts and recommendations with the request that you will accord them your full and sympathetic consideration.

Respectfully submitted,
Masaru Narahara, Chairman

ALL CENTER CONFERENCE

Approved:

Delegate for Gila Project   Delegate for Granada Project
Delegate for Minidoka Project   Delegate for Heart Mountain Project
Delegate for Poston Project   Delegate for Rohwer Project
Delegate for Topaz Project

STATEMENT OF FACTS

1. Mental sufferings caused by the forced mass evacuation.

2. Almost complete destruction of financial foundation built over half a century.

3. Especially for the duration the war has created fears of prejudices, persecution, also violence towards lives and properties.

4. Many Isseis, whose average age is between 60–65, were depending upon their sons for their livelihood but these sons are serving in the United States Armed Forces. Now these Isseis have nothing to go back to so they are reluctant to consider relocation.

5. Residents feel insecure and apprehensive to many changes and modifications of W.R.A. policies.

6. The residents have prepared to remain for the duration because of many statements made by W.R.A. that relocation centers will be maintained for the duration of the war.

7. Many residents were forced to dispose of their personal and real properties, business and agricultural equipment at mere trifle of their cost,

and also drew leases for the "duration." At present they have no definite place to return.

8. Practically every Buddhist priest is now excluded from the West Coast. Buddhism has substantial following and the members obviously prefer to remain where the religion centers.

9. There is an acute shortage of housing, which is obviously the basic need for resettlement. The residents fear that adequate housing is not available.

10. Many persons of Japanese ancestry have difficulty of obtaining insurance coverage on life, fire, automobiles, etc.

RECOMMENDATIONS

We recommend:

1. That special governmental agencies or units be established solely for providing assistance to evacuees who might require funds in re-establishing themselves.

   a. Resettlement aid (grants).

   b. Loans.

2. That the present relocation grant be increased. It should be given to every relocatee. The penalty clause on the present form should be deleted.

We further recommend that federal aid be granted according to every individual's particular needs until such time as he is re-established.

3. That long term loans at a low rate of interest be made available, without security, to aid the residents in re-establishing themselves as near as possible to their former status in private enterprises, such as business, agriculture fisheries, etc.

4. That W.R.A. use their good offices so that consideration may be given on priority by O.P.A. Because of evacuation, residents were forced to dispose of their equipments, trucks cars and etc., many of which at present require the approval of O.P.A. Board. These equipments are essential to many residents in order to re-establish themselves in former enterprises.

5. That government give financial aid as might be necessary to prevent the loss of property being purchased on installment.

6. That W.R.A. give financial aid to residents with definite plans, for the purposes of defraying the expenses, of investigating specific relocation possibilities.

7. That W.R.A. establish its full offices in important areas and employ persons of Japanese ancestry, who is acquainted with Japanese psychology and also to establish in these field offices legal advisory and employment departments.

8. That WRA continue the operation of evacuee property offices for the duration to fulfill the needs of relocatees.

9. That WRA reinduct into centers without redtape those persons who find themselves unable to completely resettle.

10. That WRA establish hostels and other facilities in various areas; and furthermore, build new homes through the F.H.A. with WRA assistance.

11. That WRA provide transportation of evacuee property to their home.

12. That old people's home exclusively for persons of Japanese ancestry be established.

13. That arrangements be concluded so that former civil service employees be reinstated and various former business licenses.

14. That short term leave regulation be changed to permit an absence to two months with one month extension privileges. Also, that the evacuee investigating relocation possibilities be permitted to become employed without change of status.

15. That when an evacuee relocates or returns to his former home, WRA should make every effort to release frozen assets, both in cases of individual or organization.

16. That the WRA negotiate for the concluding of arrangements whereunder alien parents may be able to operate or manage properties with powers of attorney issued to their children particularly by sons in the United States Armed Forces.

17. That WRA make an effort to secure an outright release in the case of a parolee who have relocated.

18. That the federal government assure adequate compensation for personal injuries and property damages sustained by evacuees at the hands of individual or group of individuals.

19. That the federal government assure adequate compensation against losses to evacuee property by fire, theft, etc., while in government or private storage or while in transit.

20. That the WRA make every effort to provide students of Japanese ancestry with adequate protection in case of need and opportunities equal to those enjoyed by Caucasian students.

21. That the WRA make every effort to secure work opportunities for returnees and relocatees on equal basis with Caucasian citizens and particularly in reference to the joining of labor unions.

Anti-Japanese sentiment was reported in Nevada, Idaho, Washington and Oregon. When a survey published in January 1943 asked Hood River Valley, Oregon residents whether Japanese Americans should return to the area after the war, 84 percent said no Japanese Americans should return, 9 percent felt only citizens should return, 5 percent believed all Japanese Americans should return, while 2 percent were undecided. A Gallup poll in California, Washington, Nevada, Arizona and other parts of Oregon asked the same question, and 31 percent said no, 24 percent citizens only, 29 percent yes, and 16 percent were undecided. Chicago and Des Moines were favorite places to relocate because there was substantially less community hostility to the Japanese.

Although the exploits of the 442nd and 100th Battalion were publicized during the war, returning veterans still faced harassment. In a few cases, military service led directly to community acceptance. In August 1946, *The Houston Press* ran a story about Sergeant George Otsuka, who had helped rescue the Lost Battalion, a Texas outfit, and was now being told to "keep away" from a farm he planned to purchase. Public response to the story was strong, and Sergeant Otsuka had no further trouble moving to his farm. Even on the West Coast, it was difficult to continue abusing veterans with an excellent record.

As late as August 1945, 44,000 people still had not left the camps. A WRA survey on reluctance to leave voluntarily showed that the leading reasons were 1) uncertainty of public sentiment; 2) lack of money and familiarity with other parts of the country; and 3) housing concerns. Two of the most difficult problems were housing and transportation. There was a housing shortage in all parts of the country, but it was acute on the West Coast in 1945. It was hard for the few evacuees who owned homes on the West Coast to regain possession. Transportation was a critical situation as well. Plans were formulated to use special train cars to transport evacuees to their destinations.

The administration conducted the final eviction with a three-day notice—after this grace period the campers were escorted out to the train station by the WRA. With the closing of the tenth and last camp, 109,300 people had departed the concentration camps, including 2,355 men who went into armed services from camp; 25,778 men and women who had been inducted as of December 31, 1945; about 50,000 living in areas away from the West Coast; and 57,000 who returned to regions from which they were evacuated. In non-Pacific states with more than 1,500 resettlers, 11,200 went to Illinois; 2,800 to Michigan; 2,300 to New York; 2,200 to New Jersey; 1,700 to Minnesota. A comparison of 1946 Chicago Japanese American labor force with 1941 labor force in Los Angeles revealed that 60 percent of Chicago Japanese Americans lived in Los Angeles before evacuation and most were agricultural workers. A total 4,724 were repatriated or expatriated. Of 5,766 who renounced citizenship, 5,409 asked for return of citizenship by 1950.

The internment deeply affected the Japanese American community. As stated by Amy Iwasaki Mass:

> The truth was that the government we trusted, the country we loved, the nation to which we had pledged loyalty had betrayed us, had turned against us. Our natural human feelings of rage, fear, and helplessness were turned inward and buried. Experiencing and recognizing betrayal by a trusted source leads to a deep depression, a sense of shame, a sense there must be something wrong with me. We were ashamed and humiliated; it was too painful for us to see that the government was not helping us, but was, in fact, against us. . . .

> [We experienced] the same psychological defense that beaten and abused children use. . . . Like the abused child who still wants his parents to love him and hopes that by acting right, he will be accepted, the Japanese Americans chose the cooperative, obedient, and quite American facade to cope with an overtly hostile, racist America.

> By trying to prove that we were 100 percent super patriotic Americans, we hoped to be accepted. The problem is that acceptance by submission exacts a very high price. It is at the expense of an individual's sense of true self-worth. Although we may have been seen by others as model Americans, we have paid a tremendous psychological price for this acceptance. On the

surface we do not look like former concentration camp victims, but we are still vulnerable. Our scars are permanent and deep.

Leslie Hatamiya, RIGHTING A WRONG: JAPANESE AMERICANS AND THE PASSAGE OF THE CIVIL LIBERTIES ACT OF 1988 97 (1993).

MAY K. SASAKI, INTERVIEW BY LORI HOSHINO
Oct. 28, 1997, Densho: Japanese American Legacy Project

MS: I'd leave, when people would call me Kimi-chan, I would pretend not to hear them. I could hear them muttering and everything but I wouldn't hear them, and I figured that's the way I'm going to do it. I'm not going to be Kimiko anymore. I'm going to be May because that is my name also. And I never used my name Kimiko after.

LH: So you were equating the Japanese Kimiko-chan or Kimi-chan, you were equating that with there was something wrong with being Japanese.

MS: Yeah. I think there was lady who challenged me at one point because I didn't use my name Kimiko, and we were doing some cultural awareness kind of activity and she was Japanese.

LH: This was when you were older?

MS: Yeah, this was when I was doing some training. And she had said, "I don't know why you're doing this when you don't even use your Japanese name." And I just started crying. And here I was an adult and you'd think . . . and then later I explained to her how I lost that name and then she . . . but I thought, "Gee, why am I crying about that?" It doesn't seem like anything that I should just get mad at her, but I couldn't. Because I was ashamed that I gave up that name. Anyway, here we go. [Cries]

R.W. KENNY, FORMER ATTORNEY GENERAL OF CALIFORNIA, INTERVIEW BY JANET STEVENSON
20 American Heritage 22–25 (June 1969)

Once the Japanese had been evacuated, did the feeling against them die down?

Not everywhere. . . . You see, there were all these organizations dedicated to keeping it up. Like the California Joint Immigration Committee. That's "joint" because it was composed of the American Legion, the Native Sons of the Golden West, the state Grange, and—for a while, at least—the state Federation of Labor. Their program had always been "Get the Japanese out of California." Now they had what they wanted, and they were working over-time to make sure it stuck.

Even a liberal newspaper like the Sacramento *Bee* was involved. All during the war I remember really shocking advertisements appearing in the *Bee*. Some outfit that called itself the Home Front Commandoes was offering to pay "volunteers" to work on their "Deport the Jap" campaigns.

It wasn't just the lunatic fringe, either. I was no longer in the senate by this time, but I remember being told that a Presbyterian minister had testified that after prayer and fasting he'd concluded it was our Christian duty to keep the Japanese out of the Western world. He was for deporting them right off the continent!

One of the first things we did, now that we knew the Japanese were coming back, was to . . . ease the path of the returning Japanese and to curb the professional patriots.

What were the professional patriots doing?

All sorts of weird and shocking things. You may recall that up in Hood River, Oregon, the American Legion post had voted to remove the names of Nisei servicemen from its honor roll. Well, the city fathers in Gardena, California, did the same thing.

And there were more serious things—vandalism, dynamitings, fires. Oil lanterns were thrown at the windows of an old Buddhist temple in San Francisco where a group of returning Japanese were being sheltered. There was vandalism in a Japanese cemetery in Salinas. They were announcing up in Placer County that there would be no relief for indigent Japanese. And there were scare shootings. I remember seeing Nisei homes where bullets had gone right through the thin walls and passed within inches of sleeping children. One of the worst was an incident in Placer County, where it was perfectly well known who had shot up the house of a recently returned couple, but the local jury simply tapped them on the wrist and the judge suspended sentence.

Then there was that really dreadful incident in a little town called Loomis. A family of Japanese returned, mother, father, and three daughters, and found their home burned to the ground. That time the vigilantes overreached themselves. The War Relocation people let it be known that this family had four sons in the armed services, one of them already dead overseas, and three of the four decorated for bravery. The town conscience was touched. Money was collected, and I believe one of the churches undertook to see to it that a new house was built.

But there's no question that there was a real attempt, with organizational backing, to drive these people out of California. The motives were interesting. We conducted quite an investigation around Fresno, where there was a great deal of anti-Japanese sentiment, and we found that much of it was generated by a village banker who had been a great friend of the Japanese when they were being evacuated—when there had been no time to make arrangements. What happened in this little town must have been fairly typical. Our friendly banker said, "I'll take care of your property for you while you're gone." But now the Japanese, whom he had probably never expected to see again, were returning, and they would be asking for an accounting. We had pretty good evidence against this "worthy steward"; unfortunately, before we could proceed he had a heart attack and died. If we had been able to develop it, it might have gone a long way to explain the economic motives of patriotism in that corner of California. . . .

Japanese Americans lost more than property; they sustained tremendous damage to their lives. The Issei experienced a loss of authority and power. Incarceration dealt a major blow to the family as a social institution. Much of the economic ground gained by Japanese immigrants since the 1920s was lost. Many of the first generation had moved up the social ladder from farm laborer to entrepreneur, poised to let Nisei take over. Life savings of many families were wiped out. Community institutions were dissolved that would take years to rebuild.

Travel permits were required for all alien evacuees before any travel within the country was actually undertaken. The WRA granted 5,541 travel permits between January 1945 and February 1946, as many evacuees moved to resettle in other states; 10 percent of those moving to California were from other states where they had initially resettled, and more than one-third returned to Los Angeles County.

Resettlement hastened change in ethnic communities and caused population shifts. Before the evacuation, California had a Japanese American population of 93,717; afterwards, 48,600. Oregon had 4,071 before, 2,800 after; Washington 14,565 before, 5,900 after.

At its 1946 convention, the JACL launched an ambitious campaign to petition Congress for reparations. Support for a redress proposal based on the number of days spent in the camps was rejected in favor of individual claims for financial losses sustained because of the evacuation.

A number of factors spurred a widespread movement to compensate Japanese Americans for losses suffered due to the internment: a collective sense of guilt and moral obligation to make amends, national pride in the celebrated Nisei fighting units and increased international scrutiny. The Department of Interior also urged the passage of an evacuation claims bill. President Truman endorsed the proposal in the same month that he awarded the seventh presidential Distinguished Unit Citation to members of the 442nd Regimental Combat Team at a parade in Washington D.C.

Once the 1948 Evacuation Claims Act was passed, Congress appropriated $38 million for the program and Pacific Coast offices were established to process the claims. By the January 2, 1950, deadline, approximately 24,000 claims totaling almost $130 million had been filed: one-third of the total loss, as estimated by Federal Reserve Bank. The smallest claim was for a child's tricycle and the largest was for a little over $1 million. Sixty percent of the claims were for less than $2,500, so-called pots and pans claims for loss of household items. By the end of 1950, only 210 claims were cleared, and only seventy-three people actually received any money. Processing was slow and expensive. Only four claims were processed a month, and a $450 claim generally cost the government $1,000 to settle. Moreover, the Act compensated only those property losses that were well documented, and corroboration of oral testimony was required.

In August 1951, an amendment was passed in order to make the process more efficient. A new procedure allowed the Attorney General to settle all claims up to $2,500, "compromise claims," without a lengthy investigation. This expedited the previously lengthy process, and by November 1958, 26,552 compromise claims had been settled for approximately $37 million. Former internees were advised by their attorneys to settle for 50 percent of their loss, and because compensation was made on the basis of pre-war prices, applicants received on average no more than ten cents on the dollar.

Some Japanese Americans wondered if the result was worth the effort. Many Nisei, who had been trying to keep a low profile since the war, believed it was better to leave well enough alone. The Issei were more concerned with the timing of possible redress. A ninety-two-year-old man who claimed losses of $75,000 decided to accept $2,500 because it was reasonably certain that he would not survive the year-long adjudication proceeding. One proceeding had to be dropped when a claimant who had sole knowledge of his business losses died prior to adjudication. Many lawyers pleaded that their clients in their seventies and eighties should be given priority.

The program was well-intentioned, but it was not designed to offer reparations for all wrongs suffered by Japanese Americans during the war. The law was not flexible enough to cover all possible contingencies and did not take into account intangible losses such as the cost of human anguish, the damage to reputation, the missed opportunities and years of captivity lost forever. Further criticisms include the law's failure to include loss of earned income and earning power, the requirement of documentation in support of claims and the other relatively onerous evidentiary requirements, such as the sworn testimony of witnesses regarding ownership of property.

LEONARD BROOM AND RUTH RIEMER, REMOVAL AND RETURN: THE SOCIO-ECONOMIC EFFECTS OF THE WAR ON JAPANESE AMERICANS

125–26 (1949)

The experience of Masao Hirano was typical of these families. Hirano was a 25-year-old Nisei who operated 55 acres in the coastal site with his elderly father, his mother, and his 15-year-old brother. They employed about twenty-five seasonal workers and had realized a net income of $2,000 a year over a period of several years. When the cooperative moved, in February, they had to abandon the house, the garage, and the packing shed (estimated at a total value of $2,300) which they had built on the leased land, their underground pipe and irrigation equipment (valued at $1,000), a crop of peas they expected to harvest and sell for $3,000 in a few weeks, less mature crops of tomatoes and beans, and about $1,300 worth of farm tools and fertilizer which they were unable to sell or to move to the new location. The cooperative sold some of its tractors. The Hiranos took a loss of $700 in their equity in the equipment and of $350 in selling their horses. They sold their 1940 pickup and 1936 truck at 25 per cent below Blue Book value, entailing an additional loss of $300. Household furniture, some tools, and the family passenger car were taken to the new location; the cost of moving was $300. When Area No. 2 was evacuated in July, the Hiranos were able to store only a part of their household furniture. They lost $300 on furniture, $100 on tools, five months of labor, and all their savings ($500) which they had invested in this new venture. In selling their car they lost $400. Not including bad debts and insurance losses, their total assets of at least $10,550 were wiped out. The Hiranos did not have the financial resources to attempt relocation and left the relocation center only when it became mandatory in the fall of 1945. On the basis of noninflated prewar earnings, they would have earned $6,000 during the time they were in the center.

NOTES AND QUESTIONS

1. Migration back "home": Richard Drinnon documents that about half of the former internees returned to the West Coast. What factors might lead some internees to choose to return to their former residences, and others to go elsewhere? What do you make of the generational differences in these choices?

2. Migration away from "home": THE SALVAGE is the second volume of the UC Berkeley's Japanese Evacuation and Resettlement Study, published in 1952. Companion to THE SPOILAGE, this study focuses on those internees who left the camps and relocated in Chicago. The data used in the study derived from official censuses of evacuees, from transcripts of segregation transfers and of leave permits, from participant observation, and from interviews with resettlers in the Chicago area.

What might be some of the effects of being, for example, the only Japanese American in one's high school in Chicago? Can you imagine or do you know of any benefits of being the *only* family in a community that is Asian American? Some of the burdens of that status? Is assimilation a net positive? Or is there a loss associated with the passing of ethnic communities such as the Japantowns that existed before World War II? Professor Keith Aoki describes the impact of being raised Sansei in Detroit, Michigan in the post-war period. Keith Aoki, *Critical Legal Studies, Asian Americans in U.S. Law & Culture, Neil Gotanda, and Me*, 4 ASIAN L.J. 19 (1997).

3. Legal versus moral basis for redress: The Evacuation Claims Act did not acknowledge that a legal wrong had been done to the internees, but rather, resulted out of a moral restitutionary impulse. But didn't the internees suffer legal wrongs? And did the program offer sufficient financial compensation to the claimants even as a limited government act of accountability?

4. Limits of proof: As Broom and Riemer point out, the lack of evidence available to corroborate losses was attributable to cultural factors as well as the circumstances surrounding the evacuation. They concluded:

> The lack of documentary evidence for the details of how, when, and where each item of loss occurred will surprise no one familiar with the prewar Japanese American community and with the history of the Evacuation. Oral contracts in business were the rule. Violations by other Japanese Americans were handled within the community; dealings with non-Japanese were mostly on a cash basis. When evacuee debtors defaulted on contracts because their income was cut off by Evacuation, Japanese American creditors often had no written documents for their claims. Panic sales and even well-considered sacrifice sales of furniture, equipment, businesses, and farms were often made without itemized receipts, so that no written evidence exists to prove each instance of sale made below real value. Property was often left with non-Japanese friends or neighbors for protection or administration under informal oral agreements. And although some of these agreements worked well, many resulted in theft, misappropriation, fraud, and other violations of trust so aptly summarized by evacuees as "swindle." Others turned out badly not because of malicious intent but because of changes in the lives of the caretakers themselves. Inevitably, much of the documentary evidence evacuees did have immediately after Evacuation was

lost or misplaced in the years of movement and makeshift living arrangements.

Broom and Riemer, *supra* at 155-56.

b. THE RIGHT TO WORK REVISITED

As related in Chapter 2, Asian Americans were not treated as equals with regard to their right to work. Prior to evacuation, the JACL actively lobbied against California initiatives to restrict the rights of aliens to engage in commercial fishing. But with the Japanese American advocates out of the way, two measures that denied Japanese aliens the right to obtain fishing licenses were passed in 1943 and 1945. The regulations were an added effort to dissuade evacuees from returning to California from the internment camps. The licensing laws severely affected the Japanese Americans likely to return to the industry, particularly many Issei whose pre-internment livelihood was fishing. Torao Takahashi was an Issei who had engaged in commercial fishing in California from 1915 to 1941. After he left Manzanar in 1945, he sought to resume his lifelong occupation but was denied his fishing license. Takahashi filed suit against the Fish and Game Commission.

TAKAHASHI V. FISH AND GAME COMMISSION
334 U.S. 410 (1948)

Mr. Justice BLACK delivered the opinion of the Court.
The question presented is whether California can, consistently with the Federal Constitution and laws passed pursuant to it, use this federally created racial ineligibility for citizenship as a basis for barring Takahashi from earning his living as a commercial fisherman in the ocean waters off the coast of California.

Prior to 1943 California issued commercial fishing licenses to all qualified persons without regard to alienage or ineligibility to citizenship.... In 1943, during the period of war and evacuation, an amendment to the California Fish and Game Code was adopted prohibiting issuance of a license to any "alien Japanese." In 1945, the state code was again amended by striking the 1943 provision for fear that it might be "declared unconstitutional" because directed only "against alien Japanese," the new amendment banned issuance of licenses to any "person ineligible to citizenship," which classification included Japanese.[*] Because of this state provision barring issuance of com-

---

[*] As amended the code section now reads: "*Persons required to procure license: To whom issuable.* Every person who uses or operates or assists in using or operating any boat, net, trap, line, or other appliance to take fish, mollusks or crustaceans for profit, or who brings or causes fish, mollusks or crustaceans to be brought ashore at any point in the State for the purpose of selling the same in a fresh state, shall procure a commercial fishing license.

"A commercial fishing license may be issued to any person other than a person ineligible to citizenship. A commercial fishing license may be issued to a corporation only if said corporation is authorized to do business in this State, if none of the officers or directors thereof are persons ineligible to citizenship, and if less than the majority of each class

mercial fishing licenses to persons ineligible for citizenship under federal law, Takahashi, who met all other state requirements, was denied a license by the California Fish and Game Commission upon his return to California in 1945.

First. The state's contention that its law was passed solely as a fish conservation measure is vigorously denied. The petitioner argues that it was the outgrowth of racial antagonism directed solely against the Japanese, and that for this reason alone it cannot stand. *See Korematsu* v. *United States, Yick Wo* v. *Hopkins*. We find it unnecessary to resolve this controversy concerning the motives that prompted enactment of the legislation. Accordingly, for purposes of our decision we may assume that the code provision was passed to conserve fish in the California coastal waters, or to protect California citizens engaged in commercial fishing from competition by Japanese aliens, or for both reasons.

Second. It does not follow, as California seems to argue that because the United States regulates immigration and naturalization in part on the basis of race and color classifications, a state can adopt one or more of the same classifications to prevent lawfully admitted aliens within its borders from earning a living in the same way that other state inhabitants earn their living. The Federal Government has broad constitutional powers in determining what aliens shall be admitted to the United States, the period they may remain, regulation of their conduct before naturalization, and the terms and conditions of their naturalization. State laws which impose discriminatory burdens upon the entrance or residence of aliens lawfully within the United States conflict with this constitutionally derived federal power to regulate immigration, and have accordingly been held invalid. Moreover, Congress, in the enactment of a comprehensive legislative plan for the nation-wide control and regulation of immigration and naturalization, has broadly provided:

> All persons within the jurisdiction of the United States shall have the same right in every State and Territory to make and enforce contracts, to sue, be parties, give evidence, and to the full and equal benefit of all laws and proceedings for the security of persons and property as is enjoyed by white citizens, and shall be subject to like punishment, pains, penalties, taxes, licenses, and exactions of every kind, and to no other.

16 Stat. 140, 144, 8 U.S.C. § 41.

The protection of this section has been held to extend to aliens as well as to citizens. Consequently the section and the Fourteenth Amendment on which it rests in part protect "all persons" against state legislation bearing unequally upon them either because of alienage or color. The Fourteenth Amendment and the laws adopted under its authority thus embody a general policy that all persons lawfully in this country shall abide "in any state" on an equality of legal privileges with all citizens under non-discriminatory laws.

---

of stockholders thereof are persons ineligible to citizenship." Cal. Fish and Game Code, § 990. In 1947 the code was amended to permit "any person, not a citizen of the United States," to obtain hunting and sport fishing licenses, both of which had been denied to "alien Japanese" and to persons "ineligible to citizenship" under the 1943 and 1945 amendments. Cal.Stats.1947, c. 1329, Cal. Fish and Game Code §§ 427, 428.

All of the foregoing emphasizes the tenuousness of the state's claim that it has power to single out and ban its lawful alien inhabitants, and particularly certain racial and color groups within this class of inhabitants, from following a vocation simply because Congress has put some such groups in special classifications in exercise of its broad and wholly distinguishable powers over immigration and naturalization. The state's law here cannot be supported in the employment of this legislative authority because of policies adopted by Congress in the exercise of its power to treat separately and differently with aliens from countries composed of peoples of many diverse cultures, races, and colors. For these reasons the power of a state to apply its laws exclusively to its alien inhabitants as a class is confined within narrow limits.

Mr. Justice MURPHY, with whom Mr. Justice RUTLEDGE agrees, concurring.

The opinion of the Court, in which I join, adequately expresses my views as to all but one important aspect of this case. That aspect relates to the fact that § 990 of the California Fish and Game Code, barring those ineligible to citizenship from securing commercial fishing licenses, is the direct outgrowth of antagonism toward persons of Japanese ancestry. Even the most cursory examination of the background of the statute demonstrates that it was designed solely to discriminate against such persons in a manner inconsistent with the concept of equal protection of the laws. Legislation of that type is not entitled to wear the cloak of constitutionality.

The statute in question is but one more manifestation of the anti-Japanese fever which has been evident in California in varying degrees since the turn of the century. *See* dissenting opinion in *Korematsu*. That fever, of course, is traceable to the refusal or the inability of certain groups to adjust themselves economically and socially relative to residents of Japanese ancestry. For some years prior to the Japanese attack on Pearl Harbor, these protagonists of intolerance had been leveling unfounded accusations and innuendoes against Japanese fishing crews operating off the coast of California. These fishermen numbered about a thousand and most of them had long resided in that state. It was claimed that they were engaged not only in fishing but in espionage and other illicit activities on behalf of the Japanese Government. As war with Japan approached and finally became a reality, these charges were repeated with increasing vigor. Yet full investigations by appropriate authorities failed to reveal any competent supporting evidence; not even one Japanese fisherman was arrested for alleged espionage. Such baseless accusations can only be viewed as an integral part of the long campaign to undermine the reputation of persons of Japanese background and to discourage their residence in California.

More specifically, these accusations were used to secure the passage of discriminatory fishing legislation. But such legislation was not immediately forthcoming. The continued presence in California of the Japanese fishermen without the occurrence of any untoward incidents on their part served for a time as adequate and living refutation of the propaganda. Then came the evacuation of all persons of Japanese ancestry from the West Coast. *See Korematsu*. Once evacuation was achieved, an intensive campaign was begun to prevent the return to California of the evacuees. All of the old charges, including the ones relating to the fishermen, were refurbished and augmented. This time the Japanese were absent and were unable to provide effective opposition. The winds of racial animosity blew unabated.

During the height of this racial storm in 1943, numerous anti-Japanese bills were considered by the California legislators. Several amendments to the Alien Land Law were enacted. And § 990 of the Fish and Game Code was altered to provide that "A commercial fishing license may be issued to any person other than an alien Japanese." No pretense was made that this alteration was in the interests of conservation. It was made at a time when all alien Japanese were excluded from California, with no immediate return indicated; thus the banning of fishing licenses for them could have no early effect upon the conservation of fish.

These circumstances only confirm the obvious fact that the 1943 amendment to § 990 was intended to discourage the return to California of Japanese aliens. By taking away their commercial fishing rights, the lives of those aliens who plied the fisherman's trade would be made more difficult and unremunerative. And the non-Japanese fishermen would thereby be free from the competition afforded by these aliens. The equal protection clause of the Fourteenth Amendment, however, does not permit a state to discriminate against resident aliens in such a fashion, whether the purpose be to give effect to racial animosity or to protect the competitive interests of other residents.

The 1945 amendment to § 990 which is now before us stands in no better position than the 1943 amendment. This later alteration eliminated the reference to "alien Japanese" and substituted therefor "a person ineligible to citizenship." Adoption of this change also occurred during a period when anti-Japanese agitation in California had reached one of its periodic peaks. The announcement of the end of the Japanese exclusion orders, plus this Court's decision in *Ex parte Endo*, made the return to California of many of the evacuees a reasonable certainty. The prejudices, the antagonisms and the hatreds were once again aroused, punctuated this time by numerous acts of violence against the returning Japanese Americans. Another wave of anti-Japanese proposals marked the 1945 legislative session. It was in this setting that the amendment to § 990 was proposed and enacted in 1945.

It is of interest and significance that the amendment in question was proposed by a legislative committee devoted to Japanese resettlement problems, not by a committee concerned with the conservation of fish.

We should not blink at the fact that § 990, as now written, is a discriminatory piece of legislation having no relation whatever to any constitutionally cognizable interest of California. It was drawn against a background of racial and economic tension. It is directed in spirit and in effect solely against aliens of Japanese birth. It denies them commercial fishing rights not because they threaten the success of any conservation program, not because their fishing activities constitute a clear and present danger to the welfare of California or of the nation, but only because they are of Japanese stock, a stock which has had the misfortune to arouse antagonism among certain powerful interests. We need but unbutton the seemingly innocent words of § 990 to discover beneath them the very negation of all the ideals of the equal protection clause. No more is necessary

protection clause. No more is necessary to warrant a reversal of the judgment below.

NOTES AND QUESTIONS

1. Aliens and legal restrictions on work: As seen in Chapter 2, Asian Americans repeatedly have encountered formal legal barriers to pursuing employment opportunities in the United States. Yet both the *Yick Wo* and the *Takahashi* decisions vindicate the right of Asians in America to be free of government restrictions on earning livelihoods.

In both cases, the language of the law was not facially race-based: In *Yick Wo*, the city ordinance was directed toward wooden laundries and in *Takahashi* the state code addressed "persons ineligible for citizenship." Yet the Court both times was willing to pierce the plain text of the law in order to find the race-based animus underlying the restrictions. In *Takahashi* the Court was aided by an earlier version of the same statute that included the term "alien Japanese." If this earlier version had not existed, would it have been proper for the Court to find a racial basis to the California state code barring a "person ineligible for citizenship" from obtaining a fishing license? Put another way, how much historical context should the Court consider when analyzing a legal restriction based on race? Does the majority opinion rely too little or too much on historical context, as opposed to technical legal reasoning? Does Justice Murphy's concurrence properly draw upon social and political context to support his legal conclusions? Do the differences in their approaches matter, given that they reached the same bottom line?

2. Economic motivations: Justice Murphy's concurring opinion suggests that the actions to prevent land ownership and fishing by Japanese aliens were motivated by greed, economic competition, and desire to keep resources out of the hands of Japanese residents. What evidence supports that view, other than that in his opinion?

3. The fourteenth amendment and judicial interests: What may have motivated the Court to engage in an expansive reading of the fourteenth amendment, given its contracted interpretation in the earlier internment decisions? In retrospect, how critical should we be of the Court's about-face here? In answering this question, you may want to review the notes and questions following the right to work study module in Chapter 2, *supra*.

4. Aliens and government benefits: Should aliens in the United States generally receive the same treatment as citizens or only as to earning a livelihood? What about welfare benefits? Subsidized health care? Public education? Is there a valid distinction between aliens and citizens with regard to government benefits?

Both the California alien land law and the more recent Proposition 187 were the result of voter initiatives. A federal court struck down California's Proposition 187, a ballot initiative that restricted or completely denied government services to illegal immigrants. *League of United Latin Am. Citizens v. Wilson*, 906 F. Supp. 755 (C.D. Cal. 1995), *aff'd.*, 131 F.3d 1297 (9th Cir. 1997). After a five-year-long legal and political struggle, California's Governor Gray Davis announced that he has agreed not to appeal the court's decision. In the interim, he had angered some Proposition 187 supporters by mediating a settlement of the litigation that challenged the ballot initiative, leading to the charge that the people's will was being thwarted by executive action.

c. THE RIGHT TO OWN PROPERTY REVISITED

Life was difficult for the reintegrating Japanese Americans. Many were unable to go back to their land and communities, but they still faced lingering suspicion and economic hardship. The tensions only gradually dissipated. Some found the atmosphere just as hostile as when the evacuation was first initiated. Most Issei and Nisei acted cautiously, tried to keep a low profile within their community and stayed clear of anything Japanese. Some vigorously sought to become involved in what they perceived as typical American activities. As Valerie J. Matsumoto notes, "[l]oss of confidence, denial, and internalized anger, all compounded by the government's assimilationist policies of resettlement and by public suspicion, spurred many Japanese Americans to make strenuous efforts to prove themselves loyal, nonthreatening citizens."

In addition to numerous acts of violence, harassment and intimidation, returnees faced antagonistic economic actions such as boycotts. Signs proclaiming "No Jap Trade Wanted" appeared. Hostility was rampant in Northern Utah, considered off limits to new resettlers as the number of Japanese Americans pushed the limit of locals' tolerance. Many in California opposed the return of the evacuees, based on fear as well as on economics. Terrorism was so rampant in some rural areas that Dillon Myer believed there might be some planned campaign to frighten Japanese American agriculturalists away, making their lands available for European American competitors. However, returning evacuees received no concrete protection or aid from the WRA.

The WRA Property Officer estimated that about $200 million worth of personal and real property was owned by the evacuees at the time of evacuation. What happened to most of that real property while the owners were interned? For most of the population, less then a week elapsed between notice of evacuation and their forced removal. Sometimes only forty-eight hours were allowed for the sale, rental, loan, storage or even gift of real property and possessions. The condition of the returning internees' homes and farms varied according to the good will of the tenants. Some evacuees who had good friends running their farms found their belongings intact and their lands well kept. But more often, they returned to jimmied locks, stolen possessions, overgrown weeds and run-down land. Farmers who had leased lands before the war often lost their leases and had to do farm labor for other operators. Many landless farmers were forced to move to the cities to do gardening work.

In cases involving property interests in land, many evacuees lost valuable leases for farming acres or faced fraudulent contract terms. Many were forced to defend against government-initiated lawsuits to revert property ownership to the state under the alien land laws. According to a leading treatise writer, the term "escheat"... "refers to several bodies of law that provide for the transfer of property formerly owned by individuals or entities to the state or another designated governmental entity."

In 1940, the value of the 5,135 farms in California owned by people of Japanese descent was approximately $66 million. The war brought an increase in the value of land and crops, so those who could prove the deeds were illegal enjoyed a windfall. At least forty cases were filed by the end of 1945. Some Nisei viewed these actions as legal intimidation to discourage evacuee farmers from returning to the California agricultural industry. Many escheat actions went uncontested, as some of the owners were interned and without the funds to defend against the proceedings. In all, seventy-nine escheat proceedings were instituted after Pearl Harbor.

When the evacuation order was rescinded, many of the West Coast states responded by strengthening or enforcing existing alien land laws, discussed earlier in Chapter 2. For example, the Oregon legislature amended its law in March of 1945 to prevent Japanese aliens from living on or using land purchased in the name of a citizen relative. (In that same month, however, a Portland court was the first to order the return to a Nisei lands leased to a European American during the evacuation period.) With voter approval via referendum, the California attorney general continued a vigorous program to remove Japanese farmers by instigating escheat proceedings.

In defending actions based on alien land laws, Japanese Americans relied heavily on the fourteenth amendment and its guarantee of due process and of equal protection. *Yick Wo v. Hopkins*, discussed in Chapter 2, had already established that the guarantees of that amendment extended to all persons within the territorial jurisdiction of the United States, without regard to differences of race, color or nationality. And *Hirabayashi* and *Korematsu*, discussed in Chapter 3, marked the beginning of the strict scrutiny doctrine. But these principles were not consistently applied to race-based classifications until the late 1940s.

After the evacuees began returning to the West Coast, the JACL, with the help of other sympathetic attorneys, began to defend their property rights against land seizure proceedings.

Oyama v. California
332 U.S. 633 (1948)

Mr. Chief Justice Vinson delivered the opinion of the Court.

Petitioners challenge the constitutionality of California's Alien Land Law as it has been applied in this case to effect an escheat of two small parcels of agricultural land. One of the petitioners is Fred Oyama, a minor American citizen in whose name title was taken. The other is his father and guardian, Kajiro Oyama, a Japanese citizen not eligible for naturalization, who paid the purchase price. Petitioners press three attacks on the Alien Land Law as it has been applied in this case: first, that it deprives Fred Oyama of the equal protection of the laws and of his privileges as an American citizen; secondly, that it denies Kajiro Oyama equal protection of the laws; and, thirdly, that it contravenes the due process clause by sanctioning a taking of property after expiration of the applicable limitations period.

In broad outline, the Alien Land Law forbids aliens ineligible for American citizenship to acquire, own, occupy, lease, or transfer agricultural land. It also provides that any property acquired in violation of the statute shall escheat as of the date of acquisition and that the same result shall follow any transfer made with "intent to prevent, evade or avoid" escheat. In addition, that intent is presumed, *prima facie*, whenever an ineligible alien pays the consideration for a transfer to a citizen or eligible alien.

The first of the two parcels in question, consisting of six acres of agricultural land in southern California, was purchased in 1934, when Fred Oyama was six years old. Kajiro Oyama paid the $4,000 consideration, and the seller executed a deed to Fred.

Some six months later, the father petitioned the Superior Court for San Diego County to be appointed Fred's guardian, stating that Fred owned the six acres. After a hearing, the court found the allegations of the petition true and Kajiro Oyama "a competent and proper person" to be appointed Fred's guardian.

The second parcel, an adjoining two acres, was acquired in 1937, when Fred was nine years old. It was sold by the guardian of another minor, and the court supervising that guardianship confirmed the sale "to Fred Oyama" as highest bidder at a publicly advertised sale. A copy of the court's order was recorded. Fred's father again paid the purchase price, $1,500.

In 1942, Fred and his family were evacuated from the Pacific Coast along with all other persons of Japanese descent. And in 1944, when Fred was sixteen and still forbidden to return home, the State filed a petition to declare an escheat of the two parcels on the ground that the conveyances in 1934 and 1937 had been with intent to violate and evade the Alien Land Law.

The trial court filed no written opinion but indicated orally that its findings were based primarily on four inferences: (1) the statutory presumption that any conveyance is with "intent to prevent, evade or avoid" escheat if an ineligible alien pays the consideration; (2) an inference of similar intent from the mere fact that the conveyances ran to a minor child; (3) an inference of lack of bona fides at the time of the original transactions from the fact that the father thereafter failed to file annual guardianship reports; and (4) an inference from the father's failure to testify that his testimony would have been adverse to his son's cause. No countervailing inference was warranted by the exhibits in Fred's name, the judge said, "because there are many instances where there is little in a name."

In holding the trial court's findings of intent fully justified by the evidence, the Supreme Court of California pointed to the same four inferences. It also ruled that California could constitutionally exclude ineligible aliens from any interest in agricultural land, and that Fred Oyama was deprived of no constitutional guarantees since the land had passed to the State without ever vesting in him.

We agree with petitioners' first contention, that the Alien Land Law, as applied in this case, deprives Fred Oyama of the equal protection of California's laws and of his privileges as an American citizen. In our view of the case, the State has discriminated against Fred Oyama; the discrimination is based solely on his parents' country of origin; and there is absent the compelling justification which would be needed to sustain discrimination of that nature.

In the first place, for most minors California has the customary rule that where a parent pays for a conveyance to his child there is a presumption that a gift is intended; there is no presumption of a resulting trust, no presumption that the minor takes the land for the benefit of his parent. When a gift is thus presumed and the deed is recorded in the child's name, the recording suffices for delivery, and, absent evidence that the gift is disadvantageous, acceptance is also presumed. Thus the burden of proving that there was in fact no completed bona fide gift falls to him who would attack its validity.

Fred Oyama, on the other hand, faced at the outset the necessity of overcoming a statutory presumption that conveyances financed by his father and recorded in Fred's name were not gifts at all. Something very akin to a resulting trust *was* presumed and, at least *prima facie*, Fred *was* presumed to hold title for the benefit of his parent.

In the second place, when it came to rebutting this statutory presumption, Fred Oyama ran into other obstacles which, so far as we can ascertain, do not beset the path of most minor donees in California.

The cumulative effect, we believe, was clearly to discriminate against Fred Oyama. He was saddled with an onerous burden of proof which need not be borne by California children generally. The statutory presumption and the two ancillary inferences, which would not be used against most children, were given such probative value as to prevail in the face of a deed entered in the public records, four court orders recognizing Fred Oyama as the owner of the land, several newspaper notices to the same effect, and testimony that business transactions regarding the land were generally understood to be on his behalf. In short, Fred Oyama lost his gift, irretrievably and without compensation, solely because of the extraordinary obstacles which the State set before him.

The only basis for this discrimination against an American citizen, moreover, was the fact that his father was Japanese and not American, Russian, Chinese, or English. But for that fact alone, Fred Oyama, now a little over a year from majority, would be the undisputed owner of the eight acres in question.

There remains the question of whether discrimination between citizens on the basis of their racial descent, as revealed in this case, is justifiable. Here we start with the proposition that only the most exceptional circumstances can excuse discrimination on that basis in the face of the equal protection clause and a federal statute giving all citizens the right to own land. In *Hirabayashi v. United States*, this Court sustained a war measure which involved restrictions against citizens of Japanese descent. But the Court recognized that, as a general rule, "Distinctions between citizens solely because of their ancestry are by their very nature odious to a free people whose institutions are founded upon the doctrine of equality."

Since the view we take of petitioners' first contention requires reversal of the decision below, we do not reach their other contentions: that the Alien Land Law denies ineligible aliens the equal protection of the laws, and that failure to apply any limitations period to escheat actions under that law takes property without due process of law.

Reversed.

Mr. Justice BLACK, with whom Mr. Justice DOUGLAS agrees, concurring.

If there is any one purpose of the Fourteenth Amendment that is wholly outside the realm of doubt, it is that the Amendment was designed to bar States from denying to some groups, on account of their race or color, any rights, privileges, and opportunities accorded to other groups. I would now overrule the previous decisions of this Court that sustained state land laws which discriminate against people of Japanese origin residing in this country.

Mr. Justice MURPHY, with whom Mr. Justice RUTLEDGE joins, concurring.

To me the controlling issue in this case is whether the California Alien Land Law on its face is consistent with the Constitution of the United States. Can a state prohibit all aliens ineligible for American citizenship from acquiring, owning, occupying, enjoying, leasing or transferring agricultural land? Does such a prohibition square with the language of the Fourteenth Amendment that no state shall "deny to any person within its jurisdiction the equal protection of the laws"?

The negative answer to those queries is dictated by the uncompromising opposition of the Constitution to racism, whatever cloak or disguise it may assume. The California statute in question, as I view it, is nothing more than an outright racial discrimination. As such, it deserves constitutional condemnation. And since the very core of the statute is so defective, I consider it necessary to give voice to that fact even though I join in the opinion of the Court.

In its argument before us, California has disclaimed any implication that the Alien Land Law is racist in its origin, purpose or effect. Reference is made to the fact that nowhere in the statute is there a single mention of race, color, creed or place of birth or allegiance as a determinant of who may not own or hold farm land. The discrimination established by the statute is said to be entirely innocent of the use of such factors, being grounded solely upon the reasonable distinctions created by Congress in its naturalization laws. However, an examination of the circumstances surrounding the original enactment of this law in 1913, its reenactment in 1920 and its subsequent application reveals quite a different story.

The flood of anti-Japanese proposals continued in the 1911 session, at which more than twenty such measures were introduced. Among them, of course, was still another alien land bill. It provided that "no alien who is not eligible to citizenship" should hold real property in California. The prospects for the passage of this bill seemed good, for by this time all political parties in the state had anti-Japanese planks in their platforms. But Presidential intervention was once again successful and the bill died in committee.

In 1913, however, nothing could stop the passage of the original version of what is now the Alien Land Law. This measure, though limited to agricultural lands, represented the first official act of discrimination aimed at the Japanese.

The intention of those responsible for the 1913 law was plain. The "Japanese menace" was to be dealt with on a racial basis. The immediate purpose, of course, was to restrict Japanese farm competition.

Further evidence of the racial prejudice underlying the Alien Land Law is to be found in the events relating to the reenactment and strengthening of the statute by popular initiative in 1920. More severe and effective than the 1913 law, the initiative measure prohibited ineligible aliens from leasing land for agricultural purposes; and it plugged various other loopholes in the earlier provisions. A spirited campaign was waged to secure popular approval, a campaign with a bitter anti-Japanese flavor.

No mention was made by the statute's proponents of the Hindus or the Malay and Polynesian aliens who were . . . so numerically insignificant as to arouse no interest or animosity. Only the Japanese aliens presented the real problem. It was they, the "yellow horde," who were the object of legislation.

That fact has been further demonstrated by the subsequent enforcement of the Alien Land Law. At least 79 escheat actions have been instituted by the state since the statute became effective. Of these 79 proceedings, 4 involved Hindus, 2 involved Chinese and the remaining 73 involved Japanese. Curiously enough, 59 of the 73 Japanese cases were begun by the state subsequent to Pearl Harbor, during the period when the hysteria generated by World War II magnified the opportunities for effective anti-Japanese propaganda. Vigorous enforcement of the Alien Land Law has been but one of the cruel discriminatory actions which have marked this nation's treatment since 1941 of those residents who chanced to be of Japanese origin.

The Alien Land Law, in short, was designed to effectuate a purely racial discrimination, to prohibit a Japanese alien from owning or using agricultural land solely because he is a Japanese alien. It is rooted deeply in racial, economic and social antagonisms. The question confronting us is whether such a statute, viewed against the background of racism, can mount the hurdle of the equal protection clause of the Fourteenth Amendment. Can a state disregard in this manner the historic ideal that those within the borders of this nation are not to be denied rights and privileges because they are of a particular race? I say that it cannot.

Hence the basic vice, the constitutional infirmity, of the Alien Land Law is that its discrimination rests upon an unreal racial foundation. It assumes that there is some racial characteristic, common to all Japanese aliens, that makes them unfit to own or use agricultural land in California. There is no such characteristic. None has even been suggested. The arguments in support of the statute make no attempt whatever to discover any true racial factor. They merely represent social and economic antagonisms which have been translated into false racial terms. As such, they cannot form the rationalization necessary to conform the statute to the requirements of the equal protection clause of the Fourteenth Amendment. Accordingly, I believe that the prior decisions of this Court giving sanction to this attempt to legalize racism should be overruled.

FUJII V. STATE

38 Cal. 2d 718, 242 P.2d 617 (Supreme Court of California 1952)

Chief Justice GIBSON

Plaintiff, an alien Japanese who is ineligible to citizenship under our naturalization laws, appeals from a judgment declaring that certain land purchased by him in 1948 had escheated to the state. There is no treaty between this country and Japan which confers upon plaintiff the right to own land, and the sole question presented on this appeal is the validity of the California alien land law [under the] Fourteenth Amendment of the Federal Constitution.

The next question is whether the alien land law violates the due process and equal protection clauses of the Fourteenth Amendment. Plaintiff asserts, first, that the statutory classification of aliens on the basis of eligibility to citizenship is arbitrary for the reason that discrimination against an ineligible alien bears no reasonable relationship to promotion of the safety and welfare of the state. He points out that the land law distinguishes not between citizens and aliens, but between classes of aliens, and that persons eligible to citizenship are given all the rights of citizens regardless of whether they desire or intend to become naturalized. Secondly, he contends that the effect of the statute, as well as its purpose, is to discriminate against aliens solely on the basis of race and that such discrimination is arbitrary and unreasonable.

The issue of the constitutionality of the alien land law is thus again presented to this court, and we are met at the outset with the contention that a re-examination of the question is foreclosed by decisions of the United States Supreme Court rendered in 1923 upholding the statute. [C]f. *Terrace v. Thompson*[, 263 U.S. 197 (1923).] This objection is a serious one, and we have rejected it only after the most careful deliberation.

It appears that the decisions of the United States Supreme Court do not foreclose, but rather invite, further consideration of the constitutional issues which have been raised.

There can be no question that the rights to acquire, enjoy, own and dispose of property are "among the civil rights intended to be protected from discriminatory state action by the Fourteenth Amendment," and that the power of a state to regulate the use and ownership of land must be exercised subject to the controls and limitations of that amendment. *Shelley v. Kraemer*[, 334 U.S. 1 (1948)]; see *Terrace v. Thompson*.

The California act, in the absence of treaty, withholds all interests in real property from aliens who are ineligible to citizenship under federal naturalization laws, and the Nationality Code limits the right of naturalization to certain designated races or nationalities, excluding Japanese and a few racial groups comparitively [sic] small in numbers. 8 U.S.C.A. § 703. Congress, however, at least prior to 1924, saw fit to permit aliens who are ineligible for citizenship to enter and reside in the United States despite the fact that they could not become naturalized, and such aliens are entitled to the same protection as citizens from arbitrary discrimination. *Yick Wo v. Hopkins*[, 118 U.S. 356 (1886)]. Accordingly, the statute cannot be sustained unless it can be shown that the public interest requires limitation of their rights to acquire and enjoy interests in real property. . . .

Subsequent to the *Oyama* case the Supreme Court condemned the enforcement by state courts of covenants which restrict occupancy of real property on the basis of race or color, and it expressly pointed out that statutes incorporating such restrictions would violate the Fourteenth Amendment. *Shelley v. Kraemer.* While the persons discriminated against in the *Shelley* and *Oyama* cases were citizens, it is clear, as we have seen, that the Fourteenth Amendment protects aliens as well as citizens from arbitrary discrimination. *Yick Wo v. Hopkins.*

As a general rule a legislative classification will be sustained if it is reasonable and has a substantial relation to a legitimate object, and the existence of any reasonably conceivable state of facts sufficient to uphold the legislation will be presumed. Where, however, as here, the classification is on the basis of race, it is "immediately suspect" and will be subjected "to the most rigid scrutiny." *Korematsu v. United States.* In *Perez v. Sharp*, [32 Cal. 2d 711; 198 P.2d 17 (1948)] Justice Traynor pointed out that "Race restrictions must be viewed with great suspicion, for the Fourteenth Amendment 'was adopted to prevent state legislation designed to perpetuate discrimination on the basis of race or color' and expresses 'a definite national policy against discrimination because of race or color.'" Any state legislation discriminating against persons on the basis of race or color has to overcome the strong presumption inherent in this constitutional policy.

The clear import of the statements quoted above from the *Korematsu*, *Oyama* and *Perez* cases is that the presumption of validity is greatly narrowed in scope, if not entirely dispelled, whenever it is shown, as here, that legislation actually discriminates against certain persons because of their race or nationality. . . .

In the light of the foregoing discussion, we have concluded that the constitutional theories upon which the *Porterfield* [*v. Webb*, 263 U.S. 225 (1923)] case was based are today without support and must be abandoned. The California alien land law is obviously designed and administered as an instrument for effectuating racial discrimination, and the most searching examination discloses no circumstances justifying classification on that basis. There is nothing to indicate that those alien residents who are racially ineligible for citizenship possess characteristics which are dangerous to the legitimate interests of the state, or that they, as a class, might use the land for purposes injurious to public morals, safety or welfare. Accordingly, we hold that the alien land law is invalid as in violation of the Fourteenth Amendment.

NOTES AND QUESTIONS

1. **Definition of "escheat":** According to Powell on Real Property, escheat "is generally invoked in two circumstances: 1) when the owner of the property dies with no heirs; or 2) when the property has been abandoned." Did either of those situations exist in the *Oyama* case?

2. Constitutionality of the alien land laws: This was not the first time alien land laws had come before the Supreme Court. As Chapter 2 points out, *Terrace v. Thompson*, 263 U.S. 197 (1923), upheld the validity of a Washington state statute applicable to ineligible aliens. The Court ruled that the law was not repugnant to the due process clause or a violation of equal protection, and further stated that "each state . . . has the right to deny to aliens the right to own land within its borders." The same day that the Court handed down *Terrace v. Thompson*, it decided *Porterfield v. Webb*, 263 U.S. 225 (1923), which upheld California's version of the alien land law. Soon thereafter, the Court upheld as constitutional the judicial squelching of various creative end runs attempted by Japanese Americans. *See, e.g., Webb v. O'Brien*, 263 U.S. 313 (1923) (share-cropping agreements with Japanese tenant farmers); *Frick v. Webb*, 263 U.S. 326 (1923) (Japanese ownership of shares in agribusiness); *Cockrill v. California*, 268 U.S. 258 (1925) (purchase of land through a White agent for the citizen children of Japanese aliens).

What caused the Court to do an apparent about-face in *Oyama*? The Supreme Court of Oregon asked itself this question when considering its alien land law in *Kenji Namba v. McCourt*, 204 P.2d 569 (1949): "A quarter of a century has passed since the decision in *Terrace v. Thompson* . . . and its companion cases were announced. In that score and five years significant changes took place in our understanding of constitutional law, in our governmental structure, in our relationship with other nations and their people, in the number of ineligible aliens within our borders, and in the attitude of the American citizen toward others who do not have his individual color, creed or racial background." The Oregon court went on to strike down its state's law as violating the equal protection clause of the fourteenth amendment.

Drawing on all the materials discussed in previous chapters, as well as in this study module, assess the Oregon court's reasoning. What crucial changes—legal, social and political—occurred in the twenty years between *Terrace* and *Oyama*? Do the results in *Oyama* and *Fujii* surprise you? Why or why not?

The *Oyama* majority invokes *Hirabayashi's* earlier language concerning the "odious" nature of "distinctions based on ancestry." Does the end of wartime hostilities, the passage of five years or some other factor explain the very different results in these two cases that turn on the same principle of repugnance toward discrimination?

3. Race and property law: Professor Randall Kennedy says this of Justice Murphy's concurring opinion in *Oyama*: "Justice Murphy's willingness to display anger, to embarrass publicly officials engaging in despicable conduct, and to educate readers about the social, political, and cultural background from which a legal controversy arises are all aspects of his judicial persona that emerge in his concurrence in *Oyama*. They make this opinion outstanding and admirable."

Do you agree with this assessment? Are the alien land laws really about racial discrimination? Or are there some non-race-based government interests (whether compelling or not) that might underlie these forms of regulation? Was escheat used as a political weapon against a racial minority group, as charged by Justice Murphy? How does race affect property rights in this country?

Justice Murphy, as you have seen, authored one of the dissenting opinions in *Korematsu* as well as one of the cautionary concurring opinions in *Hirabayashi*. Thus his *Oyama* concurrence is consistent with his earlier opinions regarding the constitutional rights of Japanese Americans.

4. Race and property rights: In *Shelley v. Kraemer*, 334 U.S. 1 (1948), the Supreme Court struck down a covenant that restricted ownership of property on the basis of race, including "Mongolians" and "Negroes." Enforcing the restrictive covenant through the courts against the African American petitioners constituted "state action," and therefore violated the fourteenth amendment equal protection rights. This case is still viewed as a major victory against racial discrimination, and is cited extensively throughout the *Oyama* opinion. (However, as Professor Derrick Bell notes, "while the commentators were concerned with the principle in *Shelley*, whites, determined to bar blacks from their neighborhoods, devised a seemingly inexhaustible list of restrictions, many of which took advantage of the *Shelley* holding that restrictions were valid between the parties. All manner of self-operating cooperatives, associations, and leasing arrangements were devised to protect the racial exclusiveness of white areas.")

Shelley is important for two reasons. Practically, it struck a blow against residential segregation. Doctrinally, it stands as the high watermark for a broad definition of "state action." The *amicus* brief filed by the Justice Department in *Shelley v. Kraemer* included a 1946 letter by Dean Acheson, then the Acting Secretary of State:

> The existence of discrimination against minority groups in this country has an adverse effect upon our relations with other countries. We are reminded over and over by some foreign newspapers and spokesmen, that our treatment of various minorities leaves much to be desired. . . . Frequently we find it next to impossible to formulate a satisfactory answer to our critics in other countries. . . .
>
> An atmosphere of suspicion and resentment in a country over the way a minority is being treated in the United States is a formidable obstacle to the development of mutual understanding and trust between the two countries. We will have better international relations when these reasons for suspicion and resentment have been removed.

46 Landmark Briefs and Arguments of the Supreme Court of the United States: Constitutional Law 19-20 (Philip B. Kurland and Gerhard Casper, eds., 1975).

The California Supreme Court in *Perez v. Sharp*, 32 Cal. 2d 711 (1948), was the first state court to strike down antimiscegenation laws. In *Fujii*, that same court relies on its own precedent, *Perez*, as well as on the U.S. Supreme Court cases *Korematsu* and *Oyama*, for finding a strong legal presumption against government racial classifications.

This development in the law raises a similar question to the one asked above regarding *Oyama* and *Terrace*: What happened in the eight years between *Korematsu* and *Fujii* that explains the difference in results? What difference does the U.S. Supreme Court's 1948 ruling in *Shelley* make?

5. Property law trends: Other Western states with alien land laws filed similar actions against Japanese American property owners during this period. However, most state courts followed the lead of the *Oyama* concurrences and those decisions of their neighboring states and struck down these laws as unconstitutional. *See State of Montana v. Oakland,* 129 Mont. 347 (1955), *Kenji Namba v. McCourt,* 185 Or. 579 (1949), *Masaoka v. People,* 39 Cal. 2d 883 (1952).

In 1952, the same year California struck down its alien land law as unconstitutional, Issei ceased to be classified as aliens ineligible for citizenship. Thus state alien land laws became less significant. However, Washington state did not repeal its law until 1966 through a ballot initiative won by an underwhelming majority vote of 413,996 to 391,216.

As of the beginning of 2001, alien land laws were still on the books in Florida, Wyoming and New Mexico. Joseph Hong, "Racism Still on the Law Books," ASIAN WEEK, February 16, 2001. However, students at the Alien Land Law Project of the University of Cincinnati Immigration and Nationality Law Review were successful in lobbying the Wyoming legislature to pass a bill to repeal the act, which was then signed into law. Students at the University of New Mexico School of Law, Southwest Indian Law Clinic were similarly successful in having a bill pass both houses of the New Mexico legislature. This action will have to be approved by voters in the 2002 election. E-mail from Professor Gabriel J. Chin to YLOPEARL (Asian Pacific American Law Professors listserver) (March 14, 2001).

4. POSTSCRIPT: DEMOGRAPHIC AND CULTURAL SHIFTS IN ASIAN AMERICA FROM WORLD WAR II TO THE VIETNAM WAR

a. INTRODUCTION

What changes occurred in the Japanese American population after the experience of the internment? The decades following the closing of the camps were marked by significant changes in the social patterns of Japanese Americans. Having lost some footing as the heads of households while incarcerated, the Issei watched their American-born children became partially integrated into American life. Armed with educational backgrounds, language proficiency, cultural familiarity, and other advantages missed by their parents, the Nisei made great strides in resettlement communities. Job opportunities, higher income levels, entry into managerial positions and civil service careers gave Nisei entry into the middle class.

Dramatic changes in post-war immigration laws, policy and patterns had a profound effect on the "face" of all Asians in America, including the Japanese. Japanese Americans went from being one of the largest Asian ethnic groups in the United States before the war to the fifth largest in 1980, as newer immigrants arrived from the Philippines, Korea, China, Vietnam and India. As the third-generation Sansei came into adolescence and adulthood, Japanese Americans saw further changes among their population. Sansei continued the upward mobility of their parents but also experienced some of the same barriers faced by their parents—discrimination and prejudice.

The "model minority" label saddled Japanese and all Asian Americans with expectations and stereotypes that were simultaneously positive and problematic. This and other stereotypes about Asian Americans removed from popular view the ongoing poverty, racism and violence faced by many Asian Americans. The political, social and cultural turbulence of the 1960s also had a marked effect on Japanese Americans. Cleavages and coalitions were created by the civil rights and anti-war movements. A new Asian American identity across ancestral backgrounds created unity among previously divergent groups. Within the Japanese American community, these social movements led to the quest for redress and, ultimately, reparations.

b. CHANGING DEMOGRAPHICS

(i) THE EMERGENCE OF THE NISEI MIDDLE CLASS AND THE POST-WAR SANSEI GENERATION

By 1940, the American-born children of the first-generation Issei made up 62.7 percent of the Japanese American population. This marked a change from a predominately immigrant, Japanese-speaking community to an English-speaking, American-educated second generation. During the 1950s, the Nisei worked diligently to be viewed as hardworking employees, solid family units and model citizens. Even after their harsh treatment by representatives and institutions of the U.S. government, Issei and Nisei remained for the most part firm believers in the American dream. Japanese Americans trusted that by engaging in a lifestyle of modesty and honest work, they would be rewarded with acceptance by neighbors and colleagues in their resettlement cities and suburbs.

Scholars and commentators have observed the notable speed with which Japanese Americans, following World War II, assimilated with other Americans in schools, workplace and neighborhoods—and even through dating and marriage. Nisei moved into educational and occupational areas from which they had been excluded previously. The post-war economic boom meant great demand for Nisei skills and less competition with White Americans for desirable jobs. Aspects of Japanese values, such as educational and work ethics, played a role in this social integration. The second generation Nisei attained higher educational levels than their parents. Whereas typical Issei had primary school educations and some secondary schooling, their offspring were high school graduates and attended at least some college. However, as described below, the educational achievement of the Nisei did not always translate into economic attainment equal to that of European Americans.

The shift from Issei to Nisei thus led away from occupations such as agriculture, trades and service industries toward professional, technical and managerial occupations. With more education, Nisei were allowed to move into higher-status jobs with better pay. The number of Nisei who went into professional services and public administration increased. By 1980, almost

22 percent of the Japanese American populace was involved in professional services.

A 1960 study of Japanese American education, occupation and income levels in Washington State documented the simultaneous economic achievements and limited mobility of Japanese Americans. While Japanese Americans had by far the highest educational levels of any ethnic group in the state, White Americans had a large economic edge over Japanese Americans in similar occupational categories. A study in California yielded similar results: "[O]f American-born men in California in 1970, for each additional year of education, whites earned $522 more, compared to $438 for Japanese, $320 for Chinese, $340 for Mexican Americans, and $284 for blacks."

As the Nisei settled into their post-war lifestyles, a new generation was born, the third-generation "Sansei." The Sansei, and eventually the fourth-generation "Yonsei," continued the upward educational trend of their parents and attended college and graduate school, including some of the best schools in the country. By 1970, 15.9 percent of persons of Japanese ancestry had completed college, compared to 11.3 percent of European Americans. By 1980, the gap widened to 26.4 percent versus 17.4 percent, respectively.

While the average Japanese American family income was higher than the average income for White American families, Japanese American families were larger than the latter. Individual earnings still lagged behind those for comparably educated White Americans. The disparity between educational level and income that existed for the Nisei thus continued with their offspring.

A significant change in the post-World War II family life of Japanese Americans has been the increase in the amount of intermarriage with White Americans. Antimiscegenation laws were in effect in many states until the mid-20th century. For example, between 1905 and 1948 in California, Japanese Americans could not marry White Americans. Thus Issei and Nisei rates of intermarriage were quite low—2 percent and 4 percent respectively. By the 1970s, intermarriage among the third-generation Sansei had jumped to 60 percent of all new marriages, despite strong social norms against outmarrying.

Some scholars have commented on a "decline in community" among Japanese Americans. Others, however, point out that Japanese Americans have maintained an involvement in ethnic community affairs at a rate ten times higher than European immigrant groups, with a majority of Japanese Americans involved in some voluntary association (not including churches). Japanese American involvement in ethnic community activities is proportionally higher in places with a lower density of ethnic group members.

Discrimination against Japanese Americans persisted but became less overt and more subtle. As Stephen Fugita and David O'Brien have noted,

> The role of discrimination in maintaining the involvement of Japanese Americans in their ethnic community can be viewed as operating on several levels. The number of actual experiences with visible and demeaning kinds of discrimination differ[s] considerably by generation. At this level, most Nisei have vivid memories of the evacuation and incarceration as well as being discriminated against in their youth when they attempted to use public facili-

ties such as swimming pools and theaters. The Sansei, on the other hand, have grown up in the more benign postwar era and have not had nearly as many personal experiences with the more visible forms of discrimination.

At another level, however, the vast majority of Japanese Americans perceive the persistence of less dramatic but nonetheless real incidences of prejudice and discrimination. . . . There is widespread feeling among Japanese Americans in corporate and governmental settings that it is difficult to become a full fledged member of the "old boy network" and to make it into upper management. [S]everal studies suggest that Japanese Americans cannot convert their educational attainment into income and high status jobs as well as whites with comparable backgrounds. On the other hand, white managers have argued that the small number of Japanese Americans and other Asian Americans in upper management is largely due to their lack of "aggressiveness" and the necessary "leadership" qualities.

David O'Brien and Stephen S. Fugita, THE JAPANESE AMERICAN EXPERIENCE (MINORITIES IN MODERN AMERICA) 103, 104–05 (1991).

(ii) IMMIGRATION

Chapter 2 provided an historical background of immigration laws and policies as they affected Asians in America. Beginning in the 1940s, some liberalization of immigration laws toward other Asian ethnic groups occurred. The major changes to the immigration and naturalization laws occurred in 1952, with the passage of the McCarran-Walter Immigration and Nationality Act, and with the 1965 amendments to the Act.

POST-WAR AMENDMENTS

During World War II, China and the United States were allies against the Japanese. Despite opposition from the American Federation of Labor and some veterans' groups, in 1943 Congress gave China a minimum quota for immigrants and allowed Chinese to naturalize. This was known as the "Chinese Repealer." The Repealer, however, gave persons of Chinese descent an annual quota of only 105 immigrants. In 1945, Congress passed the War Brides Act and two years later, amended the Act to admit Chinese wives of citizens without regard to the 105-quota limit and to allow citizens to petition for their spouses to join them.

Post-World War II changes in U.S. immigration laws and policies had profound effects on other Asian subgroups as well. In 1946, the United States conferred the same naturalization rights upon Filipinos and Indians and established immigration quotas of 100 for each country and also extended non-quota status to wives and children of citizens. Commentators note that Asian wars and international relations motivated these reforms. As Professor Bill Ong Hing writes:

> The legislation was actually introduced to strengthen ties with India, which during World War II the United States began to regard as a prominent political and military force and as a potentially valuable ally. . . . After India won independence in 1946 and the two countries grew closer, the relaxation of exclusion became important to their new alliance. Although the legislation was originally intended to benefit only nationals of India, the Philippines were

added at the last minute for similar political reasons. In 1942, Filipinos who joined the armed forces in the Pacific were extended citizenship opportunities.

Bill Ong Hing, MAKING AND REMAKING ASIAN AMERICA THROUGH IMMIGRATION POLICY, 1850–1990 36–37 (1993).

THE McCARRAN-WALTER ACT

In 1952, Congress passed the Immigration and Nationality Act known as "McCarran-Walter." McCarran-Walter eliminated the 1917 Immigration Act's Asiatic Barred Zone but created a new restrictive zone, the Asia-Pacific Triangle. This zone consisted of countries from India to Japan and all the Pacific Islands north of Australia and New Zealand. A maximum of 2,000 Asians from the triangle were allowed to immigrate annually; small quotas were set for each country within the triangle. The bill retained the quota system for immigration under which Great Britain, Germany and Ireland were allotted over two-thirds of the total quotas. The special quota of 105 for Chinese persons, set up in 1943, was retained. A notable feature of McCarran-Walter was the requirement that a person of half-Asian ancestry had to be charged to the quota of the Asian country, rather than to the area from which he or she was emigrating. That feature clearly had a prejudicial effect on Asian immigrants. Generally, under the 1952 Act, quota immigrants were charged against the quota for their birth country. Thus, an immigrant from Germany whose parents were British and Swedish would be charged to the German quota. For Asians, however, an immigrant whose ethnic ancestry could be traced to the triangle on the side of either parent would be charged against the Asian country. In the German immigrant example, if one parent were Japanese, the immigrant would be charged against Japan's quota, not Germany's. The quota for the Japanese was set at 185.

On the other hand, McCarran-Walter is credited with eliminating remaining bars against Asian naturalization. As a result, the "ineligible for citizenship" prohibition of the 1924 Act was removed. Thus, for the first time Japanese immigrants as well as other Asians previously barred were allowed to become naturalized citizens of the United States. Some touted the statute as progress toward racial equality. The House Judiciary Committee Report stated:

> The bill would make all persons, regardless of race, eligible for naturalization, and would set up minimum quotas for aliens now barred for racial reasons. Thus, persons of Japanese, Korean, Indonesian, etc., ancestry could be admitted and naturalized as any other qualified alien. No doubt this will have a favorable effect on our international relations, particularly in the Far East. American exclusion policy has long been resented there and, in the eyes of qualified observers, was an important factor in the anti-American feeling in Japan prior to the last World War.

H.R. Rep. No. 82-1365 at 28-29 (1952), reprinted in 1952 U.S.C.C.A.N. 1653, 1679.

McCarran-Walter had a significant impact on Japanese Americans. Professor Hing notes:

> Between 1952 and 1961, Japanese Americans were the largest group of Asian naturalization applicants. Once they became citizens they were able to petition for their spouses on an unlimited, nonquota basis. In fact, between 1956 and 1965, the relatively large numbers of Japanese who immigrated were primarily these nonquota wives. In 1959, for example, 5,012 Japanese women immigrated, compared to 839 men; in 1961, 3,665 women and only 648 men entered. By 1965 the community consisted of more women than men (approximately 85 males for every 100 females)—the only Asian American group at the time with such a profile. Between the 1952 and 1965 acts, far more Japanese immigrated than any other Asian nationality. After overtaking Chinese Americans in 1910, they remained America's largest Asian group through 1970.

Hing, *supra* at 56.

Despite the McCarran-Walter Act's removal of the racial bar on naturalization, Asian American legal scholars challenge whether McCarran-Walter reflected a complete shift in the public's attitude toward Asian immigrants. Consider the following quote, again from Professor Hing:

> [T]he act demonstrated the consistent desire of Congress to keep Asian immigration tightly in check. Once again Congress proved schizophrenic. Foreign policy dictated an end to absolute exclusion, but exclusionist ideology at home would not permit immigration beyond the token quota of two thousand immigrants a year from the entire Asia-Pacific region.

Hing, *supra* at 38. In evaluating Professor Hing's claim, consider the following post-World War II case, decided just before the 1965 immigration revisions. Hitai, a native-born Brazilian citizen, was found deportable. He applied for adjustment of status, at a time when the Japanese quota was 185 persons a year.

HITAI V. IMMIGRATION AND NATURALIZATION SERVICE
343 F.2d 466 (2d Cir. 1965)

Circuit Judge HAYS

Although as an "immigrant who was born in . . . an independent country of Central or South America," petitioner would otherwise be classified as a "nonquota immigrant," the special inquiry officer assigned petitioner to the quota area for Japan because of Section 202(b)(4) of the Act. Under the terms of that section an

> immigrant born outside the Asia-Pacific triangle (defined by geographic boundaries including Japan) who is attributable by as much as one-half of his ancestry to a people or peoples indigenous to not more than one separate quota area, situate wholly within the Asia-Pacific triangle, shall be chargeable to the quota of that quota area. . . .

A visa is not available under the Japanese quota.

We are constrained to reject petitioner's claim that Section 202(b)(4) as here applied is unconstitutional. The exclusion and deportation of aliens pursuant to [the] statute falls within that category of policy decisions, which, "so far as the subjects affected are concerned, are necessarily conclusive upon all . . . (the government's) departments and officers," including "the judiciary." The Chinese Exclusion Case, 130 U.S. 581, 606, 9 S.Ct. 623, 630, 32 L.Ed. 1068 (1889).

Petitioner also bases his argument on Article 55 of the United Nations Charter which provides for the promotion of "universal respect for, and observance of, human rights and fundamental freedoms for all without distinction as to race, sex, language, or religion." This provision of the Charter is not self-executing and therefore did not ex proprio vigore repeal or invalidate any of the laws, including the immigration laws, of the member states.

The petitioner makes no claim that he was not accorded a full hearing with adequate notice pursuant to Section 242(b) nor that the statutes were misapplied or that the facts were incorrectly found in his case. Therefore the petition must be denied.

(iii) THE 1965 IMMIGRATION ACT

BILL ONG HING, MAKING AND REMAKING ASIAN AMERICA THROUGH IMMIGRATION POLICY

1850–1990 39–40 (1993)

Truman and other critics did not relent. Soon after the enactment of the 1952 law, he appointed a special Commission on Immigration and Naturalization to study the system. A 319-page report issued in 1953 strongly urged the abolition of the national-origins system and recommended quotas without regard to national origin, race, creed, or color. President Eisenhower embraced the findings, but his push for corrective legislation failed. Despite repeated attempts at new legislation, no major action was taken on any of the commission's recommendations until more than ten years later.... President Kennedy submitted a comprehensive program that provided the impetus for ultimate reform. His proposals reflected his long-standing interest in immigration reform. Kennedy called for the repeal of racial exclusion from the Asia-Pacific triangle, and he assailed the nativism that led to the Chinese exclusion laws as well as the national-origins system of the 1924 law....

President Kennedy's hopes for abolishing the quota system were realized when the 1965 amendments were enacted. But his vision of visas on a first-come, first-served basis gave way to a narrower and more historically parochial framework that provided few, if any, obvious advantages for prospective Asian immigrants. The new law allowed twenty thousand immigrant visas for every country not in the Western Hemisphere ... regardless of the size of a country, so that mainland China had the same quota as Tunisia. Of the 170,000 visas set aside for the Eastern Hemisphere, 75 percent were for specified "preference" relatives of citizens and lawful permanent residents, and an unlimited number was available to immediate relatives of United States citizens.

For the first time since the United States began regulating immigration, race was radically reduced as a factor. The 1965 Act removed the McCarran-Walter's Asia-Pacific triangle provisions. As in 1943 and 1952, proponents of the amendments cited foreign policy repercussions of having racially discriminatory immigration laws. With the civil rights movement demanding an end to discrimination at home, other legislators called McCarran-Walter's ethnicity-based provisions racist and inconsistent with anti-discrimination goals. The legislative history of the 1965 Act reveals that

> [t]he principal purpose of the bill, as amended, [was] to repeal the national origin quota provisions . . . and to substitute a new system for the selection of immigrants to the United States. . . . A new system of preferential admissions based upon the existence of a close family relationship with U.S. citizens or permanent resident aliens, and upon the advantage to the United States of the special talents and skills of the immigrant [was created]. In place of the national origins system, the bill established a new system of selection designed to be fair, rational, humane, and in the national interest. Under this system emphasis in the selection from among those eligible to be immigrants within the annual numerical ceiling of 170,000 (inclusive of 10,200 refugees) will be based upon the existence of a close family relationship to U.S. citizens or lawful resident aliens regardless of the birthplace of the alien. . . . The closer the family relationship the higher the preference. . . . The bill provides an ample preference for the members of the professions with personal qualifications whose admission will be substantially beneficial to the national economy, cultural interests, or welfare of the United States. Aliens, both skilled and unskilled, who are capable of filling labor needs in the United States are provided a lesser preference.

H.R. Rep. No. 89-745 (1965), reprinted in 1965 U.S.C.C.A.N. 3328, 3328-29, 3332.

Scholars have debated whether Congress anticipated that large numbers of Asians would immigrate. Intended or not, these changes caused a huge increase in the number of Asian immigrants, from 1 million in 1965 to more than 7 million in 1990. Professor Hing reports that "[b]etween 1931 and 1965, [Asians] were a mere 5 percent of all those who entered the country legally. . . . [B]y the late 1980s and early 1990s, they were nearly half . . . of all legal entries." However, even with the huge influx of Asian immigrants, less than 3 percent of the entire U.S. population was of Asian ancestry. In addition to sheer numbers, the 1965 amendments altered residential patterns and employment. More Asian immigrants settled in the East and South; every Asian group experienced an injection of more professionals as a result of the skills-based preference system.

However, the impact on Japanese America was limited. Again, according to Professor Hing, "[f]rom 1965 to 1990 the Japanese American population increased by only 59 percent, from about 500,000 to a little over 847,500. During this period only 116,000 Japanese immigrated. Japanese Americans were in an excellent position to petition for relatives under the 1965 amendments' kinship provisions, yet they did not take advantage of this opportunity as other Asian American groups did." Japanese Americans were the largest Asian community at the time of the 1965 reforms; by 1980 they had slipped to third. The following table tracks increases in the number of Japanese Americans as a result of U.S. immigration laws.

Table 1: Comparison of Japanese American Population with Immigration by Decade and the Immigration Law in Effect, 1888–1985

Decade Ending	Population	Immigration in prior decade	Law in effect in prior decade
1890		2,270	Open immigration
1900	85,716	25,942	Open immigration
1910	152,745	129,797	Open immigration until Gentlemen's Agreement
1920	220,596	83,837	Gentlemen's Agreement
1930	278,743	33,462	Gentlemen's Agreement until 1924 Act
1940	285,115	1,948	1924 Act
1950	326,379	1,555	1924 Act
1960	464,332	46,250	1924 Act until 1952 Act
1970	591,290	39,988	1952 Act until 1965 amendments
1980	716,331	49,775	1965 amendments
1990	847,562	44,800	1965 amendments

SOURCE: INS Annual Reports and Statistical Yearbooks; Gardner et al., 1985.

Hing, *supra* at 54.

Asian American populations other than Japanese grew dramatically between 1965 and the present. The four most important sending countries (after Mexico, which sends the most) are the Philippines, Korea, China, and Vietnam. The Filipino American population grew seven-fold to become the second largest group. The Korean American and Asian Indian communities grew eighteen times and sixteen times respectively. Chinese Americans increased by four and a half times to remain the largest group to immigrate since 1980. As noted by Professor Hing, "[I]n the 1980's . . . the Asian and Pacific Islander population grew 107.8 percent compared to only 9.8 percent for the entire nation." The 1975 Indochina Migration and Refugee Assistance Act, the 1980 Refugee Act and the 1987 Amerasian Homecoming Act amended the 1965 Act, and further added to the reshaping of Asian America.

As with the earlier McCarran-Walter Act, post-1965 immigration law and policy has simultaneously benefited and burdened Asian Americans. After a thorough examination of legislative history and interviews with the players about their current recollections, Professor Gabriel Chin concludes that "sincere anti-racism" motivated sympathetic members of Congress to end racial distinctions in immigration policy. He argues that "the 1965 bill was a genuine repudiation of the discriminatory laws of the past, for Asians as well as for the African and southern and eastern European nationals whose opportunities to immigrate were limited by the national origins quota system."

However, Professor Jan Ting states that "vestiges of anti-Asian exclusion remain in current immigration law and immigration law enforcement." He argues that the 7 percent limitation on the number of visas assigned to any country regardless of size reduces legal immigration from Asia and Mexico. He also notes that the 1986 "diversity" program and its expansion in 1990 were intended to ensure more visas to European immigrants and that enforcement policies reflect "yellow peril" fears.

c. CHANGING STEREOTYPES AND EMERGING IDENTITIES

(i) THE MODEL MINORITY: REALITY OR MYTH?

Japanese American achievement and upward mobility led some social commentators to label them a "model minority." Sociologist William Petersen stated:

> By any criterion of good citizenship that we chose, the Japanese Americans are better than any other group in our society, including native-born whites. They have established this remarkable record, moveover, by their almost totally unaided effort. Every attempt to hamper their progress resulted only in enhacing their determination to succeed. Even in a country whose patron saint is the Horatio Alger hero, there is no parallel to this success story.

William Peterson, *Success Story, Japanese American Style*, NEW YORK TIMES MAGAZINE 21, January 9, 1966.

This popular image suggests that Japanese American achievement is primarily attributable to quiet perseverance, and that other minority groups can attain the same success in occupational and residential assimilation by sheer hard work. The model minority rationale is offered to explain the academic and other achievements not only of Japanese Americans, but also of Asian Americans in general. Professor Natsu Taylor Saito observes the double-edged quality of this facially laudatory stereotype:

> Those of Asian descent are sometimes portrayed as the "model minority," people who are succeeding in America despite their status as minorities by working and studying, saving and sacrificing for the future. However, as the "yellow peril," Asians and Asian Americans are also depicted as military, cutural or economic enemies and unfair competitors for education and jobs. The positive versions of these stereotypes include images of Asian Americans as hardworking, industrious, thrifty, family-oriented, and even mysterious or exotic. It is striking that the negative images almost invariably involve the same traits. Hardworking and industrious become unfairly competitive; family-oriented becomes clannishness; mysterious becomes dangerously inscrutable.

Natsu Taylor Saito, *Model Minority, Yellow Peril: Functions of "Foreignness" in the Construction of Asian American Legal Identity*, 4 Asian L.J. 71, 71-72 (May, 1997).

In the employment realm, the model minority stereotype ignores the fact that Asian Americans are often educationally overqualified for their jobs. Professor Pat Chew's study of Asian American employment reveals that Asian Americans are underrepresented in many occupations, such as the legal profession, in relation to their percentage of the total population. For example, the table below demonstrates that the "'glass ceiling' to supervisory positions that hampers other minority groups applies to Asian Americans as well. The data for managerial occupations substantiate the relative lack of Asian

Americans in executive roles." In each of these occupations, the percentage of each racial minority group is less than 1 percent of the total.

Table 2: Representation of Minority Groups in Selected Occupations

Occupations (in Percentages)	Asian Americans	African Americans	Latinos
Public administrators and officials	.65	.93	.40
Administrators in education and related fields	.67	.70	.46
Lawyers	.49	.21	.18
Psychologists	.49	.64	.42
Social workers	.59	1.81	.80
Elementary teachers	.44	.73	.37
Secondary teachers	.36	.60	.38
Counselors	.64	1.28	.41
Actors and directors	.49	.87	.53
Editors and reporters	.70	.37	.31
Announcers	.41	.52	.58

Pat K. Chew, ASIAN AMERICANS: THE "RETICENT" MINORITY AND THEIR PARA-DOXES, 36 Wm. and Mary L. Rev. 1, 30–32 (1994).

Continuing the trend noted in the 1960s and 1970s, Asian Americans are often underpaid relative to White Americans with comparable educational levels. Published reports that the 1990 median annual income for Asian American households ($42,250) exceeded that of the White American population ($36,920) failed to note that there are more workers per Asian American household, resulting in lower per capita income. Moreover, in areas with high concentrations of Asian Americans, the percentage of Asian Americans in low-status, low-income jobs—service workers, laborers, farm laborers, private household workers—is considerably higher than among White Americans. And the low unemployment rate among Asian Americans masks a high underemployment rate. Studies show they are clustered in occupations that pay less than other jobs in the same industries. The model minority stereotype also overlooks the rising poverty rate among Asian Americans, which increased from 13 percent in 1979 to 16 percent in 1988, a rate twice as high as the 8 percent rate for non-Hispanic whites.

Finally, the model minority image fails to take into account the effects of discrimination on Asian Americans. Professor Chew writes:

> Many Americans believe that society does not discriminate against Asian Americans and that Asian Americans enjoy social equality. The reality is that Asian Americans have been the target of both historical and ongoing discrimination. ... [N]umerous federal government reports confirm that racist actions against Asian Americans are ongoing. As stated in a recent report, "many Asian Americans are forced to endure anti-Asian bigotry, ranging from ignorant and insensitive remarks, to stereotypical portrayals of Asians in the media, to name-calling, on a regular basis. Asian Americans are also frequent victims of hate crimes, including vandalism, assault, and sometimes even murder."

Chew, *supra* at 8, 18–19.

The level of intimidation and harassment faced by Americans of Asian ancestry is also obscured by the model minority myth. A 1996 study by the National Asian Pacific American Legal Consortium reports a 17 percent increase in reported violent expressions of animus (motivated by anti-Asian bias or prejudice) against Asian Pacific Americans over the previous year, a figure "particularly significant because the FBI reported a 7 percent decrease in violent crime for 1996."

Leslie Hatamiya argues that the model minority myth factored into the redress movement as an argument against reparations. The perception of many in Congress was that Japanese Americans did well and needed formal government recognition of the injuries incurred during the internment. These arguments are considered in more detail in the following chapter.

(ii) THE ASIAN AMERICAN MOVEMENT AND PAN-ASIAN ETHNICITY

In the late 1960s, college students of Asian descent led the charge for "Asian Power" or "Yellow Power," a call to radicalism. A combination of the civil rights, Black Power, and anti-war movements, as well as the activist cry for global Third World liberation contributed to the mobilization of Asian Americans on campuses and in communities.

The 1969 strike of Third World students at the University of California-Berkeley and San Francisco State University to establish ethnic studies programs were notable events. The San Francisco State strike was the longest student strike in United States history and the first campus uprising involving Asian Americans as a collective force. Professor William Wei argues that a permanent state of "otherness" assigned to Asian Americans by mainstream America was a great impetus in the movement's concern over identity:

> In a rude awakening, Asian Americans became acutely aware that they had more in common with African Americans than with European Americans, that racial injustice had been visited upon them as well. As individuals, they too had experienced prejudice and discrimination; as a group, they too had been victims of mainstream society. They became aware that the discrimination they suffered was more than the work of individual bigots who should know better; it was in fact an intrinsic feature of American society. This new awareness generated not only an ambivalence about their own identity but also disillusionment with a society that failed to live up to its principles of equality and justice for all.

William Wei, THE ASIAN AMERICAN MOVEMENT 13 (1993). During the height of this movement, Amy Uyematsu urged:

> Asian Americans can no longer afford to watch the black-and-white struggle from the sidelines. They have their own cause to fight, since they are also victims—with less visible scars—of the white institutionalized racism. A yellow movement has been set into motion by the black power movement. Addressing itself to the unique problems of Asian Americans, this "yellow power" movement is relevant to the black power movement in that both are part of the Third World struggle to liberate all colored people. The yellow power movement has been motivated largely by the problem of self-identity in Asian Americans. . . . Precisely because Asian Americans [the main body

being Chinese and Japanese] have become economically secure, they face serious identity problems. Asian Americans still try to gain complete acceptance by denying their yellowness. Mentally, they have adjusted to the white man's culture by giving up their own languages, customs, histories, and cultural values. . . . Next, they have rejected their physical heritages, resulting in extreme self-hatred. Yellow people share with blacks the desire to look white.

Amy Uyematsu, The Emergence of Yellow Peril in America in ROOTS: AN ASIAN AMERICAN READER 9 (Amy Tachiki et al., eds. 1971). As this quote suggests, cultural nationalism and pan-Asian ethnicity fueled the Asian power movement. Third-generation Sansei rejected the Nisei assimilationist philosophy of trying to blend in with the White majority culture. The movement inspired writers, artists, performers and others to focus on cultural heritage. Asian American studies programs and curricular initiatives stressing Asian American history and perspective proliferated on campuses.

By the late 1960s, there was a second generation of American-born Asian Americans. Two-thirds of the Asian population in California in 1960 was born in the United States. As the population became increasingly native-born, linguistic and cultural differences became less meaningful and old-world ties faded.No language problem existed because they shared English as their first language. Many, in fact, were unable to speak the native tongue of their ancestors, further attenuating ties to ethnic homelands in Asia. Unlike the first generation, there were few feelings of historical animosity with others of Asian descent. Sansei were much more likely than Nisei to see themselves as Asian American rather than Japanese American. The decline in ethnic segregation and enhanced awareness of common problems such as exploitation, oppression and discrimination contributed to this pan-Asian solidarity. Through organizations, publications, educational and community programs and media outlets, activists built upon this inclusive pan-Asian identification.

Asian Americans' racial similarity to the "enemy" throughout each of the major wars in Asia beginning with World War II led to the dehumanizing "gook" stereotype. Asian Americans in the service complained of ill treatment of all soldiers of Asian descent by the U.S. military. The racial aspects of the Viet Nam war and anticolonial sentiments fostered demonstrations against racism and U.S. imperialism abroad. A strong anti-racist sentiment set Asian American activists apart from their White activist counterparts. In 1971, the Asian American contingent refused to join the main anti-war march in Washington because the coordinating committee failed to adopt the contingent's anti-racist statement.

The Asian American movement advocated a rejection of passivity and acquiescence, even in language. The term "oriental" was rejected as identifying Asians only in relation to Europeans. For example, in 1969, a UCLA student group changed its name from the Oriental Concern to the Asian American Political Alliance. In the late 1960s and early 1970s, Asian Americans created their own organizations across the country in the areas of health, law, education, culture, labor, media and business.

This expansion of racial awareness and broader Asian American identity among the Sansei had a profound effect on their parents and grandparents as well. Jere Takahashi describes the "generational convergence" around political and social issues that resulted from this era:

> The political and racial transformations of the 1960's simultaneously produced a political space enabling Sansei activists to align themselves with Nisei and Kibei who practiced a progressive political style and espoused similar concerns. The intergenerational linking that resulted from this period of protest and movement for racial equality reconnected Japanese Americans with the struggles and unresolved debates that occupied Nisei activists, intellectuals, and artists in the 1930's about their position and role in American life. Equally important, second-generation Japanese Americans who did not fit the main currents of the Nisei generation began to express their social and political concerns during this period of racial destabilization and political change. As Nisei and Sansei shared new cultural and political spaces enabling them to discuss and expand upon previous notions of identity, community, and political orientation, they forged a unity that had been previously absent.

Jere Takahashi, NISEI/SANSEI: SHIFTING JAPANESE AMERICAN IDENTITIES AND POLITICS 203 (1997).

The reparations and redress movement described in the next chapter provided one focal point for this multigenerational activism.

C. ADDITIONAL READINGS

BOOKS

Derrick A. Bell Jr., RACE, RACISM, AND AMERICAN LAW (1992).

Allan R. Bosworth, AMERICA'S CONCENTRATION CAMPS (1967).

Leonard Broom and John I. Kitsuse, THE MANAGED CASUALTY: THE JAPANESE-AMERICAN FAMILY IN WORLD WAR II (1973).

Leonard Broom and Ruth Riemer, REMOVAL AND RETURN: THE SOCIOECONOMIC EFFECTS OF THE WAR ON JAPANESE AMERICANS (1949).

Sucheng Chan, ASIAN AMERICANS, AN INTERPRETIVE HISTORY (1991).

Frank F. Chuman, THE BAMBOO PEOPLE: THE LAW AND JAPANESE-AMERICANS (1976).

Donald E. Collins, NATIVE AMERICAN ALIENS: DISLOYALTY AND THE RENUNCIATION OF CITIZENSHIP BY JAPANESE AMERICANS DURING WORLD WAR II (1985).

EAST ACROSS THE PACIFIC: HISTORICAL AND SOCIOLOGICAL STUDIES OF JAPANESE IMMIGRATION AND ASSIMILATION (Hilary Conroy and T. Scott Miyakawa eds., 1972).

Roger Daniels, CONCENTRATION CAMPS, NORTH AMERICA: JAPANESE IN THE UNITED STATES AND CANADA DURING WORLD WAR II (1981).

JAPANESE AMERICANS: FROM RELOCATION TO REDRESS (Roger Daniels et al. eds., c.1986, 1991).

Yen Le Espiritu, Asian American Panethnicity: Bridging Institutions and Identities (1992).

Paul F. Gerhart, The Plight of the Japanese Americans During World War II: A Study of Group Prejudice: Its History and Manifestations.

Audrie Girdner and Anne Loftis, The Great Betrayal: The Evacuation of the Japanese-Americans During World War II (1969).

Leslie T. Hatamiya, Righting A Wrong: Japanese Americans and the Passage of the Civil Liberties Act of 1988 (1993).

Bill Ong Hing, Making and Remaking Asian America Through Immigration Policy, 1850-1990 (1993).

Bill Hosokawa, Nisei: The Quiet Americans (1969).

Russell Warren Howe, The Hunt For "Tokyo Rose" (1990).

Lawson Fusao Inada, Only What We Could Carry: The Japanese American Internment Experience (2000).

Ellen Levine, A Fence Away from Freedom: Japanese Americans and World War II (1995).

Valerie J. Matsumoto, Farming the Home Place: A Japanese American Community in California, 1919-1982 (1993).

Dillon S. Myer, Uprooted Americans: The Japanese Americans and the War Relocation Authority During World War II (1971).

Mei T. Nakano, Japanese American Women: Three Generations, 1890-1990 (1990).

Richard S. Nishimoto, Inside An American Concentration Camp: Japanese American Resistance at Poston, Arizona (1995).

David J. O'Brien and Stephen S. Fugita, The Japanese American Experience (1991).

Paul R. Spickard, Japanese Americans: The Formation and Transformations of an Ethnic Group (1996).

Amy Tachiki, Roots: An Asian American Reader (1971).

Jere Takahashi, Nisei/Sansei: Shifting Japanese American Identities and Politics (Asian American History and Culture) (1997).

Dorothy Swaine Thomas, The Salvage: Japanese American Evacuation and Resettlement (1952).

Dorothy Swaine Thomas and Richard S. Nishimoto, The Spoilage (1946).

United States Commission on Wartime Relocation and Internment of Civilians, Personal Justice Denied: Report of the Commission on Wartime Relocation and Internment of Civilians (1997).

Michi Weglyn, Years of Infamy: The Untold Story of America's Concentration Camps (1976).

William Wei, The Asian American Movement (1993).

LAW REVIEW ARTICLES AND OTHER SOURCES

Keith Aoki, *Critical Legal Studies, Asian Americans in U.S. Law & Culture, Neil Gotanda, and Me*, 4 ASIAN L.J. 19 (1997).

Pat K. Chew, *Asian Americans: The "Reticent" Minority and Their Paradoxes*, 36 WM. AND MARY L. REV. 1 (1994).

Gabriel J. Chin, *The Civil Rights Revolution Comes to Immigration Law: A New Look at the Immigration and Nationality Act of 1965*, 75 N.C. L. REV. 273 (1996).

DENSHO: THE JAPANESE AMERICAN LEGACY PROJECT, <www.densho.org>.

Joseph Hong, *Racism Still on the Law Books*, ASIAN WEEK, February 16, 2001.

H.R. Rep. No. 82-1365 (1952).

H.R. Rep. No. 89-745 (1965).

Immigration and Nationality Act Amendments, Pub. L. No. 89-236 (1965).

Kenneth L. Karst, *The Pursuit of Manhood and the Desegregation of the Armed Forces*, 38 UCLA L. REV. 499 (1991).

Randall Kennedy, *Justice Murphy's Concurrence in Oyama v. California: Cussing Out Racism*, 74 TEX. L. REV. 1245 (1996).

Ken Masugi, *The Duties of Citizenship*, 18 NEW PERSPECTIVES 3 (1996).

Mari J. Matsuda, *Looking to the Bottom: Critical Legal Studies and Reparations*, 22 HARV. C.R.-C.L. L. REV. 323 (1987).

Lawrence Kent Mendenhall, *Misters Korematsu and Steffan: The Japanese Internment and the Military's Ban on Gays in the Armed Forces*, 70 N.Y.U. L. REV. 196 (1995).

National Asian Pacific American Consortium, 1996 Audit of Violence Against Asian Pacific Americans.

William Peterson, *Success Story, Japanese American Style*, NEW YORK TIMES MAGAZINE, January 9, 1966, at 21.

Natsu Taylor Saito, *Model Minority, Yellow Peril: Functions of "Foreignness" in the Construction of Asian American Legal Identity*, 4 ASIAN L.J. 71 (1997).

Rene Sanchez, *Proposition 187*, WASHINGTON POST, July 30, 1999.

Janet Stevenson, *Before the Colors Fade: Return of the Exiles, Interview of R.W. Kenny, Former Attorney General of California*, 20 AMERICAN HERITAGE 22 (1969).

Peter T. Suzuki, *The University of California Japanese Evacuation and Resettlement Study: A Prolegomenon*, DIALECTIC ANTHROPOLOGY 10 (1986).

Jan C. Ting, *Other Than a Chinaman: How U.S. Immigration Law Resulted from and Still Reflects a Policy of Excluding and Restricting Asian Immigration*, 4 TEMPLE POL. & CIV. RTS. L. REV. 301 (1995).

War Relocation Authority, U.S. Department of Interior, *Legal and Constitutional Phases of the WRA Program, Part II: Legal Considerations in the Development of Center Management Policies*, 18-36 (1946).

T. Yatsushiro, I. Ishino, and Y. Matsumoto, *Japanese Americans Look at Resettlement*, 8 PUB. OPINION Q. 188-201 (1944).

Part III: Redress

Looking at Center
Picoie
3-25-45 1:15 PM.
97.106.2EU

Chapter 5 THE *CORAM NOBIS* CASES

This chapter addresses the legal dimensions of redress for Japanese Americans interned during World War II. It starts by examining in detail the *coram nobis* litigation of the mid-1980s that reopened the infamous *Korematsu, Hirabayashi* and *Yasui* cases of the 1940s. A *coram nobis* proceeding is an "extraordinary" process that enables a person who was long ago convicted of a crime to reopen his or her "completed" case and to have the conviction set aside if he or she can prove "manifest injustice." The *coram nobis* proceeding is extraordinary because it is rarely used and because proving manifest injustice in the original prosecution of a case is exceedingly difficult. Fred Korematsu, Gordon Hirabayashi and Minoru Yasui succeeded in the 1980s litigation of their *coram nobis* petitions. The trial courts that originally convicted them "vacated" (or nullified) these convictions forty years later. These *coram nobis* decisions formed the judicial cornerstone for the Japanese American reparations effort.

In addition to cases and commentaries, we include in this chapter rich documentary material, much of which is reproduced in its original form, to aid the study of lawyering strategy and judicial decision-making in the *coram nobis* cases. The following chapter explores other attempted legal avenues of redress, including the *Hohri* class action damages litigation and the federally enacted Civil Liberties Act of 1988, which authorized a presidential apology and monetary reparations.

A. JUDICIAL DECLARATION OF INJUSTICE: AN OVERVIEW

How does a government repair serious harm it inflicts upon its own citizens, particularly when those citizens are members of a minority racial group targeted because of their race? In particular, what kinds of remedies were sought and given for the internment of 120,000 Japanese Americans during World War II? Earlier chapters focused on how law and legal institutions affected the demographic and life possibilities of Asian Americans. This chapter explores how Asian Americans challenged, used and changed American law through political struggle and litigation. The legal struggles for redress addressed here can be viewed in many ways: as the efforts of dreamers initially tilting at windmills; as hard-nosed practical lawyering and political organizing; as serendipity or hardheadedness, or both; as grassroots community work; as mass media events. Or the legal effort could encompass all of these meanings. At bottom, both the successes and the failures of litigation and political organizing reflect acts of group agency by those suffering from serious governmental injustice—acts worthy of thoughtful study.

Chapter 4 ended with a description of the demographic effect of the 1952 and 1965 amendments to U.S. immigration laws. While the Japanese American population remained small and mostly non-immigrant, the numbers of Asian Americans rose dramatically by 1990—to 3 percent of the U.S. population. Although concentrated in the Pacific states (California, Hawai'i, Oregon, Washington) and New York City and Chicago, Asian Americans now reside in noticeable numbers in most major cities.

Asian American political participation is largely a post-World War II phenomenon. Hawai'i's Japanese Americans, active in the statehood movement, achieved national visibility after Hawai'i became a state in 1959. Hawai'i Senators Daniel Inouye and Spark Matsunaga (along with Hiram Fong), Congresspersons Patsy Mink and Pat Saiki and Governor George Ariyoshi provided the first national Asian American political presence. In the 1970s, California Japanese Americans Robert Matsui (of Sacramento) and Norman Mineta (of San Jose) won elections to Congress and played pivotal roles in legislation affecting Asian Americans. These politicians were crucial to the passage of the Civil Liberties Act in 1988.

Electoral politics was only one of the catalysts for the redress movement. Redress also was fueled by American college students of Asian descent whose "Yellow Power" radicalism in the 1960s contributed to the establishment of Asian American Studies programs and community service and social justice activism. The civil rights, Black Power, anti-war and Third World liberation movements mobilized many Asian Americans on university campuses and in ethnic communities. In earlier historical periods Asian Americans of different ethnic groups often tried to distance themselves from one another. During the civil rights era, Asian American activists found common ground in resisting White American domination. By the late 1960s, Sansei (third-generation Japanese Americans) were much more likely than the Nisei (second-generation) to see themselves as Asian American rather than Japanese American. Through organizations, publications, educational and community programs, and media outlets, activists (including civil rights lawyers) built upon an inclusive pan-Asian identity. These newly identified "Asian Americans" embraced a strong anti-racist agenda. For example, in 1971 an Asian American contingent refused to join the main anti-war march in Washington, D.C., because the coordinating committee failed to adopt anti-racism as one of its tenets.

From this social ferment arose the quest for redress. The redress movement was started informally in the late 1960s by Edison Uno, a Nisei, who began a campaign of public education and legislative lobbying in support of reparations for former internees. This personal effort gradually gained group momentum, with sometimes splintered and reluctant support within the Nisei and Sansei communities. The movement proceeded along all three political channels: executive, legislative and judicial, and each prong of this effort influenced the others. On the executive level, for example, intense lobbying culminated in President Ford's 1976 repeal of Executive Order 9066 during the nation's bicentennial. In the legislative arena, Congresspersons from California and Hawai'i successfully pushed through federal legislation creating a study commission, the Commission on Wartime Relocation and Internment of Civilians (CWRIC). Excerpted in various chapters of this book, the CWRIC's 1983 report PERSONAL JUSTICE DENIED is a penetrating historical investigation of governmental racism and a sensitive exploration of the continuing personal harms of the internment. On the judicial front, Japanese Americans initiated two different kinds of lawsuits. In one, former internees filed a class action damages suit in an attempt to obtain monetary reparations for the material and psychological harms of the internment. This suit, the *Hohri* case, was ultimately dismissed by the federal courts as untimely.

The other litigation, known as the *coram nobis* cases, reopened the original internment decisions themselves: *Korematsu, Yasui* and *Hirabayashi*. The petitioners, Fred Korematsu, Minoru Yasui and Gordon Hirabayashi, did not seek monetary relief. Instead, they asked three different federal courts to rule, based on newly discovered evidence from World War II that (1) no military necessity existed to justify the internment, and (2) the government knew this and suppressed and destroyed evidence in its arguments to the U.S. Supreme Court in the 1940s. As relief, they requested that the courts vacate their original convictions. Although the various courts handled the petitions differently, each of the three *coram nobis* petitions was successful.

Examined in detail in this chapter, the redress litigation illustrates many of the characteristic qualities of the movement as a whole. One problem facing the movement was how to claim remedies for harms that had occurred long ago. Another problem lay in reopening cases that had been decided by the Supreme Court with seeming finality in the 1940s. Finally, the sheer enormity of the legal tasks was daunting. How do volunteer teams of legal workers compete with a U.S. Justice Department committed in its opposition? How does a litigant obtain documents pointing to government misconduct when those documents rest in government file cabinets? How much is success dependent on aggressive inquiry and how much on sheer luck?

Collectively, the *coram nobis* and class action cases helped to galvanize a renewed reparations movement in the mid-1980s. They contributed to the passage of the Civil Liberties Act of 1988, which legislated reparations for all surviving internees and instructed then-President Ronald Reagan to apologize. As described by Professor Eric Yamamoto, a member of the Korematsu legal team, "One woman in her sixties, stated that she always felt the internment was wrong, but that, after being told by the military, the President and the Supreme Court that it was a necessity, she had come seriously to doubt herself. Redress and reparations and the recent successful court challenges, she said, had now freed her soul."

1. BACKGROUND

PETER IRONS, JUSTICE DELAYED: THE RECORD OF THE JAPANESE AMERICAN INTERNMENT CASES

3–26, 225, 27–45 (1989)

"They did me a great wrong."

With these few words, spoken in a quiet but firm voice, Fred Korematsu launched an unprecedented legal effort in January 1982. . . .

With the agreement of Fred Korematsu, [Gordon Hirabayashi and Min Yasui], the campaign to reopen and reverse the wartime internment cases began. Never before in American legal history had an effort been launched— let alone succeeded—to overturn convictions in cases that had been finally decided by the Supreme Court. Beyond the criminal records imposed on the three defendants, the Court's adoption of the government's "racial disloyalty" claims had imposed a collective stigma on Japanese Americans that many internment camp survivors still bore as a mark of shame. . . .

The legal procedure was so obscure and seldom used that few lawyers, let alone laypeople, had even heard of it. . . . [The writ of] *coram nobis* is limited to those who have been released from custody after conviction and final judgment by the courts. Those who invoke *coram nobis*, limited by the Supreme Court to instances of "fundamental error" or "manifest injustice," face a high burden of proof: [O]nly defendants who can prove the most outrageous and obvious governmental or prosecutorial misconduct have any real chance of winning in a *coram nobis* case.

[The identical *coram nobis* petitions filed in three separate federal district courts by Korematsu, Hirabayashi and Yasui in 1983 indeed alleged, and supported with government documents from World War II, claims of outrageous misconduct in the government's efforts to legally justify the curfew and internment. Excerpts from the *coram nobis* petitions and key government documents are reproduced in the next section.]

[KOREMATSU]

The morning of January 19, [1983], the legal team gathered at the office of the federal district court clerk in San Francisco to file the Korematsu petition. Cases were assigned to judges by computer, and the lawyers had some apprehension they might draw one of the more conservative judges from the fifteen who were available for assignment. [A]n assistant clerk []punched a docket number into a computer terminal, waited a minute [ ] and then turned to the waiting lawyers with a wide smile on his face. "Congratulations," he announced. "You got Judge Patel." The lawyers exploded with whoops of joy and hand-slapping. Judge Marilyn Patel was probably the most sympathetic member of the district court bench. . . .

Petitions in the remaining two cases were filed at the end of January [for Yasui in Portland and for Hirabayashi in Seattle]. . . .

In mid-February, the [Congressional] Commission on Wartime Relocation released a 467-page report of its internment investigation, entitled *Personal Justice Denied*. As the title suggested, the commission labeled the internment a "grave injustice" to Americans of Japanese ancestry. The commissioners agreed without dissent that the internment resulted from "race prejudice, war hysteria and a failure of political leadership.". . .

The release of the long-awaited recommendations of the Commission on Wartime Relocation came on June 16, and set off a new round of disputes between [Justice Department lawyer Victor] Stone and the *coram nobis* lawyers. . . .

[In addition to recommending $20,000 reparations for each surviving internee, the Commission] unanimously proposed "that the President pardon those who were convicted of violating the statutes imposing a curfew on American citizens on the basis of their ethnicity and requiring the ethnic Japanese to leave designated areas of the West Coast or to report to assembly centers.". . .

The pardon recommendation gave the Justice Department a way to avoid answering the petitions on their merits unless one of the judges forced an answer to the misconduct charges. . . . After discussions with their respective clients, the lead attorneys on each legal team decided that any formal pardon offer from the government would be rejected in any form. . . .

[As a result,] Stone filed the government's response [to the Korematsu petition] on October 4, 1983. Covering less than two pages of text, the response tried to shift the initiative from the petitioner to the government by asking Judge Patel to vacate Korematsu's conviction on the government's motion. Confessing that the internment of Japanese Americans "was part of an unfortunate episode in our nation's history," the response stated that "the government has concluded—without any intention to disparage those persons who made the decisions in question—that it would not be appropriate to defend this forty year old misdemeanor conviction." Cast as an act of executive grace, much like the pardon Korematsu had scorned, the response argued that Judge Patel had no reason "to convene hearings or make findings about petitioner's allegations of governmental wrong-doing in the 1940s." Almost as an afterthought, the government concluded, "the petition should be dismissed." A tone of apology but not contrition pervaded the brief document.

Judge Patel scheduled the hearing on the Korematsu petition for November 10, 1983, in the ceremonial courtroom of the federal courthouse in San Francisco. Well before the courtroom was opened, a crowd gathered in an atmosphere of emotion and anticipation. Many of those who attended were elderly Japanese Americans who had endured three years of imprisonment in barren internment camps in the desert and mountains. Cries of recognition broke the hallway chatter as former internees met campmates they had not seen for forty years. . . .

Over three hundred spectators crowded the chamber when Judge Patel entered and took the bench. Judge Patel opened the session with a brisk review of history of the case and the *coram nobis* petition, and she quickly announced that she did not consider the government's motion to vacate the conviction and dismiss the petition as a proper vehicle for judicial action. . . .

Concluding that Stone's motion was "inappropriate," Judge Patel stated she would "treat it as essentially non-opposition to the petition and deal with the petition on the merits.". . .

[Attorney Dale] Minami [presented] the charges raised in the *coram nobis* petition. "The allegations we put forth are perhaps unique in legal history, charging that high government officials suppressed, altered and destroyed information and evidence in order to influence the outcome of a Supreme Court decision," he claimed. . . . Fred Korematsu, he said, "lived forty years with the conviction while carrying the burden of losing the case which sanctioned the mass imprisonment of his people. For him to fight as a representative of all Japanese Americans virtually alone, when his community was either too young, too tired, too old, or too frightened to fight and risking imprisonment and a criminal record entitles him to some consideration. Surely after forty years of fighting, Fred Korematsu's interest is part of the public interest. For the Japanese American community, Fred's fight was their fight."

Minami had cast his statement not as a legal argument but to voice the hopes of an entire community: "For those Japanese Americans interned, for those ex-internees in the audience, for Fred Korematsu and for this court, this is the last opportunity to finally achieve the justice denied forty years ago." He ended with a request that Fred Korematsu be allowed to address the court, and Judge Patel agreed.

Korematsu spoke quietly to a hushed courtroom. "Your Honor," he began, "I still remember forty years ago when I was handcuffed and arrested as a criminal here in San Francisco." Speaking for all those who endured the "concentration camps" he had defied, Korematsu asked for the vindication he sought for himself and for those who suffered with him. "As long as my record stands in federal court, any American citizen can be held in prison or concentration camps without a trial or a hearing." He concluded with a simple request. "I would like to see the government admit that they were wrong and do something about it so this will never happen again to any American citizen of any race, creed or color."

[Government attorney Stone] hurried through a brief statement. His only reference to the misconduct charges was to deny any "acts of suppression by the government that might have occurred when the cases were litigated" during wartime. Suggesting the petition had no legal ground, Stone ended by stating as a "symbolic matter" that acknowledgment of the internment as a national mistake "justifies vacating the conviction and dismissing the petition.". . . .

Judge Patel paused for a moment, then began reading the opinion she had composed before the hearing. She cited [not only] the documents [Korematsu's lawyers] had presented [with the petition, but also] the report of the Commission on Wartime Relocation as grounds for her decision. Labeling the government's petition response as "tantamount to a confession of error," she stated that a *coram nobis* petition was the appropriate vehicle "for the Court to correct fundamental errors in its record."

Judge Patel reminded her listeners of the limited scope of her authority as a district judge. She could not reverse the Supreme Court opinion of 1944 or correct any errors of law the justices may have made. Robbed by later cases of any value as legal precedent, she continued, the Court's opinion "stands as a constant caution that in times of war or declared military necessity our institutions must be vigilant in protecting constitutional guarantees." Judge Patel paused again, then stated firmly that "the petition for a writ of *coram nobis* is granted." She rose from the bench without further comment and left for her chambers.

The abrupt conclusion of the hearing left the courtroom in momentary silence. As the audience realized the impact of the judge's historic decision, silence turned to jubilation and tears. Several wept with long-suppressed tears, while others crowded around Fred Korematsu and his lawyers, pumping hands and clapping backs, adding words of gratitude. . . .

[O]n April 19, Judge Patel issued her written opinion on the Korematsu petition. . . . She held that "there is substantial support in the record that the government deliberately omitted relevant information and provided misleading information" to the Supreme Court in the 1940s. . . . [Conceding that "it cannot now be said what result would have obtained had the information been disclosed," she found this question irrelevant to the *coram nobis* proceeding, which turned on whether government lawyers had failed "to provide a full and accurate" factual record to the Supreme Court. Judge Patel added. . . .] "The judicial process is seriously impaired when the government's law enforcement officers violate their ethical obligations to the court.". . .

[YASUI]

Yasui's lawyers were not surprised when Victor Stone, assigned to all three *coram nobis* cases, asked Judge Belloni [of the U.S. district court in Portland] to vacate Yasui's conviction and dismiss his petition, the same motion Judge Patel had denied. [However, differing from the *Korematsu* case,] Stone filed with Judge Belloni a lengthy legal memo that supported the government's claim of power to dismiss criminal prosecutions after convictions had been entered. . . .

Judge Belloni took only ten days to decide the case. He granted the government's motion in a two-page order issued on January 26, 1984. He agreed with Stone that the two sides had asked for the "same relief" in vacating the conviction. "The only difference is that petitioner asks me to make findings of governmental acts of misconduct that deprived him of his Fifth Amendment rights." Listing the requested findings that no military necessity existed for the internment and that "the government knew about and withheld evidence refuting military necessity," Judge Belloni concluded that "I decline to make such findings forty years after the events took place." Yasui wanted to have "the court engage in fact finding which would have no legal consequences," he added. "Courts should not engage in that kind of activity." Before they decided his appeal, Yasui's time on earth expired in November 1986. . . .

[HIRABAYASHI]

Judicial action began in the *Hirabayashi* case when Judge [Donald S.] Voorhees [of the U.S. district court in Seattle] scheduled a hearing for May 18, 1984, on the government's motion to dismiss the petition. . . . The *coram nobis* lawyers had asked Judge Voorhees to hold a full-scale evidentiary hearing at a later date, while the government heatedly opposed this request. Stone urged Judge Voorhees to apply the "laches" defense to the petition as an analogy to the civil statute of limitations. . . .

Judge Voorhees . . . denied the government's motion to dismiss the petition. Noting that Stone had addressed the misconduct charges at length, while denying their legal significance, the judge told the audience he believed Hirabayashi had a right to seek a hearing on his petition. . . .

More than forty years after he entered the federal courthouse in Seattle as a criminal defendant, Gordon Hirabayashi returned on June 17, 1985, to put his former prosecutors on trial. Close to a hundred spectators crowded the courtroom, with former internment camp inmates sharing the wooden benches with a small contingent of the local "Remember Pearl Harbor" group. Faced with a standing-room audience, Judge Voorhees opened the jury box to spectators and set a relaxed tone for the unprecedented hearing. . . .

"This case is an American case," [attorney] Rod Kawakami began. "This is not just Gordon Hirabayashi's case, and this is more than just a Japanese American case. This is a case where an American citizen with a deep and abiding faith in American principles stood up and was one of the few voices to proclaim that as an American, evacuation and incarceration based solely on ancestry was contrary to the most fundamental concept of what being an American is all about.". . .

Stone first denied that "this is a unique case, a Japanese American case," and described it as no different than "hundreds of kinds of criminal cases that are prosecuted every day" in the courts. He went on to denounce allegations that Japanese Americans had been deprived of their rights on racial grounds as "not only spurious but also almost incredible.". . .

Attention shifted from the lawyers when Edward Ennis, white-haired and dapper at seventy-seven, entered the courtroom and took the witness stand. Led by [attorney] Cam Hall through an account of his lengthy government service, Ennis then confirmed the "suppression of evidence" charge he made to Solicitor General Charles Fahy in 1943, the central misconduct charge in Hirabayashi's petition. "And does that remain your view today?" Hall asked. Ennis answered with a firm "yes.". . .

Stone's cross-examination of Ennis spanned two days. . . .

Gordon Hirabayashi took the stand as the hearing moved to a second week of testimony. He added to an account of his wartime arrest and trial some of the reasons his criminal record left him "personally handicapped" after four decades. . . .

The government began its defense when Hirabayashi left the stand. William Hammond, a retired Army officer with wartime combat intelligence service, was the first of four military and FBI officials called by the government to testify about official fears that Japanese Americans posed a potential threat of espionage and sabotage on the West Coast. . . . Hammond conceded under cross-examination by Cam Hall that he had no personal knowledge or recollection of any connection between Japanese Americans and espionage. None of the government's remaining wartime witnesses—Richard Hamm of the Army and Richard Hood and Robert Mayer of the FBI—could recall any evidence of such a connection. . . .

More than seven months passed before Judge Voorhees issued his written opinion on February 10, 1986 . . . [finding] "an error of the most fundamental character" [that] required the vacation of Hirabayashi's conviction on the evacuation charge[.] . . Judge Voorhees [] declined to vacate Hirabayashi's curfew conviction. . . .

[On appeal, the Ninth Circuit issued] in September 1987 a unanimous, thirty-nine-page opinion that Judge [Mary M.] Schroeder wrote. She first observed that the Supreme Court's wartime opinions "have never occupied an honored place in our history." She cited numerous books and articles documenting that "the convictions were unjust," that they were based not on military necessity but on "racial stereotypes," and that General DeWitt's orders "caused needless suffering and shame for thousands of American citizens." Judge Schroeder reviewed the record presented before Judge Voorhees and agreed that "the information now in the public record constitutes objective and irrefutable proof of the racial bias that was the cornerstone of the internment orders."

Judge Schroeder also agreed that "the United States government doctored the documentary record" that was submitted to the Supreme Court. Had the "suppressed material been submitted to the Supreme Court," she wrote, "its decision probably would have been materially affected." Based on these findings of misconduct, . . . [the court reversed] Judge Voorhees on the curfew conviction and [] remand[ed] the case to him with orders to "vacate both convictions."

[In January 1988 the Justice Department abandoned its courtroom defense of the internment.]

2. PRIMARY DOCUMENTS—PETITION FOR WRIT OF ERROR *CORAM NOBIS*, GOVERNMENTS' RESPONSE AND EXHIBITS TO THE PETITION

PETITION FOR WRIT OF ERROR *CORAM NOBIS*— KOREMATSU V. UNITED STATES

Excerpts from Fred Korematsu's *coram nobis* petition, filed with the U.S. District Court for the Northern District of California on January 19, 1983, are reproduced on the next few pages. The first three pages are photocopies of the actual petition. The remaining pages, mainly the summary of argument and prayer for relief, are transcribed. This document reveals the legal strategies ultimately advanced by Korematsu's *coram nobis* legal team, after hundreds of hours of document analysis, legal research and discussion.

```
 1   Dale Minami
     Minami, Tomine & Lew
 2   370 Grand Avenue
     Oakland, California  94610
 3   (415) 893-9100

 4   Peter Irons
     429 Parkwood Lane
 5   Leucadia, California  92024
     (619) 753-0403
 6
     Attorneys for Petitioner
 7
 8              UNITED STATES DISTRICT COURT

 9             NORTHERN DISTRICT OF CALIFORNIA

10
11   FRED TOYOSABURO KOREMATSU,     )
                                    )
12                  Petitioner,     )   Crim. No. 27635-W
                                    )
13   v.                             )   PETITION FOR WRIT OF
                                    )   ERROR CORAM NOBIS
14   UNITED STATES OF AMERICA,      )
                                    )
15                  Respondent.     )
     ─────────────────────────────  )
16
17
18           Fred T. Korematsu ("Petitioner") alleges as follows:
19
20   PARTIES
21       A.    Petitioner
22           Petitioner FRED TOYOSABURO KOREMATSU is a citizen of
23   the United States and a resident of San Leandro, California.
24       B.    Respondent
25           Respondent is the UNITED STATES OF AMERICA.
26   - - - - -
27   - - - - -
28   - - - - -
```

1 JURISDICTION
2   Jurisdiction is conferred on this Court by 28 U.S.C.
3 §1651. Included in the powers conferred on federal district
4 courts by this section of the United States Code, known as the
5 All-Writs Act, is the authority to issue writs of error coram
6 nobis and thus to vacate the criminal convictions of defendants
7 who have completed the sentences imposed on them after conviction,
8
9 CONVICTION BY THIS COURT OF PETITIONER
10   Petitioner was convicted in this Court on September
11 8, 1942 of one count of violation of Public Law 503, 56 Stat.
12 173. Petitioner was sentenced to a term of five years of
13 probation and imposition of sentence was suspended. Following
14 an order of the United States Supreme Court and subsequent
15 decision by the United States Court of Appeals for the Ninth
16 Circuit and the United States Supreme Court, Petitioner com-
17 pleted service of his probationary sentence.
18 - - - - -
19 - - - - -
20 - - - - -
21 - - - - -
22 - - - - -
23 - - - - -
24 - - - - -
25 - - - - -
26 - - - - -
27 - - - - -
28 - - - - -

```
 1                        INTRODUCTION
 2           By this petition for writ of error coram nobis,
 3    Petitioner seeks to vacate his conviction in 1942 before this
 4    court for violation of Public Law 503.  His conviction was
 5    upheld by the United States Supreme Court in 1944.  Petitioner
 6    has recently discovered evidence that his prosecution was
 7    tainted, both at trial and during the appellate proceedings
 8    that followed, by numerous and related acts of governmental
 9    misconduct.  Both separately and cumulatively, these acts of
10    misconduct constituted fundamental error and resulted in
11    manifest injustice to Petitioner, depriving him of rights
12    guaranteed by the Fifth Amendment to the Constitution of the
13    United States.
14         A.    Relation of This Petition to Those Filed on
                 Behalf of Gordon Hirabayashi and Minoru Yasui
15
16           This is an extraordinary petition in many ways.
17    First, it seeks to vacate a conviction that led to a historic
18    and widely cited and debated opinion of the Supreme Court.
19    Second, the allegations of governmental misconduct made below
20    raise the most fundamental questions of the ethical and legal
21    obligations of government officials.  Third, the alleged
22    misconduct was committed not only before this court but also
23    before the United States Supreme Court.  Fourth, this petition
24    is identical to separate petitions being filed on behalf of
25    Gordon Hirabayashi and Minoru Yasui in the federal district
26    courts in Seattle, Washington and Portland, Oregon, respective-
27    ly.  Hirabayashi and Yasui were also convicted in 1942 of
28    - - - - -
```

(continuation of text inside box):

violation of Public Law 503 and their convictions were upheld by the Supreme Court in 1943. . . .

(petition continued) *

C. SUMMARY OF ACTS OF GOVERNMENTAL MISCONDUCT ALLEGED BY PETITIONERS

Point One: Officials of the War Department altered and destroyed evidence and withheld knowledge of this evidence from the Department of Justice and the Supreme Court. In April 1943, General John L. DeWitt, who headed the Western Defense Command and issued the military orders at issue in Petitioners' cases, submitted an official report to the War Department on the evacuation and incarceration program. Justice Department officials had requested access to this Final Report for use in the government's Supreme Court briefs in *Hirabayashi* and *Yasui*. When War Department officials discovered that the report contained statements contradicting representations made by the Justice Department to the courts, they altered these statements. They subsequently concealed records of the report's receipt, destroyed records of its preparation, created records that falsely identified a revised version as the only report, and withheld the original version from the Justice Department. These acts were committed with knowledge that the contents of this report were material to the cases pending before the Supreme Court.

Point Two: Officials of the War Department and the Department of Justice suppressed evidence relative to the loyalty of Japanese Americans and to the alleged commission by them of acts of espionage. The government relied in Petitioners' cases on purported evidence of widespread disloyalty among the Japanese Americans and the alleged commission by them of acts of espionage. Presented to the courts as justification of the curfew and exclusion orders at issue, these claims were made in the Final Report of General DeWitt. Responsible officials knew that these claims were false. Reports of the Office of Naval Intelligence directly refuted DeWitt's disloyalty claims, while reports of DeWitt's own intelligence staff and of the Federal Bureau of Investigation and the Federal Communications Commission directly refuted DeWitt's espionage claims. Although the Final Report was before the Supreme Court in Petitioners' cases, these exculpatory reports were withheld from the Court despite the protest of government attorneys that such action constituted "suppression of evidence."

Point Three: Government officials failed to advise the Supreme Court of the falsity of the allegations in the Final Report of General DeWitt. When certain Justice Department attorneys learned of the exculpatory evidence discussed in Point Two, [*supra*], they attempted to alert the Supreme Court to its existence and the falsity of the Final Report of General DeWitt. Their effort took the form of a crucial footnote in the government's *Korematsu* brief to the Court. This footnote explicitly repudiated DeWitt's espionage claims and advised the Court of the existence of countering evidence. Before submission of the brief, War Department officials intervened with the Solicitor General and urged removal of the footnote. As a result of this intervention, the Solicitor General halted printing of the brief and directed that the footnote be revised to the War Department's satisfaction. The *Korematsu* brief

---

* Peter Irons, JUSTICE DELAYED: THE RECORD OF THE JAPANESE AMERICAN INTERNMENT CASES 128-130, 174 (1989).

accordingly failed to advise the Court of the falsity of DeWitt's claims and thus misled the Court.

Point Four: The government's abuse of the doctrine of judicial notice and the manipulation of amicus briefs constituted a fraud upon the courts. Justice Department and War Department officials undertook separate but related efforts to present a false and misleading record to the courts in Petitioners' cases.

Even before trial of these cases, Justice Department officials decided to utilize the doctrine of judicial notice in presenting "evidence" that the "racial characteristics" of Japanese Americans predisposed them to disloyalty. Despite the rebuff of one trial judge, and knowledge by Justice Department attorneys that countering evidence existed, such tainted "evidence" was included in the Supreme Court briefs in Petitioners' cases. In addition, War Department officials made available to the attorneys general of the West Coast states the Final Report withheld from the Justice Department, and delegated a military officer to assist in preparing the amicus briefs submitted by these states to the Supreme Court. Justice Department attorneys later learned of these acts and concluded they were unlawful, but failed to report these acts to the Supreme Court.

Point Five: Petitioners are also entitled to relief on the ground that their convictions are based on governmental orders that violate current constitutional standards. The acts of misconduct alleged in the preceding Points provide ample ground for the vacation of Petitioners' convictions. With Petitioners' cases before this Court through the instant petition, the application of current constitutional standards provides an additional ground for vacation. The racial classification involved in the military orders at issue is subject to the "strict scrutiny" standard laid out in subsequent Supreme Court opinions. The government now has the task of proving that such a racial classification is essential to fulfill a compelling governmental interest and that no less restrictive alternative is available. Petitioners argue that application of this standard requires vacation of their convictions. . . .

PRAYER FOR RELIEF

Petitioners respectfully submit that it would be impossible to find any other instance in American history of such a long standing, pervasive and unlawful governmental scheme designed to mislead and defraud the courts and the nation. By the misconduct set forth in detail above, the United States deprived petitioners of their rights to fair judicial proceedings guaranteed by the Fifth Amendment to the United States Constitution. Although successful to date, this fundamental and egregious denial of civil liberties cannot be permitted to stand uncorrected.

Wherefore, petitioner Fred Toyosaburo Korematsu respectfully prays:

1. That judgment of conviction be vacated;
2. That the military orders under which he was convicted be declared unconstitutional;
3. That his indictment be dismissed;
4. For costs of suit and reasonable attorneys' fees;
5. For such other relief as may be just and proper.

Dated: January 19, 1983
Respectfully submitted,
By: Peter Irons
By: Dale Minami
Minami, Tomine & Lew

GOVERNMENT'S RESPONSE TO PETITION FOR
WRIT OF ERROR *CORAM NOBIS*

Peter Irons, JUSTICE DELAYED: THE RECORD OF THE JAPANESE AMERICAN INTERNMENT CASES
210–12 (1989)

In 1942, petitioner was one of a very few standard bearers who chose to challenge the propriety of World War II military orders which resulted in the mass evacuation of over one-hundred thousand persons of Japanese ancestry from the west coast.

Although the judiciary questioned the wisdom of those military orders, *Korematsu v. United States*, 323 U.S. 214,225 (Frankfurter, J., concurring), it affirmed petitioner's misdemeanor conviction because it upheld the very broad discretionary authority of the Legislative and Executive Branches of government acting together in wartime. *Korematsu v. United States*, 323 U.S. 214, 217–218 (1944).

Both of those branches of government have long since concluded that the mass evacuation was part of an unfortunate episode in our nation's history. In the 1976 presidential proclamation formally rescinding Executive Order 9066, President Ford praised the sacrifice and contributions of Japa-nese-Americans and called upon the American people to affirm with him the lesson "learned from the tragedy of that long-ago experience forever to treas-ure liberty and justice for each individual American, and resolve that this kind of action shall never again be repeated." Proclamation No. 4417, 41 Fed. Reg. No. 35 p. 7741 (Feb. 20, 1976).

The Legislative Branch has acted likewise. Even before the creation in 1980 of the Commission on Wartime Relocation and Internment of Civilians, Congress enacted 18 U.S.C. 4001(a) in 1971 which provides that "no citizen shall be . . . detained by the United States except pursuant to an Act of Con-gress." The only Act of Congress which had allowed such action, Public Law 77–503, then codified at 18 U.S.C. 1383 (which petitioner was convicted of violating in 1942), has been explicitly repealed. P.L. 94-412, Title V, § 501(e), 90 Stat.1258 (1976).

In this specific context, the government has concluded—without any in-tention to disparage those persons who made the decisions in question—that it would not be appropriate to defend this forty year old misdemeanor convic-tion. Because we believe that it is time to put behind us the controversy which led to the mass evacuation in 1942 and instead to reaffirm the inherent right of each person to be treated as an individual, it is singularly appropriate to vacate this conviction for non-violent civil disobedience. It is also the in-tention of the government to extend the same relief to other similarly situated individuals who request it.

There is, therefore, no continuing reason in this setting for this court to convene hearings or make findings about petitioner's allegations of govern-mental wrongdoing in the 1940's. Moreover, as the Commission found after spending three years and more than one-million dollars, no completely satis-factory answer can be reached about these emotion laden issues from this vantage point in history. See Addendum and Additional Views to Commis-sion's Report.

Having recited above the current valid national interests to be served by vacating this misdemeanor conviction and dismissing the indictment at this time, the government hereby moves to vacate petitioner's conviction and dismiss the underlying indictment. See *Rinaldi v. United States*, 434 U.S. 22 (1978); and *United States v. Hamm*, 659 F. 2d 624, 631 (5th Cir. 1981)(en banc).

Thereupon, petitioner having received all the relief which this Court can render, the petition should be dismissed.

Dated: October 4,1983

Respectfully submitted,
Stephen S. Trott, Assistant Attorney General, Criminal Division Joseph P. Russoniello, United States Attorney
By: William T. McGivern, Jr., Chief Assistant United States Attorney
Victor Stone, Counsel for Special and Appellate Matters, General Litigation and Legal Advice Section, U.S. Department of Justice
Attorneys for Respondent

EXHIBITS TO PETITION FOR WRIT OF ERROR *CORAM NOBIS*

The Korematsu legal team submitted thirty-two exhibits with the *coram nobis* petition. The exhibits included governmental memoranda, letters, telegrams and reports and transcripts of conversations. The documents were prepared during World War II by government officials and were, at the time, confidential. Some documents are marked with handwritten comments. The excerpted photocopies of the actual documents are organized below in four groups. Each group addresses the misconduct alleged in the petition.

The first group of documents speaks to the deliberate alteration of evidence presented to the Supreme Court. The second group addresses the charge that the prosecution knowingly suppressed crucial exculpatory evidence that contradicted the government's legal position. The third group of documents supports the contention that high-level Justice Department attorneys altered an important footnote in the draft of the *Korematsu* brief that was designed to advise the Supreme Court of the falsity of key factual statements in the DeWitt Final Report. The documents in each of these groups are labeled with the exhibit numbers used with the *coram nobis* petitions.

The fourth section consists of excerpts from the transcript of oral argument before the Supreme Court in *Korematsu*. That oral argument, in varying ways, contextualizes both the other sets of documents and the petitioners' claims. It provides evidence of direct misrepresentations by the highest-ranking government lawyer, the Solicitor General of the United States. The transcript was not found until after the conclusion of the *Korematsu coram nobis* proceeding; nonetheless, it was part of the record of the *Hirabayashi coram nobis* appeal.

As you read these documents, refer back to the *Korematsu* petition's "Summary of Governmental Misconduct," *infra*, to assess how the documents supported the specific arguments of the *coram nobis* petition.

a. THE ALTERED EVIDENCE

Exhibit D consists of excerpts from the original version of General DeWitt's Final Report, including handwritten comments. The report was finalized and selectively distributed. It was then recalled when its contents were found to conflict with the Justice Department's position in its *Korematsu* brief to the Supreme Court. All copies of the original Final Report, save one, were deliberately destroyed.* Take note of the paragraph on page 297, beginning with "To return again for the moment to the situation confronting the Commanding General. . . ." Note also the language in the last two sentences of the ensuing paragraph. These parts were originally on page 9 of the original report.

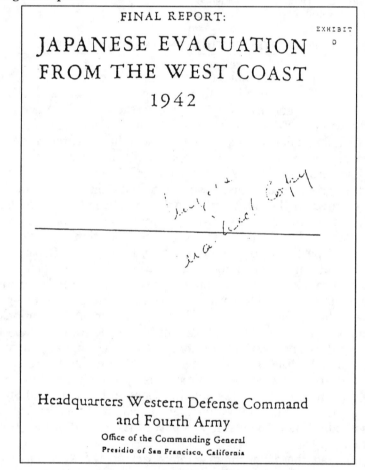

FINAL REPORT:

JAPANESE EVACUATION FROM THE WEST COAST

1942

EXHIBIT
D

Headquarters Western Defense Command
and Fourth Army
Office of the Commanding General
Presidio of San Francisco, California

---

* Government archivist Aiko Herzig-Yoshinaga discovered the last remaining copy of the original Final Report in 1981, in response to a request made by legal historian (and eventual *coram nobis* team member) Peter Irons while he was researching for a book on the internment cases, eventually published as JUSTICE AT WAR.

HEADQUARTERS WESTERN DEFENSE COMMAND
AND FOURTH ARMY
OFFICE OF THE COMMANDING GENERAL
PRESIDIO OF SAN FRANCISCO, CALIFORNIA

April 15, 1943

SUBJECT: Final Report on the Evacuation of Japanese from Certain Military Areas in Western Defense Command.

TO: Chief of Staff, United States Army, War Department, Washington, D. C.

1. I transmit herewith my final report on the evacuation of Japanese from the Pacific Coast.

2. The evacuation was impelled by military necessity. The security of the Pacific Coast continues to require the exclusion of Japanese from the area now prohibited to them and will continue for the duration of the present war. The continued presence of large numbers of persons of an unassimilated, tightly knit racial group, bound to an enemy nation by strong ties of race, culture, customs and religion, along a frontier vulnerable to attack, could not have been countenanced. The rapacious temper of the enemy, quickened and emboldened by the methods of modern war, would have made it worse than folly to have left any stone unturned in building the strength of our defenses. It is better to have had this protection and not to have needed it, than to have needed this protection and not to have had it—as we have learned to our sorrow.

3. On February 13, 1942, I recommended to the War Department that the military security of the Pacific Coast required the establishment of broad civil control, anti-sabotage and counter-espionage measures, including the evacuation therefrom of all persons of Japanese ancestry. In pursuance of my recommendation, the President issued Executive Order No. 9066 on February 19, 1942, authorizing the accomplishment of these and any other necessary security measures. By letter dated February 20, 1942, the Secretary of War authorized me to effectuate my recommendations and to exercise all of the powers which the Executive Order conferred upon him and upon any military commander designated by him. A number of separate and distinct security measures have been instituted under the broad authority thus delegated. Military necessity requires their continuance and may demand the initiation of others. Among the steps taken was the evacuation of Japanese from western Washington and Oregon, California, and southern Arizona. Transmitted herewith is the final report of that evacuation.

* * *

11. This report has been classified as confidential at the direction of the Secretary of War. I recommend that the classification be removed and the report immediately published. The original printing has been confined to a total of ten copies. In anticipation of its publication I have arranged that the type remain set so that the distribution of this report to many Federal and State agencies, public libraries, colleges and universities who have requested it can be readily and quickly effected.

***

CHAPTER I
Action Under Alien Enemy Proclamations

The ultimate decision to evacuate all persons of Japanese ancestry from the Pacific Coast under Federal supervision was not made coincidentally with the outbreak of war between Japan and the United States. It was predicated upon a series of intermediate decisions, each of which formed a part of the progressive development of the final decision. At certain stages of this development, various semi-official views were advanced proposing action less embracing than that which finally followed.

On December 7th and 8th, 1941, the President issued proclamations declaring all nationals and subjects of the nations with which we were at war to be enemy aliens.

***

On the night of December 7th and the days that followed, certain enemy aliens were apprehended and held in detention pending the determination whether to intern. Essentially, the apprehensions thus effected were based on lists of suspects previously compiled by the intelligence services, the Federal Bureau of Investigation, the Office of Naval Intelligence, and the Military Intelligence Service. During the initial stages of this action, some 2,000 persons were apprehended. Japanese aliens were included in their number. ——— ·———

Beyond this, little was done forcefully to implement the presidential proclamations. No steps were taken to provide for the collection of contraband and no prohibited zones were proclaimed.

The Commanding General, during the closing weeks of December, requested that the War Department induce the Department of Justice to take vigorous action along the Pacific Coast. He sought steps looking toward the enforcement of the contraband prohibitions contained in the proclamations and toward the declaration of certain prohibited zones surrounding "vital installations" along the coast. The Commanding General had become convinced that the military security of the coast required these measures.

His conclusion was in part based upon the interception of unauthorized radio communications which had been identified as emanating from certain areas along the coast. Of further concern to him was the fact that for a period of several weeks following December 7th, substantially every ship leaving a West Coast port was attacked by an enemy submarine. This seemed conclusively to point to the existence of hostile shore-to-ship (submarine) communication.

***

CHAPTER II

Need for Military Control and for Evacuation

* * *

In the Monterey area in California a Federal Bureau of Investigation spot raid made about February 12, 1942, found more than 60,000 rounds of ammunition and many rifles, shotguns and maps of all kinds. These raids had not succeeded in arresting the continuance of illicit signaling. Most dwelling places were in the mixed occupancy class and could not be searched promptly upon receipt of reports. It became increasingly apparent that adequate security measures could not be taken unless the Federal Government placed itself in a position to deal with the whole problem.

The Pacific Coast had become exposed to attack by enemy successes in the Pacific. The situation in the Pacific theatre had gravely deteriorated. There were hundreds of reports nightly of signal lights visible from the coast, and of intercepts of unidentified radio transmissions. Signaling was often observed at premises which could not be entered without a warrant because of mixed occupancy. The problem required immediate solution. It called for the application of measures not then in being.[1]

Further, the situation was fraught with danger to the Japanese population itself. The combination of spot raids revealing hidden caches of contraband, the attacks on coastwise shipping, the interception of illicit radio transmissions, the nightly observation of visual signal lamps from constantly changing locations and the success of the enemy offensive in the Pacific, had so aroused the public along the West Coast against the Japanese that it was ready to take matters into its own hands. Press and periodical reports of the public attitudes along the West Coast from December 7, 1941, to the initiation of controlled evacuation clearly reflected the intensity of feeling. Numerous incidents of violence involving Japanese and others occurred; many more were reported but were subsequently either unverified or were found to be cumulative.

To return again for the moment to the situation confronting the Commanding General. When the Attorney General advised that his Department was not in a position to declare as prohibited to enemy aliens the extensive areas recommended for such action in Oregon and Washington, he did not thereby establish the need for military control. It had become apparent that even those measures would not have satisfied the military necessities facing the Commanding General. For, by these means, no control would have been exerted over nearly two-thirds of the total Japanese population. Only about one-third were aliens, subject to enemy alien regulations.

Because of the ties of race, the intense feeling of filial piety and the strong bonds of common tradition, culture and customs, this population presented a tightly-knit racial group. It included in excess of 115,000 persons deployed along the Pacific Coast. Whether by design or accident, virtually always their communities were adjacent to very vital shore installations, war plants, etc. While it was believed that some were loyal, it was known that many were not. It was impossible to establish the identity of the loyal and the disloyal with any degree of safety. It was not that there was insufficient time in which to make such a determination; it was simply a matter of facing the realities that a positive determination could not be made, that an exact separation of the "sheep from the goats" was unfeasible.

---

1. It is interesting to note that following the evacuation, interceptions of suspicious or unidentified red signals and shore-to-ship lights were virtually eliminated and attacks on outbound shipping from west coast ports appreciably reduced.

It could not be established, of course, that the location of thousands of Japanese adjacent to strategic points verified the existence of some vast conspiracy to which all of them were parties. Some of them doubtless resided there through mere coincidence. It seemed equally beyond doubt, however, that the presence of others was not mere coincidence. It was difficult to explain the situation in Santa Barbara County, for example, by coincidence alone.

Throughout the Santa Maria Valley in that County, including the cities of Santa Maria and Guadalupe, every utility, air field, bridge, telephone and power line or other facility of importance was flanked by Japanese. They even surrounded the oil fields in this area. Only a few miles south, however, in the Santa Ynez Valley, lay an area equally as productive agriculturally as the Santa Maria Valley and with lands equally available for purchase and lease, but without any strategic installations whatever. There were no Japanese in the Santa Ynez Valley.

Similarly, along the coastal plain of Santa Barbara County from Gaviota south, the entire plain, though narrow, had been subject to intensive cultivation. Yet, the only Japanese in this area were located immediately adjacent to such widely separated points as the El Capitan Oil Field, Elwood Oil Field, Summerland Oil Field, Santa Barbara airport and Santa Barbara lighthouse and harbor entrance. There were no Japanese on the equally attractive lands between these points. In the north end of the county is a stretch of open beach ideally suited for landing purposes, extending for 15 or 20 miles, on which almost the only inhabitants were Japanese.

Such a distribution of the Japanese population appeared to manifest something more than coincidence. In any case, it was certainly evident that the Japanese population of the Pacific Coast was, as a whole, ideally situated with reference to points of strategic importance, to carry into execution a tremendous program of sabotage on a mass scale should any considerable number of them have been inclined to do so.

There were other very disturbing indications that the Commanding General could not ignore. He was forced to consider the character of the Japanese colony along the coast. While this is neither the place nor the time to record in detail significant pro-Japanese activities in the United States, it is pertinent to note some of these in passing. Research has established that there were over 124 separate Japanese organizations along the Pacific Coast engaged, in varying degrees, in common pro-Japanese purposes. This number does not include local branches of parent organizations, of which there were more than 310.

***

Exhibit G is a memorandum by Captain Hall suggesting alterations to the DeWitt Final Report. The excerpt includes key additional suggestions by Herbert Wechsler, Assistant Attorney General, that were incorporated in the subsequent version of the DeWitt Final Report. These included striking out the entire paragraph in the original report that began with "To return again for the moment. . . ." He also recommended changing two key sentences in the subsequent paragraph., beginning with "It was impossible to establish. . . ."

EXHIBIT

***   G

26. Page 9, strike out the first complete paragraph on that page, and Insert "The acceptance by the Attorney General of the Washington and Oregon recommendations would not have provided the security which the military situation then required. More than two-thirds of the total Japanese population on the West Coast were not subject to alien enemy regulations. The action ultimately taken was based upon authority not then existing. It had become essential to provide means which would remove the potential menace to which the presence of this group under all the circumstances subjected the West Coast. It is pertinent now to examine the situation with which the military authorities were then confronted."

27. Page 9, second complete paragraph, substitute for the fifth and sixth sentences the following: "To complicate the situation, no ready means existed for determining the loyal and the disloyal with any degree of safety."

***

[Transcription of script above: It was necessary to face the realities, that a positive determination could not be made. —Ed.]

b. THE SUPPRESSED EVIDENCE

Exhibit N is a memorandum from the Office of Naval Intelligence, prepared by Lieutenant Commander K.D. Ringle, reporting on the ONI's investigation of the West Coast "Japanese Problem" and recommending against mass internment.

BIO/NB11/EF37/A8-5

BRANCH INTELLIGENCE OFFICE
ELEVENTH NAVAL DISTRICT
FIFTH FLOOR, VAN NUYS BUILDING
SEVENTH AND SPRING STREETS
LOS ANGELES, CALIFORNIA

Serial LA/1055 /re

CONFIDENTIAL SSIFIED

26 JAN 1942

SUBJECT: Japanese Question, Report on.

- -

government to act as agents. In spite of their legal citizenship and the protection afforded them by the Bill of Rights, they should be looked upon as enemy aliens and many of them placed in custodial detention. This group numbers between 600 and 700 in the Los Angeles metropolitan area and at least that many in other parts of Southern California.

(g) That the writer heartily agrees with the reports submitted by Mr. Munson, (reference (b) of this report.)

(h) That, in short, the entire "Japanese Problem" has been magnified out of its true proportion, largely because of the physical characteristics of the people; that it is no more serious than the problems of the German, Italian, and Communistic portions of the United States population, and, finally that it should be handled on the basis of the <u>individual</u>, regardless of citizenship, and <u>not</u> on a racial basis.

(i) That the above opinions are and will continue to be true just so long as these people, Issei and Nisei, are given an opportunity to be self-supporting, but that if conditions continue in the trend they appear to be taking as of this date; i.e., loss of employment and income due to anti-Japanese agitation by and among Caucasian Americans, continued personal attacks by Filipinos and other racial groups, denial of relief funds to desperately needy cases, cancellation of licenses for markets, produce houses, stores, etc., by California State authorities, discharges from jobs by the wholesale, unnecessarily harsh restrictions on travel, including discriminatory regulations against all Nisei preventing them from engaging in commercial fishing—there will most certainly be outbreaks of sabotage, riots, and other civil strife in the not too distant future.

Exhibit W is an interoffice memorandum from J. Edgar Hoover, Director of the Federal Bureau of Investigation, to the Attorney General of the United States. It reports the FBI's inability to substantiate statements in General DeWitt's Final Report about espionage on the West Coast.

Office Memorandum • UNITED STATES GOVERNMENT

PERSONAL AND CONFIDENTIAL

TO   :   The Attorney General

FROM   :   J. Edgar Hoover — Director, Federal Bureau of Investigation   DATE: FEB - 7 .44

SUBJECT: Reported Bombing and Shelling of the West Coast

There is attached a memorandum relative to Lieutenant General DeWitt's final report on the Japanese evacuation of the West Coast.

Certain statements were made in the report indicating that immediately after the attack on Pearl Harbor there was a possible connection between the sinking of United States ships by Japanese submarines and alleged Japanese espionage activity on the West Coast. It was also indicated that there had been shore-to-ship signaling, either by radio or lights, at this time.

As indicated in the attached memorandum, there is no information in the possession of this Bureau as the result of investigations conducted relative to submarine activities and espionage activity on the West Coast which would indicate that the attacks made on ships or shores in the area immediately after Pearl Harbor have been associated with any espionage activity ashore or that there has been any illicit shore-to-ship signaling, either by radio or lights.

Attachment

EXHIBIT
W

OFFICE OF THE
RECEIVED
FEB 7 - 1944

MEMORANDUM

Reported Bombing and Shelling of the West Coast

In the Washington Post under dateline of January 20, 1944, an article appeared entitled "Japs Attack All Ships Leaving Coast", wherein Lieutenant General DeWitt was quoted on the disclosures made by him in a final report on the Japanese evacuation of the West Coast. This report, which is a 618-page bound volume, has been reviewed relative to any possible connection between Japanese espionage activity on the West Coast and shore-to-ship signaling, either by lights or radio. The only references relative to such statements are those included in Part I, in which various reasons are stated in an apparent attempt to justify the Japanese evacuation plan. As will be noted, all allegations are substantially the same as those appearing in the Washington Post news article previously mentioned.

Part I.   Evacuation--Its Military Necessity

* * *

With reference to General DeWitt's statement that after Pearl Harbor Japanese activity on the West Coast was so effective that "substantially every ship leaving a West Coast port was attacked by an enemy submarine", it should be noted that no information is possessed relative to the number or percentage of ships attacked immediately after Pearl Harbor, nor is there any information to indicate that these attacks were associated with any espionage activity ashore. However, it is pointed out that undoubtedly the Japanese Navy had made preparations for submarines to proceed to the West Coast immediately after Pearl Harbor and, quite, naturally, if such preparations were made these attacks would follow.

As to General DeWitt's statement that "there were many evidences of the successful communication of information to the enemy, information regarding positive knowledge on his part of our installations", it is generally known that the Japanese had for years prior to the outbreak of the war collected information as to locations of military and naval installations, as well as data relative to the coast lines of the United States, but it should not be assumed that any part of this information came to the Japanese through shore-to-ship signaling by lights or illicit radio operation. Every complaint in this regard has been investigated, but in no case has any information been obtained which would substantiate the allegation that there has been illicit signaling from shore-to-ship since the beginning of the war.

Relative to the comment made in this report to the effect that "It is interesting to note that following the evacuation, interceptions of suspicious or unidentified radio signals and shore-to-ship signal lights were virtually eliminated and attacks on outbound shipping from west coast ports appreciably reduced", it is noted that numerous reports concerning allegations pertaining to flashing lights, radio transmissions, et cetera, have been received. However, all such reports have been investigated with negative results. It might also be said that there has been no material reduction in the number of complaints received pertaining to submarine activities on the West Coast as a result of persons of Japanese ancestry having been removed from the coast.

Exhibit V is a letter from James Fly, Chairman of the Federal Communications Commission, to Attorney General Francis Biddle. This letter undercuts the factual statements in the DeWitt Final Report concerning illegal communications on the West Coast.

FEDERAL COMMUNICATIONS COMMISSION

Washington 25, D. C.

EXHIBIT
V

April 4, 1944

Honorable Francis Biddle
Attorney General
Washington, D.C.

My dear Mr. Attorney General

This is in reply to your letter of February 26, 1944 with reference to Lieutenant General John L. DeWitt's Final Report on Japanese Evacuation from the West Coast, which was recently made public by the War Department.

You state that you are interested in the accuracy of General DeWitt's account, in the first two chapters of the Report, of the events leading to his decision that military necessity required the evacuation, and you note that prevention of signaling by persons, presumably of Japanese descent, on shore to enemy surface vessels or submarines off the coast apparently was a very considerable part of the problem with which General DeWitt was concerned during the period between December 1941 and July 1, 1942, when the evacuation was substantially complete. You direct attention particularly to his reference to hundreds of reports of such signaling by means of signal lights and unlawful radio transmitters and state that investigation by the Department of Justice of great numbers of rumors concerning signal lights and radio transmitters proved them, without exception, to be baseless.

You inquire, first, whether during the period from December 1941 to July 1, 1942, the Commission was engaged on the West Coast in monitoring and identifying signals reported to be from unlawful transmitters and in locating any such transmitters; and, if so, the number of reports received by the Commission during this period of unlawful or unidentified signals, with a detailed break-down of the results of its investigations:

Throughout this period on the West Coast as elsewhere throughout the United States and its territories, the Commission's Radio Intelligence Division was engaged in a comprehensive 24-hour surveillance of the entire radio spectrum to guard against any unlawful radio activity.

Soon after December 7, 1941, at the request of General DeWitt, the monitoring facilities described above were supplemented by patrols of mobile direction-finding intercept units along the West Coast from Canada to Mexico. These patrols were instituted for the particular purpose of detecting any radio transmissions from shore to ships off the coast.

In the early months of the war, the Commission's field offices and stations on the West Coast were deluged with calls, particularly from the Army and Navy, reporting suspicious radio signaling and requesting the identification of radio signals. In hundreds upon hundreds of cases, identification of the signal was made by Radio Intelligence Division personnel merely by listening to it right at the monitoring station. In no case was the transmission other than legitimate.

In the case of 760 reports of unidentified or unlawful radio signals within the evacuated area during the period in question, which could not be heard or identified by listening at the monitoring station, a field investigation was conducted by mobile direction-finding units. In 641 of the cases it was found that no radio signaling at all was involved. Of the 119 cases remaining, 116 were found to involve lawful transmissions by the following stations:

United States Army Stations	– 21
United States Navy Stations	– 8
Local Police Stations	– 12
United States and Foreign Commercial Licensed Stations	– 65
Japanese Stations in Japanese Territory	– 10
	116

The final 3 were found to involve the very short-range transmissions of the ordinary commercial type phonograph oscillator used in playing recordings for home amusement.

There were no radio signals reported to the Commission which could not be identified, or which were unlawful. Like the Department of Justice, the Commission knows of no evidence of any illicit radio signaling in this area during the period in question.

You also ask the extent to which General DeWitt or his subordinates were informed of the operations of the Commission's Radio Intelligence Division. The General and his staff were kept continuously informed of the Commission's work, both through occasional conferences and day-to-day liaison.

***

You direct attention, further, to the statement in General DeWitt's
Report that following the evacuation, interception of suspicious or
unidentified radio signals and shore-to-ship signal lights was virtually eliminated. You state it was the experience of the Department of Justice that, although no unlawful radio signaling or any unlawful shore-to-ship signaling with lights was discovered, a great
number of reports of such activity were received, and that these did
not diminish in number following the evacuation. It is likewise the
Commission's experience that reports of unlawful radio signaling
along the West Coast – which in each case were unfounded – were not
affected by the evacuation. In fact, throughout the year 1942, the
number of reports of unlawful radio operation requiring investigation by mobile units which were received in the States along the
West Coast varied in close parallel with the number of such reports
received throughout the whole country.

* * *

Sincerely

/s/ JAMES LAWRENCE FLY
Chairman

   Exhibit Q is a memorandum by Edward Ennis, head of the Alien Enemy
Control Unit in the Justice Department, and co-author of the government's
Korematsu brief. The memorandum is addressed to Solicitor General Fahy.
It argues for disclosure of the Justice Department's knowledge of intelligence
service reports contradicting key factual statements in the DeWitt Final Re-
port.

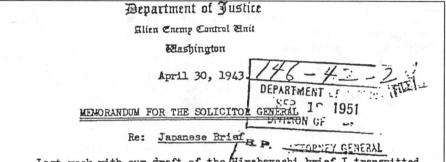

Department of Justice

Alien Enemy Control Unit

Washington

                    April 30, 1943

MEMORANDUM FOR THE SOLICITOR GENERAL

          Re: Japanese Brief

        Last week with our draft of the Hirabayashi brief I transmitted
to Mr. Raum some material which I thought he would find helpful in obtaining a background view of the context of this case. In particular,
I sent him a copy of Harpers Magazine for October 1942, which contains
an article entitled The Japanese in America, The Problem and Solution,
which is said to be by "An Intelligence Officer". Without attempting
to summarize this article, it stated among other things that:

        1. The number of Japanese aliens and citizens who would act as
saboteurs and enemy agents was less than 3,500 throughout the entire
United States.

        2. Of the Japanese aliens, "the large majority are at least
passively loyal to the United States".

        3. "The Americanization of Nisei (American-born Japanese)
is far advanced."

        4. With the exception of a few identified persons who were
prominent in pro-Japanese organizations the only important group of
dangerous Japanese were the Kibei (American-born Japanese predominantly
educated in Japan).

        5. "The identity of Kibei can be readily ascertained from United
States Government records."

        6. "Had this war not come along at this time, in another ten or
fifteen years there would have been no Japanese problem, for the Issei
would have passed on, and the Nisei taken their place naturally in
American communities and national life."

        This article concludes: "To sum up: The 'Japanese Problem' has
been magnified out of its true proportion largely because of the physical
characteristics of the Japanese people. It should be handled on the basis
of the individual, regardless of citizenship and not on a racial basis."
(Emphasis in original.)

        I thought this article interesting even though it was substantially
anonymous. I now attach much more significance to it because a memorandum
prepared by Lt. Com. K. D. Ringle, who has until very recently been Assis-

tant District Intelligence Officer, 11th Naval District, in charge of
naval intelligence in that district (which includes Los Angeles), and
who was formerly Assistant District Intelligence Officer in Hawaii,
has come to my attention. A comparison of this memorandum with the
article leaves no doubt that the author of the Harpers article is
Lt. Com. K. D. Ringle. There are many long passages in the first person
relating to personal experiences which are identical in the two writings.

In addition, I am informed entirely unofficially by the persons
in the Office of Naval Intelligence that Lt. Com. Ringle in fact was lent
to War Relocation Authority to prepare a manual on the background of the
Japanese who were being evacuated from an Intelligence or security viewpoint, for the use of the WRA personnel. After this memorandum was prepared permission was obtained to abstract it and publish it anonymously
in Harpers. Thus the Harpers article, which clearly indicates that the
method of evacuation was wrong and that it would have been sufficient
to evacuate not more than 10,000 known Japanese and that it would now
be safe to release all but not more than 10,000 presently identified
Japanese, was written by a Naval Intelligence officer who was on duty
from 1940 until very recently in the Los Angeles area, from which approximately one-third of the evacuation came.

I have furthermore been most informally, but altogether reliably,
advised that both the article and the WRA memorandum prepared by
Lt. Com. Ringle represent the views, if not of the Navy, at least of
those Naval Intelligence officers in charge of Japanese counter-intelligence
work. It has been suggested to me quite clearly that it is the view of
these officers that the whole evacuation scheme was carried on very badly
and that it would have been sufficient to evacuate the following three
groups:

1. The Kibei.
2. The parents of Kibei.
3. A known group of aliens and citizens who were
   active members of pro-Japanese societies such
   as the Japanese Navy League, the Military Virtue Society, etc.

Since the naval officers believe that it was necessary to evacuate only
about 10,000 people they could have identified by name, they did not
feel that it was necessary to evacuate all of the Japanese. Presumably,
they did not make this view known fourteen months ago for the reasons
that Secretary Knox was at that time greatly exercised about the Japanese Fifth Column and that; since it was the Army's problem, it was safer
to keep quiet than to brave the political storm then raging.

In retrospect it appears that this Department made a mistake fourteen months ago in not bringing the Office of Naval Intelligence into the

controversy. I suppose that the reason that it did not occur to any of us to do this was the extreme position then taken by the Secretary of the Navy.

To have done so would have been wholly reasonable, since by the terms of the so-called delimitation agreement it was agreed that Naval Intelligence should specialize on the Japanese, while Army Intelligence occupied other fields. I have not seen the document, but I have repeatedly been told that Army, before the war, agreed in writing to permit the Navy to conduct its Japanese intelligence work for it. I think it follows, therefore, that to a very considerable extent the Army, in acting upon the opinion of Intelligence officers, is bound by the opinion of the Naval officers in Japanese matters. Thus, had we known that the Navy thought that 90% of the evacuation was unnecessary, we could strongly have urged upon Gen. DeWitt that he could not base a military judgment to the contrary upon Intelligence reports, as he now claims to do.

Lt. Com. Ringle's full memorandum is somewhat more complete than the version published in Harpers and I think you will be interested in reading it. In the past year I have looked at great numbers of reports, memoranda, and articles on the Japanese, and it is my opinion that this is the most reasonable and objective discussion of the security problem presented by the presence of the Japanese minority. In view of the inherent reasonableness of this memorandum and in view of the fact that we now know that it represents the view of the Intelligence agency having the most direct responsibility for investigating the Japanese from the security viewpoint, I feel that we should be extremely careful in taking any position on the facts more hostile to the Japanese than the position of Lt. Com. Ringle. I attach the Department's only copy of this memorandum.

Furthermore, in view of the fact that the Department of Justice is now representing the Army in the Supreme Court of the United States and is arguing that a partial, selective evacuation was impracticable, we must consider most carefully what our obligation to the Court is in view of the fact that the responsible Intelligence agency regarded a selective evacuation as not only sufficient but preferable. It is my opinion that certainly one of the most difficult questions in the whole case is raised by the fact that the Army did not evacuate people after any hearing or on any individual determination of dangerousness, but evacuated the entire racial group. The briefs filed by appellants in the Ninth Circuit particularly pressed the point that no individual consideration was given, and I regard it as certain that this point will be stressed even more, assuming that competent counsel represent appellants, in the Supreme Court. Thus, in one of the crucial points of the case the Government is forced to argue that individual, selective evacuation would have been impractical and insufficient when we have positive knowledge that the only Intelligence agency responsible for advising Gen. DeWitt gave him advice directly to the contrary.

In view of this fact, I think we should consider very carefully whether we do not have a duty to advise the Court of the existence of the Ringle memorandum and of the fact that this represents the view of the Office of Naval Intelligence. It occurs to me that any other course of conduct might approximate the suppression of evidence.

As I have said, my information that the Ringle memorandum represents the view of the Office of Naval Intelligence has come to me informally. I feel, therefore, that we have an obligation to verify my informal information. I believe that we should address an inquiry to the Secretary of the Navy, making reference to the Ringle memorandum, and stating that we have been advised that this represents the Navy's view and asking the Secretary if in fact the views of ONI, at the time of the evacuation, coincided with Com. Ringle's.

The Ringle memorandum originally came into my possession from WRA and we noticed the parallel between the memorandum and the article in this office. Attorneys for WRA furthermore are among the persons who have advised us that the Ringle memorandum represents the official Navy view. In view of the fact that any other information which I have obtained is highly confidential, I would prefer to refer in a letter to Secretary Knox only to WRA.

I have prepared for your consideration a draft of a letter which you might wish to send to Mr. Knox.

Edward J. Ennis
Director, Alien Enemy Control Unit

Attachment

c. THE FOOTNOTE

Exhibit AA is a memorandum from J.L. Burling, Assistant Attorney General, dated September 11, 1944, quoting the language of the original footnote and then the proposed revision by Mr. Fahy.

M—— J.L. BURLING   SEP 11 1944

UJECT: Korematsu v. U.S.   Assistant Attorney General
                                                         War Division

       The Solicitor General has gone over the revised page proof of the brief and has made certain additional changes. I desire to invite your attention particularly to the footnote which appears on page 11 of the revised page proof. As set out in the first page proof at page 26, the footnote read:

       "The Final Report of General DeWitt (which is dated June 5, 1943, but which was not made public until January 1944) is relied on in this brief for statistics and other details concerning the actual evacuation and the events that took place subsequent thereto. The recital of the circumstances justifying the evacuation as a matter of military necessity, however, is in several respects, particularly with reference to the use of illegal radio transmitters and to shore-to-ship signalling by persons of Japanese ancestry, in conflict with information in the possession of the Department of Justice. In view of the contrariety of the reports on this matter we do not ask the Court to take judicial notice of the recital of those facts contained in the Report."

As Mr. Fahy has revised it, it reads:

       "The Final Report of General DeWitt (which is dated June 5, 1943, but which was not made public until January 1944) hereinafter cited as Final Report, is relied on in this brief for statistics and other details concerning the actual evacuation and the events that took place subsequent thereto. The recital in the Final Report of circumstances justifying the evacuation as a matter of military necessity, however, is in several respects, particularly with reference to the use of illegal radio transmitters and shore-to-ship signalling by persons of Japanese ancestry, in conflict with the views of this Department. We, therefore, do not ask the Court to take judicial notice of the recital of those facts contained in the Report."

       You will recall that General DeWitt's report makes flat statements concerning radio transmitters and ship-to-shore signalling which are categorically denied by the FBI and by the Federal Communications Commission. There is no doubt that these statements were intentional falsehoods, inasmuch as the Federal Communications Commission reported in detail to General DeWitt on the absence of any illegal radio transmission.

       146-42-7

       DEPARTMENT
             1951
       DIVISION

addition, there are other misstatements of fact which seek to blame
his Department with the evacuation by suggesting that we were derelict
in our duties. These are somewhat more complicated but they are nevertheless demonstrably false.

In view of the fact that General DeWitt in his official report
on the evacuation has sought to justify it by making important misstatements
of fact, I think it important that this Department correct the record
insofar as possible and certainly we should not ask the Court to take
judicial notice of those facts.

The War Department has no proper complaint as to our disavowal
of the recital of the facts. When we were preparing the Hirabayashi brief
we heard that the report had been made and asked for a copy of it for
our use. We were told that it was secret but that the Army would temporarily
lend us certain pages torn out of the report. We did examine these pages
in May 1943 and then returned them to the War Department. (Some of these
pages then turned up in a brief filed in the Hirabayashi case, without our
knowledge, by the States of California, Oregon and Washington as amicii
curiae) Mr. McCloy advised Mr. Ennis at this time that DeWitt's Final
Report would not be made public.

We next heard of the report in January 1944. At Mr. Ennis'
direction, I called Captain Hall, who was Captain Fisher's predecessor,
and asked that the publication of the report be withheld until this
Department might examine the full report and make comments concerning
the report's discussion of the role played by this Department. Captain
Hall stated that the report had already been published and it was too late
to do anything about it. The report, however, was not published until two
weeks later when it was released to the press. I verified this through the
Army's Publications and Public Relations officers and there was no question
but that Captain Hall's statement on this subject was untrue and that there
would have been time to permit this Department to make representations
with respect to the publication of a report placing the responsibility on
it in part for the necessity of the evacuation, had the War Department seen
fit to permit this Department to inspect the report prior to publication.

In view of all these circumstances, it seems to me that the present
bowdlerization of the footnote is unfortunate. There is in fact a
contrariety of information and we ought to say so. The statements made
by General DeWitt are not only contrary to our views but they are contrary
to detailed information in our possession and we ought to say so.

I press the point not only because I would like to see the footnote restored to its earlier form, if possible, but because it is now
contemplated that the revised brief be submitted again to the War Department.
I assume that the War Department will object to the footnote and I think we
should resist any further tampering with it with all our force.

Exhibit B is a memorandum by Edward Ennis to Herbert Wechsler, dated September 30, 1944, arguing against the proposed alteration of the Burling footnote in the government's *Korematsu* brief.

𝔇epartment of 𝔍ustice

𝔄lien 𝔈nemy 𝔆ontrol 𝔘nit

𝔚ashington

EXHIBIT

B   September 30, 1944

Noted
C. 7.

MEMORANDUM FOR MR. HERBERT WECHSLER

Re: Korematsu v. United States

        I understand that the War Department is currently discussing with the Solicitor General the possibility of changing the footnote in the Korematsu brief in which it is stated that this Department is in possession of information in conflict with the statements made by General DeWitt relating to the causes of the evacuation. Mr. Burling and I feel most strongly that three purposes are to be served by keeping the footnote in its present form. (1) This Department has an ethical obligation to the Court to refrain from citing it as a source of which the Court may properly take judicial notice if the Department knows that important statements in the source are untrue and if it knows as to other statements that there is such contrariety of information that judicial notice is improper. (2) Since the War Department has published a history of the evacuation containing important misstatements of fact, including imputations and inferences that the inaction and timidity of this Department made the drastic action of evacuation necessary, this Department has an obligation, within its own competence, to set the record straight so that the true history may ultimately become known. (3) Although the report deals extensively with the activities of this Department and with the relationship of the War Department to this Department, the report was published without its being shown to us. In addition, when we learned of its existence, we were on one occasion advised that the report would never be published and, on another occasion when we asked that release be held up so that we could consider it, we were told that the report had already been released although in fact the report was not released until two weeks thereafter. In view of the War Department's course of conduct with respect to the report, we are not required to deal with the report very respectfully.

·I

        As to the propriety of taking judicial notice of the contents of the report, it will be sufficient to point out that (1) the report makes an important misstatement concerning our published alien enemy procedures;

- 2 -

(2) the report makes statements concerning radio transmissions directly
contradicted by a letter from the Federal Communications Commission, and
(3) the report makes assertions concerning radio transmissions and ship-
to-shore signaling directly contradicted by a memorandum from the Federal
Bureau of Investigation.

II

The wilful historical inaccuracies of the report are objectionable
for two different reasons. (1) The chief argument in the report as to the
necessity for the evacuation is that the Department of Justice was slow in
enforcing alien enemy control measures and that it would not take the
necessary steps to prevent signaling whether by radio or by lights. It
asserts that radio transmitters were located within general areas but this
Department would not permit mass searches to find them. It asserts that
signaling was observed in mixed occupancy dwellings which this Department
would not permit to be entered. Thus, because this Department would not
allow the reasonable and less drastic measures which General DeWitt wished,
he was forced to evacuate the entire population. The argument is untrue
both with respect to what this Department did and with respect to the radio
transmissions and signaling, none of which existed, as General DeWitt at
the time well knew. (2) The report asserts that the Japanese-Americans
were engaged in extensive radio signaling and in shore-to-ship signaling.
The general tenor of the report is not only to the effect that there was a
reason to be apprehensive, but also to the effect that overt acts of treason
were being committed. Since this is not so it is highly unfair to this
racial minority that these lies, put out in an official publication, go
uncorrected. This is the only opportunity which this Department has to correct
them.

-3-

III.

As to the relations of this Department to the report, the
first that we knew of its existence was in April, 1942, when we requested
Judge Advocate General Cramer to supply any published material in the
War Department's possession on the military situation on the West Coast
at the time of the evacuation to be used in the Hirabayashi brief in the
Supreme Court. Colonel Watson, General DeWitt's Judge Advocate, stated
that General DeWitt's report was being rushed off the press and would be
available for consideration. I was then advised, however, that the
printed report was confidential and I could not see it but I was given
40 pages torn out of the report on the understanding that I return them
which, unfortunately, I have done. Because these excerpts misstated the

facts as I knew them and misstated the relations between the Department
of Justice and the War Department, I suggested to the Solicitor General
that he might wish to discuss with the Attorney General the matter of
the Attorney General taking up with the Secretary of War the question of
showing us this report before it was released. Colonel Watson then advised
me that Mr. McCloy was treating the report as a draft and my personal recollection is that Mr. McCloy stated in Mr. Biddle's presence that it was
not intended to print this report. We did not hear about this report again
until over six months later when I learned accidentally from Mr. Myer of
WRA that he had a copy of the report which the War Department was going to,
publish. I borrowed his copy and then Mr. Burling called Captain Hall,
Mr. McCloy's Assistant Executive Officer, and pointed out to him that the
report undertook to discuss relations between the War and Justice Departments without giving us a chance to examine it and it was my understanding
that Mr. McCloy did not intend to have the report released. Captain Hall
admitted that Mr. McCloy had stated that the report was not to be issued
but stated that he was sorry but the report had already been released and
there was nothing that could be done. We accepted his statement as true
and did not check on it until two weeks had passed without any publicity
and then when the report was discussed in the newspapers we checked with
the public relations office of the War Department and they advised that
the report had just been released and had not been released at the time
Captain Hall said it had.

It is also to be noted that parts of the report which, in April
1942 could not be shown to the Department of Justice in connection with the
Hirabayashi case in the Supreme Court, were printed in the brief amici
curiae of the States of California, Oregon and Washington. In fact the
Western Defense Command evaded the statutory requirement that this Department represent the Government in this litigation by preparing the erroneous
and intemperate brief which the States filed.

It is entirely clear that the War Department entered into an arrangement with the Western Defense Command to rewrite demonstrably erroneous items in the report by reducing to implication and inference what

-4-

had been expressed less expertly by the Western Defense Command and then contrived to publish this report without the knowledge of this Department by the use of falsehood and evasion.

For your information I annex copies of (a) my memorandum of April 20, 1943 to the Solicitor General, (b) my memorandum of January 21, 1944 to the Solicitor General, (c) my memorandum of February 26, 1944 to the Attorney General, and (d) a transcript of Mr. Burling's conversation of January 7, 1944 with Captain Hall which clearly brings out the evasion and falsehood used in connection with the publication of the report.

I also annex copies of memoranda from the FBI and of an exchange of correspondence between the Attorney General and the Chairman of the Federal Communications Commission which establish clearly that the facts are not as General DeWitt states them in his report and also that General DeWitt knew them to be contrary to his report.

RECOMMENDATION: In view of the Attorney General's personal participation in, and final responsibility for, this Department's part in the broad administrative problem of treatment of the Japanese minority, I urge that he be consulted personally on this problem. Much more is involved than the wording of the footnote. The failure to deal adequately now with this Report cited to the Supreme Court either by the Government or other parties, will hopelessly undermine our administrative position in relation to this Japanese problem. We have proved unable to cope with the military authorities on their own ground in these matters. If we fail to act forthrightly on our own ground in the courts, the whole historical record of this matter will be as the military choose to state it. The Attorney General should not be deprived of the present, and perhaps only, chance to set the record straight.

Edward J. Ennis

Exhibit CC is a memorandum from A.S. Fisher to John McCloy, Assistant Secretary of War, dated October 2, 1944, quoting the revised footnote and quoting two options for further revisions of the last two sentences.

EXHIBIT   2 October 1944
CC

MEMORANDUM FOR MR. McCLOY:

    Subject: Footnote at bottom of Page 11 in Draft Brief in
             the Korematsu case.

The footnote at the bottom of page 11 in the draft brief
in the Korematsu case reads as follows:

    "The Final Report of General DeWitt (which is dated
    June 5, 1943, but which was not made public until
    January 1944), hereinafter cited as Final Report, is
    relied on in this brief for statistics and other details
    concerning the actual evacuation and the events that
    took place subsequent thereto."

The remaining two sentences of the footnote, in which the
Solicitor General does not ask the court to take judicial notice
of the Final Report insofar as it deals with matters as to the
use of radio transmitters and shore-to-ship signalling, is
objectionable to the War Department for obvious reasons.

    Today Mr. Wechsler called me up and stated that the Depart-
ment of Justice was willing to strike the last two sentences
of the footnote and substitute one or the other of the following
alternatives:

    1. "We have specifically recited in this brief the facts
    relating to the justification for the evacuation, of.
    which we ask the court to take judicial notice; and we
    rely upon the Final Report only to the extent that it
    relates to such facts."

    2. "We do not ask the court to notice judicially such
    particular details recited in the report as justification
    for the evacuation as the use of illegal radio transmitters
    and shore-to-ship signalling by persons of Japanese
    ancestry, which conflict with information derived from
    other sources."

After considering the matter I phoned them and said that although
the War Department did not agree to either alternative, nevertheless
the first would be preferable.

                                         A.S. Fisher
                                       FISHER

Korematzu

d. THE DIRECT MISREPRESENTATIONS

The following is an excerpt of the transcript of oral argument to the Supreme Court in *Korematsu v. United States*, on October 12, 1944. As explained by legal historian and *coram nobis* legal team member Peter Irons in *Fancy Dancing in the Marble Palace*, this transcript was recovered from government archives after the *coram nobis* litigation was already underway.

The intense interactions between Solicitor General Charles Fahy, Chief Justice Stone and Justice Jackson address rumors of altered and suppressed evidence and the impropriety of judicial notice of the Dewitt Final Report.

THE CHIEF JUSTICE: The act itself refers to exclusion.

MR. FAHY: The act itself refers specifically to exclusion. . . .

That brings us to the question of the nature of the order in relation to the military situation, and the efforts made in this manner to protect the West Coast, under the threat of invasion, from espionage and sabotage. . . .

The final report of General DeWitt was held up to your Honors . . . as proving that he himself had no rational basis on which to make a military judgment. . . . I do assert that there is not a single line, a single word, or a single syllable in that report which in any way justifies the statement that General DeWitt did not believe he had, and did not have a sufficient basis, in honesty and good faith, to believe that the measures which he took were required as a military necessity in protection of the West Coast. . . .

It is even suggested that because of some foot note in our brief in this case indicated that we do not ask the Court to take judicial notice of the truth of every recitation or instance in the final report of General DeWitt, that the Government has repudiated the military necessity of the evacuation. It seems to me, if the Court please, that that is a neat little piece of fancy dancing. There is nothing in the brief of the Government which is any different in this respect from the position it has always maintained since the Hirabayashi case—that not only the military judgment of the general, but the judgment of the United States, has always been in justification of the measures taken; and no person in any responsible position has ever taken a contrary position, and the Government does not do so now. . . .

MR. JUSTICE JACKSON: And in certain instances in which the [DeWitt] report is silent as to dates, it is pointed out that the occurrences stated in the report were after the Japanese had all been evacuated. What is our duty in a case of that kind? Where do we get the facts, if the facts become important?

MR. FAHY: I do not think Your Honor can rely upon the facts other than those which are matters of common knowledge, or which come from sources of which the Court can take judicial notice, and from which such facts can be made available to the Court. If it should become important, we would make every effort to do that.

THE CHIEF JUSTICE: As I understood the argument of the other side, it was that this report, taken as a whole, could be taken to exclude the possibility of a basis for military judgment to continue these exclusion orders. We are dealing now only with exclusion orders.

MR. FAHY: Yes; that is their position.

THE CHIEF JUSTICE: Do you challenge that position?

MR. FAHY: We say that the report proves the basis for the exclusion orders. There is not a line in it that can be taken in any other way. It is a complete justification and explanation of the reasons which led to [DeWitt's] judgment. . . .

Peter Irons, *Fancy Dancing in the Marble Palace*, 3 CONST. COMM. 35, 48–49 (1986)

3. THE *CORAM NOBIS* OPINIONS

Forty years later, the same World War II government documents were pivotal to the three separate *coram nobis* filings in *Korematsu, Hirabayashi* and *Yasui*. Although the documents and petitions were identical for all three cases, the federal courts in San Francisco, Portland and Seattle handled the cases quite differently. Moreover, although the government filed identical motions to dismiss the indictment, vacate the conviction and dismiss the petition as moot in each case, the courts responded to these government requests in very different ways.

The *Korematsu coram nobis* petition, litigated first, was a victory at the federal district (trial) court level in northern California. The court granted the petition and rejected the government's motion to dismiss. The government filed a notice of appeal to the U.S. Court of Appeals for the Ninth Circuit, but then withdrew it.

The *Yasui coram nobis* petition also succeeded, but in a different fashion. The Oregon district court issued a brief order vacating Yasui's conviction without ruling on the issue of prosecutorial misconduct. In granting the government's motion to dismiss Yasui's *coram nobis* petition, Judge Belloni's order stated,

> I decline to make findings [of fact] forty years after the events took place. There is no case nor controversy since both sides are asking for the same relief but for different reasons. The Petitioner would have the court engage in fact finding which would have no legal consequences. Courts should not engage in that kind of activity.

Through this ruling, Yasui achieved the ultimate legal relief he had requested, *i.e.*, the nullification of his conviction, based on the government's agreement that the conviction "was part of an unfortunate episode in our nation's history." Despite granting the ultimate relief sought, however, the ruling did not provide a revised factual record about the validity of the curfew or internment. As stated in a letter to *Korematsu* attorney Dale Minami, Yasui's feelings about a possible appeal were contingent on what he felt would be good for the entire trilogy of cases:

> As far as continuing efforts on the "*coram nobis*" cases, I wanted to again reassure you, and others, that my personal position is that I am willing to do whatever is necessary to advance the cause of justice. . . .
>
> As I publicly stated, if in the interests[] of winning a continuing victory in these[] cases, it becomes necessary for me to back away from an appeal in my case, I am willing to do so. . . .

> Nevertheless, . . . I will not back away from an appeal in my case, until it appears certain that such appeal of my case would jeopardize success in the other cases. . . .

Letter from Minoru Yasui to Dale Minami (April 20, 1984), *Korematsu v. United States Coram Nobis* Case Collection, UCLA Asian American Studies Center, Asian American Movement Archives. Yasui's desire to appeal reflected his view that the district court should have reached the merits of his petition in the course of vacating the conviction.

Yasui's legal team did in fact appeal this order to the U.S. Court of Appeals for the Ninth Circuit, resulting in a published opinion and decision on technical appellate jurisdictional grounds. The appellate court remanded the case to the trial court, but Yasui died during the interim.

Finally, the Seattle-based *Hirabayashi* district court decided in favor of Hirabayashi on the evacuation but not on the curfew issue. The U.S. Court of Appeals for the Ninth Circuit affirmed the district court on the evacuation charge and reversed on the curfew charge. In doing so, it issued a strongly worded opinion that both condemned the government's litigation strategies during the original internment cases and criticized the government's approach to the *coram nobis* litigation itself.

Reproduced here are the *Korematsu* district court and *Hirabayashi* court of appeals *coram nobis* case opinions. Read these cases together, observing similarities and differences in judicial treatment. While reading, recall the historical setting for the original decisions discussed in earlier chapters. Imagine the impact of those original decisions on the lives of still-interned Japanese Americans, and then how former internees may have experienced the judicial hearings forty years later. After reading the opinions, you will be ready to engage the study modules that examine the complex and interrelated issues of ethics, procedure, evidence and political lawyering raised by these cases.

KOREMATSU V. UNITED STATES

584 F. Supp. 1406 (N.D. Cal. 1984)

PATEL, District Judge.

Fred Korematsu is a native born citizen of the United States. He is of Japanese ancestry. On September 8, 1942[,] he was convicted in this court of being in a place from which all persons of Japanese ancestry were excluded pursuant to Civilian Exclusion Order No. 34 issued by Commanding General J. L. DeWitt. His conviction was affirmed. *Korematsu v. United States*, 323 U.S. 214 (1944).

Mr. Korematsu now brings this petition for a writ of *coram nobis* to vacate his conviction on the grounds of governmental misconduct. His allegations of misconduct are best understood against the background of events leading up to his conviction.

On December 8, 1941[,] the United States declared war on Japan.

Executive Order No. 9066 was issued on February 19, 1942 [,] authorizing the Secretary of War and certain military commanders "to prescribe military areas from which any persons may be excluded as protection against espionage and sabotage."

Congress enacted § 97a of Title 18 of the United States Code, enforcing the exclusions promulgated under the Executive Order. Section 97a made it a misdemeanor for anyone to enter or remain in any restricted military zone contrary to the order of a military commander.

In the meantime, General DeWitt was designated Military Commander of the Western Defense Command which consisted of several western states including California.

On March 2, 1942[,] General DeWitt issued Public Proclamation No. 1 pursuant to Executive Order 9066. The proclamation stated that "the entire Pacific Coast . . . is subject to espionage and acts of sabotage, thereby requiring the adoption of military measures necessary to establish safeguards against such enemy operations."

Thereafter, several other proclamations based upon the same justification were issued placing restrictions and requirements upon certain persons, including all persons of Japanese ancestry. As a result of these proclamations and Exclusion Order No. 34, providing that all persons of Japanese ancestry be excluded from an area specified as Military Area No. 1, petitioner, who lived in Area No. 1, could not leave the zone in which he resided and could not remain in the zone unless he were in an established "Assembly Center." Petitioner remained in the zone and did not go to the Center. He was charged and convicted of knowingly remaining in a proscribed area in violation of § 97a.

It was uncontroverted at the time of conviction that petitioner was loyal to the United States and had no dual allegiance to Japan. He had never left the United States. He was registered for the draft and willing to bear arms for the United States.

In his papers petitioner maintains that evidence was suppressed or destroyed in the proceedings that led to his conviction and its affirmance. He also makes substantial allegations of suppression and distortion of evidence which informed Executive Order No. 9066 and the Public Proclamations issued under it. While the latter may be compelling, it is not for this court to rectify. However, the court is not powerless to correct its own records where a fraud has been worked upon it or where manifest injustice has been done.

The question before the court is not so much whether the conviction should be vacated as what is the appropriate ground for relief. A description of the procedural history of these proceedings explains this posture.

PROCEDURAL HISTORY OF THESE PROCEEDINGS

Petitioner filed his petition for a writ of *coram nobis* on January 19, 1983. The first scheduled status conference was conducted on March 14, 1983, when all parties appeared before the court. At that time the petition was deemed a motion and the government was ordered to respond by August 29, 1983. Petitioner's reply to the government's response was set for September 26, 1983, and a hearing on the petition was scheduled for October 3, 1983. Informal discovery was conducted in accordance with the agreement arrived at during the conference. Thereafter, the government moved for an extension

based upon the forthcoming report of the Commission on Wartime Relocation and Internment of Civilians ("Commission"), which it anticipated would
have a substantial bearing on these proceedings. The motion for a continuance was opposed. The court granted the motion, giving the government until September 27, 1983 to respond, and setting October 25, 1983 for
petitioner's reply and November 4, for a hearing on the petition. Thereafter,
the government was given a further extension, to October 4, for the filing of
its response. On October 4, 1983, a document entitled "Government's Response and Motion Under L.R. 220–6" ("Response") was filed. The substance of the Response consists of less than four pages. In fact, it is not an
opposition to the petition, but a counter-motion to vacate the conviction and
dismiss the underlying indictment.

On October 31, petitioner filed his reply and Request for Judicial Notice.
The government filed its Preliminary Response to the Request for Judicial
Notice on November 7, 1983. A hearing on the petition and counter-motion
was conducted on November 10, 1983.

Because the government maintains that the court should grant its motion
and not reach the merits of the petition, the counter-motion is considered
first.

THE GOVERNMENT'S COUNTER-MOTION

The government does not specifically designate in its memorandum the
grounds for its motion. At the hearing the government acknowledged (Fed.
R. Crim. P.) Rule 48(a) as the premise for its motion.

Rule 48(a) has its antecedents in the common law doctrine of *nolle prosequi*. An understanding of that doctrine is necessary to a discussion of the
Rule's application here. As the literal translation of *nolle prosequi*—"I am
unwilling to prosecute"—makes clear, the primary purpose of the doctrine
was to allow the government to cease active prosecution. At common law,
and before Rule 48(a) was enacted, prosecution was within the exclusive jurisdiction of the prosecuting attorney at the early stages of the proceedings
and a *nolle prosequi* could be entered at any time before the jury was empan-
eled.

However, as the case progressed, the prosecuting attorney lost the unilateral right to enter a *nolle prosequi*. After the jury was sworn and evidence
heard, the defendant had the right to object to the entry of a *nolle prosequi*
and the effect of the entry at that stage was a verdict of acquittal. While the
prosecutor's unilateral power to enter a *nolle prosequi* apparently revived just
after the verdict was returned, once a sentence had been handed down or final judgment entered, that unilateral right of the prosecutor was again extin-
guished.

With the adoption of Rule 48(a), the absolute authority of the prosecutor
was tempered and leave of court was required for dismissal of an indictment,
information or complaint at *any* stage of the proceedings. Although there is a
substantial body of case law dealing with the scope of the court's authority to
grant or deny leave to dismiss, little has been written about the time within
which a Rule 48(a) dismissal may be brought.

There is nothing to suggest that the Rule was intended to extend the *nolle prosequi* privilege beyond that allowed at common law. In fact, the purpose of the Rule was to place some fetters on prosecutorial discretion. The plain language of the section is also instructive. The Rule allows for dismissal, with leave, of an indictment, information or complaint, whereupon "the prosecution shall . . . terminate." As the Rule provides that upon the court's approval of a *nolle prosequi*, the prosecution will terminate, it clearly contemplates action by the prosecuting agency only while control of the prosecution still lies, at least in part, with it. By contrast, the prosecutor has no authority to exercise his *nolle prosequi* prerogatives at common law or to invoke Rule 48(a) after a person has been subject to conviction, final judgment, imposition of sentence and exhaustion of all appeals and, indeed, after a lapse of many years. At that stage, there is no longer any prosecution to be terminated. . . .

The court finds no authority for the proposition that a Rule 48(a) motion may be made long after the prosecution has come to rest, the judgment is final, appeals have been exhausted, judgment imposed and the sentence served.

THE PETITION FOR A WRIT OF *CORAM NOBIS*

A writ of *coram nobis* is an appropriate remedy by which the court can correct errors in criminal convictions where other remedies are not available. Although Rule 60(b), Fed. R. Civ. P., abolishes various common law writs, including the writ of *coram nobis* in civil cases, the writ still obtains in criminal proceedings where other relief is wanting. *United States v. Morgan*, 346 U.S. 502 (1954).

While the *habeas corpus* provisions of 28 U.S.C. § 2255 supplant most of the functions of *coram nobis*, particularly in light of the federal courts' expanded view of custody, *habeas corpus* is not an adequate remedy here. Petitioner's sentence has been served. He cannot meet the "in custody" requirements of § 2255 under any interpretation of that section.

The source of the court's power to grant *coram nobis* relief lies in the All Writs Act, 28 U.S.C. § 1651(a). The petition is appropriately heard by the district court in which the conviction was obtained. This is so even though the judgment has been appealed and affirmed by the Supreme Court. Appellate leave is not required for a trial court to correct errors occurring before it.

Coram nobis being the appropriate vehicle for petitioner to seek relief, I turn to the question of how the court shall proceed in this unusual case.

While the government would have this court grant its motion and look no further, petitioner asks this court to look behind the conviction, view the "evidence" that has now come to light and make findings of fact. The court concludes that the first alternative, although easy, is not available; the second alternative is unnecessary.

Even were the government in a position to move under Rule 48(a) of the Fed. R. Crim. P., the court would not automatically grant dismissal. A limited review by the court is necessary, even where the defendant consents. The purpose of this limited review is to protect against prosecutorial impropriety or harassment of the defendant and to assure that the public interest is not disserved.

This Circuit has resolved that petitions for a writ of *coram nobis* should be treated in a manner similar to § 2255 *habeas corpus* petitions. Thus, the nature of the court's inquiry is substantially more expansive than under Rule 48(a). For example, § 2255 considerations apply in determining whether an evidentiary hearing is required. . . .

On a motion under § 2255, the government must establish that there is no genuine issue of material fact; the petitioner is entitled to the benefit of favorable inferences. Where, as here, the government offers no opposition and, in effect, joins in a similar request for relief, an expansive inquiry is not necessary. In fact, the government agrees petitioner is entitled to relief and concedes: "There is, therefore, no continuing reason in this setting for the court to convene hearings or make findings about petitioner's allegations of governmental wrongdoing in the 1940's." However, even where the government has acknowledged that the conviction should be set aside, albeit on different grounds, the court must conduct some review to determine whether there is support for the government's position.

Ordinarily, in cases in which the government agrees that a conviction should be set aside, the government's position is made clear because it confesses error, calling to the court's attention the particular errors upon which the conviction was obtained. A confession of error is generally given great deference.

In this case, the government, joining in on a different procedural footing, is not prepared to confess error. Yet it has not submitted any opposition to the petition, although given ample opportunity to do so. Apparently the government would like this court to set aside the conviction without looking at the record in an effort to put this unfortunate episode in our country's history behind us.

The government has, however, while not confessing error, taken a position tantamount to a confession of error. It has eagerly moved to dismiss without acknowledging any specific reasons for dismissal other than that "there is no further usefulness to be served by conviction under a statute which has been soundly repudiated." In support of this statement, the government points out that in 1971, legislation was adopted requiring congressional action before an Executive Order such as Executive Order 9066 can ever be issued again; that in 1976, the statute under which petitioner was convicted was repealed; and that in 1976, all authority conferred by Executive Order 9066 was formally proclaimed terminated as of December 31, 1946. While these are compelling reasons for concluding that vacating the conviction is in the best interests of this petitioner, respondent and the public, the court declines the invitation of the government to treat this matter in the perfunctory and procedurally improper manner it has suggested.

On the other hand, this court agrees that it is not necessary to reopen the partially healed wounds of an earlier period in order to perform its role of conducting independent judicial review. Fortunately, there are few instances in our judicial history when courts have been called upon to undo such profound and publicly acknowledged injustice. Such extraordinary instances require extraordinary relief, and the court is not without power to redress its own errors.

Because the government has not acknowledged specific errors, the court will look to the original record and the evidence now before it to determine whether there is support for the petition and whether manifest injustice would be done in letting the conviction stand.

EVIDENTIARY ISSUES

The "evidence" before this court consists of certain documents and reports of which petitioner asks the court to take judicial notice. The posture of this request is curious. In response to the request, the government filed a "Preliminary Response." This was filed three days before the hearing on the petition. In its "Preliminary Response," the government did not take issue with the merits of petitioner's request for judicial notice. Its response was merely "designed to convey our general objections" and the government offered to file a full response if requested by the court.

The matters which petitioner asks the court to judicially notice are the Report of the Commission on Wartime Relocation and Internment of Civilians, entitled *"Personal Justice Denied"* (Washington, D.C., 1982) ("Report") and certain government documents, the authenticity of which is not in dispute.

Judicial notice may be taken of adjudicative facts in accordance with Fed. R. Evid. 201, as well as of legislative facts. The distinction between the two is not always readily apparent. Adjudicative facts are usually those facts that are in issue in a particular case. Judicial notice of adjudicative facts dispenses with the need to present other evidence or for the factfinder to make findings as to those particular facts. Rule 201 provides that only those adjudicative facts which are not subject to reasonable dispute because they are generally known or "capable of accurate and ready determination by resort to sources whose accuracy cannot reasonably be questioned" may be judicially noticed.

Legislative facts are "established truths, facts or pronouncements that do not change from case to case but [are applied] universally, while adjudicative facts are those developed in a particular case." Legislative facts are facts of which courts take particular notice when interpreting a statute or considering whether Congress has acted within its constitutional authority. For example, courts frequently take judicial notice of legislative history, including committee reports. . . .

Two factors make the particular stance of this case unusual. The government has neither interposed any specific objection nor put any facts in controversy. Furthermore, this is not a matter which will ultimately be decided by a jury. Where the function of the court is to act as a factfinder or exercise its discretion, more leeway to take judicial notice is justified. Still, the court should be careful in deciding whether to take judicial notice of the records proffered.

In light of these concerns, the court finds it proper to take judicial notice of the purpose of the Commission, the manner in which it was established and, subject to a finding of trustworthiness, the general nature and substance of its conclusions. Judicial notice of these facts may be used to inform the court's determination of whether denial of the motion would result in manifest injustice, of the public interest to be served by the granting of the motion, and of whether there is support for the government's acquiescence.

The court concludes it is not proper or necessary to take judicial notice of the specific Commission findings and conclusions as adjudicative facts under § 201, despite the government's failure to adequately object.[5]

THE COMMISSION REPORT

The Commission on Wartime Relocation and Internment of Civilians was established in 1980 by an act of Congress. It was directed to review the facts and circumstances surrounding Executive Order 9066 and its impact on American citizens and permanent resident aliens; to review directives of the United States military forces requiring the relocation and, in some cases, detention in internment camps of American citizens, including those of Japanese ancestry; and to recommend appropriate remedies.

The Commission was composed of former members of Congress, the Supreme Court and the Cabinet as well as distinguished private citizens. It held approximately twenty days of hearings in cities across the United States, taking the testimony of over 720 witnesses, including key government personnel responsible for decisions involved in the issuance of Executive Order 9066 and the military orders implementing it. The Commission reviewed substantial numbers of government documents, including documents not previously available to the public.

In light of all these factors, the Report carries substantial indicia of trustworthiness. Indeed, as noted above, the government conceded at the March 1983 status conference that the Report was an appropriate subject of judicial notice.

The findings and conclusions of the Commission were unanimous. In general, the Commission concluded that at the time of the issuance of Executive Order 9066 and implementing military orders, there was substantial credible evidence from a number of federal civilian and military agencies contradicting the report of General DeWitt that military necessity justified exclusion and internment of all persons of Japanese ancestry without regard to individual identification of those who may have been potentially disloyal.

The Commission found that military necessity did not warrant the exclusion and detention of ethnic Japanese. It concluded that "broad historical causes which shaped these decisions [exclusion and detention] were race prejudice, war hysteria and a failure of political leadership." As a result, "a

---

[5] It should be noted that the report appears to meet the requirements of Rule 803(8) of the Federal Rules of Evidence as findings resulting from an investigation made pursuant to authority granted by law. Under the Rule, it would be deemed admissible absent a showing of lack of trustworthiness. Advisory Committee Notes to Exceptions 803(8). There is nothing to suggest the report lacks trustworthiness. Admission of the report under 803(8) would allow it to be weighed along with other evidence, if any, and permit the court to make its own findings. Were the court to take judicial notice of the findings under Rule 201, by contrast, the findings would become conclusive.

grave injustice was done to American citizens and resident aliens of Japanese ancestry who, without individual review or any probative evidence against them, were excluded, removed and detained by the United States during World War II."

The Commission's Report provides ample support for the conclusion that denial of the motion would result in manifest injustice and that the public interest is served by granting the relief sought.

GOVERNMENT MEMORANDA

Petitioner offers another set of documents showing that there was critical contradictory evidence known to the government and knowingly concealed from the courts. These records present another question regarding the propriety of judicial notice. They consist of internal government memoranda and letters. Their authenticity is not disputed. Yet they are not the kind of documents that are the proper subject of judicial notice, and they are offered on the ultimate issue of governmental misconduct.

The internal memoranda and letters may, however, be considered by the court as evidence under Rule 803(1) or 803(16). Alternatively, because they are not actually offered for the truth of the statements contained in them, but rather as evidence that the statements were made (*i.e.*, verbal conduct), they may be admitted as non-hearsay within the purview of 801(c).

The substance of the statements contained in the documents and the fact the statements were made demonstrate that the government knowingly withheld information from the courts when they were considering the critical question of military necessity in this case. A series of correspondence regarding what information should be included in the government's brief before the Supreme Court culminated in two different versions of a footnote that was to be used to specify the factual data upon which the government relied for its military necessity justification. The first version read as follows:

> The Final Report of General DeWitt (which is dated June 5, 1943, but which was not made public until January 1944) is relied on in this brief for statistics and other details concerning the actual evacuation and the events that took place subsequent thereto. *The recital of the circumstances justifying the evacuation as a matter of military necessity, however, is in several respects,* particularly with reference to the use of illegal radio transmitters and to shore-to-ship signalling by persons of Japanese ancestry, *in conflict with information in the possession of the Department of Justice. In view of the contrariety of the reports on this matter we do not ask the Court to take judicial notice of the recital of those facts contained in the Report.*

Petitioner's Exhibit AA, Memorandum of John L. Burling to Assistant Attorney General Herbert Wechsler, September 11, 1944 (emphasis added) [*supra* section A.2.c at 310].

After revision, it read:

> The Final Report of General DeWitt (which is dated June 5, 1943, but which was not made public until January 1944) hereinafter cited as Final Report, is relied on in this brief for statistics and other details concerning the actual evacuation and the events that took place subsequent thereto. *The recital in the Final Report of circumstances justifying the evacuation as a matter of*

military necessity, however, is in several respects, particularly with reference to the use of illegal radio transmitters and shore-to-ship signalling by persons of Japanese ancestry, *in conflict with the views of this Department. We, therefore, do not ask the Court to take judicial notice of the recital of those facts contained in the Report.*

Id. (emphasis added).

The footnote that appeared in the final version of the brief merely read as follows:

The Final Report of General DeWitt (which is dated June 5, 1943, but which was not made public until January 1944), hereinafter cited as Final Report, is relied on in this brief for statistics and other details concerning the actual evacuation and the events that took place subsequent thereto. *We have specifically recited in this brief the facts relating to the justification for the evacuation, of which we ask the Court to take judicial notice, and we rely upon the Final Report only to the extent that it relates to such facts.*

Brief for the United States, *Korematsu v. United States*, October Term, 1944, No. 22, at 11. The final version made no mention of the contradictory reports. The record is replete with protestations of various Justice Department officials that the government had the obligation to advise the courts of the contrary facts and opinions. Petitioner's Exhibits A-FF. In fact, several Department of Justice officials pointed out to their superiors and others the "wilful historical inaccuracies and intentional falsehoods" contained in the DeWitt Report.

These omissions are critical. In the original proceedings, before the district court and on appeal, the government argued that the actions taken were within the war-making powers of the Executive and Legislative branches and, even where the actions were directed at a particular class of persons, they were beyond judicial scrutiny so long as they were reasonably related to the security and defense of the nation and the prosecution of the war.

Indeed, this emphasis on national security was reflected in the standard of review laid down in *Hirabayashi v. United States*: "We think that constitutional government in time of war, is not so powerless and does not compel so hard a choice if those charged with the responsibility of our national defense have reasonable ground for believing that the threat is real." The Court acknowledged that it could not second guess the decisions of the Executive and Congress but was limited to determining whether all of the relevant circumstances "within the knowledge of those charged with the responsibility for maintaining the national defense afforded a rational basis for the decisions which they made."

The government relied on the rationale of *Hirabayashi* in its memoranda in *Korematsu*. That rationale was adopted in *Korematsu*.

In *Hirabayashi* and *Korematsu*, the courts at each level engaged in an extensive examination of the facts known to the Executive and Legislative Branches. The facts which the government represented it relied upon and provided to the courts were those contained in a report entitled "Final Report, Japanese Evacuation from the West Coast" (1942), prepared by General DeWitt. His evaluation and version of the facts informed the courts' opinions. Yet, omitted from the government's representations was any reference to contrary reports which were considered reliable by the Justice Department and military officials other than General DeWitt.

A close reading of the briefs filed in the District Court by the government and amicus curiae State of California shows they relied heavily on the DeWitt Report for the facts justifying their military necessity arguments.[9]

There is no question that the Executive and Congress were entitled to reasonably rely upon certain facts and to discount others. The question is not whether they were justified in relying upon some reports and not others, but whether the court had before it all the facts known by the government. Was the court misled by any omissions or distortions in concluding that the other branches' decisions had a reasonable basis in fact? Omitted from the reports presented to the courts was information possessed by the Federal Communications Commission, the Department of the Navy, and the Justice Department which directly contradicted General DeWitt's statements. Thus, the court had before it a selective record.

Whether a fuller, more accurate record would have prompted a different decision cannot be determined. Nor need it be determined. Where relevant evidence has been withheld, it is ample justification for the government's concurrence that the conviction should be set aside. It is sufficient to satisfy the court's independent inquiry and justify the relief sought by petitioner.

OTHER REQUIREMENTS FOR *CORAM NOBIS* RELIEF

The government has . . . failed to rebut petitioner's showing of timeliness. It appears from the record that much of the evidence upon which petitioner bases his motion was not discovered until recently. In fact, until the discovery of the documents relating to the government's brief before the Supreme Court, there was no specific evidence of governmental misconduct available.

There is thus no barrier to granting petitioner's motion for *coram nobis* relief.

CONCLUSION

The Supreme Court has cautioned that *coram nobis* should be used "only under certain circumstances compelling such action to achieve justice" and to correct "errors of the most fundamental character." It is available to correct errors that result in a complete miscarriage of justice and where there are exceptional circumstances.

---

[9] The upper echelons of the Justice Department were well aware of the unjustified reliance being placed on the DeWitt Report by the amici curiae. "It is also to be noted that parts of the [DeWitt] report which, in April 1942 could not be shown to the Department of Justice in connection with the Hirabayashi case in the Supreme Court, were printed in the brief amici curiae of the States of California, Oregon and Washington. In fact the Western Defense Command evaded the statutory requirement that this Department represent the Government in this litigation by preparing the erroneous and intemperate brief which the States filed." Memorandum from Edward J. Ennis, Director of the Alien Enemy Control Unit, Department of Justice to Assistant Attorney General Herbert Wechsler, September 30, 1944 [*supra* section B.2.c—ED.].

Coram nobis also lies for a claim of prosecutorial impropriety. This Circuit noted in *United States v. Taylor* [(648 F.2d 565 (9th Cir.)),] *cert. denied*, 454 U.S. 866, 102 S.Ct. 329 (1981)], that the writ "strikes at the veracity *vel non* of the government's representations to the court" and is appropriate where the procedure by which guilt is ascertained is under attack. The *Taylor* court observed that due process principles, raised by *coram nobis* charging prosecutorial misconduct, are not "strictly limited to those situations in which the defendant has suffered arguable prejudice; . . . [but also designed] to maintain public confidence in the administration of justice."

At oral argument the government acknowledged the exceptional circumstances involved and the injustice suffered by petitioner and other Japanese-Americans. Moreover, there is substantial support in the record that the government deliberately omitted relevant information and provided misleading information in papers before the court. The information was critical to the court's determination, although it cannot now be said what result would have obtained had the information been disclosed. Because the information was of the kind peculiarly within the government's knowledge, the court was dependent upon the government to provide a full and accurate account. Failure to do so presents the "compelling circumstance" contemplated by *Morgan*[, *supra*]. The judicial process is seriously impaired when the government's law enforcement officers violate their ethical obligations to the court.[10]

This court's decision today does not reach any errors of law suggested by petitioner. At common law, the writ of *coram nobis* was used to correct errors of fact. It was not used to correct legal errors and this court has no power, nor does it attempt, to correct any such errors.

Thus, the Supreme Court's decision stands as the law of this case and for whatever precedential value it may still have. Justices of that Court and legal scholars have commented that the decision is an anachronism in upholding overt racial discrimination as "compellingly justified." "Only two of this Court's modern cases have held the use of racial classifications to be constitutional." *Fullilove v. Klutznick*[, 448 U.S. 448, 507 (1980)] (Powell, J., concurring and referring to *Korematsu* and *Hirabayashi*). The government acknowledged its concurrence with the Commission's observation that "today the decision in *Korematsu* lies overruled in the court of history."

Korematsu remains on the pages of our legal and political history. As a legal precedent it is now recognized as having very limited application. As historical precedent it stands as a constant caution that in times of war or declared military necessity our institutions must be vigilant in protecting constitutional guarantees. It stands as a caution that in times of distress the shield of military necessity and national security must not be used to protect governmental actions from close scrutiny and accountability. It stands as a cau-

---

[10] Recognizing the ethical responsibility to make full disclosure to the courts, Director Ennis pointed out to the Assistant Attorney General that "[t]he Attorney General should not be deprived of the present, and perhaps only, chance to set the record straight." Exhibit B, p. 4 [*supra* section B.2.c—ED.].

tion that in times of international hostility and antagonisms our institutions, legislative, executive and judicial, must be prepared to exercise their authority to protect all citizens from the petty fears and prejudices that are so easily aroused.

ORDER

In accordance with the foregoing, the petition for a writ of *coram nobis* is granted and the counter-motion of the respondent is denied.

Unlike Judge Patel's ruling, the decision on the *Hirabayashi coram nobis* petition followed a full trial.

HIRABAYASHI V. UNITED STATES

828 F.2d 591 (9th Cir. 1987)

SCHROEDER, Circuit Judge.

I. INTRODUCTION

Gordon Hirabayashi is an American citizen who was born in Seattle, Washington, in 1918, and is currently Professor Emeritus of Sociology at the University of Alberta. He is of Japanese ancestry. In 1942 he was living in Seattle and was therefore subject to wartime orders requiring all persons of Japanese ancestry, whether citizens or not, to remain within their residences between 8:00 p.m. and 6:00 a.m. He was also subject to subsequent orders to report to a Civilian Control Station for processing requisite to exclusion from the military area. Hirabayashi refused to honor the curfew or to report to the control station because he believed that the military orders were based upon racial prejudice and violated the protection the Constitution affords to all citizens. The Supreme Court reviewed his conviction for violating the curfew order and unanimously affirmed. In an opinion by Chief Justice Stone, the Court accepted the government's position that the curfew was justified by military assessments of emergency conditions existing at the time. *Hirabayashi v. United States*, 320 U.S. 81 (1943). Because Hirabayashi had received a concurrent sentence for violating the exclusion order, the Court affirmed that conviction as well. The following year, a majority of what was by then a sharply divided Court applied the same military emergency rationale to uphold explicitly the exclusion of all citizens of Japanese ancestry from the West Coast. *Korematsu v. United States*. 323 U.S. 214 (1944).

The *Hirabayashi* and *Korematsu* decisions have never occupied an honored place in our history. In the ensuing four and a half decades, journalists and researchers have stocked library shelves with studies of the cases and surrounding events. These materials document historical judgments that the convictions were unjust. They demonstrate that there could have been no reasonable military assessment of an emergency at the time,[1] that the orders were based upon racial stereotypes,[2] and that the orders caused needless suffering and shame for thousands of American citizens.[3] The legal judgments of the courts reflecting that Hirabayashi and Korematsu had been properly convicted of violating the laws of the United States, however, remained on their records. Petitioner filed this lawsuit in 1983 to obtain a writ of error *coram nobis* to vacate his convictions and thus to make the judgments of the courts conform to the judgments of history.

The event which triggered the lawsuit occurred in 1982, when an archival researcher discovered the sole remaining copy of the original report prepared by the general who issued the curfew and exclusion orders. This report was intended to explain the basis for those orders. War Department officials revised the report in several material respects and tried to destroy all of the original copies before issuing the final report. The Justice Department did not know of the existence of the original report at the time its attorneys were preparing briefs in the *Hirabayashi* and *Korematsu* cases.

In his *coram nobis* petition Hirabayashi contended that the original report, the circumstances surrounding its alteration, and recently discovered related documents provided the proof, unavailable at the time of his conviction, that the curfew and exclusion orders were in fact based upon racial prejudice rather than military exigency. Hirabayashi further alleged that the government concealed these matters from his counsel and the Supreme Court, and that had the Supreme Court known the true basis for the orders, the ultimate decision in the case would probably have been different.

The district court held a full evidentiary proceeding on Hirabayashi's claims. It reviewed hundreds of documents and heard the testimony of several witnesses. They included Edward Ennis, who had been the Director of the Alien Enemy Control Unit at the Department of Justice and a principal author of the government's briefs in both the *Hirabayashi* and *Korematsu* cases; William Hammond, who had been the Assistant Chief of Staff for the entire Western Defense Command; Aiko Herzig-Yoshinaga, a researcher for the Commission on Wartime Relocation and Internment of Civilians from 1981 to 1983 and the person who discovered the original version of the final report.

---

[1] *See, e.g.,* P. Irons, *Justice at War* (1983); R. Daniels, *The Decision to Relocate the Japanese Americans* (1975); M. Grodzins, *Americans Betrayed* (1949); Yamamoto, *Korematsu Revisited—Correcting the Injustice of Extraordinary Government Excess and Lax Judicial Review: Time for a Better Accommodation of National Security Concerns and Civil Liberties,* 26 SANTA CLARA L. REV. 1 (1986).

[2] *See, e.g.,* A. Fisher, *Exile of a Race* (1970); C. McWilliams, *Prejudice* (1944); Rostow, *The Japanese American Cases—A Disaster,* 54 Yale L.J. 489 (1954); Dembitz, *Racial Discrimination and the Military Judgment: The Supreme Court's Korematsu and Endo Decisions,* 45 COLUM. L. REV. 175 (1945).

[3] *See, e.g.,* R. Daniels, S. Taylor & H. Kitano, *Japanese Americans: From Relocation To Redress* (1986); M. Weglyn, *Years of Infamy* (1976); D. Myer, *Uprooted Americans* (1971).

In a careful opinion containing detailed findings of fact, the district court confirmed Hirabayashi's contentions in virtually every factual respect. *See Hirabayashi v. United States*, 627 F. Supp. 1445 (W.D. Wash. 1986). It rejected as factually and legally unsupported the government's arguments that Hirabayashi had not been prejudiced by the concealment of the newly discovered material, that Hirabayashi could and should have made the same claims years earlier, and that there was no remaining case or controversy because Hirabayashi suffered no continuing adverse consequences from the original convictions.

The district court held that Hirabayashi's conviction for violating the exclusion order resulted in a violation of due process and ordered it vacated. Another district court has reached the same result in the *Korematsu* case, *Korematsu v. United States*, 584 F. Supp. 1406 (N.D. Cal. 1984), and there has been no appeal. The district court in this case, however, concluded as a matter of law that the curfew conviction should not be vacated. It ruled that because the curfew order less significantly infringed Hirabayashi's freedom, the Supreme Court would have distinguished it from the exclusion order and would have affirmed the conviction even if it had known the racial basis of the order.

Both Hirabayashi and the government appeal. We agree with the district court's factual and legal analysis leading to its vacation of the exclusion conviction. We disagree with the court's conclusion that the curfew conviction rests upon a legal foundation different from the exclusion conviction. We therefore hold that both convictions should be vacated.

II. FACTUAL BACKGROUND

This proceeding is a collateral attack upon convictions for violating military orders promulgated in 1942. The facts underlying this litigation thus form a very small part of the great mosaic of American participation in World War II. . . .

A grand jury indicted petitioner on May 28, 1942. Count I charged that he had failed to report pursuant to Civilian Exclusion Order 57. Count II charged the curfew violation. He was tried by a jury in October 1942, found guilty, and sentenced to three months on each count to be served concurrently. On appeal, this court certified issues to the Supreme Court, and the Supreme Court on April 5, 1943, certified the entire record to it. . . .

B. THE SUPREME COURT PROCEEDINGS

. . . In his brief, Hirabayashi argued that there was no emergency justifying a racially based classification and that the orders had been issued upon invidious racial prejudice. . . .

The Justice Department justified the exclusion and curfew orders upon what it said was a reasonable judgment of military necessity. It argued that because of cultural characteristics of the Japanese Americans, including religion and education, it was likely that some, though not all, American citizens of Japanese ancestry were disloyal. It then argued that because of the military exigencies, the government did not wait to segregate the loyal from the disloyal. The government's brief stated:

The classification was not based upon invidious race discrimination. Rather, it was founded upon the fact that the group as a whole contained an unknown number of persons who could not readily be singled out and who were a threat to the security of the nation; and in order to impose effective restraints upon them it was necessary not only to deal with the entire group, but to deal with it at once.

Later in its brief, the government stated that "[w]hat was needed was a method of removing at once the unknown number of Japanese persons who might assist a Japanese invasion, and not a program for sifting out such persons in the indefinite future."

The government claimed that the "operative fact" on which the classification was made was the danger arising from the existence of over 100,000 persons of Japanese descent on the West Coast. It acknowledged, however, that the "record in this case does not contain any comprehensive account of the facts which gave rise to the exclusion and curfew measures here involved." The government therefore made extensive use of judicial notice in order to convey its position that those responsible for the orders reasonably regarded an emergency situation to exist. It argued that "historical facts" and "facts appear[ing] in official documents . . . are peculiarly within the realm of judicial notice."

The government's argument that the urgency of the situation made individual hearings to determine loyalty impossible was the subject of special concern. Solicitor General Charles Fahy filed a post-argument memorandum stressing that the hearings could not have been utilized because the "situation did not lend itself, in the *unique and pressing* circumstances, to solution by individual loyalty hearings."

The Supreme Court decided the case on June 21, 1943. The government's view prevailed; Chief Justice Stone deferred to the military assessment of necessity. The Court saw the racial classification as justifiable only as a matter of military expediency, and indicated that it had to accept the judgment of the military authorities that the exigencies of time required the entire Japanese population to be treated as a group. The Court concluded:

> Whatever views we may entertain regarding the loyalty to this country of the citizens of Japanese ancestry, we cannot reject as unfounded the judgment of the military authorities and of Congress that there were disloyal members of that population, whose number and strength could not be precisely and quickly ascertained. We cannot say that the war making branches of the Government did not have ground for believing that in a critical hour such persons could not readily be isolated and separately dealt with. . . .

C. THE *CORAM NOBIS* PROCEEDINGS: GENERAL DEWITT'S REPORT AND OTHER MATTERS DEVELOPED IN THE RECORD BELOW

Hirabayashi filed this *coram nobis* proceeding early in 1983, alleging that new material had come to light in this decade which showed that the Department of War had suppressed evidence from both Hirabayashi and the Justice Department during the crucial period when the case was being presented to the Supreme Court, and that this material required the court to grant the unusual writ of *coram nobis* to vacate the convictions. The government, recognizing that the circumstances surrounding Hirabayashi's convictions may have been unjust, nevertheless asked the district court to refrain from considering the facts, and to dismiss the petition for *coram nobis*. It asked the court instead to utilize the provisions of Fed. R. Crim. P. 48, permitting termination of a prosecution by dismissal of the indictment, to vacate the conviction. The district court denied the government's motion to dismiss and held a full evidentiary hearing on Hirabayashi's claims.

The principal factual matter developed at the trial concerned the suppressed report of General DeWitt. This report set forth the basis for his promulgation of the orders of which Hirabayashi stood convicted. At the time General DeWitt issued his series of orders regarding curfew and exclusion in 1942, neither he nor the War Department provided any factual explanation of the reasons for the orders. After they were issued, General DeWitt prepared such a report. The official version of the report, *Final Report: Japanese Evacuation from the West Coast 1942*, was dated June 5, 1943, but was not made public until January 1944. Recent historical research, however, has uncovered in the National Archives a previously unknown copy of an original version of that report. That copy reflects that General DeWitt transmitted his original report to the War Department in Washington on April 15, 1943.

The original version differed materially from the official version. Most significantly, the original report did not purport to rest on any military exigency, but instead declared that because of traits peculiar to citizens of Japanese ancestry it would be impossible to separate the loyal from the disloyal, and that all would have to be evacuated for the duration of the war. Other documents in the record below show that officials in the War Department were alarmed when they received the original report. The district court observed that Assistant Secretary of War John J. McCloy was "more than a little exercised because the Final Report had been printed in final form and distributed without any prior consultation by the Western Defense Command with the War Department about its contents."

McCloy and Colonel Karl Bendetsen, who was in charge of the Wartime Civil Control Administration of the Western Defense Command, had a number of communications with General DeWitt in order to persuade him to change the report. At first intransigent, DeWitt stated "[I] [h]ave no desire to compromise in any way govt [sic] case in Supreme Court." He eventually capitulated. The result was that the report was changed in several substantive respects after the War Department suggested some fifty-five alterations. The changes most relevant to this case were summarized by the district court as follows:

> Page iii, paragraph 2, second sentence: Eliminate the words "and will continue for the duration of the present war." Page iii, paragraph 2, end of the second sentence: Insert "The surprise attack at Pearl Harbor by the enemy crippled a major portion of the Pacific Fleet and exposed the West Coast to an attack which could not have been substantially impeded by defensive fleet operations. More than 120,000 persons of Japanese ancestry resided in colonies adjacent to many highly sensitive installations. Their loyalties were unknown, and time was of the essence."

Page 9. Strike the following: "It was impossible to establish the identity of the loyal and the disloyal with any degree of safety. It was not that there was insufficient time in which to make such a determination; it was simply a matter of facing the realities that a positive determination could not be made, that an exact separation of the 'sheep from the goats' was unfeasible."

And replace with the following: "To complicate the situation, no ready means existed for determining the loyal and the disloyal with any degree of safety. It was necessary to face the realities—a positive determination could not have been made."

The revised, official version of the report was dated June 5, 1943. The War Department tried to destroy all copies of the original report when the revised version was prepared. This record contains a memo by Theodore Smith of the Civil Affairs Division of the Western Defense Command, dated June 29, 1943, certifying that he witnessed the burning of "the galley proofs, galley pages, drafts and memorandums of the original report of the Japanese Evacuation."

Edward Ennis, the Director of the Alien Enemy Control Unit of the Justice Department and a principal author of the government's 1942 brief, testified extensively in these proceedings. He testified as to his efforts in 1943 and 1944 in briefing both the *Korematsu* and *Hirabayashi* cases, and other efforts on the part of the Justice Department to obtain the full materials from the War Department supporting General DeWitt's decisions. While preparing the government's brief in *Hirabayashi*, Ennis learned that a report had been written but when he asked for a copy, the War Department gave him only a few selected pages. The district court observed, in denying the Government's Petition for Rehearing in this case, that it found Ennis entirely credible and that it believed that had Ennis had the original report showing the true rationale of DeWitt, he would have informed the Supreme Court of its contents.

On the basis of the evidence before it, the district court entered an extensive opinion setting forth the reasons for its decision to vacate the exclusion conviction. Judge Voorhees based that decision upon the factual record developed before him. He found first, that while the Supreme Court based its decision in *Hirabayashi* upon deference to military judgment of the need for expediency, General DeWitt, the person responsible for the racially based confinement of American citizens, had made no such judgment. The district court further found that the United States government doctored the documentary record to reflect that DeWitt had made a judgment of military exigency. Finally, the court found that had the suppressed material been submitted to the Supreme Court, its decision probably would have been materially affected. The government appeals the grant of relief.

The district court refused, however, to grant *coram nobis* relief with respect to the curfew conviction. It based that decision upon its conclusion that the Supreme Court would have drawn a legal distinction between the curfew and exclusion orders. It is from that denial of relief that Hirabayashi appeals. We consider first the contentions of the government.

III. THE GOVERNMENT'S CONTENTIONS IN ITS APPEAL

The government's contentions in its appeal from the district court's decision to vacate the exclusion conviction can be classified in four general categories. They are, first, that certain factual determinations of the district court are clearly erroneous; second, that the claims are barred by laches; third, that the case is moot because Hirabayashi does not continue to suffer from any adverse consequences from the convictions; and, finally, that the district court abused its discretion in reaching the merits of the petition by not granting the government's motion to vacate the convictions pursuant to Fed. R. Crim. P. 48.

A. FACTUAL CHALLENGES

We turn to the government's challenge to certain of the district court's factual findings. The government first takes issue with the district court's finding that it was General DeWitt who made the decision that exclusion of all persons of Japanese ancestry from the West Coast was required by military necessity. Support for the finding that the decision was General DeWitt's is abundant in this record. Secretary of War Stimson delegated his authority to General DeWitt pursuant to the power delegated to Stimson by the President.

The government points to uncontroverted evidence in the record that there were those in the War Department who did not agree with the reasons given by General DeWitt for the order and would have justified the order on other grounds. This evidence, however, merely underscores the critical nature of General DeWitt's decision and his report. It was because General DeWitt had exercised the authority, and because his judgment was essential, that the War Department suppressed the original version of his report in the first place. Indeed, Solicitor General Fahy in his oral argument in 1944 in *Korematsu* conceded that it was the views of the Commanding General which counted, and that if his orders had been based upon racist precepts, they would have been invalid. The following colloquy took place in which Justice Frankfurter and the Solicitor General discussed the revised version of DeWitt's report without knowledge of the existence of the original version.

MR. JUSTICE FRANKFURTER: Suppose the commanding general, when he issued Order No. 34, had said, in effect, "It is my judgment that, as a matter of security, there is no danger from the Japanese operations; but under cover of war, I had authority to take advantage of my hostility and clear the Japanese from this area." Suppose he had said that, with that kind of crude candor. It would not have been within his authority, would it?

MR. FAHY: It would not have been.

MR. JUSTICE FRANKFURTER: As I understand the suggestion, it is that, as a matter of law, the report of General DeWitt two years later proved that that was exactly what the situation was. As I understand, that is the legal significance of the argument.

MR. FAHY: That is correct, Your Honor; and the report simply does nothing of the kind. . . .

The district court's finding that it was General DeWitt who decided that the curfew and exclusion orders were required is not clearly erroneous.

The government next challenges as factually erroneous the district court's finding that the Supreme Court in 1943 would probably have reached a different result in the exclusion case if it had known the true basis for the General's decision. The government disagrees with the following portions of the district court's opinion:

> Had the statement of General DeWitt been disclosed to petitioner's counsel, they would have been in a position to argue that, contrary to General DeWitt's belief, there were in fact means of separating those who were loyal from those who were not; that the legal system had developed through the years means whereby factual questions of the most complex nature could be answered with a high degree of reliability. Counsel for petitioner could have pointed out that with very little effort the determination could have been made that tens of thousands of native-born Japanese Americans—infants in arms, children of high school age or younger, housewives, the infirm and elderly—were loyal and posed no possible threat to this country.

> * * * * * *

> Had counsel for petitioner known and been able to present to the Supreme Court the [initial] reason stated by General DeWitt for the evacuation of all Japanese, [and] . . . [i]f the military necessity for exclusion was the impossibility of separating the loyal from the disloyal, the Supreme Court would not have had to defer to military judgment because this particular problem, separating the loyal from the disloyal, was one calling for judicial, rather than military, judgment.

In making [its] challenge, the government agrees with petitioner and the district court that the Supreme Court in *Hirabayashi* deferred to a military judgment that circumstances required the prompt evacuation of all Japanese Americans, and that there was not enough time to attempt to separate the loyal from the disloyal. The government also agrees with petitioner and the district court that General DeWitt acted on the basis of his own racist views and not on the basis of any military judgment that time was of the essence. What the government contends in this appeal is that on the basis of the record before it, the Supreme Court should have known both that General DeWitt was a racist, and that he made no military judgment of emergency. The government asks us to hold, therefore, that the Supreme Court probably would have reached the same erroneous result even if the government had not suppressed the evidence and had accurately represented to the Court the basis of General DeWitt's decision.

There are several problems with this position. First, as the district court observed when it denied rehearing, the material in the record before the Supreme Court showing General DeWitt's racism was limited primarily to a newspaper clipping. More importantly, it was principally Hirabayashi and those amici who supported him, not the government, who presented the evidence of racial bias to the Court and who argued that the decisions must have been based upon racism rather than military necessity. By contrast, the information now in the public record constitutes objective and irrefutable proof of the racial bias that was the cornerstone of the internment orders.

The basis for General DeWitt's decision was a very crucial issue which divided the government and Hirabayashi. For illustration, Hirabayashi's brief referred to testimony by DeWitt indicating that "prejudice dominated his thinking," and quoted him as stating: "It makes no difference whether the Japanese is theoretically a citizen. . . . A Jap is a Jap.". . .

The government, on the other hand, through the device of judicial notice asked the Supreme Court to recognize that the judgment made was one of exigency; the "principal danger to be apprehended was a Japanese invasion." [Solicitor General Fahy] argued that the "situation did not lend itself, in the unique and pressing circumstances, to solution by individual loyalty hearings." In deciding the case against Hirabayashi, the Supreme Court obviously accepted the government's view of the facts as the government presented them in 1943, and rejected Hirabayashi's.

In asking us to hold that the Supreme Court would have reached the same result even if the Solicitor General had advised Hirabayashi and the Court of the true basis for General DeWitt's orders, the government ignores the fact that in 1943 it was clearly in a better position to know that basis than was the defense. It also ignores the traditionally special relationship between the Supreme Court and the Solicitor General which permits the Solicitor General to make broad use of judicial notice and commands special credence from the Court.[10]

The record here shows that Ennis, in preparing the government's brief, felt that responsibility keenly.[11]

The importance which the Supreme Court attached to the statements of the government regarding the factual situation at the time was brought out during the course of the proceedings in *Korematsu*, decided a year after *Hirabayashi*. By the time *Korematsu* was briefed and argued, the revised version of DeWitt's report had been made public. Justice Department attorneys with access to contemporaneous intelligence reports had had misgivings about the accuracy of even that version. This apprehension was reflected in a footnote to the government's brief in *Korematsu* limiting reliance on the report.[12] The footnote came up during oral argument, the transcript of which is

[10] Traditionally, the Supreme Court has shown great respect for the views of the Solicitor General—"an advocate whom the Court can trust." Thus, he owes a special obligation to the Court as well as his client.

[11] As the Justice Department prepared its brief, Ennis came into possession of the intelligence work of Lt. Commander Kenneth D. Ringle, an expert on Japanese intelligence in the Office of Naval Intelligence. Ringle had reached conclusions directly contradicting the two key premises in the government's argument. Ringle found (1) that the cultural characteristics of the Japanese Americans had *not* resulted in a high risk of disloyalty by members of that group, and (2) that individualized determinations *could* be made expeditiously. Ennis therefore concluded:

> I think we should consider very carefully whether we do not have a duty to advise the Court of the existence of the Ringle memorandum and of the fact that this represents the view of the Office of Naval Intelligence. It occurs to me that any other course of conduct might approximate the suppression of evidence.

Memorandum from Ennis to Solicitor General Re: Japanese Brief, April 30, 1943 [Exhibit Q, *supra* section B.2.b—ED.]. Notwithstanding Ennis' plea, the Justice Department's brief in *Hirabayashi* made no mention of Ringle's analysis.

[12] The footnote actually inserted in the government's brief was as follows:

in this record. Solicitor General Fahy denied that the footnote was a repudiation of the military necessity of the evacuation and reaffirmed the government's position in *Hirabayashi*.[13]

The Court's divided opinions in *Korematsu* demonstrate beyond question the importance which the Justices in *Korematsu* and *Hirabayashi* placed upon the position of the government that there was a perceived military necessity, despite contrary arguments of the defendants in those cases. The majority in *Korematsu* reaffirmed the Court's deference in *Hirabayashi* to military judgments. Justice Murphy's dissent highlighted the difference between his position and the majority's. He expressly faulted the majority's acceptance of the government's justification that "time is of the essence." We now know this very phrase was inserted by the War Department into DeWitt's final report and was not a concept upon which DeWitt himself based his decision. Justice Murphy [dissenting] said:

> The Final Report of General DeWitt (which is dated June 5, 1943, but which was not made public until January 1944), hereinafter cited as Final Report, is relied on in this brief for statistics and other details concerning the actual evacuation and the events that took place subsequent thereto. We have specifically recited in this brief the facts relating to the justification for the evacuation, of which we ask the Court to take judicial notice, and we rely upon the Final Report only to the extent that it relates to such facts.

Based upon the revised report, and without knowledge of the existence of the original version, lawyers within the Justice Department had pushed for a stronger footnote which would have at least partially discredited the report. The proposal for this footnote was contained in a memorandum from John L. Burling to Assistant Attorney General Herbert Wechsler dated September 11, 1944 [Exhibit AA, *supra* section B.2.c—Ed.]. The full text of the footnote he proposed was:

> The Final Report of General DeWitt (which is dated June 5, 1943, but which was not made public until January 1944) is relied on in this brief for statistics and other details concerning the actual evacuation and the events that took place subsequent thereto. The recital of the circumstances justifying the evacuation as a matter of military necessity, however, is in several respects, particularly with reference to the use of illegal radio transmitters and to shore-to-ship signaling by persons of Japanese ancestry, in conflict with information in possession of the Department of Justice. *In view of the contrariety of the reports on this matter we do not ask the Court to take judicial notice of the recitals of those facts contained in the Report.*

[13] After being asked to make copies of the DeWitt report available to the Court, Solicitor General Fahy agreed and said:

> It is even suggested that because of some foot note in our brief in this case indicating that we do not ask the Court to take judicial notice of the truth of every recitation or instance in the final report of General DeWitt, that the Government has repudiated the military necessity of the evacuation. It seems to me, if the Court please, that that is a neat little piece of fancy dancing. There is nothing in the brief of the Government which is any different in this respect from the position it has always maintained since the Hirabayashi case—that not only the military judgment of the general, but the judgment of the Government of the United States, has always been in justification of the measures taken; and no person in any responsible position has ever taken a contrary position, and the Government does not do so now. Nothing in its brief can validly be used to the contrary. [*Supra* section B.2.d—Ed.]

No adequate reason is given for the failure to treat these Japanese Americans on an individual basis by holding investigations and hearings to separate the loyal from the disloyal, as was done in the case of persons of German and Italian ancestry. *It is asserted merely that the loyalties of this group "were unknown and time was of the essence."*

Justice Jackson's dissent zeroed in on the majority's acceptance of General DeWitt's revised report. He stated:

So the Court, having no real evidence before it, has no choice but to accept General DeWitt's own unsworn, self-serving statement, untested by any cross-examination, that what he did was reasonable. And thus it will always be when courts try to look into the reasonableness of a military order.

The majority decision in *Korematsu* was a reaffirmation that it would defer to a military judgment of necessity in upholding first the curfew and then the exclusion orders. . . .

The claimed emergency preventing the separation of loyal from disloyal Japanese Americans was critical to the Supreme Court's decisions upholding the internment of Hirabayashi and Korematsu. This was clearly evidenced when the Court subsequently held that detention of a concededly loyal Japanese American citizen was unlawful. *See Ex Parte Endo*, 323 U.S. 283 (1944).

We cannot hold that the district court erred in deciding that the reasoning of the Supreme Court would probably have been profoundly and materially affected if the Justice Department had advised it of the suppression of evidence which established the truthfulness of the allegations made by Hirabayashi and Korematsu concerning the real reason for the exclusion order. . . .

IV. HIRABAYASHI'S APPEAL OF THE DISTRICT COURT'S REFUSAL TO VACATE THE CURFEW CONVICTION

The district court vacated Hirabayashi's conviction for violation of the exclusion order but left standing the conviction for violation of the curfew order. This was a result which neither side sought and which neither strenuously defends in this court.

The district court based its distinction on the premise that the curfew was a lesser restriction on freedom than the exclusion. It does not follow, however, that the Supreme Court would have made such a distinction had it been aware of the suppressed evidence. The Supreme Court in 1943 reviewed only the curfew order and clearly saw it as a serious deprivation of liberty. The Court therefore held that it would be justified only on the basis of a reasonable military judgment of necessity. . . .

The district court erred in distinguishing between the validity of the curfew and exclusion convictions.

CONCLUSION

The judgment of the district court as to the exclusion conviction is affirmed. The judgment as to the curfew conviction is reversed and the matter is remanded with instructions to grant Hirabayashi's petition to vacate both convictions.

B. STUDY MODULES: *CORAM NOBIS* LITIGATION

The following study modules focus on several key issues raised by the three *coram nobis* cases (referred to herein as *Korematsu II*, *Yasui II* and *Hirabayashi II*). These issues include lawyering ethics, civil and criminal civil procedure (including judicial review of constitutionality), evidence and political lawyering practice. Before delving into any of the study modules, you should read the petition for writ of error *coram nobis,* the government's response and the case opinions. Where indicated, also refer to specific documentary exhibits.

1. ETHICS: TRUTH-TELLING BY GOVERNMENT LAWYERS

At the heart of the *coram nobis* cases lay allegations of egregious Justice Department and War Department misconduct. The *coram nobis* petitioners alleged misconduct by attorneys and other officials at the highest levels of the federal government in their prosecution of the Japanese American internment cases. Petitioners supported their allegations with documents obtained from the government's own files.

You have read the petition's argument summary and seen excerpts of key documents. You have also read about the courts' findings of serious prosecutorial misconduct in the *Korematsu II* and *Hirabayashi II* cases. With these texts in mind, delve more deeply into the ethical issues raised by the cases.

- **War Department Officials.** According to the courts, War Department officials played a significant role in fabricating evidence. The original version of the DeWitt Final Report, bound and selectively distributed, was recalled by high-level War Department officials when they realized that DeWitt's actual justification for the exclusion orders undermined the government's legal position. As you have seen by reviewing Exhibits D and G (section A.2.a, *supra* at 294 and 299), a key passage of the report was altered to bolster the government's legal position. (And all documents relating to the recall and alteration were then ordered to be destroyed.)

- **Justice Department Attorneys in 1943–1944.** In addition, the *coram nobis* petition charges of prosecutorial misconduct focused on the actions of Justice Department attorneys. As Exhibits N, W and V (section A.2.b, *supra* at 300, 301 and 303) demonstrate, there were various reports from the Office of Naval Intelligence, the Federal Bureau of Investigation, and the Federal Communications Commission that directly contradicted the government's claim that Japanese Americans' disloyalty justified the exclusion and curfew orders. As Exhibits Q (section A.2.b, *supra* at 306), AA, B and CC (section A.2.c, *supra* at 310, 312 and 312) show, Justice Department attorneys in charge of the case refused to inform the Supreme Court of these contradictory reports.

This deliberate refusal was significant in several respects. First, the Justice Department was preparing to ask the Supreme Court to take judicial notice of salient facts in the DeWitt Final Report that its attorneys knew to be untrue. This is discussed at greater length in the evidence study module, *infra* section B.3.a at 358. In addition, other lower-level attorneys responsible for drafting the government's *Korematsu* brief to the Supreme Court had vigorously protested the hiding of key evidence from the Court. They had argued that such attorney conduct might constitute a suppression of evidence. In ruling on the *Hirabayashi coram nobis* petition, the Ninth Circuit observed:

> As the Justice Department prepared its brief, [Edward] Ennis[, then Director of the Alien Enemy Control Unit at the Department of Justice] came into possession of the intelligence work of Lt. Commander Kenneth D. Ringle, an expert on Japanese intelligence in the Office of Naval Intelligence. Ringle had reached conclusions directly contradicting the two key premises in the government's argument. Ringle found (1) that the cultural characteristics of the Japanese Americans had not resulted in a high risk of disloyalty by members of that group, and (2) that individualized determinations could be made expeditiously. See K. Ringle, Report on the Japanese Question 3 (Jan. 26, 1942). Ennis therefore concluded:
>
>> I think we should consider very carefully whether we do not have a duty to advise the Court of the existence of the Ringle memorandum and of the fact that this represents the view of the Office of Naval Intelligence. It occurs to me that any other course of conduct might approximate the suppression of evidence.
>
> Memorandum from Ennis to Solicitor General [Fahy] Re: Japanese Brief, April 30, 1943 [Exhibit Q, section A.2.b, *supra* at 306]. Notwithstanding Ennis' plea, the Justice Department's brief in *Hirabayashi* made no mention of Ringle's analysis.

Hirabayashi II, supra at n. 11.

The Justice Department attorneys drafting the *Korematsu* brief also tried to apprise the Supreme Court about the false factual justification for military necessity presented in DeWitt's Final Report. Both the *Korematsu II* and *Hirabayashi II* courts referred to this compelling evidence of suppressed evidence in the original proceedings. A footnote in the draft brief read:

> The recital of the circumstances justifying the evacuation as a matter of military necessity, however, is in several respects, particularly with reference to the use of illegal radio transmitters and to shore-to-ship signaling by persons of Japanese ancestry, in conflict with information in possession of the Department of Justice. *In view of the contrariety of the reports on this matter we do not ask the Court to take judicial notice of the recitals of those facts contained in the Report.*

Korematsu II, supra; Hirabayashi II, supra at n. 12 (quoting memorandum to J.L. Burling from Edward Ennis (Sept. 11, 1944); Exhibit AA, section A.2.c, *supra* at 310).

The Justice Department, however, at the urging of Assistant Attorney General Herbert Wechsler and others, ultimately altered the footnote in the government's brief to conceal credible information directly refuting key factual statements in the DeWitt Report. Exhibits AA, B and CC (section A.2.c, *supra* at 310, 312 and 312) illustrate the internal Justice Department decision-making process.

The cumulative evidence of willful misrepresentations by government attorneys at the highest levels led Judge Patel in *Korematsu II* to conclude

> there is substantial support in the record that the government deliberately omitted relevant information and provided misleading information in papers before the court. The information was critical to the court's determination, although it cannot now be said what result would have obtained had the information been disclosed. Because the information was of the kind peculiarly within the government's knowledge, the court was dependent upon the government to provide a full and accurate account. Failure to do so presents the "compelling circumstance" contemplated by *Morgan*. The judicial process is seriously impaired when the government's law enforcement officers violate their ethical obligations to the court.

Korematsu II, supra.

The Ninth Circuit in *Hirabayashi II* reached similar conclusions, based also in part on the direct misrepresentations made by Solicitor General Charles Fahy during oral argument before the Supreme Court in *Korematsu* (ironically, the full transcript of this argument was discovered after *Korematsu II* was decided). Despite his knowledge of official reports to the contrary, Fahy asked the Court to take judicial notice of the factual foundations for military necessity recited in the DeWitt Report. During the argument, Justice Jackson challenged the government's use of the DeWitt Report to prove military necessity—a report not admitted into evidence by the trial court and therefore untested by cross-examination. Fahy responded that

> not only the military judgment of the general, but the judgment of the Government of the United States, has always been in justification of the measures taken, and no person in any responsible position has ever taken a contrary position, and the Government does not do so now.

See the Transcript of Oral Argument in *Korematsu v. United States* (U.S. Supreme Ct., Oct. 12, 1944), reproduced above in section A.2.d, *supra* at 316 ("The Direct Misrepresentations").

- **Justice Department Attorneys in the 1980s.** The Justice Department's responses to the *coram nobis* petitions advanced differing and sometimes clearly inconsistent positions with respect to the authenticity, relevance and meaning of the key government documents. In *Korematsu II*, the government did not oppose the petition and all but conceded, in its responsive brief, the wrongfulness of the internment—"the mass evacuation was part of an unfortunate episode in our nation's history" and "it would not be appropriate to defend this forty year old misdemeanor conviction." Government's Response, *supra*, section A.2 at page 292.

In *Hirabayashi II*, however, the government argued that (1) the underlying cases raised ordinary military necessity issues that were not unique to Japanese Americans; (2) the Supreme Court was well aware of its options and simply chose not to require the government to prove its claims; (3) the situation after forty years could not be presented accurately because much of the evidence was lost; and (4) the War Department had available independent highly secret intelligence information that justified the government's wartime "necessity" argument. This latter argument is addressed in more detail in the Evidence study module concerning the "Magic Cables."

NOTES AND QUESTIONS

1. How zealous the government advocacy?: Should government attorneys be zealous advocates for the United States in the same way that criminal defense attorneys advocate for their private clients? What ethical obligations might Justice Department attorneys owe to defendants and the public at large about truth-telling, particularly in cases of national significance?

2. An exception for national security cases?: Should the Justice Department attorneys be given broad ethical leeway in light of the political importance of wartime issues? What about the importance of national security issues during peacetime?

3. Solicitor General's duty of candor: The Solicitor General of the United States argues before the Supreme Court on appeals directly involving the United States. He or she is entrusted with the responsibility of advancing the cause of justice, representing the government not only as a party to a case but also as the embodiment of the public. The Solicitor General is therefore sometimes called the "tenth justice" of the Supreme Court.

What does it mean when the Solicitor General deliberately misleads the Court in response to a justice's question about the evidentiary basis of the government's position in a case challenging the continuing imprisonment of thousands of people?

4. Split strategies: Do the differing arguments by the Justice Department in each of the *coram nobis* cases raise any ethical issues? Are the differences simply strategic choices? Does it matter that the different arguments were made on behalf of the same Justice Department, and therefore presumably the same "client"? Note that the government's position hardened between *Korematsu II*, litigated first, and *Hirabayashi II*.

5. Then and now: Judged by today's ethical standards, would the Justice Department's attorneys, including the Solicitor General, be subject to disciplinary sanctions for their conduct in 1943–1944? For what reasons? Is it fair now to make such judgments? Consider Rule 3.3 on "Candor toward the tribunal" in the American Bar Association (ABA) Model Rules of Professional Conduct:

> A lawyer shall not knowingly: (1) make a false statement of material fact or law to a tribunal; . . . or (4) offer evidence that the lawyer knows to be false.

This rule had a rough counterpart in the older ABA Canon 22 on "Candor and Fairness" (existing at the time of the original *Korematsu* case), which states that "[i]t is not candid or fair for the lawyer knowingly . . . in argument to assert as a fact that which has not been proved." The comment to Rule 3.3 states that "[t]here are circumstances where failure to make a disclosure is the equivalent of an affirmative misrepresentation."

Were these ethical standards violated by the Solicitor General's argument to the Supreme Court in *Korematsu* and by the Justice Department's disguising of the Burling footnote? What could the attorneys drafting the *Kore-*

matsu brief, Ennis and Burling, have done after they lost the footnote battle and heard the Solicitor General's argument?

6. Then and now (II): What are the ethical responsibilities of non-attorney government officials in attempting to justify the constitutionality of a government action? And what are the responsibilities of government attorneys in preventing unethical conduct by non-attorney officials? Consider Rule 3.4 on "Fairness to opposing party and counsel" in the ABA Model Rules of Professional Conduct:

> A lawyer shall not: (a) unlawfully obstruct another party's access to evidence or unlawfully alter, destroy or conceal a document or other material having potential evidentiary value. A lawyer shall not counsel or assist another person to do any such act.

There is no exact counterpart in the ABA Canons that was in effect at the time of the original internment litigation. Does this rule shed any light on the propriety of the Justice Department lawyers' actions at that time? On what they should do in similar circumstances today?

7. Codes of Professional Responsibility: In addition to more common-sense notions of fairness and propriety, the government's prosecution of the *coram nobis* cases may be analyzed in the context of the following sets of rules of professional conduct:

    ABA Model Rules of Professional Conduct:
3.3   Candor toward the tribunal.
3.4   Fairness to opposing party and counsel.
3.8   Special responsibilities of a prosecutor.
8.3   Reporting professional misconduct.
8.4   Misconduct.
ABA Standards Relating to the Administration of Criminal Justice, Chapter 3.

    The Prosecution Function:
3–1.2(c)   Function of the Prosecutor.
3–1.5   Duty to respond to misconduct.
3–2.8   Relations with the courts and bar.
3–3.1   Investigative function of prosecutor.
3–5.6   Presentation of Evidence.
Federal Bar Association's Model Rules of Professional Conduct for Federal Lawyers. (Similar to ABA Model Rules.)

2. LEGAL PROCESS: AN INTERSECTION OF LAW AND POLITICS

The *coram nobis* litigation raised a host of legal process issues. By "legal process" we mean the methods by which judicial decisions are made, both at the trial and appellate levels. The formulation, interpretation and application of specific rules of procedure (such as those that govern the filing of a civil complaint) are an integral part of legal process. Also central to that process are the methods of legal inquiry (such as standards of judicial review) and reasoning (for example, the resort to precedent).

This *coram nobis* litigation module explores two general issues of legal process: the reopening of the completed case (via both criminal and civil procedure) and judicial review of the constitutionality of national security restrictions of civil liberties. Each of these general inquiries generates an array of specific questions about the methods and politics of judicial decision-making in major cases.

a. Reopening the Completed Case: Civil and Criminal Procedure

The defendants in the Japanese American internment cases reopened their wartime convictions through an obscure procedural vehicle—the writ of error *coram nobis*. They did so based on evidence of the government's prosecutorial misconduct uncovered thirty-five years after the Supreme Court's affirmance of their convictions. As the 1946 Advisory Committee notes to Rule 60 of the Federal Rules of Civil Procedure observe, "the generally accepted view is that the [*coram nobis*] remedies are still available, although the precise relief obtained in a particular case by use of these ancillary remedies is shrouded in ancient lore and mystery."

In *United States v. Morgan*, 346 U.S. 502, 511 (1953), the Court observed that a writ of error *coram nobis* lies in the federal courts "after final judgment and exhaustion or waiver of any statutory right of review . . . only under circumstances compelling such action to achieve justice." No statute or rule expressly authorizes the writ. In 1987, Rule 60 of the Federal Rules of Civil Procedure was amended to abolish the writ for purposes of reopening civil cases, apparently to ensure that Rule 60 is the primary procedural device for reopening civil judgments. Federal district courts may nevertheless entertain the writ to reopen criminal cases under the general authority granted by the all-writs sections of the Judicial Code, 28 U.S.C. § 1651, which provides: "the Supreme Court and all courts established by Act of Congress may issue all writs necessary or appropriate in aid of their respective jurisdictions and agreeable to the usages and principles of law."

The *Morgan* Court explained the writ's purpose:

> Although the [defendant's] term has been served, the results of the conviction may persist. Subsequent convictions may carry heavier penalties, civil rights may be affected. As the power to remedy an invalid sentence exists, we think, respondent is entitled to an opportunity to attempt to show that this conviction was invalid.

Morgan, 346 U.S. at 512–513. As the vehicle for correcting belatedly discovered prosecutorial abuses, the writ serves the interests of the criminal justice system by maintaining public confidence in the fairness of the criminal prosecution process. The writ, however, does not function simply as another avenue of appeal. The writ is issued only in extraordinary situations. Thus a petitioner bears the burden of demonstrating that major trial defects or egregious prosecutorial misconduct subverted the fundamental fairness of the original trial and that the petitioner still suffers some form of legally recognized harm.

The writ of error *coram nobis* thus addresses fundamental fairness in the original criminal trial. The petition triggers a proceeding that is both similar to and different from the much more common *habeas corpus* proceeding. The proceedings are similar in that they both seek relief after conviction and appeal. Relief is also limited to situations of manifest injustice. Both allow the judge to make a summary determination on the petition or to hold a full evidentiary hearing. Perhaps most important, the *coram nobis* and *habeas corpus* petitions generally are treated as a civil rather than criminal filings. To afford former criminal defendants the opportunity to prove serious prosecutorial misconduct, where further discovery is needed, the judge usually instructs the parties to use the liberal discovery rules of the Federal Rules of Civil Procedure rather than the more restrictive discovery rules of the Federal Rules of Criminal Procedure. (Judge Patel did this in the *Korematsu coram nobis* case.) Petitioners generally consider their access to civil litigation discovery tools (depositions, interrogatories and document requests) a tactical advantage because evidence of prosecutorial misconduct often lies in the government's files.

Coram nobis and *habeas corpus* proceedings also differ in important respects. First, the *habeas corpus* writ operates to liberate a defendant still in government custody (as was Mitsuye Endo when she was detained in the internment camps). By contrast, the *coram nobis* writ operates to clear a defendant's record—sometimes many years after serving one's prison term. Second, although both writs have common law roots, the *habeas corpus* writ is now substantially shaped by federal statute. *See* 28 U.S.C. § 2255. Congress has diminished the writ's availability in an effort to curtail prisoner litigation, particularly in death penalty cases. The *coram nobis* writ, although authorized generally by the All Writs Act, is still a creature of common law.

In sum, (1) the *coram nobis* writ is available to reopen criminal proceedings alleged to have been fundamentally unfair at the time and that continue to have adverse effects; it is unavailable to reopen civil cases (that is handled by Federal Rule of Civil Procedure 60(b)); and (2) the *coram nobis* proceeding itself usually is treated as civil litigation governed by the rules of civil procedure.

(i) *REOPENING THE INTERNMENT CASES: THE CORAM NOBIS PETITIONS*

Fred Korematsu's petition for writ of *coram nobis* identified its extraordinary nature:

> First, [the petition] seeks to vacate a conviction that led to a historic and widely cited and debated opinion of the Supreme Court. Second, the allegations of governmental misconduct made below raise the most fundamental questions of ethical and legal obligations of government officials. Third, the alleged misconduct was committed not only before this court but also before the United States Supreme Court. Fourth, [the] petition is identical to separate petitions being filed on behalf of Gordon Hirabayashi and Minoru Yasui in the federal district courts in Seattle, Washington and Portland, Oregon.

Petition for Writ of Error *Coram Nobis, supra*, section A.2 at 301.

The petition asked the court to find egregious prosecutorial misconduct, to vacate Korematsu's conviction, to declare the unconstitutionality of the underlying military orders, to dismiss his indictments and to award costs and attorneys' fees.

(ii) THE GOVERNMENT'S COUNTER-MOTION TO DISMISS

The Justice Department, representing the United States, responded to each of the *coram nobis* petitions by filing what it called a "counter-motion" to vacate the petitioner's conviction and dismiss his indictment and also to dismiss his petition on grounds of mootness. Although the government did not state the grounds for its motion, the courts treated it as a motion pursuant to Federal Rule of Criminal Procedure 48 (Rule 48). Rule 48 provides:

> The Attorney General or the United States attorney may by leave of court file a dismissal of an indictment, information or complaint and the prosecution shall thereupon terminate. Such a dismissal may not be filed during the trial without the consent of the defendant.

According to the district court in *Korematsu*, the basis for Rule 48(a) lies in the common law doctrine of *nolle prosequi* (dismissal of prosecution). Rule 48(a), however, limits common law prosecutorial discretion:

> With the adoption of Rule 48(a), the absolute authority of the prosecutor was tempered and leave of court was required for dismissal of an indictment, information or complaint at *any* stage of the proceedings.

Korematsu II, supra (emphasis in original).

The government's counter-motion acknowledged that the "mass evacuation [of the Japanese Americans was an] unfortunate episode in our nation's history." It added, however, that the executive and legislative branches had already rescinded the statute and orders authorizing the internment and argued that therefore the petitions were superfluous.

> [I]t would not be appropriate to defend this forty year old misdemeanor conviction. Because we believe that it is time to put behind us the controversy which led to the mass evacuation in 1942 and instead to reaffirm the inherent right of each person to be treated as an individual, it is singularly appropriate to vacate this conviction for non-violent civil disobedience. . . .

> There is, therefore, no continuing reason in this setting for this court to convene hearings or make findings about petitioner's allegations of governmental wrongdoing in the 1940s.

Government's Response and Motion, *Korematsu v. United States* (Oct. 4, 1983); *supra*, section A.2.

Despite the government's offer to stipulate to the vacation of petitioners' convictions "to put this behind us," Korematsu, Hirabayashi and Yasui contested the government's motions. As Marc Hideo Iyeki has noted,

> [t]he government's objective . . . was not to make an admission of wrongdoing, but rather to avoid an independent assessment of the factual and constitutional issues raised in the petition. In essence, the government wanted the court to set aside [the convictions] without consideration of the record in an effort to forget "this unfortunate episode in our country's history."

Marc Hideo Iyeki, *The Japanese American Coram Nobis Cases: Exposing the Myth of Disloyalty*, 13 N.Y.U. REV. OF L. & SOC. CHANGE 199, 210 (1985).

Korematsu's counsel argued vigorously against the government's motion, first discounting the government's stated reasons as "excuses for not admitting error and for refusing to confront the real public interest" at stake:

> This is not just a 40-year-old misdemeanor, as the government characterizes it. This is a monumental precedent which affected deeply and irrevocably the lives of a hundred thousand Japanese-Americans, and countless numbers of friends and neighbors by mass banishment of a single racial minority group.

> The total in lost property, lost opportunities, broken families and human suffering was staggering. This case also established some of the most criticized and controversial precedents in legal history.

> First, the mass exclusion of an identifiable minority based on race without notice, without hearing, without an attorney was justified.

Korematsu's counsel then cited the prospect of leaving intact damaging legal precedent:

> Secondly, military judgments in times of crises are virtually unreviewable by the courts, even though the courts are functioning and no martial law has been declared.

> *Korematsu* has never been overruled and has never been reversed. Today we know that this Supreme Court decision rests on a non-existent factual foundation.

Finally, Korematsu's counsel argued for a full hearing on the petitions in the interest of genuine racial healing:

> The government . . . is arguing . . . that we should put the controversy behind us, . . . let old wounds heal.

> But whose wounds need healing? The Japanese-Americans who have lived with the stigma of this decision for 40 years and who never received a judicial declaration of wrongfulness or wrongdoing or adequate compensation for their suffering, or is it the wounds of guilt, of high government officials who were responsible for this great civil rights disaster?

> The government's approach turns the idea of public interest on its head. The government, in effect, is advocating letting the guilty go free and keeping the innocent imprisoned in the shame and suffering they endured for 40 years . . . keeping the public imprisoned in the ignorant notion that this was an "unfortunate" incident.

Transcript of oral argument in *Korematsu v. United States* (N.D. Cal., Nov. 10, 1983); *reprinted in* Peter Irons, JUSTICE DELAYED: THE RECORD OF THE JAPANESE AMERICAN INTERNMENT CASES 216–17 (1989).

Faced with the *coram nobis* petitions and the government's Rule 48(a) motions to dismiss, how should the federal district courts in San Francisco, Seattle and Portland have ruled? Consider the courts' differing responses and ponder why the courts diverged in their treatment of the three identical petitions.

(iii) DIFFERING DECISIONS ON THE PETITIONS

• **Korematsu II**. Judge Patel denied the government's motion in *Korematsu II*, finding no authority for the prosecution's filing of a Rule 48(a) motion to dismiss, subsequent to the completion of the prosecution.

> [Rule 48(a)] allows for dismissal . . . whereupon "the prosecution shall . . . terminate." . . . [T]he prosecutor has no authority to exercise his *nolle prosequi* prerogatives . . . after a person has been subject to conviction, final judgment, imposition of sentence and exhaustion of all appeals and . . . after a lapse of many years. At that stage, there is no longer any prosecution to be terminated.

Korematsu II, supra, section A.3. Her opinion further observed that under these circumstances a Rule 48(a) motion did not shield the government misconduct from public scrutiny. The scrutiny triggered by a *coram nobis* petition, like the inquiry for a *habeas corpus* filing, is

> substantially more expansive than under Rule 48(a). . . . Even were the government in a position to move under Rule 48(a) . . . the court would not automatically grant dismissal. A limited review by the court is necessary, even where the defendant consents. The purpose of this limited review is to protect against prosecutorial impropriety or harassment of the defendant and to assure that the public interest is not disserved.

Id.

After reviewing Korematsu's petition and exhibits and the government's minimal response, and without a full evidentiary trial, Judge Patel concluded that the government in 1944 withheld critical evidence, presented a selective record and provided misleading information to the Supreme Court. These acts of misconduct satisfied the "compelling circumstances" *coram nobis* test in *Morgan*.

• **Yasui II**. The *Yasui II* court did not follow Judge Patel's lead. Instead, Judge Belloni issued a brief order vacating Yasui's conviction but granting the government's motion to dismiss Yasui's *coram nobis* petition. His order stated,

> I decline to make such findings [of fact] forty years after the events took place. There is no case nor controversy since both sides are asking for the same relief but for different reasons. The Petitioner would have the court engage in fact finding which would have no legal consequences. Courts should not engage in that kind of activity.

Judge Belloni's hands-off approach has been criticized by Marc Hideo Iyeki:

> Japanese Americans regard the judicial finding of governmental misconduct to be as significant as the vacating of Korematsu's conviction. . . . The entire community has a stake in the *coram nobis* lawsuits since favorable opinions would diminish the stigma attached to it by the suspicion of wartime disloyalty.
>
> [T]he *coram nobis* lawsuits are analogous to a class action waged on a behalf of all former internees. . . . A meaningful remedy requires no less than writ-

ten opinions explicitly stating that the government's misconduct, not its be-
nevolence, compelled the courts to vacate the convictions.... Justice requires the judicial declaration of facts which would set the record straight
with respect to the loyalty of Japanese Americans to the United States during
World War II.

Iyeki, *supra* at 214.

• ***Hirabayashi II***. The *Hirabayashi II* court took a different tack. The
federal district court heard fully and denied the government's motion to dismiss, determining that "where petitioner seeks to have his petition considered on the merits, the Court is of the opinion that it is not in the public
interest, over the objections of the petitioner, to grant the government's motion." The court then held a full evidentiary trial on the merits of the petition.
Hirabayashi v. United States, 627 F. Supp. 1445 (W.D. Wash. 1986). The
Ninth Circuit affirmed the ruling denying the government's motion, in the
opinion found here. *Hirabayashi v. United States*, *supra*, section A.3; 828
F.2d 591 (9th Cir. 1987) ("There is no precedent for applying Rule 48 to vacate a conviction after the trial and appellate proceedings have ended.").

NOTES AND QUESTIONS

1. **Procedural hoops:** Under what circumstances can a convicted defendant petition for a writ of error *coram nobis*? Pursuant to what legal authority? Filed in which court? Seeking what relief? Was the relief requested
by Korematsu, Yasui and Hirabayashi available under the writ? How is this
relief different from other forms of relief available through civil actions?
Work through the requirements for *coram nobis* filings.

Imagine that you had just graduated from law school and had to answer
all these questions without the benefit of the introductory material in this
study module. Where would you look for answers? *Coram nobis* petitions
are not garden-variety pleadings. Professor Lorraine Bannai, a *Korematsu*
coram nobis team member, recounts that she was selected to file the petition
in the court. When she handed the petition to the court clerk, the clerk did
not know whether the petition should be filed as a civil action or criminal action. When Professor Bannai began working on the *Korematsu II* case, she
was a new law graduate who never dreamed when she took civil procedure
that she soon would be researching the obscure procedural intricacies of *coram nobis* petitions. The experience seared into her consciousness the importance of procedure.

2. **Manifest injustice or fundamental error:** Review again the
documentary exhibits accompanying the *coram nobis* petitions, reproduced
above in section A.2. Which documents supported the courts' finding of
manifest injustice or fundamental unfairness needed to grant the writ? Why?

In *Hirabayashi II*, the Ninth Circuit Court of Appeals upheld the district
court's finding that Hirabayashi was "prejudiced" by the government's misconduct in the prosecution of his case. Specifically, the court stated, "we cannot hold that the district court erred [after full evidentiary hearing] in
deciding that the reasoning of the Supreme Court would probably have been

profoundly and materially affected if the Justice Department had advised it of the suppression of evidence . . . concerning the real reason for the exclusion order."

What if there had been no suppression of evidence at the original criminal trials? Could the *coram nobis* petitioners have demonstrated manifest injustice or fundamental error in the original proceedings? If so, why? If not, why not? Should there be a distinction between what some call "procedural injustice" and "substantive injustice"? Review Judge Patel's *Korematsu II* opinion.

3. Federal Rule of Civil Procedure 60 compared: How does the civil rules analog to the *coram nobis* writ operate? *See* Fed. R. Civ. P 60(b) ("Relief from Judgment: Mistakes; Inadvertence; Excusable Neglect, Fraud, etc."). Is the concept of finality deployed differently in Rule 60 than it is in a *coram nobis* petition? Note that courts read into Rule 60(b)(6) ("any other reason justifying relief") an "extraordinary circumstances" requirement.

In *Ackermann v. United States*, 340 U.S. 193 (1950), German citizens were denaturalized during WWII and did not appeal, and then sought to re-open the denaturalization proceedings. The Supreme Court affirmed the denial of their 60(b)(6) motion, reasoning that the Ackermanns had not shown extraordinary circumstances to justify reopening their case, despite the fact that they were detained in an internment camp for the duration of the war.

What is the significance of some district courts' treatment of the petition as a "civil" filing for purposes of pleadings, motions and discovery? Consider that pretrial discovery of relevant information is much more restricted in criminal cases (*e.g.*, neither party may take depositions).

4. Federal Rules of Criminal Procedure: Interestingly, the government failed to cite to Rule 48(a) of the Federal Rules of Criminal Procedure, or any other rule, in support of its motion to dismiss the petitions. Why did the judges in *Korematsu II* and *Hirabayashi II* deny the Rule 48(a) motions and the judge in *Yasui* grant the motion? What do these differences tell you about the certainty of litigation outcomes? What might have been some of the larger political considerations underlying the differing court decisions?

5. Prior adjudication: What might have been the strategic considerations behind the government's offer to agree to vacate the petitioners' convictions? Might the doctrine of issue preclusion (or collateral estoppel) have played a part in the government's offer in 1983, especially in light of the pending *Hohri* class action damage case? (*See* Chapter 6 for further details.) The doctrine of issue preclusion (or collateral estoppel) prevents the loser in the first case from relitigating in the second case those issues (such as the absence of military necessity) that were already litigated and necessary to the first judgment. Note that it was not until 1984 that the Supreme Court ruled that "non-mutual collateral estoppel" could not be employed "offensively" (that is, by a new plaintiff to establish liability) against the U.S. government. *See United States v. Mendoza*, 464 U.S. 154 (1984).

6. Vacating a conviction or pardoning the defendant: Shortly before the hearing on the merits of the *Korematsu II* petition, the Justice Department offered to pardon Korematsu, Hirabayashi and Yasui. Speculate why the government adopted this strategy. What is the practical difference between a presidential pardon and *coram nobis* judicial relief? The legal significance? Speculate about why the three *coram nobis* petitioners unequivocally rejected the government's pardon offer.

7. Public perception of the justice system: How, if at all, might the procedural skirmishing have affected (a) the litigation of the "merits"; and (b) the petitioners' and the public's perception about the legal system? Why would it be important to use the civil justice system to reopen the questions raised forty years earlier?

8. Finality versus fairness: When should the policy in favor of finality of judgments give way to the interests of vindicating the legal rights of a minority group? If the reparation is limited and easily measurable? If, measured in hindsight, the original decision was wrong on the merits? If, even by the legal and moral standards of the time of the original decision, that decision was on shaky grounds? If a community was disempowered at the time of the judgment but now has political and legal clout?

The Seattle Post-Intelligencer recently reported on the Washington State Supreme Court's decision to admit Takuji Yamashita posthumously to the bar on March 1, 2001, almost one hundred years after he had been denied admission. The original case, litigated by Yamashita all the way up to the U.S. Supreme Court, was based on the Washington Supreme Court's decision to bar him from practicing law because he was a member of the "yellow race." *In Re Yamashita*, 30 Wash. 234 (1902) (cited in *Ozawa v. United States*, 260 U.S. 178 (1922)). Is this situation similar to the *coram nobis* cases? What actions are the courts taking? What roles are the courts playing besides decision-making roles?

b. JUDICIAL REVIEW: THE CONSTITUTIONALITY OF NATIONAL SECURITY RESTRICTIONS OF CIVIL LIBERTIES

When the Supreme Court decided *Hirabayashi* in 1943 and *Korematsu* in 1944, its equal protection jurisprudence did not embrace the three-tiered standard of means-ends analysis generally in place today (strict scrutiny, intermediate scrutiny, rational basis). The threshold issue in the war-time cases, therefore, was the appropriate degree of judicial scrutiny of the government's "military necessity" justification for the curfew, exclusion and internment. How did the Court handle that issue? In answering this question, the following materials review key aspects of the original internment decisions discussed in Chapter 3, as well as the *coram nobis* petition reproduced earlier in this chapter.

(i) STANDARD OF REVIEW IN THE INTERNMENT CASES

The military's curfew and exclusion orders targeted persons of Japanese ancestry, including many American citizens. For that reason, the Court in *Korematsu* stated that the military orders were "suspect" and were to be subjected to the "most rigid scrutiny." *Korematsu v. United States*, 323 U.S. 214, 216 (1944). But did the Court in *Hirabayashi*, *Korematsu* and *Yasui* thoroughly scrutinize the government's proffered military necessity justification?

Or did the Court largely defer to the judgment of military and political leaders? Consider that in *Hirabayashi*, the Court explicitly limited its inquiry.

> Our investigation here does not go beyond the inquiry whether, in the light of all the relevant circumstances preceding and attending their promulgation, the challenged orders and statute afforded a reasonable basis for the action taken in imposing the curfew. . . . In this case it is enough that circumstances within the knowledge of those charged with the responsibility for maintaining the national defense afforded a rational basis for the decision they made.

Hirabayashi, supra.

In *Korematsu* the Court appeared to apply a similarly deferential standard of review. First, the majority acknowledged that "legal restrictions which curtail the civil rights of a single racial group . . . must [be] subject . . . to the most rigid scrutiny." It then, however, undertook something far less than the "most rigid scrutiny" to determine whether the contested military orders were based on "pressing public necessity." The *Korematsu* majority deferred to military judgment, reiterating its statement in *Hirabayashi* that "'we cannot reject as unfounded the judgment of the military authorities.'" The Court's majority explained that it would not closely examine the military's actions in hindsight:

> [Fred Korematsu] was excluded because we are at war with the Japanese Empire, because the properly constituted military authorities feared an invasion of our West Coast and felt constrained to take proper security measures, because they decided that the military urgency of the situation demanded that all citizens of Japanese ancestry be segregated from the West Coast temporarily, and finally, because Congress, reposing its confidence in this time of war in our military leaders—as inevitably it must—determined that they should have the power to do just this. There was evidence of disloyalty on the part of some, the military authorities considered that the need for action was great, and time was short. We cannot—by availing ourselves of the calm perspective of hindsight—now say that at that time these actions were unjustified.

Korematsu, supra.

The Court divided sharply over the propriety of the majority's deferential approach. *Id.* (Justices Roberts, Murphy and Jackson dissenting). According to Justice Jackson, the majority's approach would always validate military control over civilians.

> How does the Court know that these orders have a reasonable basis in necessity? No evidence whatever on that subject has been taken by this or any other court. There is sharp controversy as to the credibility of the DeWitt report. So the Court, having no real evidence before it, has no choice but to accept General DeWitt's own unsworn, self-serving statement, untested by any cross examination, that what he did was reasonable.

Id. Justice Jackson's dissent also warned of the serious consequences of the majority's decision to uphold the exclusion order without proof of military necessity.

> [A] judicial construction of the due process clause that will sustain this order is a far more subtle blow to liberty than the promulgation of the order itself. A military order, however unconstitutional, is not apt to last longer than the

military emergency. . . . But once a judicial opinion rationalizes such an order to show that it conforms to the Constitution, or rather rationalizes the Constitution to show that the Constitution sanctions such an order, the Court for all time has validated the principle of racial discrimination in criminal procedure and of transplanting American citizens. The principle then lies about like a loaded weapon ready for the hand of any authority that can bring forward a plausible claim of an urgent need.

Id. (emphasis added). Finally, Justice Jackson asserted that the courts, as the enforcement branch of government, should not defer to military views of "reasonableness" but should instead apply the exacting standards required by the Constitution.

I should hold that a civil court cannot be made to enforce an order which violates constitutional limitations even if it is a reasonable exercise of military authority. The courts can exercise only the judicial power, can apply only law, and must abide by the Constitution, or they cease to be civil courts and become instruments of military policy.

Id.

(ii) EMPLOYING TODAY'S STANDARD OF REVIEW TO REVISIT THE CONSTITUTIONAL QUESTION

Through their *coram nobis* petitions, Korematsu, Hirabayashi and Yasui sought to vacate their wartime convictions not only on grounds of government misconduct in the prosecution of these cases, but also on the grounds of the unconstitutionality of the orders. Point five of Fred Korematsu's petition, reproduced above in section B of this chapter, summarizes the argument. The petitioners asserted that the military orders were unconstitutional according to standards then in place and, in addition, according to the current standard of constitutional review:

Petitioners further allege that their convictions are based on governmental orders that violate current substantive constitutional standards. Nearly forty years ago, the Supreme Court sustained the constitutionality of the government's decision to impose a curfew on and then to evacuate all Japanese Americans living on the West Coast. In doing so, however, the Court did not in fact apply the same type of "strict scrutiny" of suspect classifications that would be applied today.

Petition for Writ of Error *Coram Nobis, supra*, section A.2.

In making this argument, the petitioners asserted that "[i]n racial discrimination cases decided after *Korematsu*, the Court demanded far more from the government to justify the use of a racial classification that burdened or stigmatized a racial minority" and argued that, in light of the suppressed evidence, the government should now have to prove that "it [was] essential to use [the race-based] classification to fulfill a compelling government interest and that no less restrictive alternative [was] available."

NOTES AND QUESTIONS

1. Strict scrutiny then: Should the Court have subjected the government's proffered military necessity justification to the "most rigid scrutiny"?

If the Court in 1943 and 1944 had employed a strict scrutiny standard of review, what would have been the likely result? Would that result have changed if the recently discovered World War II government documents had been available?

2. Strict scrutiny now: In ruling on the *coram nobis* petitions, could the district courts have revisited the underlying constitutional issue? In her *Korematsu coram nobis* opinion, Judge Patel declared that the district court could not assess errors of law in the case because the purpose of the *coram nobis* writ is to correct only "errors of fact"; the court lacked power to correct any legal errors made by the U.S. Supreme Court. What was the impact of this declaration on the petitioners' request that the court reassess the underlying constitutional issue?

3. Judicial error?: The earlier Ethics and later Evidence study modules suggest that the Supreme Court not only based its decisions on a faulty factual record, but also improperly took judicial notice of key facts not in the record on appeal. If the government deliberately misled the Court into doing so, did the Court commit an error of fact or an error of law? Or, since the Court has the final word on questions of federal law, did the Court commit no error at all? This raises the related question: When, if ever, should a district court modify or reverse a higher court's ruling of "law" in the same case?

4. Reconciling national security and civil liberties: Do the *Hirabayashi* and *Korematsu coram nobis* opinions address Justice Jackson's "loaded weapon" warning about the original *Korematsu* opinion? Review the essays on national security and equal protection in Chapters 1 and 3. In what ways, if at all, did the *coram nobis* decisions alter the courts' role in reconciling the national security interests of government and the civil liberties of citizens?

These questions about standards of judicial review raise the issue of court competence. To what extent would "strict scrutiny" review actually deter government officials and attorneys from serious misconduct in attempting to justify the legality of the national security or military necessity measures? More specifically, in assessing government actions taken during times of apparent crisis, can the courts, which move deliberately and operate in hindsight, fairly adjudge the legitimacy of often chaotic executive and legislative national security measures that are restrictive of civil liberties? What if proof of "necessity" entails disclosure of highly confidential information? In other words, how effective will heightened judicial scrutiny be if the legal process, including appeals, may take several years, and the exigency itself requires a quick response? *Cf.* National Security Act (establishing a confidential agency panel to consider challenges to a limited range of national security actions), 66 F.R. 9185, 32 C.F.R. Part 2001 Appendix (Interagency Security Classification Appeals Panel).

5. Retroactive application of current constitutional standards: Does it make legal (or moral) sense to invalidate military orders from 1942 under current constitutional standards? Would it be more persuasive to argue that the Supreme Court misapplied the standard of constitutional review it articulated at the time? But then what does it mean for the Supreme Court to misapply its own doctrine? Is what the Supreme Court does, by definition of positive law, the law? None of the courts in the *coram nobis* cases reached these questions.

6. Constitutional scrutiny of Japanese American reparations: The U.S. Court of Appeals for the D.C. Circuit rejected a constitutional challenge to the Civil Liberties Act of 1988 on behalf of German Americans. *Jacobs v. Barr*, 959 F.2d 313 (D.C. Cir. 1992). Considering a claim by Arthur Jacobs that he too should receive compensation, the Court stated that the congressional decision about the scope of reparations to Japanese Americans could pass strict scrutiny, "let alone the intermediate scrutiny that the Supreme Court requires us to apply."

In his class action complaint, Jacobs had alleged that he had been interned in February 1945 with his German father. His counsel conceded that Jacobs's father had been allowed an individualized hearing before the family was sent to Crystal City, Texas, for seven months. Jacobs had learned "how to 'eat sushi' and make 'sandals and kites'" while there. Jacobs's strategy in the litigation deserves attention. Jacobs argued that he should be allowed wide-ranging discovery through government archives "to prove that there was a military justification for the large-scale exclusion of individuals of Japanese descent" while there had been no such justification for the treatment he had been accorded. While his lawyers withdrew the argument and it should not be attributed to others who make the same basic contentions, it remains troubling.

7. International law and Japanese Latin Americans: For some observers the United States violated not only the civil rights of citizens, under the mantle of national security, but international human rights as well. As discussed *supra*, section A.4 in Chapter 4, 2,200 Japanese Latin Americans were kidnapped by the United States from Peru and other Latin American countries and interned as hostages during World War II. Professor Natsu Taylor Saito examines the experience of these internees in the context of U.S. foreign policy and disregard of international law:

> The harm caused to the thousands of interned Japanese Latin Americans, their families and their communities was the result of the United States' willingness to disregard well-established international law prohibiting the kidnapping and forced deportation of civilians, the holding of hostages, the indefinite internment without charge or hearing, and the forced repatriation and/or deportation at the end of the war. [That] the internment of Japanese Latin Americans was allowed to happen, over some objections from the Justice Department, but with very little resistance from U.S. authorities, unreported to the general public, and without triggering any subsequent intragovernmental review revealing the flawed nature of the program as a whole, illustrates how important it is to create an oversight system designed to assure congruence between American foreign policy and international law.

> Had the executive branch, through the President and the Cabinet officials, made international law a priority and then communicated this policy to each department and the agency thereunder; had Congress enacted legislation to enforce international law; or had federal courts, particularly the Supreme Court, incorporated international law into their decisions—this situation could have been avoided altogether.

Natsu Taylor Saito, *Justice Held Hostage: U.S. Disregard for International Law in the World War II Internment of Japanese Peruvians—A Case Study*, 19 B.C. THIRD WORLD L.J., 40 B.C. L. REV. 275, 347 (1999). Chapter 6 treats these issues in greater detail.

Professor Saito identifies the silence of all branches of government in the face of clear international law violations. What role should the court play when the executive branch and military violate these international law mandates?

Published in the same symposium issue* as Professor Taylor's article is Professor Gil Gott's interpretation of the internment cases through the lens of foreign affairs law. He reads the majority opinion in *Hirabayashi* as revealing the Supreme Court's deference to executive war power in all situations. He argues that the Court has essentially adopted a stance of absolute nonreviewability. *See* Gil Gott, *A Tale of New Precedents: Japanese American Internment as Foreign Affairs Law*, 19 B.C. THIRD WORLD L.J., 40 B.C. L. REV. 179 (1999). If Professor Gott is correct, what are the implications of the Supreme Court's deference? Whose responsibility should it be to ensure that the United States complies with international law? Reconsider the alternative approach, a judiciary "provid[ing] 'watchful care' over personal liberties of executive and military excess, especially during apparent crises," described in Chapters 1 and 3, and explored further in Chapter 7.

3. EVIDENCE: WHAT MATTERS TO THE COURT

The *coram nobis* litigation raised two evidentiary issues: (1) the propriety of the Supreme Court's "judicial notice" of Japanese Americans' propensity toward disloyalty, and (2) the evidentiary relevance of the intercepted Japanese Magic Cables. The Court's judicial notice of these racial characteristics are examined in the context of legal requirements of the rules of evidence.

a. MISUSE OF THE DOCTRINE OF JUDICIAL NOTICE?

The government justified the military's curfew and exclusion orders in *Korematsu* and *Hirabayashi* on grounds of Japanese American disloyalty. The government's only "factual" evidence of disloyalty was contained in General DeWitt's Final Report. The government asked the Supreme Court to take judicial notice of the report and its key statements of fact: The report, however, was not part of the lower courts' evidentiary record and thus could not be considered as evidence on appeal, unless the high court invoked the judicial notice doctrine. Review point four of Korematsu's *coram nobis* petition, reproduced *supra*, section A.2. That part of the petition asserted that "Justice Department officials decided to utilize the doctrine of judicial notice in presenting 'evidence' that the 'racial characteristics' of Japanese Americans predisposed them to disloyalty."

---

* *Symposium: The Long Shadow of Korematsu*, 19 B.C. THIRD WORLD L.J., 40 B.C. L. REV. (1998).

The doctrine of judicial notice is now codified in federal and state statutes as a rule of evidence. Rule 201(b) of the Federal Rule of Evidence sets forth the conditions for judicial notice of "adjudicative facts":

[a] judicially noticed fact must be one not subject to reasonable dispute in that it is either (1) generally known within the territorial jurisdiction of the trial court or (2) capable of accurate and ready determination by resort to sources whose accuracy cannot reasonably be questioned.[*]

A common illustration of an adjudicative fact is: "The sun sets in the west."

The *coram nobis* petitioners asserted that the Justice Department abused the doctrine of judicial notice as part of "an intentional and contrived program to mislead the Court."

The doctrine [of judicial notice], which provides a process of streamlining the presentation of adjudicative facts, is reserved for those points which are unquestionably true. If there is a bona fide dispute about the truth of the fact and the court believes that the truth is not or cannot be established to a convincing degree, the court should refuse judicial notice and remand for further evidence.

Memorandum of Points and Authorities in Support of Petition for Writ of Error *Coram Nobis* in *Korematsu v. United States* (Jan. 19, 1983), *reprinted in* Peter Irons, JUSTICE DELAYED: THE RECORD OF THE JAPANESE AMERICAN INTERNMENT CASES 207 (1989).

The petitioners first argued that the DeWitt Report was not suitable for judicial notice because it contained statements about the "racial characteristics of Japanese Americans which [were] prejudicial, racially biased, irrelevant and of dubious credibility," statements of "fact" that were used to infer a disposition towards disloyalty.

In its brief . . . the Government first asked the Court to take judicial notice of "facts" such as: concentration of Japanese population on the West Coast . . . ; religion . . . ; attendance at Japanese language schools . . . ; membership in cultural or social organizations . . . ; dual citizenship . . . ; and Japanese Americans who were educated in Japan. . . . The Government then argued that these "racial characteristics" proved that a great number of Japanese Americans were very likely to be disloyal . . . despite evidence indicating the "facts" were in dispute.

Petitioner's Post-Hearing Brief in *Hirabayashi v. United States* (April 19, 1984), *reprinted in* Irons, *supra* at 296–97.

The petitioners also contended that the government sought judicial notice of the factual statements in the DeWitt Report concerning espionage and

---

[*] Judge Patel in the *Korematsu coram nobis* decision distinguished "adjudicative facts" from "legislative facts."

Legislative facts are "established truths," facts or pronouncements that do not change from case to case but [are applied] universally, while adjudicative facts are those developed in a particular case. Legislative facts are facts of which courts take particular notice when interpreting a statute or considering whether Congress has acted within its constitutional authority. For example, courts frequently take judicial notice of legislative history, including committee reports. So, too, historical facts, commercial practices and social standards are frequently noticed in the form of legislative facts.

sabotage when it knew that those statements about actual acts of Japanese American disloyalty were directly contradicted by the reports of all of the intelligence services responsible for investigating potential disloyalty.

> The government [also] used the doctrine of judicial notice to prove facts [of disloyalty] which it could not establish by other means. Given the government's knowledge of contradictory evidence, the use of judicial notice illustrates clearly the extent to which the government manipulated both the facts and the court's processes to win Petitioner's case at all costs.

Memorandum of Points and Authorities in Support of Petition for Writ of Error *Coram Nobis* in *Korematsu v. United States* (Jan. 19, 1983), *reprinted in* Irons, *supra* at 207-208.

The petitioners also faulted Solicitor General Fahy for refusing to inform the Court about the impropriety of judicial notice of the DeWitt Report, both in the Justice Department's brief and in his oral argument. They asserted that the Solicitor General knew that the factual statements of the DeWitt Report were not only controverted but were in fact untrue and that he ignored vehement protests by Justice Department attorneys. In support of this claim, the petitioners quoted from a memorandum to the Solicitor General written by Edward Ennis, one of the Justice Department attorneys drafting the Korematsu brief:

> This Department has an ethical obligation to the Court to refrain from citing [the DeWitt Report] as a source of which the Court may properly take judicial notice if the Department knows that important statements in the source are untrue and if it knows as to other statements that there is such contrariety of information that judicial notice is improper.

Exhibit B, *supra* section A.2.c at 312.

Ennis's position was not accepted by his superiors at the Justice Department. In oral argument to the Court in *Korematsu*, Solicitor General Fahy attested to the government's complete confidence in the DeWitt Report.

> We say that the report proves the basis for the exclusion orders. There is not a line in it that can be taken in any other way. It is a complete justification and explanation of the reasons which led to [General DeWitt's] judgment. The Solicitor General concluded by saying that "no person in any responsible position has ever taken a contrary position."

Oral argument, *supra*, section A.2.d at 316.

Without an established evidentiary record, and in apparent reliance on the judicially noticed "factual" statements of the DeWitt Report, the *Korematsu* majority upheld the military orders, concluding that "[t]here was evidence of disloyalty on the part of some [Japanese Americans]" to justify the orders. In her *coram nobis* review, Judge Patel found in *Korematsu* that the Justice Department, in arguing for judicial notice, wrongly ignored its own attorneys' vehement protests.

> The final version [of the *Korematsu* brief] made no mention of the contradictory reports. The record is replete with protestations of various Justice Department officials that the government had the obligation to advise the courts of the contrary facts and opinions. . . . In fact, several Department of

Justice officials pointed out to their superiors and others the "willful historical inaccuracies and intentional falsehoods" contained in the DeWitt Report.[*]

Korematsu II, supra.

b. RELEVANCE OF THE "MAGIC CABLES"

Courts are prohibited from admitting into evidence "irrelevant" information. Federal Rule of Evidence 401 provides:

> "Relevant evidence" means evidence having any tendency to make the exis-
> tence of any fact that is of consequence to the determination of the action
> more probable or less probable than it would be without the evidence.

At the *Hirabayashi coram nobis* evidentiary hearing, in defense of the
military's claim of necessity, the government for the first time raised the
"Magic Cables" defense.   The government contended that decoded official
Japanese communications supported the military's position.

> [P]rior to the bombing of Pearl Harbor, the Office of Naval Intelligence (ONI)
> and the Military Intelligence Division (MID) of the Army secretly intercepted
> and decrypted Japanese diplomatic cables.... These cables reveal that in
> 1941 the Japanese government believed that it had recruited some "second
> generation" Japanese Americans in West Coast airplane factories and in the
> United States Army in order to learn about the disposition in the United
> States of critical war materials and manpower.

Government's Post-Hearing Brief, *Hirabayashi v. United States* (Sept. 5,
1985), *reprinted in* Irons, *supra* at 296–97.

Hirabayashi asserted in his post-hearing brief that the "Magic Cables"
evidence was irrelevant and showed no actual involvement of Japanese
Americans in acts of espionage for Japan.

> The Government's last main argument was ... that secret information in its
> possession proved military necessity ... that diplomatic intercepts provided
> the basis for the decision to evacuate. There is no evidence which even sug-
> gests that DeWitt utilized ... the information from the intercepts as a basis
> for his decision to order evacuation.

> The intercepts ... are totally irrelevant to the issues of governmental mis-
> conduct and violation of Petitioner's due process.... [T]he intercepts ... at
> most contain a request from Tokyo to the consulate to recruit second genera-
> tion Japanese for information collecting....

> However, there is not a single cable nor group of cables taken collectively,
> which can reasonably demonstrate that recruitment efforts were successful.

Petitioner's Post-Hearing Brief, *Hirabayashi v. United States* (July 31, 1985),
reprinted in Irons, *supra* at 299.

---

[*] Judge Patel took judicial notice of the purpose of the Commission on Wartime Relocation and Internment of Civilians, the manner in which it was established and the general
nature and substance of its conclusions, but did not take judicial notice of the Commission's specific findings and conclusions; the court did not deem those findings "conclusive."

General DeWitt made no reference to the Magic Cables in his Final Report. District Judge Voorhees and Circuit Judge Schroeder also ignored the Magic Cables in their opinions.

The CWRIC did address the Magic Cables in the addendum to its report. After lengthy analysis of the Magic Cables, the CWRIC concluded that there was no evidence in the cables of actual espionage by Japanese Americans.

> Much has been made of the sentence in *Personal Justice Denied* which states that "not a single documented act of espionage, sabotage or fifth column activity was committed by an American citizen of Japanese ancestry or by a resident Japanese alien on the West Coast." This statement stands. The "Magic" cables do not identify individuals in those groups who committed demonstrable acts of espionage, sabotage or fifth column activity.

Commission on Wartime Relocation and Internment of Civilians, PERSONAL JUSTICE DENIED: REPORT OF THE COMMISSION ON WARTIME RELOCATION AND INTERNMENT OF CIVILIANS 475 (1983).

NOTES AND QUESTIONS

1. Judicial notice of racial characteristics: As Professor Lorraine Bannai and Dale Minami point out, "[t]he Japanese American internment cases illustrate a highly unusual use of the doctrine of judicial notice." The U.S. Supreme Court eventually accepted the education of Japanese children in Japanese language schools as reliable evidence that Japanese Americans were predisposed to espionage and sabotage. Think about the possible inferences that could be drawn regarding the attendance by Japanese American children at Japanese language school. If one inference is that the children are more likely to be exposed to Japanese culture, does this necessarily lead to the further inference of predisposition to espionage or of disloyalty? If there are several possible inferences, is disloyalty one "whose accuracy could not reasonably be questioned"? Would judicial notice of these possible inferences be proper?

If the answers to the above questions are "no," then what led the U.S. Supreme Court to draw and rely on those inferences without demanding more evidence? What ideologies of race were circulating at the time that might have made the Court more willing to accept race-based arguments with less than compelling evidence? Did the sparse trial record on the question of military necessity and the importance of the issues justify the Supreme Court's apparent resort to judicial notice of apparently disputed "adjudicative facts"? Do general concerns about national security justify attenuation of strict judicial notice requirements? And what does it mean for a constitutional system of checks and balances if the Court bends evidentiary rules to uphold military orders curtailing fundamental freedoms of civilians?

2. Judicial notice strategy: Professor Gil Gott, quoting historian and *Korematsu coram nobis* legal team member Peter Irons, sheds light on how the government planned to use judicial notice in the internment cases to establish Japanese American disloyalty through a genetic theory:

> Charles Burdell, a Justice Department lawyer working on the *Yasui* case, who adopted the judicial notice strategy, drafted a memorandum for submission

to the trial judge that contained a straightforward statement of the argument. . . .

> "Jap citizens are inevitably bound, by intangible ties, to the people of the Empire of Japan," [Burdell] wrote. "They are alike, physically and psychologically." Burdell then elaborated his genetic theory of loyalty. "Even now, though we have been separated from the English people for over 100 years, we still take pride in the exploits of the R.A.F. over Berlin, and the courageous fighting of the Aussies in Northern Africa. Why? Because they are people like us. They are Anglo-Saxons." Burdell's theory equally fit the Japanese Americans. "Who can doubt that these Japs in this country, citizens as well as aliens, feel a sense of pride in the feats of the Jap Army—this feeling of pride is strong in some, weak in others, but the germ of it must be present in the mind of every one of them.

There is no proof that the memorandum was delivered to the judge in the trial of Minoru Yasui, but it shows how the lawyers imagined judicial notice would work in the test cases.

Gil Gott, *A Tale of New Precedents: Japanese American Internment as Foreign Affairs Law*, 19 B.C. THIRD WORLD L.J. 179, 40 B.C. L. REV. 239 (1999).

Was this proposed use of judicial notice to prove Japanese American disloyalty by way of biological predisposition any better or worse than the "cultural characteristics" strategy actually employed by the Justice Department? How did the government's genetic theory differ from its cultural theory of disloyalty? Why might the Justice Department have rejected one approach and embraced the other in its legal arguments?

3. Evidence, ethics and government lawyers: Nanette Dembitz was another member of the government's original litigation team who urged the strategy of relying on racial characteristics of the Japanese Americans. An astute lawyer, she zeroed in on a tactic that ultimately persuaded the U.S. Supreme Court via the government's Hirabayashi brief. A year after the Korematsu decision, she published a law review article repudiating the Court's acceptance of this strategy:

> Though it is of course correct that governmental authorities "have constitutional power to appraise the danger in the light of facts of public notoriety," here the opinion itself shows that the danger was appraised not in the light of "facts" reasonably established by consideration of an adequate amount of data but of widely held suspicions, such as may be possessed by every group of society with respect to every other group. A typical instance is the statement, frequently and positively made, that the children of persons of Japanese ancestry have close filial ties and are thus easily dominated by their parents, as contrasted with the findings by reputable sociologists that the second-generation generally strive to disassociate themselves from the ways of their parents even more than in the usual immigrant families.

> The Court has in other decisions stated that especial attention must be given to the basis for a measure affecting fundamental liberties, and insisted on a strong affirmative showing in support of such a measure rather than merely the absence of a showing against it. The need for this principle is particularly sharp in the field of racial discrimination.

Nanette Dembitz, *Racial Discrimination and the Military Judgment: The Supreme Court's Korematsu and Endo Decisions*, 45 COLUM. L. REV. 175 (1945).

As a lawyer representing the government, could she have avoided the question of whether to take advantage of negative racial stereotyping in arguing the government's position before the Court? Could she have decided upon a different, more ethical course of action? What does a lawyer do when he or she identifies an argument that might be winning from the client's point of view but is personally distasteful? When is reliance on racial stereotypes defensible as a legal tactic? Is it ever? Does the answer depend on whether the argument is being made on behalf of the government or on behalf of an individual resisting a government's race-based classification?

What do you make of Circuit Judge Schroeder's reference in the *Hirabayashi coram nobis* decision to "the traditionally special relationship between the Supreme Court and the Solicitor General which permits the Solicitor General to make broad use of judicial notice and commands special credence from the Court?" In cases such as this, who does the Solicitor General represent, and what are his or her ethical obligations in terms of factual accuracy?

5. Evidence and the CWRIC report: Despite the government's failure to object to the petitioner's request, Judge Patel declined to take judicial notice of the findings of the official government commission established to review the events surrounding the internment, in the CWRIC report PERSONAL JUSTICE DENIED.

Did Judge Patel correctly refuse to take judicial notice of the CWRIC's findings regarding the government's misconduct and racial discrimination? Is there an irony or an inconsistency in having a judge refuse to take judicial notice of a government report in a case that relied so heavily in the first instance on judicial notice of a previous government report?

6. Relevance: Of what evidentiary value were the Magic Cables in the *Hirabayashi coram nobis* case? Is it significant that neither the DeWitt Final Report nor the Justice or War Department mentioned the Magic Cables during the original *Korematsu, Hirabayashi* and *Yasui* litigation?

What would have been the evidentiary impact of the Magic Cables if they had identified Japanese Americans committing espionage? Observing that neither German Americans nor Italian Americans were interned as a group despite disloyalty convictions of persons of German and Italian descent during World War II, the CWRIC report cautioned:

> Since it is always possible that such an identification of [a Japanese American or alien] might one day be made, it is worth underscoring that espionage or sabotage by a small group does not justify excluding and detaining the entire ethnic group to which they belong.

PERSONAL JUSTICE DENIED, *supra* at 475.

4. POLITICAL LAWYERING: IN THE PUBLIC INTEREST

Who litigated the *Korematsu, Hirabayashi* and *Yasui coram nobis* cases? Where did the attorneys come from? What kind of legal training did they have? How could they afford to volunteer their time? How did the legal teams coordinate their efforts with each other, with supportive lawyers, community organizations and student volunteers? And where did they obtain funding for the substantial litigation costs?

Perhaps most important, what philosophical and strategic judgments about the court system and legal justice did the legal teams make? And how did those judgments account for public education forums and interactions with the media?

The three *coram nobis* legal teams in San Francisco, Seattle and Portland were comprised primarily of third-generation Japanese Americans (Sansei), although White Americans and several Chinese Americans also served on the core teams.[*] Most came from West Coast families whose parents and grandparents had been interned (although two members of the *Korematsu* team from Hawai'i had no interned family members). Most received their legal training at law schools on the West Coast (one team member was still a law student). Most worked as legal services attorneys after graduation, doing both legal and political work for low-income Asian American communities (one member was the executive director of the Asian Law Caucus). One member was a political science professor and scholar. One was lead partner in a small law firm. A few others worked for larger law firms (one such firm provided substantial logistical and technical support gratis). All participated in some fashion in public education about and fundraising for the cases. Most had direct contact with journalists and media personalities.

And despite differences in experience, outlook and style, the legal team members shared one feeling in common—that they had trained themselves legally and politically to do something for their communities, something special—and this was it.

The following account provides a glimpse of some of the political lawyering dynamics of the *coram nobis* litigation.

PETER IRONS, JUSTICE DELAYED: THE RECORD OF THE JAPANESE AMERICAN INTERNMENT CASES

11–14 (1989)

The most urgent task at the first meetings of the *Korematsu* legal team was to develop a structure for the overall *coram nobis* effort. Dale Minami was the natural choice to direct the group and serve as "lead counsel" in the courtroom. His experienced guidance, offered with self-deprecating humor,

---

[*] Core members of the *Korematsu* legal team were Lorraine Bannai, Marjie Barrows, Ed Chen, Dennis Hayashi, Peter Irons, Karen Kai, Dale Minami (team leader), Leigh-Ann Miyasato, Robert Rusky, Don Tamaki, Akira Togasaki and Eric Yamamoto. Members of the *Hirabayashi* legal team were Nettie Alvaraz, Kathryn Bannai (team leader), Arthur Barnett, Jeffrey Beaver, Camden Hall, Daniel Ichinaga, Gary Iwamoto, Rod Kawakami (team leader), Craig Kobayashi, Michael Leong, Nina Mar, Diane Narasaki, Karen Narasaki, Richard Ralston, Sharon Sakamoto, Roger Shimizu and Benson Wong. The *Yasui* legal team was comprised of Russell Aoki, Jeffrey Beaver, Frank Chuman, Fern Eng, Bert Fukumoto, Stephen Griffith, Scott Meisner, Mary Mori, Peggy Nagae (team leader), Clayton Patrick and Don Willner. Aiko Herzig-Yoshinaga and Jack Herzig were researchers and consultants crucial to the efforts of all the legal teams.

eased the legal team through conflicts over strategy and tactics. Aided by Lorraine Bannai, [Peter Irons] assumed responsibility for factual research and further document searches. In looking for additional documents to bolster [the] petitions, Lori and [Peter] relied heavily on Aiko Herzig-Yoshinaga, the CWR's chief researcher, . . . and her husband, Jack Herzig, a retired lieutenant colonel in Army counterintelligence. After Aiko left the commission, she and Jack had turned their Washington apartment into an archive of internment files. Bob Rusky and Karen Kai, along with Dennis Hayashi, a lawyer at the Asian Law Caucus in Oakland, headed the legal research effort. More than a dozen lawyers and law students helped this group in plowing through cases in the search for legal precedent to buttress our misconduct charges.

Legal and factual research was only half the task of the *coram nobis* effort. Equally important, the lawyers agreed, was mounting as broad and intensive a public education campaign as possible. The primary goals of [the] campaign were to clear the criminal records of the three defendants and to obtain strong judicial findings on the misconduct charges. We also hoped for judicial findings that the internment program itself had been unlawful and unconstitutional. Even if achieved, these goals would lose their impact if the public failed to learn about the cases, the internment, and the continuing need to rectify this national mistake. The legal team devoted much time to plans for an outreach and education program to include media relations, liaison with the Japanese American community, contacts with church, labor, political, and civic groups, and funding.

Donald Tamaki volunteered to direct the education and outreach program. Don was a graduate of Boalt Hall Law School at the University of California, Berkeley, and then served as executive director of the Asian Law Caucus, which provided free legal services to the Asian community in areas such as housing, employment, and health care. Virtually from scratch, he mastered the skills of writing press releases, arranging press conferences, and juggling the demands of the media for interviews, photographs, and "exclusive" news. He also raised funds to cover the legal team's expenses and built a network of support from a wide spectrum of groups that endorsed [the team's] efforts. . . .

The legal team had initially planned to file the petitions in October 1982, but as work progressed over the summer it became obvious the date would have to be pushed back. Bay Area law students and undergraduates volunteered their services for legal and factual research, and a blizzard of memoranda swirled about the legal team meetings. One group of Berkeley undergraduates, students in a course on Asian American legal issues taught by Dale Minami and Don Tamaki, prepared a giant chart, some ten feet long, that matched all the important statements in the government documents, court briefs, and Supreme Court opinions, tracing their origins and connections. . . .

Two events in October created concern and consternation within the legal team. Late that month, someone provided the Japanese American press with a copy of an October 1 letter from Arthur J. Goldberg to Judge William Marutani. As a former Supreme Court justice and member of the Commission on

Wartime Relocation, Goldberg had an aura of influence and a reputation as a judicial liberal. In his letter, Goldberg criticized the *coram nobis* effort as unnecessary and potentially damaging. . . .

The press of work in completing the petitions, and doubts about December as a time to launch them, led to a final choice of January 19, 1983, as the filing date for the *Korematsu* petition in San Francisco. After consultation with the Portland and Seattle legal teams, we decided that their separate petitions would be filed two weeks later. Hectic meetings to polish the petitions, and several all-night sessions at the word processors by Bob Rusky's law office, preceded the filing date. Don Tamaki spent hours on the telephone, urging newspaper and television people to attend the press conference scheduled after the court filing and patiently explaining the details of the cases and the *coram nobis* procedure to dozens of callers.

NOTES AND QUESTIONS

In light of the original criminal prosecutions and *coram nobis* litigation in *Korematsu*, *Hirabayashi* and *Yasui*, think about the problems and possibilities of political lawyering practice.

1. Rejecting former Justice Goldberg's advice: Reproduced here is page two of former Justice Goldberg's original letter strongly advising against the *coram nobis* litigation. Goldberg sent the letter to Judge William Marutani, a member of the congressional commission investigating the internment. Marutani in turn forwarded the letter to the *coram nobis* legal team.

Korematsu is a thoroughly discredited decision. Its rationale
that by an Executive Order,based on alleged military necessity,
the constitutional rights of Americans can be trampled upon
is completely at variance with the Court's decision in the
famous steel seizure case, Youngstown vs. Sawyer, 343 U.S. 579
(1952).

     Further, at the time Korematsu was decided the prevail-
ing doctrine was that since the Fifth Amendment to the
Constitution guaranteeing due process of law does not contain
an Equal Protection Clause, as does the Fourteenth Amendment,
denial of equal protection could not be invoked in a suit in
attacking federal action. On this basis, the Court in
Korematsu rejected the Petitioner's argument that Japanese-
Americans were discriminated against since German-Americans
and Italian-Americans were not subject to relocation. However, this construction of the Fifth Amendment was overruled
in Bolling vs. Sharpe, 347 U.S. 497 (1954).

     Bolling vs. Sharpe involved racial segregation in the
public schools of the District of Columbia. The applicable
constitutional provision, therefore, was the Fifth and not
the Fourteenth Amendment which applies only to state action.
Notwithstanding, Chief Justice Warren writing for a unanimous
Court said that the Fifth Amendment, although not containing
an equal protection clause, subsumes such a clause under the
general ambit of due process. Bolling vs. Sharpe, therefore,
overrules Korematsu on the equal protection issue.

     In sum, it is my considered opinion that it is not
necessary and indeed not procedurally possible to mount a
legal attack to overrule Korematsu. Moreover, it is also my
opinion that Korematsu is one of the most ill conceived
decisions handed down by the Supreme Court, perhaps second
only to Dred Scott vs. Sanford, 19 Howard 393 (1857).
Korematsu has been overruled in the court of history.

     The correct constitutional doctrine applicable to the
evacuation of Japanese-Americans in World War II was stated
by the Supreme Court in Ex Parte Milligan, 4 Wall 2, 120-121
(1866): "The Constitution of the United States is a law for
rules and people, equally in war and in peace, and covers
with the shield of its protection all classes of man, at all
times, and under all circumstances."

                                        Sincerely,

                                        Arthur J. Goldberg

Korematsu v. United States Coram Nobis Case Collection, UCLA Asian American Studies Center,
Asian American Movement Archives.

What lay behind Justice Goldberg's advice? Why did the *coram nobis* team reject it?

2. Rejecting the government's offer of a pardon: Another issue that confronted the team was whether to accept the government's offer of a pardon. If you were a member of the *coram nobis* litigation team, how would you handle this offer? Would you have a different view if you were not a political lawyer, but simply focused on the most efficient way to end the litigation? Consider *Korematsu* team member Lorraine Bannai's perspective:

> Eventually [the government] contacted us, and asked if Fred would be willing to accept a pardon. Again, we viewed this as an effort not to squarely address the allegations of prosecutorial misconduct in the petition, but a way for them to sneak out of any responsibility and end up still looking good. So they offered a pardon, and of course, our obligation as attorneys was to communicate that offer to our client. And we talked about the offer of pardon amongst ourselves first. We did some research on the issue of the effect of the pardon, and amongst ourselves, the attorneys felt quite strongly that a pardon would be unacceptable because a pardon implies that you committed a crime, and that you were guilty. . . .

> But, of course, we took this to Fred and to Kathryn [Korematsu], and presented it to him as a way to terminate the litigation. . . . We advised him about what the pardon meant, and after a pause, Fred looked at us, and said, "Why should I accept a pardon? [] I should be pardoning the government." And we all were incredibly relieved that he felt that way and th[at] he understood that the pardon would not be a victory for him.

Lorraine K. Bannai, interview by Margaret Chon (March 23–24, 2000) DENSHO: JAPANESE AMERICAN LEGACY PROJECT.

3. Conflicting views of legal justice: In terms of philosophical and strategic judgment calls, how could the *coram nobis* legal teams embrace, or at least work within, the very same legal system that visited such injustice upon Japanese Americans (not to mention their clients) in the first place? Was it ignorance, or faith, or careful calculation or some combination? What views of the legal system and racial justice did the legal teams hold? Consider the following account by another one of the *Korematsu* legal team members:

> Minorities [have] dichotomous views of law arising out of minority litigation experiences. [They] have experienced the influence exercised by powerful economic and political interests upon judicial decisions. In a social milieu tolerant of biased attitudes and discriminatory acts, judicial outcomes tend to denigrate minority interests. [Yet] minorities also have "passionately invoked legal doctrine, legal ideals, and liberal theory in the struggle against" discrimination and have succeeded partially due to the "passionate response that conventional legalism can at time elicit."

> Can the embrace and the distrust coexist? [Prof. Mari] Matsuda suggests that they can and do, that "minority experience of dual consciousness accommodates both the idea of legal indeterminacy as well as the core belief in a liberating law that transcends indeterminacy." Responding to the "charge from the right that rights promote conflict rather than community" and to the charge from the "left that rights reinforce individualism at the expense of community," scholars are forging a view of rights assertion that encompasses "debate over legal and political choices without pretending a social harmony

that does not exist and without foreclosing social changes as yet unimagined.". . .

Especially for minorities, courts can [sometimes] . . . contribute to and stimulate the process of "cultural transformation" by encouraging those without established forms of power or social status to "assemble, associate and articulate positions publicly on the terrain of civil society."

This view of rights assertion and courts tempers theory with experience and responds to the call for ways in which law can contribute to . . . better social conditions. It is a view of rights assertion that was viscerally accepted and strategically adopted by the *Korematsu* legal team in filing the *coram nobis* petition in 1983. The legal team's analysis of the original *Korematsu* litigation led it to believe that the Supreme Court's ruling in 1944 was largely political rather than principled. The team asserted this in its petition, drawing support from the newly discovered World War II government documents. . . . At the same time, the legal team decided to rely upon the indeterminate and discretionary principle of fairness embodied in the concept of due process in asking the same court that had convicted Korematsu forty years earlier to vacate his conviction.

Korematsu's attorneys acknowledged the false cultural assumptions and political values at play in the Supreme Court's 1944 decision, recognized the shifting of attitudes towards the internment and focused on the expanded role of the federal courts in addressing civil liberties. Despite predictions of failure from many corners, the legal team decided to employ the traditional language of rights as the mechanism for confronting apparent anti-civil rights policies of the Reagan Administration, for expanding the support base for a legislative reparations movement, for publicly challenging lingering racial stereotypes and for rebuilding the self-image of an ethnic group still suffering from a grievous governmental wrong. The legal team adopted political and social goals beyond the specific outcome of the litigation—goals directed both inward at the social group and outward toward the public.

Eric K. Yamamoto, *Efficiency's Threat to the Value of Accessible Courts for Minorities*, 25 Harv. C.R.-C.L. L. Rev. 341, 424 (1990). Are Professors Yamamoto and Matsuda correct that minorities, society's outsiders, have a dualistic experience with the legal system? Did the *coram nobis* lawyers approach the cases with "multiple consciousness"?

   4. Civil rights strategies: How might political lawyers representing members of disadvantaged communities most productively view the American legal system? How should their clients (whether individuals or community organizations) most realistically view "rights"—particularly the judicial recognition and enforcement of civil rights? To what extent are the definition and enforcement of civil rights tied to society's political and economic climate? Consider again Professor Lorraine Bannai's thoughts:

> [Fred] was a really supportive, encouraging client. He trusted our opinion. Again, I think he might have started out a little skeptical about us because we were so young, but I think that he quickly grew to trust us and rely on us. . . .
>
> We certainly consulted with him every step of the way. It was an unusual situation because we had a client, Fred Korematsu, and as a lawyer, your first obligation is to your client. . . . But . . . aside from having Fred as a client, we in some ways had the entire Japanese American community as a client because this case, for us at least, represented the trial they never had. Certainly

as lawyers, we never let our concerns about how the community would feel about the case get in the way of our representation of our client. Fortunately, there was never any deviation between what Fred wanted and what we wanted to do politically.

Lorraine K. Bannai, *supra*.

In what ways do courts and legal process offer opportunities to communicate with and educate nonparticipants? What kind of organizing, analyzing and funding is needed make effective educational use of the legal process? What is the role of the media? Again, in Professor Bannai's words:

> The biggest significance of the case for me [] is that it was really not just one legal case . . . but it really was one part of a much larger political effort. It was our case being brought at the same time redress was being sought before Congress, at the same time NCJAR [National Council for Japanese American Redress] was bringing its class action, at the same time there was media coming out, media covering the story, plays being written. . . . The issue of redress and the experience of Japanese Americans was a whole movement brought by and pushed by numerous different segments within the community itself. And not only that, but also it was a powerful example of the value of coalition work. The Jewish American organizations got behind redress. Other civil rights organizations got involved in it. So numerous . . . communities outside of the Japanese American community getting behind this issue on the basis of principle. . . .

Id.

5. Practical lawyering skills: In contemplating the larger questions just posed, keep in mind the importance of day-to-day practical lawyering skills. The *coram nobis* lawyers filed pleadings, drafted motions and memoranda of points and authorities, took depositions, organized large numbers of documents, met with judges in pretrial conferences, strategized about procedural opportunities, researched the admissibility of evidence and argued positions in open court. In filing the obscure *coram nobis* petition to reopen a historic case and in taking on the United States, the lawyers believed that they had to be not only good political lawyers but also first-rate lawyers, period.

Probing interrogation during depositions, for instance, revealed some startling information. John McCloy, Assistant Secretary of War during the internment, played a key role in the alteration of the original DeWitt Final Report. During his deposition in 1984, McCloy maintained that the Japanese Americans had not been interned, that they only had been ordered away from defense facilities on the West Coast. When Justice Department attorney Edward Ennis was asked during his deposition why he had not resigned when the Burling footnote had been revised into oblivion, he responded simply that Watergate had not yet happened.

Review the following original document setting forth the agenda for a typical *Korematsu* legal team work-group meeting.

```
   TO:  Western Defense Commandos
 FROM:  Dale
   RE:  Minutes of January 25 meeting
 DATE:  January 27, 1983
```

A. MECHANICS
    1. Petitions are being copied and will be returned to
        Caucus.
    2. We will send out petitions to all amici.
    3. For all other requests, we will charge $20-$25.

B. FUNDING
    1. We have just about exhausted all funds. Zero.
        Zip. Goose egg. Circles. Donuts. Tap
        city.
    2. We will request several people to assist us in
        fundraising including Frank Chuman in Southern
        California and Marshall Sumida in Northern
        California.
    3. Russell Matsumoto will draft a pursuasive press
        release to the Japanese press begging for help.
    4. Don will still continue work on the foundation
        proposal.
    5. Lori will make contacts in Los Angeles and Russell
        Matsumoto will make contacts in San Francisco.
    6. Don Tamaki will go to Los Angeles to talk with
        fundraisers in early Februar.

C. EDUCATION
    1. Some misunderstanding arose over the Committee to
        Reverse the Japanese American Wartime Cases. This
        is not a legal committee but an educational/funding
        committee to educate the public about the cases.
    2. The brochure is almost done but we don't have
        enough money to print or distribute it so we must
        wait until some more funding comes in.
    3. Russell Matsumoto will look into incorporation.
    4. We have been requested to speak at the San Mateo
        JACL Day of Remembrance, and to do an interview
        with a Tokyo reporter.

D. LEGAL ORGANIZATION

    1. Research Coordinator (Bob Rusky/Dennis Hayashi) --
        will coordinate all research assignments relating
        to all aspects of the cases including motions,
        discovery, evidence, substantive law, procedural
        questions and coordinate research among various
        jurisdictions.
    2. Evidence/document control/discovery (Karen Kai,
        Lorraine Bonnai, Akira Togasaki, Russell Matsumoto)
            a. Will computerize indexing and cataloging of
                evidence and documents.
            b. Will attempt to match evidence to particular
```
```

points or elements required to prove in our case.
- c. Will draft a discovery plan.
- d. Experts/consultants (Peter Irons) -- will coordinate compilation of any historical materials and contact possible expert witnesses for testimony and/or consultation.

E. RESEARCH TO BE DONE/THINGS TO DO

1. Suppression/Standard of Review/Corum Novis
2. Constitutional challenge
3. Hearsay
4. Official records
5. Ancient documents
6. Governmental privilege
7. Official reports of governmental agencies
8. Code of ethics
9. Civil vs. criminal discovery
10. Retroactive law/legal standard at the time
11. Due diligence
12. Send copies of all evidence and documents (Peter Irons)
13. Contact U.C. Berkeley person in charge of Bancroft Library.
14. Request status conference?

Korematsu v. United States Coram Nobis Case Collection, UCLA Asian American Studies Center, Asian American Movement Archives.

Imagine the dynamics of coordinating this kind of work of a core group of a dozen volunteer lawyers and researchers and 30 to 40 volunteer assistants. What are the attributes and problems of a successful collaboration of this type?

Note that the agenda item of funding the legal team's costs came from donated money to finance the costly litigation ("zip" "goose egg"). Where does the money come from to finance litigation like this? Court fees, discovery expenses, copying and distribution costs and publicity can easily exceed $50,000, as they did in the *Korematsu coram nobis* litigation (and this was with legal team member Robert Rusky's law firm absorbing substantial copying, secretarial and related costs).

6. Integration of law, politics and practical skills: To what extent does "political lawyering" practice, or public interest law practice, require a blend of insightful political analysis and skilled lawyering? How do new lawyers and law students develop that mix? Certainly, in mentor-mentee relationships with experienced political lawyers, the answer is when they are available. But what about other sources? What is the role of law schools' clinical law practice programs? The role of theory courses in law school curriculum? The effect of work with legal services and civil rights organizations?

And what are the problems and risks of political lawyering practice? In terms of job opportunities, pay, status, burn-out?

In pondering these questions, consider the strategic decisions made by the *coram nobis* legal teams about media mobilization as an educational tool for the court of public opinion. For all legal events, the teams used press conferences (with press releases and information packets) to reach television, radio and print media. Media coverage was nationwide, including a segment on CBS's "60 Minutes." The teams' public education effort also had a significant grassroots direct-contact component. Legal team members and supporters met with community people at innumerable events and spoke at many forums—in universities, high schools, community centers, churches and political events.

Korematsu legal team member Lorraine Bannai expresses "how strongly the team felt about the public education aspect of the case, [getting] the media to thrust the issue before the public."

> The team . . . felt very strongly that the case had to be retried in the court of public opinion, just as much, if not more, than . . . in a court of law. Statutes and court opinions, despite the doctrine of stare decisis, are only pieces of paper that can be changed at any time given enough public pressure or other changes in the political winds. If the goal was to ensure that such an event would never happen again, and truly that was the goal of the community, the public needed to know what happened to Japanese Americans and know that the public has the power and responsibility to ensure that such an event will not happen again.

Lorraine K. Bannai, interview by Margaret Chon, *supra*.

The *coram nobis* legal teams, as a matter of political lawyering strategy, embraced public education with two goals in mind: to bring the actual history of the internment to public light (separate from the legal outcome); and to help shape the public perceptions of and influence the litigation process itself. Are all politically significant legal cases approached in this manner? How should we assess the practicality and ethics of this kind of strategy?

7. Dynamics within the legal teams: Consider the following correspondence between *Korematsu* legal team leader Dale Minami and *Yasui* legal team leader Peggy Nagae. What insights does it give you about the challenging dynamics of political lawyering practice?

May 22, 1984

Peggy Nagae
University of Oregon Law School
Eugene, OR   79403

Dear Peggy,

Remember when you told me that you would never give up on this
relationship until we went ten rounds? Well the bell has rung
and now is the time for us to start fighting. Before we get into
it, however, I want to tell you what I told Min as reflected in
the enclosed letter -- that whatever you decide about the appeal
we will back you 100% whether it involves legal research,
fundraising, educational work or whatever.

Actually, before we begin the main event, I wanted to apologize
for the tone of the position paper we sent you. In reviewing it
after the Hirabayashi hearing, I realized the tone was strong,
condescending and not helpful to discussion. The history is
this: I drafted it when there appeared to be little
communication between our workgroup and even less respect for
decisions I felt we had made jointly. I won't bore (nor anger)
you with details as we can talk about this some time later when
we are both of advanced age and more mellow. It was supposed to
be edited and since I was involved in other legal work at the
time, the draft was sent out virtually without review and without
any further input from myself. In any event, the bad news is
that the paper was somewhat insulting; the good news is that with
the Hirabayashi decision, most of the content is irrelevant at
this point.

But I stray from my purpose in writing you. I just wanted to let
you know that despite the several rounds we have gone before and
the several rounds we have yet to go through, I want to offer you
my support, legal assistance and friendship. And so, if we try
to knock each other's head off in the next few months, at least
our fights will be out of love and not hostility.

In spirit,

Dale

enc
DM:tm

Korematsu *v. United States Coram Nobis* Case Collection, UCLA Asian American Studies Center, Asian American Movement Archives.

8. What is the public interest?: On behalf of Fred Korematsu, Dale Minami made a powerful argument to Judge Patel at the hearing on Korematsu's *coram nobis* petition. Minami's original handwritten outline for that historic argument is reproduced below.

Korematsu v. United States Coram Nobis Case Collection, UCLA Asian American Studies Center, Asian American Movement Archives.

In 2001, Minami has this reflection on his argument:

Almost twenty years later. Almost a generation. But the "public interest" our legal team argued for in November 1983 is still the same "public interest" we honor today. An individual fighting for his own rights and his community's dignity, representing the pain and hope of all Americans. A nation struggling with the racism of a past. A court acknowledging what the United States government would not. All converged on the day when Judge Marilyn Hall Patel overturned Fred Korematsu's 40 year-old conviction with the declaration that Japanese Americans were victimized by racism during World War II. Her warning about the fragility of our civil rights resonates even louder 20 years later in the face of concerted attacks on the civil rights of people of color. "Public interest" today must surely include this history of discrimination for us to move forward as a nation.

E-mail message from Dale Minami to Margaret Chon (March 27, 2001).

Peggy Nagae, team leader for the *Yasui coram nobis* team, reflects on what these cases meant to her as a Sansei female lawyer:

I remember sitting in con law class my third year in law school and reading the *Korematsu* case. I said, "If there was anything I could do to right that case, it would make these three years of torture (actually I used the word "hell") worthwhile. My second thought was that there's nothing that could be done because they had already gone to the Supreme Court and the next court was God, and I wasn't ready to go there.

When at Vassar, I was an East Asian Studies major and I had wanted to do my senior thesis on the cases, and my advisor responded, "After you say they were racist decisions, then what else is there to say?" That was in 1972. So I changed my thesis subject.

Here I was again in law school in 1976, thinking similar thoughts. Little did I realize that five years later, I would have that chance. It was the opportunity of my legal career: to work on a case that meant so much to my community, robbed my father of his dreams and held my mother captive, and more than that, created a world for me in which I grew up ashamed of being Japanese American and wanting to be white. I first had a meeting with Min and a group of lawyers from Portland, several of whom said they didn't think it was a very good case. I was so surprised. I thought that regardless of whether it's good, bad or indifferent, this is our case, this is for our community, this is the case from which we all shared a common past. I was committed to taking the case regardless of whether any one else thought it was a good idea or not.

I remember saying to [then-dean] Derrick Bell, "I'd love to accept the position as assistant dean [of the University of Oregon law school], but I have this case that I'm working on, and if it doesn't fit within my job description, I can't accept the position." He said, "Come on and bring the case with you. If my community asked me to undertake that case, I would do it anywhere." He was wonderful.

Finally, I think as an Asian American woman lawyer, it meant many things to me: an expression of the leadership ability of Asian American women as well as the opportunity to be at the table and to be a part of righting an injustice. Every time we wrote a brief we asked ourselves, "If this was the last brief we were allowed to write on this case, what would we want to say? What would we want to leave as a legacy?" There was no path to follow, only a trail to leave.

It was a trial in many ways because it was a group process. It was a trial to work together; to see the common vision; to work out the issues; and to move forward with a greater purpose in mind. I remember keeping separate from the redress movement because we wanted to make sure the legal issues were not intertwined. I remember working out the differences with Dale and then meeting again on the CLPEF [Civil Liberties Public Education] board and anchoring our relationship. I really am quite fond of him because he did listen and I did push and we did end up together. That's more than I might say about others. Dale and I reached a level of trust, respect and love for each other.

So, in a long-winded nutshell, that's what it meant for me. It was the height of my legal career. To give something back to my parents and grandparents, who had suffered so that I might achieve; to honor Minoru Yasui and the courage he had to step forward; to play a part in justice in a country that oftentimes goes for injustice. It was a privilege, an honor and a time of great trial and triumph, all at the same time.

E-mail from Peggy Nagae to Margaret Chon (April 10, 2001).

C. ADDITIONAL READINGS

BOOKS

Kenneth S. Brown, et al., MCCORMICK ON EVIDENCE (3rd 1984).

Daniel R. Coquillette, LAWYERS AND FUNDAMENTAL MORAL RESPONSIBILITY (1995).

Peter Irons, JUSTICE DELAYED: THE RECORDS OF THE JAPANESE AMERICAN INTERNMENT CASES (1989).

Peter Irons, JUSTICE AT WAR: THE STORY OF THE JAPANESE AMERICAN INTERNMENT CASES (1983).

THE POLITICS OF LAW: A PROGRESSIVE CRITIQUE (David Kairys ed., 3rd ed., 1998).

Lorraine K. Bannai & Dale Minami, *Internment During World War II and Litigations, in* ASIAN AMERICANS AND THE SUPREME COURT (Hyung-Chan Kim ed., 1992).

Richard Kluger, SIMPLE JUSTICE: THE HISTORY OF BROWN V. BOARD OF EDUCATION AND BLACK AMERICA'S STRUGGLE FOR EQUALITY (1975).

Gerald Lopez, REBELLIOUS LAWYERING: ONE CHICANO'S VISION OF PROGRESSIVE LAW PRACTICE (1993).

David Luban, LAWYERS AND JUSTICE: AN ETHICAL STUDY (1988).

William H. Rehnquist, ALL THE LAWS BUT ONE: CIVIL LIBERTIES IN WARTIME (1998).

United States Commission on Wartime Relocation and Internment of Civilians, PERSONAL JUSTICE DENIED: REPORT OF THE COMMISSION ON WARTIME RELOCATION AND INTERNMENT OF CIVILIANS (1997).

United States, Final Report: JAPANESE EVACUATION FROM THE WEST COAST 1942 (1943).

LAW REVIEW ARTICLES AND OTHER SOURCES

Sumi Cho, *Whiteness Redeemed: Earl Warren, Internment and Brown v. Board of Education*, 19 B.C. THIRD WORLD L.J., 40 B.C. L. REV. 73 (1999).

Nanette Dembitz, *Racial Discrimination and the Military Judgments: The Supreme Court's Korematsu and Endo Decisions*, 45 COLUM. L. REV. 177 (1945).

M. Diane Duszak, *Note, Post-McNally Review of Invalid Convictions Through the Writ of Coram Nobis*, 58 FORDHAM L. REV. 979 (1990).

Heath Foster, *Victim of Racism Will Gain Posthumous Bar Membership*, SEATTLE POST-INTELLIGENCER (February 5, 2001).

Gil Gott, *A Tale of New Precedents: Japanese American Internment as Foreign Affairs Law*, 19 B.C. THIRD WORLD L.J. 179 (1999).

Morton Horwitz, *Symposium: National Conference on Judicial Biography "Contracted" Biographies and other Obstacles to "Truth" Commentary*, 70 N.Y.U. L. REV. 714 (1995).

Peter Irons, *Fancy Dancing in the Marble Palace*, 3 CONST. COMMENTARY 35 (1986).

Marc Hideo Iyeki, *The Japanese American Coram Nobis Cases: Exposing the Myth of Disloyalty*, 13 N.Y.U. REV. OF L. & SOC. CHANGE 199 (1985).

John A. Jenkins, *The Solicitor General's Winning Ways*, 69 ABA J. 734 (1983).

Jennifer Mee, *Comment, Petitioners for Writ of Error Coram Nobis Must Show "Lingering Disabilities" from Erroneous Conviction*, 70 WASH. U.L.Q. 665 (1992).

Natsu Taylor Saito, *Justice Held Hostage: U.S. Disregard for International Law in the World War II Internment of Japanese Peruvians—A Case Study*, 19 B.C. THIRD WORLD L.J., 40 B.C. L. REV. 275 (1999).

Note, *Government Litigation in the Supreme Court: The Roles of the Solicitor General*, 78 YALE L.J. 1442 (1969).

Reggie Oh & Frank Wu, *Essay, The Evolution of Race in the Law: The Supreme Court Moves From Approving Internment of Japanese Americans to Disapproving Affirmative Action for Asian Americans*, 1 MICH. J. RACE & L. 165 (1996).

Brendan W. Randall, *Comment, United States v. Cooper: The Writ of Error Coram Nobis and the Morgan Footnote Paradox*, 74 MINN. L. REV. 1063 (1990).

Eugene Rostow, *The Japanese American Cases—A Disaster*, 54 YALE L.J. 489 (1945).

Eric K. Yamamoto, *Efficiency's Threat to the Value of Accessible Courts for Minorities*, 25 HARV. C.R.-C.L. L. REV. 341 (1990).

Eric K. Yamamoto, *Korematsu Revisited—Correcting the Injustice of Extraordinary Government Excess and Lax Judicial Review: Time for a Better Accommodation of National Security Concerns and Civil Liberties*, 26 SANTA CLARA L. REV. 1 (1986).

Alfred C. Yen, *Introduction: The Importance of Korematsu Studies*, 19 B.C. Third World L.J., 40 B.C. L. REV. 1 (1999).

Fred Korematsu family photo (young Fred is second from right), circa 1940.
Courtesy of Fred Korematsu and Donald Tamaki.

Press conference announcing the reopening of the Supreme Court cases of Fred Kore-
matsu, Gordon Hirabayashi and Minoru Yasui, (left to right seated lead counsel Dale
Minami, Donald Tamaki and attorney and researcher Peter Irons, (standing left to
right) Fred Korematsu, Gordon Hirabayashi and Minoru Yasui).
San Francisco Press Club, 1983.

Courtesy of Chris K. D. Huie and the National Japanese American Historical Society.

*Some of the legal team at a press conference for Fred Korematsu after the government
conceded the case (standing left to right, Donald Tamaki, Dennis Hayashi, Lorraine
Bannai; seated left to right, Dale Minami—lead counsel, litigant Fred Korematsu,
Peter Irons—attorney and researcher).
San Francisco Press Club, 1983.*

Courtesy of Chris K. D. Huie and the National Japanese American Historical Society.

Fred Korematsu and Professor Peter Irons with Professor Lorraine Bannai at
Seattle University School of Law, Spring 1997.
Courtesy of Ross Mulhousen and Seattle University School of Law.

*Kathryn and Fred Korematsu speaking at UCLA conference
"Of Civil Wrong and Rights," November 16, 2000.*

Courtesy of Prof. Laura Gómez.

Fred Korematsu chatting with UCLA students.
Courtesy of Leigh Iwanaga.

The UCLA School of Law Critical Race Studies/Concentration Asian American Studies Center and the California Civil Liberties Public Education Program present...

OF CIVIL WRONGS AND RIGHTS

The Fred Korematsu Story

A film by Eric Fournier

November 16, 2000
3:30 p.m.
1102 Perloff Hall, UCLA

Los Angeles Premiere

discussion with the director Eric Fournier, Fred Korematsu, and Katherine Korematsu followed by a reception.

Courtesy of Frank Lopez, UCLA School of Law.

Chapter 6 REPARATIONS

A. JAPANESE AMERICAN REDRESS, CONTINUED: AN OVERVIEW

In the previous chapter, we asked: *how does a government repair serious harm it inflicts upon its own citizens, particularly when those citizens are members of a minority racial group who are targeted because of their race? In particular, what kinds of remedies were sought and given for the internment of 120,000 Japanese Americans during World War II?* Chapter 5 explored in detail the first of four types of possible government redress: judicial declaration of injustice. This chapter looks at three other types of reparations.

As the last chapter revealed, the Japanese American redress and reparations movement targeted each branch of the federal government. On the judicial front, Japanese Americans initiated two different kinds of lawsuits. The first, discussed in the last chapter, was the *coram nobis* litigation brought by the three individuals who had been convicted of violating the wartime curfew and exclusion orders. This litigation sought a judicial declaration of injustice and did not seek monetary relief. The second was a class action damages lawsuit, filed by former internees in an attempt to obtain monetary compensation for the material and psychological harms of the internment. Discussed below, this case, *Hohri v. United States*, was ultimately dismissed by the federal courts as untimely filed.

On the executive level, intense lobbying culminated in President Ford's 1976 repeal of Executive Order 9066 during the nation's bicentennial. In the legislative arena, Congresspersons from California and Hawai'i successfully pushed through federal legislation creating a study commission, the Commission on Wartime Relocation and Internment of Civilians (CWRIC). Excerpted below and in various other chapters of this book, the CWRIC's 1983 report PERSONAL JUSTICE DENIED is a penetrating historical investigation of government racism and an in-depth exploration of the continuing harms of the internment. In response to the various redress efforts—the lawsuits, the CWRIC hearings and report and extensive lobbying by diverse groups—Congress passed the Civil Liberties Act of 1988. The Act committed the President to apologize to the former internees and established a $1.25 billion trust fund for reparations payments of $20,000 to each surviving internee.

The first study module explores the reparations theory that is now emerging from worldwide redress efforts. The second two study modules in Section B address the compensatory aspect of reparations: time bars to lawsuits for compensation, as well as the money damage claims of African Americans and Native Americans for historical injustices. In the third study module, the implications of nonjudicial forms of redress are examined—including their effects on Japanese American internees and their simultaneous uplifting and unsettling potential for other groups suffering historical injustice. The section concludes with inquiries into the claims for reparations by Japanese Latin Americans, African Americans, Native Hawaiians, South Africans and Korean sex slaves.

1. BACKGROUND

Grassroots organizing and education for reparations included an early

APPEAL FOR ACTION TO OBTAIN REDRESS[*]

Shosuke Sasaki, Mike Nakata and Henry Miyatake, Seattle JACL Chapter (Nov. 19, 1975)

When Japanese Americans obviously have done nothing against those who systematically vilified and libeled them during the first half of this century, have meekly submitted to mass imprisonment by the Government without receiving a formal statement of charges or trial; and thereafter have failed thus far even to ask for redress from the Government for that unjustified imprisonment, the white majority living on the Pacific Coast can hardly be blamed for looking upon the Japanese Americans as actually having been espionage agents and saboteurs at the start of World War II.

No amount of docile submission to white officials or "demonstrations of loyalty" to the United States by the Nisei can ever "disprove" the false accusations in the minds of most white Americans. That can only be done when the Government of the U.S. either through Congress or through its courts publicly declares that the wartime uprooting and imprisonment of Japanese Americans was totally without justification and awards the victims of its wartime outrage proper and reasonable redress.

Government recognition of and payment for wrongs done to their ancestors several generations ago have been secured by a number of Native American Indian tribes and Alaskan Natives in recent years. There can be little doubt that someday Americans of Japanese descent will press for and obtain reparations for the World War II uprooting and imprisonment of the Issei and Nisei. And while it is better to obtain redress of wrongs even generations late than not at all, for most Issei, justice delayed would in effect mean justice denied. In fact, many of the Issei who were most seriously hurt by the evacuation and imprisonment are already dead and gone and within five or ten years most of the remaining Issei will have passed away. Even some of the older Nisei are starting to die in slowly increasing numbers.

Except for approximately 10% of the Nisei who are convinced that they "have it made" or have been "accepted by the whites" and are opposed to any action which would "rock the boat," there is general agreement among Japanese Americans that action to obtain redress for the evacuation and related injustices is needed. Recent surveys show that a heavy majority want any payments made directly to each individual claimant. The surveys also reveal almost total agreement that the Issei should be given first priority in receiving such payments.

If redress and justice are to be gotten for the Issei and Nisei, strong and determined efforts must immediately be initiated and pushed to a successful conclusion. Most Americans believe in justice and it is unlikely that their elected officials in the United States Government would now deny a just set-

---

[*] For the World War II Evacuation and Imprisonment of Japanese Americans.

tlement if the true facts of our unjustified maltreatment at the hands of the Government during World War II were properly presented.

HENRY MIYATAKE, INTERVIEW BY TOM IKEDA
October 28, 1999, Densho: Japanese American Legacy Project

But if you look at the constitutionality of the issue, to me, if you round up 115,000, 120,000 people, and you put 'em into enforced incarceration process without due process of law, without martial law being declared, we're talking about a constitutional issue. You can't do that. So it becomes, whether you could get 51 or 50+ percent of the 435 Members of the House of Representatives and fifty people in the Senate to go along with this kind of issue[. I]f they can't go along with it, then the Constitution doesn't mean a damn thing to me. And the way they thre[w] us into the camp[s], they disregarded the Constitution. So the monkey's on their back also because they, they wrote Public Law 503, and they banged it through Congress in two days flat. And that's the real bill that put us into the camp. And that was part of Congress's action. . . .

To me, this whole thing about Japanese American redress, to me, is a[n] issue of what possibly can be done by individuals that's dedicated to a, for a cause and a mission. And to think of this group that we had, which is one Issei and one Kibei and the rest of us Niseis, and we tried, in my time period, I tried to get the legal services of Japanese Americans, and they shut the door on me. For one thing, it's pro bono work. Secondly, they weren't interested in raising Cain with the public. It's too much of a controversial issue. But to have a bunch of engineers and one economist do this is a kind of a[n] interesting case study. First of all, why wouldn't a politician be the spearhead of this kind of effort? Especially a Japanese American politician, somebody in Congress that has the right and the ability to write a bill for Congress and get it enacted?

2. JUDICIAL ACTION: THE *HOHRI* CLASS ACTION DAMAGES CASE

PETER IRONS, JUSTICE DELAYED: THE RECORD OF THE JAPANESE AMERICAN INTERNMENT
27–32 (1989)

Spurred by William Hohri of Chicago, the National Council for Japanese American Redress had filed a suit [in Washington, D.C.] in March 1983, after the *coram nobis* petitions were filed, on behalf of all internment camp survivors as a class. The suit listed twenty-one separate legal injuries the government had caused the internees and asked that each class member be awarded damages of $10,000 for each violation, a total potential award of some $24 billion. The injuries claimed by the camp survivors included "summary removal from their homes, imprisonment in racially segregated prison camps, and mass deprivations of their constitutional rights" by the government.

Although the *coram nobis* petitions and class action suit had no legal connection, both were facets of the overall "redress" movement and lawyers in the two efforts maintained contact. Several of the documents from the *coram nobis* petition were included in the class action suit as "direct evidence that the government knew of the falsity of its claim of military necessity" in defending the internment before the Supreme Court.

[On May 17, 1984, Federal District] Judge Louis Oberdorfer dismissed the class action suit [as untimely], holding that the government records refuting the Army's "military necessity" claim had been available in the 1940s.

The Court of Appeals for the District of Columbia revived the class action redress suit.

The *Hohri* case was litigated in two different federal district courts and reviewed in three separate appellate courts. The two most important judicial opinions follow. They are labeled here *Hohri I* and *Hohri II*.

HOHRI v. UNITED STATES
782 F.2d 227 (D.C. Cir. 1986) (*Hohri I*)

WRIGHT, Circuit Judge.

In the spring of 1942 the government of the United States forcibly removed some 120,000 of its Japanese-American citizens from their homes and placed them in internment camps. There they remained for as long as four years. When the constitutionality of this action was challenged in the Supreme Court the government justified its actions on the grounds of "military necessity." The Supreme Court deferred. Nearly forty years later, a congressional commission concluded that the government's asserted justification was without foundation. It is now alleged that this fact was concealed from the Supreme Court when it rendered its historic decision in *Korematsu v. United States*. Yet today, now that the truth can be known, the government says that the time for justice has passed. We cannot agree.

This suit was brought by nineteen individuals, former internees or their representatives, against the United States.[1] They seek money damages and a declaratory judgment on twenty-two claims, based upon a variety of constitutional violations, torts, and breach of contract and fiduciary duties. The United States moved to dismiss for lack of subject matter jurisdiction under Federal Rule of Civil Procedure 12(b)(1). In support of its motion the United States cited the applicable statutes of limitations, sovereign immunity, and the alleged exclusivity of the American-Japanese Evacuation Claims Act. The District Court granted appellee's motion to dismiss. *Hohri v. United States*, 586 F. Supp. 769 (D. D.C. 1984) (*Hohri*). We now affirm in part and reverse

---

[1] Although appellants had moved for class certification, a decision on this motion was postponed pending resolution of appellee's motion to dismiss.

in part, remanding the Takings Clause claims of those appellants who never received awards under the Claims Act for further proceedings. . . .

I.C. EXTENSION OF THE RULE IN *KOREMATSU* TO CLAIMS FOR COMPENSATION

In 1948 Congress enacted the American-Japanese Evacuation Claims Act, 50 U.S.C. App. § 1981 *et seq.* (1982) (hereinafter the Claims Act). Under the Act the Attorney General was given jurisdiction to determine claims for "damage to or loss of real or personal property" filed by former evacuees that were a "reasonable and natural consequence of the evacuation." The Act provided for specific limitations on the types of compensable losses for which claims could be filed.[23] All awards were deemed "final and conclusive for all purposes."

The Claims Act, however, was not passed in recognition of a legal wrong inflicted on the evacuees. On the contrary, the history of the Act reveals that Congress believed it was acting out of moral impulse, not legal obligation. Congress thereby signified its belief that although the *Korematsu* holding may only have applied to the validity of a criminal conviction, the *Korematsu* rationale effectively barred all claims for compensation as well. . . .

IV. SOVEREIGN IMMUNITY

It is well settled that the United States is amenable to suit only in those instances where it has specifically waived its immunity. Two such waivers are alleged in this case: the Tucker Act and the Federal Tort Claims Act. Although we find that the Tucker Act does provide a waiver for appellants' claims founded upon the Takings Clause and upon contract, it appears that sovereign immunity bars the residue of appellants' monetary claims.

V. STATUTE OF LIMITATIONS

28 U.S.C. § 2401(a) (1982) is the statute of limitations governing appellants' Taking Clause and contract claims. It provides that a claim must be filed within six years of the time that the "right of action first accrues." Appellee argues that appellants' cause of action first "accrued" when appellants' were first subjected to the evacuation program. For their part appellants argue that because the government fraudulently concealed essential elements of their cause of action the statute of limitations was tolled until they actually discovered the facts that had been concealed. The law of this circuit supports neither view. Instead, our cases hold that when a defendant fraudulently conceals the basis of a plaintiff's cause of action, the statute of limitations is tolled until the time that a reasonably diligent plaintiff could have discovered the elements of his claim. Applying this standard to the case at bar, we hold

---

[23] *See, e.g.,* 50 U.S.C. App. § 1982(b)(5) (denying compensation for loss of anticipated profits). Similar limits were interpolated through subsequent adjudications. *See, e.g., Claim of Mary Sogawa* (1950), (denying compensation for expenses of the evacuation); *Claim of George M. Kawaguchi* (1950) (limiting compensation to purchase price, implicitly denying any interest increment).

that although appellants' contract claims are barred by the statute of limitations, appellants' Takings Clause claims were timely filed.

When the government appealed to the Supreme Court in April of 1987, Solicitor General Charles Fried argued that the class action damage claims were barred by sovereign immunity and the statute of limitations. He also argued that the Circuit Court of Appeals for the District of Columbia lacked jurisdiction to entertain the appeal and that the appropriate court was the recently created Federal Circuit Court of Appeals. In 1987 the Supreme Court agreed with Fried's jurisdictional argument, vacated the lower court decision, and remanded the case to the new court.

After the D.C. Court of Appeals decision in *Hohri I*, the Supreme Court determined that the appeal was lodged in the wrong court and transferred the case to Court of Appeals for the Federal Circuit. That court issued the following opinion.

HOHRI V. UNITED STATES
847 F.2d 779 (Fed. Cir. 1988) (*Hohri II*)

Per Curiam

This appeal comes to this court following the decision of the Supreme Court in *United States v. Hohri*, 482 U.S. 64 (1987) (vacating judgment of District of Columbia Circuit and remanding with instructions to transfer to this court pursuant to 28 U.S.C. § 1631 (1982)). In *Hohri*, the Supreme Court held that a case which presents both a nontax claim under the "Little Tucker Act," and a claim under the Federal Tort Claims Act, as here, may be appealed only to the Court of Appeals for the Federal Circuit.

The appeal here is from the judgment of the United States District Court for the District of Columbia, 586 F. Supp. 769 (D.D.C. 1984) (Oberdorfer, J.), dismissing the claims of nineteen individuals and an organization of Japanese-Americans which sought damages and declaratory relief for injuries resulting from the internment of Japanese-Americans during World War II. The district court held, *inter alia*, that appellants' claims were barred by applicable statutes of limitations.

Each of the numerous issues raised to this court is fully addressed in the opinion of Judge Oberdorfer. After a meticulous review of that opinion, we are unpersuaded of any error. We see no need to restate or elaborate on the district court's careful and scholarly analysis, nor to burden appellants with further delay. Accordingly, we affirm for the reasons stated in the district court opinion.

Affirmed.

BALDWIN, Senior Circuit Judge, dissenting-in-part.

The majority adopts, *in toto*, the District Court's opinion. Although I agree with much of what the trial judge says, I respectfully dissent because I

believe he erred in concluding that appellants' takings claims are barred by
the statute of limitations. . . .

The trial judge correctly determined that appellants had stated a takings
claim, and that the portion of appellants' takings claims concerning constitutional rights other than property rights were unfounded. I believe, however,
that the trial judge incorrectly decided that appellants' remaining takings
claims were barred by the applicable six year statute of limitations. The trial
judge rejected appellants' contention that the statute of limitations was tolled
as a result of the government's fraudulent concealment of information relating to the military necessity for relocating and interning Japanese-Americans
during World War II. Instead, he found that appellants failed to exercise due
diligence in asserting their claims. He found that a reasonably diligent plaintiff would have discovered sufficient evidence to state a claim as early as the
late 1940's. I cannot agree that the government's fraudulent concealment of
vital information did not toll the statute.

The statute of limitations to which appellants' claims are subject is enumerated in 28 U.S.C. § 2401(a) (1982):

> Every civil action commenced against the United States shall be barred
> unless the complaint is filed within six years after the right of action first *ac-*
> *crues* (emphasis added).

The question, therefore, is when appellants' right of action first "accrued."
The trial judge decided that appellants' claims accrued, at the latest, some
time in the late 1940's, following publication of the Ringle, Fly, and Hoover
documents.

As a general rule, a statute of limitations is tolled where a defendant
fraudulently or deliberately conceals material facts relevant to a plaintiff's
claim, *provided* the plaintiff could not, through the exercise of due diligence,
have discovered the basis of the claim. As the trial judge pointed out, the parties do not dispute that appellee concealed various intelligence reports which
contradicted the claim of military necessity raised in *Hirabayashi* and *Korematsu*. The parties do dispute, however, the effect this concealment had on
the accrual of appellants' claims, and the duration of the effective concealment of sufficient matter to delay such accrual.

Appellants argue that their claims did not accrue until the completion of
work by the Commission on Wartime Relocation and Internment of Civilians
(CWRIC), and the publication of the CWRIC Report of its investigations entitled *Personal Justice Denied* in 1982. Appellants' position is that the Supreme Court erected an insurmountable legal barrier with its decisions in
Hirabayashi and *Korematsu* when it upheld the internment policy in deference to the military. This barrier could be removed they assert only by an
affirmative statement by one of the "war-making" branches that military necessity did not require the internment policy. They argue that the creation of
CWRIC and the publication of *Personal Justice Denied* is the first event constituting such a statement. This conclusion is premised upon the disclosure
in *Personal Justice Denied* that the government fraudulently concealed significant and vital information concerning its role in the *Korematsu* and *Hirabayashi* decisions. Appellants say that this fraudulent behavior precluded
them from seeking relief in the courts because the level of deference shown by

the Supreme Court in *Korematsu* and *Hirabayashi* to military decision making rendered any claim virtually frivolous. Thus, the statute of limitations should, they assert, be tolled until 1980 or 1982.

In opposition, appellee asserts that appellants' claims accrued at the time of the taking because that is when appellants knew of the injury and its cause. In the alternative, appellee argues appellants' claims accrued at one of several later dates: (1) when the Ringle, Fly, and Hoover documents first appeared; (2) when other books about the interning of Japanese-Americans appeared in the 1950's; or (3) at the latest, when President Ford signed Presidential Proclamation 4417 in 1976 declaring the incident a "mistake." The basis for this position is that the facts concealed concerned a potential affirmative defense of military necessity and not the appellants' cause of action. This is, as the trial judge realized, a mere technical distinction, especially where, as here, the Supreme Court sanctioned this affirmative defense as a bar to cases questioning the propriety of the internment policy. Appellee's assessment of the impact of *Hirabayashi* and *Korematsu* is a faulty one. These cases had the effect of validating the exclusion orders *in toto* as compelled by military necessity. . . .

The Supreme Court's decision to defer to military authorities was constitutionally based. Even though it stated in *Korematsu* that racial classifications were "immediately suspect," the Court left little room for judicial evaluation of the propriety of the orders when it agreed with its earlier position in *Hirabayashi* that the authority vested in the military by the exclusion orders was "not wholly beyond the limits of the Constitution," and that "Congress, and the military authorities acting with its authorization, have constitutional power to appraise the danger in the light of facts of public notoriety." Once the courthouse doors were effectively closed, it did not matter that appellants knew of the existence of their injury and the identity of the defendant. Appellants may have been on notice to inquire, but this knowledge left them in no better position where the available information and Supreme Court decisions precluded them from filing a good faith claim. . . .

Where a defendant fraudulently conceals information, and that concealment has the effect of dooming a plaintiff's claims at the outset, the statute of limitations should be tolled until such time as the plaintiff discovers or should have discovered, through due diligence, the facts concealed. . . .

Appellee's actions during the War clearly constituted fraudulent concealment. The district court found, based on the pleadings and the historical evidence, that appellee did, in fact, conceal critical evidence during the prosecution of *Hirabayashi* and *Korematsu* before the Supreme Court. But the court found that once the Hoover, Fly, and Ringle documents, all objects of concealment, were leaked, the statute began to run. I disagree that these documents were sufficient to rebut the presumption of military deference provided by the Supreme Court in *Hirabayashi* and *Korematsu*. These documents constituted only a small portion of the information concealed, and by no means the most important information. . . .

The statute having been tolled by appellee's fraudulent concealment, the question remaining is when did it begin to run? The traditional standard applied by this court is that appellants "must either show that [appellee] has concealed its acts with the result that [appellants were] unaware of their existence or [appellants] must show that [their] injury was 'inherently unknowable' at the accrual date." Generally, it would be sufficient that appellants were on notice to inquire that they had a potential claim, and it is "irrelevant for limitations purposes that [appellants did not] learn[] until later that [they] had *further* support for [their] decision."

Strict application of this rule without regard for appellants' peculiar circumstance would yield the result reached by the trial court and majority. Appellants were readily aware that their property had been taken at the time they were excluded and interned. There was no question as to who had committed the acts against them. According to the trial court, the only obstacle in their way was a pair of Supreme Court decisions upholding appellee's actions and granting complete deference to the military's judgment. Under this logic, appellants, had they acted with due diligence, should have filed their claims in the forties or fifties. At that time, however, with the information available, they were destined for dismissal on the pleadings.

Application of this rule in appellants' situation is, I believe, inappropriate and inequitable. Instead, I would judge appellants' diligence according to whether they acted reasonably under the circumstances. Our decisions suggest holding that appellants had knowledge of their claims when they were on notice to inquire about their *potential* claims. In a situation such as this, this standard should be applied in such a way that appellants are not barred until such time as they were able to obtain sufficient knowledge of the factual basis of their claims to allow them to file a *good faith* complaint.[6] Before the statute could begin to run against appellants, there had to be sufficient evidence in the public domain to permit appellants to state a claim. In the peculiar facts of this case, this means that appellants needed enough facts to potentially rebut the Supreme Court's presumption of deference. Thus, the evidence concealed by appellee must have been sufficient to provide appellants with enough facts to make a good faith determination that they could *potentially* rebut this presumption.

The leaked documents, as noted earlier, could not suffice to defeat the presumption erected. It was not until CWRIC exposed and declassified a wealth of intelligence information that appellants became aware of the existence of adequate facts indicating that sufficient concealment had occurred to cast sincere doubt upon the Supreme Court's *Hirabayashi* and *Korematsu* holdings.

The additional information was available to the Justice Department at the time it prepared the briefs in those cases. Appellee did not present evidence indicating that appellants should have, or could have, known of the existence of this additional information solely because of the presumed knowledge of

---

[6] The filing of frivolous claims (and appeals) is a serious matter in today's judicial system. Rule 11 of the Federal Rules of Civil Procedure has evolved into a strong judicial weapon against claims which do not have a good faith basis. . . .

Even though Rule 11 did not have the bite it now has in the 1940s and 1950s, appellants should not be penalized for failure to file a timely claim which could not then be substantiated.

the Ringle, Fly, and Hoover documents. There were only two means for appellants to obtain this information: (1) by Executive declassification;[7] or (2) by Act of Congress. In this case, the latter occurred before the former. . . .

Our nation has evolved tremendously since the incidents which gave rise to this action occurred. So, too, our government institutions have matured since that time. Unfortunately, we have not yet erased the possibility of abuse of individual citizens or groups of citizens. Fortunately, we have adequate means in our laws and our Constitution for those harmed by governmental actions to seek recompense in the courts. While the statute of limitations seeks justly to protect the United States from endless claims that may be age old, it does not behoove our society to sanction the perpetration of fraud by the sovereign. Appellants are, I believe, entitled to their day in court to attempt to prove their allegations that their property was taken, and that they are entitled to relief for that taking. Whether they will succeed is irrelevant at this point. In my opinion, appellee's actions before this nation's highest Court, and its long concealment of the factual basis of appellants' claims entitles appellants to the opportunity to try. I would therefore reverse that portion of the trial judge's opinion dismissing the takings clause claims for those appellants who did not receive payment under the American-Japanese Evacuation Claims Act.

3. EXECUTIVE ACTION

For Japanese American internees, presidential action entailed both the rescission of Executive Order 9066 and a formal governmental apology.

a. REPEAL OF EXECUTIVE ORDER 9066

President Roosevelt's executive action in 1942—Executive Order 9066—initiated the internment. President Ford's repeal of that order in 1976, the year of America's bicentennial, marked the beginning of the lengthy redress process. In his proclamation, President Ford acknowledged that "We now know what we should have known then—not only was the evacuation wrong, but Japanese Americans were and are loyal Americans." The proclamation is reproduced on the next page in original form.

---

[7] It is unnecessary to consider whether a Freedom of Information Act request would have yielded these documents, although it is unlikely because of their continued classification, because appellee made no showing that appellants should have known of their existence.

THE PRESIDENT

PROCLAMATION 4417

An American Promise

By the President of the United States of America

A Proclamation

In this Bicentennial Year, we are commemorating the anniversary dates of many of the great events in American history. An honest reckoning, however, must include a recognition of our national mistakes as well as our national achievements. Learning from our mistakes is not pleasant, but as a great philosopher once admonished, we must do so if we want to avoid repeating them.

February 19th is the anniversary of a sad day in American history. It was on that date in 1942, in the midst of the response to the hostilities that began on December 7, 1941, that Executive Order No. 9066 was issued, subsequently enforced by the criminal penalties of a statute enacted March 21, 1942, resulting in the uprooting of loyal Americans. Over one hundred thousand persons of Japanese ancestry were removed from their homes, detained in special camps, and eventually relocated.

The tremendous effort by the War Relocation Authority and concerned Americans for the welfare of these Japanese-Americans may add perspective to that story, but it does not erase the setback to fundamental American principles. Fortunately, the Japanese-American community in Hawaii was spared the indignities suffered by those on our mainland.

We now know what we should have known then—not only was that evacuation wrong, but Japanese-Americans were and are loyal Americans. On the battlefield and at home, Japanese-Americans—names like Hamada, Mitsumori, Marimoto, Noguchi, Yamasaki, Kido, Munemori and Miyamura—have been and continue to be written in our history for the sacrifices and the contributions they have made to the well-being and security of this, our common Nation.

The Executive order that was issued on February 19, 1942, was for the sole purpose of prosecuting the war with the Axis Powers, and ceased to be effective with the end of those hostilities. Because there was no formal statement of its termination, however, there is concern among many Japanese-Americans that there may yet be some life in that obsolete document. I think it appropriate, in this our Bicentennial Year, to remove all doubt on that matter, and to make clear our commitment in the future.

NOW, THEREFORE, I, GERALD R. FORD, President of the United States of America, do hereby proclaim that all the authority conferred by Executive Order No. 9066 terminated upon the issuance of Proclamation No. 2714, which formally proclaimed the cessation of the hostilities of World War II on December 31, 1946.

I call upon the American people to affirm with me this American Promise—that we have learned from the tragedy of that long-ago experience forever to treasure liberty and justice for each individual American, and resolve that this kind of action shall never again be repeated.

IN WITNESS WHEREOF, I have hereunto set my hand this nineteenth day of February in the year of our Lord nineteen hundred seventy-six, and of the Independence of the United States of America the two hundredth.

Gerald R. Ford

[FR Doc.76-5141 Filed 2-19-76;1:27 pm]

b. PRESIDENT'S APOLOGY TO JAPANESE AMERICANS

A presidential apology accompanied reparations payments authorized by Congress to former internees. President George Bush sent a letter to each of the surviving internees, apologizing on behalf of the United States in the following words:

> A monetary sum and words alone cannot restore lost years or erase painful memories; neither can they fully convey our Nation's resolve to rectify injustice and to uphold the rights of individuals. We can never fully right the wrongs of the past. But we can take a clear stand for justice and recognize that serious injustices were done to Japanese Americans during World War II.

> In enacting a law calling for restitution and offering a sincere apology, your fellow Americans have, in a very real sense, renewed their traditional commitment to the ideals of freedom, equality, and justice. You and your family have our best wishes for the future.

For some former internees the apology was paramount. For others the apology and monetary reparations, in combination, both word and deed, began a process of healing. For still others neither the apology nor reparations were enough to do justice. For them, justice also meant government restructuring of the military, political and judicial institutions that contributed to the internment in the first place.

4. CONGRESSIONAL ACTION

Another type of government response to group redress claims for historical injustice is legislatively authorized monetary reparations.

a. THE COMMISSION ON WARTIME RELOCATION AND INTERNMENT OF CIVILIANS

As mentioned in the chapter's overview, the CWRIC played a pivotal role in the Japanese American redress process. It held broad scale public hearings during which internees told their stories of suffering then and their continuing pain. Its findings of no military necessity for and governmental misconduct in justifying the internment laid the foundation for the court rulings in the *Korematsu* and *Hirabayashi coram nobis* cases. Equally important, the Commission's unexpected recommendations that the government apologize and provide monetary reparations for surviving internees galvanized the Japanese American reparations movement.

The Commission's main recommendations from its 1983 report, *Personal Justice Denied*, are reproduced below.

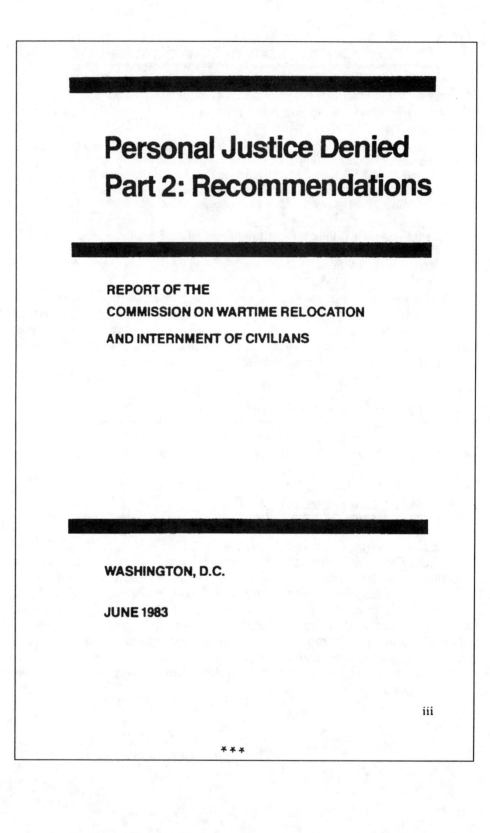

Personal Justice Denied
Part 2: Recommendations

REPORT OF THE
COMMISSION ON WARTIME RELOCATION
AND INTERNMENT OF CIVILIANS

WASHINGTON, D.C.

JUNE 1983

iii

* * *

Recommendations

In 1980 Congress established a bipartisan Commission on Wartime Relocation and Internment of Civilians, and directed it to:

1. review the facts and circumstances surrounding Executive Order Numbered 9066, issued February 19, 1942, and the impact of such Executive Order on American citizens and permanent resident aliens.

2. review directives of United States military forces requiring the relocation and, in some cases, detention in internment camps of American citizens, including Aleut civilians, and permanent resident aliens of the Aleutian and Pribilof Islands; and

3. recommend appropriate remedies.

The Commission fulfilled the first two mandates by submitting to Congress in February 1983 a unanimous report, *Personal Justice Denied*, which extensively reviews the history and circumstances of the fateful decisions to exclude, remove and then to detain Japanese Americans and Japanese resident aliens from the West Coast, as well as the treatment of Aleuts during World War II. The remedies which the Commission recommends in this second and final part of its report are based upon the conclusions of that report as well as upon further studies done for the Commission, particularly an analysis of the economic impact of exclusion and detention.

* * *

The Commission makes the following recommendations for remedies in several forms as an act of national apology.

1. The Commission recommends that Congress pass a joint resolution, to be signed by the President, which recognizes that a grave injustice was done and offers the apologies of the nation for the acts of exclusion, removal and detention.

2. The Commission recommends that the President pardon those who were convicted of violating the statutes imposing a curfew on American citizens on the basis of their ethnicity and requiring the ethnic Japanese to leave designated areas of the West Coast or to report to assembly centers. The Commission further recommends that the Department of justice review other wartime convictions of the ethnic Japanese and recommend to the President that he pardon those whose offenses were grounded in a refusal to accept treatment that discriminated among citizens on the basis of race or ethnicity. Both recommendations are made without prejudice to cases currently before the courts.

3. The Commission recommends that Congress direct the Executive agencies to which Japanese Americans* may apply for the restitution of positions, status or entitlements lost in whole or in part because of acts or events between December 1941 and 1945 to review such applications with liberality, giving full consideration to the historical findings of this Commission. For example, the responsible divisions of the Department of Defense should be instructed to review cases of less than honorable discharge of Japanese Americans from the armed services during World War II over which disputes remain, and the Secretary of Health and Human Services should be directed to instruct the Commissioner of Social Security to review any remaining complaints of inequity in entitlements due to the wartime detention.

4. The Commission recommends that Congress demonstrate official recognition of the injustice done to American citizens of Japanese ancestry and Japanese resident aliens during the Second World War, and that it recognize the nation's need to make redress for these events, by appropriating monies to establish a special foundation.

The Commissioners all believe a fund for educational and humanitarian purposes related to the wartime events is appropriate, and all agree that no fund would be sufficient to make whole again the lives damaged by the exclusion and detention. The Commissioners agree that such a fund appropriately addresses an injustice suffered by an entire ethnic group, as distinguished from individual deprivations.

Such a fund should sponsor research and public educational activities so that the events which were the subject of this inquiry will be remembered, and so that the causes and circumstances of this and similar events may be illuminated and understood. A nation which wishes to remain just to its citizens must not forget its lapses. The recommended foundation might appropriately fund comparative studies of similar civil liberties abuses or of the effect upon particular groups of racial prejudice embodied by government action in times of national stress; for example, the fund's public educational activity might include preparing and distributing the Commission's findings about these events to textbook publishers, educators and libraries.

5. The Commissioners, with the exception of Congressman Lungren, recommend that Congress establish a fund which will provide personal redress to those who were excluded, as well as serve the purposes set out in Recommendation 4. Appropriations of $1.5 billion should be made to the fund over a reasonable period to be determined by Congress. This fund should be used, first, to provide a one-time per capita compensatory payment of $20,000 to each of the approximately 60,000 surviving persons excluded from their places of residence pursuant to

---

* This recommendation and those that follow apply to all ethnic Japanese excluded or detained during World War II without regard to the explicit legal authority under which the government acted.

Executive Order 9066[1]. The burden should be on the government to locate survivors, without requiring any application for payment, and payments should be made to the oldest survivors first. After per capita payments, the remainder of the fund should be used for the public educational purposes discussed in Recommendation 4 as well as for the general welfare of the Japanese American community. This should be accomplished by grants for purposes such as aid to the elderly and scholarships for education, weighing, where appropriate, the effect of the exclusion and detention on the descendants of those who were detained. Individual payments in compensation for loss or damage should not be made.

The fund should be administered by a Board, the majority of whose members are Americans of Japanese descent appointed by the President and confirmed by the Senate. The compensation of members of the Board should be limited to their expenses and per diem payments at accepted governmental rates.

II. THE ALEUTS[2]

* * *

1. The Commissioners, with Congressman Lungren dissenting, recommend that Congress establish a fund for the beneficial use of the Aleuts in the amount of $5 million. The principal and interest of the fund should be spent for community and individual purposes that would be compensatory for the losses and injuries Aleuts suffered as a result of the evacuation. These injuries, as *Personal Justice Denied* describes, include lasting disruption of traditional Aleut means of subsistence and, with it, the weakening of their cultural tradition. The Commissioners therefore foresee entirely appropriate expenditures from the proposed fund for community educational, cultural or historical rebuilding in addition to medical or social services.

2. The Commissioners, with Congressman Lungren dissenting, recommend that Congress appropriate funds and direct a payment of $5,000 per capita to each of the few hundred surviving Aleuts who were evacuated from the Aleutian or Pribilof Islands by the federal government during World War II.

3. The Commission recommends that Congress appropriate funds and direct the relevant government agency to rebuild and restore the churches damaged or destroyed in the Aleutian Islands in the course of World War II; preference in employment should be given to Aleuts in

---

[1] Commissioner William M. Marutani formally renounces any monetary recompense either direct or indirect.

[2] Commissioner Joan Z. Bernstein recuses herself from participation in recommending remedies for the Aleuts because of a potential conflict of interest involving representation by the law firm of which she is a member.

performing the work of rebuilding and restoring these buildings, which were community centers as well as houses of worship.

4. The Commission recommends that Congress appropriate adequate funds through the public works budget for the Army Corps of Engineers to clear away the debris that remains from World War II in and around populated areas of the Aleutian Islands.

5. The Commission recommends that Congress declare Attu to be native land and that Attu be conveyed to the Aleuts through their native corporation upon condition that the native corporation is able to negotiate an agreement with the Coast Guard which will allow that service to continue essential functions on the island.

b. CIVIL LIBERTIES ACT OF 1988

The coalescence of mainstream elective politics, grassroots community organizing and education, the CWRIC's investigation and report and the *coram nobis* and *Hohri* cases culminated in the passage of the Civil Liberties Act of 1988. President Ronald Reagan signed the Act into law. That Act created the Office of Redress Administration to administer the reparations program. It also committed the president to a formal apology and authorized reparations in the amount of $20,000 for each surviving internee who was a U.S. citizen or legal resident alien at the time of internment. Securing congressional funding over subsequent years required additional rounds of intense political maneuvering. Reparations payments, along with the presidential letter of apology, commenced in 1991 and continued (as new eligibility was determined) through the Act's sunset in 1998.

President Signs Law to Redress Wartime Wrong

By JULIE JOHNSON
Special to The New York Times

WASHINGTON, Aug. 10 — President Reagan, moving to "right a grave wrong," signed legislation today that apologizes for the Government's forced relocation of 120,000 Japanese-Americans in World War II and establishes a $1.25 billion trust fund to pay reparations to those who were placed in camps and to their families.

"Yes, the nation was then at war, struggling for its survival," Mr. Reagan said at the White House. "And it's not for us today to pass judgment upon those who may have made mistakes while engaged in that great struggle. Yet we must recognize that the internment of Japanese-Americans was just that, a mistake."

Under the law, the Government will issue individual apologies for all violations of civil liberties and constitutional rights. And, through the office of the United States Attorney General, an award of $20,000 in tax-free payments will be given to each eligible intern or the designated beneficiary of the approximately 60,000 surviving Japanese-Americans who were driven from their homes and placed in internment camps in the war. Legislation providing the money still must be enacted.

Veto Had Been Threatened

Mr. Reagan had threatened to veto the measure but went ahead and signed it today. The White House spokesman, Marlin Fitzwater, said that the president had been concerned about the price tag of the bill, not its concept. In signing the legislation, Mr. Reagan endorsed the position that Vice President Bush staked out in June on the eve of the California primary.

About 40 percent of those affected by the legislation live in California, according to Congressional estimates.

The White House denied, as it has frequently done in recent weeks, that Mr. Reagan's initial opposition to the measure was reversed in part to help Mr. Bush in California.

When asked whether Mr. Bush's

Continued on Page A8, Column 2

Read the Civil Liberties Act of 1988 partially reproduced below. Pay particular attention to the provisions concerning the apology, restitution and public education. How does the Act justify the apology and reparations? What is the importance of public education? As you read further, speculate about the importance to redress of the Congressional Commission and community organizing efforts.

PUBLIC LAW 100–383—AUG. 10, 1988   102 STAT. 903

Public Law 100–383
100th Congress

An Act

To implement recommendations of the Commission on Wartime Relocation and Internment of Civilians.

Aug. 10, 1988
[H.R. 442]

Be it enacted by the Senate and House of Representatives of the United States of America in Congress assembled,

Human rights.

SECTION 1. PURPOSES.

50 USC app. 1989.

The purposes of this Act are to—

(1) acknowledge the fundamental injustice of the evacuation, relocation, and internment of United States citizens and permanent resident aliens of Japanese ancestry during World War II;

(2) apologize on behalf of the people of the United States for the evacuation, relocation, and internment of such citizens and permanent resident aliens;

(3) provide for a public education fund to finance efforts to inform the public about the internment of such individuals so as to prevent the recurrence of any similar event;

Public information.

(4) make restitution to those individuals of Japanese ancestry who were interned;

(5) make restitution to Aleut residents of the Pribilof Islands and the Aleutian Islands west of Unimak Island, in settlement of United States obligations in equity and at law, for—

(A) injustices suffered and unreasonable hardships endured while those Aleut residents were under United States control during World War II;

(B) personal property taken or destroyed by United States forces during World War II;

Real property.

(C) community property, including community church property, taken or destroyed by United States forces during World War II; and

(D) traditional village lands on Attu Island not rehabilitated after World War II for Aleut occupation or other productive use;

(6) discourage the occurrence of similar injustices and violations of civil liberties in the future; and

(7) make more credible and sincere any declaration of concern by the United States over violations of human rights committed by other nations.

SEC. 2. STATEMENT OF THE CONGRESS.

50 USC app. 1989a.

(a) WITH REGARD TO INDIVIDUALS OF JAPANESE ANCESTRY.—The Congress recognizes that, as described by the Commission on Wartime Relocation and Internment of Civilians, a grave injustice was done to both citizens and permanent resident aliens of Japanese ancestry by the evacuation, relocation, and internment of civilians during World War II. As the Commission documents, these actions were carried out without adequate security reasons and without any acts of espionage or sabotage documented by the Commission, and were motivated largely by racial prejudice, wartime hysteria, and a failure of political leadership. The excluded individuals of Japanese ancestry suffered enormous damages, both material and intangible, and there were incalculable losses in education and job training, all of which resulted in significant human suffering for which appropriate compensation has not been made. For these fundamental violations of the basic civil liberties and constitutional rights of these individuals of Japanese ancestry, the Congress apologizes on behalf of the Nation.

(b) WITH RESPECT TO THE ALEUTS.—The Congress recognizes that, as described by the Commission on Wartime Relocation and Internment of Civilians, the Aleut civilian residents of the Pribilof Islands and the Aleutian Islands west of Unimak Island were relocated during World War II to temporary camps in isolated regions of southeast Alaska where they remained, under United States control and in the care of the United States, until long after any potential danger to their home villages had passed. The United States failed to provide reasonable care for the Aleuts, and this resulted in widespread illness, disease, and death among the residents of the camps; and the United States further failed to protect Aleut personal and community property while such property was in its possession or under its control. The United States has not compensated the Aleuts adequately for the conversion or destruction of personal property, and the conversion or destruction of community property caused by the United States military occupation of Aleut villages during World War II. There is no remedy for injustices suffered by the Aleuts during World War II except an Act of Congress providing appropriate compensation for those losses which are attributable to the conduct of United States forces and other officials and employees of the United States.

* * *

SEC. 105. RESTITUTION.

(a) LOCATION AND PAYMENT OF ELIGIBLE INDIVIDUALS.—

(1) IN GENERAL.—Subject to paragraph (6), the Attorney General shall, subject to the availability of funds appropriated to the Fund for such purpose, pay out of the Fund to each eligible individual the sum of $20,000, unless such individual refuses, in the manner described in paragraph (4), to accept the payment.

50 USC app. 1989b-4.

* * *

(5) PAYMENT IN FULL SETTLEMENT OF CLAIMS AGAINST THE UNITED STATES.—The acceptance of payment by an eligible individual under this section shall be in full satisfaction of all claims against the United States arising out of acts described in section 108(2)(B). This paragraph shall apply to any eligible

individual who does not refuse, in the manner described in paragraph (4), to accept payment under this section within 18 months after receiving the notification from the Attorney General referred to in paragraph (3).

* * *

<table>
<tr><td>50 USC app.
1989b-5.</td><td>SEC. 106. BOARD OF DIRECTORS OF THE FUND.

(a) Establishment.—There is established the Civil Liberties Public Education Fund Board of Directors, which shall be responsible for making disbursements from the Fund in the manner provided in this section.

(b) Uses of Fund.—The Board may make disbursements from the Fund only—</td></tr>
<tr><td>Research and development.
Education.
Public information.</td><td>(1) to sponsor research and public educational activities, and to publish and distribute the hearings, findings, and recommendations of the Commission, so that the events surrounding the evacuation, relocation, and internment of United States citizens and permanent resident aliens of Japanese ancestry will be remembered, and so that the causes and circumstances of this and similar events may be illuminated and understood; and

(2) for reasonable administrative expenses of the Board, including expenses incurred under subsections (c)(3), (d), and (e).</td></tr>
</table>

* * *

B. Study Modules: Reparations

The United States' apology to and reparations for interned Japanese Americans galvanized reparations movements in America and abroad. It also helped stimulate development of reparations theory—that is, the philosophical and strategic bases for governmental redress.

1. Emerging Reparations Theory

Reparations theory is at its early stages of development. The worldwide explosion of reparations efforts, discussed below, largely commenced in the late 1980s. One aspect of emerging reparations theory is highly conceptual: It draws upon law, political theory, social psychology, theology and community studies. With this backdrop, Martha Minow's excerpted article provides an illuminating conceptual framework. She explores vengeance and forgiveness as two opposing ends on a spectrum of responses to historic group injustice. She also opens possible reparatory paths in between.

A second aspect of developing reparations theory is practical: It describes conditions necessary for the achievement of group redress and guides redress movements through political and legal shoals. Roy Brooks' excerpt examines practical dimensions of apologies and reparations and the range of government and societal responses.

Both dimensions of reparations are raised in subsequent study modules in this chapter.

MARTHA MINOW, *BETWEEN VENGEANCE AND FORGIVENESS*
9–23 (1998)

VENGEANCE AND FORGIVENESS

Perhaps there simply are two purposes animating societal responses to collective violence: justice and truth. Justice may call for truth but also demands accountability. And the institutions for securing accountability—notably, trial courts—may impede or ignore truth. Democratic guarantees protecting the rights of defendants place those rights at least in part ahead of truth-seeking; undemocratic trials may proceed to judgment and punishment with disregard for particular truths or their complex implications beyond particular defendants. Then the question becomes: Should justice or truth take precedence? Of what value are facts without justice? If accountability is the aim, does it require legal proceedings and punishment? Do legal proceedings generate knowledge? One answer calls for "[a]ll the truth and as much justice as possible"; another would stress punishment for wrongdoing, especially horrific wrongdoing. Only if we make prosecution a duty under international law will we ensure that new regimes do not lose courage, overstate the obstacles they face, and duck their duties to punish perpetrators of mass violence, argue experts such as Diane Orentlicher. Yet only if we acknowledge that prosecutions are slow, partial, and narrow, can we recognize the value of independent commissions, investigating the larger patterns of atrocity and complex lines of responsibility and complicity.

Even this debate is too partial. Truth and justice are not the only objectives. At least, they do not transparently indicate the range of concerns they may come to comprise. There is another basic, perhaps implicit pair of goals or responses to collective violence—vengeance and forgiveness.

Vengeance: Although this word may sound pejorative, it embodies important ingredients of moral response to wrongdoing. We should pursue punishment because wrongdoers should get what is coming to them; this is one defense—or perhaps restatement—of vengeance. Vengeance is the impulse to retaliate when wrongs are done. Through vengeance, we express our basic self-respect. . . .

The danger is that precisely the same vengeful motive often leads people to exact more than necessary, to be maliciously spiteful or dangerously aggressive, or to become hateful themselves by committing the reciprocal act of violence. The core motive may be admirable but it carries with it potential insatiability. Vengeance thus can set in motion a downward spiral of violence, or an unquenchable desire that traps people in cycles of revenge, recrimination, and escalation. . . .

Finding some alternative to vengeance—such as government-managed prosecutions—is a matter, then, not only of moral and emotional significance. It is urgent for human survival.

Forgiveness: Reaching for a response far from vengeance, many people, from diverse religious traditions, call for forgiveness. The victim should not seek revenge and become a new victimizer but instead should forgive the offender and end the cycle of offense. When we have been injured by another's offense, we should seek to reconnect and recognize the common humanity of the other, and grant forgiveness to underscore and strengthen our commonality. Through forgiveness, we can renounce resentment, and avoid the self-destructive effects of holding on to pain, grudges, and victimhood. The act of forgiving can reconnect the offender and the victim and establish or renew a relationship; it can heal grief; forge new, constructive alliances; and break cycles of violence.

These aspirations may seem especially compelling following a period of mass atrocity. Finding a way to move on, as individuals and as a society, takes central stage. If the nation is turning or returning to democracy, forging new relationships of trust and foundations for collective self-government become urgent goals. Those very goals may be jeopardized by backward-looking, finger-pointing prosecutions and punishments.

José Zalaquett, a Chilean human rights activist, maintains that underneath truth, justice, and forgiveness lie the "twin goals of prevention and reparation in the process of moral reconstruction." This formulation acknowledges that vengeance can be excessive or unquenchable, and that preoccupation with harms in the past can be debilitating for victims and bystanders. Instead, through forgiveness, victims can reassert their own power and reestablish their own dignity while also teaching wrongdoers the effects of their harmful actions. They can seek the reintegration of oppressors into society for their own sake, and for the sake of the larger projects of reconciliation and the rebuilding of a more fair and more humane world.

In theory, forgiveness does not and should not take the place of justice or punishment. Forgiveness marks a change in how the offended feels about the person who committed the injury, not a change in the actions to be taken by a justice system. . . . Forgiveness in this sense need not be a substitute for punishment. Even the traditional Christian call to forgive rather than avenge accompanies faith that vengeance will come—through the Divine.

Yet, in practice, forgiveness often produces exemption from punishment. Especially when a governmental body adopts a forgiving attitude toward offenders, the instrument often takes the form of amnesty or pardon, preempting prosecution and punishment. This institutionalizes forgetfulness, and sacrifices justice in a foreshortened effort to move on. Moreover, such an effort to move on often fails because the injury is not so much forgiven but publicly ignored, leaving it to fester. . . .

Human rights activist Aryeh Neier warns that public forgiveness in particular runs the risk of signaling to everyone the need to forget. When governments or their representatives "usurp the victim's exclusive right to forgive his oppressor," they thereby fail to respect fully those who have suffered. Governmental forgiveness that means exemption from punishment also forecloses the communal response, the acknowledgment of harm, that vengeance, and indeed justice, demand. Even if the rigor of prosecution and punishment are not pursued, some other form of public acknowledgment, overcoming communal denial, is the very least that can be done to restore dignity to victims. . . .

Perhaps forgiveness should be reserved, as a concept and a practice, to instances where there are good reasons to forgive. To forgive without a good reason is to accept the violation and devaluation of the self. Some acts of for-giveness raise questions about whether the victim has enough self-respect or strength to view the injury as a violation. If forgiveness involves letting go of warranted resentment, then the forgiver needs a good reason to let go. If the offense injured and devalued the victim, then the victim must have some very good reason to overcome the anger and hatred toward a person who commit-ted such unjustified and inexcusable harm. Expressing outrage, making clear what is unacceptable, and refusing relationships with those who commit evil are responses especially justifiable after mass violence. There may be no good reason to forego blame and condemnation. "[H]ow could one even *con-sider* reconciling oneself with people such as Hitler or Stalin or Charles Man-son, who really may not have any decency left in them—nor even any possibility of decency?"

In ordinary, everyday instances of wrongdoing, a reason to forgive arises, for some, when a wrongdoer changes, becomes "a new person" who repents his or her wrongs. But repentance for participation in a mass atrocity may simply be insufficient. Because no subsequent change of heart or regret could begin to be commensurate with the violations done, forgiveness seems out of place. . . .

Victims have much to gain from being able to let go of hatred, even when the perpetrator is unrepentant. Rabbi Harold Kushner argues that victims should forgive not because the other deserves it but because the victim does not want to turn into a bitter resentful person. Victims should release the anger for their own sake. Indeed, especially after mass atrocities, life could seem so precious that not a moment should be wasted in grudges or hatred toward the perpetrators. Dumisa Ntsebeza, a commissioner of the South Af-rica Truth and Reconciliation Commission who himself spent years incarcer-ated under the apartheid regime, explained that there could be generosity toward perpetrators because "there is so much to do in the time that remains of one's freedom.". . .

Vengeance and forgiveness are marks along the spectrum of human re-sponses to atrocity. Yet they stand in opposition: to forgive is to let go of vengeance; to avenge is to resist forgiving. Perhaps justice itself "partakes of both revenge and forgiveness. . . ."

I suggest a similar spirit but—an expanded—scope of possibilities. What responses do or could lie between vengeance and forgiveness, *if legal and cultural institutions offered other avenues for individuals and nations?* For nations recovering from periods of massive atrocity, the stakes are high, the dangers enormous. Members of those societies need to ask not only what should count as a good reason to forgive, and not only what are the appropri-ate limits to vengeance. They need to ask, what would it take, and what do our current or imagined institutions need to do, to come to terms with the past, to help heal the victims, the bystanders, and even the perpetrators? What would promote reconstruction of a society devastated by atrocities? What could build a nation capable of preventing future massacres and inci-dents or regimes of torture?

One path between vengeance and forgiveness pursues therapeutic goals. Promoting healing for individual victims, bystanders, and even offenders points to potential aims in response to mass atrocity. Recognizing healing as a value prompts new questions. What relative importance should the therapeutic goals have for victims, bystanders, and offenders, and what weight should therapeutic purposes bear in relation to the search for truth, the demand for justice, the urge for retribution, and the call of forgiveness? What place should a psychological frame of analysis have in assessing alternative responses to collective atrocities by individuals and societies? What if any sense is there in drawing analogies between the psychological needs and therapeutic responses appropriate to individuals, and issues involving entire groups of people, and even societies? . . .

Political concerns are often aimed at another set of goals, also lying somewhere between vengeance and forgiveness. The first is creating a climate conducive to human rights, a democratic process that seems to many a crucial rejoinder to mass violence. To mark the defeat of terror; to set in place safeguards against future collective atrocity; to communicate the aspiration that "never again" will such abominations happen—these are all significant human rights accomplishments that may be set in motion by political means. When terror was state sponsored, vital responses would establish the legitimacy and stability of a new regime.

Promoting reconciliation across divisions created by, or themselves causing, the collective violence is still another goal. Such reconciliation would assist stability, and democracy, but it also would require other measures: restoring dignity to victims would be part of this process, but so would dealing respectfully with those who assisted or were complicit with the violence. Otherwise, new rifts and resentments are likely to emerge and grow.

ROY BROOKS, *THE AGE OF APOLOGY*, IN WHEN SORRY ISN'T ENOUGH

3–9 (ROY BROOKS ED., 1999)

"Man's inhumanity to man makes countless thousands mourn." So wrote the poet Robert Burns two centuries ago. . . .

With apologies coming from all corners of the world—Britain's Queen Elizabeth apologizing to the Maori people; Australia to the stolen aboriginal children; the Canadian government to the Canadian Ukrainians; President Bill Clinton to many groups, including native Hawaiians and African American survivors of the Tuskegee, Alabama, syphilis experiment; South Africa's former president F. W. de Klerk to victims of Apartheid; and Polish, French, and Czech notables for human injustices perpetrated during World War II— we have clearly entered what can be called the "Age of Apology."

What is happening is more complex than "contrition chic," or the canonization of sentimentality. The apologies offered today can be described as "a matrix of guilt and mourning, atonement and national revival." Remorse improves the national spirit and health. It raises the moral threshold of a society. German society is a much better place today because Germans have been forced, and have forced themselves, to face their guilt with deep humility and penitence. So painful and enduring is the moral stain on the German soul that it may lend some truth to Socrates' argument that it is better to be the victim than the perpetrator of an injustice.

Heartfelt contrition just might signify a nation's capacity to suppress its next impulse to harm others. The significance of this point cannot be overstated. Before working on this book, I was not conscious of the undercurrent of fear that exists among survivors of human injustices that the very same atrocity might be revisited upon them. Jews fear that the Holocaust could be repeated, if not in Germany then in some other nation in the "civilized world," and Japanese Americans worry that relocation and internment could happen again on American soil, given the right set of circumstances. Head-bowed apologies from the leaders of Germany and the United States have only quieted the survivors' apprehension. But without such apologies, there would be greater concern, perhaps not just among the survivors, that those shameful acts might be repeated. . . .

Many of the most heinous acts can be attributed to the military gone amok during times of war. Examples include Japanese soldiers raping and torturing three hundred thousand civilians within a three-month period in Nanking, China, during World War II; American GIs slaughtering 504 women, children, and old men in four hours at the Vietnamese village of My Lai during the Vietnam War. . . .

Most human injustices, however, can be tied directly to conscious political choice. Millions of Jews, Gypsies, and others were murdered as a result of Nazi policy before and during World War II. Millions of blacks were killed and millions more enslaved under three centuries of American domestic policy. Thousands of Native Americans were killed and mistreated under similar policies. And millions of blacks were killed and subjugated by a ruling white minority through Apartheid policies in South Africa.

Women seem to occupy an especially precarious position during times of war. Not only are women victims of the same injustices as men (*e.g.*, slavery, assault, torture, looting, burning), but they are often singled out for additional sexual and reproductive brutalities (rape, sexual mutilation, and forced prostitution, sterilization, impregnation, and maternity). Throughout history, men have sexually abused women during times of war (and to an alarming extent during times of peace). Seen as an inevitability of war—a sort of "boys will be boys" extreme—rape is a historically well-documented war strategy that is highly effective for terrorizing the enemy. . . .

Rather than relying on the community of nation-states to bring criminal proceedings against perpetrators of human injustices, the victims can take matters into their own hands by seeking civil redress—money or other forms of relief—from the perpetrators under certain conditions. . . . However, some victims of human injustices find such redress morally objectionable. They see it as little more than "blood money." While one must, of course, be sensitive to the concerns of the victims, I do not equate redress with "blood money," nor do the many victims who seek monetary redress. True, a price cannot and should not be placed on suffering exacted by the Holocaust, Japanese American internment, African American slavery, and the like. But when rights are ripped away, the victim or his family is entitled to compensation and much more.

[There are] various conditions . . . necessary for successful redress of human injustices. These conditions can be woven into a *theory of redress*, which has four elements. First, the demands or claims for redress must be placed in the hands of legislators rather than judges. Legislators, quite simply, can do more than judges. . . .

Courts do, however, play a useful role in the redress process. They can and have been used to interpret and enforce extant rights and laws handed down by the legislature. Sometimes the legislature will create a court or quasijudicial body for the specific purpose of resolving redress claims. This happened in the United States with the creation of the now-defunct Indian Claims Commission. But most of the time, the highest court in the land can only apply existing rights and remedies; it cannot create new ones.

Within the legislative realm, successful redress movements have been able to reach the hearts and minds of lawmakers and citizens alike. But the success of any redress movement has depended largely on the degree of pressure (public and private) brought to bear upon the legislators—that is, politics—than with matters of logic, justice, or culture. Political pressure, then, is the second condition necessary for successful redress. . . .

Strong internal support is a third element of successful redress. The victims themselves must exhibit unquestioned support for the claims being pressed. Redress must be a top priority within the group. Indeed, it is the absence of this element from the African American redress movement that, in my judgment, is most responsible for the refusal of American political leaders (including President Clinton, who has been more attentive to African American concerns than any other American president) to offer even an apology for slavery or Jim Crow. The redress movement is growing. . . . But it has yet to reach the level of passion and necessity displayed in the successful Japanese American redress movement.

Although the politics of redress claims overshadow their merits, such claims still must be meritorious. There must be something of substance for lawmakers to promote. This is the fourth and final element of my theory of redress. The critical question, of course, is what constitutes a meritorious claim.

Mari Matsuda has identified several prerequisites for a meritorious redress claim. These requirements find support in this book, if modified into the following factors: (1) a human injustice must have been committed; (2) it must be well-documented; (3) the victims must be identifiable as a distinct group; (4) the current members of the group must continue to suffer harm; and (5) such harm must be causally connected to a past injustice. The first and last prerequisites warrant further discussion.

The definition of human justice can be formulated from the concept of "human rights." The place to begin is international law, the United Nations Charter in particular. Article 55(c) of the Charter reads in relevant part: "The United Nations shall promote . . . universal respect for, and observance of, human rights and fundamental freedoms for all without distinction as to race, sex, language, or religion. . . ."

Once a meritorious claim for redress is presented, how should a government respond? What is the proper *form of redress*? . . . The list of responses is dizzying. Some governments have issued sincere apologies; others have not. Some have followed up their apologies with payments to victims or their families; others have paid money to victims without issuing an apology. And still others have invested money, services, or both in the victims' community in lieu of compensating victims individually.

Although the forms of redress are diverse, they can be subsumed under conceptual categories for deeper understanding. First, we can distinguish between responses that are remorseful (some more so than others) and those that are not. Reponses that seek atonement for the commission of an injustice are properly called *reparations*. Responses in which the government does not express atonement are more suitably called *settlements*. The latter can be analogized to their use in American law. . . .

Reparations and settlements can be subdivided into *monetary* and *non-monetary* responses. Examples of the latter include amnesty, affirmative action, and municipal services such as the construction of new medical facilities or the creation of new educational programs. Nonmonetary reparations or settlements can be more effective than cash in responding to the victims' individual or collective current needs.

Monetary or nonmonetary reparations and settlements can be directed toward the victims individually or collectively. A reparation or settlement directed toward the individual is intended to be *compensatory*—in other words, to return the victim to the status quo ante. One directed toward the group is designed to be *rehabilitative* of the community—in other words, to nurture the group's self-empowerment or the community's cultural transformation, or at least to improve the conditions under which the victims live.

NOTES AND QUESTIONS

1. Between vengeance and forgiveness: Professor Martha Minow describes the struggle of individuals, groups and countries to deal with large-scale social atrocities. She posits that in many instances a socially productive path lies somewhere between seeking vengeance and simply forgiving. What are the potential limits of international criminal tribunals, truth commissions and civil reparations?

2. Age of apology: The excerpt from Roy Brooks explores practical aspects of redress: legislation rather than judicial decrees, reparations versus settlements, monetary and nonmonetary redress, compensatory versus rehabilitative rationales. Think about these distinctions as you review the reparations for Japanese Americans and read about the efforts of other groups in the next study modules, *infra*. What type of redress have the Japanese Latin Americans, African Americans, Native Hawaiians, South Africans and Korean comfort women sought and received to date? Is redress for any of these groups meaningful? If yes, what actions made redress meaningful? If no, what actions are needed to achieve meaningful redress?

2. PROCEDURE: TIME BARS OVER SUBSTANCE?

A relatively rare type of remediation for historical government wrongdo-ing is a court's award of "monetary damages" to the injured parties as com-pensation. This type of judicial remedy is rare because the United States government cannot be sued for damages unless it explicitly waives its "sover-eign immunity" from suit. The federal government has waived its immunity only in limited situations—for example, where the government is a party to a contract, where its employees are guilty of ordinary negligence (in driving a government car), or where the government violates the Constitution by tak-ing private property without fair compensation. The *Hohri* class action case asserted, among other things, the latter type of claim—the taking of internees' property without compensation.

Claims for judicially awarded compensation for historic injustice are also rare because even if those who are injured can assert a claim that is not pro-hibited by the government's sovereign immunity, that claim may be too old. A court may declare that the claim is "time-barred" by statutes of limitations, which require the prompt filing of claims. The statutory time bar became a major obstacle in the *Hohri* class action.

The *Hohri I* and *II* opinions address the shield defendants sometimes raise to prevent an adjudication on the merits: the statutory time bar. A stat-ute of limitations designates the time period within which a plaintiff can make a legal claim upon a defendant. Policy reasons for statutes of limita-tions include the need to ensure that crucial witnesses are not missing or de-ceased and that evidence has not grown stale from the passage of time. These statutes encourage the plaintiff to be vigilant about claiming an injury, and they protect a defendant by putting old claims to rest.

Although limitations periods are not specifically mentioned in the Federal Rules of Civil Procedure, they lurk within the language of Rule 3. According to that rule, an action is "commenced" by filing of the plaintiff's complaint with the court. The commencement of an action "tolls" the statute of limita-tions—that is, filing a complaint stops the clock. But when does a statute of limitations "accrue"—that is, when does the clock start?

A key issue in both *Hohri I* and *II* was the starting point of the six-year statute of limitations applicable to the action against the United States. Ac-crual could be measured when the injury first occurred or when the plaintiff first could have reasonably discovered the injury. For example, American soldiers, who were sprayed with Agent Orange insecticide by the U.S. Army, sustained relatively unnoticed superficial injuries almost immediately, but their serious injuries often were not noticeable until years later in the form of cancerous tumors. If the statute of limitations had started to run at the time the injury actually occurred, the limitations period for filing suit may have expired for many soldiers even before they knew of their serious injuries. If, however, the limitations period began only when the soldiers noticed their injuries, claims they asserted shortly thereafter would not be time-barred.

The *Hohri* cases highlight significant procedural barriers to monetary re-dress. When the injuries occurred in the distant past and if the limitations period accrues from the date of the initial injury, then claimants seeking redress for constitutional violations will not have access to a court of law. If the limitations period is not tolled by the fraudulent or stone-walling tactics of the defendant (who often controls the information that the plaintiff needs to make a claim), then again the plaintiff is out of luck.

Note that the *Hirabayashi coram nobis* court addressed the government's "late filing" argument and reached a result very different from the *Hohri II* court. It found that the government's suppression of key evidence, including the original unaltered DeWitt report, prevented the doctrine of laches, which is analogous to the statute of limitations, from barring Hirabayashi's claim.

NOTES AND QUESTIONS

1. **When does the claim accrue?:** Federal Circuit Judge Baldwin vigorously dissented on the statute of limitations issue in *Hohri II*. His dissent tracked the District of Columbia Court of Appeals' earlier opinion finding no time bar to plaintiffs' property takings claims. How persuasive was Judge Baldwin's dissent? Consider the following excerpt from the Ninth Circuit's opinion in the *Hirabayashi coram nobis* case.

> The district court's decision to grant the writ was clearly based upon material which was not known until very recently. The key document upon which the district court relied was the suppressed report of General DeWitt. The district court squarely confronted the government's laches contention:
>
> > [T]he government argues that all of the factual material presented on behalf of petitioner has been a matter of public record for nearly forty years and that petitioner is hence bound by the doctrine of laches from seeking to overturn his convictions.... At no place [] is there any reference to the statements made by General DeWitt in the initial version of his Final Report. In none of the other publications submitted by the government is there any such reference.
>
> These findings are clearly supported.
>
> The suppressed DeWitt Report is not the only evidence which has surfaced as a result of research during this decade. There are memos, which have only recently come to light, by Justice Department lawyers Ennis and Burling relating to the War Department's suppression of the revised report, and their doubts about the accuracy of the report. The discovery of these materials recently caused the District of Columbia Circuit to hold that the government's fraudulent concealment tolled the statute of limitations in cases brought by Japanese Americans for civil damages arising out of their internment.
>
> As to the diligence of Hirabayashi in finding the material, we must agree with the district judge who heard direct evidence on this issue and found that "petitioner cannot be faulted for not finding and relying upon [the only surviving copy of the initial version of the report] long before he brought this action in early 1983." Professional historians had failed to discover it as well, and the difficulty for a lay person to locate the initial version was documented in the record by testimony concerning its discovery.

Hirabayashi II, supra, chapter 5; 828 F.2d at 605.

2. **When is the statute tolled?:** The *Hohri II* majority adopted the district court's analysis and rejected summarily the plaintiffs' fraudulent con-

cealment argument. Tolling of the statute of limitations occurs not only upon the plaintiff's filing of the complaint with the court, but also by the defendant's concealment of the plaintiff's injury. The district court found that once "the Hoover, Fly, and Ringle documents, all objects of concealment, were leaked, [sometime in the late 1940s] the statute began to run." The government's further concealment of additional evidence of misconduct was deemed insufficient to toll the limitations period. But could the plaintiffs have stated a legal claim then without the later-uncovered original DeWitt Report and the internal Justice Department memoranda surrounding the Burling footnote?

3. *Hohri* and *Hirabayashi* compared: Why did the *Hohri* courts apply the time bar to the civil class action lawsuit? The *Hirabayashi coram nobis* court did the opposite. Could different outcomes be attributable to the difference between criminal and civil adjudication? Could it be attributable to the fact that the *Hohri* class action asked for billions of dollars in damages? By contrast, the *Hirabayashi coram nobis* suit requested specific non-monetary relief—that the judgment of conviction be vacated, the military orders declared unconstitutional and the indictment dismissed. If so, was this "distinguishing feature" a product of legal or political judgment?

4. **Assessing damages:** If the plaintiffs in *Hohri* had succeeded, how might former internees have established viable constitutional claims for the taking of property? What about claims for emotional injury? What kinds of proof would be required?

5. **Procedure over substance?:** Did the federal courts ultimately avoid a decision on the merits of the former internee's claims by resort to a procedural device—the statute of limitations? If so, was this appropriate in light of the timing of the availability of some of the incriminating documents, or was it more akin to a judicial feint—a dismissal on a "mere technicality" to prevent a possible huge damage award against the federal government? Or something else?

6. **Class action certification:** As discussed briefly in Chapter 4, in 1948 Congress passed legislation allowing former internees to recover limited amounts for internment-related property losses. If the district court in *Hohri* had certified a class action, would the former internees who had received a limited "property settlement" via the Evacuation Claims Act of 1948 (discussed in Chapter 4, *supra*) be barred from joining in the class action? Given the limited scope of the earlier Act and the limited amount of most settlements, should those internees have been given a second bite of the apple?

7. **Litigation and legislation:** The Federal Circuit affirmed the *Hohri* district court's dismissal in 1988, the same year President Reagan signed the Civil Liberties Act authorizing reparations for surviving former internees. The legislation provided that the legislative reparations foreclosed other reparations claims. What might have been the overall impact of the *Hohri* and *coram nobis* cases on the political movement for reparations?

3. REMEDIES: COMPENSATORY DAMAGES FOR AFRICAN AMERICAN AND NATIVE AMERICAN CLAIMS

What about other groups' legal claims for monetary damages for historic wrongs? African Americans and Native Americans have contemplated, and in several instances initiated, lawsuits for money damages for past injustices.

African Americans have filed damage claims in federal court for the harms of slavery, including the loss of freedom, property and income. Those claims, cast under the thirteenth amendment, reconstruction-era civil rights statutes and the Federal Tort Claims Act, have met with quick dismissal on grounds of governmental immunity, lack of standing and the statute of limitations. For instance, in *Cato v. United States*, 70 F.3d 1103 (9th Cir. 1997), the class of plaintiffs sought compensation of $100,000,000 for "forced, ancestral indoctrination into a foreign society; kidnapping of ancestors from Africa; forced labor; breakup of families; removal of traditional values; deprivations of freedom; and the imposition of oppression." The Ninth Circuit affirmed dismissal .of the class action damages claims, pointing African American claimants toward legislative solutions.

> Discrimination and bigotry of any type is intolerable, and the enslavement of Africans by this country is inexcusable. This Court, however, is unable to identify any legally cognizable basis upon which [these] claims may proceed against the United States. While plaintiff[s] may be justified in seeking redress for past and present injustices, it is not within the jurisdiction of this court to grant the requested relief.

70 F.3d 1103, 1105 (9th Cir. 1997).

America's indigenous peoples have fared somewhat better with their legal damages claims. The federal government settled land claims by Native Alaskans in the early 1970s (providing large sums of money and tracts of land as a prelude to the building of the Alaska pipeline). Native American tribes received monetary awards most often for the government's violation of treaties, including $81 million to the Klamaths of Oregon, $105 million to the Sioux of South Dakota, $12.3 million to the Seminoles of Florida, $31 million to the Chippewas of Wisconsin, and $32 million to the Ottowas of Michigan. Under instructions of the Hawai'i Supreme Court, Native Hawaiians are negotiating with the State of Hawai'i to settle their billion dollar damages claim based on the state's misappropriation of Hawaiian land trust funds. Whether the monetary payments just described ultimately reflect justice done is, in some instances, an open question.

NOTES AND QUESTIONS

1. **Differing treatment of African Americans?:** Are the courts treating African American legal claims for damages for slavery and Jim Crow segregation in one way and Native American claims for treaty and trust violations in another? How does one account for the several judicial damage awards to Native American tribes and Native Hawaiians and no similar damage awards to African Americans?

2. Problems with the legal framing of claims: As you contemplate the questions just posed, review the Ninth Circuit's ruling in *Cato* and consider the following view of the problem with the legal framing of compensation/damage claims for historic injustice.

> African American groups seeking broad redress for slavery and Jim Crow segregation have encountered considerable difficulty in casting their reparations claims in terms of individual rights and remedies. Legally framed claims for lost wages, liberty and property meet the slew of standard legal objections. . . . Opponents of African American reparations point to: (1) the statute of limitations ("this all happened over one hundred and thirty years ago"); (2) the absence of directly harmed individuals ("all ex-slaves have been dead for at least a generation"); (3) the absence of individual perpetrators ("white Americans living today have not injured African Americans and should not be required to pay for the sins of their slave master forbearers"); (4) the lack of direct causation ("slavery did not cause the present ills of African American communities"); (5) the indeterminacy of compensation amounts ("it is impossible to determine who should get what and how much").

Eric K. Yamamoto, *Racial Reparations: Japanese American Redress and African American Claims*, 19 B.C. THIRD WORLD L.J., 40 B.C. L. REV. 477, 490-91 (1999).

3. Framing African American reparations claims: How might African American reparations claims be most productively framed? For what decision-making bodies? With what legal and psychological effects? According to what kinds of political strategies? This topic is addressed in more detail *infra* in study module 5.b.

4. SOCIAL JUSTICE: IMPLICATIONS OF JAPANESE AMERICAN REDRESS

The 1988 Civil Liberties Act and the apology and reparations that followed were viewed by many as a tremendous victory for Japanese Americans. Many rejoiced. Some felt a sense of personal relief, of healing, for the first time. Some felt a renewed sense of commitment to the United States and its legal and political institutions. As discussed in the next section, Japanese American redress has had profound effects beyond the internment. But some view the legacy of the Japanese American reparations as incomplete.

Ten years have passed since the Civil Liberties Act. The Office of Redress Administration has closed its doors. We can now step back and begin to assess the questions posed above about Japanese American redress. Consider the following inquiries about the possible catalytic affect of Japanese American reparations internationally and about its potentially mixed social legacy in the United States.

Read the following excerpts from three related essays, with a constructively critical eye on the social meanings of Japanese American redress. Then compare the points raised with the fourth essay's strategic assessment of the benefits and risks of reparations, particularly in the context of reparations for

Native Hawaiians. Consider also the final essay's claim that Japanese American redress is related to the model minority stereotype.

a. NATIONAL AND WORLDWIDE TRENDS

ERIC K. YAMAMOTO, *RACE APOLOGIES*

1 J. GENDER, RACE & JUST. 47, 49 (1997)

Since the United States' 1988 apology to and monetary reparations for Japanese Americans wrongfully interned during World War II, America has experienced a spate of race-related apologies. The apologies range from Congress' apology to indigenous Hawaiians in 1993 for the illegal United States-aided overthrow of the sovereign Hawaiian nation, to the Southern Baptists' apology to African American church members for the denomination's endorsement of slavery, to the Florida legislature's $2 million reparations to black survivors [and descendants] of the government-backed murder and mayhem in the black town of Rosewood, to Ice Cube's apology to Korean American merchants for his rap "Black Korea" that threatened the burning of Korean stores, to Rutgers University president's apology for indicating that blacks lacked the "genetic background" to perform well on standardized tests, to Senator D'Amato's pseudo-apology for his linguistic mocking of Judge Lance Ito's Japanese ancestry. Several racial justice grievances with pending claims for apologies and reparations included African American claims for reparations for the harms of slavery, a suit for reparations by Peruvian Japanese abducted from Peru by the United States during World War II and interned in America's concentration camps, and Native Hawaiian claims for reparations from the United States.

These recent past and potential future race apologies in the United States are part of a worldwide phenomenon that includes Queen Elizabeth's apology to and reparations for New Zealand's Maoris for British-initiated nineteenth-century bloody race wars, French President Chirac's recognition of French complicity in the deportation of 76,000 Jews to Nazi concentration camps, the Catholic church's apology for its assimilationist policy in Australia that contributed to Aborigines' spiritual and cultural destruction, and the Evangelical Lutheran Church of America's apology for founder Martin Luther's damaging anti-Semitism.

What potential does the wave of race apologies hold for the redress of justice grievances among racial groups in the United States? For, where appropriate, interracial reconciliation? When do apologies lead to meaningful restructuring of intergroup relations? When are they simply masks for continuing status quo oppression?

b. The Legacy of Japanese American Redress

Eric K. Yamamoto, *Friend, Foe or Something Else: Social Meanings of Redress and Reparations*

20 Denv. J. Int'l L. and Pol'y 223, 223-224 (1992)

Who has benefited from redress and reparations; who has been ignored? What freedoms have been protected; what obligations forsaken? What promises have been fulfilled; what illusions fostered? In what diverse ways may society come to understand redress and reparations for WWII Japanese American internees? Put another way: What are the evolving social meanings of the United States government's reparations law and program?

Some of the meanings are salutary. Former WWII internees have benefited in myriad ways—financially, culturally, emotionally. Some also say government and all of society have benefited. Reparations are proof that the United States constitution works, that government is self-correcting, and that the American legal and political systems are essentially just. Still others say the United States has bolstered its moral foundation [for commanding] international allegiance to human rights. Its reparations program may be a model for other countries concerned about redemption for past wrongs.

But are these salutary views overstated? Or misguided? Do reparations laws inevitably engender institutional and attitudinal changes reflecting "lessons learned?" Or [by letting out some social steam and diminishing the pressure for change] might redress and reparations ultimately aid in the perpetuation of institutional power structures and public attitudes that suppress freedom for those society views as different and vulnerable?

[Perhaps] a reparations law's salient meanings lie not in the achievement of payments and apologies to a particular group or in symbolic constitutional victories, but in the commitment of recipients and others to build upon the reparations process' inter-group linkages and political insights to contribute to broad-based institutional and attitudinal restructuring [for the benefit of all facing group discrimination or oppression]. Whether those commitments are made and acted upon may, and should, in principal part determine enduring social meanings of reparations.

c. The Potential Underside of the Reparations Process

Eric K. Yamamoto, *Racial Reparations: Japanese American Redress and African American Claims*

19 B.C. Third World L.J., 40 B.C. L. Rev. 477, 487, 494, 496-97 (1999)

Reparations, if thoughtfully conceived, offered and administered, can be transformative. They can help change material conditions of group life and send political messages about societal commitment to principles of equality. When reparations stimulate change, however, they also generate resistance. Proponents suffer backlash. Thus, when reparations claims are treated seriously, they tend to recreate victimhood by inflaming old wounds and triggering regressive reactions. This is the dilemma of reparations.

Seeing these dual possibilities in all redress movements, Joe Singer describes the potential for further victimization. . . . He recounts Jews' highly publicized demands in 1997 that Swiss banks account for and restore Jewish money and gold held by the banks for Nazis during World War II. Bank acknowledgment and restitution treats Jews as worthy human beings with rights, including the right to own property. Restitution counters the anti-Semitic myth of Jews misappropriating the property of others. . . .

One problem, however, is that Jewish demands for monetary restitution resurrect for some the harsh historical stereotypes of Jews "as money-grubbing, as having both accumulated secret bank accounts in the past and caring now about nothing more than money. . . ." Another, and broader, problem is that additional Jewish reparations claims may spark resentment among other groups whose reparations claims have gone unmet (such as Hungarian gypsies who were exterminated by Nazis in Auschwitz and elsewhere). . . .

The dilemma also played out—but in a different way—after Japanese American redress. Since past governmental sin had been absolved, Asian Americans were once again permissible targets for the government and mainstream America. The President and Congress criticized Japanese competition in the auto industry and extensive Japanese real estate purchases in the United States. Asian immigrants became a target of popular initiatives like California's Proposition 187 and federal welfare reforms. They were blamed for America's depressed economy, inadequate public education and other social ills. The recent congressional investigation into campaign finance tarred with the taint of "yellow peril" not only Asian nationals and immigrants, but also all Americans of Asian ancestry. Some believe that although the redress process educated many about the historical injustice, reparations, combined with a feeling that "now the system works," also let the government off the hook so that it no longer needed to vigorously oppose racism against Asian Americans.

The transformative potential of reparations is therefore linked, ironically, to dissatisfaction and risk. Reparations for some does not necessarily presage reparations for deserving others. Reparations for one group may stretch the resources or political capital of the giver, precluding immediate reparations (or enough reparations) for others. The very dynamic of reparations process, even where salutary for recipients can generate backlash and disappointment. . . .

My thesis is not that this underside diminishes the significance of achieving reparations or forecloses future redress efforts. Rather, I suggest that the risks caution careful strategic framing of debate and action and anticipatory grappling with a reparations movement's both bright and darker potential.

d. STRATEGIES

MARI J. MATSUDA, *LOOKING TO THE BOTTOM: CRITICAL LEGAL STUDIES AND REPARATIONS*

22 HARV. C.R.-C.L. L. REV. 323, 393-96 (1987)

Reparations is a "critical legalism," a legal concept that has transformative power and that avoids the traps of individualism, neutrality and indeterminancy that plague many mainstream concepts of rights or legal principles. Reparations avoids standard liberal pitfalls because, first, it is a concept directed at remedying wrongs committed against the powerless. Unlike "free speech" or "due process," payment for past injustice is a one-way value. Those on the bottom—minority group members, political outsiders, the exploited—will receive reparations.

Second, reparations doctrine supports group rights rather than individual rights and thus escapes some of the ideological traps of traditional rights thinking.

Finally, reparations is at its heart transformative. It recognizes the crimes of the powerful against the powerless. It condemns exploitation and adopts a vision of a more just world. The reparations concept has the aspirational, affirming, idealistic attraction of rights rhetoric, without the weak backbone. While rights rhetoric turns to dust time and again, reparations theory, should we accept and internalize it, may prove more dependable.

This progressive tilt of reparations, however, can mask lurking dangers. Some detect a certain commodifying vulgarity in throwing money at injured people. . . . Reparations, one could argue, promotes the idea that everyone has a price, that every wound is salved by cash, that success merely means more money.

The practical shortage of resources in the injured communities weighs against the commodification risk. Monetary grants will not compensate for the terrible losses sustained. No sum can make up for loss of freedom or sovereignty. . . . The judgment states, "Something terrible has happened for which we are responsible. While no amount can compensate for your loss, we offer here a symbol of our deep regret and our continuing obligation."

Resistance to commodification is important. If reparations are viewed as an equivalent exchange for past wrongs, continuing claims are terminated. Any obligation to victim-groups would end since their injury is transformed into a commodity and the price paid. A reparations claim would become a dangerous gamble for victims, and a welcome res judicata (barring future claims) opportunity for perpetrators. One generation could sell away their claim at bargain-basement prices, to the detriment of future generations, in an effort to cash in at the earliest opportunity. Commodification must be resisted if reparations is to be more than a coercive quit-claim mechanism.

A related and indeed troubling objection to reparations comes from looking to the bottom. Some thoughtful victim group members are inclined to reject reparations because of the political reality that any reparations award will come only when those in power decide it is appropriate. Hayden Burgess, a native Hawaiian nationalist lawyer, suggests that any award of cash reparations is inadequate, for it ignores the Hawaiian's primary need: restoration of the Hawaiian government and removal of the United States presence in Hawai'i. Rather than a top-down model of reparations granted by the United States, Burgess prefers negotiations between the Hawaiians and the United States as equals, perhaps mediated by a neutral third party in an international forum, to determine an appropriate remedy for the overthrow of the Hawaiian government.

CHRIS IIJIMA, *REPARATIONS AND THE "MODEL MINORITY" IDEOLOGY OF ACQUIESCENCE: THE NECESSITY TO REFUSE THE RETURN TO ORIGINAL HUMILIATION*

19 B.C. THIRD WORLD L.J., 40 B.C. L. REV. 385, 392-95, 397-99 (1998)

[It is] postulated that the "model minority" stereotype conveyed a number of silent messages which in turn conveyed the notion that if other minorities were the same as Japanese Americans and had overcome hardship without Government aid, they would be "rewarded" as well. Indeed, these fears are also well founded. Contemporaneous stories in the national and local popular press about how Asian Americans were a "model minority" were prevalent during the time of debate and passage of the redress bill. It is no accident that there is ample evidence in the record of allusions to the "model minority" image of Asian Americans, and particularly of Japanese Americans. . . .

There is a particular irony about the debate on the redress bill. While there was general agreement, at least rhetorically, on the injustice of the internment, all of the glowing historical references centered around those contemporary political and ideological positions that *justified* and *accommodated* the decision to intern Japanese Americans. Those who, at the time of internment, saw it for the injustice and outrage that it was and chose to dissent continue to be silenced and unheralded even during the process of acknowledging their prescience. In essence, the idea that Americans were being told by Congress to celebrate by giving of redress to Japanese Americans was that patriotism—the kind of patriotism that does not resist injustice—get rewarded. Thus the ideological baggage of the decision to redress the injustice of internment is the celebration of the "superpatriotic" response to it. It is this response—the ideological component of the model minority stereotype—and its celebration by Congress that contains great lessons and holds great dangers for Japanese Americans in particular and Asian Americans in general. . . .

[R]eference to the heroism and success of the segregated Japanese-American Army unit, the 442nd Regimental Combat Team, is . . . typical. The accolades were much deserved, celebrated achievements about which all Americans, particularly Japanese Americans, are proud. Yet, the congressional debate was barren of favorable, indeed any, references to those heroic "others"—Japanese-American draft resisters who refused to fight for the United States until their families were freed from the camps.

An example of this resistance was the Fair Play Committee at Heart Mountain Relocation Center, which was organized to protest the violation of constitutional rights. In March 1944, it published a leaflet protesting the injustice of ordering Japanese Americans to join a segregated unit in the Army without restoration of their constitutional rights.... The seven leaders of the Heart Mountain draft resistance movement, Kiyoshi Okamoto, Paul Nakadate, Ben Wakaye, Ken Yanagi, Frank Emi, Minoru Tamesa, and Sam Horino were convicted later that year on draft conspiracy charges. Yet these men and others, who also sacrificed for hallowed democratic principles, went unnoticed during the congressional debate.

NOTES AND QUESTIONS

1. Evaluating claims for redress: How are we to assess the national and worldwide trend of race apologies? How do we fashion and evaluate specific redress efforts? What determines if redress in a given situation is "meaningful" (and for whom) or the perpetuator of "status quo oppression"? In what ways does a government (or private entity) conferring reparations itself benefit? And what are the obligations of reparations beneficiaries in terms supporting the redress movements of others?

How might other Asian Americans groups, African Americans, Native Hawaiians and Native Americans respond to Japanese American reparations?

2. Interracial healing: To what extent, and under what circumstances, do group-based apologies and reparations foster racial healing? In practical day-to-day terms, what does racial healing between groups once in conflict look like? For an insightful account, *see* Harlan Dalton, RACIAL HEALING: CONFRONTING THE FEARS BETWEEN BLACKS AND WHITES (1995).

3. The model minority myth and reparations: What role did the model minority myth play in Japanese American redress? What are the implications of that myth for other minority groups seeking reparations? Why were the Japanese Latin Americans marginally successful in securing reparations, while other groups, African Americans in particular, are still awaiting even minimal reparations.

4. The Evacuation Claims Act of 1948: Shortly after the war, Congress passed the Evacuation Claims Act of 1948 authorizing the Attorney General to "adjudicate certain claims resulting from evacuation of certain persons of Japanese Ancestry under military orders." The Act, however, specifically excluded compensation for "loss on account of death or personal injury,... or mental suffering" and for "loss of anticipated profits... or earnings." The Act, as implemented with these limitations, provided minimal compensation for property losses, and only covered those losses that could be proven (actual recovery was estimated at ten cents on the dollar). Because pain and suffering, as well as loss of business profits and worker earnings, were excluded, the Claims Act resulted in no compensation for most and limited compensation for the others. See Chapter 4, *supra* at section B.3.a.

In light of these realities, how do you respond to reasons for the Act set forth in the 1947 House Report on the Claims Act: "Not to redress these loyal Americans in some measure for the wrongs inflicted upon them would provide ample material for attacks by the followers of foreign ideologies on the

American way of life, and to redress them would be simple justice"? How much of the impetus for the limited government redress was to undermine criticism of "followers of foreign ideologies" (that is, the Soviet Union), and how much was "simple justice" for those interned? Opponents of the 1988 Japanese American reparations legislation maintained that the United States had already proffered reparations, referring to the 1948 Evacuation Claims Act. To what extent did the Claims Act confer reparations? In whose eyes did the Act "repair" the internment's damage? With what effects on Japanese Americans and on American society?

5. **Americans stranded in Japan:** In his article *Stranded in Japan and the Civil Liberties Act of 1988: Recognition for an Excluded Group of Japanese Americans*, 6 Asian L.J. 151 (May 1999), Mark Hanasona argues that the "strandees" should be deemed eligible for reparations under the Civil Liberties Act.

5. REDRESS: OTHER RACIAL AND INDIGENOUS GROUPS

In what ways are Japanese American reparations connected to redress movements by other racial groups? What lessons might be drawn by contemporary reparations advocates?

a. JAPANESE LATIN AMERICANS

The Civil Liberties Act limited reparations to citizens and legal resident aliens. This limiting language created a bizarre anomaly. Japanese Latin Americans (JLAs)—that is, persons of Japanese ancestry who were citizens of Latin American countries—failed to qualify for reparations even though they had been kidnapped in those countries by the United States and taken to the United States and placed in internment camps. Professor Natsu Taylor Saito describes the Japanese Latin American treatment:

NATSU TAYLOR SAITO, *JUSTICE HELD HOSTAGE: U.S. DISREGARD FOR INTERNATIONAL LAW IN THE WORLD WAR II INTERNMENT OF JAPANESE PERUVIANS—A CASE STUDY*

19 B.C. THIRD WORLD L.J., 40 B. C.L. REV. 275, 276-79, 316, 325 (1999)

More than 2,200 Latin Americans, most of them of Japanese ancestry and a majority from Peru, forcibly were brought to the United States during the war.

After Pearl Harbor was bombed, the U.S. government, hoping to use Japanese Latin Americans as exchange prisoners for U.S. POWs, collaborated with the Peruvian government and other Central and South American countries to round them up and ship them to the United States. During the war, an estimated 550 Latin American Japanese were sent to Japan in exchange for U.S. POWs. When the war was over, 900 more were deported to Japan, even though they didn't want to go.

Neither the administration of President Franklin D. Roosevelt nor later administrations gave an official explanation for the removals and internment. . . .

[After the war and closure of the internment camps, many of the Japanese Latin Americans were designated "illegal aliens" in the United States. Angered by the government's refusal to pay reparations in the 1990s, the JLAs filed suit against the United States, alleging denial of the equal protection of the laws. The *Mochizuki v. United States* suit was settled in 1998, shortly before the expiration of the Act. That settlement, however, satisfied few. Although all class members were to receive an apology, monetary payments were limited to $5,000 per internee, and payments were to occur only if sufficient funds remained after all other eligible internees were paid. (The fund's interest ran out before payment.) Professor Saito compares the JLA and Japanese American internees' experiences and examines the differing legal and political treatment:]

The . . . settlement in *Mochizuki* . . . is most notable for what it does not offer. The plaintiffs lost homes and possessions; some were forced to clear jungle in the Canal Zone; and men, women and children were transported under armed guard to prison camps in the Texas desert where they were incarcerated indefinitely without charge or hearing. Families were torn apart and scattered across the globe. Held as hostages, some Japanese Latin Americans were exchanged for U.S. citizens, and others were imprisoned past the end of the war, when the INS declared them to be "illegal aliens" and deported them, against their will, to Japan. . . .

The [Civil Liberties Act compensation] . . . symbolizes this country's recognition of the injustices inflicted upon Japanese Americans during World War II. The CLA restricts compensation to those who were U.S. citizens or permanent residents at the time of the internment, thus excluding interned Japanese Latin Americans. The *Mochizuki* settlement neither expands the terms of the CLA to incorporate the Japanese Latin Americans, nor does it provide for compensation comparable to that received by Japanese Americans. . . . Under such terms, it is hard to say whether the settlement constitutes acknowledgment and apology or symbolizes disrespect for the harm suffered by the Japanese Latin American claimants.

Most importantly, the settlement does not acknowledge that the United States violated any domestic or international law by interning Japanese Latin Americans. While the precedent set by *Korematsu v. United States* has never been overturned, it is widely accepted that the incarceration of Japanese Americans from the West Coast violated the constitutional rights of U.S. citizens and permanent residents. The terms of the *Mochizuki* settlement imply that the harm inflicted on Japanese Latin Americans, because they were nonresident aliens, was less significant than that inflicted upon Japanese Americans. Similarly, unacknowledged are the gross violations of international law committed. . . . If the *Mochizuki* settlement is the only U.S. acknowledgment of these actions, its central message may be that the U.S. government can disregard international law and violate human rights with impunity.

Japanese Latin American internees were subjected to conditions similar to those inflicted upon the Japanese American internees and, in addition, suffered the trauma of being uprooted from their countries. Why, then, would the government offer them only a fraction of the compensation given Japanese Americans? . . .

Congress provided compensation to Japanese Americans as a matter of discretion. Accordingly, there need only be a rational basis for their legislative distinctions made in the legislation. In addition, considerable precedent authorizes distinguishing between people on the basis of citizenship or immigration status when the benefit at issue constitutes a privilege as opposed to a right. As a result, it is extremely difficult to make a compelling legal argument that the failure to include Japanese Latin Americans under the Civil Liberties Act constitutes national origin discrimination in violation of the Fifth Amendment's guarantee of due process.

b. AFRICAN AMERICANS

Compare Japanese American redress to African American reparations claims. One African American said that she believed that Japanese American redress was very appropriate, yet she was left with the uneasy feeling, "why them and not us?" The Civil Liberties Act itself stated that it did not set a precedent for reparations for any other group suffering injustice at the hands of the U.S. government. Does the legislation impede or aid African American and Native American reparations claims?

Professor Robert Westley explores African American reparations in light of recent setbacks for affirmative action:

ROBERT WESTLEY, *MANY BILLIONS GONE: IS IT TIME TO RECONSIDER THE CASE FOR BLACK REPARATIONS?*

19 B.C. THIRD WORLD L.J., 40 B.C. L. REV. 429, 429-30, 433-45 (1999).

Affirmative action for Black Americans as a form of remediation for perpetuation of past injustice is almost dead. Due to a string of Supreme Court decisions . . ., the future possibility of using affirmative action to redress the perpetuation of past wrongs against Blacks is now in serious doubt. . . .

[I] argue that a program of reparations . . . benefits subordinated communities in ways that avoid some of the pitfalls and drawbacks of affirmative action. Moreover, a glimmer of promise can be taken from the recent revival of the reparations principle in the case of Holocaust survivors whose assets were illegally confiscated by Swiss banks in the wake of World War II. Through legislation the positive law of some countries has slowly and painfully evolved towards recognition of reparations claims in extreme cases of group injustice, casting aside judicially imposed doctrinal limits such as time bar, sovereign immunity, and denial of jurisdiction. This evolving position, which has been taken in some cases, may serve as an enforceable norm for all subordinated groups under which Blacks may seek reparations. The fact that reparations have been more effectively obtained through legislation than through litigation offers an opportunity to circumvent a court system grown hostile to the remedial claims of Blacks arising under the very constitutional rights enacted to protect Black rights.

ERIC K. YAMAMOTO, *RACIAL REPARATIONS: JAPANESE AMERICAN REDRESS AND AFRICAN AMERICAN CLAIMS*

19 B.C. THIRD WORLD L.J., 40 B.C. L. REV. 477, 488-89, 521-22 (1999)

African Americans seeking reparations for slavery have tended to frame their arguments according to traditional remedies law—that reparations are a form of both payment for individual losses (just compensation) and divestiture of ill-gotten gain (preventing unjust enrichment). This resort to traditional legal remedies makes some sense at first glance. Compensation and unjust enrichment are well-recognized remedial principles, and they generally appear to fit the circumstances of African American slavery-based claims.

In practical legal application, however, those traditional principles erect inordinately high barriers. For instance, according to Vincenne Verdun, by casting reparations as a "claim for compensation based on slavery," present-day African Americans are required to prove "that all African Americans were injured by slavery and that all white Americans caused the injury or benefited from the spoils of slave labor." The courts legally, and mainstream America politically, have been unwilling to accept this group victim/group perpetrator proposition. They continue to look instead for individual wrongdoers who inflict harm on identifiable individuals, resulting in quantifiable damages. This search, framed by the common law paradigm, undermines historical group-based claims for the wrongs of slavery and Jim Crow segregation.

Without a marked shift away from the individual rights/remedies paradigm, reparations claims face formidable obstacles—unless the circumstances, particulars and timing of the claims allow for recasting those claims in traditional legal garb. . . .

Reparations, as repair, . . . aim for more than temporary monetary salve for those hurting. Reparations are a vehicle, along with an apology, for groups in conflict to rebuild their relationships through attitudinal changes and institutional restructuring. . . .

This repair paradigm of reparations redirects attention from individual rights (recognized by law) and legal remedies (monetary compensation). It focuses instead on (1) historical wrongs committed by one group, (2) which harmed, and continue to harm, both the material living conditions and psychological outlook of another group, (3) which, in turn, has damaged present-day relations between the groups, and (4) which ultimately has damaged the larger community, resulting in divisiveness, distrust, social disease—a breach in the polity. Within this framework, reparations by the polity and for the polity are justified on moral and political grounds—healing social wounds by bringing back into the community those wrongly excluded.

c. NATIVE HAWAIIANS

The situation of the Native Hawaiians reflects a century-old wrong. Specifically, that "wrong" began in 1893, when the U.S. government illegally overthrew the sovereign Hawaiian monarchy. With the overthrow, Native Hawaiians lost their independence as citizens of a sovereign nation. Much of the land held in trust by the Hawaiian monarchy was seized by the provisional government in 1894 and later ceded to the U.S. government. The

United States annexed Hawai'i as a territory in 1898 over vehement protest of almost all Native Hawaiians. Hawai'i became the fiftieth state of the union in 1959.

Professor Mari J. Matsuda describes the contemporary Native Hawaiian sovereignty movement and its claim for reparations:

MARI J. MATSUDA, *LOOKING TO THE BOTTOM: CRITICAL LEGAL STUDIES AND REPARATIONS*

22 HARV. C.R.-C.L. L. REV. 323, 371-73 (1987)

Native Hawaiians seek reparations for the overthrow of the Hawaiian government and loss of land. They request a formal recognition of the illegal destruction of Hawaiian sovereignty and an apology from the United States. They also seek resumption of Hawaiian rule, return of at least part of the lands presently held by the federal and state governments, and monetary compensation. In one survey of Hawaiian opinion, a majority of respondents favored reparations in the form of land and programs benefiting Hawaiians collectively, as well as individual monetary awards.

Non-Hawaiian opponents of reparations argue that the American take-over was an historical inevitability, and that present-day taxpayers are not responsible for the wrongdoing of government officials of 100 years ago. Yet the recent judicial and congressional recognition of moral and legal obligations for treaty violations and uncompensated takings of the land of Native North Americans has encouraged Hawaiians to press their claims.

One hundred years after the overthrow of the Kingdom of Hawai'i, on November 23, 1993, Congress adopted and President Clinton signed into law Public Law 103–150, or the "Apology Resolution." The Apology Resolution's purpose was "To acknowledge the 100th anniversary of the January 17, 1893 overthrow of the Kingdom of Hawaii, and to offer an apology to Native Hawaiians on behalf of the United States for the overthrow of the Kingdom of Hawaii."

PUBLIC LAW 103-150

S.J. RES. 19, 103D CONG., 1ST SESS., 107 STAT. 1510 (1993)

Whereas the health and well-being of the Native Hawaiian people is intrinsically tied to their deep feelings and attachment to the land;

Whereas the long-range economic and social changes in Hawaii over the nineteenth and early twentieth centuries have been devastating to the population and to the health and well-being of the Hawaiian people;

Whereas the Native Hawaiian people are determined to preserve, develop and transmit to future generations their ancestral territory, and their cultural identity in accordance with their own spiritual and traditional beliefs, customs, practices, language, and social institutions; . . .

Whereas it is proper and timely for the Congress on the occasion of the impending one hundredth anniversary of the event, to acknowledge the historic significance of the illegal overthrow of the Kingdom of Hawaii, to express its deep regret to the Native Hawaiian people, and to support the reconciliation efforts of the State of Hawaii and the United Church of Christ with Native Hawaiians;. . .

Section 1. Acknowledgment and Apology.

The Congress—

(1) on the occasion of the 100th anniversary of the illegal overthrow of the Kingdom of Hawaii on January 17, 1893, acknowledges the historical significance of this event which resulted in the suppression of the inherent sovereignty of the Native Hawaiian people;

(2) recognizes and commends efforts of reconciliation initiated by the State of Hawaii and the United Church of Christ with Native Hawaiians;

(3) apologizes to Native Hawaiians on behalf of the people of the United States for the overthrow of the Kingdom of Hawaii on January 17, 1893 with the participation of agents and citizens of the United States, and the deprivation of the rights of Native Hawaiians to self-determination;

(4) expresses its commitment to acknowledge the ramifications of the overthrow of the Kingdom of Hawaii, in order to provide a proper foundation for reconciliation between the United States and the Native Hawaiian people; and

(5) urges the President of the United States to also acknowledge the ramifications of the overthrow of the Kingdom of Hawaii and to support reconciliation efforts between the United States and the Native Hawaiian people.

d. SOUTH AFRICAN RECONCILIATION

Although they are the majority race in South Africa, Black South Africans experienced overt racial oppression by Whites for most of the latter part of the 20th century. In 1993, however, the tide of racial oppression turned when the African National Congress, after fierce international and domestic protests, negotiated a political settlement with the ruling White National Party to end apartheid. Following that settlement, South Africans participated in the country's first nonracial presidential election. Nelson Mandela, a Black South African politically imprisoned for twenty-seven years, was elected. His election marked the beginning of a social and economic transition period in South Africa. Key to that transition is a process of "reconciliation" as outlined by the African National Congress Statement to the Truth and Reconciliation Committee.

Consider the following account of the reconciliation process:

ERIC K. YAMAMOTO, *RACE APOLOGIES*

1 J. GENDER, RACE & JUSTICE 4, 49-52 (1997)

Following the fall of apartheid, Nelson Mandela joined hands with F.W. de Klerk and declared, "Let's forget the past! What's done is done!" Mandela, head of South Africa's new government and former prisoner of de Klerk's white National Party regime, sent a clear message: Reconciliation between whites and blacks is a fundamental first step toward healing historic wounds and rebuilding the nation. Since this optimistic proclamation, the process of interracial healing has lurched forward.

Among his first presidential acts, Mandela signed the Promotion of National Unity and Reconciliation Bill and established the Truth and Reconciliation Commission. Headed by Nobel Peace Laureate Archbishop Desmond Tutu, the seventeen-member Commission includes psychologists, lawyers and scholars selected by experts and appointed by Mandela. Its staff numbers 150 and its two-year budget is $40 million. The Commission is composed of three committees with distinct but related functions: the first function is to investigate gross violations of human rights; the second, to consider amnesty for those who confess to political crimes; and the third, to recommend nonmonetary reparations for victims.

According to Justice Minister Dullah Omar, an author of the Reconciliation Bill, the Commission's larger task is to initiate a healing process that fosters genuine reconciliation between the races. "There is a need for understanding, but not for vengeance, a need for reparation, but not for retaliation." Commission proponents believe that healing is achievable and that South African society can move beyond apartheid if those who inflicted racial wounds acknowledge the suffering they wrought and accept appropriate responsibility. The Commission's work is deemed to be especially important by many in light of the perceived failure of the current South African courts and criminal laws to bring apartheid abusers to justice—as evidenced by the recent acquittal of former apartheid Defense Minister Magnus Malan and others on charges of ordering a massacre in a black township.

A first step in the Commission's process is storytelling by those physically and emotionally scarred. For Archbishop Tutu, the catharsis of personal storytelling is as necessary to South Africa's healing as the broader legal and governmental changes: "The consequences of apartheid cannot be wiped away simply by democratic decisionmaking structures or even by large sums of money for housing, education, health, and job creation." Saths Cooper, director of the Family Institute in Johannesburg, agrees, maintaining that "a broad commission allowing the victims to articulate their suffering is essential for reconciliation. 'The degree of hurt, bitterness, and anger is still palpable. . . . No amount of legislation will remove that.'"

A second step in the Commission's process is acknowledgement of harm by wrongdoers. The Commission "hopes to encourage political criminals on all sides to confess in detail their acts." Criminal confessions are fostered by assurances of amnesty, offering "perpetrators of human-rights abuses a kind of giant national plea bargain." Their stories and apologies, Commission proponents hope, will lead to a sense of closure for those who suffered. Commission supporters believe that perpetrator storytelling and amnesty will also prevent protracted litigation and adversarialness in reconstructing the nation.

In light of storytelling by both perpetrators and those suffering, Archbishop Tutu echoes Justice Minister Omar's view of the Commission and emphasizes that the Commission's goal is reconciliation, not retribution. Telling stories is a beginning step toward forgiveness, and therefore, nation-building: "It's realpolitick, this forgiveness thing. It's not just something in the realm of religion or the spiritual. If [retributive] justice is your last word, you've had it. You've got to go beyond it." According to Tutu, retributive justice is "largely Western. . . . The justice we hope for is restorative of the dignity of the people." This kind of restorative justice is reflective of the African notion of "ubuntu," or interconnectedness. Ubuntu is the idea that no one can be healthy when the community is sick. "Ubuntu says I am human only because you are human. If I undermine your humanity, I dehumanise myself." It characterizes justice as community restoration—the rebuilding of the community to include those harmed or formerly excluded.

EMILY H. McCARTHY, *WILL THE AMNESTY PROCESS FOSTER RECONCILIATION AMONG SOUTH AFRICANS?*

WHEN SORRY ISN'T ENOUGH 487 (Roy L. Brooks, ed. 1999)

South Africans across the political and racial spectrum have been voicing doubt about the Commission's ability to foster reconciliation and national unity. At the same time that members of the Black community are finding their sense of justice sorely tested by the seemingly indiscriminate grants of amnesty to White applicants, much of the White and conservative populations in South Africa are accusing the Commission of "bias" against Whites. While the Commission is doing a formidable job of uncovering the truth about the apartheid-era crimes, it is having far less success in promoting reconciliation. Although there is logic in the argument that the ANC [African National Congress] government "must temper its reaction to the past, given how it came to power and the continuing importance of the white population to the economy and in the security forces," the Truth Commission must pay heed to the complaints about promoting reconciliation in the vast majority of South Africans. For the amnesty process to succeed, the Commission must focus more of its attention on fostering reconciliation and less of its attention on exposing the painful "truth" at the expense of justice.

e. KOREAN SEX SLAVES

"I can no longer tolerate the lies of the Japanese government."[*]
—Kim Hak-Sun

During World War II, Japan established a coercive system of military brothels called "comfort stations." The Japanese Imperial Military authorized the abduction of women and girls into sexual servitude for the Japanese Imperial Army throughout Asia. Of the estimated 100,000 to 200,000 "jugun ianbu,"[†] or military comfort women (ianfu), 80 percent were from Korea. The others were from China, Taiwan, the Philippines, Malaysia and the Netherlands. Conditions were horrific. Women and children were forced to

---

[*] Jugun Ianfu Mondai Uri-Yosong Network (1992), ed., Kono han o toku (To liberate this bitterness) (Tokyo, Jugun Ianfu Mondai Uriyosong Nettowaku, 1992).

[†] Translation: in Korean, "jugun" means deceased and "ianbu" means comfort woman or women. "Ianfu" is the Japanese version of "ianbu."

have sex with as many as 20 soldiers a day. Defiant women were brutally beaten. Some were killed. Strict surveillance made escape impossible.

While enslaved, the ianfu were further subjected to a racial hierarchy. For instance, Japanese women (few in number) were superior—reserved for the highest ranking Japanese soldiers. Korean women were inferior—available for the ordinary soldiers.

The hierarchy was no accident. The Japanese people generally, and government and military officials specifically, denigrated Koreans as an inferior race of people. The annexation of Korea compounded with the general attitude of Korean inferiority made them easy targets for exploitation.

As the war progressed, women and girls were "recruited" from all of Japan's colonies and its captured territories—China, Taiwan, the Philippines and Indo-China. These women, too, were treated both as sex slaves and as racial inferiors.

For nearly half a century, the Japanese government not only denied its central role in the sex slaves system, it denied the very existence of sex slaves. These denials rendered the ianfu invisible, and it shrouded their suffering in silence. Fueled in part by the Japanese American redress, the "comfort women" redress movement emerged in the early 1990s. Angered by the Japanese government's denial of its role in the ianfu system, Kim Hak-Sun, a former comfort woman from Korea, first broke the silence. In December 1991, Kim and two other former Korean comfort women filed suit for damages in the Tokyo District Court. They sought compensation, reparations, official apologies and a revision of Japanese historical records. The lawsuit demanded that Japan confront its post-war responsibility for the ianfu system and the suffering it caused. The governments of North and South Korea, Taiwan, China and the Philippines joined in, later demanding reparations on behalf of their citizens. Kim's lawsuit galvanized the comfort women. For the first time, they testified publicly about their experiences.

Initially, the Japanese government continued to deny involvement in the ianfu system—maintaining that private operators recruited women and girls into frontline brothels. During litigation, however, official government documents surfaced that undermined the government's denial. In July of 1992, the Japanese government responded by formally acknowledging its official role in organizing the sex stations. However, it still denied that the women were forcibly recruited. It also declined to offer an official apology or to acknowledge the authenticity of the women's testimonies. Most important, the government remained silent on reparations.

After further litigation and mounting international protests, in 1993 the Japanese government finally confessed to forcibly recruiting comfort women. Even this acknowledgment was qualified, however, by limiting language ("in many cases" women were "recruited against their own will.") The government's continual attempts to escape full responsibility exacerbated a raw fifty-year wound. Despite its military's direct involvement in the operation of comfort stations, the government continued to deny requests for compensation and an official apology. In doing so, it rejected redress recommendations by the UN Human Rights Commission and other international organizations, arguing that government compensation had already been paid to war victims generally pursuant to post-war peace treaties.

Japan's response to the demands of the ianfu paralleled its response to the compensation demands of World War II slave laborers. During the war, Japan constructed dozens of slave labor camps. Individuals were first imprisoned and then exploited to provide needed labor for Japan's spiraling war efforts. Surviving slave laborers have now filed lawsuits to confront the Japanese government and the private companies that benefited from slave labor practices. As it did when confronted with claims of the ianfu, Japan has refused to pay compensation or give an official apology to World War II slave laborers.

In response to escalating international criticism, in 1995 the Japanese government helped create an Asian Women's Fund (AWF) financed solely by private donations. The AWF is premised on the idea that Japan is not the government alone but a nation of citizens that must collectively deal with Japan's past. Managed by the Japanese Red Cross Society, the AWF offered to pay 2 million yen ($18,957) to each former sex slave and provide a general letter of apology from the prime minister. The Japanese government did not contribute to the AWF's reparation fund.

Did the AWF provide appropriate reparation? From its inception, the AWF engendered fierce criticism. Many survivors declined to accept money from the fund. Japan, they said, created the private AWF to shirk, not accept, responsibility. Others perceived the fund payments as sympathy money—as charity and a one-time settlement in lieu of full monetary reparations. One group referred to the fund as "an insult to the war victims and a desecration." Without direct compensation from the Japanese government, questions linger: Who was the perpetrator? and who is now accepting responsibility?

The Japanese government's recalcitrance also raised this larger question: To what extent can the Japanese courts provide meaningful reparations for the ianfu? Judicial powers are limited.

> Even if the Japanese courts rule favorably for the former comfort women, a full resolution of the comfort women issue may require supplemental executive or legislative action. The plaintiffs in the recent litigation seek numerous remedies in addition to monetary compensation, including Japan's acknowledgment of its moral and legal culpability, a formal apology, full disclosure of all facts, and accurate revision of Japanese history textbooks to reflect Japan's conduct during World War II. But as in other civil law systems, Japanese courts do not enjoy the equitable powers of common law courts to fashion remedies. The Japanese courts thus may not be able to provide such non-monetary remedies. The other branches, however, do have the capacity to meet these demands.

Tong Yu, *Reparations for Former Comfort Women of World War II*, 36 HARV. INT'L L.J. 528, 537 (1995).

Japan, however, fares poorly in terms of legislative redress for historical injustice. Other countries, like Germany, have assumed responsibility for war crimes by issuing apologies and granting reparations. Germany has paid victims more than $50 billion in post-war reparations. The U.S. government has also paid over $4 billion in reparations to its own citizens, Japanese

Americans, for their unlawful wartime internment. By contrast, Japan has paid less than $1.5 billion in reparations to all war victims.

The ianfu's healing will come, if at all, in many stages. A first stage will likely involve the government's forthright recognition of the wounds it inflicted and a genuine expression of contrition. Recently, the Japanese officials issued several modest blanket apologies to war victims. The apologies were modest because the high officials apologized as individuals, not on behalf of the government. The apologies were "blanket apologies" because they did not specifically address the circumstances and suffering of the ianfu; they instead covered all war atrocities.

In many respects, Japan's minimalist path toward reparations appears to have salted rather than healed the wounds of the ianfu and their survivors. The Japanese government has conferred no direct reparations, has not fully acknowledged its role and has not undertaken educational programs. Instead, it has attempted to dilute its responsibility by creating the nongovernmental AWF and encouraging "private" reparations. The Fund's dearth of private donations has rendered it practically meaningless to most—a truth readily apparent to the ianfu.

Resistance by the Japanese government and difficulties in the Japanese courts—and the absence of ianfu healing—have compelled comfort women survivors to look elsewhere for justice. The survivors have filed suits in other countries, including the United States. Most recently, fifteen ianfu sued in a U.S. court on behalf of all comfort women and their heirs for "multiple rapes by soldiers, confinement in squalid conditions, physical abuse, and death threats." They filed suit under the Federal Alien Tort Claims Act. (That Act enables individuals to sue in U.S. courts on the basis of certain human rights violations. It was under this act that survivors of torture and inhumane treatment successfully sued the late Philippine President Ferdinand Marcos.) As long as Japan refuses to apologize and confer meaningful reparations, more "foreign" lawsuits are likely.

Slave labor lawsuits filed in California by Korean, Chinese, Filipino and other Asian victims illustrate the continuing sense of injustice for those conscripted. In September 2000, thirty individual plaintiffs filed lawsuits in the United States against major Japanese corporations. The plaintiffs, including former American and allied prisoners of war, had been forced to work for Japanese industries. A 1999 California law authorized war survivors to sue. However, the California court dismissed the suits, reasoning that the Treaty of Peace with Japan prohibited reparation claims by former soldiers. *In re World War II Era Japanese Forced Labor Litigation*, 114 F. Supp. 2d 939 (N.D. Cal. 2000) ("And while full compensation for plaintiffs' hardships, in the purely economic sense, has been denied these former prisoners and countless other survivors of the war, the immeasurable bounty of life for themselves and their posterity in a free society and in a more peaceful world services the debt.")

NOTES AND QUESTIONS

1. Immigration status: Although Japanese Americans and Japanese Latin Americans shared the same national origin, reparations for the two groups were distinguished according to their immigration status. Professor Saito concludes that "[d]omestic law thus provides no effective avenues for redress" for the latter group. Are there other explanations aside from immigration status for the different treatment of the JLAs? On what alternative grounds might JLAs seek reparation? Should international law provide some sort of avenue for redress?

2. Legislative v. judicial action: Professor Westley suggests that legislatures may go where courts fear to tread. However, as Professor Chris Iijima points out, legislative attempts at reparation for African Americans thus far have fared no better than the court claims:

> The simple notion of a national apology for slavery has raised much controversy. On June 12, 1997, Congressman Tony Hall introduced a house resolution calling for an apology to those who suffered as slaves under the Constitution and laws of the United States. The response was quick, and overwhelmingly negative. A national poll found that 61% of the people polled disfavored a congressional apology for slavery, even as Blacks favored the apology by a two-to-one margin. Even Congressman Hall, the sponsor of the resolution, was "stunned" at the amount and level of criticism of his proposal. Perhaps what was most striking about the reaction to the apology proposal was the immediate dismissal by Congress and the President of any consideration of Black reparations.

Chris K. Iijima, *Reparations and the "Model Minority" Ideology of Acquiescence: The Necessity to Refuse the Return to Original Humiliation*, 19 B.C. THIRD WORLD L.J. 385, 389 (1999). Which route to reparations seems more likely to succeed, in your view?

What are some of the specific obstacles encountered by the African American redress movement? Does a narrow legal framing of reparations claims rooted in slavery and Jim Crow segregation contribute to current difficulties?

3. Compensation to repair: Professor Yamamoto suggests shifting from a compensation to a repair paradigm. What would be the likely effect on African American reparations of such a paradigm shift?

4. Native Hawaiian reparations: What are the likely effects of the Congressional Apology Resolution? For many Native Hawaiians, this apology is a start, but only a start. Land is central to the debate over sovereignty.

> More than anything, Hawaiian sovereignty leaders say, their movement is about land—or rather the effort to regain land that they believe was taken away when the monarchy was overthrown. The immediate issue is over rights to some portion of revenue or control of some 1.8 million acres of public lands—about half the total land on all the islands—ceded to the United States at the time of annexation, then returned to Hawaii when it became a state. . . . Considering that some of those lands have been leased for shopping malls, hotels and the Honolulu International Airport, [the Office of Hawaiian Affairs ("OHA"), a state agency created for the support of Native Hawaiians,] almost immediately became one of the most lucrative agencies in the state; it has been fighting with the state to gain full access to those

funds ever since. . . . But the bond between Native Hawaiians and the land goes much deeper than revenues. Many believe that ancient practices, such as gathering ti leaves, tending fish ponds and maintaining religious ceremonial sites, are part of the essence of their cultural heritage. And most sovereignty movement leaders agree that any form of self-government for Hawaiians must involve control over at least part of the public lands.

James Podgers, *Greetings from Independent Hawaii*, A.B.A. J. 83, 74, 78 (June 1997).

For a discussion of recent Native American reparations, *see* study module B.3. *supra* at 420.

5. Long term effects of the TRC process: How have South Africans responded to the work of the Truth and Reconciliation Commission (TRC)? Some have criticized the TRC because it provides amnesty for political oppressors who simply confess, however, others support the TRC's work because of its "realpolitick" approach to racial healing by a new democratic South African government.

> Perhaps the best response to this deeply felt opposition to an aspect of the TRC's work is, firstly, to . . . acknowledge openly that amnesty is unjust. This acknowledgement should also involve a recognition of the reality and legitimacy of the feelings of anger and frustration, the deep sense of injustice at stake.
>
> However, this is not the end of the story. It can then be made clear, in the second place, that this kind of criticism is misdirected: the Truth and Reconciliation Commission is not trying to achieve justice. Guaranteeing amnesty is the price we, unfortunately, have to pay for peace, for the common good, for a negotiated settlement in 1994 which led to a democratic South Africa. . . .
>
> The important point is, however, that (criminal) justice is not the only social goal, nor always the ultimate value. And sometimes one will be faced with difficult choices between these values, sometimes one must make judgements about their relative importance. In the context of a fragile transition to a stable democracy, for example, political compromises, such as amnesty, might be justified for the sake of, say, the common good and peace.

Wilhelm Verwoerd, *Justice After Apartheid? Reflections on the South African TRC*, WHEN SORRY ISN'T ENOUGH 479 (WHEN SORRY ISN'T ENOUGH).

To respond to criticisms and meet human needs, in October 1997, the TRC formally announced its reparation and rehabilitation policies. Hlengiew Mkhize, the chairperson of the Reparation and Rehabilitation Committee of the TRC, explained the necessity of reparations:

> The conflicts of the past in our country produced many casualties, as a result of which there are a range of needs [such as health, mental health, psychosocial burdens for communities and society at large, and education and training needs].
>
> Reparation and rehabilitation measures are necessary to counter-balance the amnesty process; R&R measures and services will offer South African society as a whole a systematic way of re-visiting and dealing with the memories of the apartheid years, and of entrenching a human rights culture.

Remembering suffering is important to ensure that the mistakes of the past are not forgotten.... Our own political leaders have challenged future generations not to forget the pain and suffering of those who liberated South Africans.

There is also a legal basis for reparations: the Preamble to the Act which gives us our mandate says one of our objectives is to provide for the "taking of measures aimed at the granting of reparation to, and the rehabilitation and the restoration of the human and civil dignity of, victims of violations of human rights."

Hlengiwe Mkhize, *Introductory Notes to the Presentation of the Truth and Reconciliation Commission's Proposed Reparation and Rehabilitation Policies,* October 23, 1997, in WHEN SORRY ISN'T ENOUGH 501–02.

What will be the long-term effects of the TRC process? How can we assess the success or failure of South Africa's "reconciliation" efforts? Consider the following view:

An apology and some form of reparation are often necessary for reconciliation. Yet, they may not be enough to foster psychic healing.... The proposed payments alone are not compensation for suffering: "None of us labours under any delusions—you cannot put a monetary value to a person's suffering." Nevertheless, as the Reparations and Rehabilitation Committee recognized, "while such [reparations] measures can never bring back the dead, nor adequately compensate for pain and suffering, they can and must improve the quality of [victims'] lives." When victims and survivors see reconstruction of socioeconomic conditions and institutional structure—in addition to recognition and acceptance of responsibility—then those long disenfranchised in South Africa may sense a kind of justice that liberates, that contributes to intergroup healing....

What is clear ... is that the often wrenching reconciliatory process thus far has fostered healing for some but not others, that some groups have grasped the opportunity for beginning rapprochement and others have not. In terms of prospects for long-term transformation, amid the success and failures, collective reframing has yet to occur concerning "what happened," "who is responsible" and "how we are to get on with the new South Africa."... Whether new collective memories will lead to collective forgiveness and a release of the "baggage of past wrongs"—repair—is the question of South Africa's future.

Eric K. Yamamoto and Susan K. Serrano, *Healing Racial Wounds? The Final Report of South Africa's Truth and Reconciliation Commission,* in WHEN SORRY ISN'T ENOUGH 498–99.

6. Apologies for other wartime activities: In March 2001, on the basis that no serious constitutional violation had occurred, the Hiroshima High Court overturned a 1998 district court ruling that ordered the government to pay a total of $7,260 to three Korean comfort women. Time for the ianfu is running out. During her fight for reparations, Kim Hak-Sun died. What will remain of Kim's story? To what extent will it serve as a lasting reminder of the need for reparatory justice to heal historical wounds?

C. ADDITIONAL READINGS

BOOKS

Boris J. Bittker, THE CASE FOR BLACK REPARATIONS. New York (1973).

Roy L. Brooks (ed.), WHEN SORRY ISN'T ENOUGH: THE CONTROVERSY OVER APOLOGIES AND REPARATIONS FOR HUMAN INJUSTICE. New York (1999).

Harlan Dalton, RACIAL HEALING: CONFRONTING THE FEARS BETWEEN BLACKS AND WHITES (1995).

Ustina Dolgopol & Snehal Paranjape, COMFORT WOMEN: AN UNFINISHED ORDEAL (1994).

George L. Hicks, THE COMFORT WOMEN: THE SEX SLAVES OF THE IMPERIAL JAPANESE FORCES (1994).

Peter Irons (ed.), JUSTICE DELAYED: THE RECORD OF THE JAPANESE AMERICAN INTERNMENT CASES. Middleton, Conn. (1989).

Mitchell T. Maki, Harry H.L. Kitano, and Megan S. Berthold, ACHIEVING THE IMPOSSIBLE DREAM: HOW JAPANESE AMERICANS OBTAINED REDRESS. Urbana (1999).

Martha Minow, BETWEEN VENGEANCE AND FORGIVENESS: FACING HISTORY AFTER GENOCIDE AND MASS VIOLENCE. Boston (1998).

Randall Robinson, THE DEBT: WHAT AMERICA OWNS TO BLACKS (2000)

United States Commission on Wartime Relocation and Internment of Civilians, PERSONAL JUSTICE DENIED: REPORT OF THE COMMISSION ON WARTIME RELOCATION AND INTERNMENT OF CIVILIANS (1997).

LAW REVIEW ARTICLES AND OTHER SOURCES

African National Congress Statement to the Truth and Reconciliation Committee (August 1996) (*reprinted in* WHEN SORRY ISN'T ENOUGH 451 (Roy L. Brooks, ed. 1999)).

American-Japanese Evacuation Claims Act, 50 U.S.C. APP. § 1981 et seq. 1982.

Apology Resolution, Pub. L. No. 103–150, 107 Stat. 1510 (1993).

Civil Liberties Act of 1988, Pub. L. No. 100–383, 102 Stat. 903.

Executive Order 9066 (1942).

Mark Hanasona, *Stranded in Japan and the Civil Liberties Act of 1988: Recognition for an Excluded Group of Japanese Americans*, 6 ASIAN L.J. 151 (May 1999).

Chris K. Iijima, *Reparations and the "Model Minority" Ideology of Acquiescence: The Necessity to Refuse the Return to Original Humiliation*, 19 B.C. THIRD WORLD L.J., 40 B.C. L. REV. 385 (1999).

The Seattle Times, *Court Denies Payment to Sex Slaves*, March 30, 2001.

Sharon La Franiere and George Larner, *U.S. Set to Photograph, Fingerprint All New Iraqi and Kuwaiti Visitors: Unusual Move Taken to Try to Counter Possible Terrorist Attacks*, THE WASHINGTON POST, January 11, 1991.

Susan Lope, *Indian Giver: The Illusion of Effective Legal Redress for Native American Land Claims*, 23 SW. U. L. REV. 331 (1994).

Rhonda V. Magee, *The Master's Tools, From the Bottom Up: Responses to African-American Theory in Mainstream and Outsider Remedies Discourse*, 79 VA. L. REV. 863 (1993).

Mari J. Matsuda, *Looking to the Bottom: Critical Legal Studies and Reparations*, 22 HARV. C.R.-C.L. L. REV. 323 (1987).

Natsu Taylor Saito, *Justice Held Hostage: U.S. Disregard for International Law in the World War II Internment of Japanese Peruvians—A Case Study*, 19 B.C. THIRD WORLD L.J., 40 B.C. L. REV. 275 (1999).

Vincene Verdun, *If the Shoe Fits, Wear It: An Analysis of Reparations to African Americans*, 67 TUL. L. REV. 597 (1993).

John F. Walsh, *Settling the Alaska Native Claims Settlement Act*, 38 STAN. L. REV. 227 (1985).

Robert Westley, *Many Billions Gone: Is It Time to Reconsider the Case for Black Reparations?*, 19 B.C. THIRD WORLD L.J., 40 B.C. L. REV. 429 (1999).

Eric K. Yamamoto, *Racial Reparations: Japanese American Redress and African American Claims*, 19 B.C. THIRD WORLD L.J., 40 B.C. L. REV. 477 (1999).

Eric K. Yamamoto, *Race Apologies*, 1 J. GENDER, RACE AND JUST. 47 (1997).

Eric K. Yamamoto, *Friend, Foe Or Something Else: Social Meanings of Redress and Reparations*, 20 DENV. J. INT'L L. & POL'Y 223 (1992).

Tong Yu, *Reparations for Former Comfort Women of World War II*, 36 HARV. INTL'L L.J. 528, 537 (1995).

Chapter 7 RACE, RIGHTS AND LIBERTY: CONTEMPORARY ISSUES

Τ his final chapter and its accompanying study modules focus on contemporary legal issues illuminated by the Japanese American internment and redress experience. Section A addresses *Korematsu* as precedent: whether *Korematsu* is still a "loaded weapon" with significant effects on current equal protection and national security law. The accompanying study modules in section B consist of four distinct case studies. The first provides a glimpse of the connections between the internment and 1950s McCarthyism (the prosecution and persecution of Americans on often tenuous or completely false charges of communist affiliations or of being sympathizers). The second case study, the 1990s Haitian Immigrant Interdiction, extends the analysis of national security and civil liberties tensions into the contemporary international realm. The third addresses the treatment of Arab Americans during the Gulf War in 1991. The final module covers the Wen Ho Lee prosecution, or persecution from some perspectives, based on unsubstantiated charges of nuclear science spying for China. These study modules raise afresh many of the issues addressed throughout this book.

In working through the sections below, keep in mind the following questions:

• If the U.S. Supreme Court were faced today with a challenge to the internment of a group of American civilians, or immigrants, how would it decide?

• If the executive branch were faced today with the same kinds of tensions between national security concerns and the protection of civil liberties, what choices would it make?

• If faced today with requests for reparations from other groups suffering from government acts of historical injustice, how would Congress act?

• And how would diverse American peoples respond in these situations?

A. *KOREMATSU* AS PRECEDENT: AN OVERVIEW

1. "LIMITED APPLICATION" OR "LOADED WEAPON"?

In *Korematsu II*, *Hirabayashi II* and *Yasui II*, the petitioners filed in the federal district courts in their respective states to reopen their cases, even though their convictions had been affirmed by the Supreme Court forty years earlier.

The filing of a *coram nobis* petition in district court raises an interesting legal process question: If the district court grants the petition, setting aside the petitioner's conviction, what is the effect of that decision on the precedential value of the earlier Supreme Court ruling in the very same case? For example, what is the effect of the district court's 1984 decision to vacate Korematsu's conviction on the Supreme Court's 1944 *Korematsu* holding? A district court cannot overrule the Supreme Court. Moreover, a *coram nobis* proceeding is not an "appeal," so the district court lacks the authority to "reverse." Yet the factual foundations upon which the Supreme Court precedent is based are swept away by the district court's later ruling. Review the conclusion of Judge Patel's *Korematsu coram nobis* opinion:

> *Korematsu* remains on the pages of our legal and political history. As a legal precedent it is now recognized as having very limited application. As historical precedent it stands as a constant caution that in times of war or declared military necessity our institutions must be vigilant in protecting constitutional guarantees. It stands as a caution that in times of distress the shield of military necessity and national security must not be used to protect governmental actions from close scrutiny and accountability. It stands as a caution that in times of international hostility and antagonisms our institutions, legislative, executive and judicial, must be prepared to exercise their authority to protect all citizens from the petty fears and prejudices that are so easily aroused.

Korematsu, 584 F. Supp. at 1420, *supra* Chapter 5.

What is the contemporary significance of Judge Patel's comment? Is Judge Patel correct in concluding that the 1944 *Korematsu* decision now carries limited constitutional weight? Is *Korematsu* an "anachronism"? Or is Justice Jackson's warning still apt: *Korematsu* "lies about like a loaded weapon"? Or, given the many subsequent cases citing *Korematsu* as the progenitor of the strict scrutiny standard of review, does *Korematsu* stand for something else?

How do you assess whether the *Korematsu* decision may still carry substantial weight, notwithstanding subsequent *coram nobis* decisions? Consider Federal Judge Harry Edwards' view of the continuing relevance of *Korematsu*.

> Other costs of the *Korematsu* decision, though less grievous in human terms, demand consideration. Difficult to quantify, but nonetheless compelling, is the price paid in terms of judicial stature. From the day it was announced over the dissents of three Justices, at least two of which were unusually vehement, *Korematsu* was roundly condemned by legal scholars and observers as a tragic miscarriage of justice. Though lower federal courts have since vacated the convictions of individual Japanese Americans who violated curfew and internment orders during World War II, the Supreme Court has yet to overrule or repudiate *Korematsu*. The case stays with us, "an evil blotch upon our national legal conscience and our law," and each subsequent generation's perceptions of the judicial system, its competence and its integrity, are undoubtedly shaped accordingly.

Harry T. Edwards, *The Judicial Function and the Elusive Goal of Principled Decisionmaking*, 1991 WISC. L. REV. 837, 843.

Do you agree with Judge Edwards' observation that *Korematsu* and other legal precedents shape each generation's view of the justice system? If you were a judge, how would you respond to parties' citations to *Korematsu* as still "good law"?

Professor Alfred C. Yen perceives that "[e]ven if those who openly support the internment remain few in number, those who 'praise it with faint damnation' are likely to increase, thereby making it respectable to overlook or even deny the racism that made internment possible." Professor Yen continues:

> A prime example of the way in which *Korematsu* may be "praised with faint damnation" is a recent essay by no less than the Chief Justice of the United States Supreme Court, William H. Rehnquist. In *When the Laws Were Silent*,* the Chief Justice considers the internment and the criticisms advanced against the Supreme Court. Rehnquist never endorses the internment, nor does he claim that the *Korematsu* decision was unproblematic. At the same time, however, the Chief Justice is curiously muted in his criticism of the internment and those responsible for it. . . .

> The Chief Justice defends the military for exaggerating the alleged threat posed by Japanese Americans:

>> In defense of the military it should be pointed out that these officials were not entrusted with the protection of anyone's civil liberty; their job was making sure that vital areas were as secure as possible from espionage or sabotage. The role of General DeWitt was not one to encourage nice calculation of the costs in civil liberty as opposed to the benefits of national security.

> The Chief Justice is similarly kind to Henry Stimson and John McCloy, the civilians charged with military oversight as Secretary and Assistant Secretary of War respectively. His assertion that these men felt no need to defend civil liberties, which seems odd given the fact that Stimson and McCloy took oaths "to support and defend the Constitution of the United States."

> The Chief Justice then completely omits the Justice Department's complicated role in the internment, especially the behavior of the Solicitor General's office. This lapse is particularly unfortunate given the Chief Justice's defense of the military. Even if the entire Department of War felt no obligation to guard the constitutional rights of Japanese Americans, this claim cannot, by mere extension, apply to the Justice Department, whose function was the enforcement of the constitutional rights violated by internment.

> Furthermore, to the extent that the case for internment stood on misrepresentations about the threat posed by Japanese Americans, Justice Department lawyers—including the Solicitor General's office—owed an ethical obligation to correct those falsehoods before the Supreme Court. . . . It is therefore not possible to defend the Justice Department by simply asserting that the Department (like the military) was simply "doing its job." The Chief Justice's failure to discuss the Justice Department is significant because it creates the impression that nobody in the executive branch of government had responsibility for protecting the constitutional rights of Japanese Americans. By extension, it insinuates that the executive branch of our government, from the military to the Solicitor General, behaved correctly by carrying out and defending the internment of Japanese Americans.

> The Chief Justice's analysis leaves the Supreme Court as the only organ of government that might be charged with responsibility for stopping the injustice of internment. Here too, Rehnquist takes great pains to avoid criticism. . . .

---

* William H. Rehnquist, *When the Laws Were Silent*, AMERICAN HERITAGE 77-89 (Oct. 1998).

Rehnquist concludes his essay by calling *Korematsu* "the least justified" —as opposed to unjustified—curtailment of civil liberty during wartime. His words show why it is important for scholars to study carefully *Korematsu* and its legal legacy.... [T]he passage of time and healing of wounds make it easy to forget the injustice of internment. If "it wasn't that bad," the climate becomes ripe for rewriting the history that so rightly condemns internment. Perhaps Chief Justice did not intend to rehabilitate *Korematsu*. Nevertheless, his reluctance to clearly criticize the internment and those responsible for it makes that rehabilitation more likely.

Alfred C. Yen, *Introduction: The Importance of Korematsu Studies*, 19 B.C. THIRD WORLD L.J. 1, 40 B.C. L. REV. 1–5, 7 (1999).

In the same symposium issue, Professor Sumi Cho observes in former Chief Justice Earl Warren a similar "reluctance to clearly criticize the internment and those responsible for it," despite sincere misgivings about his pivotal role in initiating it.

[I]n a 1962 law review article... [Warren] defend[ed] the Court's decisions in *Hirabayashi* and *Korematsu* [in the following fashion]:

Where the circumstances are such that the Court must accept uncritically the Government's description of the magnitude of the military need, actions may be permitted that restrict individual liberty in a grievous manner. Consequently, if judicial review is to constitute a meaningful restraint upon unwarranted encroachments upon freedom in the name of military necessity, situations in which the judiciary refrains from examining the merit of the claim of necessity must be kept to an absolute minimum.

Twenty years after the internment order and nine years after *Brown*, the Chief Justice suggests that the same result would ensue if he were presiding over the case in 1962. Warren's invocation of "freedom" and "military necessity" rationalizes the Court's *de minimis* review of the military's case for internment, while obscuring the documented racial hysteria and stereotypes that pervaded the military's flawed assessment of "necessity.".... Under such an "absolute minimum" standard of review, Warren uncritically reproduces the legal structure of internment's injustice and prefigures its future recurrence.

Sumi K. Cho, *Redeeming Whiteness in the Shadow of Internment: Earl Warren, Brown, and a Theory of Racial Redemption*, 19 B.C. THIRD WORLD L.J. 73, 40 B.C. L. REV. 131 (1999).

Professor Cho contextualizes Warren's essay by examining Warren's often overlooked involvement in the internment itself. She emphasizes that her research seeks not to disparage the legacy of Earl Warren and his contributions to civil rights jurisprudence, but to question why his internment activity is so rarely discussed and what that means about our understanding of internment.

Earl Warren is a civil rights/civil liberties icon. During his reign as Chief Justice of the U.S. Supreme Court from 1953–69, the Court set standards of liberal judicial activism on race issues by which future Courts would be judged. Chief Justice Warren presided over momentous decisions that outlawed segregation in public education and public facilities, invalidated Jim

Crow laws designed to prevent African Americans from exercising the vote, and found anti-miscegenation laws to be unconstitutional. . . .

Despite this iconography, there is another less-detailed aspect of Warren's career that looms. . . . This aspect predates his work on the Supreme Court, going back to the days of World War II when Warren was Attorney General of California and a gubernatorial candidate in the 1942 elections. During this time period, Warren counted himself among California's anti-Asian "native sons and daughters." In fact, Warren was a key actor in the anti-Asian movement that culminated in the 1942 internment of over 120,000 persons of Japanese ancestry, two-thirds of which were U.S. citizens. . . .

Id. at 73–75.

How might Warren's active participation in internment politics have influenced his subsequent civil rights jurisprudence? Some scholars such as Morton Horwitz believe that Warren, through his later decisions, was attempting to redeem himself. Others, such as Professor Cho, offer a more complex explanation of Warren's civil rights decisions, viewing them as part of "racial redemption"—the "transformation [but not elimination] of contemporary white supremacy."

2. NATIONAL SECURITY AND CIVIL LIBERTIES?

Consider the following view of the vitality of *Korematsu* as precedent on the judicial standard of review of national security restrictions of the civil liberties of civilians:

[The Supreme Court] has not overruled or formally discredited the *Korematsu* decision or its principle of judicial deference to government claims of military necessity. Nor has the Court announced in principle that the demanding standards of review now normally applicable to government restrictions of constitutionally protected liberties are unaltered by the government's claim of military necessity or national security. At best, the decisions on these issues reflect an acceptance of the Court's role as guardian of constitutional liberties during times of war and upheaval, with notable exceptions. At worst, they reflect ambiguity and vacillation. Indeed, reminiscent of *Korematsu*, the Supreme Court's recent opinions in *Rostker v. Goldberg, Haig v. Agee, Regan v. Wald,* and *United States v. Albertini* have fueled perception of a trend towards diminished government accountability for national defense and national security restrictions of civil liberties.

Eric K. Yamamoto, *Korematsu Revisited—Correcting the Injustice of Extraordinary Government Excess and Lax Judicial Review: Time for a Better Accommodation of National Security Concerns and Civil Liberties,* 26 SANTA CLARA L. REV. 1, 31-33 (1986).

And think about the following observation of the importance of Justice Jackson's "loaded weapon" warning in the context of recent international events:

[I]t bears repeating that the "loaded weapon" of the internment as precedent for racial repression in the name of national interest is still available. Two recent examples suggest that the authorities that Justice Jackson feared, those who would avail themselves of the loaded weapon, are not just a thing of the past. In the late 1980s it was reported that the Reagan administration had begun to plan for suspension of the Constitution and martial detention of dissidents, targeting in particular Central American refugees. Then, in 1991 during the Gulf War the FBI engaged in sweeping investigations of Arab Americans that were likened to the initial steps taken prior to the internment.

Gil Gott, *A Tale of New Precedents: Japanese American Internment as Foreign Affairs Law*, 19 B.C. THIRD WORLD L.J., 40 B.C. L. REV. 179, 260 (1999). See also study module B.2.b in Chapter 5, *supra*.

What about other situations in which the civil liberties of American civilians apparently have been restricted in the ostensible interest of national security or military necessity? You may want to research the government's treatment of Arab Americans during the Iranian hostage crisis in the 1980s and immediately following the bombing of the Oklahoma City federal building in 1995. As you do that research, ask how the original *Korematsu* decision, in light of the *coram nobis* ruling, might influence a district court's ruling on the propriety of similar government treatment of American citizens today?

3. EQUAL PROTECTION?

In *Adarand Constructors v. Pena*, 515 U.S. 200 (1995), the Supreme Court presented its lengthiest explication of strict scrutiny mechanics since *Korematsu*. The Court held that the strict scrutiny standard of review is also to be applied to evaluate federal affirmative action programs—that is, racial classifications *beneficial* to minorities.

In the majority opinion, which under the fifth amendment invalidated race-based set-asides for federal contractors, Justice Sandra Day O'Connor discussed the internment cases in detail. Her treatment warrants full quotation here.

> Through the 1940s, this Court had routinely taken the view in non-race-related cases that, "unlike the Fourteenth Amendment, the Fifth contains no equal protection clause and it provides no guaranty against discriminatory legislation by Congress." When the Court first faced a Fifth Amendment equal protection challenge to a federal racial classification, it adopted a similar approach, with most unfortunate results. In *Hirabayashi*, the Court considered a curfew applicable only to persons of Japanese ancestry. The Court observed—correctly—that "distinctions between citizens solely because of their ancestry are by their very nature odious to a free people whose institutions are founded upon the doctrine of equality," and that "racial discriminations are in most circumstances irrelevant and therefore prohibited." But it also cited the proposition that the Fifth Amendment "restrains only such discriminatory legislation by Congress as amounts to a denial of due process," and upheld the curfew because "circumstances within the knowledge of those charged with the responsibility for maintaining the national defense afforded a rational basis for the decision which they made."

> Eighteen months later, the Court again approved wartime measures directed at persons of Japanese ancestry. *Korematsu* concerned an order that completely excluded such persons from particular areas. The Court did not address the view, expressed in cases like *Hirabayashi*, that the Federal Government's obligation to provide equal protection differs significantly

from that of the States. Instead, it began by noting that ["the most rigid scrutiny" was appropriate]. But in spite of the "most rigid scrutiny" standard it had just set forth, the Court then inexplicably relied on "the principles we announced in the *Hirabayashi* case," to conclude that, although "exclusion from the area in which one's home is located is a far greater deprivation than constant confinement to the home from 8 p.m. to 6 a.m.," the racially discriminatory order was nonetheless within the Federal Government's power.

In [the 1954 decision] *Bolling v. Sharpe*, the Court for the first time explicitly questioned the existence of any difference between the obligations of the Federal Government and the States to avoid racial classifications. . . .

Bolling's facts concerned school desegregation, but its reasoning was not so limited. The Court's observations that "distinctions between citizens solely because of their ancestry are by their very nature odious," *Hirabayashi*, and that "all legal restrictions which curtail the civil rights of a single racial group are immediately suspect," *Korematsu*, carry no less force in the context of federal action than in the context of action by the States—indeed, they first appeared in cases concerning action by the Federal Government.

We think that requiring strict scrutiny is the best way to ensure that courts will consistently give racial classifications that kind of detailed examination, both as to ends and as to means. *Korematsu* demonstrates vividly that even "the most rigid scrutiny" can sometimes fail to detect an illegitimate racial classification. [Citing congressional finding that "These actions . . . were carried out without adequate security reasons . . . and were motivated largely by racial prejudice, wartime hysteria, and a failure of political leadership."] Any retreat from the most searching judicial inquiry can only increase the risk of another such error occurring in the future.

Adarand Constructors v. Pena, 515 U.S. 200, 213-16, 236 (1995).

Scholars sharply criticized Justice O'Connor's construction of the internment cases in *Adarand*. They asserted that the internment cases were understood then as justified by the wartime context and cannot be readily extended to other situations.

Is the *Adarand* Court's interpretation of the internment cases persuasive? Is your response informed at all by the *Adarand* majority's disavowal of a distinction deemed significant to several justices in prior cases—that "invidious" racial classifications (*e.g.*, school segregation, which is harmful to racial minorities) and "benign" classifications (*e.g.*, affirmative action, which is beneficial to racial minorities) should be treated differently by the courts?

In answering these questions, think about the following critique of *Adarand's* use of *Korematsu* by Professor Frank Wu and Reginald Oh.

Reggie Oh & Frank Wu, *Essay, The Evolution of Race in the Law: The Supreme Court Moves from Approving Internment of Japanese Americans to Disapproving Affirmative Action for Asian Americans*

1 Mich. J. Race & L. 165, 176-78 (1996)

Korematsu echoes throughout *Adarand* in the formalist "fit" analysis of racial classifications. Justice O'Connor asserted that equal protection standards have always embraced three principles: (1) "skepticism" toward "any preference" based on racial classifications, (2) "consistency," meaning that the same skepticism applied regardless of the context of the classification, and (3) "congruence" in equal protection analysis under the Fifth and Fourteenth Amendments. Justice O'Connor applied these principles in deriving three results that bear on earlier cases: (1) "despite the surface appeal of holding 'benign' racial classifications to a lower standard [than 'strict scrutiny'] . . . 'it may not always be clear that a so-called preference is . . . benign"; (2) "all racial classifications . . . must be strictly scrutinized"; and (3) the pronouncement that "we wish to dispel the notion that strict scrutiny" automatically leads to invalidation of the official use of racial classifications.

With each of these statements, *Adarand* altered [*Regents of University of California v.*] *Bakke*[, 438 U.S. 265 (1978)], *Croson*[, 488 U.S. 469 (1989)] and *Metro Broadcasting*[, 497 U.S. 547 (1990)]. By equating benign racial classifications with invidious ones, *Adarand* effectively overrules *Bakke*—i.e., the Powell opinion as well as any part of the other opinions more favorable to affirmative action. In stating that "strict scrutiny" applies to all racial classifications, *Adarand* extended *Croson* from the state and local level to the federal level, achieving a consistency with respect to racial classifications, but not necessarily with conservative notions of federalism. By explaining that some statutes could conceivably pass "strict scrutiny," *Adarand* renders the *Metro Broadcasting* analysis superfluous because government entities no longer need to support affirmative action by making the distinction that it is helpful rather than harmful; rather they need to support it by empirical data. Under *Adarand*, however, the government can continue to consider race. The judicial branch also participates in the process as it evaluates whether an affirmative action plan is supported by sufficient evidence of discrimination and need.

In reaching its holding, the *Adarand* majority relied heavily on the *Korematsu* case. The Court treated *Korematsu* as analytic support for its holding as well as a rhetorical example of the dangers of relying on race to prove other characteristics. In two relatively lengthy passages, the Court discussed the *Korematsu* statements setting up the "strict scrutiny" test.

In the first section, the contemporary Court observed of its wartime counterpart that "in spite of the 'most rigid scrutiny' standard it had just set forth, the Court then inexplicably . . . conclude[d] that . . . the racially discriminatory [internment] order was nonetheless within the Federal Government's power." The Court reiterated that the internment was "motivated largely by racial prejudice, wartime hysteria, and a failure of political leadership." In *Adarand*, at last, the dissenting Justices in *Korematsu* were vindicated. The *Adarand* majority recognized that the *Korematsu* minority had challenged a law that "falls into the ugly abyss of racism."

In the second section, beyond disapproving the earlier decision, the *Adarand* Court continued with its powerful dicta on *Korematsu*. After all, *Korematsu* served a purpose, as a warning against judicial laxity in reviewing racial classifications. The Court states, "*Korematsu* demonstrates vividly that even 'the most rigid scrutiny' can sometimes fail to detect an illegitimate racial classification." And, "[a]ny retreat from the most searching judicial inquiry can only increase the risk of another such error occurring in the future."

What is remarkable is the type of judicial inquiry which is required after *Adarand*.

B. STUDY MODULES: IS IT HAPPENING AGAIN?

A common refrain is that "it" (the internment) could never happen again, or at least we need to ensure that "it" never happens again. But is "it" (recast as the racial restriction of civil liberties for ostensible national security reasons) already happening? The next study module, on the internment and McCarthyism, and the following three studies of contemporary legal-political problems speak to this question. To what extent do *Korematsu*, *Hirabayashi* and *Yasui* still resonate?

1. DOMESTIC POLITICS AND NATIONAL SECURITY: 1950S MCCARTHYISM

In the Forward to a recent symposium law review issue on the "Long Shadow of *Korematsu*," Professor Mari Matsuda compares the falsified justifications of the Japanese American internment with the national security rationale offered to buttress the interrogations of the 1950s House Committee on Un-American Activities. She describes similar rhetorical maneuvers—turning a group into a "monolithic, fearsome, inhuman enemy"—in both the McCarthy investigation and the internment.

MARI J. MATSUDA, *MCCARTHYISM, THE INTERNMENT, AND THE CONTRADICTIONS OF POWER*

19 B.C. THIRD WORLD L.J., 40 B.C. L. REV. 9, 17-21, 15-16 (1999)

[T]he internment was justified by widely believed lies. First was the lie of inherent racial being, part of the lie of race. The Japanese Americans were a distinct species, marked by the inability to Americanize. Second was the lie of military necessity. The Japanese Americans were part of a secret fifth column situated to destroy America from within, such that there was neither time nor ability to discern individual loyalty. . . . Third was the lie concealing true purpose. Military necessity masked the real impetus of lust for Japanese American land holdings and fear of Japanese American competition in the highly profitable West Coast farming industry. . . .

Japanese Americans were rhetorically transformed into a monolithic, fearsome, inhuman enemy. Japanese-Americans were called "mad dogs," "yellow vermin," "treacherous," "war-like," "fifth column," and the ubiquitous "J__p." . . .

In testimony before the House Committee on Un-American Activities (HUAC), communists were referred to as "worldwide organization of gangsters," "disease spreading" and "a worldwide conspiratorial movement." [Historian Ellen] Schrecker cites references to Communists as "poisonous germs," "snakes," "tigers," "rats," "termites," and "slime." Professional red-baiters described a hidden, inhuman threat that would destroy America from within. . . .

In the case of both HUAC and the internment, class interests were at once obvious and denied. Evicting Japanese Americans from their communities, and denying the Japanese Americans equal participation in California's economy, advantaged white growers and land speculators. . . .

Similarly, the lasting legacy of McCarthyism was the purging of Communists, who were often tireless and effective organizers. . . . This gift to the capitalist class—the emaciation of the labor movement and the chilling of public criticism, accompanied by the legitimization of greed and of the income gap—was not a mere by-product of anti-communist witch hunting. It was the goal, albeit never the acknowledged one. . . . The threat of the outside invader was used to mask class interests in [both] the cases of McCarthyism and the internment. . . .

The lens of internment is exactly what we need to illuminate grand themes, connections, and deep understanding of American consciousness. . . . How do we understand the role of nativism and racism in distribution of land ownership if we fail to connect the internment to its precursor, the Alien Land Laws? . . . What does the treatment of interned Japanese-Peruvians tell us about the ability of international human rights law to constrain states as dominant as the United States? . . . How are we to understand the great Chief Justice Earl Warren's legacy if we don't push hard on the question of how his support for the internment was consistent with his world view? . . . And perhaps most importantly, where do we go from here—what does the internment and reparations for Japanese Americans suggest about the path to justice for all? . . .

To use the internment as a lens is to take the denial of human rights directed against Japanese Americans as a starting point for understanding the bigger picture of repression in America.

What is your assessment of Professor Matsuda's proposal that one see the internment not as an aberrational moment in U.S. history, but as a lens for viewing anew other instances and patterns of government oppression in the name of national security? To what extent is the Japanese American internment a civil liberties aberration? Professor Gil Gott's research reveals how "national security" has been employed throughout America's history to justify restrictions of individual and group liberties including freedoms of speech, assembly and association, and imprisonment without charges or trial. Gott explains this phenomenon in part by closely inspecting the elastic understanding of "national security" asserted by the government and used by the courts. In particular, he critiques national security as an artificial construct that is both politically malleable and exclusionary.

> Postwar erosions of personal liberties, undertaken in the name of state interest, are legion and well known. In a series of Supreme Court cases of the early Cold War era, communism . . . assumed constitutionally taboo-status as

the Court began authorizing a regime of guilt by association: free speech and association restrictions, ideological grounds for deportation, and loyalty oaths were approved by the Court. . . . [In *Dennis v. United States*, 339 U.S. 494, 422 (1951), Justice Jackson] suggested going so far as to sanction, *ipso facto*, restriction of any Communist speech, whether or not it met the established "clear and present danger" standard. Thus, even the most revered of individual rights, such as First Amendment freedoms, were truncated by the Court in light of national security demands. . . .

National security is . . . a metaphor that ascribes to "the nation" the ability to perceive of safety and well-being in the same way individual subjects presumably do in their "survival struggles." The metaphor collapses the multiplicity of society in to a monolithic sameness of nation. . . . National interest, and thus determinations of national security, assumed to be legitimate and rational, are valorized when set over against their Other. . . .

Gil Gott, *A Tale of New Precedents: Japanese American Internment as Foreign Affairs Law*, 19 B.C. THIRD WORLD L.J., 40 B.C. L. REV. 179, 211-12, 252 (1999).

2. IMMIGRATION AND NATIONAL SECURITY: 1990S HAITIAN INTERDICTION

With the *coram nobis* cases as a backdrop, many now are convinced that something like the internment could never happen again in this country. Are they correct? Examine the following excerpted article by human rights lawyer Cheryl Little about recent events affecting Haitian immigrants. Her account is interspersed with our comments and questions in italics.

CHERYL LITTLE, *INTERGROUP COALITIONS AND IMMIGRATION POLITICS: THE HAITIAN EXPERIENCE IN FLORIDA*

53 U. MIAMI L. REV. 717 (1999)

Refugees from Haiti have been singled out for special discriminatory treatment. Between June 1983 and March 1991, [the INS granted asylum to] only 1.8% of Haitian applicants [claiming persecution] in the U.S., the lowest approval rate among nationalities submitting the largest number of applications.

Haitians in the U.S.

In the early 1980s, a suit was filed on behalf of 4,000 Haitians requesting political asylum [as a result of the INS's denial of all 4,000 applications]. [In *Haitian Refugee Center v. Civiletti*, 503 F. Supp. 442 (S.D. Fla. 1980)] the court found that government agencies had set up a [process] designed to deny, as quickly as possible, the asylum claims of Haitians, a program which "in its planning and executing [was] offensive to every notion of constitutional due process and equal protection." Moreover, the court concluded that the INS was engaging in scare tactics, noting that the INS Deputy Commissioner encouraged government attorneys to point out "THE DIMENSIONS OF THE HAITIAN THREAT" and called the Haitian cases a threat to the community's social and economic well-being. . . . [On appeal in a similar case,] an Eleventh Circuit Court of Appeals panel found that the federal government had engaged in a "stark pattern" of discrimination against the Haitian asylum seekers.[*] The Court of Appeals *en banc* later vacated the decision on the grounds that Haitians had no constitutional rights [but did not disturb] the factual findings of the panel opinion. . . .[†]

The Haitian Program

Haitians outside the U.S. who wished to apply for refugee status or who tried to reach the U.S. to apply for asylum faced even greater obstacles. [In 1981, President Reagan found that aliens without visas in the United States was "a serious national problem detrimental to the interests of the United States." The government entered into an agreement with Haiti which allowed U.S. authorities to board a Haitian vessel and return it and its passengers if a violation of U.S. or Haitian law was suspected.] This interdiction program was established because undocumented Haitians had "threatened the welfare and safety of [our] communities," even though Haitians comprised less than two percent of the undocumented population of the U.S. at that time. Haiti was the only foreign government with which the U.S. had such an agreement, and it was entered into under U.S. threats to remove economic aid to Haiti. . . .

Haitian Refugee Center, Inc. v. Baker

Shortly after the 1991 coup d'etat in Haiti, amid widespread reports of brutal attacks on Aristide supporters [and rumors of rampant AIDS and disease among Haitian immigrants], attorneys at the Haitian Refugee Center (HRC) learned that the U.S. Coast Guard was about to forcibly return 538 Haitians. HRC filed a lawsuit, challenging the forced repatriation of Haitians without any meaningful consideration of their asylum claims.[‡]

Testimony revealed that the pre-screening interviews were a complete sham—a formal validation of a predetermined result. The interviews often lasted no more than five minutes, and the INS officers interviewing the Haitians had virtually no knowledge of Haitian politics or culture. . . . One politically active Haitian, who was interdicted and returned to Haiti in March 1989, told of Haitian soldiers [shooting] him four times in the legs at the time of his arrest in January 1988 and ten anguishing months in prison. Referring to his interview aboard the Coast Guard cutter, after he managed to flee Haiti, he stated: "I told them of my circumstances and specifically said that I preferred to kill myself instead of returning to Haiti. They returned me anyway."

Recall that no individual assessments were made of any potential threat to national security for Japanese Americans. Would such assessments merely have been perfunctory? If the government had made efforts to conduct individual screening of Japanese Americans, would the practical and legal result have been any different?

---

[*] *See Jean v. Nelson*, 711 F.2d 1455 (11th Cir. 1983).

[†] *See Jean v. Nelson*, 727 F.2d 957 (11th Cir. 1984).

[‡] *See Haitian Refugee Center, Inc. v. Baker*, 789 F. Supp. 1552 (S.D. Fla. 1991).

Although District Court Judge Clyde C. Atkins issued three separate restraining orders in favor of the Haitians, three times the Eleventh Circuit Court of Appeals stayed or vacated the judge's orders. The Appeals Court found that the Haitians had no legally enforceable rights in the United States because they were outside United States territory. The catch-22 nature of this finding was not lost on Judge Hatchett who remarked in a dissenting opinion: "Haitians, unlike other aliens from anywhere in the world, are *prevented* from freely reaching the continental United States." In a brief sentence order issued without comment on January 31, 1992, the Supreme Court voted to permit repatriations.

Judge Hatchett pointed out that "agencies of the United States captured the refugees and [held] them on United States vessels and leased territory." Was it appropriate to deny the interdicted Haitians asylum rights that they would have had but for the United States interdiction?

More important, should the judiciary defer to judgments by the political branches in dealing with immigrant "threats to national security" or the view of a judiciary providing "watchful care" over constitutional liberties, especially during apparent crises?

The [HRC] argued that legal issues took a back seat to political maneuvering. Indeed, the then Solicitor General Kenneth W. Starr argued before the District Court, although Solicitors General generally only argued in particularly important U.S. Supreme Court cases, signaling the effort U.S. officials would engage in to keep Haitians out of the United States. . . . [In addition,] in their brief to the Supreme Court, the [HRC] referred to the government's reliance on the declaration of Robert K. Wolthuis [concerning national security], whom the government presented as the Assistant Secretary of Defense. Mr. Wolthuis, according to the [HRC], had assumed that position for one day only—the day he signed the declaration. Mr. Wolthuis readily admitted that most of the facts he swore to in his declaration were what the lawyers who had drafted it told him. The declaration was so defective that the [HRC] filed a separate memorandum [challenging] it.

More specifically, the HRC argued that government lawyers manufactured affidavits, rushed courts to judgments, and deliberately misled the courts with false claims of national emergency and military necessity. On January 28, 1992, for example, the government filed an emergency petition for a stay of the ban on repatriations, alleging that 20,000 Haitians "were massed" on the Haitian beaches and waiting to head for Guantanamo, and that the naval base could not accommodate such numbers. The HRC argued that this was a "self created" crisis and that Guantanamo had a far greater capacity to hold people than the Administration claimed. They charged that Undersecretary Bernard Aronson admitted that the term "massing" was ambiguous and retracted his use of the word; contrary to the statements in his declaration to the Supreme Court, he admitted that he was quite unsure of the number of Haitians preparing to leave. . . .

Similarly, in denying the HRC access to Guantanamo and the Coast Guard cutters, the government claimed that it would seriously interfere with military operations. Judge Atkins noted, however, the portions of the military base to which the attorneys sought access were not used for military purposes. Furthermore, Coast Guard Admiral William P. Leahy acknowledged in his deposition that press members, VIPs, and many others had access to Guantanamo and admitted that family members of the Coast Guard periodically traveled on Coast Guard cutters.

Recall in the internment cases how high-level War Department officials altered key evidence and how Justice Department attorneys deliberately withheld exculpatory evidence on questions of disloyalty and military necessity. Review the study module B.1 of Chapter 5, and reflect on the ethical responsibilities of attorneys and other government officials. If the HRC's charges were accurate, did the government lawyers break any ethical rules in "constructing" Mr. Wolthuis' testimony? In proffering "facts" concerning military necessity? Or was this simply zealous lawyering in the broad interest of national security? What are the responsibilities of government attorneys in preventing unethical conduct by non-attorney officials?

The injunction granted by Judge Atkins was dissolved by the appellate court on grounds that the interdicted Haitians lacked any right to invoke judicial review of the government's actions. Should a court be skeptical or deferential when the government raises the specter of national security as justification for restricting the liberties of non-citizens seeking asylum? Should your answer depend on whether those non-citizens are on U.S. soil seeking asylum or are at sea? Can a court competently subject the government's proffered military necessity justification for interdiction and repatriation to the most rigid scrutiny?

The HRC also charged that summary dismissals on critical decisions were issued, affidavits not a part of the record were treated as if they were, and key parts of the record were ignored. [Appeals] Judge Hatchett [maintained] that the majority was deciding the case under "some procedures here before unknown to the law" and that "[t]he majority's actions, ruling, and holdings . . . are inconsistent with its actions, holdings and rulings of two days ago." Government officials claimed their effort to forcibly return the Haitians was inspired by the desire to save the lives of those who would otherwise be encouraged to take to the sea in unworthy vessels. But as Judge Hatchett pointed out: "The primary purpose of the [interdiction] program was, and has continued to be, to keep Haitians out of the United States."

What was the appeals court grappling with? How convincing was the government's claim? Should the government be given broad leeway in light of the political importance of military necessity? If so, how much? Was it appropriate in Korematsu? Is it appropriate here? How should the Court reconcile national security interests and civil liberties?

Response by Others and Ultimate Outcome

Amnesty International and the United Nations High Commissioner for Refugees condemned the repatriations, expressing fear that those returned would be exposed to real danger. To exacerbate matters, testimony revealed that the INS had lost at least 2500 files and even repatriated previously "screened-in" Haitians. . . . [On May 24, 1992,] President Bush issued [the "Kennebunkport Order"] stopping *all* Haitian interviews and permitting the INS to repatriate Haitians interdicted at sea without *any* investigation into the likelihood of their persecution in Haiti. The government's response to the widespread condemnation of the Order was to claim that Haitians could apply for asylum at the U.S. Embassy in Port-au-Prince and in January, 1992, announced the opening of an office to process refugee applications.

U.S. Treatment of Other Refugees

These government policies aptly call attention to the disparities in the treatment of Haitian [and other] refugees. Immigration policy toward Cubans tends to be generous and humanitarian while immigration policy towards Haitians tends to be stringent and inhumane. [For instance,] while Cubans were routinely paroled in the U.S. and freed from detention, Haitians were not. . . . [Furthermore,] it is estimated that 153,000 Nicaraguans and Cubans will get their green cards as a result of [the Nicaraguan Adjustment and Central American Relief Act].

What explains the government's differential treatment of Haitian and Cuban refugees? Lamar Smith, a Republican from Texas who chairs the House Immigration Subcommittee, argued that Nicaraguans and Cubans were granted amnesty because they were allies in the Cold War fight against communism. Is this convincing? Should it make a difference in the application of asylum laws?

To what extent might race have been a factor in the differential treatment? Recall that, unlike Japanese Americans, German Americans and Italian Americans were not subject to blanket removal from their homes and imprisonment in internment camps. How does one account for the government's difference in treatment?

[In the end,] the [government] did an excellent job of diverting attention away from the legal issues and convincing the courts and the public that denying the Haitians their legal rights was in the best interest of everyone. . . . The Reverend Jesse Jackson aptly described the plight of the Haitians when he claimed that they have been "trapped between the tyranny at home and the abandonment and rejection of the American people."

What light do the Korematsu, Hirabayashi *and* Yasui coram nobis *cases shed on the executive and judicial branches' handling of the Haitian controversy?*

3. WAR AND NATIONAL SECURITY: ARAB AMERICANS AND THE GULF WAR

How were Arab Americans, especially Arab immigrants, treated by the United States during the Persian Gulf War of 1991? The following newspaper account indicates that Arab Americans came under suspicion, apparently as a racial group, and were subjected to official investigations. Law enforcement agencies also used race-based profiles of "suspicious" travelers.

The Justice Department yesterday ordered immigration authorities to begin photographing and fingerprinting anyone entering the United States with an Iraqi or Kuwaiti passport as part of an effort to counter what the administration views as a mounting threat of terrorism.

The new procedures, effective immediately, come two days after the FBI began nationwide interviews of 200 Arab-American business and community leaders.

The agency said it wanted to collect information about possible terrorist threats and inform the Arab Americans that it wants to protect them from any backlash here.

At a meeting in Detroit, home to North America's largest Arab-American community, Arab Americans called the FBI initiative discriminatory and offensive.

Some civil rights attorneys were critical as well, saying it appears to violate constitutional and privacy act rights of Arab Americans.

"If we were on the verge of going to war with Nigeria, and the FBI started interviewing black Americans, I don't think anybody would stand for it," said David Cole, a constitutional law professor at the Georgetown University Law Center. "This kind of selection violates the principles of the [Constitution's] equal protection clause . . . that you be treated as an individual and not singled out by the government on account of your race or ethnic origin."

An administration official, who asked not to be identified, said the initiative was clearly within the FBI's legal authority. "Basic constitutional law is that a law-enforcement officer can direct an inquiry to any person and that person has the option of either speaking to them or not.

"It's only logical if you are asking about the activities within a particular ethnic group to ask people who are members of that ethnic group what they know about it," he said.

Officials declined to comment on what other measures might be taken to stem the possibility of terrorist attacks in the United States, but both FBI and INS spokesmen denied reports that members of suspected pro-Iraqi cells who have been under surveillance since August will be rounded up if war breaks out.

The Wall Street Journal reported earlier this week that such roundups, aimed at harassing and disrupting terrorist groups, would take place here and in countries around the world in the event of hostilities.

Civil rights attorneys said the FBI's interviewing of Arab Americans, because it is directed at U.S. citizens, is more open to legal challenge than the policy of fingerprinting visitors.

Still, Cole said, "I don't think that a court is going to enjoin the FBI from engaging in this kind of activity. The courts, particularly in times like this, bend over backwards to accommodate the federal government's national security claims."

Kate Martin, an attorney with the American Civil Liberties Union, said "the presumption" behind the FBI's activity is "outrageous" and "clearly unconstitutional."

"The presumption is that because you are of Arab descent, you might have some connection to terrorism," she said.

Civil rights attorneys said the FBI and the INS have harassed and closely watched Arab Americans in the name of national security since the 1979–80 hostage crisis in Iran.

Sharon La Franiere and George Larner, *U.S. Set to Photograph, Fingerprint All New Iraqi and Kuwaiti Visitors: Unusual Move Taken to Try to Counter Possible Terrorist Attacks*, THE WASHINGTON POST, January 11, 1991.

Inspiring a fictionalized big-budget Hollywood thriller, "The Siege," in which Arab American men in New York City are placed in prison camps by an Army general, the INS actually prepared an internal memorandum discussing such plans. The 1986 document, entitled ALIEN TERRORISTS AND UNDESIRABLES: A CONTINGENCY PLAN, calls for a "limited targeting" strategy. Following a more limited program executed during the 1979–80 Iranian hostage crisis, which focused on Iranian students in the United States, the document recounted:

> Close cooperation and an exchange of information will be required between INS and other governmental agencies with national intelligence and security functions, including but not limited to the FBI and CIA.
>
> The Service will likely be required to concentrate its counterterrorism efforts against particular nationalities or groups known to be composed primarily of certain nationalities, most probably those citizens of states known to support terrorism.
>
> INS should distinguish and isolate those members of the nationality group whose presence is inimical to national security interests, from those who have fled to this country seeking asylum or are dissidents from the regime in power.
>
> Corollary to the above, INS should distinguish between the broad categories of aliens of the nationality group, *i.e.* immigrants and nonimmigrants, due to the differing standards which exist in law for processing and initiation of proceedings against these two classes.

U.S. Department of Justice, Immigration and Naturalization Service, Central Office, INVESTIGATIONS DIVISION: ALIEN TERRORISTS AND UNDESIRABLES: A CONTINGENCY PLAN (May 1986).

The document further advocated that the INS pursue development of a "general registry" for a "clear picture of the number and kind of aliens within the designated class that are in the United States" as well as to "act[] as a logical precursor to further actions for those who do not comply with the registry or are found to be in violation of law at the time of registry." It also indicated that such a listing "has the benefit of being tested in administrative tribunals, district courts and courts of appeal, and [have] been found constitutional and within the power of the government." *Id.*

In the event that a "general registry" was not acceptable, the INS "recommend[ed] the following steps:" an executive order that the INS, CIA and FBI provide "lists of names, nationalities, and other identifying data and evidence relating to alien undesirables and suspected terrorists believed to be in, or likely to enter the United States." It advocated investigation by "Special Agents . . . with an eye toward location and apprehension of those identified." The INS would then pursue deportation under amended regulations defining "international terrorism" broadly, to be "immediately published as a final rule in the Federal Register without resort to proposed rule-making procedures, as a matter of national security." Then, aliens would be "routinely [held] without bond" and prosecuted using confidential information in hearings from which the public was excluded. In addition to summary exclusion procedures (adopted a decade later), more stringent entry and departure controls, suspension of entry, and prevention of status adjustments from non-immigrant to immigrant status, the document called for use of "the recently re-opened Oakdale, Louisiana processing facility" for mass detention. Depending on the number of aliens, "in emergent conditions, or faced with the need to obtain maximum security facilities, the Service would seek the cooperation of the Bureau of Prisons to assist in providing appropriate detention space." *Id.*

The same Washington Post story quoted above indicated that the INS disavowed this plan in 1987 after it became public. A spokeperson said, " 'It was summarily discarded.'"

Some observers were highly critical of Arab American civil liberties protests. Commenting in his magazine, THE NEW REPUBLIC, a moderate-to-liberal periodical covering politics, publisher Martin Peretz wrote,

> No one in his right mind would allude to Jewish terror in the United States. It just doesn't exist. No one except, predictably, The Washington Post, which, in its customary desperation to find moral equivalents for everything, explains the controversy surrounding Ed Zwick's new movie, The Siege, this way: "To understand the objections of Arab Americans and Muslims to 20th Century Fox's new film, "The Siege" . . . picture the following scenario: a nefarious rabbi exhorts his extremist, ultra-Orthodox followers to plant bombs against Arab sympathizers in America. . . ." The problem with picturing this is that nothing remotely like it has ever happened. It is true that one Palestinian was killed in California out of sheer hatred. Otherwise, the one rabbi—not ultra-Orthodox but ultra-nationalist—who did try to stir up actionable hatred of Arabs among U.S. Jews utterly failed. He moved to Israel, where he was barred from running for public office. In the end, Meir Kahane was assassinated in New York by just the sort of Arab terrorist depicted in Zwick's true-to-life film.

> What the filmmaker knows and what he says is that the prospect of Muslim terror in America is real, very real. We have already experienced dozens of attacks on American targets, and we have had our dead and maimed. And there are terrorist incidents that did not come off quite as planned or that were headed off by law enforcement. All of this constitutes the factual basis for the movie. It is also the factual basis that the Council on American Islamic Relations and the American-Arab Anti-Discrimination Committee and their hand-wringing allies in the media want to wish out of our view. With this pretext and pretense, they are trying to close down a film by a director who is so scrupulous with the facts and so fair that he has given the complainants much more than even a very extensive definition of probity would require. . . .

> It would be one thing if it were conceivable that the United States might imprison thousands of innocent people simply on the basis of ethnicity, religion, or skin pigment in order to catch a few guilty ones. But this country is no longer capable of an internment like that of the Japanese-Americans during World War II—and thank God we are so disabled.

Martin Peretz, Cambridge Diarist: *The Siege*, THE NEW REPUBLIC (NOVEMBER 30, 1999).

The suspicion of Arab Americans following instances of domestic terror-ism such as the bombing of the Oklahoma City federal building in 1995, which killed 168 people, similarly has prompted criticism of racial profiling in law investigation. Although Timothy McVeigh, a Caucasian ex-serviceman, ultimately was convicted in the worst case of domestic terrorism in U.S. his-tory, initial suspicions focused on individuals of Arab descent.

Moreover, the American-Arab Anti-Discrimination Committee (AADC) claimed that the FBI and CIA initiated "Operation Boulder" in 1972 to "screen" Arabs in the United States, defined as anyone with Arab parentage or ancestry. According to the AADC, "the CIA and the FBI agreed to coordi-nate intelligence information on the whereabouts and activities of Arab lead-ers, groups, associations, and individuals, as well as any non-Arab who voiced support for Arab causes."

Given the many divergent views of Arab American civil liberties, "secu-rity risks" and government and media responses, in what ways does the Japanese American internment provide a lens for asserting the govern-ment's treatment of Arab Americans following the Iran hostage crisis and during the Gulf War? Or is the treatment of Arab Americans comparable to that of Japanese Americans?

4. RACE, RIGHTS AND NATIONAL SECURITY: THE WEN HO LEE PROSECUTION

What follows is an account of recent events surrounding allegations of nuclear technology spying for China by a Chinese American scientist. As you read this composite account, based primarily on news reports, ask yourself:

- What are the prevailing stereotypes circulating in the media and what are their sources?
- What are the linkages of race to disloyalty?
- Do Wen Ho Lee and the Cox Report bear any resemblance to Fred Korematsu and the DeWitt Report?
- Is this recent episode comparable to the internment of Japanese Americans during World War II, as asserted in a recent ABC News Nightline report?

a. THE ALLEGATIONS

Born in Taiwan and a naturalized American citizen for 25 years, nuclear scientist Wen Ho Lee was the target of a four-year federal investigation os-tensibly for "nuclear weapons spying." In 1996, U.S. officials worried that the Chinese government may have received design information for a U.S. nuclear warhead. They circulated an allegation that Dr. Lee surreptitiously gave China secret information about the W-88 miniaturized nuclear warhead used on Trident submarines. The government, however, never charged Dr. Lee with espionage, and FBI investigators later admitted there was no evidence to support such a charge.

They did prosecute Dr. Lee for transferring legacy codes from a classified computer system to his unsecured office computer—a not uncommon occurrence (the former CIA director did the same thing). Secretary of Energy Bill Richardson fired Dr. Lee from his Los Alamos job in March of 1999 for failure to report his security breach and for failure to report contact during a public conference with Chinese scientists. Dr. Lee was held without bail for ten months in a New Mexico jail on the basis of FBI assertions that Lee had stolen the "crown jewels" of the United States' nuclear war program. The FBI limited Dr. Lee's family contact in prison to one hour per day and required that all conversations be in English.

The FBI had interrogated Dr. Lee one day before he was fired from the Los Alamos lab. He unequivocally denied passing nuclear weapons secrets to the Chinese government. During an earlier lie detector test, Dr. Lee made the same statements. An independent polygraph interpreter observed that Dr. Lee's score for honesty was among the highest he had seen. FBI agents nevertheless misled Dr. Lee into believing that he had failed the polygraph test in an unsuccessful effort to induce a confession of espionage.

Throughout the March 1999 interrogation, FBI agents pressed Dr. Lee to admit that he had passed secrets to the Chinese scientists. The agents suggested that unless he confessed, he would be arrested for espionage and possibly executed. "Do you know who the Rosenbergs are?" one of the agents asked Dr. Lee. "The Rosenbergs are the only people that never cooperated with the federal government in an espionage case. You know what happened to them? They electrocuted them, Wen Ho."

b. Unequal Treatment?

At the same time the government targeted Dr. Lee, it learned that former CIA Director John M. Deutch similarly mishandled classified information by using his unsecured home computer to store sensitive government security information. Deutch used that same computer to access the Internet and to receive and send e-mail, including e-mail from a Russian scientist.

Chalking it up to Deutch's "sloppiness," the CIA rejected any similarity between Deutch's and Dr. Lee's cases. Initially, the Justice Department deferred to the CIA and declined to prosecute Deutch. Asian American groups, however, charged that Deutch's security violations were more serious than Dr. Lee's and that Deutch received special treatment—CIA investigators never even questioned him. CIA Director George Tenet responded vaguely, saying he didn't think the cases were similar.

In December of 1999, Dr. Lee sued the FBI and the Justice and Energy Departments, alleging that they engaged in racial profiling, violated his privacy and wrongly portrayed him as a Chinese spy.

In February of 2000, Attorney General Janet Reno announced that she was "particularly concerned" with the similarity of Deutch's and Dr. Lee's cases and decided to reopen the Justice Department's investigation of Deutch and the CIA's failure to promptly report his possible crimes to the Justice Department. The Justice Department, however, has not prosecuted or even charged, Deutch.

c. ONCE AGAIN, DOES THE ENEMY HAVE AN ASIAN FACE?

In a spectacular disclosure, Robert S. Vrooman, the former Chief of Counterintelligence at Los Alamos, charged that Dr. Lee was singled out by the government for prosecution because of his ethnicity. Vrooman spoke out after Energy Department Secretary Bill Richardson recommended that Vrooman and two other former Los Alamos executives be disciplined for allegedly failing to carry out properly the spying investigation that focused on Dr. Lee. Vrooman asserted that the case was "screwed up" because there was nothing there—it was "built on thin air." Vrooman concluded that Dr. Lee's ethnicity was a major factor in the investigation.

Did the Wen Ho Lee investigation and the Cox Report revive stereotypes of a "yellow peril" threatening the nation's security? Consider the following account of reactions by conservative politicians.

Presidential candidate Pat Buchanan called Wen Ho Lee the epicenter of the most dangerous penetration of America's nuclear labs since the Rosenbergs were condemned to the electric chair in 1953. Senator Don Nickles said that Dr. Lee was responsible for the most serious case of espionage in U.S. history. Senator Frank Murkowski stated that Dr. Lee perpetrated "the greatest loss of nuclear military secrets in our nation's history," secrets that, in the words of Senator Richard Lugar, will place the United States "at a significantly greater risk from a Chinese ballistic missile attack." These and related statements so tainted public beliefs that NBC's Brian Williams described the decision not to prosecute Dr. Lee for espionage as "amazing."

As facts emerged during the four-month media frenzy, Dr. Lee looked less like a master spy and more like a victim of government racial profiling and Republican witch-hunting.

d. THE COX REPORT AND ITS PARALLELS TO THE DEWITT REPORT

Soon after Dr. Lee was fired, a special committee headed by Representative Christopher Cox (R-Cal.) reported that China had gained crucial design information for all U.S. nuclear weapons. The committee's widely publicized report made sweeping unsubstantiated assertions about suspected espionage among Chinese in America. That committee, the Congressional Select Committee on U.S. National Security and Military/Commercial Concerns with the People's Republic of China, released its findings in June 1999. It concluded, without supporting details, that Chinese American scientists, businessmen and students are recruited as "sleeper agents" or "walk-in spies."

> The PRC [People's Republic of China] . . . tries to identify ethnic Chinese in the United States who have access to sensitive information, and sometimes is able to enlist their cooperation in illegal technology or information transfers.

> Espionage played a central part in the PRC's acquisition of classified U.S. thermonuclear warhead design secrets. In several cases, the PRC identified lab employees, invited them to the PRC, and approached them for help, sometimes playing upon ethnic ties to recruit individuals.

House Report 105-851, Report of the Select Committee on U.S. National Security and Military/Commercial Concerns with the People's Republic of China (June 1999) (Cox Report).

While thinking about this passage in the Cox Report, recall the following excerpts from the report by General DeWitt in his investigation regarding national security risk posed by persons of Japanese ancestry in the United States.

> Because of the ties of race, the intense feeling of filial piety and the strong bonds of common tradition, culture and customs, this population [of 115,000 Japanese Americans] presented a tightly-knit racial group. . . . Whether by design or accident, virtually always their communities were adjacent to very vital shore installations, war planes, etc. While it was believed that some were loyal, it was known that many were not. It was impossible to establish the identity of the loyal, and the disloyal with some degree of safety. It was not that there was insufficient time in which to make such a discrimination; it was simply a matter of facing the realities that a positive determination could not be made, that an exact separation of the "sheep from the goats" was unfeasible.

Office of the Commanding General, FINAL REPORT: JAPANESE EVACUATION FROM THE WEST COAST 1942 (1943).

Is there a similar assumption of ethnicity and disloyalty in the two reports? The Cox Report maintained Chinese Americans are susceptible to spying because the PRC targets them, implying their loyalty to their "motherland." Does this sound similar to DeWitt's report that Japanese Americans had "strong bonds of common tradition, culture and customs"? DeWitt's report also gleaned disloyalty from the fact that some Japanese American communities were located near defense installations (it was later determined that these undesirable areas were the only tracts available to Japanese Americans because of discrimination in land occupancy and housing). Does the Cox Report rely on evidence of "location"—that Chinese Americans "gravitate" toward technology centers, including nuclear labs?

The Cox Report also drew connections between illegal Chinese American campaign contributions and Chinese espionage.

> Johnny Chung, a Chinese-American at the heart of the campaign finance controversy, was given $300,000 by two Chinese military officials in an apparent effort to establish one of them, [a lieutenant colonel in the Chinese Army and] the daughter of a Chinese general, in the United States so she could acquire American technology.

Cox Report, *supra.*

e. THE COX REPORT REFUTED

Soon after its release, both the CIA and prominent nuclear weapons experts rejected the Cox Report's key findings. Harold Agnew, a former director of Los Alamos, stated that the allegedly stolen warhead information would have "limited value" for the Chinese. And the CIA released a damage assessment concluding it was impossible to tell how comprehensive the information was, and how much had been obtained through espionage rather than careful research.

> This is completely overblown, Spurgeon Keeney, president of the privately funded Arms Control Association, [said]. A lot of the [supposedly secret] stuff they are making a big deal about you will find in the *Nuclear Weapons Databook* that was put out [in the 1980s] by the Natural Resources Defense Council, including pictures.

James Risen, *Fund-Raising Figure Had Spy Case Role,* N.Y. TIMES, May 26, 1999.

The most detailed criticism of the Cox Report came in the form of a ninety-nine-page report released in December of 1999 by scientists and scholars at Stanford University's Center for International Security and Cooperation (CISC). The CISC report charged that the Cox Report failed to support a number of "spectacular accusations" against China and several U.S. research facilities, and that the Report reached unwarranted conclusions. Among the CISC authors' findings:

> Regarding the Cox Report's assertion that China has stolen sensitive nuclear information, [. . .] "While China may spy on the U.S. nuclear program, the allegations are generally unproven. The broad accusations of spying has cast a cloud of suspicion on both foreign and Asian-born U.S. citizens. . . . The report never makes clear how much China learned on its own and from unclassified sources, as distinct from spying." . . . [As for FBI investigators' conclusion that classified information regarding nuclear warheads had been stolen,] investigators wrongly concluded that information could only have come from an inside source at the labs.

Sam Chu Lin, *Stanford Experts Criticize Cox Report, China Probe,* THE RAFU SHIMPO, Dec. 20, 1999, at 1.

Lewis Franklin, a career intelligence expert on Sino-Soviet missile and space programs, agreed with the CISC. Referring to the Cox Report's findings, Franklin stated, "they are quite wrong, . . . they allege technology theft at the launch sites in China for which their [sic] is no evidence. They claim the PRC missiles are predominantly based on stolen technology, much as they say for their nuclear weapons."

Wolfgang K.H. Panofsky, a high-energy physicist and director emeritus of the Stanford Linear Accelerator Center, warned that the Cox Report may have an adverse effect on U.S. research programs:

> Asian American students and scientists won't come near or make any applications to the laboratories, which is damaging to the laboratories . . . . Asian Americans make up a significant faction of the weapons laboratories. I don't know if that was the intent of the Cox Report, but I hope we can repress it.

Sam Chu Lin, *supra.*

f. SUSPECTED PARTISAN POLITICS BEHIND THE COX REPORT

Stephen Schwartz, publisher of the *Bulletin of the Atomic Scientists,* wrote in an editorial entitled "A Very Convenient Scandal" that the story emerged at the perfect time for advocates of legislation promoting the swift deployment of ballistic missile defenses. Schwartz also noted that the first public allegations that China had stolen U.S. nuclear weapons technology had been published in 1990, when George Bush was president, and resulted in no similar outcry—and no improvement in security at the labs.

> "This is the case of a pretty sexy group of things coming together," says Stan Norris, senior analyst at the Natural Resources Defense Council. "You've got nuclear bombs, espionage. Throw in a dash of political campaign contributions and an upcoming election, and you have the perfect Washington story. He might have done some things he shouldn't have done, like mishandling computer information. But he wasn't alone in doing those things. It is beginning to look like Wen Ho Lee was a scapegoat."

Bill Mesler, *The Spy Who Wasn't,* THE NATION, Aug. 9, 1999.

g. MEDIA RESPONSE TO THE WEN HO LEE INVESTIGATION

The day after Fred Korematsu was arrested for violating military Exclusion Order 34, a newspaper headline read, "Jap Spy Arrested in San Leandro." After the allegations against Dr. Lee and the release of the Cox Report, the New York Times' coverage in a series of articles painted Dr. Lee as guilty of espionage. Asian Americans reacted to what they perceived as harsh and unfair media treatment.

> The Asian American Journalist Association [AAJA] . . . is alarmed that the allegations of espionage at Los Alamos National Laboratory have sparked numerous press reports, editorials and cartoons that promote racist stereotypes. If coverage does not improve, AAJA is concerned that these media accounts will do more harm to the Asian Pacific community than some of the poor coverage stemming from allegations of fundraising by Asian nationals during the 1996 presidential campaign. . . . [A tip to ensure fair and accurate coverage is to] avoid stereotypes, overgeneralizations and outdated terms. Loaded words such as "inscrutable," "clever," and "shrewd," as well as seemingly complimentary adjectives such as "industrious," can reinforce stereotypes that have become associated with the Asian Pacific community.

Asian American Journalists Association, *Coverage of Spying Allegations at Nuclear Labs,* <http://www.aaja.org/html/news_html/news_arch99_5.html>.

What do you make of the following "friendly" comments by a non-Asian media writer?

> We have to start remembering what great, capable, artistic people the Chinese are. We shouldn't let our opinion of them be dominated by . . . the suspected spy, Wen Ho Lee. The influx of Chinese into this country is a good addition to the all-American mix we have. Their kids are doing better-than-well in our schools, and the Chinese are contributing to our society on every level. It would be a sad thing if, because of the Chinese leaders who make this stupid decision to spy and infiltrate our political system, we started looking suspiciously at every ethnic Chinese man, woman or child in America.

Andy Rooney, *Who Can Figure Out the Inscrutable Chinese,* THE BUFFALO NEWS, May 30, 1999, at 3H.

Rooney makes a cautionary statement against brushing all Chinese Americans with the tar of disloyalty. But does he also perpetuate stereotypes of "the Chinese" as "great, capable, [and] artistic,"—"doing better than well in our schools"? To what extent are these "model minority" stereotypes the flip side of the stereotypes of Chinese in America that the AAJA advises the media from using?

Some believed that overall the media resisted racial profiling of Asian Americans and have avoided "feeding anti-Asian hysteria." According to Karen Narasaki, Executive Director of the National Asian Pacific American Legal Consortium, the coverage was fairly responsible—not quite the "alarmist coverage" surrounding the Asian finance campaign fiasco." Many Asian Americans also applauded ABC Nightline's series of televised reports examining the Asian American communities' reactions and fears in the wake of the campaign-finance scandal, the Cox Report, and the investigation of Dr. Lee.

h. ARE ASIANS IN AMERICA MALIGNED OR OVERREACTING?

The Cox Report and media frenzy led many Chinese Americans and other Asian Americans to perceive a revival of the linkage of Asian ethnicity to disloyalty.

> During and after [World War II], too many Americans forgot the difference between Japanese citizens and Americans of Japanese descent. . . . Who would have thought it would be necessary to revisit the issues in 1999? Yet, in light of growing sensitivity over the question of Chinese espionage, there is no avoiding the questions of ethnicity, citizenship, nationhood and, yes, loyalty. . . .
>
> Ethnicity wrongly is starting to be seen as a predictor of disloyalty regardless of citizenship.

Richard Estrada, *Familiarity Doesn't Always Breed Friendship,* THE DALLAS MORNING NEWS, May 28, 1999, at 29A.

Did people forget the difference between Chinese citizens and American citizens of Chinese decent? Did the "friendly" commentator attempt to distinguish the two? To what extent did ethnicity again become a "predictor" of disloyalty? Recall that the FBI apparently targeted only Dr. Lee, even though there were other identically situated "security risks."

Reporter Jim Donovan observed that to "white Americans," it is not "obvious" why Asian Americans feel vulnerable at this time. But to some Asian Americans, the link between disloyalty and national origin is only obvious.

> Most news accounts about Lee, a naturalized U.S. citizen born in Taiwan, describe him as a "Chinese spy." That ambiguous characterization suggests not only that he is a spy for China, but also a spy of Chinese ethnicity. The implication is that his national origin is an important clue to his conduct.
>
> As a result, others of Asian descent may face the slander about "dual loyalties."

Frank H. Wu, *Spying Case Shouldn't Lead to Racial Stereotyping,* SUN-SENTINEL, May 10, 1999, at 19A.

In one account, snickering and hushed laughter broke out in a roomful of computer users as a person with a Chinese surname was introduced to lead a session on computer security. In another, a lab manager told an Asian American employee that "personal characteristics" would determine a person's career opportunities in the wake of recent disclosures of security breaches, implying that ethnicity was one such characteristic. Jeff Garberson, spokesman for Lawrence Livermore nuclear weapons lab, revealed to the Los Angeles Times that he recently received a request from a national news magazine for a generic photo of an Asian American employee at work "to illustrate a story on espionage."

Are Asian American groups appropriately concerned about fears of a resurgence of "yellow peril"—that their ethnicity determines their loyalty? In a recent editorial, Angela Oh, a member of President Clinton's Advisory Board on Race, reported "hostility" toward Chinese Americans in the sciences after the Cox Report:

> For Chinese Americans who have chosen scientific research as a career, the current climate in the professional arena has become hostile. The irony is that those who have made significant contributions to the nation's preeminence in international intelligence and satellite technology cannot say a word to counteract the rhetoric that raises suspicion. This is due to the "classified" nature of their work and the awareness that national security requires silence. This silence has been interpreted by at least one senator as "crafty." ... The images of Asian Pacific Americans as corrupt political operatives, spies and a foreign threat have been reinforced in the media coverage of the Lee case. ... The history, leadership, contributions and struggles common to the bicultural and intergenerational relationships are largely unreported and, frankly, non-Asians don't even seem to notice.

Angela E. Oh, *Spy Charges Fueled Search for Scapegoats,* L.A. TIMES, June 21, 1999, at B5.

Consider also the charges of nine Asian-American lab workers against the University of California, alleging racial discrimination in their December 1999 lawsuit. Kalina Wong worked in the university's nuclear energy lab for twenty-one years. Although she is a fifth generation Chinese American, Wong reportedly still experiences discrimination:

> She's been passed up for promotions, gets paid less than her white counterparts, and sees no opportunities for advancement—all because she is Asian. And since Wen Ho Lee has come under fire, she believes the discrimination and disparaging treatment has become more blatant. "It's the same kind of mentality. We are the target. They can't get behind my Asian face and they don't see American. They see Asian, and all Asians steal data."

Janet Dang, *API Lab Employees File Suit,* ASIAN WEEK, Jan. 27, 2000, at 12.

However, Energy Secretary Bill Richardson, who fired Dr. Lee, believes that Asian Americans' perceptions of discrimination are overblown.

Are those voicing opinions about an Asian American backlash correct? Are Asian Americans unfairly maligned, or are they overreacting?

i. FOREVER FOREIGN

For some observers, the evidence against Dr. Lee was so thin that it was always clear he would never face criminal charges for espionage. Nevertheless, they believed Dr. Lee had been "convicted in parts of the press."

To what extent did the Cox Report raise legitimate concerns? To what extent did it pander to public fears and prejudices about threats to national security in order to undermine President Clinton and his administration?

Dr. George Koo, in his address at the UNITY 99 Journalists of Color Convention, lamented the government's disinterest in constitutional rights of individuals in its pursuit of ostensible threats of national security.

> It's hard to know what if anything Wen Ho Lee is guilty of, but one thing is certain. He did not get anything that comes close to the due process, something that is supposed to be the sacred right of every American citizen.... Of course when the campaign scandal hit about two years ago, due process was the last thing anyone had in mind. Innuendoes flew thick and fast unimpeded by any hard facts or evidence.... Asian Americans who thought they were joining the mainstream political process by becoming active fund raisers for political campaigns were suddenly pariahs in America. The Democratic National Committee couldn't return checks with Asian surnames fast enough.

Jun Shan, *Asian Americans Victimized?*, <http://chineseculture.about.com/culture/chineseculture/library/weekly/aa071499.htm?terms=wen+ho+lee>

Finally, Angela Oh reflected on the larger implications of the Lee controversy:

> When a problem such as the Lee case arises ... [t]he hope is that the nation will not be misled by stereotypes in a search for scapegoats. But the experiences of Asian Pacific Americans support all too well their concerns about the potential for tragedy. The World War II internment of patriotic Americans of Japanese descent, the denial of honorable treatment of Filipino war veterans, the stabbing death of a 15-year-old Vietnamese high school student in retribution for deaths during the Vietnam war, the targeting of immigrant Koreans in Los Angeles in 1992 and the recent shooting of a Japanese American grocer in Chicago for his apparent "foreignness" are just a few examples.

> The rhetoric of nativism and hegemony are anachronistic remnants of the Cold War era.... Negotiating solutions that keep a balance between national security and accountability with individual rights and integrity will be no easy task.

Angela Oh, *supra*.

j. CASE CLOSED—OR IS IT?: *KOREMATSU* REVISITED

In September of 2000, after nine months in solitary confinement and of villification as a spy so dangerous that he couldn't be granted bail, the government set Dr. Lee free. The Justice Department had charged Dr. Lee with fifty-nine counts of downloading secret computer information. Dr. Lee pled guilty to one count of unlawful gathering of information. He was never charged with spying or passing nuclear secrets. After all the government's posturing and public denunciations of Dr. Lee as a spy intent on severely harming the United States, how did this minimal plea agreement become a reality?

In July of 2000, the government's prosecution began to collapse on multiple fronts. First, Judge Parker "allowed Wen Ho Lee's lawyers to subpoena internal government documents that might shed light on whether racial profiling had been used to target Lee in the first place."* The Justice Department had fought vigorously to prevent Dr. Lee's defense team from viewing these documents.

Second, as the trial approached, the government's factual case disintegrated. Reports surfaced that the government had suppressed four internal FBI investigative memos stating that Dr. Lee was not guilty of espionage. In addition, a principal FBI investigator in the case, Robert Messemer, acknowledged that he "misstated" key facts to federal Judge Parker about Dr. Lee's danger to national security during the earlier bail hearing. (Judge Parker relied on those misstated facts in denying bail and approving Dr. Lee's placement in solitary confinement.) Messemer also acknowledged, contrary to his earlier sworn testimony, that Dr. Lee never said he was downloading the information to aid his search for overseas employment. Messemer also conceded that Dr. Lee had passed his first lie detector test in which he was questioned about spying for China, and that an independent analyst so informed the FBI. In fact, independent experts at the time confirmed to the FBI that Dr. Lee's score reflected a high degree of honesty—one of the highest possible scores for credibility. The FBI, however, lied to Dr. Lee and others about this.

Third, several nuclear scientists confirmed that the information Dr. Lee downloaded was not the "crown jewel" of the U.S. nuclear war program; rather, ninety-nine percent of the information was already in the public domain. Moreover, at the time of downloading, the information had been merely designated as "restricted"; the government changed its status to "secret" only after the investigation commenced. Finally, Judge Parker unsealed the affidavits of Charles Vrooman, the original investigator in charge, and another investigator. Their affidavits stated under oath that the government had engaged in racially discriminatory targeting of Dr. Lee.

With these emerging facts, the government's claim of necessity under the mantle of national security crumbled and its denial of racial profiling met with judicial as well as public disbelief. With the impending public disclosure of internal Justice Department documents on the racial profiling issue, the government negotiated the plea bargain agreement. (Dr. Lee pled guilty to one felony count of having unauthorized possession of national defense materials (the other fifty-eight counts were dismissed); agreed to cooperate with the FBI concerning downloaded files; and was sentenced to time served.)

---

*Asian American legal organizations, led by Victor Hwang of the Asian Law Caucus, filed an *amici curiae* brief in support of Dr. Lee's position. These organizations included Chinese for Affirmative Action, Committee of 100, Japanese American Citizens League, National Asian Pacific American Bar Association, National Asian Pacific American Legal Consortium, National Lawyers Guild and Organizations of Chinese Americans.

At the hearing on the plea agreement, Judge Parker rebuked the government and apologized to Dr. Lee. He stated he was "angered over having been misled into believing the sixty-year old nuclear scientist was a danger to national security." "I sincerely apologize to you, Dr. Lee, for the unfair manner in which you were held in custody by the executive branch." "[The prosecution has] embarrassed our entire nation and each of us who is a citizen of it." Judge Parker also stated that he wished he were not bound by the plea agreement to refrain from commenting about the real reasons for the prosecution and treatment of Dr. Lee. Some interpreted that statement to imply the existence of evidence of government racial profiling and its fueling of public stereotypical fears of dangerous and always-foreign Chinese Americans.

Despite the prolonged public relations campaign against Dr. Lee in Congress and by the Justice Department, the government in the end could not point to a single piece of evidence showing that Dr. Lee passed nuclear secrets to China, engaged in any form of nuclear espionage or was otherwise disloyal to the United States. Attorney General Janet Reno nevertheless refused to apologize to Dr. Lee. "Lee was at fault for not providing the information [about the downloaded tapes] sooner." "I think Dr. Lee, from the beginning, had the opportunity to answer this and I think now he needs to look himself, rather than expect an apology from the US government."

The Justice Department declined to prosecute former CIA Director Deutsch for computer security violations that were apparently far more serious than Dr. Lee's. Just in case, as one of his last executive acts, President Clinton pardoned Deutsch for those violations.

In September of 2000, in an unprecedented move, the New York Times publically apologized for its uneven coverage of the Wen Ho Lee investigation and prosecution. The paper acknowledged that its unbalanced coverage may have unfairly tainted public perceptions of Dr. Lee.

One way to characterize the Wen Ho Lee investigation is that good faith fears for the nation's security turned into overzealous government prosecution. Another, perhaps more compelling way, is to examine the Wen Ho Lee controversy through the lens of the internment cases: empty charges of espionage; prolonged incarceration without trial and without evidence of national security necessity; the suppression of exculpatory evidence; media innuendo of Asian American disloyalty; the reemergence of racial stereotypes in the public imagination—"Yellow Peril"; racially discriminatory profiling by government officials; and retrospective U.S. embarrassment.

What have we learned about race, rights, liberty and reparation from Korematsu, Hirabayashi *and* Yasui?

C. ADDITIONAL READINGS

BOOKS

Peter Irons, JUSTICE AT WAR: THE STORY OF THE JAPANESE INTERNMENT CASES. New York (1983).

Hyung-Chan Kim (ed.), ASIAN AMERICANS AND THE SUPREME COURT: A DOCUMENTARY HISTORY. New York (1992).

U.S. Department of Justice, Immigration and Naturalization Service, Central Office, Investigations Division: ALIEN TERRORISTS AND UNDESIRABLES: A CONTINGENCY PLAN (May 1986).

United States, Final Report: JAPANESE EVACUATION FROM THE WEST COAST, 1942 (1943).

LAW REVIEW ARTICLES AND OTHER SOURCES

Nick Anderson, *Spy Scare Taints Lab's Atmosphere, Asian Americans Say Discrimination: Insensitive Remarks, Warnings Raises Fear of "Ethnic Profiling" Following Allegations of Chinese Espionage, Employees Say*, L.A. TIMES, May 21, 1999, at A12.

Lorraine K. Bannai & Dale Minami, *Internment During World War II and Litigations*, in ASIAN AMERICANS AND THE SUPREME COURT (Hyung-Chan Kim, ed., 1992).

Sumi Cho, *Whiteness Redeemed: Earl Warren, Internment and Brown v. Board of Education*, 19 B.C. THIRD WORLD L.J., 40 B.C. L. REV. 73 (1999).

Janet Dang, *API Lab Employees File Suit*, ASIAN WEEK, Jan. 27, 2000, at 12.

Richard Estrada, *Familiarity Doesn't Always Breed Friendship*, THE DALLAS MORNING NEWS, May 28, 1999, at 29A.

Gil Gott, *A Tale of New Precedents: Japanese American Internment as Foreign Affairs Law*, 19 B.C. THIRD WORLD L.J. 179 (1999).

Morton Horwitz, Symposium: National Conference on Judicial Biography "Contracted" Biographies and Other Obstacles to "Truth" Commentary, 70 N.Y.U. L. REV. 714 (1995).

Elizabeth M. Iglesias, *Out of the Shadow: Marking Intersections In/Between Asian Pacific American Critical Legal Scholarship and Latina/o Critical Legal Theory*, 19 B.C. THIRD WORLD L.J. 349 (1999).

Sam Chu Lin, *Stanford Experts Criticize Cox Report, China Probe*, THE RAFU SHIMPO, Dec. 20, 1999, at 1.

Cheryl Little, *InterGroup Coalitions and Immigration Politics: The Haitian Experience in Florida*, 3 U. MIAMI L. REV. 717 (1999).

Mari J. Matsuda, *McCarthyism, the Internment, and the Contradictions of Power*, 19 B.C. THIRD WORLD L.J. 9 (1999).

Bill Mesler, *The Spy Who Wasn't*, THE NATION, Aug. 9, 1999.

Angela E. Oh, *Spy Charges Fueled Search for Scapegoats,* L.A. TIMES, June 21, 1999, at B5.

Reggie Oh & Frank Wu, *The Evolution of Race in the Law: The Supreme Court Moves from Approving Internment of Japanese Americans to Disapproving Affirmative Action for Asian Americans,* 1 MICH. J. RACE & L. 165 (1996).

James Risen, *Fund-Raising Figure Had Spy Case Role,* N.Y. TIMES, May 26, 1999.

Andy Rooney, *Who Can Figure Out the Inscrutable Chinese,* THE BUFFALO NEWS, May 30, 1999, at 3H.

Eugene Rostow, *The Japanese American Cases—A Disaster,* 54 YALE L.J. 489 (1945).

Frank H. Wu, *Spying Case Shouldn't Lead to Racial Stereotyping,* SUN-SENTINEL, May 10, 1999, at 19A.

Frank H. Wu and Francey Lim Youngberg, *People from China Crossing the River: Asian American Political Empowerment and Foreign Influence,* in ASIAN AMERICANS AND POLITICS: PERSPECTIVES, EXPERIENCES, PROSPECTS (Gordon H. Chang, ed., 2000).

Eric K. Yamamoto, *Korematsu Revisited—Correcting the Injustice of Extraordinary Government Excess and Lax Judicial Review: Time for a Better Accommodation of National Security Concerns and Civil Liberties,* 26 SANTA CLARA L. REV. 1 (1986).

ONLINE RESOURCES

Asian American Journalists Association, *Coverage of Spying Allegations at Nuclear Labs*
<http://www.aaja.org/html/news_html/news_arch99_5.html>.

Jun Shan, *Asian Americans Victimized?*
<http://chineseculture.about.com/culture/chineseculture/library/weekly/aa071499.htm?terms=wen+ho+lee>.

Nightline Agenda, ABC News <http://abcnews.go.com/onair/nightline>

Vincent Law, *Chinagate and Chinagoats* <http://asianamculture.about.com>

Table of Cases

Index